P9-CRZ-997

CLASSICS *of the* MODERN THEATER

Realism and After

CLASSICS *of the*

MODERN THEATER

Realism and After

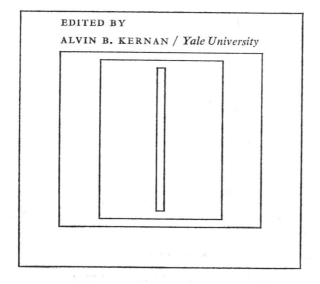

EDITED BY

ALVIN B. KERNAN / *Yale University*

HARCOURT, BRACE & WORLD, INC.

New York · Chicago · San Francisco · Atlanta

© 1965 by Harcourt, Brace & World, Inc.
All rights reserved. No part of this publication may
be reproduced or transmitted in any form or by any means,
electronic or mechanical, including photocopy, recording,
or any information storage and retrieval system, without
permission in writing from the publisher.
Library of Congress Catalog Card Number: 65-14541
Printed in the United States of America

CONTENTS

INTRODUCTION

A great dramatic tradition impresses itself on the mind not as a series of dates or plot outlines, but as a montage of vivid scenes and arrested gestures, over which human voices hang suspended: asserting, threatening, explaining, questioning. To think of the Elizabethan theater is to see an old man standing on a bare heath in a great thunderstorm shouting at the elements, a young man at night in a walled garden below a balcony looking upward at a beautiful girl, a prince dressed in seafarer's clothing standing in a graveyard holding a skull in his hand. It is to hear such voices as "Thou art the thing itself. Unaccommodated man is no more but such a poor, bare, forked animal as thou art"—"But soft! What light through yonder window breaks? It is the east, and Juliet is the sun!"—"To what base uses we may return, Horatio! Why may not imagination trace the noble dust of Alexander till he find it stopping a bunghole?"

Such scenes as these come to define a theater because each provides a sharply focused image of man in some crucial area of his existence. The modern theater also has its great definitive scenes which sum up man as he has come to sense himself in the nineteenth and twentieth centuries—his most fundamental hopes and fears, his understanding of the shape and currents of the world, and his intuition of his stance in relation to that world. At daybreak in a dark Norwegian valley at the head of a gloomy fiord a helpless madman, who has struggled vainly through his life for light and happiness, sees the astronomically distant sun hurling bright light on the snow-covered peaks far above. He speaks flatly to a woman who a moment ago had thought that a decision to face the truth guaranteed happiness: "Mother, give me the sun."

On a bare stage in an empty Italian theater a middle-aged gentleman, who is not a person but a "character," stands trying with great effort to explain the truth of his nature to an uncomprehending director and group of actors whom he *must* persuade to stage his own personal reality in a play. As he speaks, the dreadful truth slowly overwhelms him:

Each one of us has within him a whole world of things, each man of us his own special world. And how can we ever come to an understanding if I put in the words I utter the sense and value of things as I see them, while you who listen to me must inevitably translate them according to the conception of things each one of you has within himself. We think we understand each other, but we never really do.

A group of Russians sitting by a decayed wayside shrine in a cherry orchard, which had once been their support and justification but is now about to be sold, hear a sound like a breaking harp string, sad and faraway. They speculate aimlessly about whether they have heard the cry of some nameless bird or a lift cable snapping in some distant mineshaft. A moment of silence follows, and then they drift away, each isolated from the others and from a world they no longer understand.

High in the Swedish forests, deep with snow, an old nurse slips a straitjacket on a distraught man, a father, scientist, and one-time army officer, who had thought his authority invincible and his range unlimited, until he entered a death struggle with his wife for control of the family. The man who had once dreamed of a vast world entirely intelligible to the human intellect and manageable by reason sees his dream dissolve into the old, dark nightmare of blind struggle, containment, and death:

So when we thought the sun should have risen for us, we found ourselves back among the ruins in the full moonlight, just as in the good old times. Our light morning sleep had only been troubled by fantastic dreams—there had been no awakening.

In Central Park, near the zoo, two men quarrel over a bench. Jerry, who speaks for all of the disorders, loneliness, and personal disasters which are censored in the official versions of our affluent society, attempts to force himself on, communicate in some manner with, Peter, a man who consistently approximates middle-class statistical norms. It is as if two half-lives, private man and public man, were coming together for a moment and attempting to join. But no communication is possible, and in the end Jerry stands impaled on the knife held defensively at arm's length by the frightened Peter.

Lost somewhere deep in a labyrinthine "Palace of Justice" built around archives in which everything is neatly filed but nothing can be found, and in an eerie quietness, a group of judges face the intricate and elusive problems of guilt and responsibility which confront modern man working within an insulated administrative hierarchy. As they search, a greater emptiness is opened up until "the guilty one is frightened by the non-reaction of the universe: 'But then, if I, too, could sit back and forget: this would be more terrifying than all the rest.' " [1]

Such gloomy images and sounds as these dominate the modern theater, though occasionally scenes of hope and the sound of laughter flash out. Bernard Shaw's supermen, the instruments of the life force, such as Bluntschli in *Arms and the Man,* stand exposing and mocking various kinds of stupidity, cruelty, and romantic sentimentalism which threaten, but do not interrupt, the onward movement of life to its unknown goal. Thornton Wilder's less heroic, comic figures contrive somehow to escape by the skin of their teeth the traps of an apparently hostile or indifferent universe and the dangers of their own natures.

Even such a brief collection of scenes as this reveals one peculiarity of the modern theater, its international quality. The other great theaters of the West were the products of a single language and a single culture, even though that culture faced a crisis at the time it produced its great drama—fifth-century Athens, the London of Elizabeth and James I, and the France of Cardinal Richelieu and Louis XIV. But the modern theater is the product of nearly all the languages of the Western world, and its settings have ranged from the isolated country houses of the Russian upper-middle class to the fiords and forests of Scandinavia, from the arid plains of Andalusia to a bench in Central Park.

The subject matter of this theater has been as diverse as its languages and settings. Beginning as it does in the mid-nineteenth century, it has embodied at one time or another each of the major theories to explain the nature and destiny of man which have emerged in the last one hundred or so years. The realistic settings and the natural speech of plays by Ibsen, Chekov, and Hauptmann give solid form to the general philosophy of naturalism which is, roughly, the view that man's life is shaped entirely by his social and physical environment. Brecht's characters, struggling with the demands of earning bread and seeking shelter, constantly engaged in economic warfare, dramatize the world view of Marx. Relativism, the view that nothing, neither space nor morals, is absolute, finds its theatrical voice in the characters of Pirandello who try futilely to explain to others their personal sense of themselves, while the others interpret those explana-

---

[1] Ugo Betti, "Essays, Correspondence, Notes," trans. by William Meriwether and Gino Rizzo, *Tulane Drama Review,* 8, 1964, p. 78.

tions according to their own particular sense of things. The constant war between men and women, the grotesque sexual antagonisms, of Strindberg's plays give dramatic form to the theory of biological determinism and the social Darwinism which developed from the scientific views. Fabian socialism and a tempered belief in progress become the answer to the injustices and confusions of nineteenth-century imperialist politics, laissez-faire economics, and Victorian morality in the plays of Shaw. The existentialist belief that man is an absurd creature loose in a universe empty of real meaning finds expression in the plays of Ionesco, Sartre, and Camus. Finally, the psychology of Freud, which was anticipated in the plays of Strindberg, has in the last twenty or thirty years very nearly replaced traditional theories of motivation in such plays as those of Betti, Williams, and O'Neill.

These new ideas have by no means entirely usurped the modern stage, but continue to exist in uneasy mixture or in violent opposition with older, more traditional views of man and nature. While Yeats wrote poetic plays for the Abbey Theater dealing with the ancient Gaelic legends in which ideals triumphed over vulgar reality, Sean O'Casey wrote grimly realistic plays for the same theater dealing with slum life in Dublin during the Irish Rebellion—plays which demonstrated the sham of such ideals as patriotism and duty because they destroyed life rather than fostered it. Similarly, playwrights such as Lorca, Cocteau, and Fry have continued to see in poetry ("poetry of the theater" in Cocteau's case) the power to open up new and unsuspected areas of reality, while Ionesco has devoted himself entirely to showing the emptiness of language because of its inability to communicate even the most simple facts. And while T. S. Eliot has written several verse plays that turn on the miraculous changes wrought in some lives by grace and Christian vision, Samuel Beckett's characters wait, vainly, on a nearly bare stage for some saving power whose name is uncertain and who never appears, who may have come and gone unnoticed, or who may not even exist.

The styles in which modern dramatists have written are nearly as varied as their settings and the ideas which have informed their plays. A Greek tragic dramatist of the fifth century B.C. wrote in a tradition which prescribed the use of certain poetic meters, limited the number of characters who could appear on stage at one time, made obligatory the provision of odes and dances for a chorus, and directed that the plot must be drawn from heroic legend and the myths of the distant past. Modern dramatists work in no such dramatic tradition, and they have been left entirely free to choose subjects and invent new dramatic styles. The result has been a bewildering number of styles: realism, naturalism, poetic drama, symbolism, expressionism, the epic theater, the theater of the absurd, and surrealism, to name only the most prominent among them. As a result of this freedom, modern plays have taken nearly every possible shape, ranging from imitations of Elizabethan tragedy in blank verse to modified Japanese Noh plays; from sprawling plays which take half a day to perform and seek to encompass all of human life (Ibsen's *Emperor and Galilean,* Strindberg's *To Damascus,* O'Neill's *Mourning Becomes Electra*), to brief one-act "anti-plays" which prove the impossibility of finding any meaning in life except its meaninglessness (Ionesco's *The Chairs* or Albee's *The Sand Box*).

What is true of the dramatic form and style of the modern theater is equally true of the acting styles. The dominant mode of acting has been some modification of the Stanislavsky method (developed around the turn of the century at the Moscow Art Theater), which trains an actor, in effect, to lose his own personality while on the stage and become the character he is playing. This is the extension into the player's art of the realistic style, for just as the realistic stage is thought to become not a symbolic representation of reality but an actual place, so the Stanislavsky actor ceases to be a player representing someone else and is transformed into the character. But while this has been the dominant acting style, the reactions against it have been constant and extreme: Brecht trained the actors of his *Berliner Ensemble* to remember always that they were on stage playing a part, and actors at the Abbey Theater in Dublin, it is said, were frequently rehearsed in barrels in order to restrict their movements and to force them to concentrate on speaking their poetic lines, thus reminding them that they were no more than voices for the poetry, necessary but ultimately unimportant instruments of the author.

Attitudes toward stage designs and sets have been similarly various. One end of the range is marked by the meticulously realistic drawing-room sets of Ibsen, where the furniture, rugs, and draperies on the stage were chosen to create the illusion of rooms as real as those the audience had just left in coming to the theater. The general concern for realism led ultimately to such extremes as getting every detail on the costumes, down to the last button, historically accurate for period pieces, and the introduction of water taps that really worked, real doors, genuine gravel for walks, and television sets that showed the same program you would have seen if you hadn't come to the theater. This drive to make the stage a photographic imitation of the actual world remains in many ways the main current of the modern theater, though it has been resisted from the beginning by those who have argued that the stage is by nature a symbolic place, not an illusion of reality, and that settings and costumes should be designed with their symbolic function in mind. This view, most properly termed expressionism, has led to the construction of improbable sets in which skeletal structures represent houses, where the world is reduced to a bare stage with a single tree, where a few folding chairs stand for an automobile and household furnishings. On the expressionistic stage the world may be symbolized by a few angular pieces of abstract statuary, by a color alone, or by a few boards made into platforms of different levels; tall buildings may lean over a house to express menace, stables may flower at their peak to express hope, men may walk through mirrors to express their insubstantiality. The laws of nature and probability are suspended on the expressionistic stage, and their place is taken by the laws of poetry, which state that the writer is free to reshape the natural world in order to make his point clear.

In every area of the modern theater—language, setting, dramatic style, acting technique, theme, stage decor—we seem to find diversity, heterogeneity, and open conflict. Instead of a smoothly developing tradition, a continuing exploitation of a limited number of theatrical resources, and an ever narrowing and finer focus on a few key ethical and metaphysical questions—all the marks of the great theatrical traditions of the past—the theater of the modern age seems to jump nervously and without progression from extreme to extreme, from one bizarre experiment to its opposite, and from one explanation of human nature to its reverse. So great is this diversity that Francis Fergusson has been able to argue most persuasively that what we have is not a true "theater," which focuses "at the center of the life of the community the complementary insights of the whole culture," [2] but only a collection of plays loosely related by the accident of having been written in the same historical period, the late nineteenth and the twentieth centuries. Fergusson explains that this is so because our age lacks any common view of life and man and history:

Human nature seems to us a hopelessly elusive and uncandid entity, and our playwrights (like hunters with camera and flash-bulbs in the depths of the Belgian Congo) are lucky if they can fix it, at rare intervals, in one of its momentary postures, and in a single bright, exclusive angle of vision.[3]

If Fergusson is right, there is no hope of seeing modern drama as a significant whole. The best that can be done is to gather together a group of modern plays and to allow each to present its peculiar view of man and his world. Across one stage let Freudian man move in a painful attempt to exorcise his own and his family's psychic history;

[2] Francis Fergusson, *The Idea of a Theater* (Princeton, 1949), p. 2.
[3] *The Idea of a Theater*, p. 1.

on another stage let Marxist man move in the search for the means of production and the socialist utopia; on still another stage let existentialist man move toward that free and irremediable act which will establish his identity. Taken at this level, the views of man which our theater has offered us are difficult if not impossible to reconcile as complementary visions of the same man and the same world. But while the characters who appear on our stage may seem so different, they stand always in the same place, in front of a common background which reflects some shared sense of the human condition. To understand this fact, we must turn to the physical arrangements of our playing houses, and a word of explanation is needed here about the view of the physical theater I am about to offer.

We know that social situations and technological ability affect the architectural style and buildings of a period, but we also know by now that a style, such as the Gothic or the Baroque—embodied in buildings such as Chartres or St. Peter's—is an index to far more than the labor available in a given time and the ability to carve stones or work in plaster. These styles and buildings are, finally, the reflection in stone and space of a people's most fundamental values: their basic sense of themselves and the world they live in. What is true of a cathedral or a palace is likely to be true of a theater, which, at least at some times, has focused man's sense of himself and his world as finely as his churches or his civic buildings. As the drama of a great age tells us as much about that culture as its theology and its laws, so its theaters tell us as much as do its cathedrals and palaces.

Description of the physical theater (the size of the theater, the location of the stage, the costuming, machinery, and sets) has been the province of theater historians. They have tended to give us objective measurements in feet and inches and factual descriptions of the outstanding features of various theaters. Most often they have treated the change in theaters over a period of time and the development of new theatrical arrangements as evolutionary processes driven along by social events and technological advances. For example, the large indoor theaters built in the eighteenth and nineteenth centuries might be described as the result of improved engineering skill which allowed builders to span greater spaces without supporting pillars, and of an increase in the wealth and size of the middle class, which resulted in an increase in the number of people who would pay to go to the theater because they had leisure time for culture or because they wished to advertise their new prosperity in public.

As a result of the patient researches of theater historians, however, it has become apparent that each age and culture builds a particular *type* of theater, the external and decorative elements of which it may modify a great deal while leaving the basic form untouched. Consider for a moment the theater of classical Greece, where the plays of Aeschylus, Sophocles, and Euripides were performed. It was an open theater built along an axis. At one end, on seats going up the hillside, the population of the city was seated. Directly in front of them, and partly within the arms formed by the seats, was the circular orchestra or dancing floor, where the chorus of some twelve dancers chanted their odes and moved in intricate but orderly dances. This chorus, in the tragedies but not the comedies, was bewildered by trouble, usually incapable of direct action, and its members voiced the most conservative opinions about the actions which took place on the low stage directly before them. Here on this stage—we know little about its details—stood the two or three actors, the *doers*. Their costumes made them larger than life size, as befitted the heroes who met and challenged the mysterious powers, the will of Zeus and the other gods, which resided in the great blue sky which arched over the entire theater and formed the permanent backdrop for an Agamemnon, an Oedipus, or a Phaedra. From this mystery came curses on great houses, plagues on great cities, and frightening oracles for great men. But these terrors were met at the stage by great men who acted, suffered, and persevered until at last the mystery was clarified, the weight of ignorance was lifted, and the gods themselves, on some occasions, were forced to materialize on the stage and explain themselves. As the heroes by their pride and pain and loss gradually penetrated the mystery, the chorus behind them absorbed the new knowledge, embodied it in odes, and transmitted it by way of language and dance back to the audience which, always visible, was the human backdrop, the body of society, at the end of the theater opposite the great sky.

To move from the Greek to the modern theater is to move from a vast lighted space organized along a line to a small, isolated area located in the midst of an infinitely extended darkness. At the front of the covered auditorium, elevated above the seats, is a rectangular opening, the proscenium arch, varying in size from theater to theater. The opening in the arch is covered with a curtain while the auditorium is filling and the house lights are on. When the audience has been seated, a switch is thrown, the house lights go out, and the audience has been obliterated. There no longer is a community present, as there was in the Greek and Elizabethan theaters, where the assembled citizens were a passive but very real part of the theatrical symbolism. The curtain rises, the stage lights go on, and before us is our theater: an illuminated box with a few objects in it, floating in a darkness which extends to infinity in every direction. Out of this darkness and into the spotlights come a few actors to speak and struggle for a brief time and then retire, or be carried, back into the darkness out of which they came. The business transacted, the curtain falls and the theater ceases to exist.

In the past hundred years this basic theater has been modified in many ways. Projecting platforms have been thrown forward of the arch into the audience, the physical arch has been removed and the entire stage has been made into a circle in the center of the audience, actors have entered and exited through the auditorium in an attempt to extend the stage to the entire theater. Each of these changes has been an attempt to reach the audience, to bring the community back into the theater, but each has failed, and the actor remains isolated in the small area defined for a brief time by the stage lights. The changes do modify the symbolic values of theater in some ways: so long as the actors remain behind the proscenium arch, in that room with the fourth wall removed created by the box set, there are definite boundaries to their situation, their world is as small but very solid; once they move onto a platform in the center of the audience with their acting area defined only by spotlights, their space becomes more vague, the surrounding darkness presses closer and menaces the area of light more constantly.

This theater is well known to all of us, so well known that we have lost all sense of its strangeness and ceased to wonder, as with most familiar things, about what it suggests. But here in this arrangement of light, space, and actors is focused a basic sense of the universe and man's position in it which has been shared for some time now by men who otherwise hold violently opposite views. Obviously the existentialist playwright, a Sartre or a Camus, finds himself very much at home in a theater which states by its very arrangements that man with all his "absurd" longings for meaning and validation by some transcendent power is, in fact, isolated in an empty and meaningless universe where he must carve out his own justification and even his own being by a series of acts. But can a religious playwright adjust himself to such a bleak image of time and space? Apparently he cannot if he wishes to show a world in which some certain metaphysical order exists outside man and fills that darkness beyond the narrow confines of the illuminated stage. T. S. Eliot's attempts to dramatize visions and bring spirits into the theater are a history of the awkwardness and frustration inevitable in any attempt to say in our theater what that theater seems designed to deny. But there are religious views, perhaps more common in our times than simple piety, which see the age of miracles as past and regard the life of the spirit as one of constant anxiety and a struggle to maintain a faith which flickers intermittently in a universe which

never answers it unequivocally. Religious views of this kind—and by
"religion" I mean here all beliefs in some metaphysical power—have
found our theater well suited to their sense of the human condition.
Robert Bolt in his *Man for All Seasons* and John Osborne in his
Luther have, for example, recently given us presentations of men of
powerful religious convictions, Thomas More and Martin Luther, whose
sense that they were in touch with and acting in the name of some
divine power derived much of its tragic intensity from the great darkness surrounding those stages where they were forced, unsupported,
to defy mighty princes and great states. Whatever certainty they found
came only from their own hearts. If the same theater and the basic
world view it manifests can contain approaches to life as widely
separated as existentialism and Christian humanism, it can without
difficulty also contain Freudian psychology and conventional morality, explanations of life based on Marxian economic analysis and those
based on the meaninglessness of money and possessions, and the host of
other rational theories which have been advanced in plays as explanations of and solutions to the basic human condition posited by the
form of our theater.

So far we have looked at only the larger dimensions of the modern
theater, but we need now to take a closer look at the stage, for if this
small illuminated island lost in the vastness of space is our acting
ground, what is placed on this stage is of crucial importance. It will
represent the substance of the world. We can begin again by a com-
parison with the Greek and Elizabethan stages. The Greek actor at
the Theater of Dionysus in Athens acted, most frequently, in front of
a stage house with pillars and portals which represented the palace
of the rulers of the city or a temple of its gods. The ground in front
of the stage, the dancing floor, thus became the city square, where
the chorus, perhaps the elders of the city, assembled to appeal to their
rulers, the princes and the gods. In the center of the orchestra was
an altar for sacrifices to the gods. Behind the stage house was the sky
and the landscape from which the gods might appear at any time,
lowered onto the stage by a machine or, less spectacularly, walking on
to mingle with the actors. Thus most actions in the Greek theater took
place in the context of the principal symbols, the ultimate foundations,
of the Athenian world—the social and the heavenly order, the city,
the palace, the temple, the abode of the mysterious gods.

Something of the same kind of symbolism was built into the Elizabethan stage. The canopy over the stage was gorgeously painted on
the underside to represent the order of the heavenly bodies, a trap in
the floor led to an area below the stage known as the cellarage or

hell. The area at the back of the stage was splendidly decorated and could represent, with its upper balconies, the palace of a king or his throne room, the walls of a city or the house of a citizen. One writer has argued that the entire acting area was so constructed that it symbolized simultaneously "a castle, a throne, a city gate, and an altar. It was a symbol of social order and of divine order—of the real ties between man and king, between heaven and earth." [4] If this is so, no matter how much the actions and speeches of the characters might question the meaning and order of life, these solid symbols would stand to remind the audience of the unchanging social and religious order which their theater was built to affirm.

Our theater, however, has no such built-in symbols. At the back of the stage there is only a blank wall or occasionally a cyclorama. It is left to our authors and stage designers to fill the space and mark the boundaries of the stage in any way they wish, and they have done this in some very strange ways; indeed one might even say that each of the dramatic styles mentioned earlier—realism, expressionism, symbolism, epic theater, theater of the absurd—has given us a different kind of setting; but in general we can distinguish two major styles, again realism and expressionism, and trace a general trend in our theater from one to the other—though both have existed side by side from the beginning of the modern theater.

Realism, like all other styles, has had its excesses: real forests planted in tubs to provide the actors with living trees to climb, entire houses complete with brick chimneys constructed by carpenters and masons, and—summit of paradox!—gauzy curtains hung over the stage to provide a "realistic illusion" of such places as the forest outside Athens where the elves and fairies dance in *A Midsummer Night's Dream.* But the characteristic set of realism has been more modest and more sensible. It has been most often an interior set, such as that in Ibsen's *Ghosts* or Strindberg's *The Father,* with painted flats to suggest side walls in proper perspective, doors and windows that open and close, and the type of furnishings which would be found in a room of the same kind outside the theater. When the realistic set tries to reflect the outdoors, it offers, by means of paint and objects, the same sense of familiar reality. If at the edges of the realistic stage we see a most unsettling cosmic and temporal darkness, inside we see a most ordinary and familiar world of tables, chairs, and rugs, or of bushes and trees. And the actors who move within this set increase our sense of familiarity by wearing clothes such as we wear, speaking

[4] George R. Kernodle, "The Open Stage: Elizabethan or Existentialist?" *Shakespeare Survey,* 12, 1959, p. 3.

not in blank verse but in the kind of prose we think we might hear on the street, and revealing motives very like those we expect in ordinary life.

When this realistic set first began to appear in the modern theater, around 1870, it was a great relief from the painted sets of Swiss chalets and far-away castles in Spain which had been (and still are) the staple of the popular romantic drama and opera. The exotic Bulgarian mountains and village in which *Arms and the Man* is set are a spoof of this romantic tradition, and as Shaw's play proceeds it becomes clear that the setting of moonlight and balconies is as unrealistic as are the attitudes toward life held by the figures from musical comedy with whom Shaw peoples his play. Only Bluntschli, the hard-headed Swiss soldier of fortune and hotelkeeper, is out of place in this operatic world. His solid, realistic approach to personal problems, his plain language which cuts through pretense, and his common sense belong, properly, in the new realistic sets where the realism of the stage setting signaled a realistic approach to life and a concern not with romance but with actual social problems. Even today the realistic set is thought to stand for a solid, sensible, down-to-earth treatment of life, and dramatists are praised for their "realism."

No doubt some dramatists do use realistic sets simply as appropriate places in which to locate their plays about the ordinary lives of ordinary people, but the great masters of the realistic style—Ibsen, Chekov, Strindberg, Shaw—seem to have considered their sets, which appear to have been assembled at random out of the prop room to imitate day-to-day reality, as symbolic forms, carefully chosen and arranged to define the material world in which their characters must live and through which they must struggle to achieve their ends. Some sense of this can be gained by noting the extreme care with which Ibsen creates and places on his stage such ordinary objects as stoves, pictures, bric-a-brac shelves, and tables. He is not merely constructing a typical Norwegian room in an upper middle-class home of the late nineteenth century—any property-room man could do this. He is arranging his set to symbolize the social and material world in which his characters are so trapped and deadened. Overstuffed chairs which seem to swallow up the character who sits in them, heavy draperies which blot the outside light, furniture which in its very weight and richness seems to deny the existence of the spirit, and in its cluttered placement on the stage constantly interrupts the free movement of the characters who try to stride directly and purposefully through it. The movement of Ibsen's characters has been described as an attempted dance "the opening steps of which are constantly being broken off and replaced by something else"[5] as the character encounters some solid object such as a table, a bookcase, a paper, a photograph album, an armchair, or a stove. This happens constantly in Ibsen's plays, and can be seen to advantage in *Ghosts*, where the heavy, dark rooms of the Alving house are but the most solid manifestation of the social and material facts, the realities, which everywhere impede Mrs. Alving in her "dance" toward truth and the "joy of life." Just as the furniture impedes her free physical movements on stage, so those other more sinister realities which the play portrays—the smoke of Oswald's pipe, his taste for liquor, Engstrand's carelessness with matches, the pressures of society for conformity, and, finally, the inherited syphilis—impede her efforts to be done with the Alving inheritance and the ghosts of old ideas and old crimes. Ibsen was fascinated with the way in which social and material realities, realized by his set, channel and thwart the human spirit with what very nearly amounts to malevolence, and his realistic set is always a representation of the social and material prison in which the free spirit struggles. Chekov, another master of the realistic style, was peculiarly interested in the indifference of the material world to men and their clownish clumsiness in trying to deal with it. *The Cherry Orchard* opens in a realistic Russian room, and within the first five minutes of the play two of the characters demonstrate again and again their inability to deal with the simplest facts of reality: one falls asleep over a book and fails to meet a train he had sat up purposely to meet; another enters with a vase of flowers, which he drops, and bumps into a chair—all this in new boots which he can't keep from squeaking. Throughout the play the characters show in a variety of ways their utter helplessness in dealing with the solid facts of life—with the furniture, frost, gravity, time, and death. In the end all that they have valued, all that is focused in the delicate, fragile cherry orchard, goes down before the indifferent processes of nature, just as their shins are broken by indifferent tables and their backsides by indifferent floors.

Once it is understood that the realistic set, and the realistic style in general, has been used to symbolize the solidity of the material and social worlds in which modern man is isolated, the way is clear to understand in still another way the oneness of the modern theater. While realism remains the dominant style, from the time of Ibsen to the present there have been a great many experiments in other directions, and frequently an author will fluctuate from style to style, as Strindberg did. In general, these experiments constituted a rejection

[5] Daniel Haakonsen, "Ibsen the Realist," in *Discussions of Henrik Ibsen,* ed. by J. W. McFarlane (Boston, 1962), p. 71.

of realism's basic tenet that the stage should be set to look like the familiar face of the everyday world, that the characters should speak a prose something like that spoken on the streets, and that their motives and actions should be much like those we normally think we see daily. But a large number of playwrights have constructed their plays on the premise that the function of drama, or any other art, is not to hold the mirror up to objective nature, but rather to provide an "image" of the world, to show it as it appears to our imagination rather than to our senses. For example, a realistic playwright who wished to show the inability of human beings to communicate with one another would create a group of characters moving around a conventional drawing room and talking in a normal way; but as they moved toward one another the furniture would get in their way, as they talked their speech would trail away in nervousness or ineptitude, they would be unable to find appropriate words, and they would express incredulity or fail to understand what another said. The result of their failure to communicate directly would be that the unions— love affairs, business agreements, marriages, friendships—which they had hoped to achieve would trail away into nothing, like their words and gestures.

An expressionistic playwright might go to work directly to express the same theme. He might have his characters pour out spates of nonsense, words without meaning, while at the same time they maintained grammatical form and looked as if they understood the nonsense uttered by others and expected their own to be understood. He might fill the stage with empty chairs, as Ionesco does, and have the characters babble on thinking they are talking to real people sitting in them. As a climax Ionesco has a dumb and illiterate orator deliver some "great" message to these same empty chairs. Writing of this latter kind has had many names, but it can most simply be called expressionism, the style in which the artist dispenses with probability in order to express directly his sense of life in images. Poetry is the most familiar form of expressionism, and all expressionistic drama is in some sense an extension of poetry, depending as it does on visual metaphors to establish its meaning. Man ceases to be *like* some strange monster and is actually presented as a rhinoceros or a bug; life ceases to be *like* a wearying circle and is presented as an endless bicycle race in which characters peddle faster and faster to win prizes which are never awarded.

Expressionism existed in the early years of the modern theater with the symbolic plays of Ibsen, the "dream plays" of Strindberg, and the strange subjective plays of Maeterlinck; but since about 1920 it has become much more prominent. Pirandello, Cocteau, O'Neill, and the postwar German expressionists such as Brecht were but the beginnings of a tide that has run ever more strongly down to the plays of Beckett, Albee, Ionesco, Genet, Arrabal, and many others who write for the theater of the absurd. Even the realistic drama has been strongly influenced by expressionism, and the plays of such realists as Shaw, Sartre, Miller, and Williams have been affected. Expressionism has, in fact, been so powerful that many have argued that we have not one theater but two: the theater of realism, which was dominant in the years 1870-1920, and the expressionistic or absurd theater, from about 1920 to the present. The fact that the physical theater with its symbolic arrangement of the world has not changed essentially argues against such a division, but it can be demonstrated in another way that our expressionistic drama is but an intensified, a more openly poetic, form of the realistic drama which preceded and still accompanies it.

Six Characters in Search of an Author is, in my opinion, the pivotal play in the modern theater. It reveals in the starkest terms possible the meaning of the realistic drama of Ibsen, Strindberg, and Chekov which leads into it and the theater of the absurd which leads out of it. The earlier realistic plays depict man as caught in an alien and hostile environment with which he struggles to achieve his peculiarly human aims with only limited success. Pirandello picked up and intensified this theme, but he perceived that the full meaning of this "human condition" could best be dramatized by showing man as trapped in the theater itself. Given the premises stated by the modern theater, that the world which appears within the illuminated box has meaning only in its own terms, that it is not backed up by metaphysical realities existing outside and beyond it, it follows that the lives of men and the events of history have a stagelike or theatrical quality. We are but actors for a brief time on the stage of the world, and our actions and creations endure for only a moment and pass on into history, just as theater sets go to property rooms and plays into anthologies or oblivion. Men are no more than characters in a play, or not even so much, since characters are at least permanently whatever they are, while real men are forever changing. Yet in this world which resembles a theater men struggle desperately to express themselves, to find for themselves a play (or a life) which will reveal their true natures adequately and give their lives a satisfactory shape, as a skillful playwright does his plot. But where the heroes of the earlier realistic drama sought to achieve some such realistic aim as to be rid of the ghosts of old ideas or to control the future as they wished, Pirandello *goes to the root of things* and shows his heroes *trying to be in a play*. And where the earlier heroes found their efforts thwarted by reality, by the nature of things represented by the solid, realistic set, Pirandello's heroes find themselves thwarted by the theater of realism. If Epihodov in *The Cherry Orchard* cannot cross a room without bumping into a table, or Mrs. Alving in *Ghosts* finds herself so trammeled by the demands of society that she can act only in certain accepted ways, the characters of Pirandello's play discover that the realistic theater interferes with and finally prohibits any expression of what they conceive to be their full reality, their true nature. For the step-daughter the presence of a yellow couch in the room where she was nearly seduced is essential, and for the father it is absolutely necessary that he be given time to explain his very complex motives, but the prop room in the theater has only a green couch, and the requirement that the plot continue to move does not allow the father time to explain himself. At every turn the "realism" of the theater denies the "reality" of the characters.

Pirandello has stated in expressionistic terms the same conflict between *realism* and *reality* which Ibsen, Chekov, and Strindberg stated in realistic terms. In so doing, he clarified the meaning of the realistic plays and showed the way to a host of later expressionistic plays in which reality is presented as some bizarre form of prison with man at once a heroic and a ludicrous struggler. It may seem a very long way from a realistic play like *Ghosts* to an expressionistic play like *The Ghost Sonata,* but the strange room in Strindberg's play with its mummy, its death screen, its cook who steals all the goodness out of the broth, and the ink pot which always spills is the same place as that room where Mrs. Alving is locked with her hopelessly insane son. And the flowering hyacinth in the conservatory is but a visual expression of the same transcendent hope which drives Mrs. Alving and her son Oswald toward the light and "joy of life." The difference between the two plays is that in the expressionistic *Ghost Sonata* the situation is expressed through a variety of unusual and bizarre stage images which combine to suggest the grotesque and killing restraints society and life impose on man, while in *Ghosts* the terror of the human condition is perhaps blurred in one way and heightened in another, by being presented in the familiar surroundings of the bourgeois parlor where everything seems so normal and natural.

While each modern set may reflect reality from a particular vantage point, they all seem to say that man finds the material universe they represent to be antagonistic to his transcendent hopes and the aspirations of his spirit. In other words, where man is sustained and his social world substantiated by the great symbols of the Greek and Elizabethan stages, man on the modern stage finds himself hemmed in and opposed by the symbols of ours. The sense of entrapment in society and nature which the sets and arrangement of our theater express is, of course, a focused form of a general sense of entrapment in nature and time which has grown steadily in Western culture in the nineteenth and twentieth centuries. There is no need to recapitulate the history of thought since the Romantic revolution, but reference to a few of the leading ideas will serve to make the point that our theater stands as close to the center of our culture as the Greek and Elizabethan theaters apparently did to theirs.

Once faith in a supernatural order weakened under the pressure of scientific rationalism, and the belief in an established hierarchical society began to break up under the attack of democratic revolutions and the doctrine of absolute equality, individual man was freed to face nature, society, and himself, and to make them into what he wanted them to be. Or so it seemed. Yet each great discovery of the free, inquiring mind, while it promised control over the accidents of nature and history, turned out, paradoxically, to show more clearly the isolation of man in time and nature. Darwin's great statement on the origin, differentiation, and evolution of the species cut man adrift from his metaphysical origins and placed him in a world where survival belongs to the strong, the ruthless, and the biologically lucky; not to the moral and the just. Marx's investigations of society revealed economic man, the producer and the buyer of goods and services, who bands together with other men only for his own economic advantage and who is caught in a historical movement which pits the have-nots against the haves. Freud's explorations of the mind seemed to extend nature's tyranny over man inward, making him the very nearly helpless victim of unconscious drives and libidinal forces, an automaton dancing to a tune called by internal forces or a compulsive neurotic twisting into strange shapes in the attempt to repress powers he is not even aware of repressing. Physical science broke up the familiar face of creative nature, with its traditional intimations of some orderly, regenerative force, into quantities which can only be measured mathematically and into electrified particles. The last familiar markers disappeared when the theory of relativity told us that speed and direction existed only in relation to where we stood.

All these discoveries can be viewed optimistically, of course, and were so viewed by their discoverers, as demonstrations of the power of the human mind to uncover the truth of things and thus lay the grounds for some understanding of the world and life. To believe in this way is to believe in progress. But it is possible to believe in the necessity of knowing these hard facts and at the same time to recognize that each of them is frightening because it imprisons us in a nature which limits and denies those essential qualities which we feel to be uniquely ours:

in theological terms, our souls; in humanistic terms, our true natures as men. If we are no more than strugglers for survival adapting to a constantly changing environment; exploiters or exploited caught up in a predetermined class struggle for control of the means of production; walking instruments of inescapable psychological forces, chemical reactions, and social conditioning; if we are all these in a universe we cannot even see truly, where there are no absolute directions or movements, how are we to validate our consciousness, our suffering, our sense of dignity, our demand that life have meaning, our ability to look at all the forces which control us and still withdraw into some area peculiarly ourselves?

For some, these last are simply illusions, fostered by outmoded ways of thinking. For them, the sooner man accepts himself as an object moved about by an interaction of forces and natural laws, the better. But our dramatists have never shared this view. The modern theater has not denied the existence of the deterministic and morally irresponsible universe; rather it has accepted it and embodied it in the construction of its stage, in its sets, and in its plays, where the standard plot shows the entrapment of man in history, society, economics, psychology, and in some form of environment. A history of the modern drama could be written using scenes of entrapment ranging from Old Firs locked in the dying house of *The Cherry Orchard,* or the captain in *The Father* sitting still while his old nurse slips the straitjacket on him, to Mother Courage harnessed to her wagon and Blanche du Bois in *Streetcar Named Desire* trying desperately to call a number she doesn't know for help, while Stanley Kowalski stands grinning in his red pajamas, blocking the door. But two scenes will do to make the point here in its largest and its smallest forms.

The first is the concluding scene of *Ghosts.* Throughout the play Mrs. Alving and her son Oswald have struggled to free themselves from the gray, dim world forced on them by society, nature, and heredity. Using the play's chief symbols, one could say they have struggled to escape from the darkness into the truth of light. But they thought, like the great rebels and formulators of truth in the nineteenth century, that light and truth would bring "joy of life." When Mrs. Alving rejects the demands of society that unpleasant truths be hidden under a cover of well-seeming, and tells her son that his sickness and the drunken debauchery of his father were the results of heredity and an unfavorable environment, not of moral failing, she breaks into the world of truth. But the truth proves unendurable. Oswald, who is in the last stages of syphilis, goes insane before her eyes, his fear unassuaged and his madness no less terrible for being not his own fault but the result of his heredity. The son and mother stand at last in the full light of truth, and as the sun rises, shining on the icy peaks far above the dark valley in which they stand, the insane son's cry, "Mother, give me the sun," distills modern man's sense of isolation and helplessness in the midst of alien nature. Clarity of vision reveals only the desperateness of the situation in which we long like children for light and heat which originate ninety million miles away and send only their dimmest emanations into our homes.

The other scene is from Lorca's *Blood Wedding,* in which the violent, uncontrollable power of blood and passion, represented by the horse, has destroyed an entire family and wasted a country. Her husband and son dead, a mother sits wondering how it can be that so small a thing as a knife, a mere piece of steel, can destroy so great a thing as a man:

> Neighbors: with a knife,
> with a little knife,
> on their appointed day, between two and three,
> these two men killed each other for love.
> With a knife,
> with a tiny knife
> that barely fits the hand,
> but that slides in clear
> through the astonished flesh
> and stops at the place
> where trembles, enmeshed,
> the dark root of a scream.

There is no question in our theater that life is subject to objects so small as a knife in such strange places as "between two and three," but the peasant mother's astonishment that this is so is an astonishment that has kept our theater alive.

When William Butler Yeats first saw a performance of *Ghosts,* he remarked:

All the characters seemed to be less than life-size; the stage, though it was but the little Royalty stage, seemed larger than I had ever seen it. Little whimpering puppets moved here and there in the middle of that great abyss. Why did they not speak with louder voices or move with freer gestures? What was it that weighed upon their souls perpetually? Certainly they were all in prison, and yet there was no prison.[6]

Yeats is being disingenuous here, for he knew very well what the prison was—his poetry is a record of a heroic struggle with it—and he knew that it is as real as the stage says it is. But he was right in one way

---

[6] W. B. Yeats, "The Irish Dramatic Movement," *Plays and Controversies* (New York, 1924), p. 122.

about the figures in this prison: they are small and ineffective. It is a commonplace of criticism that our dramatic heroes are but shadows of those of previous days. The figures of Greek tragedy were demigods, titans, founders of kingdoms, and rulers of great cities. When they, or the kings and queens of Elizabethan drama, rose or fell, kingdoms rose or fell with them, and all mankind shared in their fortunes. But the heroes of modern tragedy are neither so great nor so powerful in the scheme of things. They are likely to be a group of ineffective, middle-class Russians in some isolated country house, a salesman who tries to sell himself in a territory where no one wants to buy, two tramps waiting on a bare stage, an old woman trying to pull a tattered wagon about, or two old people who think they have something of importance to say to the world but don't really know what it is they have to say. Where the fate of kingdoms turned on the actions of earlier heroes, much less is involved in the actions of our heroes: they try to save a cherry orchard, pay for a house and raise their children, wait for someone who will probably never come, or just find someone who will be kind to them.

As their statures and their aims are diminished, so are their voices. Playwrights are frequently exhorted by modern critics to give their characters poetry, and some of our dramatists have tried, without much success. A type of realistic prose, a heightened version of the speech of everyday life, seems to be the most congenial form of speech for our heroes. One of the principal themes of modern drama has been the inability of language to convey the full meanings desired by the speakers, and this theme has been carried in large part by the characters' struggle with the flat, realistic prose they most often speak. I am not arguing that Ibsen or Chekov could have written poetry of a quality equal to Shakespeare's had they wished to do so; rather I am suggesting that these and other dramatists of our theater were led away from attempting dramatic poetry of the older variety by the nature of their theme, the isolation of man in a universe where all his environment, including the very language he speaks, thwarts his efforts to express what he feels to be his essential self. Behind the mumbling, inarticulate dying voices of Chekov's characters there is a passion and depth of feeling something like Romeo's or Hamlet's, but these feelings are first qualified and lose their force in the mind and are then finally dissipated in the awkward, flat phrases which are the only language available to modern man. The failure of language to express the fullness of self which is implicit in the realistic drama becomes explicit in the expressionistic drama—*The Chairs, Zoo Story*—where we are shown characters who cannot convey any sense of their own reality by words, who babble on in long speeches which sound very serious but mean nothing, who spout open nonsense, or who stand mutely on stage.

But with all the limitations which are imposed on him on the modern stage, man has not given up the struggle on that stage and accepted the role of a machine moved in a predictable manner by a variety of unchanging forces, which his world tries to force on him. No matter how close the darkness may creep toward him—and it has come very close in the most recent plays—he continues to occupy a place in the center of the stage and at least one light still shines on him. His desires remain "spacious." [7] Unsupported by any visible metaphysical order, thwarted by society, at odds with external nature and his own being, he still continues to act and to try to tear from the world those things without which he feels he cannot live as a human being: his freedom, his dignity, his reality. In this persistent effort he becomes one with the great strugglers of the older drama who moved toward these same goals, but his chances of success are greatly diminished. Not only is his environment more hostile, but the fact that he is a salesman or a tattered tramp, whose voice no longer fills the theater and batters at the world which denies him, suggests that his chances of success are far less than those of older heroes, and that his success or failure will not disturb the order of things greatly.

Our theater does not underestimate the dangers of the universe in which man lives, but it has not lost faith in man either. When pressed to the extremes, in the bleak place where almost everything has lost its meaning, man on the modern stage at least still waits:

What are we doing here, *that* is the question. And we are blessed in this, that we happen to know the answer. Yes, in this immense confusion one thing alone is clear. We are waiting for Godot to come—

This waiting is as likely to be the height of foolishness as the absolute of virtue: an ambiguity which haunts most actions on the modern stage. But man, no matter how tattered and inarticulate, is still *there;* he has not yet walked off and left the stage to darkness.

By no means all, or even a majority, of the plays written for the modern theater have realized the meaning implicit in that theater; but the greatest have, and the plays printed in this volume have been selected from the group which have fully exploited and enlarged that image of the human condition built into our places of dramatic performance. They are for this reason entitled to the name "Classics of

[7] "Ibsen the Realist," p. 75.

the Modern Theater." This selection has also been made to illustrate various experiments with style made by modern dramatists. The bulk of the book is given to realism, since this has been the most important single tendency in modern drama, but there are examples of the major departures from realism: poetic drama, epic theater, expressionism, and theater of the absurd. While this selection of plays may be used to illustrate the variety of styles of the modern drama, it can also be used to show the oneness of the modern theater, the continuing view of the human condition which underlies the great plays of our age. Pirandello's *Six Characters* provides the bridge between realism and the other styles, and also focuses clearly, in both realistic and expressionistic terms, the essential quality of our theater.

ALVIN B. KERNAN

New Haven, Connecticut
June, 1964

GHOSTS [1881]

by Henrik Ibsen

translated by William Archer

Characters

MRS. ALVING, *a widow*
OSWALD ALVING, *her son, an artist*
MANDERS, *the pastor of the parish*
ENGSTRAND, *a carpenter*
REGINA ENGSTRAND, *his daughter, in* MRS. ALVING'S *service*

The action takes place at MRS. ALVING'S *house on one of the larger fjords of western Norway.*

ACT ONE

Scene. A large room looking upon a garden. A door in the left-hand wall, and two in the right. In the middle of the room, a round table with chairs set about it, and books, magazines, and newspapers upon it. In the foreground on the left, a window, by which is a small sofa with a work-table in front of it. At the back the room opens into a conservatory rather smaller than the room. From the right-hand side of this a door leads to the garden. Through the large panes of glass that form the outer wall of the conservatory, a gloomy fjord landscape can be discerned, half obscured by steady rain.

ENGSTRAND *is standing close up to the garden door. His left leg is slightly deformed, and he wears a boot with a clump of wood under the sole.* REGINA, *with an empty garden-syringe in her hand, is trying to prevent his coming in.*

REGINA (*below her breath*). What is it you want? Stay where you are. The rain is dripping off you.

ENGSTRAND. God's good rain, my girl.

REGINA. The Devil's own rain, that's what it is!

ENGSTRAND. Lord, how you talk, Regina. (*Takes a few limping steps forward.*) What I wanted to tell you was this——

REGINA. Don't clump about like that, stupid! The young master is lying asleep upstairs.

ENGSTRAND. Asleep still? In the middle of the day?

REGINA. Well, it's no business of yours.

ENGSTRAND. I was out on the spree last night——

REGINA. I don't doubt it.

ENGSTRAND. Yes, we are poor weak mortals, my girl——

REGINA. We are indeed.

ENGSTRAND. —and the temptations of the world are manifold, you know—but, for all that, here I was at my work at half-past five this morning.

REGINA. Yes, yes, but make yourself scarce now. I am not going to stand here as if I had a rendezvous with you.

ENGSTRAND. As if you had a what?

REGINA. I am not going to have any one find you here: so now you know, and you can go.

ENGSTRAND (*coming a few steps nearer*). Not a bit of it! Not before we have had a little chat. This afternoon I shall have finished my job down at the school house, and I shall be off home to town by to-night's boat.

REGINA (*mutters*). Pleasant journey to you!

ENGSTRAND. Thanks, my girl. To-morrow is the opening of the Orphanage, and I expect there will be a fine kick-up here and plenty of good strong drink, don't you know. And no one shall say of Jacob Engstrand that he can't hold off when temptation comes in his way.

REGINA. Oho!

ENGSTRAND. Yes, because there will be a lot of fine folk here to-morrow. Parson Manders is expected from town, too.

REGINA. What is more, he's coming to-day.

ENGSTRAND. There you are! And I'm going to be precious careful he doesn't have anything to say against me, do you see?

REGINA. Oh, that's your game, is it?

ENGSTRAND. What do you mean?

REGINA (*with a significant look at him*). What is it you want to humbug Mr. Manders out of, this time?

ENGSTRAND. Sh! Sh! Are you crazy? Do you suppose *I* would want to humbug Mr. Manders? No, no—. Mr. Manders has always been too kind a friend for me to do that. But what I wanted to talk to you about, was my going back home to-night.

REGINA. The sooner you go, the better I shall be pleased.

ENGSTRAND. Yes, only I want to take you with me, Regina.

REGINA (*open-mouthed*). You want to take me——? What did you say?

ENGSTRAND. I want to take you home with me, I said.

REGINA (*contemptuously*). You will never get me home with you.

ENGSTRAND. Ah, we shall see about that.

REGINA. Yes, you can be quite certain we *shall* see about that. I, who have been brought up by a lady like Mrs. Alving?—I, who have been treated almost as if I were her own child?—do you suppose I am going home with *you?*—to such a house as yours? Not likely!

ENGSTRAND. What the devil do you mean? Are you setting yourself up against your father, you hussy?

REGINA (*mutters, without looking at him*). You have often told me I was none of yours.

ENGSTRAND. Bah!—why do you want to pay any attention to that?

REGINA. Haven't you many and many a time abused me and called me a——? For shame!

ENGSTRAND. I'll swear I never used such an ugly word.

REGINA. Oh, it doesn't matter what word you used.

ENGSTRAND. Besides, that was only when I was a bit fuddled—hm! Temptations are manifold in this world, Regina.

REGINA. Ugh!

ENGSTRAND. And it was when your mother was in a nasty temper. I had to find some way of getting my knife into her, my girl. She was always so precious genteel. (*Mimicking her*) "Let go, Jacob! Let me be! Please to remember that I was three years with the Alvings at Rosenvold, and they were people who went to Court!" (*Laughs.*) Bless my soul, she never could forget that Captain Alving got a Court appointment while she was in service here.

REGINA. Poor mother—you worried her into her grave pretty soon.

ENGSTRAND (*shrugging his shoulders*). Of course, of course; I have got to take the blame for everything.

REGINA (*beneath her breath, as she turns away*). Ugh—that leg, too!

ENGSTRAND. What are you saying, my girl?

REGINA. Pied de mouton.

ENGSTRAND. Is that English?

REGINA. Yes.

ENGSTRAND. You have had a good education out here, and no mistake; and it may stand you in good stead now, Regina.

REGINA (*after a short silence*). And what was it you wanted me to come to town for?

ENGSTRAND. Need you ask why a father wants his only child? Ain't I a poor lonely widower?

REGINA. Oh, don't come to me with that tale. Why do you want me to go?

ENGSTRAND. Well, I must tell you I am thinking of taking up a new line now.

REGINA (*whistles*). You have tried that so often—but it has always proved a fool's errand.

ENGSTRAND. Ah, but this time you will just see, Regina! Strike me dead if——

REGINA (*stamping her feet*). Stop swearing!

ENGSTRAND. Sh! Sh!—you're quite right, my girl, quite right! What I wanted to say was only this, that I have put by a tidy penny out of what I have made by working at this new Orphanage up here.

REGINA. Have you? All the better for you.

ENGSTRAND. What is there for a man to spend his money on, out here in the country?

REGINA. Well, what then?

ENGSTRAND. Well, you see, I thought of putting the money into something that would pay. I thought of some kind of an eating-house for seafaring folk——

REGINA. Heavens!

ENGSTRAND. Oh, a high-class eating-house, of course,—not a pigsty for common sailors. Damn it, no; it would be a place ships' captains and first mates would come to; really good sort of people, you know.

REGINA. And what should I——?

ENGSTRAND. You would help there. But only to make a show, you know. You wouldn't find it hard work, I can promise you, my girl. You should do exactly as you liked.

REGINA. Oh, yes, quite so!

ENGSTRAND. But we must have some women in the house; that is as clear as daylight. Because in the evening we must make the place a little attractive—some singing and dancing, and that sort of thing. Remember they are seafolk—wayfarers on the waters of life! (*Coming nearer to her*) Now don't be a fool and stand in your own way, Regina. What good are you going to do here? Will this education, that your mistress has paid for, be of any use? You are to look after the children in the new Home, I hear. Is that the sort of work for you? Are you so frightfully anxious to go and wear out your health and strength for the sake of these dirty brats?

REGINA. No, if things were to go as I want them to, then——. Well, it may happen; who knows? It may happen!

ENGSTRAND. What may happen?

REGINA. Never you mind. Is it much that you have put by, up here?

ENGSTRAND. Taking it all round, I should say about forty or fifty pounds.

REGINA. That's not so bad.

ENGSTRAND. It's enough to make a start with, my girl.

REGINA. Don't you mean to give me any of the money?

ENGSTRAND. No, I'm hanged if I do.

REGINA. Don't you mean to send me as much as a dress-length of stuff, just for once?

ENGSTRAND. Come and live in the town with me and you shall have plenty of dresses.

REGINA. Pooh!—I can get that much for myself, if I have a mind to.

ENGSTRAND. But it's far better to have a father's guiding hand, Regina. Just now I can get a nice house in Little Harbour Street. They don't want much money down for it—and we could make it like a sort of seamen's home, don't you know.

REGINA. But I have no intention of living with you! I have nothing whatever to do with you. So now, be off!

ENGSTRAND. You wouldn't be living with me long, my girl. No such

luck—not if you knew how to play your cards. Such a fine wench
as you have grown this last year or two——

REGINA. Well——?

ENGSTRAND. It wouldn't be very long before some first mate came
along—or perhaps a captain.

REGINA. I don't mean to marry a man of that sort. Sailors have no
savoir-vivre.

ENGSTRAND. What haven't they got?

REGINA. I know what sailors are, I tell you. They aren't the sort of
people to marry.

ENGSTRAND. Well, don't bother about marrying them. You can make
it pay just as well. (*More confidentially*) That fellow—the Englishman—the one with the yacht—he gave seventy pounds, he
did; and she wasn't a bit prettier than you.

REGINA (*advancing towards him*). Get out!

ENGSTRAND (*stepping back*). Here! here!—you're not going to hit me,
I suppose?

REGINA. Yes! If you talk like that of mother, I *will* hit you. Get out, I
tell you! (*Pushes him up to the garden door.*) And don't bang the
doors. Young Mr. Alving——

ENGSTRAND. Is asleep—I know. It's funny how anxious you are about
young Mr. Alving. (*In a lower tone*) Oho! is it possible that it is
he that——?

REGINA. Get out, and be quick about it! Your wits are wandering, my
good man. No, don't go that way; Mr. Manders is just coming
along. Be off down the kitchen stairs.

ENGSTRAND (*moving towards the right*). Yes, yes—all right. But have
a bit of a chat with him that's coming along. He's the chap to
tell you what a child owes to its father. For I am your father,
anyway, you know. I can prove it by the Register.

(*He goes out through the farther door which* REGINA *has opened.
She shuts it after him, looks hastily at herself in the mirror, fans
herself with her handkerchief and sets her collar straight, then
busies herself with the flowers.* MANDERS *enters the conservatory
through the garden door. He wears an overcoat, carries an umbrella and has a small travelling-bag slung over his shoulder on
a strap.*)

MANDERS. Good morning, Miss Engstrand.

REGINA (*turning round with a look of pleased surprise*). Oh, Mr.
Manders, good morning. The boat is in, then?

MANDERS. Just in. (*Comes into the room.*) It is most tiresome, this
rain every day.

REGINA (*following him in*). It's a splendid rain for the farmers, Mr. Manders.

MANDERS. Yes, you are quite right. We town-folk think so little about that. (*Begins to take off his overcoat.*)

REGINA. Oh, let me help you. That's it. Why, how wet it is. I will hang it up in the hall. Give me your umbrella, too; I will leave it open, so that it will dry.

(*She goes out with the things by the farther door on the right.* MANDERS *lays his bag and his hat down on a chair.* REGINA *re-enters.*)

MANDERS. Ah, it's very pleasant to get indoors. Well, is everything going on well here?

REGINA. Yes, thanks.

MANDERS. Properly busy, though, I expect, getting ready for to-morrow?

REGINA. Oh, yes, there is plenty to do.

MANDERS. And Mrs. Alving is at home, I hope?

REGINA. Yes, she is. She has just gone upstairs to take the young master his chocolate.

MANDERS. Tell me—I heard down at the pier that Oswald had come back.

REGINA. Yes, he came the day before yesterday. We didn't expect him till to-day.

MANDERS. Strong and well, I hope?

REGINA. Yes, thank you, well enough. But dreadfully tired after his journey. He came straight from Paris without a stop—I mean, he came all the way without breaking his journey. I fancy he is having a sleep now, so we must talk a little bit more quietly, if you don't mind.

MANDERS. All right, we will be very quiet.

REGINA (*while she moves an armchair up to the table*). Please sit down, Mr. Manders, and make yourself at home. (*He sits down; she puts a footstool under his feet.*) There! Is that comfortable?

MANDERS. Thank you, thank you. That is most comfortable. (*Looks at her.*) I'll tell you what, Miss Engstrand, I certainly think you have grown since I saw you last.

REGINA. Do you think so? Mrs. Alving says, too, that I have developed.

MANDERS. Developed? Well, perhaps a little—just suitably.

(*A short pause.*)

REGINA. Shall I tell Mrs. Alving you are here?

MANDERS. Thanks, there is no hurry, my dear child.—Now tell me, Regina my dear, how has your father been getting on here?

REGINA. Thank you, Mr. Manders, he is getting on pretty well.

MANDERS. He came to see me, the last time he was in town.

REGINA. Did he? He is always so glad when he can have a chat with you.

MANDERS. And I suppose you have seen him pretty regularly every day?

REGINA. I? Oh, yes, I do—whenever I have time, that is to say.

MANDERS. Your father has not a very strong character, Miss Engstrand. He sadly needs a guiding hand.

REGINA. Yes, I can quite believe that.

MANDERS. He needs someone with him that he can cling to, someone whose judgment he can rely on. He acknowledged that freely himself, the last time he came up to see me.

REGINA. Yes, he has said something of the same sort to me. But I don't know whether Mrs. Alving could do without me—most of all just now, when we have the new Orphanage to see about. And I should be dreadfully unwilling to leave Mrs. Alving, too; she has always been so good to me.

MANDERS. But a daughter's duty, my good child——. Naturally we should have to get your mistress' consent first.

REGINA. Still I don't know whether it would be quite the thing, at my age, to keep house for a single man.

MANDERS. What!! My dear Miss Engstrand, it is your own father we are speaking of!

REGINA. Yes, I dare say, but still——. Now, if it were in a good house and with a real gentleman——

MANDERS. But, my dear Regina——

REGINA. ——one whom I could feel an affection for, and really feel in the position of a daughter to——

MANDERS. Come, come—my dear good child——

REGINA. I should like very much to live in town. Out here it is terribly lonely; and you know yourself, Mr. Manders, what it is to be alone in the world. And, though I say it, I really am both capable and willing. Don't you know any place that would be suitable for me, Mr. Manders?

MANDERS. I? No, indeed I don't.

REGINA. But, dear Mr. Manders—at any rate don't forget me, in case——

MANDERS (*getting up*). No, I won't forget you, Miss Engstrand.

REGINA. Because, if I——

MANDERS. Perhaps you will be so kind as to let Mrs. Alving know I am here?

REGINA. I will fetch her at once, Mr. Manders.

(*Goes out to the left.* MANDERS *walks up and down the room once or twice, stands for a moment at the farther end of the room with his hands behind his back and looks out into the garden. Then he comes back to the table, takes up a book and looks at the title page, gives a start and looks at some of the others.*)

MANDERS. Hm!—Really!

(MRS. ALVING *comes in by the door on the left. She is followed by* REGINA, *who goes out again at once through the nearer door on the right.*)

MRS. ALVING (*holding out her hand*). I am very glad to see you, Mr. Manders.

MANDERS. How do you do, Mrs. Alving? Here I am, as I promised.

MRS. ALVING. Always punctual!

MANDERS. Indeed, I was hard put to it to get away. What with vestry meetings and committees——

MRS. ALVING. It was all the kinder of you to come in such good time; we can settle our business before dinner. But where is your luggage?

MANDERS (*quickly*). My things are down at the village shop. I am going to sleep there to-night.

MRS. ALVING (*repressing a smile*). Can't I really persuade you to stay the night here this time?

MANDERS. No, no; many thanks all the same; I will put up there, as usual. It is so handy for getting on board the boat again.

MRS. ALVING. Of course you shall do as you please. But it seems to me quite another thing, now we are two old people——

MANDERS. Ha! ha! You will have your joke! And it's natural you should be in high spirits today—first of all there is the great event to-morrow, and also you have got Oswald home.

MRS. ALVING. Yes, am I not a lucky woman? It is more than two years since he was home last, and he has promised to stay the whole winter with me.

MANDERS. Has he, really? That is very nice and filial of him, because there must be many more attractions in his life in Rome or in Paris, I should think.

MRS. ALVING. Yes, but he has his mother here, you see. Bless the dear boy, he has got a corner in his heart for his mother still.

MANDERS. Oh, it would be very sad if absence and preoccupation with such a thing as Art were to dull the natural affections.

MRS. ALVING. It would, indeed. But there is no fear of that with him,

I am glad to say. I am quite curious to see if you recognize him
again. He will be down directly; he is just lying down for a little
on the sofa upstairs. But do sit down, my dear friend.

MANDERS. Thank you. You are sure I am not disturbing you?

MRS. ALVING. Of course not. (*She sits down at the table.*)

MANDERS. Good. Then I will show you——. (*He goes to the chair
where his bag is lying and takes a packet of papers from it, then
sits down at the opposite side of the table and looks for a
clear space to put the papers down.*) Now first of all, here is—
(*breaks off*). Tell me, Mrs. Alving, what are these books doing
here?

MRS. ALVING. These books? I am reading them.

MANDERS. Do you read this sort of thing?

MRS. ALVING. Certainly I do.

MANDERS. Do you feel any the better or the happier for reading books
of this kind?

MRS. ALVING. I think it makes me, as it were, more self-reliant.

MANDERS. That is remarkable. But why?

MRS. ALVING. Well, they give me an explanation or a confirmation of
lots of different ideas that have come into my own mind. But
what surprises me, Mr. Manders, is that, properly speaking, there
is nothing at all new in these books. There is nothing more in
them than what most people think and believe. The only thing
is that most people either take no account of it or won't admit it
to themselves.

MANDERS. But, good heavens, do you seriously think that most people——?

MRS. ALVING. Yes, indeed, I do.

MANDERS. But not here in the country at any rate? Not here amongst
people like ourselves?

MRS. ALVING. Yes, amongst people like ourselves too.

MANDERS. Well, really, I must say——!

MRS. ALVING. But what is the particular objection that you have to
these books?

MANDERS. What objection? You surely don't suppose that I take any
particular interest in such productions?

MRS. ALVING. In fact, you don't know anything about what you are
denouncing?

MANDERS. I have read quite enough about these books to disapprove
of them.

MRS. ALVING. Yes, but your own opinion——

MANDERS. My dear Mrs. Alving, there are many occasions in life
when one has to rely on the opinion of others. That is the way

in this world, and it is quite right that it should be so. What would become of society otherwise?

MRS. ALVING. Well, you may be right.

MANDERS. Apart from that, naturally I don't deny that literature of this kind may have a considerable attraction. And I cannot blame you, either, for wishing to make yourself acquainted with the intellectual tendencies which I am told are at work in the wider world in which you have allowed your son to wander for so long. But——

MRS. ALVING. But——?

MANDERS (*lowering his voice*). But one doesn't talk about it, Mrs. Alving. One certainly is not called upon to account to every one for what one reads or thinks in the privacy of one's own room.

MRS. ALVING. Certainly not. I quite agree with you.

MANDERS. Just think of the consideration you owe to this Orphanage, which you decided to build at a time when your thoughts on such subjects were very different from what they are now—as far as I am able to judge.

MRS. ALVING. Yes, I freely admit that. But it was about the Orphanage——

MANDERS. It was about the Orphanage we were going to talk; quite so. Well—walk warily, dear Mrs. Alving! And now let us turn to the business in hand. (*Opens an envelope and takes out some papers.*) You see these?

MRS. ALVING. The deeds?

MANDERS. Yes, the whole lot—and everything in order. I can tell you it has been no easy matter to get them in time. I had positively to put pressure on the authorities; they are almost painfully conscientious when it is a question of settling property. But here they are at last. (*Turns over the papers.*) Here is the deed of conveyance of that part of the Rosenvold estate known as the Solvik property, together with the buildings newly erected thereon—the school, the masters' houses, and the chapel. And here is the legal sanction for the statutes of the institution. Here, you see—(*reads*) "Statutes for the Captain Alving Orphanage."

MRS. ALVING (*after a long look at the papers*). That seems all in order.

MANDERS. I thought "Captain" was the better title to use, rather than your husband's Court title of "Chamberlain." "Captain" seems less ostentatious.

MRS. ALVING. Yes, yes; just as you think best.

MANDERS. And here is the certificate for the investment of the capital in the bank, the interest being earmarked for the current expenses of the Orphanage.

MRS. ALVING. Many thanks; but I think it will be most convenient if you will kindly take charge of them.

MANDERS. With pleasure. I think it will be best to leave the money in the bank for the present. The interest is not very high, it is true; four per cent at six months' call. Later on, if we can find some good mortgage—of course it must be a first mortgage and on unexceptionable security—we can consider the matter further.

MRS. ALVING. Yes, yes, my dear Mr. Manders, you know best about all that.

MANDERS. I will keep my eye on it, anyway. But there is one thing in connection with it that I have often meant to ask you about.

MRS. ALVING. What is that?

MANDERS. Shall we insure the buildings, or not?

MRS. ALVING. Of course we must insure them.

MANDERS. Ah, but wait a moment, dear lady. Let us look into the matter a little more closely.

MRS. ALVING. Everything of mine is insured—the house and its contents, my livestock—everything.

MANDERS. Naturally. They are your own property. I do exactly the same, of course. But this, you see, is quite a different case. The Orphanage is, so to speak, dedicated to higher uses.

MRS. ALVING. Certainly, but——

MANDERS. As far as I am personally concerned, I can conscientiously say that I don't see the smallest objection to our insuring ourselves against all risks.

MRS. ALVING. That is exactly what I think.

MANDERS. But what about the opinion of the people hereabouts?

MRS. ALVING. Their opinion——?

MANDERS. Is there any considerable body of opinion here—opinion of some account, I mean—that might take exception to it?

MRS. ALVING. What, exactly, do you mean by opinion of some account?

MANDERS. Well, I was thinking particularly of persons of such independent and influential position that one could hardly refuse to attach weight to their opinion.

MRS. ALVING. There are a certain number of such people here, who might perhaps take exception to it if we——

MANDERS. That's just it, you see. In town there are lots of them. All my fellow-clergymen's congregations, for instance! It would be so extremely easy for them to interpret it as meaning that neither you nor I had a proper reliance on Divine protection.

MRS. ALVING. But as far as you are concerned, my dear friend, you have at all events the consciousness that——

MANDERS. Yes, I know, I know; my own mind is quite easy about it, it is true. But we should not be able to prevent a wrong and injurious interpretation of our action. And that sort of thing, moreover, might very easily end in exercising a hampering influence on the work of the Orphanage.

MRS. ALVING. Oh, well, if that is likely to be the effect of it——

MANDERS. Nor can I entirely overlook the difficult—indeed, I may say, painful—position I might possibly be placed in. In the best circles in town the matter of this Orphanage is attracting a great deal of attention. Indeed the Orphanage is to some extent built for the benefit of the town too, and it is to be hoped that it may result in the lowering of our poor-rate by a considerable amount. But as I have been your adviser in the matter and have taken charge of the business side of it, I should be afraid that it would be I that spiteful persons would attack first of all——

MRS. ALVING. Yes, you ought not to expose yourself to that.

MANDERS. Not to mention the attacks that would undoubtedly be made upon me in certain newspapers and reviews——

MRS. ALVING. Say no more about it, dear Mr. Manders; that quite decides it.

MANDERS. Then you don't wish it to be insured?

MRS. ALVING. No, we will give up the idea.

MANDERS (*leaning back in his chair*). But suppose, now, that some accident happened—one can never tell—would you be prepared to make good the damage?

MRS. ALVING. No; I tell you quite plainly I would not do so under any circumstances.

MANDERS. Still, you know, Mrs. Alving—after all, it is a serious responsibility that we are taking upon ourselves.

MRS. ALVING. But do you think we can do otherwise?

MANDERS. No, that's just it. We really can't do otherwise. We ought not to expose ourselves to a mistaken judgment; and we have no right to do anything that will scandalize the community.

MRS. ALVING. You ought not to, as a clergyman, at any rate.

MANDERS. And, what is more, I certainly think that we may count upon our enterprise being attended by good fortune—indeed, that it will be under a special protection.

MRS. ALVING. Let us hope so, Mr. Manders.

MANDERS. Then we will leave it alone?

MRS. ALVING. Certainly.

MANDERS. Very good. As you wish. (*Makes a note.*) No insurance, then.

MRS. ALVING. It's a funny thing that you should just have happened to speak about that to-day——

MANDERS. I have often meant to ask you about it——

MRS. ALVING. ——because yesterday we very nearly had a fire up there.

MANDERS. Do you mean it?

MRS. ALVING. Oh, as a matter of fact it was nothing of any consequence. Some shavings in the carpenter's shop caught fire.

MANDERS. Where Engstrand works?

MRS. ALVING. Yes. They say he is often so careless with matches.

MANDERS. He has so many things on his mind, poor fellow—so many anxieties. Heaven be thanked, I am told he is really making an effort to live a blameless life.

MRS. ALVING. Really? Who told you so?

MANDERS. He assured me himself that it is so. He's a good workman, too.

MRS. ALVING. Oh, yes, when he is sober.

MANDERS. Ah, that sad weakness of his! But the pain in his poor leg often drives him to it, he tells me. The last time he was in town, I was really quite touched by him. He came to my house and thanked me so gratefully for getting him work here, where he could have the chance of being with Regina.

MRS. ALVING. He doesn't see very much of her.

MANDERS. But he assured me that he saw her every day.

MRS. ALVING. Oh well, perhaps he does.

MANDERS. He feels so strongly that he needs some one who can keep a hold on him when temptations assail him. That is the most winning thing about Jacob Engstrand; he comes to one like a helpless child and accuses himself and confesses his frailty. The last time he came and had a talk with me——. Suppose now, Mrs. Alving, that it were really a necessity of his existence to have Regina at home with him again——

MRS. ALVING (*standing up suddenly*). Regina!

MANDERS. ——you ought not to set yourself against him.

MRS. ALVING. Indeed, I set myself very definitely against that. And, besides, you know Regina is to have a post in the Orphanage.

MANDERS. But consider, after all he is her father——

MRS. ALVING. I know best what sort of father he has been to her. No, she shall never go to him with my consent.

MANDERS (*getting up*). My dear lady, don't judge so hastily. It is very sad how you misjudge poor Engstrand. One would really think you were afraid——

MRS. ALVING (*more calmly*). That is not the question. I have taken Regina into my charge, and in my charge she remains. (*Listens.*)

Hush, dear Mr. Manders, don't say any more about it. (*Her face brightens with pleasure.*) Listen! Oswald is coming downstairs. We will only think about him now.

(OSWALD ALVING, *in a light overcoat, hat in hand and smoking a big meerschaum pipe, comes in by the door on the left.*)

OSWALD (*standing in the doorway*). Oh, I beg your pardon, I thought you were in the office. (*Comes in.*) Good morning, Mr. Manders.

MANDERS (*staring at him*). Well! It's most extraordinary——

MRS. ALVING. Yes, what do you think of him, Mr. Manders?

MANDERS. I—I—no, can it possibly be——?

OSWALD. Yes, it really is the prodigal son, Mr. Manders.

MANDERS. Oh, my dear young friend——

OSWALD. Well, the son come home, then.

MRS. ALVING. Oswald is thinking of the time when you were so opposed to the idea of his being a painter.

MANDERS. We are only fallible, and many steps seem to us hazardous at first, that afterwards—(*grasps his hand*). Welcome, welcome! Really, my dear Oswald—may I still call you Oswald?

OSWALD. What else would you think of calling me?

MANDERS. Thank you. What I mean, my dear Oswald, is that you must not imagine that I have any unqualified disapproval of the artist's life. I admit that there are many who, even in that career, can keep the inner man free from harm.

OSWALD. Let us hope so.

MRS. ALVING (*beaming with pleasure*). I know one who has kept both the inner and the outer man free from harm. Just take a look at him, Mr. Manders.

OSWALD. (*Walks across the room.*) Yes, yes, mother dear, of course.

MANDERS. Undoubtedly—no one can deny it. And I hear you have begun to make a name for yourself. I have often seen mention of you in the papers—and extremely favorable mention, too. Although, I must admit, latterly I have not seen your name so often.

OSWALD (*going towards the conservatory*). I haven't done so much painting just lately.

MRS. ALVING. An artist must take a rest sometimes, like other people.

MANDERS. Of course, of course. At those times the artist is preparing and strengthening himself for a greater effort.

OSWALD. Yes. Mother, will dinner soon be ready?

MRS. ALVING. In half an hour. He has a fine appetite, thank goodness.

MANDERS. And a liking for tobacco too.

OSWALD. I found father's pipe in the room upstairs, and——

MANDERS. Ah, that is what it was!

MRS. ALVING. What?

MANDERS. When Oswald came in at that door with the pipe in his mouth, I thought for the moment it was his father in the flesh.

OSWALD. Really?

MRS. ALVING. How can you say so? Oswald takes after me.

MANDERS. Yes, but there is an expression about the corners of his mouth—something about the lips—that reminds me so exactly of Mr. Alving—especially when he smokes.

MRS. ALVING. I don't think so at all. To my mind, Oswald has much more of a clergyman's mouth.

MANDERS. Well, yes—a good many of my colleagues in the church have a similar expression.

MRS. ALVING. But put your pipe down, my dear boy. I don't allow any smoking in here.

OSWALD. (*Puts down his pipe.*) All right, I only wanted to try it, because I smoked it once when I was a child.

MRS. ALVING. You?

OSWALD. Yes, it was when I was quite a little chap. And I can remember going upstairs to father's room one evening when he was in very good spirits.

MRS. ALVING. Oh, you can't remember anything about those days.

OSWALD. Yes, I remember plainly that he took me on his knee and let me smoke his pipe. "Smoke, my boy," he said, "have a good smoke, boy!" And I smoked as hard as I could, until I felt I was turning quite pale, and the perspiration was standing in great drops on my forehead. Then he laughed—such a hearty laugh——

MANDERS. It was an extremely odd thing to do.

MRS. ALVING. Dear Mr. Manders, Oswald only dreamt it.

OSWALD. No indeed, mother, it was no dream. Because—don't you remember—you came into the room and carried me off to the nursery, where I was sick, and I saw that you were crying. Did father often play such tricks?

MANDERS. In his young days he was full of fun——

OSWALD. And, for all that, he did so much with his life—so much that was good and useful, I mean—short as his life was.

MANDERS. Yes, my dear Oswald Alving, you have inherited the name of a man who undoubtedly was both energetic and worthy. Let us hope it will be a spur to your energies——

OSWALD. It ought to be, certainly.

MANDERS. In any case it was nice of you to come home for the day that is to honor his memory.

OSWALD. I could do no less for my father.

MRS. ALVING. And to let me keep him so long here—that's the nicest part of what he has done.

MANDERS. Yes, I hear you are going to spend the winter at home.

OSWALD. I am here for an indefinite time, Mr. Manders.—Oh, it's good to be at home again!

MRS. ALVING (*beaming*). Yes, isn't it?

MANDERS (*looking sympathetically at him*). You went out into the world very young, my dear Oswald.

OSWALD. I did. Sometimes I wonder if I wasn't too young.

MRS. ALVING. Not a bit of it. It is the best thing for an active boy, and especially for an only child. It's a pity when they are kept at home with their parents and get spoilt.

MANDERS. That is a very debatable question, Mrs. Alving. A child's own home is, and always must be, his proper place.

OSWALD. There I agree entirely with Mr. Manders.

MANDERS. Take the case of your own son. Oh yes, we can talk about it before him. What has the result been in his case? He is six or seven and twenty, and has never yet had the opportunity of learning what a well-regulated home means.

OSWALD. Excuse me, Mr. Manders, you are quite wrong there.

MANDERS. Indeed? I imagined that your life abroad had practically been spent entirely in artistic circles.

OSWALD. So it has.

MANDERS. And chiefly amongst the younger artists.

OSWALD. Certainly.

MANDERS. But I imagined that those gentry, as a rule, had not the means necessary for family life and the support of a home.

OSWALD. There are a considerable number of them who have not the means to marry, Mr. Manders.

MANDERS. That is exactly my point.

OSWALD. But they can have a home of their own, all the same; a good many of them have. And they are very well-regulated and very comfortable homes, too.

(MRS. ALVING, *who has listened to him attentively, nods assent, but says nothing.*)

MANDERS. Oh, but I am not talking of bachelor establishments. By a home I mean family life—the life a man lives with his wife and children.

OSWALD. Exactly, or with his children and his children's mother.

MANDERS. (*Starts and clasps his hands.*) Good heavens!

OSWALD. What is the matter?

MANDERS. Lives with—with—his children's mother!

OSWALD. Well, would you rather he should repudiate his children's mother?

MANDERS. Then what you are speaking of are those unprincipled conditions known as irregular unions!

OSWALD. I have never noticed anything particularly unprincipled about these people's lives.

MANDERS. But do you mean to say that it is possible for a man of any sort of bringing-up, and a young woman, to reconcile themselves to such a way of living—and to make no secret of it, either?

OSWALD. What else are they to do? A poor artist, and a poor girl—it costs a good deal to get married. What else are they to do?

MANDERS. What are they to do? Well, Mr. Alving, I will tell you what they ought to do. They ought to keep away from each other from the very beginning—that is what they ought to do!

OSWALD. That advice wouldn't have much effect upon hot-blooded young folk who are in love.

MRS. ALVING. No, indeed it wouldn't.

MANDERS (*persistently*). And to think that the authorities tolerate such things! That they are allowed to go on, openly! (*Turns to* MRS. ALVING.) Had I so little reason, then, to be sadly concerned about your son? In circles where open immorality is rampant—where, one may say, it is honored——

OSWALD. Let me tell you this, Mr. Manders. I have been a constant Sunday guest at one or two of these "irregular" households——

MANDERS. On Sunday, too!

OSWALD. Yes, that is the day of leisure. But never have I heard one objectionable word there; still less have I ever seen anything that could be called immoral. No; but do you know when and where I *have* met with immorality in artists' circles?

MANDERS. No, thank heaven, I don't!

OSWALD. Well, then, I shall have the pleasure of telling you. I have met with it when some one or other of your model husbands and fathers have come out there to have a bit of a look round on their own account, and have done the artists the honor of looking them up in their humble quarters. Then we had a chance of learning something, I can tell you. These gentlemen were able to instruct us about places and things that we had never so much as dreamt of.

MANDERS. What? Do you want me to believe that honorable men when they get away from home will——

OSWALD. Have you never, when these same honorable men come home again, heard them deliver themselves on the subject of the prevalence of immorality abroad?

MANDERS. Yes, of course, but——

MRS. ALVING. I have heard them, too.

OSWALD. Well, you can take their word for it, unhesitatingly. Some of them are experts in the matter. (*Putting his hands to his head*) To think that the glorious freedom of the beautiful life over there should be so besmirched!

MRS. ALVING. You mustn't get too heated, Oswald; you gain nothing by that.

OSWALD. No, you are quite right, mother. Besides, it isn't good for me. It's because I am so infernally tired, you know. I will go out and take a turn before dinner. I beg your pardon, Mr. Manders. It is impossible for you to realize the feeling; but it takes me that way. (*Goes out by the farther door on the right.*)

MRS. ALVING. My poor boy!

MANDERS. You may well say so. This is what it has brought him to! (MRS. ALVING *looks at him, but does not speak.*) He called himself the prodigal son. It's only too true, alas—only too true! (MRS. ALVING *looks steadily at him.*) And what do you say to all this?

MRS. ALVING. I say that Oswald was right in every single word he said.

MANDERS. Right? Right? To hold such principles as that?

MRS. ALVING. In my loneliness here I have come to just the same opinions as he, Mr. Manders. But I have never presumed to venture upon such topics in conversation. Now there is no need; my boy shall speak for me.

MANDERS. You deserve the deepest pity, Mrs. Alving. It is my duty to say an earnest word to you. It is no longer your business man and adviser, no longer your old friend and your dead husband's old friend, that stands before you now. It is your priest that stands before you, just as he did once at the most critical moment of your life.

MRS. ALVING. And what has my priest to say to me?

MANDERS. First of all I must stir your memory. The moment is well chosen. To-morrow is the tenth anniversary of your husband's death; to-morrow the memorial to the departed will be unveiled; to-morrow I shall speak to the whole assembly that will be met together. But today I want to speak to you alone.

MRS. ALVING. Very well, Mr. Manders, speak!

MANDERS. Have you forgotten that after barely a year of married life you were standing at the very edge of a precipice?—that you forsook your house and home?—and that you ran away from

your husband—yes, Mrs. Alving, ran away, ran away—and refused to return to him in spite of his requests and entreaties?

MRS. ALVING. Have you forgotten how unspeakably unhappy I was
during that first year?

MANDERS. To crave for happiness in this world is simply to be possessed by a spirit of revolt. What right have we to happiness? No!
we must do our duty, Mrs. Alving. And your duty was to cleave
to the man you had chosen and to whom you were bound by a
sacred bond.

MRS. ALVING. You know quite well what sort of life my husband was
living at that time—what excesses he was guilty of.

MANDERS. I know only too well what rumor used to say of him; and
I should be the last person to approve of his conduct as a young
man, supposing that rumor spoke the truth. But it is not a wife's
part to be her husband's judge. You should have considered it your
bounden duty humbly to have borne the cross that a higher will
had laid upon you. But, instead of that, you rebelliously cast off
your cross; you deserted the man whose stumbling footsteps you
should have supported; you did what was bound to imperil your
good name and reputation, and came very near to imperilling the
reputation of others into the bargain.

MRS. ALVING. Of others? Of one other, you mean.

MANDERS. It was the height of imprudence, your seeking refuge with
me.

MRS. ALVING. With our priest? With our intimate friend?

MANDERS. All the more on that account. You should thank God that
I possessed the necessary strength of mind—that I was able to
turn you from your outrageous intention, and that it was vouch-
safed to me to succeed in leading you back into the path of duty
and back to your lawful husband.

MRS. ALVING. Yes, Mr. Manders, that certainly was your doing.

MANDERS. I was but the humble instrument of a higher power. And
is it not true that my having been able to bring you again under
the yoke of duty and obedience sowed the seeds of a rich blessing
on all the rest of your life? Did things not turn out as I foretold
to you? Did not your husband turn from straying in the wrong
path as a man should? Did he not, after all, live a life of love and
good report with you all his days? Did he not become a benefactor to the neighbourhood? Did he not so raise you up to his
level, so that by degrees you became his fellow-worker in all his
undertakings—and a noble fellow-worker, too, I know, Mrs.
Alving; that praise I will give you.—But now I come to the
second serious false step in your life.

MRS. ALVING. What do you mean?

MANDERS. Just as once you forsook your duty as a wife, so, since then, you have forsaken your duty as a mother.

MRS. ALVING. Oh——!

MANDERS. You have been overmastered all your life by a disastrous spirit of wilfulness. All your impulses have led you towards what is undisciplined and lawless. You have never been willing to submit to any restraint. Anything in life that has seemed irksome to you, you have thrown aside recklessly and unscrupulously, as if it were a burden that you were free to rid yourself of if you would. It did not please you to be a wife any longer, and so you left your husband. Your duties as a mother were irksome to you, so you sent your child away among strangers.

MRS. ALVING. Yes, that is true; I did that.

MANDERS. And that is why you have become a stranger to him.

MRS. ALVING. No, no, I am not that!

MANDERS. You are; you must be. And what sort of son is it that you have got back? Think over it seriously, Mrs. Alving. You erred grievously in your husband's case—you acknowledge as much, by erecting this memorial to him. Now you are bound to acknowledge how much you have erred in your son's case; possibly there may still be time to reclaim him from the paths of wickedness. Turn over a new leaf, and set yourself to reform what there may still be that is capable of reformation in him. Because (*with uplifted forefinger*) in very truth, Mrs. Alving, you are a guilty mother!—That is what I have thought it my duty to say to you. (*A short silence.*)

MRS. ALVING (*speaking slowly and with self-control*). You have had your say, Mr. Manders, and to-morrow you will be making a public speech in memory of my husband. I shall not speak to-morrow. But now I wish to speak to you for a little, just as you have been speaking to me.

MANDERS. By all means; no doubt you wish to bring forward some excuses for your behavior——

MRS. ALVING. No. I only want to tell you something.

MANDERS. Well?

MRS. ALVING. In all that you said just now about me and my husband, and about our life together after you had, as you put it, led me back into the path of duty—there was nothing that you knew at first hand. From that moment you never again set foot in our house—you, who had been our daily companion before that.

MANDERS. Remember that you and your husband moved out of town immediately afterwards.

MRS. ALVING. Yes, and you never once came out here to see us in my husband's lifetime. It was only the business in connection with the Orphanage that obliged you to come and see me.

MANDERS (*in a low and uncertain voice*). Helen—if that is a reproach, I can only beg you to consider——

MRS. ALVING. ——the respect you owed to your calling?—yes. All the more as I was a wife who had tried to run away from her husband. One can never be too careful to have nothing to do with such reckless women.

MANDERS. My dear—Mrs. Alving, you are exaggerating dreadfully——

MRS. ALVING. Yes, yes,—very well. What I mean is this, that when you condemn my conduct as a wife you have nothing more to go upon than ordinary public opinion.

MANDERS. I admit it. What then?

MRS. ALVING. Well—now, Mr. Manders, now I am going to tell you the truth. I had sworn to myself that you should know it one day —you, and you only!

MANDERS. And what may the truth be?

MRS. ALVING. The truth is this, that my husband died just as great a profligate as he had been all his life.

MANDERS (*feeling for a chair*). What are you saying?

MRS. ALVING. After nineteen years of married life, just as profligate— in his desires at all events as he was before you married us.

MANDERS. And can you talk of his youthful indiscretions—his irregularities—his excesses, if you like—as a profligate life?

MRS. ALVING. That was what the doctor who attended him called it.

MANDERS. I don't understand what you mean.

MRS. ALVING. It is not necessary you should.

MANDERS. It makes my brain reel. To think that your marriage—all the years of wedded life you spent with your husband—were nothing but a hidden abyss of misery.

MRS. ALVING. That and nothing else. Now you know.

MANDERS. This—this bewilders me. I can't understand it! I can't grasp it! How in the world was it possible——? How could such a state of things remain concealed?

MRS. ALVING. That was just what I had to fight for incessantly, day after day. When Oswald was born, I thought I saw a slight improvement. But it didn't last long. And after that I had to fight doubly hard—fight a desperate fight so that no one should know what sort of man my child's father was. You know quite well what an attractive manner he had; it seemed as if people could believe nothing but good of him. He was one of those men whose mode of life seems to have no effect upon their reputations. But at last, Mr. Manders—you must hear this too—at last something happened more abominable than everything else.

MANDERS. More abominable than what you have told me?

MRS. ALVING. I had borne with it all, though I knew only too well what he indulged in in secret, when he was out of the house. But when it came to the point of the scandal coming within our four walls——

MANDERS. Can you mean it? Here?

MRS. ALVING. Yes, here, in our own home. It was in there (*pointing to the nearer door on the right*) in the dining-room that I got the first hint of it. I had something to do in there and the door was standing ajar. I heard our maid come up from the garden with water for the flowers in the conservatory.

MANDERS. Well——?

MRS. ALVING. Shortly afterwards I heard my husband come in too. I heard him say something to her in a low voice. And then I heard—(*with a short laugh*)—oh, it rings in my ears still, with its mixture of what was heartbreaking and what was so ridiculous —I heard my own servant whisper: "Let me go, Mr. Alving! Let me be!"

MANDERS. What unseemly levity on his part! But surely nothing more than levity, Mrs. Alving, believe me.

MRS. ALVING. I soon knew what to believe. My husband had his will of the girl—and that intimacy had consequences, Mr. Manders.

MANDERS (*as if turned to stone*). And all that in this house! In this house!

MRS. ALVING. I have suffered a good deal in this house. To keep him at home in the evening—and at night—I have had to play the part of boon companion in his secret drinking-bouts in his room up there. I have had to sit there alone with him, have had to hobnob and drink with him, have had to listen to his ribald senseless talk, have had to fight with brute force to get him to bed——

MANDERS (*trembling*). And you were able to endure all this!

MRS. ALVING. I had my little boy, and endured it for his sake. But when the crowning insult came—when my own servant—then I made up my mind that there should be an end of it. I took the upper hand in the house, absolutely—both with him and all the others. I had a weapon to use against him, you see; he didn't dare to speak. It was then that Oswald was sent away. He was about seven then, and was beginning to notice things and ask questions as children will. I could endure all that, my friend. It seemed to me that the child would be poisoned if he breathed the air of this polluted house. That was why I sent him away. And now you understand, too, why he never set foot here as long as his father was alive. No one knows what it meant to me.

MANDERS. You have indeed had a pitiable experience.

MRS. ALVING. I could never have gone through with it, if I had not had my work. Indeed, I can boast that I have worked. All the increase in the value of the property, all the improvements, all the useful arrangements that my husband got the honor and glory of —do you suppose that he troubled himself about any of them? He, who used to lie the whole day on the sofa reading old Official Lists! No, you may as well know that too. It was I that kept him up to the mark when he had his lucid intervals; it was I that had to bear the whole burden of it when he began his excesses again or took to whining about his miserable condition.

MANDERS. And this is the man you are building a memorial to!

MRS. ALVING. There you see the power of an uneasy conscience.

MANDERS. An uneasy conscience? What do you mean?

MRS. ALVING. I had always before me the fear that it was impossible that the truth should not come out and be believed. That is why the Orphanage is to exist, to silence all rumors and clear away all doubt.

MANDERS. You certainly have not fallen short of the mark in that, Mrs. Alving.

MRS. ALVING. I had another very good reason. I did not wish Oswald, my own son, to inherit a penny that belonged to his father.

MANDERS. Then it is with Mr. Alving's property——

MRS. ALVING. Yes. The sums of money that, year after year, I have given towards this Orphanage make up the amount of property —I have reckoned it carefully—which in the old days made Lieutenant Alving a catch.

MANDERS. I understand.

MRS. ALVING. That was my purchase money. I don't wish it to pass into Oswald's hands. My son shall have everything from me, I am determined.

(OSWALD *comes in by the farther door on the right. He has left his hat and coat outside.*)

MRS. ALVING. Back again, my own dear boy?

OSWALD. Yes, what can one do outside in this everlasting rain? I hear dinner is nearly ready. That's good!

(REGINA *comes in from the dining-room, carrying a parcel.*)

REGINA. This parcel has come for you, ma'am. (*Gives it to her.*)

MRS. ALVING (*glancing at* MANDERS). The ode to be sung to-morrow, I expect.

MANDERS. Hm——!

REGINA. And dinner is ready.

MRS. ALVING. Good. We will come in a moment. I will just—(*begins to open the parcel*).

REGINA (*to* OSWALD). Will you drink white or red wine, sir?

OSWALD. Both, Miss Engstrand.

REGINA. Bien—very good, Mr. Alving. (*Goes into the dining-room.*)

OSWALD. I may as well help you to uncork it——. (*Follows her into the dining-room, leaving the door ajar after him.*)

MRS. ALVING. Yes, I thought so. Here is the ode, Mr. Manders.

MANDERS (*clasping his hands*). How shall I ever have the courage to-morrow to speak the address that——

MRS. ALVING. Oh, you will get through it.

MANDERS (*in a low voice, fearing to be heard in the dining-room*). Yes, we must raise no suspicions.

MRS. ALVING (*quietly but firmly*). No; and then this long dreadful comedy will be at an end. After to-morrow, I shall feel as if my dead husband had never lived in this house. There will be no one else here then but my boy and his mother.

(*From the dining-room is heard the noise of a chair falling; then* REGINA'S *voice is heard in a loud whisper.*)

REGINA. Oswald! Are you mad? Let me go!

MRS. ALVING (*starting in horror*). Oh——!

(*She stares wildly at the half-open door.* OSWALD *is heard coughing and humming, then the sound of a bottle being uncorked.*)

MANDERS (*in an agitated manner*). What's the matter? What is it, Mrs. Alving?

MRS. ALVING (*hoarsely*). Ghosts. The couple in the conservatory—over again.

MANDERS. What are you saying? Regina——? Is she——?

MRS. ALVING. Yes. Come. Not a word——! (*Grips* MANDERS *by the arm and walks unsteadily with him into the dining-room.*)

Curtain

ACT TWO

The same scene. The landscape is still obscured by mist. MANDERS *and* MRS. ALVING *come in from the dining-room.*

MRS. ALVING (*calls into the dining-room from the doorway*). Aren't you coming in here, Oswald?

OSWALD. No, thanks; I think I will go out for a bit.

MRS. ALVING. Yes, do; the weather is clearing a little. (*She shuts the dining-room door, then goes to the hall door and calls.*) Regina!

REGINA (*from without*). Yes, ma'am?

MRS. ALVING. Go down into the laundry and help with the garlands.

REGINA. Yes, ma'am.

    (MRS. ALVING *satisfies herself that she has gone, then shuts the door.*)

MANDERS. I suppose he can't hear us?

MRS. ALVING. Not when the door is shut. Besides, he is going out.

MANDERS. I am still quite bewildered. I don't know how I managed to swallow a mouthful of your excellent dinner.

MRS. ALVING (*walking up and down, and trying to control her agitation*). Nor I. But what are we to do?

MANDERS. Yes, what are we to do? Upon my word I don't know; I am so completely unaccustomed to things of this kind.

MRS. ALVING. I am convinced that nothing serious has happened yet.

MANDERS. Heaven forbid! But it is most unseemly behavior, for all that.

MRS. ALVING. It is nothing more than a foolish jest of Oswald's, you may be sure.

MANDERS. Well, of course, as I said, I am quite inexperienced in such matters; but it certainly seems to me——

MRS. ALVING. Out of the house she shall go—and at once. That part of it is as clear as daylight——

MANDERS. Yes, that is quite clear.

MRS. ALVING. But where is she to go? We should not be justified in——

MANDERS. Where to? Home to her father, of course.

MRS. ALVING. To whom, did you say?

MANDERS. To her——. No, of course Engstrand isn't——. But, great heavens, Mrs. Alving, how is such a thing possible? You surely may have been mistaken, in spite of everything.

MRS. ALVING. There was no chance of mistake, more's the pity. Joanna was obliged to confess it to me—and my husband couldn't deny it. So there was nothing else to do but to hush it up.

MANDERS. No, that was the only thing to do.

MRS. ALVING. The girl was sent away at once, and was given a tolerably liberal sum to hold her tongue. She looked after the rest herself when she got to town. She renewed an old acquaintance with the carpenter Engstrand; gave him a hint, I suppose, of how much money she had got, and told him some fairy tale about a foreigner who had been here in his yacht in the summer. So she and Engstrand were married in a great hurry. Why, you married them yourself!

MANDERS. I can't understand it———. I remember clearly Engstrand's coming to arrange about the marriage. He was full of contrition, and accused himself bitterly for the light conduct he and his fiancée had been guilty of.

MRS ALVING. Of course he had to take the blame on himself.

MANDERS. But the deceitfulness of it! And with me, too! I positively would not have believed it of Jacob Engstrand. I shall most certainly give him a serious talking to.—And the immorality of such a marriage! Simply for the sake of the money———! What sum was it that the girl had?

MRS. ALVING. It was seventy pounds.

MANDERS. Just think of it—for a paltry seventy pounds to let yourself be bound in marriage to a fallen woman!

MRS. ALVING. What about myself, then?—I let myself be bound in marriage to a fallen man.

MANDERS. Heaven forgive you! what are you saying? A fallen man?

MRS. ALVING. Do you suppose my husband was any purer, when I went with him to the altar, than Joanna was when Engstrand agreed to marry her?

MANDERS. The two cases are as different as day from night———

MRS. ALVING. Not so very different, after all. It is true there was a great difference in the price paid, between a paltry seventy pounds and a whole fortune.

MANDERS. How can you compare such totally different things? I presume you consulted your own heart—and your relations.

MRS. ALVING (*looking away from him*). I thought you understood where what you call my heart had strayed to at that time.

MANDERS (*in a constrained voice*). If I had understood anything of the kind, I would not have been a daily guest in your husband's house.

MRS. ALVING. Well, at any rate this much is certain, that I didn't consult myself in the matter at all.

MANDERS. Still you consulted those nearest to you, as was only right— your mother, your two aunts.

MRS. ALVING. Yes, that is true. The three of them settled the whole matter for me. It seems incredible to me now, how clearly they made out that it would be sheer folly to reject such an offer. If my mother could only see what all that fine prospect has led to!

MANDERS. No one can be responsible for the result of it. Anyway, there is this to be said, that the match was made in complete conformity with law and order.

MRS. ALVING (*going to the window*). Oh, law and order! I often think it is that that is at the bottom of all the misery in the world.

MANDERS. Mrs. Alving, it is very wicked of you to say that.

MRS. ALVING. That may be so; but I don't attach importance to those obligations and considerations any longer. I cannot! I must struggle for my freedom.

MANDERS. What do you mean?

MRS. ALVING (*tapping on the window panes*). I ought never to have concealed what sort of life my husband led. But I had not the courage to do otherwise then—for my own sake, either. I was too much of a coward.

MANDERS. A coward?

MRS. ALVING. If others had known anything of what happened, they would have said: "Poor man, it is natural enough that he should go astray when he has a wife that has run away from him."

MANDERS. They would have had a certain amount of justification for saying so.

MRS. ALVING (*looking fixedly at him*). If I had been the woman I ought, I would have taken Oswald into my confidence and said to him: "Listen, my son, your father was a dissolute man"——

MANDERS. Miserable woman——

MRS. ALVING. ——and I would have told him all I have told you, from beginning to end.

MANDERS. I am almost shocked at you, Mrs. Alving.

MRS. ALVING. I know. I know quite well! I am shocked at myself when I think of it. (*Comes away from the window.*) I am coward enough for that.

MANDERS. Can you call it cowardice that you simply did your duty? Have you forgotten that a child should love and honor his father and mother?

MRS. ALVING. Don't let us talk in such general terms. Suppose we say: "Ought Oswald to love and honor Mr. Alving?"

MANDERS. You are a mother—isn't there a voice in your heart that forbids you to shatter your son's ideals?

MRS. ALVING. And what about the truth?

MANDERS. What about his ideals?

MRS. ALVING. Oh—ideals, ideals! If only I were not such a coward as I am!

MANDERS. Do not spurn ideals, Mrs. Alving—they have a way of avenging themselves cruelly. Take Oswald's own case, now. He hasn't many ideals, more's the pity. But this much I have seen, that his father is something of an ideal to him.

MRS. ALVING. You are right there.

MANDERS. And his conception of his father is what you inspired and encouraged by your letters.

MRS. ALVING. Yes, I was swayed by duty and consideration for others; that was why I lied to my son, year in and year out. Oh, what a coward—what a coward I have been!

MANDERS. You have built up a happy illusion in your son's mind, Mrs. Alving—and that is a thing you certainly ought not to undervalue.

MRS. ALVING. Ah, who knows if that is such a desirable thing after all! —But anyway I don't intend to put up with any goings on with Regina. I am not going to let him get the poor girl into trouble.

MANDERS. Good heavens, no—that would be a frightful thing!

MRS. ALVING. If only I knew whether he meant it seriously, and whether it would mean happiness for him——

MANDERS. In what way? I don't understand.

MRS. ALVING. But that is impossible; Regina is not equal to it, unfortunately.

MANDERS. I don't understand. What do you mean?

MRS. ALVING. If I were not such a miserable coward, I would say to him: "Marry her, or make any arrangement you like with her —only let there be no deceit in the matter."

MANDERS. Heaven forgive you! Are you actually suggesting anything so abominable, so unheard of, as a marriage between them?

MRS. ALVING. Unheard of, do you call it? Tell me honestly, Mr. Manders, don't you suppose there are plenty of married couples out here in the country that are just as nearly related as they are?

MANDERS. I am sure I don't understand you.

MRS. ALVING. Indeed you do.

MANDERS. I suppose you are thinking of cases where possibly——. It is only too true, unfortunately, that family life is not always as stainless as it should be. But as for the sort of thing you hint at —well, it's impossible to tell, at all events with any certainty. Here, on the other hand—for you, a mother, to be willing to allow your——

MRS. ALVING. But I am not willing to allow it. I would not allow it for anything in the world; that is just what I was saying.

MANDERS. No, because you are a coward, as you put it. But, supposing you were not a coward——! Great heavens—such a
revolting union!

MRS. ALVING. Well, for the matter of that, we are all descended from
a union of that description, so we are told. And who was responsible for this state of things, Mr. Manders?

MANDERS. I can't discuss such questions with you, Mrs. Alving; you are
by no means in the right frame of mind for that. But for you to
dare to say that it is cowardly of you——!

MRS. ALVING. I will tell you what I mean by that. I am frightened and
timid, because I am obsessed by the presence of ghosts that I
never can get rid of.

MANDERS. The presence of what?

MRS. ALVING. Ghosts. When I heard Regina and Oswald in there, it
was just like seeing ghosts before my eyes. I am half inclined to
think we are all ghosts, Mr. Manders. It is not only what we
have inherited from our fathers and mothers that exists again in
us, but all sorts of old dead ideas and all kinds of old dead beliefs
and things of that kind. They are not actually alive in us; but
there they are dormant, all the same, and we can never be rid
of them. Whenever I take up a newspaper and read it, I fancy I
see ghosts creeping between the lines. There must be ghosts all
over the world. They must be as countless as the grains of the
sands, it seems to me. And we are so miserably afraid of the
light, all of us.

MANDERS. Ah!—there we have the outcome of your reading. Fine fruit
it has borne—this abominable, subversive, free-thinking literature!

MRS. ALVING. You are wrong there, my friend. You are the one who
made me begin to think; and I owe you my best thanks for it.

MANDERS. I?

MRS. ALVING. Yes, by forcing me to submit to what you called my
duty and my obligations, by praising as right and just what my
whole soul revolted against, as it would against something abominable. That was what led me to examine your teachings critically.
I only wanted to unravel one point in them; but as soon as I had
got that unravelled, the whole fabric came to pieces. And then I
realized that it was only machine-made.

MANDERS (*softly, and with emotion*). Is that all I accomplished by
the hardest struggle of my life?

MRS. ALVING. Call it rather the most ignominious defeat of your life.

MANDERS. It was the greatest victory of my life, Helen; victory over
myself.

MRS. ALVING. It was a wrong done to both of us.

MANDERS. A wrong?—wrong for me to entreat you as a wife to go back to your lawful husband, when you came to me half distracted and crying: "Here I am, take me!" Was that a wrong?

MRS. ALVING. I think it was.

MANDERS. We two do not understand one another.

MRS. ALVING. Not now, at all events.

MANDERS. Never—even in my most secret thoughts have I for a moment regarded you as anything but the wife of another.

MRS. ALVING. Do you believe what you say?

MANDERS. Helen——!

MRS. ALVING. One so easily forgets one's own feelings.

MANDERS. Not I. I am the same as I always was.

MRS. ALVING. Yes, yes—don't let us talk any more about the old days. You are buried up to your eyes now in committees and all sorts of business; and I am here, fighting with ghosts both without and within me.

MANDERS. I can at all events help you to get the better of those without you. After all that I have been horrified to hear from you to-day, I cannot conscientiously allow a young defenceless girl to remain in your house.

MRS. ALVING. Don't you think it would be best if we could get her settled?—by some suitable marriage, I mean.

MANDERS. Undoubtedly. I think, in any case, it would have been desirable for her. Regina is at an age now that—well, I don't know much about these things, but—

MRS. ALVING. Regina developed very early.

MANDERS. Yes, didn't she? I fancy I remember thinking she was remarkably well developed, bodily, at the time I prepared her for Confirmation. But, for the time being, she must in any case go home. Under her father's care—no, but of course Engstrand is not——. To think that he, of all men, could so conceal the truth from me!

(*A knock is heard at the hall door.*)

MRS. ALVING. Who can that be? Come in!

(ENGSTRAND, *dressed in his Sunday clothes, appears in the door-way.*)

ENGSTRAND. I humbly beg pardon, but——

MANDERS. Aha! Hm!——

MRS. ALVING. Oh, it's you, Engstrand!

ENGSTRAND. There were none of the maids about, so I took the great liberty of knocking.

MRS. ALVING. That's all right. Come in. Do you want to speak to me?

ENGSTRAND (*coming in*). No, thank you very much, ma'am. It was Mr. Manders I wanted to speak to for a moment.

MANDERS (*walking up and down*). Hm!—do you? You want to speak to me, do you?

ENGSTRAND. Yes, sir, I wanted so very much to——

MANDERS (*stopping in front of him*). Well, may I ask what it is you want?

ENGSTRAND. It's this way, Mr. Manders. We are being paid off now. And many thanks to you, Mrs. Alving. And now the work is quite finished, I thought it would be so nice and suitable if all of us, who have worked so honestly together all this time, were to finish up with a few prayers this evening.

MANDERS. Prayers? Up at the Orphanage?

ENGSTRAND. Yes, sir, but if it isn't agreeable to you, then——

MANDERS. Oh, certainly——but—hm!——

ENGSTRAND. I have made a practice of saying a few prayers there myself each evening——

MRS. ALVING. Have you?

ENGSTRAND. Yes, ma'am, now and then—just as a little edification, so to speak. But I am only a poor common man, and haven't rightly the gift, alas—and so I thought that as Mr. Manders happened to be here, perhaps——

MANDERS. Look here, Engstrand. First of all I must ask you a question. Are you in a proper frame of mind for such a thing? Is your conscience free and untroubled?

ENGSTRAND. Heaven have mercy on me a sinner! My conscience isn't worth our speaking about, Mr. Manders.

MANDERS. But it is just what we must speak about. What do you say to my question?

ENGSTRAND. My conscience? Well—it's uneasy sometimes, of course.

MANDERS. Ah, you admit that at all events. Now will you tell me, without any concealment—what is your relationship to Regina?

MRS. ALVING (*hastily*). Mr. Manders!

MANDERS (*calming her*). Leave it to me!

ENGSTRAND. With Regina? Good Lord, how you frightened me! (*Looks at* MRS. ALVING.) There is nothing wrong with Regina, is there?

MANDERS. Let us hope not. What I want to know is, what is your relationship to her? You pass as her father, don't you?

ENGSTRAND (*unsteadily*). Well—hm!—you know, sir, what happened between me and my poor Joanna.

MANDERS. No more distortion of the truth! Your late wife made a full confession to Mrs. Alving, before she left her service.

ENGSTRAND. What!—do you mean to say——? Did she do that after all?

MANDERS. You see it has all come out, Engstrand.

ENGSTRAND. Do you mean to say that she, who gave me her promise and solemn oath——

MANDERS. Did she take an oath?

ENGSTRAND. Well, no—she only gave me her word, but as seriously as a woman could.

MANDERS. And all these years you have been hiding the truth from me —from me, who have had such complete and absolute faith in you.

ENGSTRAND. I am sorry to say I have, sir.

MANDERS. Did I deserve that from you, Engstrand? Haven't I been always ready to help you in word and deed as far as lay in my power? Answer me! Is it not so?

ENGSTRAND. Indeed there's many a time I should have been very badly off without you, sir.

MANDERS. And this is the way you repay me—by causing me to make false entries in the church registers, and afterwards keeping back from me for years the information which you owed it both to me and to your sense of the truth to divulge. Your conduct has been absolutely inexcusable, Engstrand, and from to-day everything is at an end between us.

ENGSTRAND (*with a sigh*). Yes, I can see that's what it means.

MANDERS. Yes, because how can you possibly justify what you did?

ENGSTRAND. Was the poor girl to go and increase her load of shame by talking about it? Just suppose, sir, for a moment that your reverence was in the same predicament as my poor Joanna——

MANDERS. I!

ENGSTRAND. Good Lord, sir, I don't mean the same predicament. I mean, suppose there were something your reverence were ashamed of in the eyes of the world, so to speak. We men oughtn't to judge a poor woman too hardly, Mr. Manders.

MANDERS. But I am not doing so at all. It is you I am blaming.

ENGSTRAND. Will your reverence grant me leave to ask you a small question?

MANDERS. Ask away.

ENGSTRAND. Shouldn't you say it was right for a man to raise up the fallen?

MANDERS. Of course it is.

ENGSTRAND. And isn't a man bound to keep his word of honor?

MANDERS. Certainly he is; but——

ENGSTRAND. At the time when Joanna had her misfortune with this

Englishman—or maybe he was an American or a Russian, as they call 'em—well, sir, then she came to town. Poor thing, she had refused me once or twice before; she only had eyes for good-looking men in those days, and I had this crooked leg then. Your reverence will remember how I had ventured up into a dancing-saloon where seafaring men were revelling in drunkenness and intoxication, as they say. And when I tried to exhort them to turn from their evil ways——

MRS. ALVING (*coughs from the window*). Ahem!

MANDERS. I know, Engstrand, I know—the rough brutes threw you downstairs. You have told me about that incident before. The affliction to your leg is a credit to you.

ENGSTRAND. I don't want to claim credit for it, your reverence. But what I wanted to tell you was that she came then and confided in me with tears and gnashing of teeth. I can tell you, sir, it went to my heart to hear her.

MANDERS. Did it, indeed, Engstrand? Well, what then?

ENGSTRAND. Well, then I said to her: "The American is roaming about on the high seas, he is. And you, Joanna," I said, "you have committed a sin and are a fallen woman. But here stands Jacob Engstrand," I said, "on two strong legs"—of course that was only speaking in a kind of metaphor, as it were, your reverence.

MANDERS. I quite understand. Go on.

ENGSTRAND. Well, sir, that was how I rescued her and made her my lawful wife, so that no one should know how recklessly she had carried on with the stranger.

MANDERS. That was all very kindly done. The only thing I cannot justify was your bringing yourself to accept the money——

ENGSTRAND. Money? I? Not a farthing.

MANDERS (*to* MRS. ALVING, *in a questioning tone*). But——

ENGSTRAND. Ah, yes!—wait a bit; I remember now. Joanna did have a trifle of money, you are quite right. But I didn't want to know anything about that. "Fie," I said, "on the mammon of unright-eousness, it's the price of your sin; as for this tainted gold"—or notes, or whatever it was—"we will throw it back in the American's face," I said. But he had gone away and disappeared on the stormy seas, your reverence.

MANDERS. Was that how it was, my good fellow?

ENGSTRAND. It was, sir. So then Joanna and I decided that the money should go towards the child's bringing-up, and that's what became of it; and I can give a faithful account of every single penny of it.

MANDERS. This alters the complexion of the affair very considerably.

ENGSTRAND. That's how it was, your reverence. And I make bold to say that I have been a good father to Regina—as far as was in my power—for I am a poor erring mortal, alas!

MANDERS. There, there, my dear Engstrand——

ENGSTRAND. Yes, I do make bold to say that I brought up the child, and made my poor Joanna a loving and careful husband, as the Bible says we ought. But it never occurred to me to go to your reverence and claim credit for it or boast about it because I had done one good deed in this world. No; when Jacob Engstrand does a thing like that, he holds his tongue about it. Unfortunately it doesn't often happen; I know that only too well. And whenever I do come to see your reverence, I never seem to have anything but trouble and wickedness to talk about. Because, as I said just now—and I say it again—conscience can be very hard on us sometimes.

MANDERS. Give me your hand, Jacob Engstrand.

ENGSTRAND. Oh, sir, I don't like——

MANDERS. No nonsense. (*Grasps his hand.*) That's it!

ENGSTRAND. And may I make bold humbly to beg your reverence's pardon——

MANDERS. You? On the contrary it is for me to beg your pardon——

ENGSTRAND. Oh no, sir.

MANDERS. Yes, certainly it is, and I do it with my whole heart. Forgive me for having so much misjudged you. And I assure you that if I can do anything for you to prove my sincere regret and my goodwill towards you——

ENGSTRAND. Do you mean it, sir?

MANDERS. It would give me the greatest pleasure.

ENGSTRAND. As a matter of fact, sir, you could do it now. I am thinking of using the honest money I have put away out of my wages up here in establishing a sort of Sailors' Home in the town.

MRS. ALVING. You?

ENGSTRAND. Yes, to be a sort of Refuge, as it were. There are such manifold temptations lying in wait for sailor men when they are roaming about on shore. But my idea is that in this house of mine they should have a sort of parental care looking after them.

MANDERS. What do you say to that, Mrs. Alving?

ENGSTRAND. I haven't much to begin such a work with, I know; but Heaven might prosper it, and if I found any helping hand stretched out to me, then——

MANDERS. Quite so; we will talk over the matter further. Your project attracts me enormously. But in the meantime go back to the Orphanage and put everything tidy and light the lights, so that the occasion may seem a little solemn. And then we will spend a little edifying time together, my dear Engstrand, for now I am sure you are in a suitable frame of mind.

ENGSTRAND. I believe I am, sir, truly. Good-bye, then, Mrs. Alving, and thank you for all your kindness; and take good care of Regina for me. (*Wipes a tear from his eye.*) Poor Joanna's child —it is an extraordinary thing, but she seems to have grown into my life and to hold me by the heartstrings. That's how I feel about it, truly. (*Bows and goes out.*)

MANDERS. Now then, what do you think of him, Mrs. Alving? That was quite another explanation that he gave us.

MRS. ALVING. It was, indeed.

MANDERS. There, you see how exceedingly careful we ought to be in condemning our fellow-men. But at the same time it gives one genuine pleasure to find that one was mistaken. Don't you think so?

MRS. ALVING. What I think is that you are, and always will remain, a big baby, Mr. Manders.

MANDERS. I?

MRS. ALVING (*laying her hands on his shoulders*). And I think that I should like very much to give you a good hug.

MANDERS (*drawing back hastily*). No, no, good gracious! What an idea!

MRS. ALVING (*with a smile*). Oh, you needn't be afraid of me.

MANDERS (*standing by the table*). You choose such an extravagant way of expressing yourself sometimes. Now I must get these papers together and put them in my bag. (*Does so.*) That's it. And now good-bye, for the present. Keep your eyes open when Oswald comes back. I will come back and see you again presently. (*He takes his hat and goes out by the hall door.* MRS. ALVING *sighs, glances out of the window, puts one or two things tidy in the room and turns to go into the dining-room. She stops in the doorway with a stifled cry.*)

MRS. ALVING. Oswald, are you still sitting at table?

OSWALD (*from the dining-room*). I am only finishing my cigar.

MRS. ALVING. I thought you had gone out for a little turn.

OSWALD (*from within the room*). In weather like this? (*A glass is heard clinking.* MRS. ALVING *leaves the door open and sits down with her knitting on the couch by the window.*) Wasn't that Mr. Manders that went out just now?

MRS. ALVING. Yes, he has gone over to the Orphanage.

OSWALD. Oh.

(*The clink of a bottle on a glass is heard again.*)

MRS. ALVING (*with an uneasy expression*). Oswald, dear, you should be careful with that liqueur. It is strong.

OSWALD. It's a good protective against the damp.

MRS. ALVING. Wouldn't you rather come in here?

OSWALD. You know you don't like smoking in there.

MRS. ALVING. You may smoke a cigar in here, certainly.

OSWALD. All right; I will come in, then. Just one drop more. There! (*Comes in, smoking a cigar, and shuts the door after him. A short silence.*) Where has the parson gone?

MRS. ALVING. I told you he had gone over to the Orphanage.

OSWALD. Oh, so you did.

MRS. ALVING. You shouldn't sit so long at table, Oswald.

OSWALD (*holding his cigar behind his back*). But it's so nice and cosy, mother dear. (*Caresses her with one hand.*) Think what it means to me—to have come home; to sit at my mother's own table, in my mother's own room, and to enjoy the charming meals she gives me.

MRS. ALVING. My dear, dear boy!

OSWALD (*a little impatiently, as he walks up and down smoking*). And what else is there for me to do here? I have no occupation——

MRS. ALVING. No occupation?

OSWALD. Not in this ghastly weather, when there isn't a blink of sunshine all day long. (*Walks up and down the floor.*) Not to be able to work, it's——!

MRS. ALVING. I don't believe you were wise to come home.

OSWALD. Yes, mother; I had to.

MRS. ALVING. Because I would ten times rather give up the happiness of having you with me than that you should——

OSWALD (*standing still by the table*). Tell me, mother—is it really such a great happiness for you to have me at home?

MRS. ALVING. Can you ask?

OSWALD (*crumpling up a newspaper*). I should have thought it would have been pretty much the same to you whether I were here or away.

MRS. ALVING. Have you the heart to say that to your mother, Oswald?

OSWALD. But you have been quite happy living without me so far.

MRS. ALVING. Yes, I have lived without you—that is true.

(*A silence. The dusk falls by degrees.* OSWALD *walks restlessly up and down. He has laid aside his cigar.*)

OSWALD (*stopping beside* MRS. ALVING). Mother, may I sit on the couch beside you?

MRS. ALVING. Of course, my dear boy.

OSWALD (*sitting down*). Now I must tell you something, mother.

MRS. ALVING (*anxiously*). What?

OSWALD (*staring in front of him*). I can't bear it any longer.

MRS. ALVING. Bear what? What do you mean?

OSWALD (*as before*). I couldn't bring myself to write to you about it; and since I have been at home——

MRS. ALVING (*catching him by the arm*). Oswald, what is it?

OSWALD. Both yesterday and to-day I have tried to push my thoughts away from me—to free myself from them. But I can't.

MRS. ALVING (*getting up*). You must speak plainly, Oswald!

OSWALD (*drawing her down to her seat again*). Sit still, and I will try and tell you. I have made a great deal of the fatigue I felt after my journey——

MRS. ALVING. Well, what of that?

OSWALD. But that isn't what is the matter. It is no ordinary fatigue——

MRS. ALVING (*trying to get up*). You are not ill, Oswald!

OSWALD (*pulling her down again*). Sit still, mother. Do take it quietly. I am not exactly ill—not ill in the usual sense. (*Takes his head in his hands.*) Mother, it's my mind that has broken down—gone to pieces—I shall never be able to work any more! (*Buries his face in his hands and throws himself at her knees in an outburst of sobs.*)

MRS. ALVING (*pale and trembling*). Oswald! Look at me! No, no, it isn't true!

OSWALD (*looking up with a distracted expression*). Never to be able to work any more! Never—never! A living death! Mother, can you imagine anything so horrible?

MRS. ALVING. My poor unhappy boy! How has this terrible thing happened?

OSWALD (*sitting up again*). That is just what I cannot possibly understand. I have never lived recklessly in any sense. You must believe that of me, mother! I have never done that.

MRS. ALVING. I haven't a doubt of it, Oswald.

OSWALD. And yet this comes upon me all the same!—this terrible disaster!

MRS. ALVING. Oh, but it will all come right again, my dear precious boy. It is nothing but overwork. Believe me, that is so.

OSWALD (*dully*). I thought so too, at first; but it isn't so.

MRS. ALVING. Tell me all about it.

OSWALD. Yes, I will.

MRS. ALVING. When did you first feel anything?

OSWALD. It was just after I had been home last time and had got back to Paris. I began to feel the most violent pains in my head—

mostly at the back, I think. It was as if a tight band of iron was pressing on me from my neck upwards.

MRS. ALVING. And then?

OSWALD. At first I thought it was nothing but the headaches I always used to be so much troubled with while I was growing.

MRS. ALVING. Yes, yes——

OSWALD. But it wasn't; I soon saw that. I couldn't work any longer. I would try and start some big new picture; but it seemed as if all my faculties had forsaken me, as if all my strength were paralyzed. I couldn't manage to collect my thoughts; my head seemed to swim—everything went round and round. It was a horrible feeling! At last I sent for a doctor—and from him I learnt the truth.

MRS. ALVING. In what way, do you mean?

OSWALD. He was one of the best doctors there. He made me describe what I felt, and then he began to ask me a whole heap of questions which seemed to me to have nothing to do with the matter. I couldn't see what he was driving at——

MRS. ALVING. Well?

OSWALD. At last he said: "You have had the canker of disease in you practically from your birth"—the actual word he used was "vermoulu." *

MRS. ALVING (*anxiously*). What did he mean by that?

OSWALD. I couldn't understand, either—and I asked him for a clearer explanation. And then the old cynic said—(*clenching his fist*). Oh——!

MRS. ALVING. What did he say?

OSWALD. He said: "The sins of the fathers are visited on the children."

MRS. ALVING (*getting up slowly*). The sins of the fathers——!

OSWALD. I nearly struck him in the face——

MRS. ALVING (*walking across the room*). The sins of the fathers——!

OSWALD (*smiling sadly*). Yes, just imagine! Naturally I assured him that what he thought was impossible. But do you think he paid any heed to me? No, he persisted in his opinion; and it was only when I got out your letters and translated to him all the passages that referred to my father——

MRS. ALVING. Well, and then?

OSWALD. Well, then of course he had to admit that he was on the wrong tack; and then I learnt the truth—the incomprehensible truth! I ought to have had nothing to do with the joyous happy life I had lived with my comrades. It had been too much for my strength. So it was my own fault!

MRS. ALVING. No, no, Oswald! Don't believe that!

* Literally, "worm-eaten."

OSWALD. There was no other explanation of it possible, he said. That is the most horrible part of it. My whole life incurably ruined— just because of my own imprudence. All that I wanted to do in the world—not to dare to think of it any more—not to be *able* to think of it! Oh! if only I could live my life over again—if only I could undo what I have done!

(*Throws himself on his face on the couch.* MRS. ALVING *wrings her hands and walks up and down silently fighting with herself.*)

OSWALD. (*Looks up after a while, raising himself on his elbows.*) If only it had been something I had inherited—something I could not help. But, instead of that, to have disgracefully, stupidly, thought-lessly thrown away one's happiness, one's health, everything in the world—one's future, one's life——

MRS. ALVING. No, no, my darling boy; that is impossible! (*Bending over him*) Things are not so desperate as you think.

OSWALD. Ah, you don't know——. (*Springs up.*) And to think, mother, that I should bring all this sorrow upon you! Many a time I have almost wished and hoped that you really did not care so very much for me.

MRS. ALVING. I, Oswald? My only son! All that I have in the world! The only thing I care about!

OSWALD (*taking hold of her hands and kissing them*). Yes, yes, I know that is so. When I am at home I know that is true. And that is one of the hardest parts of it to me. But now you know all about it; and now we won't talk any more about it today. I can't stand thinking about it long at a time. (*Walks across the room.*) Let me have something to drink, mother!

MRS. ALVING. To drink? What do you want?

OSWALD. Oh, anything you like. I suppose you have got some punch in the house.

MRS. ALVING. Yes, but my dear Oswald——!

OSWALD. Don't tell me I mustn't, mother. Do be nice! I must have some-thing to drown these gnawing thoughts. (*Goes into the conserva-tory.*) And how—how gloomy it is here! (MRS. ALVING *rings the bell.*) And this incessant rain. It may go on week after week—a whole month. Never a ray of sunshine. I don't remember ever having seen the sun shine once when I have been at home.

MRS. ALVING. Oswald—you are thinking of going away from me!

OSWALD. Hm!—. (*Sighs deeply.*) I am not thinking about anything. I *can't* think about anything! (*In a low voice*) I have to let that alone.

REGINA (*coming from the dining-room*). Did you ring, ma'am?

MRS. ALVING. Yes, let us have the lamp in.

REGINA. In a moment, ma'am; it is all ready lit. (*Goes out.*)

MRS. ALVING (*going up to* OSWALD). Oswald, don't keep anything back from me.

OSWALD. I don't, mother. (*Goes to the table.*) It seems to me I have told you a good lot.

(REGINA *brings the lamp and puts it upon the table.*)

MRS. ALVING. Regina, you might bring us a small bottle of champagne.

REGINA. Yes, ma'am. (*Goes out.*)

OSWALD (*taking hold of his mother's face*). That's right. I knew my mother wouldn't let her son go thirsty.

MRS. ALVING. My poor dear boy, how could I refuse you anything now?

OSWALD (*eagerly*). Is that true, mother? Do you mean it?

MRS. ALVING. Mean what?

OSWALD. That you couldn't deny me anything?

MRS. ALVING. My dear Oswald—

OSWALD. Hush!

(REGINA *brings in a tray with a small bottle of champagne and two glasses, which she puts on the table.*)

REGINA. Shall I open the bottle?

OSWALD. No, thank you, I will do it.

(REGINA *goes out.*)

MRS. ALVING (*sitting down at the table*). What did you mean, when you asked if I could refuse you nothing?

OSWALD (*busy opening the bottle*). Let us have a glass first—or two. (*He draws the cork, fills one glass and is going to fill the other.*)

MRS. ALVING (*holding her hand over the second glass*). No, thanks—not for me.

OSWALD. Oh, well, for me then! (*He empties his glass, fills it again and empties it; then sits down at the table.*)

MRS. ALVING (*expectantly*). Now, tell me.

OSWALD (*without looking at her*). Tell me this: I thought you and Mr. Manders seemed so strange—so quiet—at dinner.

MRS. ALVING. Did you notice that?

OSWALD. Yes. Ahem! (*After a short pause*) Tell me—What do you think of Regina?

MRS. ALVING. What do I think of her?

OSWALD. Yes, isn't she splendid?

MRS. ALVING. Dear Oswald, you don't know her as well as I do—

OSWALD. What of that?

MRS. ALVING. Regina was too long at home, unfortunately. I ought to have taken her under my charge sooner.

OSWALD. Yes, but isn't she splendid to look at, mother? (*Fills his glass.*)

MRS. ALVING. Regina has many serious faults——

OSWALD. Yes, but what of that? (*Drinks.*)

MRS. ALVING. But I am fond of her, all the same; and I have made myself responsible for her. I wouldn't for the world she should come to any harm.

OSWALD (*jumping up*). Mother, Regina is my only hope of salvation!

MRS. ALVING (*getting up*). What do you mean?

OSWALD. I can't go on bearing all this agony of mind alone.

MRS. ALVING. Haven't you your mother to help you to bear it?

OSWALD. Yes, I thought so; that was why I came home to you. But it is no use; I see that it isn't. I cannot spend my life here.

MRS. ALVING. Oswald!

OSWALD. I must live a different sort of life, mother, so I shall have to go away from you. I don't want you watching it.

MRS. ALVING. My unhappy boy! But, Oswald, as long as you are ill like this—

OSWALD. If it was only a matter of feeling ill, I would stay with you, mother. You are the best friend I have in the world.

MRS. ALVING. Yes, I am that, Oswald, am I not?

OSWALD (*walking restlessly about*). But all this torment—the regret, the remorse—and the deadly fear. Oh—this horrible fear!

MRS. ALVING (*following him*). Fear? Fear of what? What do you mean?

OSWALD. Oh, don't ask me any more about it. I don't know what it is. I can't put it into words. (MRS. ALVING *crosses the room and rings the bell.*) What do you want?

MRS. ALVING. I want my boy to be happy, that's what I want. He mustn't brood over anything. (*To* REGINA, *who has come to the door*) More champagne—a large bottle.

(REGINA *goes out.*)

OSWALD. Mother!

MRS. ALVING. Do you think we country people don't know how to live?

OSWALD. Isn't she splendid to look at? What a figure! And the picture of health!

MRS. ALVING (*sitting down at the table*). Sit down, Oswald, and let us have a quiet talk.

OSWALD (*sitting down*). You don't know, mother, that I owe Regina a little reparation.

MRS. ALVING. You!

OSWALD. Oh, it was only a little thoughtlessness—call it what you like. Something quite innocent, anyway. The last time I was home——

MRS. ALVING. Yes?

OSWALD. ——she used often to ask me questions about Paris, and I told her one thing and another about the life there. And I remember saying one day: "Wouldn't you like to go there yourself?"

MRS. ALVING. Well?

OSWALD. I saw her blush, and she said: "Yes, I should like to very much." "All right," I said, "I daresay it might be managed"—or something of that sort.

MRS. ALVING. And then?

OSWALD. I naturally had forgotten all about it; but the day before yesterday I happened to ask her if she was glad I was to be so long at home——

MRS. ALVING. Well?

OSWALD. ——and she looked so queerly at me, and asked: "But what is to become of my trip to Paris?"

MRS. ALVING. Her trip!

OSWALD. And then I got it out of her that she had taken the thing seriously, and had been thinking about me all the time, and had set herself to learn French——

MRS. ALVING. So that was why——

OSWALD. Mother—when I saw this fine, splendid, handsome girl standing there in front of me—I had never paid any attention to her before then—but now, when she stood there as if with open arms ready for me to take her to myself——

MRS. ALVING. Oswald!

OSWALD. ——then I realized that my salvation lay in her, for I saw the joy of life in her.

MRS. ALVING (*starting back*). The joy of life——? Is there salvation in that?

REGINA (*coming in from the dining-room with a bottle of champagne*). Excuse me for being so long, but I had to go to the cellar. (*Puts the bottle down on the table.*)

OSWALD. Bring another glass, too.

REGINA (*looking at him in astonishment*). The mistress's glass is there, sir.

OSWALD. Yes, but fetch one for yourself, Regina. (REGINA *starts, and gives a quick shy glance at* MRS. ALVING.) Well?

REGINA (*in a low and hesitating voice*). Do you wish me to, ma'am?

MRS. ALVING. Fetch the glass, Regina.

(REGINA *goes into the dining-room.*)

OSWALD (*looking after her*). Have you noticed how well she walks?—so firmly and confidently!

MRS. ALVING. It cannot be, Oswald.

OSWALD. It is settled. You must see that. It is no use forbidding it. (REGINA *comes in with a glass, which she holds in her hand.*) Sit down, Regina.

(REGINA *looks questioningly at* MRS. ALVING.)

MRS. ALVING. Sit down. (REGINA *sits down on a chair near the dining-room door, still holding the glass in her hand.*) Oswald, what was it you were saying about the joy of life?

OSWALD. Ah, mother—the joy of life! You don't know very much about that at home here. I shall never realize it here.

MRS. ALVING. Not even when you are with me?

OSWALD. Never at home. But you can't understand that.

MRS. ALVING. Yes, indeed, I almost think I do understand you—now.

OSWALD. That—and the joy of work. They are really the same thing at bottom. But you don't know anything about that either.

MRS. ALVING. Perhaps you are right. Tell me some more about it, Oswald.

OSWALD. Well, all I mean is that here people are brought up to believe that work is a curse and a punishment for sin, and that life is a state of wretchedness and that the sooner we can get out of it the better.

MRS. ALVING. A vale of tears, yes. And we quite conscientiously make it so.

OSWALD. But the people over there will have none of that. There is no one there who really believes doctrines of that kind any longer. Over there the mere fact of being alive is thought to be a matter for exultant happiness. Mother, have you noticed that everything I have painted has turned upon the joy of life?—always upon the joy of life, unfailingly. There is light there, and sunshine, and a holiday feeling—and people's faces beaming with happiness. That is why I am afraid to stay at home here with you.

MRS. ALVING. Afraid? What are you afraid of here, with me?

OSWALD. I am afraid that all these feelings that are so strong in me would degenerate into something ugly here.

MRS. ALVING (*looking steadily at him*). Do you think that is what would happen?

OSWALD. I am certain it would. Even if one lived the same life at home here, as over there—it would never really be the same life.

MRS. ALVING (*who has listened anxiously to him, gets up with a thoughtful expression and says*). Now I see clearly how it all happened.

OSWALD. What do you see?

MRS. ALVING. I see it now for the first time. And now I can speak.

OSWALD (*getting up*). Mother, I don't understand you.

REGINA (*who has got up also*). Perhaps I had better go.

MRS. ALVING. No, stay here. Now I can speak. Now, my son, you shall know the whole truth. Oswald! Regina!

OSWALD. Hush!—here is the parson——

(MANDERS *comes in by the hall door.*)

MANDERS. Well, my friends, we have been spending an edifying time over there.

OSWALD. So have we.

MANDERS. Engstrand must have help with his Sailors' Home. Regina must go home with him and give him her assistance.

REGINA. No, thank you, Mr. Manders.

MANDERS (*perceiving her for the first time*). What——? you in here? —and with a wineglass in your hand!

REGINA (*putting down the glass hastily*). I beg your pardon——!

OSWALD. Regina is going away with me, Mr. Manders.

MANDERS. Going away! With you!

OSWALD. Yes, as my wife—if she insists on that.

MANDERS. But, good heavens——!

REGINA. It is not my fault, Mr. Manders.

OSWALD. Or else she stays here if I stay.

REGINA (*involuntarily*). Here!

MANDERS. I am amazed at you, Mrs. Alving.

MRS. ALVING. Neither of those things will happen, for now I can speak openly.

MANDERS. But you won't do that! No, no, no!

MRS. ALVING. Yes, I can and I will. And without destroying any one's ideals.

OSWALD. Mother, what is it that is being concealed from me?

REGINA (*listening*). Mrs. Alving! Listen! They are shouting outside. (*Goes into the conservatory and looks out.*)

OSWALD (*going to the window on the left*). What can be the matter? Where does that glare come from?

REGINA (*calls out*). The Orphanage is on fire!

MRS. ALVING (*going to the window*). On fire?

MANDERS. On fire? Impossible. I was there just a moment ago.

OSWALD. Where is my hat? Oh, never mind that. Father's Orphanage ——! (*Runs out through the garden door.*)

MRS. ALVING. My shawl, Regina! The whole place is in flames.

MANDERS. How terrible! Mrs. Alving, that fire is a judgment on this house of sin!

MRS. ALVING. Quite so. Come, Regina. (*She and REGINA hurry out.*)

MANDERS (*clasping his hands*). And no insurance! (*Follows them out.*)

Curtain

ACT THREE

The same scene. All the doors are standing open. The lamp is still burning on the table. It is dark outside, except for a faint glimmer of light seen through the windows at the back. MRS. ALVING, *with a shawl over her head, is standing in the conservatory, looking out.* REGINA, *also wrapped in a shawl, is standing a little behind her.*

MRS. ALVING. Everything burnt—down to the ground.

REGINA. It is burning still in the basement.

MRS. ALVING. I can't think why Oswald doesn't come back. There is no chance of saving anything.

REGINA. Shall I go and take his hat to him?

MRS. ALVING. Hasn't he even got his hat?

REGINA (*pointing to the hall*). No, there it is, hanging up.

MRS. ALVING. Never mind. He is sure to come back soon. I will go and see what he is doing.

(*Goes out by the garden door.* MANDERS *comes in from the hall.*)

MANDERS. Isn't Mrs. Alving here?

REGINA. She has just this moment gone down into the garden.

MANDERS. I have never spent such a terrible night in my life.

REGINA. Isn't it a shocking misfortune, sir!

MANDERS. Oh, don't speak about it. I scarcely dare to think about it.

REGINA. But how can it have happened?

MANDERS. Don't ask me, Miss Engstrand! How should I know? Are you going to suggest too——? Isn't it enough that your father——?

REGINA. What has he done?

MANDERS. He has nearly driven me crazy.

ENGSTRAND (*coming in from the hall*). Mr. Manders——!

MANDERS (*turning round with a start*). Have you even followed me here?

ENGSTRAND. Yes, God help us all——! Great heavens! What a dreadful thing, your reverence!

MANDERS (*walking up and down*). Oh dear, oh dear!

REGINA. What do you mean?

ENGSTRAND. Our little prayer-meeting was the cause of it all, don't you see? (*Aside to* REGINA) Now we've got the old fool, my girl. (*Aloud*) And to think it is my fault that Mr. Manders should be the cause of such a thing!

MANDERS. I assure you, Engstrand——

ENGSTRAND. But there was no one else carrying a light there except you, sir.

MANDERS (*standing still*). Yes, so you say. But I have no clear recollection of having had a light in my hand.

ENGSTRAND. But I saw quite distinctly your reverence take a candle and snuff it with your fingers and throw away the burning bit of wick among the shavings.

MANDERS. Did you see that?

ENGSTRAND. Yes, distinctly.

MANDERS. I can't understand it at all. It is never my habit to snuff a candle with my fingers.

ENGSTRAND. Yes, it wasn't like you to do that, sir. But who would have thought it could be such a dangerous thing to do?

MANDERS (*walking restlessly backwards and forwards*). Oh, don't ask me!

ENGSTRAND (*following him about*). And you hadn't insured it either, had you, sir?

MANDERS. No, no, no; you heard me say so.

ENGSTRAND. You hadn't insured it—and then went and set light to the whole place! Good Lord, what bad luck!

MANDERS (*wiping the perspiration from his forehead*). You may well say so, Engstrand.

ENGSTRAND. And that it should happen to a charitable institution that would have been of service both to the town and the country, so to speak! The newspapers won't be very kind to your reverence, I expect.

MANDERS. No, that is just what I am thinking of. It is almost the worst part of the whole thing. The spiteful attacks and accusations— it is horrible to think of!

MRS. ALVING (*coming in from the garden*). I can't get him away from the fire.

MANDERS. Oh, there you are, Mrs. Alving.

MRS. ALVING. You will escape having to make your inaugural address now, at all events, Mr. Manders.

MANDERS. Oh, I would so gladly have——

MRS. ALVING (*in a dull voice*). It is just as well it has happened. This Orphanage would never have come to any good.

MANDERS. Don't you think so?

MRS. ALVING. Do you?

MANDERS. But it is none the less an extraordinary piece of ill luck.

MRS. ALVING. We will discuss it simply as a business matter.—Are you waiting for Mr. Manders, Engstrand?

ENGSTRAND (*at the hall door*). Yes, I am.

MRS. ALVING. Sit down then, while you are waiting.

ENGSTRAND. Thank you, I would rather stand.

MRS. ALVING (*to* MANDERS). I suppose you are going by the boat?

MANDERS. Yes. It goes in about an hour.

MRS. ALVING. Please take all the documents back with you. I don't want to hear another word about the matter. I have something else to think about now——

MANDERS. Mrs. Alving——

MRS. ALVING. Later on I will send you a power of attorney to deal with it exactly as you please.

MANDERS. I shall be most happy to undertake that. I am afraid the original intention of the bequest will have to be entirely altered now.

MRS. ALVING. Of course.

MANDERS. Provisionally, I should suggest this way of disposing of it. Make over the Solvik property to the parish. The land is undoubtedly not without a certain value; it will always be useful for some purpose or another. And as for the interest on the remaining capital that is on deposit in the bank, possibly I might make suitable use of that in support of some undertaking that promises to be of use to the town.

MRS. ALVING. Do exactly as you please. The whole thing is a matter of indifference to me now.

ENGSTRAND. You will think of my Sailors' Home, Mr. Manders?

MANDERS. Yes, certainly, that is a suggestion. But we must consider the matter carefully.

ENGSTRAND (*aside*). Consider!—devil take it! Oh Lord.

MANDERS (*sighing*). And unfortunately I can't tell how much longer I may have anything to do with the matter—whether public opinion may not force me to retire from it altogether. That depends entirely upon the result of the enquiry into the cause of the fire.

MRS. ALVING. What do you say?

MANDERS. And one cannot in any way reckon upon the result beforehand.

ENGSTRAND (*going nearer to him*). Yes, indeed one can, because here stand I, Jacob Engstrand.

MANDERS. Quite so, but——

ENGSTRAND (*lowering his voice*). And Jacob Engstrand isn't the man to desert a worthy benefactor in the hour of need, as the saying is.

MANDERS. Yes, but, my dear fellow—how——?

ENGSTRAND. You might say Jacob Engstrand is an angel of salvation, so to speak, your reverence.

MANDERS. No, no, I couldn't possibly accept that.

ENGSTRAND. That's how it will be, all the same. I know some one who has taken the blame for some one else on his shoulders before now, I do.

MANDERS. Jacob! (*Grasps his hand.*) You are one in a thousand! You shall have assistance in the matter of your Sailors' Home, you may rely upon that.

(ENGSTRAND *tries to thank him, but is prevented by emotion.*)

MANDERS (*hanging his wallet over his shoulder*). Now we must be off. We will travel together.

ENGSTRAND (*by the dining-room door, says aside to* REGINA). Come with me, you hussy! You shall be as cosy as the yolk in an egg!

REGINA (*tossing her head*). Merci!

(*She goes out into the hall and brings back* MANDERS' *luggage.*)

MANDERS. Good-bye, Mrs. Alving! And may the spirit of order and of what is lawful speedily enter into this house.

MRS. ALVING. Good-bye, Mr. Manders. (*She goes into the conservatory, as she sees* OSWALD *coming in by the garden door.*)

ENGSTRAND (*as he and* REGINA *are helping* MANDERS *on with his coat*). Good-bye, my child. And if anything should happen to you, you know where Jacob Engstrand is to be found. (*Lowering his voice*) Little Harbour Street, ahem——! (*To* MRS. ALVING *and* OSWALD) And my house for poor seafaring men shall be called the "Alving Home," it shall. And, if I can carry out my own ideas about it, I shall make bold to hope that it may be worthy of bearing the late Mr. Alving's name.

MANDERS (*at the door*). Ahem—ahem! Come along, my dear Engstrand. Good-bye—good-bye!

(*He and* ENGSTRAND *go out by the hall door.*)

OSWALD (*going to the table*). What house was he speaking about?

MRS. ALVING. I believe it is some sort of Home that he and Mr. Manders want to start.

OSWALD. It will be burnt up just like this one.

MRS. ALVING. What makes you think that?

OSWALD. Everything will be burnt up; nothing will be left that is in memory of my father. Here am I being burnt up, too.

(REGINA *looks at him in alarm.*)

MRS. ALVING. Oswald! You should not have stayed so long over there, my poor boy.

OSWALD (*sitting down at the table*). I almost believe you are right.

MRS. ALVING. Let me dry your face, Oswald; you are all wet. (*Wipes his face with her handkerchief.*)

OSWALD (*looking straight before him, with no expression in his eyes*). Thank you, mother.

MRS. ALVING. And aren't you tired, Oswald? Don't you want to go to sleep?

OSWALD (*uneasily*). No, no—not to sleep! I never sleep; I only pretend to. (*Gloomily*) That will come soon enough.

MRS. ALVING (*looking at him anxiously*). Anyhow, you are really ill, my darling boy.

REGINA (*intently*). Is Mr. Alving ill?

OSWALD (*impatiently*). And do shut all the doors! This deadly fear——

MRS. ALVING. Shut the doors, Regina.

(REGINA *shuts the doors and remains standing by the hall door.* MRS. ALVING *takes off her shawl;* REGINA *does the same.* MRS. ALVING *draws up a chair near to* OSWALD'S *and sits down beside him.*) That's it! Now I will sit beside you——

OSWALD. Yes, do. And Regina must stay in here too. Regina must always be near me. You must give me a helping hand, you know, Regina. Won't you do that?

REGINA. I don't understand——

MRS. ALVING. A helping hand?

OSWALD. Yes—when there is need for it.

MRS. ALVING. Oswald, have you not your mother to give you a helping hand?

OSWALD. You? (*Smiles.*) No, mother, you will never give me the kind of helping hand I mean. (*Laughs grimly.*) You? Ha, ha! (*Looks gravely at her.*) After all, you have the best right. (*Impetuously*) Why don't you call me by my Christian name, Regina? Why don't you say Oswald?

REGINA (*in a low voice*). I did not think Mrs. Alving would like it.

MRS. ALVING. It will not be long before you have the right to do it. Sit down here now beside us, too. (REGINA *sits down quietly and hesitatingly at the other side of the table.*) And now, my poor tortured boy, I am going to take the burden off your mind——

OSWALD. You, mother?

MRS. ALVING. ——all that you call remorse and regret and self-reproach.

OSWALD. And you think you can do that?

MRS. ALVING. Yes, now I can, Oswald. A little while ago you were talking about the joy of life, and what you said seemed to shed a new light upon everything in my whole life.

OSWALD (*shaking his head*). I don't in the least understand what you mean.

MRS. ALVING. You should have known your father in his young days in the army. He was full of the joy of life, I can tell you.

OSWALD. Yes, I know.

MRS. ALVING. It gave me a holiday feeling only to look at him, full of irrepressible energy and exuberant spirits.

OSWALD. What then?

MRS. ALVING. Well, then this boy, full of the joy of life—for he was just like a boy, then—had to make his home in a second-rate town which had none of the joy of life to offer him, but only dissipations. He had to come out here and live an aimless life; he had only an official post. He had no work worth devoting his whole mind to; he had nothing more than official routine to attend to. He had not a single companion capable of appreciating what the joy of life meant; nothing but idlers and tipplers——

OSWALD. Mother——!

MRS. ALVING. And so the inevitable happened!

OSWALD. What was the inevitable?

MRS. ALVING. You said yourself this evening what would happen in your case if you stayed at home.

OSWALD. Do you mean that, that father——?

MRS. ALVING. Your poor father never found any outlet for the over-mastering joy of life that was in him. And I brought no holiday spirit into his home, either.

OSWALD. You didn't, either?

MRS. ALVING. I had been taught about duty, and the sort of thing that I believed in so long here. Everything seemed to turn upon duty—my duty, or his duty—and I am afraid I made your poor father's home unbearable to him, Oswald.

OSWALD. Why did you never say anything about it to me in your letters?

MRS. ALVING. I never looked at it as a thing I could speak of to you, who were his son.

OSWALD. What way did you look at it, then?

MRS. ALVING. I only saw the one fact, that your father was a lost man before ever you were born.

OSWALD (*in a choking voice*). Ah——! (*He gets up and goes to the window.*)

MRS. ALVING. And then I had the one thought in my mind, day and night, that Regina in fact had as good a right in this house—as my own boy had.

OSWALD (*turns round suddenly*). Regina——?

REGINA (*gets up and asks in choking tones*). I——?

MRS. ALVING. Yes, now you both know it.

OSWALD. Regina!

REGINA (*to herself*). So mother was one of that sort too.

MRS. ALVING. Your mother had many good qualities, Regina.

REGINA. Yes, but she was one of that sort too, all the same. I have even thought so myself, sometimes, but——. Then, if you please, Mrs. Alving, may I have permission to leave at once?

MRS. ALVING. Do you really wish to, Regina?

REGINA. Yes, indeed, I certainly wish to.

MRS. ALVING. Of course you shall do as you like, but——

OSWALD (*going to* REGINA). Leave now? This is your home.

REGINA. Merci, Mr. Alving—oh, of course I may say Oswald now, but that is not the way I thought it would become allowable.

MRS. ALVING. Regina, I have not been open with you——

REGINA. No, I can't say you have! If I had known Oswald was ill——. And now that there can never be anything serious between us——. No, I really can't stay here in the country and wear myself out looking after invalids.

OSWALD. Not even for the sake of one who has so near a claim on you?

REGINA. No, indeed I can't. A poor girl must make some use of her youth; otherwise she may easily find herself out in the cold before she knows where she is. And I have got the joy of life in me, too, Mrs. Alving!

MRS. ALVING. Yes, unfortunately; but don't throw yourself away, Regina.

REGINA. Oh, what's going to happen will happen. If Oswald takes after his father, it is just as likely I take after my mother, I expect. ——May I ask, Mrs. Alving, whether Mr. Manders knows this about me?

MRS. ALVING. Mr. Manders knows everything.

REGINA (*putting on her shawl*). Oh, well then, the best thing I can do is to get away by the boat as soon as I can. Mr. Manders is such a nice gentleman to deal with; and it certainly seems to me that I have just as much right to some of that money as he—as that horrid carpenter.

MRS. ALVING. You are quite welcome to it, Regina.

REGINA (*looking at her fixedly*). You might as well have brought me up like a gentleman's daughter; it would have been more suitable. (*Tosses her head.*) Oh, well—never mind! (*With a bitter glance at the unopened bottle*) I daresay some day I shall be drinking champagne with gentlefolk, after all.

MRS. ALVING. If ever you need a home, Regina, come to me.

REGINA. No, thank you, Mrs. Alving. Mr. Manders takes an interest in me, I know. And if things should go very badly with me, I know one house at any rate where I shall feel at home.

MRS. ALVING. Where is that?

REGINA. In the "Alving Home."

MRS. ALVING. Regina—I can see quite well—you are going to your ruin!

REGINA. Pooh!—good-bye. (*She bows to them and goes out through the hall.*)

OSWALD (*standing by the window and looking out*). Has she gone?

MRS. ALVING. Yes.

OSWALD (*muttering to himself*). I think it's all wrong.

MRS. ALVING (*going up to him from behind and putting her hands on his shoulders*). Oswald, my dear boy—has it been a great shock to you?

OSWALD (*turning his face towards her*). All this about father, do you mean?

MRS. ALVING. Yes, about your unhappy father. I am so afraid it may have been too much for you.

OSWALD. What makes you think that? Naturally it has taken me entirely by surprise; but, after all I don't know that it matters much to me.

MRS. ALVING (*drawing back her hands*). Doesn't matter?—that your father's life was such a terrible failure?

OSWALD. Of course I can feel sympathy for him, just as I would for anyone else, but——

MRS. ALVING. No more than that! For your own father!

OSWALD (*impatiently*). Father—father! I never knew anything of my father. I don't remember anything else about him except that he once made me sick.

MRS. ALVING. It is dreadful to think of!—But surely a child should feel some affection for his father, whatever happens!

OSWALD. When the child has nothing to thank his father for? When he has never known him? Do you really cling to that antiquated superstition—you, who are so broadminded in other things?

MRS. ALVING. You call it nothing but a superstition!

OSWALD. Yes, and you can see that for yourself quite well, mother. It is one of those beliefs that are put into circulation in the world, and——

MRS. ALVING. Ghosts of beliefs!

OSWALD (*walking across the room*). Yes, you might call them ghosts.

MRS. ALVING (*with an outburst of feeling*). Oswald—then you don't love me either.

OSWALD. You I know, at any rate——

MRS. ALVING. You know me, yes; but is that all?

OSWALD. And I know how fond you are of me, and I ought to be grateful to you for that. Besides, you can be so tremendously useful to me, now that I am ill.

MRS. ALVING. Yes, can't I, Oswald? I could almost bless your illness, as it has driven you home to me. For I see quite well that you are not my very own yet; you must be won.

OSWALD (*impatiently*). Yes, yes, yes; all that is just a way of talking. You must remember I am a sick man, mother. I can't concern myself much with anyone else; I have enough to do, thinking about myself.

MRS. ALVING (*gently*). I will be very good and patient.

OSWALD. And cheerful too, mother!

MRS. ALVING. Yes, my dear boy, you are quite right. (*Goes up to him.*) Now have I taken away all your remorse and self-reproach?

OSWALD. Yes, you have done that. But who will take away the fear?

MRS. ALVING. The fear?

OSWALD (*crossing the room*). Regina would have done it for one kind word.

MRS. ALVING. I don't understand you. What fear do you mean—and what has Regina to do with it?

OSWALD. Is it very late, mother?

MRS. ALVING. It is early morning. (*Looks out through the conservatory windows.*) The dawn is breaking already on the heights. And the sky is clear, Oswald. In a little while you will see the sun.

OSWALD. I am glad of that. After all, there may be many things yet for me to be glad of and to live for——

MRS. ALVING. I should hope so!

OSWALD. Even if I am not able to work——

MRS. ALVING. You will soon find you are able to work again now, my dear boy. You have no longer all those painful depressing thoughts to brood over.

OSWALD. No, it is a good thing that you have been able to rid me of those fancies. If only, now, I could overcome this one thing——. (*Sits down on the couch.*) Let us have a little chat, mother.

MRS. ALVING. Yes, let us. (*Pushes an armchair near to the couch and sits down beside him.*)

OSWALD. The sun is rising—and you know all about it; so I don't feel the fear any longer.

MRS. ALVING. I know all about what?

OSWALD (*without listening to her*). Mother, didn't you say this evening there was nothing in the world you would not do for me if I asked you?

MRS. ALVING. Yes, certainly I said so.

OSWALD. And will you be as good as your word, mother?

MRS. ALVING. You may rely upon that, my own dear boy. I have nothing else to live for, but you.

OSWALD. Yes, yes; well, listen to me, mother. You are very strong-minded, I know. I want you to sit quite quiet when you hear what I am going to tell you.

MRS. ALVING. But what is this dreadful thing——?

OSWALD. You mustn't scream. Do you hear? Will you promise me that? We are going to sit and talk it over quite quietly. Will you promise me that, mother?

MRS. ALVING. Yes, yes, I promise—only tell me what it is.

OSWALD. Well, then, you must know that this fatigue of mine—and my not being able to think about my work—all that is not really the illness itself——

MRS. ALVING. What is the illness itself?

OSWALD. What I am suffering from is hereditary; it—(*touches his fore-head, and speaks very quietly*)—it lies here.

MRS. ALVING (*almost speechless*). Oswald! No—no!

OSWALD. Don't scream; I can't stand it. Yes, I tell you, it lies here, waiting. And any time, any moment, it may break out.

MRS. ALVING. How horrible——!

OSWALD. Do keep quiet. That is the state I am in——

MRS. ALVING (*springing up*). It isn't true, Oswald! It is impossible! It can't be that!

OSWALD. I had one attack while I was abroad. It passed off quickly. But when I learnt the condition I had been in, then this dreadful haunting fear took possession of me.

MRS. ALVING. That was the fear, then——

OSWALD. Yes, it is so indescribably horrible, you know. If only it had been an ordinary mortal disease——. I am not so much afraid of dying, though, of course, I should like to live as long as I can.

MRS. ALVING. Yes, yes, Oswald, you must!

OSWALD. But this is so appallingly horrible. To become like a helpless child again—to have to be fed, to have to be——. Oh, it's unspeakable!

MRS. ALVING. My child has his mother to tend him.

OSWALD (*jumping up*). No, never; that is just what I won't endure! I dare not think what it would mean to linger on like that for years—to get old and grey like that. And you might die before I did. (*Sits down in* MRS. ALVING'S *chair.*) Because it doesn't necessarily have a fatal end quickly, the doctor said. He called it a kind of softening of the brain—or something of that sort. (*Smiles mournfully*.) I think that expression sounds so nice. It always makes me think of cherry-colored velvet curtains—something that is soft to stroke.

MRS. ALVING (*with a scream*). Oswald!

OSWALD. (*Jumps up and walks about the room.*) And now you have taken Regina from me! If I had only had her! She would have given me a helping hand, I know.

MRS. ALVING (*going up to him*). What do you mean, my darling boy? Is there any help in the world I would not be willing to give you?

OSWALD. When I had recovered from the attack I had abroad, the doctor told me that when it recurred—and it will recur—there would be no more hope.

MRS. ALVING. And he was heartless enough to——

OSWALD. I insisted on knowing. I told him I had arrangements to make——. (*Smiles cunningly.*) And so I had. (*Takes a small box from his inner breast-pocket.*) Mother, do you see this?

MRS. ALVING. What is it?

OSWALD. Morphia powders.

MRS. ALVING (*looking at him in terror*). Oswald—my boy!

OSWALD. I have twelve of them saved up——

MRS. ALVING (*snatching at it*). Give me the box, Oswald!

OSWALD. Not yet, mother. (*Puts it back in his pocket.*)

MRS. ALVING. I shall never get over this!

OSWALD. You must. If I had had Regina here now, I would have told her quietly how things stand with me—and asked her to give me this last helping hand. She would have helped me, I am certain.

MRS. ALVING. Never!

OSWALD. If this horrible thing had come upon me and she had seen me lying helpless, like a baby, past help, past saving, past hope—with no chance of recovering——

MRS. ALVING. Never in the world would Regina have done it.

OSWALD. Regina would have done it. Regina was so splendidly light-hearted. And she would very soon have tired of looking after an invalid like me.

MRS. ALVING. Then thank heaven Regina is not here!

OSWALD. Well, now you have got to give me that helping hand, mother.

MRS. ALVING (*with a loud scream*). I!

OSWALD. Who has a better right than you?

MRS. ALVING. I? Your mother!

OSWALD. Just for that reason.

MRS. ALVING. I, who gave you your life!

OSWALD. I never asked you for life. And what kind of life was it that you gave me? I don't want it! You shall take it back!

MRS. ALVING. Help! Help! (*Runs into the hall.*)

OSWALD (*following her*). Don't leave me! Where are you going?

MRS. ALVING (*in the hall*). To fetch the doctor to you, Oswald! Let me out!

OSWALD (*going into the hall*). You shan't go out. And no one shall come in. (*Turns the key in the lock.*)

MRS. ALVING (*coming in again*). Oswald! Oswald!—my child!

OSWALD (*following her*). Have you a mother's heart—and can bear to see me suffering this unspeakable terror?

MRS. ALVING (*controlling herself, after a moment's silence*). There is my hand on it.

OSWALD. Will you——?

MRS. ALVING. If it becomes necessary. But it shan't become necessary. No, no—it is impossible it should!

OSWALD. Let us hope so. And let us live together as long as we can. Thank you, mother.

(*He sits down in the armchair, which* MRS. ALVING *had moved beside the couch. Day is breaking; the lamp is still burning on the table.*)

MRS. ALVING (*coming cautiously nearer*). Do you feel calmer now?

OSWALD. Yes.

MRS. ALVING (*bending over him*). It has only been a dreadful fancy of yours, Oswald. Nothing but fancy. All this upset has been bad for you. But now you will get some rest, at home with your own mother, my darling boy. You shall have everything you want, just as you did when you were a little child.—There, now. The attack is over. You see how easily it passed off! I knew it would. —And look, Oswald, what a lovely day we are going to have? Brilliant sunshine. Now you will be able to see your home properly.

(*She goes to the table and puts out the lamp. It is sunrise. The glaciers and peaks in the distance are seen bathed in bright morning light.*)

OSWALD (*who has been sitting motionless in the armchair, with his back to the scene outside, suddenly says*). Mother, give me the sun.

MRS. ALVING (*standing at the table, and looking at him in amazement*). What do you say?

OSWALD (*repeats in a dull, toneless voice*). The sun—the sun.

MRS. ALVING (*going up to him*). Oswald, what is the matter with you?

(OSWALD *seems to shrink up in the chair; all his muscles relax; his face loses its expression, and his eyes stare stupidly.* MRS. ALVING *is trembling with terror.*) What is it? (*Screams.*) Oswald!

What is the matter with you? (*Throws herself on her knees beside him and shakes him.*) Oswald! Oswald! Look at me! Don't you know me?

OSWALD (*in an expressionless voice, as before*). The sun—the sun.

MRS. ALVING. (*Jumps up despairingly, beats her head with her hands, and screams.*) I can't bear it! (*Whispers as though paralyzed with fear.*) I can't bear it! Never! (*Suddenly.*) Where has he got it? (*Passes her hand quickly over his coat.*) Here! (*Draws back a little way and cries:*) No, no, no!—Yes!—no, no!

(*She stands a few steps from him, her hands thrust into her hair, and stares at him in speechless terror.*)

OSWALD (*sitting motionless, as before*). The sun—the sun.

Curtain

THE FATHER [1887]
A Tragedy in Three Acts

by *August* Strindberg

translated by Elizabeth Sprigge

Characters

THE CAPTAIN
LAURA, *his wife*
BERTHA, *their daughter*
DOCTOR ÖSTERMARK
THE PASTOR
THE NURSE
NÖJD
THE ORDERLY

The whole play takes place in the central living-room of the CAP-
TAIN'S *home. He is a cavalry officer in a remote country district of
Sweden.*

It is about 1886, shortly before Christmas.

*At the back of the room, towards the right, a door leads to the
hall. In the left wall there is a door to other rooms, and in the
right-hand corner another, smaller door, covered in the same wall-
paper as the walls, opens on to a staircase leading to the* CAPTAIN'S
room above.

*In the centre of the room stands a large round table on which
are newspapers, magazines, a big photograph album and a lamp.
On the right are a leather-covered sofa, arm chairs and a smaller
table. On the left is a writing-bureau with a pendulum clock upon
it. Arms, guns and gun-bags hang on the walls, and military coats
on pegs by the door to the hall.*

The Father, reprinted by permission of Willis Kingsley Wing. Copyright © 1955, by Elizabeth Sprigge. All rights whatsoever in this play
are strictly reserved and applications for performances, etc. should be
made to Willis Kingsley Wing, 24 East 38th Street, New York, N.Y.
10016.

ACT ONE

Early evening. The lamp on the table is lighted. The CAPTAIN *and the* PASTOR *are sitting on the sofa talking. The* CAPTAIN *is in undress uniform with riding-boots and spurs; the* PASTOR *wears black, with a white cravat in place of his clerical collar, and is smoking a pipe.*

   The CAPTAIN *rises and rings a bell. The* ORDERLY *enters from the hall.*

ORDERLY. Yes, sir?

CAPTAIN. Is Nöjd there?

ORDERLY. Nöjd's in the kitchen, sir, waiting for orders.

CAPTAIN. In the kitchen again, is he? Send him here at once.

ORDERLY. Yes, sir. (*Exit.*)

PASTOR. Why, what's the trouble?

CAPTAIN. Oh, the ruffian's been at his tricks again with one of the servant girls! He's a damn nuisance, that fellow!

PASTOR. Was it Nöjd you said? Didn't he give some trouble back in the spring?

CAPTAIN. Ah, you remember that, do you? Look here, you give him a bit of a talking to, there's a good chap. That might have some effect. I've sworn at him and thrashed him, without making the least impression.

PASTOR. So now you want me to preach to him. How much impression do you think God's word is likely to make on a trooper?

CAPTAIN. Well, my dear brother-in-law, it makes none at all on me, as you know, but . . .

PASTOR. As I know only too well.

CAPTAIN. But on him? Worth trying anyhow. (*Enter* NÖJD.) What have you been up to now, Nöjd?

NÖJD. God bless you, sir, I can't talk about that—not with Pastor here.

PASTOR. Don't mind me, my lad.

NÖJD. Well you see, sir, it was like this. We was at a dance at Gabriel's, and then, well then Ludwig said as . . .

CAPTAIN. What's Ludwig got to do with it? Stick to the point.

NÖJD. Well then Emma said as we should go in the barn.

CAPTAIN. I see. I suppose it was Emma who led you astray.

NÖJD. Well, not far from it. What I mean is if the girl's not game, nothing don't happen.

CAPTAIN. Once and for all—are you the child's father or are you not?

NÖJD. How's one to know?

CAPTAIN. What on earth do you mean? Don't you know?

NÖJD. No, you see, sir, that's what you never can know.

CAPTAIN. You mean you weren't the only man?

NÖJD. That time I was. But you can't tell if you've always been the only one.

CAPTAIN. Are you trying to put the blame on Ludwig? Is that the idea?

NÖJD. It's not easy to know who to put the blame on.

CAPTAIN. But, look here, you told Emma you would marry her.

NÖJD. Oh well, you always have to say that, you know.

CAPTAIN (*to the* PASTOR). This is atrocious.

PASTOR. It's the old story. Come now, Nöjd, surely you are man enough to know if you are the father.

NÖJD. Well, sir, it's true, I did go with her, but you know yourself, Pastor, that don't always lead to nothing.

PASTOR. Look here, my lad, it's you we are talking about. And you are not going to leave that girl destitute with a child. You can't be forced to marry her, but you must make provision for the child. That you must do.

NÖJD. So must Ludwig then.

CAPTAIN. If that's how it is, the case will have to go before the Magistrate. I can't settle it, and it's really nothing to do with me. Dismiss!

PASTOR. One moment, Nöjd. Ahem. Don't you think it's rather a dirty trick to leave a girl destitute with a child like that? Don't you think so—eh?

NÖJD. Yes, if I knew I was the father, it would be, but I tell you, Pastor, you never can know that. And it wouldn't be much fun slaving all your life for another chap's brat. You and the Captain must see that for yourselves.

CAPTAIN. That will do, Nöjd.

NÖJD. Yes, sir, thank you, sir.

CAPTAIN. And keep out of the kitchen, you scoundrel! (*Exit* NÖJD.) Why didn't you haul him over the coals?

PASTOR. What do you mean? Didn't I?

CAPTAIN. No, you just sat there muttering to yourself.

PASTOR. As a matter of fact, I scarcely knew what to say to him. It's hard on the girl, of course, but it's hard on the boy too. Supposing he's not the father? The girl can nurse the baby for four months at the orphanage, and after that it will be taken care of for good. But the boy can't nurse the child, can he? Later on, the girl will get a good place in some respectable family, but if the boy is cashiered, his future may be ruined.

CAPTAIN. Upon my soul, I'd like to be the magistrate and judge this case! Maybe the boy is responsible—that's what you can't know. But one thing you *can* know—if anybody's guilty, the girl is.

PASTOR. Well, I never sit in judgment. Now what was it we were talking about when this blessed business interrupted us? Yes, Bertha and her confirmation, wasn't it?

CAPTAIN. It's not just a question of confirmation, but of her whole future. The house is full of women, all trying to mould this child of mine. My mother-in-law wants to turn her into a spiritualist; Laura wants her to be an artist; the governess would have her a Methodist, old Margaret a Baptist, and the servant girls a Salvation Army lass. You can't make a character out of patchwork. Meanwhile I . . . I, who have more right than all the rest to guide her, am opposed at every turn. So I must send her away.

PASTOR. You have too many women running your house.

CAPTAIN. You're right there. It's like going into a cage of tigers. They'd soon tear me to pieces, if I didn't hold a red-hot poker under their noses. It's all very well for you to laugh, you blackguard. It wasn't enough that I married your sister; you had to palm off your old stepmother on me too.

PASTOR. Well, good Lord, one can't have stepmothers in one's house!

CAPTAIN. No, you prefer mothers-in-law—in someone else's house, of course.

PASTOR. Well, well, we all have our burdens to bear.

CAPTAIN. I daresay, but I have more than my share. There's my old nurse too, who treats me as if I still wore a bib. She's a good old soul, to be sure, but she shouldn't be here.

PASTOR. You should keep your women-folk in order, Adolf. You give them too much rope.

CAPTAIN. My dear fellow, can you tell me how to keep women in order?

PASTOR. To tell the truth, although she's my sister, Laura was always a bit of a handful.

CAPTAIN. Laura has her faults, of course, but they are not very serious ones.

PASTOR. Oh come now, I know her!

CAPTAIN. She was brought up with romantic ideas and has always found it a little difficult to come to terms with life. But she is my wife and . . .

PASTOR. And because she is your wife she must be the best of women. No, brother-in-law, it's she not you who wears the trousers.

CAPTAIN. In any case, the whole household has gone mad. Laura's determined Bertha shan't leave her, and I won't let her stay in this lunatic asylum.

PASTOR. So Laura's determined, is she? Then there's bound to be trouble, I'm afraid. As a child she used to lie down and sham dead until they gave in to her. Then she would calmly hand back whatever she'd set her mind on, explaining it wasn't the thing she wanted, but simply to get her own way.

CAPTAIN. So she was like that even then, was she? Hm. As a matter of fact, she does sometimes get so overwrought I'm frightened for her and think she must be ill.

PASTOR. What is it you want Bertha to do that's such a bone of contention? Can't you come to some agreement?

CAPTAIN. Don't think I want to turn her into a prodigy—or into some image of myself. But I will not play pander and have my daughter fitted for nothing but the marriage market. For then, if she didn't marry after all, she'd have a wretched time of it. On the other hand, I don't want to start her off in some man's career with a long training that would be entirely wasted if she did marry.

PASTOR. Well, what do you want then?

CAPTAIN. I want her to be a teacher. Then, if she doesn't marry she'll be able to support herself, and at least be no worse off than those unfortunate schoolmasters who have to support families on their earnings. And if she does marry, she can educate her own children. Isn't that reasonable?

PASTOR. Reasonable, yes—but what about her artistic talent? Wouldn't it be against the grain to repress that?

CAPTAIN. No. I showed her attempts to a well-known painter who told me they were nothing but the usual sort of thing learnt at school. Then, during the summer, some young jackanapes came along who knew better and said she was a genius—whereupon the matter was settled in Laura's favour.

PASTOR. Was he in love with Bertha?

CAPTAIN. I take that for granted.

PASTOR. Well, God help you, old boy, I don't see any solution. But it's a tiresome business, and I suppose Laura has supporters . . . (*indicates other rooms*) in there.

CAPTAIN. You may be sure of that. The whole household is in an uproar, and between ourselves the method of attack from that quarter is not exactly chivalrous.

PASTOR (*rising*). Do you think I haven't been through it?

CAPTAIN. You too?

PASTOR. Yes, indeed.

CAPTAIN. But to me the worst thing about it is that Bertha's future should be decided in there from motives of sheer hate. They do nothing but talk about men being made to see that women can do this and do that. It's man versus woman the whole day long

. . . Must you go? Won't you stay to supper? I don't know what there is, but do stay. I'm expecting the new doctor, you know. Have you seen him yet?

PASTOR. I caught a glimpse of him on my way here. He looks a decent, reliable sort of man.

CAPTAIN. That's good. Do you think he may be my ally?

PASTOR. Maybe. It depends how well he knows women.

CAPTAIN. But won't you stay?

PASTOR. Thank you, my dear fellow, but I promised to be home this evening, and my wife gets anxious if I'm late.

CAPTAIN. Anxious! Furious, you mean. Well, as you please. Let me help you on with your coat.

PASTOR. It's certainly very cold to-night. Thank you. You must look after yourself, Adolf. You seem a bit on edge.

CAPTAIN. On edge? Do I?

PASTOR. Yes. You aren't very well, are you?

CAPTAIN. Did Laura put this into your head? For the last twenty years she's been treating me as if I had one foot in the grave.

PASTOR. Laura? No, it's just that I'm . . . I'm worried about you. Take my advice and look after yourself. Goodbye, old man. By the way, didn't you want to talk about the confirmation?

CAPTAIN. By no means. But I give you my word this shall take its own course—and be chalked up to the official conscience. I am neither a witness to the truth, nor a martyr. We have got past that sort of thing. Goodbye. Remember me to your wife.

PASTOR. Goodbye, Adolf. Give my love to Laura.

(*Exit* PASTOR. *The* CAPTAIN *opens the bureau and settles down to his accounts.*)

CAPTAIN. Thirty-four—nine, forty-three—seven, eight, fifty-six.

LAURA (*entering from the next room*). Will you please . . .

CAPTAIN. One moment!—Sixty-six, seventy-one, eighty-four, eighty-nine, ninety-two, a hundred. What is it?

LAURA. Am I disturbing you?

CAPTAIN. Not in the least. Housekeeping money, I suppose?

LAURA. Yes, housekeeping money.

CAPTAIN. If you put the accounts down there, I will go through them.

LAURA. Accounts?

CAPTAIN. Yes.

LAURA. Do you expect me to keep accounts now?

CAPTAIN. Of course you must keep accounts. Our position's most precarious, and if we go bankrupt, we must have accounts to show. Otherwise we could be accused of negligence.

LAURA. It's not my fault if we're in debt.

CAPTAIN. That's what the accounts will show.

LAURA. It's not my fault the tenant farmer doesn't pay.

CAPTAIN. Who was it recommended him so strongly? You. Why did you recommend such a—shall we call him a scatterbrain?

LAURA. Why did you take on such a scatterbrain?

CAPTAIN. Because I wasn't allowed to eat in peace, sleep in peace or work in peace till you got him here. You wanted him because your brother wanted to get rid of him; my mother-in-law wanted him because I didn't; the governess wanted him because he was a Methodist, and old Margaret because she had known his grandmother as a child. That's why, and if I hadn't taken him I should be in a lunatic asylum by now, or else in the family vault. However, here's the housekeeping allowance and your pin money. You can give me the accounts later.

LAURA (*with an ironic bob*). Thank you so much.—By the way, do you keep accounts yourself—of what you spend outside the household?

CAPTAIN. That's none of your business.

LAURA. True. As little my business as the future of my own child. Did you gentlemen come to any decision at this evening's conference?

CAPTAIN. I had already made my decision, so I merely had to communicate it to the only friend I have in the family. Bertha is going to live in town. She will leave in a fortnight's time.

LAURA. Where, if I may ask, is she going to stay?

CAPTAIN. At Sävberg's—the solicitor's.

LAURA. That Freethinker!

CAPTAIN. According to the law as it now stands, children are brought up in their father's faith.

LAURA. And the mother has no say in the matter?

CAPTAIN. None whatever. She sells her birthright by legal contract and surrenders all her rights. In return the husband supports her and her children.

LAURA. So she has no rights over her own child?

CAPTAIN. None at all. When you have sold something, you don't expect to get it back and keep the money too.

LAURA. But supposing the father and mother were to decide things together . . . ?

CAPTAIN. How would that work out? I want her to live in town; you want her to live at home. The mathematical mean would be for her to stop at the railway station, midway between home and town. You see? It's a deadlock.

LAURA. Then the lock must be forced. . . . What was Nöjd doing here?

CAPTAIN. That's a professional secret.

LAURA. Which the whole kitchen knows.

CAPTAIN. Then doubtless you know it too.

LAURA. I do.

CAPTAIN. And are ready to sit in judgment?

LAURA. The law does that.

CAPTAIN. The law doesn't say who the child's father is.

LAURA. Well, people know that for themselves.

CAPTAIN. Discerning people say that's what one never can know.

LAURA. How extraordinary! Can't one tell who a child's father is?

CAPTAIN. Apparently not.

LAURA. How perfectly extraordinary! Then how can the father have those rights over the mother's child?

CAPTAIN. He only has them when he takes on the responsibility—or has it forced on him. But of course in marriage there is no doubt about the paternity.

LAURA. No doubt?

CAPTAIN. I should hope not.

LAURA. But supposing the wife has been unfaithful?

CAPTAIN. Well, such a supposition has no bearing on our problem. Is there anything else you want to ask me about?

LAURA. No, nothing.

CAPTAIN. Then I shall go up to my room. Please let me know when the doctor comes. (*Closes the bureau and rises.*)

LAURA. I will.

CAPTAIN (*going out by the wall-papered door*). As soon as he comes, mind. I don't want to be discourteous, you understand. (*Exit.*)

LAURA. I understand. (*She looks at the bank-notes she is holding.*)

MOTHER-IN-LAW (*off*). Laura!

LAURA. Yes, Mother?

MOTHER-IN-LAW. Is my tea ready?

LAURA (*at the door to the next room*). It's coming in a moment. (*The* ORDERLY *opens the hall door.*)

ORDERLY. Dr. Östermark.

(*Enter* DOCTOR. *Exit* ORDERLY, *closing the door.*)

LAURA (*shaking hands*). How do you do, Dr. Östermark. Let me welcome you to our home. The Captain is out, but he will be back directly.

DOCTOR. I must apologize for calling so late, but I have already had to pay some professional visits.

LAURA. Won't you sit down?

DOCTOR. Thank you.

LAURA. Yes, there is a lot of illness about just now, but I hope all the same that you will find this place suits you. It is so important for people in a lonely country district like this to have a doctor who takes a real interest in his patients. I have heard you so warmly spoken of, Dr. Östermark, I hope we shall be on the best of terms.

DOCTOR. You are too kind, dear lady. I hope, however, for your sake that my visits here will not often be of a professional nature. I take it that the health of your family is, on the whole, good, and that . . .

LAURA. Yes, we have been fortunate enough not to have any serious illness, but all the same things are not quite as they should be.

DOCTOR. Indeed?

LAURA. No, I'm afraid not really at all as one would wish.

DOCTOR. Dear, dear, you quite alarm me!

LAURA. In a family there are sometimes things which honour and duty compel one to keep hidden from the world.

DOCTOR. But not from one's doctor.

LAURA. No. That is why it is my painful duty to tell you the whole truth from the start.

DOCTOR. May we not postpone this conversation until I have had the honour of meeting the Captain?

LAURA. No. You must hear what I have to say before you see him.

DOCTOR. Does it concern him then?

LAURA. Yes, him. My poor, dear husband.

DOCTOR. You are making me most uneasy. Whatever your trouble, Madam, you can confide in me.

LAURA (*taking out her handkerchief*). My husband's mind is affected. Now you know, and later on you will be able to judge for yourself.

DOCTOR. You astound me. The Captain's learned treatise on mineralogy, for which I have the greatest admiration, shows a clear and powerful intellect.

LAURA. Does it? I shall be overjoyed if we—his relatives—are mistaken.

DOCTOR. It is possible, of course, that his mind is disturbed in other ways. Tell me . . .

LAURA. That is exactly what we fear. You see, at times he has the most peculiar ideas, which wouldn't matter much for a scientist, if they weren't such a burden on his family. For instance, he has an absolute mania for buying things.

DOCTOR. That is significant. What kind of things?

LAURA. Books. Whole cases of them, which he never reads.

DOCTOR. Well, that a scholar should buy books isn't so alarming.

LAURA. You don't believe what I am telling you?

DOCTOR. I am convinced, Madam, that you believe what you are telling me.

LAURA. Well, then, is it possible for anyone to see in a microscope what's happening on another planet?

DOCTOR. Does he say he can do that?

LAURA. Yes, that's what he says.

DOCTOR. In a microscope?

LAURA. In a microscope. Yes.

DOCTOR. That is significant, if it is so.

LAURA. If it is so! You don't believe me, Doctor. And here have I let you in to the family secret.

DOCTOR. My dear lady, I am honoured by your confidence, but as a physician I must observe and examine before giving an opinion. Has the Captain shown any symptoms of instability, any lack of will power?

LAURA. Has he, indeed! We have been married twenty years, and he has never yet made a decision without going back on it.

DOCTOR. Is he dogmatic?

LAURA. He certainly lays down the law, but as soon as he gets his own way, he loses interest and leaves everything to me.

DOCTOR. That is significant and requires careful consideration. The will, you see, Madam, is the backbone of the mind. If it is injured, the mind falls to pieces.

LAURA. God knows how I have schooled myself to meet his every wish during these long hard years. Oh, if you knew what I have been through with him, if you only knew!

DOCTOR. I am profoundly distressed to learn of your trouble, Madam, and I promise I will do what I can. You have my deepest sympathy and I beg you to rely on me implicitly. But now you have told me this, I am going to ask one thing of you. Don't allow anything to prey on the patient's mind. In a case of instability, ideas can sometimes take hold and grow into an obsession—or even monomania. Do you follow me?

LAURA. . . . You mean don't let him get ideas into his head.

DOCTOR. Precisely. For a sick man can be made to believe anything. He is highly susceptible to suggestion.

LAURA. I see . . . I understand. Yes, indeed. (*A bell rings within.*) Excuse me. That's my mother ringing. I won't be a moment . . . Oh, here's Adolf!

(*As* LAURA *goes out, the* CAPTAIN *enters by the wall-papered door.*)

CAPTAIN. Ah, so you have arrived, Doctor! You are very welcome.

DOCTOR. How do you do, Captain. It's a great honour to meet such a distinguished scientist.

CAPTAIN. Oh please! Unfortunately, my military duties don't give me much time for research . . . All the same, I do believe I am now on the brink of a rather exciting discovery.

DOCTOR. Really?

CAPTAIN. You see, I have been subjecting meteoric stones to spectrum analysis, and I have found carbon—an indication of organic life. What do you say to that?

DOCTOR. Can you see that in a microscope?

CAPTAIN. No, in a spectroscope, for heaven's sake!

DOCTOR. Spectroscope! I beg your pardon. Then you will soon be telling us what is happening on Jupiter.

CAPTAIN. Not what is happening, what *has* happened. If only that blasted Paris bookseller would send my books. I really think the whole book-trade must be in league against me. Think of it, for two months I've not had one single answer to my orders, my letters or my abusive telegrams! It's driving me mad. I can't make out what's happened.

DOCTOR. Well, what could it be but ordinary carelessness? You shouldn't let it upset you.

CAPTAIN. Yes, but the devil of it is I shan't be able to get my article finished in time.—I know they're working on the same lines in Berlin . . . However, that's not what we should be talking about now, but about you. If you would care to live here, we can give you a small suite of rooms in that wing. Or would you prefer your predecessor's house?

DOCTOR. Whichever you please.

CAPTAIN. No, whichever *you* please. You have only to say.

DOCTOR. It's for you to decide, Captain.

CAPTAIN. Nothing of the kind. It's for you to say which you prefer. I don't care one way or the other.

DOCTOR. But I really can't . . .

CAPTAIN. For Christ's sake, man, say what you want! I haven't any opinion, any inclination, any choice, any preference at all. Are you such a milksop that you don't know what you want? Make up your mind, or I shall lose my temper.

DOCTOR. If I am to choose, I should like to live here.

CAPTAIN. Good!—Thank you. (*Rings.*) Oh dear me!—I apologise, Doctor, but nothing irritates me so much as to hear people say they don't care one way or the other. (*The* NURSE *enters.*) Ah, it's you, Margaret. Look here, my dear, do you know if the rooms in the wing are ready for the doctor?

NURSE. Yes, Captain, they're ready.

CAPTAIN. Good. Then I won't detain you, Doctor, for you must be tired. Goodnight, and once again—welcome. I look forward to seeing you in the morning.

DOCTOR. Thank you. Goodnight.

CAPTAIN. By the way, I wonder if my wife told you anything about us —if you know at all how the land lies?

DOCTOR. Your good lady did suggest one or two things it might be as well for a newcomer to know. Goodnight, Captain.

(*The* NURSE *shows the* DOCTOR *out and returns.*)

CAPTAIN. What is it, old girl? Anything the matter?

NURSE. Now listen, Mr. Adolf, dear.

CAPTAIN. Yes, go on, Margaret, talk. You're the only one whose talk doesn't get on my nerves.

NURSE. Then listen, Mr. Adolf. Couldn't you go halfway to meet the mistress in all this bother over the child? Think of a mother . . .

CAPTAIN. Think of a father, Margaret.

NURSE. Now, now, now! A father has many things besides his child, but a mother has nothing but her child.

CAPTAIN. Quite so, my friend. She has only one burden, while I have three and bear hers too. Do you think I'd have been stuck in the army all my life if I hadn't had her and her child to support?

NURSE. I know, but that wasn't what I wanted to talk about.

CAPTAIN. Quite. What you want is to make out I'm in the wrong.

NURSE. Don't you believe I want what's best for you, Mr. Adolf?

CAPTAIN. I'm sure you do, my dear, but you don't know what is best for me. You see, it's not enough to have given the child life. I want to give her my very soul.

NURSE. Oh, that's beyond me, but I do think you two ought to come to terms.

CAPTAIN. Margaret, you are not my friend.

NURSE. Not your friend! Ah God, what are you saying, Mr. Adolf? Do you think I ever forget you were my baby when you were little?

CAPTAIN. Well, my dear, am I likely to forget it? You have been like a mother to me, and stood by me against all the others. But now that things have come to a head, you're deserting—going over to the enemy.

NURSE. Enemy?

CAPTAIN. Yes, enemy. You know perfectly well how things are here. You've seen it all from beginning to end.

NURSE. Aye, I've seen plenty. But, dear God, why must two people torment the lives out of each other? Two people who are so good

and kind to everyone else. The mistress never treats me wrong
or . . .

CAPTAIN. Only me. I know. And I tell you, Margaret, if you desert me
now, you'll be doing a wicked thing. For a net is closing round
me, and that doctor is no friend of mine.

NURSE. Oh, goodness, Mr. Adolf, you believe the worst of everyone!
But that's what comes of not having the true faith. That's your
trouble.

CAPTAIN. While you and the Baptists have found the one true faith,
eh? You're lucky.

NURSE. Aye, luckier than you, Mr. Adolf. Humble your heart and you
will see how happy God will make you in your love for your
neighbour.

CAPTAIN. Isn't it strange—as soon as you mention God and love, your
voice grows hard and your eyes fill with hate. No, Margaret, I'm
sure you haven't found the true faith.

MARGARET. However proud you are and stuffed with book-learning, that
won't get you anywhere when the pinch comes.

CAPTAIN. How arrogantly thou speakest, O humble heart! I'm well
aware that learning means nothing to creatures like you.

NURSE. Shame on you! Still, old Margaret loves her great big boy best
of all. And when the storm breaks, he'll come back to her, sure
enough, like the good child he is.

CAPTAIN. Forgive me, Margaret. You see, you really are the only friend
I have here. Help me, for something is going to happen. I don't
know what, but I know it's evil, this thing that's on its way. (*A
scream from within.*) What's that? Who's screaming?

(BERTHA *runs in.*)

BERTHA. Father, Father! Help me! Save me!

CAPTAIN. What is it? My darling, tell me.

BERTHA. Please protect me. I know she'll do something terrible to me.

CAPTAIN. Who? What do you mean? Tell me at once.

BERTHA. Grandmother. But it was my fault. I played a trick on her.

CAPTAIN. Go on.

BERTHA. Yes, but you mustn't tell anyone. Promise you won't.

CAPTAIN. Very well, but what happened?

(*Exit* NURSE.)

BERTHA. You see, sometimes in the evening she turns the lamp down
and makes me sit at the table holding a pen over a piece of paper.
And then she says the spirits write.

CAPTAIN. Well, I'll be damned! And you never told me.

BERTHA. I'm sorry, I didn't dare. Grandmother says spirits revenge themselves on people who talk about them. And then the pen writes, but I don't know if it's me doing it or not. Sometimes it goes well, but sometimes it doesn't work at all. And when I get tired nothing happens, but I have to make something happen all the same. This evening I thought I was doing rather well, but then Grandmother said it was all out of Stagnelius* and I had been playing a trick on her. And she was simply furious.

CAPTAIN. Do you believe there are spirits?

BERTHA. I don't know.

CAPTAIN. But I know there are not.

BERTHA. Grandmother says you don't understand, and that you have worse things that can see into other planets.

CAPTAIN. She says that, does she? And what else does she say?

BERTHA. That you can't work miracles.

CAPTAIN. I never said I could. You know what meteorites are, don't you?—stones that fall from other heavenly bodies. Well, I examine these and see if they contain the same elements as the earth. That's all I do.

BERTHA. Grandmother says there are things she can see and you can't.

CAPTAIN. My dear, she is lying.

BERTHA. Grandmother doesn't lie.

CAPTAIN. How do you know?

BERTHA. Then Mother does too.

CAPTAIN. Hm!

BERTHA. If you say Mother is a liar, I'll never believe a word you say again.

CAPTAIN. I didn't say that, so now you must believe me. Listen. Your happiness, your whole future depends on your leaving home. Will you do this? Will you go and live in town and learn something useful?

BERTHA. Oh yes, I'd love to live in town—anywhere away from here! It's always so miserable in there, as gloomy as a winter night. But when you come home, Father, it's like a spring morning when they take the double windows down.

CAPTAIN. My darling, my beloved child!

BERTHA. But, Father, listen, you must be kind to Mother. She often cries.

CAPTAIN. Hm! . . . So you would like to live in town?

BERTHA. Oh yes!

CAPTAIN. But supposing your mother doesn't agree?

BERTHA. She must.

CAPTAIN. But supposing she doesn't?

* Erik Johan Stagnelius, Swedish poet and dramatist (1793–1823).

BERTHA. Then I don't know what will happen. But she must, she must!

CAPTAIN. Will you ask her?

BERTHA. No, you must ask her—very nicely. She wouldn't pay any attention to me.

CAPTAIN. Hm! . . . Well now, if you want this and I want it and she doesn't want it, what are we to do then?

BERTHA. Oh, then the fuss will begin all over again! Why can't you both . . .

(*Enter* LAURA.)

LAURA. Ah, so you're here, Bertha! Well now, Adolf, as the question of her future is still to be decided, let's hear what she has to say herself.

CAPTAIN. The child can hardly have anything constructive to say about the development of young girls, but you and I ought to be able to sum up the pros and cons. We've watched a good number grow up.

LAURA. But as we don't agree, Bertha can give the casting vote.

CAPTAIN. No. I won't allow anyone to interfere with my rights—neither woman nor child. Bertha, you had better leave us.

(*Exit* BERTHA.)

LAURA. You were afraid to hear her opinion because you knew she would agree with me.

CAPTAIN. I know she wants to leave home, but I also know you have the power to make her change her mind.

LAURA. Oh, have I much power?

CAPTAIN. Yes, you have a fiendish power of getting your own way, like all people who are unscrupulous about the means they employ. How, for instance, did you get rid of Dr. Norling? And how did you get hold of the new doctor?

LAURA. Yes, how did I?

CAPTAIN. You ran the old doctor down until he had to leave, and then you got your brother to canvass for this one.

LAURA. Well, that was quite simple and perfectly legal. Then is Bertha to leave home?

CAPTAIN. Yes, in a fortnight's time.

LAURA. I warn you I shall do my best to prevent it.

CAPTAIN. You can't.

LAURA. Can't I? Do you expect me to give up my child to be taught by wicked people that all she has learnt from her mother is nonsense? So that I would be despised by my own daughter for the rest of my life.

CAPTAIN. Do you expect me to allow ignorant and bumptious women to teach my daughter that her father is a charlatan?

LAURA. That shouldn't matter so much to you—now.

CAPTAIN. What on earth do you mean?

LAURA. Well, the mother's closer to the child, since the discovery that no one can tell who the father is.

CAPTAIN. What's that got to do with us?

LAURA. You don't know if you are Bertha's father.

CAPTAIN. Don't know?

LAURA. How can you know what nobody knows?

CAPTAIN. Are you joking?

LAURA. No, I'm simply applying your own theory. How do you know I haven't been unfaithful to you?

CAPTAIN. I can believe a good deal of you, but not that. And if it were so, you wouldn't talk about it.

LAURA. Supposing I were prepared for anything, for being turned out and ostracised, anything to keep my child under my own control. Supposing I am telling the truth now when I say: Bertha is my child but not yours. Supposing . . .

CAPTAIN. Stop it!

LAURA. Just supposing . . . then your power would be over.

CAPTAIN. Not till you had proved I wasn't the father.

LAURA. That wouldn't be difficult. Do you want me to?

CAPTAIN. Stop.

LAURA. I should only have to give the name of the real father—with particulars of place and time, of course. For that matter—when was Bertha born? In the third year of our marriage . . .

CAPTAIN. Will you stop it now, or . . .

LAURA. Or what? Very well, let's stop. All the same, I should think twice before you decide anything. And, above all, don't make yourself ridiculous.

CAPTAIN. I find the whole thing tragic.

LAURA. Which makes you still more ridiculous.

CAPTAIN. But not you?

LAURA. No, we're in such a strong position.

CAPTAIN. That's why we can't fight you.

LAURA. Why try to fight a superior enemy?

CAPTAIN. Superior?

LAURA. Yes. It's odd, but I have never been able to look at a man without feeling myself his superior.

CAPTAIN. One day you may meet your master—and you'll never forget it.

LAURA. That will be fascinating.

(*Enter* NURSE.)

NURSE. Supper's ready. Come along now, please.

LAURA. Yes, of course. (*The* CAPTAIN *lingers and sits down in an armchair near the sofa.*) Aren't you coming?

CAPTAIN. No, thank you, I don't want any supper.

LAURA. Why not? Has anything upset you?

CAPTAIN. No, but I'm not hungry.

LAURA. Do come, or they'll start asking questions, and that's not necessary. Do be sensible. You won't? Well, stay where you are then! (*Exit.*)

NURSE. Mr. Adolf, whatever is it now?

CAPTAIN. I don't know yet. Tell me—why do you women treat a grown man as if he were a child?

NURSE. Well, goodness me, you're all some woman's child, aren't you? —All you men, big or small . . .

CAPTAIN. While no woman is born of man, you mean. True. But I must be Bertha's father. You believe that, Margaret, don't you? Don't you?

NURSE. Lord, what a silly boy you are! Of course you're your own child's father. Come along and eat now. Don't sit here sulking. There now, come along, do.

CAPTAIN (*rising*). Get out, woman! To hell with the hags! (*At the hall door*) Svärd! Svärd!

ORDERLY (*entering*). Yes, sir?

CAPTAIN. Have the small sleigh got ready at once. (*Exit* ORDERLY.)

NURSE. Now listen, Captain . . .

CAPTAIN. Get out, woman! Get out, I say!

NURSE. God preserve us, whatever's going to happen now?

CAPTAIN (*putting on his cap*). Don't expect me home before midnight. (*Exit.*)

NURSE. Lord Jesus! What *is* going to happen?

ACT TWO

The same as before, late that night. The DOCTOR *and* LAURA *are sitting talking.*

DOCTOR. My conversation with him has led me to the conclusion that your suspicions are by no means proved. To begin with, you were mistaken in saying that he had made these important astronomical discoveries by using a microscope. Now I have learnt that it was a spectroscope. Not only is there no sign in this of mental derangement—on the contrary, he has rendered a great service to science.

LAURA. But I never said that.

DOCTOR. I made a memorandum of our conversation, Madam, and I remember questioning you on this vital point, because I thought I must have misheard. One must be scrupulously accurate when bringing charges which might lead to a man being certified.

LAURA. Certified?

DOCTOR. I presume you are aware that if a person is certified insane, he loses both his civil and his family rights.

LAURA. No, I didn't know that.

DOCTOR. There is one other point I should like to be clear about. He spoke of not getting any replies from his book-sellers. May I ask whether—from the best of intentions, of course—you have been intercepting his correspondence?

LAURA. Yes, I have. It is my duty to protect the family. I couldn't let him ruin us all and do nothing about it.

DOCTOR. Excuse me, I do not think you understand the possible consequences of your action. If he realises you have been interfering with his affairs behind his back, his suspicions will be aroused and might even develop into a persecution mania. Particularly, as by thwarting his will, you have already driven him to the end of his tether. Surely you know how enraging it is to have your will opposed and your dearest wishes frustrated.

LAURA. Do I not!

DOCTOR. Then think what this means to him.

LAURA (*rising*). It's midnight and he's not back yet. Now we can expect the worst.

DOCTOR. Tell me what happened this evening after I saw him. I must know everything.

LAURA. He talked in the wildest way and said the most fantastic things. Can you believe it—he even suggested he wasn't the father of his own child!

DOCTOR. How extraordinary! What can have put that into his head?

LAURA. Goodness knows, unless it was an interview he had with one of his men about maintenance for a child. When I took the girl's part, he got very excited and said no one could ever tell who a child's father was. God knows I did everything I could to calm him, but I don't believe anything can help him now. (*Weeps.*)

DOCTOR. This can't go on. Something must be done—without rousing his suspicions. Tell me, has he had any such delusions before?

LAURA. As a matter of fact, he was much the same six years ago, and then he actually admitted—in a letter to his doctor—that he feared for his reason.

DOCTOR. I see, I see. A deep-seated trouble. But . . . er . . . the sanctity of family life . . . and so forth . . . I mustn't probe too far . . . must keep to the surface. Unfortunately what is done cannot be undone, yet the remedy should have been applied to what is done . . . Where do you think he is now?

LAURA. I can't imagine. He has such wild notions these days . . .

DOCTOR. Would you like me to stay until he comes in? I could explain my presence by saying—well, that your mother is ill and I came to see her.

LAURA. That's a very good idea. Please stand by us, Doctor. If you only knew how worried I am! . . . But wouldn't it be better to tell him straight out what you think of his condition?

DOCTOR. We never do that with mental patients, unless they bring the subject up themselves, and rarely even then. Everything depends on how the case develops. But we had better not stay here. May I go into some other room, to make it more convincing?

LAURA. Yes, that will be best, and Margaret can come in here. She always waits up for him. (*At the door*) Margaret! Margaret! She is the only one who can manage him.

NURSE (*entering*). Did you call, Madam? Is Master back?

LAURA. No, but you are to wait here for him. And when he comes, tell him that my mother is unwell and the doctor is with her.

NURSE. Aye, aye. Leave all that to me.

LAURA (*opening the door*). If you will be so good as to come in here, Doctor . . .

DOCTOR. Thank you.

(*They go out. The* NURSE *sits at the table, puts on her glasses and picks up her hymn-book.*)

NURSE. Ah me! Ah me! (*Reads softly.*)

A sorrowful and grievous thing
Is life, so swiftly passing by,
Death shadows with his angel's wing
The whole earth, and this his cry:
'Tis Vanity, all Vanity!

Ah me! Ah me!

All that on earth has life and breath,
Falls low before his awful might,
Sorrow alone is spared by Death,
Upon the yawning grave to write:
'Tis Vanity, all Vanity!

Ah me! Ah me!

(*During the last lines,* BERTHA *enters, carrying a tray with a coffee-pot and a piece of embroidery.*)

BERTHA (*softly*). Margaret, may I sit in here with you? It's so dismal up there.

NURSE. Saints alive! Bertha, are you still up?

BERTHA. Well, you see, I simply must get on with Father's Christmas present. And here's something nice for you.

NURSE. But, sweetheart, this won't do. You have to be up bright and early, and it's past twelve now.

BERTHA. Oh, that doesn't matter! I daren't stay up there all alone. I'm sure there are ghosts.

NURSE. There now! What did I tell you? Mark my words, there's no good fairy in this house. What was it? Did you hear something, Bertha?

BERTHA. Oh Margaret, someone was singing in the attic!

NURSE. In the attic? At this time of night?

BERTHA. Yes. It was such a sad song; the saddest I ever heard. And it seemed to come from the attic—you know, the one on the left where the cradle is.

NURSE. Oh dear, dear, dear! And such a fearful night too. I'm sure the chimneys will blow down. "Alas, what is this earthly life? Sorrow, trouble, grief and strife. Even when it seems most fair, Nought but tribulation there."—Ah, dear child, God grant us a happy Christmas!

BERTHA. Margaret, is it true Father's ill?

NURSE. Aye, that's true enough.

BERTHA. Then I don't expect we shall have a Christmas party. But why isn't he in bed if he's ill?

NURSE. Well, dearie, staying in bed doesn't help his kind of illness. Hush! I hear someone in the porch. Go to bed now—take the tray with you, or the Master will be cross.

BERTHA (*going out with the tray*). Goodnight, Margaret.

NURSE. Goodnight, love. God bless you.

(*Enter the* CAPTAIN.)

CAPTAIN (*taking off his overcoat*). Are you still up? Go to bed.

NURSE. Oh, I was only biding till . . .

(*The* CAPTAIN *lights a candle, opens the bureau, sits down at it and takes letters and newspapers from his pocket.*)

Mr. Adolf . . .

CAPTAIN. What is it?

NURSE. The old mistress is ill. Doctor's here.

CAPTAIN. Anything serious?

NURSE. No, I don't think so. Just a chill.

CAPTAIN (*rising*). Who was the father of your child, Margaret?

NURSE. I've told you often enough, it was that heedless fellow Johansson.

CAPTAIN. Are you sure it was he?

NURSE. Don't talk so silly. Of course I'm sure, seeing he was the only one.

CAPTAIN. Yes, but was he sure he was the only one? No, he couldn't be sure, only you could be. See? That's the difference.

NURSE. I don't see any difference.

CAPTAIN. No, you don't see it, but it's there all the same. (*Turns the pages of the photograph album on the table.*) Do you think Bertha's like me?

NURSE. You're as like as two peas in a pod.

CAPTAIN. Did Johansson admit he was the father?

NURSE. Well, he was forced to.

CAPTAIN. How dreadful!—Here's the doctor. (*Enter* DOCTOR.) Good evening, Doctor. How is my mother-in-law?

DOCTOR. Oh, it's nothing much. Just a slight sprain of the left ankle.

CAPTAIN. I thought Margaret said it was a chill. There appear to be different diagnoses of the case. Margaret, go to bed. (*Exit* NURSE. *Pause.*) Won't you sit down, Dr. Östermark?

DOCTOR (*sitting*). Thank you.

CAPTAIN. Is it true that if you cross a mare with a zebra you get striped foals?

DOCTOR (*astonished*). Perfectly true.

CAPTAIN. And that if breeding is then continued with a stallion, the foals may still be striped?

DOCTOR. That is also true.

CAPTAIN. So, in certain circumstances, a stallion can sire striped foals, and vice versa.

DOCTOR. That would appear to be the case.

CAPTAIN. So the offspring's resemblance to the father proves nothing.

DOCTOR. Oh . . .

CAPTAIN. You're a widower, aren't you? Any children?

DOCTOR. Ye-es.

CAPTAIN. Didn't you sometimes feel rather ridiculous as a father? I myself don't know anything more ludicrous than the sight of a man holding his child's hand in the street, or hearing a father say: "My child." "My wife's child," he ought to say. Didn't you ever see what a false position you were in? Weren't you ever haunted by doubts—I won't say suspicions, as a gentleman I assume your wife was above suspicion?

DOCTOR. No, I certainly wasn't. There it is, Captain, a man—as I think
Goethe says—must take his children on trust.

CAPTAIN. Trust, where a woman's concerned? A bit of a risk.

DOCTOR. Ah, but there are many kinds of women!

CAPTAIN. The latest research shows there is only one kind . . . when
I was a young fellow and not, if I may say so, a bad specimen,
I had two little experiences which afterwards gave me to think.
The first was on a steamer. I was in the saloon with some friends,
and the young stewardess told us—with tears running down her
cheeks—how her sweetheart had been drowned at sea. We con-
doled with her and I ordered champagne. After the second glass
I touched her foot, after the fourth her knee, and before morning
I had consoled her.

DOCTOR. One swallow doesn't make a summer.

CAPTAIN. My second experience was a summer swallow. I was staying
at Lysekil and got to know a young married woman who was there
with her children—her husband was in town. She was religious
and high-minded, kept preaching at me and was—or so I thought
—the soul of virtue. I lent her a book or two which, strange to
relate, she returned. Three months later, I found her card in one
of those books with a pretty outspoken declaration of love. It was
innocent—as innocent, that's to say, as such a declaration from
a married woman could be—to a stranger who had never made
her any advances. Moral: don't believe in anyone too much.

DOCTOR. Don't believe too little either.

CAPTAIN. The happy mean, eh? But you see, Doctor, that woman was
so unaware of her motives she actually told her husband of her
infatuation for me. That's where the danger lies, in the fact that
women are unconscious of their instinctive wickedness. An extenuating circumstance, perhaps, but that can only mitigate the judgment, not revoke it.

DOCTOR. You have a morbid turn of mind, Captain. You should be on
your guard against this.

CAPTAIN. There's nothing morbid about it. Look here. All steam-boilers
explode when the pressure-gauge reaches the limit, but the limit
isn't the same for all boilers. Got that? After all, you're here to
observe me. Now if I were not a man I could sniff and snivel and
explain the case to you, with all its past history. But as unfortunately I am a man, like the ancient Roman I must cross my arms
upon my breast and hold my breath until I die. Goodnight.

DOCTOR. If you are ill, Captain, there's no reflection on your manhood
in telling me about it. Indeed, it is essential for me to hear both
sides of the case.

CAPTAIN. I thought you were quite satisfied with one side.

DOCTOR. You're wrong. And I should like you to know, Captain, that when I heard that Mrs. Alving* blackening her late husband's memory, I thought what a damned shame it was that the fellow should be dead.

CAPTAIN. Do you think if he'd been alive he'd have said anything? Do you think if any husband rose from the dead he'd be believed? Goodnight, Doctor. Look how calm I am. It's quite safe for you to go to bed.

DOCTOR. Then I will bid you goodnight. I wash my hands of the whole business.

CAPTAIN. So we're enemies?

DOCTOR. By no means. It's just a pity we can't be friends. Goodnight. (*The* CAPTAIN *shows the* DOCTOR *out by the hall door, then crosses to the other and slightly opens it.*)

CAPTAIN. Come in and let's talk. I knew you were eavesdropping. (*Enter* LAURA, *embarrassed. The* CAPTAIN *sits at the bureau.*) It's very late, but we'd better have things out now. Sit down. (*She sits. Pause.*) This evening it was I who went to the post office and fetched the mail, and from my letters it is clear to me that you have been intercepting my correspondence—both in and out. The result of this has been a loss of time which has pretty well shattered the expectations I had for my work.

LAURA. I acted from the best of intentions. You were neglecting your military duties for this other work.

CAPTAIN. Scarcely the best of intentions. You knew very well that one day I should win more distinction in this field than in the army, but what you wanted was to stop me winning laurels of any kind, because this would stress your own inferiority. Now, for a change, I have intercepted letters addressed to you.

LAURA. How chivalrous!

CAPTAIN. In keeping with the high opinion you have of me. From these letters it appears that for a long time now you've been setting my old friends against me, by spreading rumours about my mental condition. So successful have your efforts been that now scarcely one person from Colonel to kitchen-maid believes I am sane. The actual facts about my condition are these. My reason is, as you know, unaffected, and I am able to discharge my duties both as soldier and father. My emotions are still pretty well under control, but only so long as my will-power remains intact. And you have so gnawed and gnawed at my will that at any moment it may slip its cogs, and then the whole bag of tricks will go to

* Reference to Mrs. Alving in Ibsen's GHOSTS.

pieces. I won't appeal to your feelings, because you haven't any —that is your strength. I appeal to your own interests.

LAURA. Go on.

CAPTAIN. By behaving in this way you have made me so full of suspicion that my judgment is fogged and my mind is beginning to stray. This means that the insanity you have been waiting for is on its way and may come at any moment. The question you now have to decide is whether it is more to your advantage for me to be well or ill. Consider. If I go to pieces, I shall have to leave the Service, and where will you be then? If I die, you get my life-insurance. But if I take my own life, you get nothing. It is therefore to your advantage that I should live my life out.

LAURA. Is this a trap?

CAPTAIN. Certainly. You can avoid it or stick your head in it.

LAURA. You say you'd kill yourself, but you never would.

CAPTAIN. Are you so sure? Do you think a man can go on living when he has nothing and nobody to live for?

LAURA. Then you give in?

CAPTAIN. No, I offer peace.

LAURA. On what terms?

CAPTAIN. That I may keep my reason. Free me from doubt and I will give up the fight.

LAURA. Doubt about what?

CAPTAIN. Bertha's parentage.

LAURA. Are there doubts about that?

CAPTAIN. Yes, for me there are, and it was you who roused them.

LAURA. I?

CAPTAIN. Yes. You dropped them like henbane in my ear, and circumstances encouraged them to grow. Free me from uncertainty. Tell me straight out it is so, and I will forgive you in advance.

LAURA. I can scarcely admit to guilt that isn't mine.

CAPTAIN. What can it matter to you, when you know I won't reveal it? Do you think any man would proclaim his shame from the housetops?

LAURA. If I say it isn't so, you still won't be certain, but if I say it is, you will believe me. You must want it to be true.

CAPTAIN. Strangely enough I do. Perhaps because the first supposition can't be proved, while the second can.

LAURA. Have you any grounds for suspicion?

CAPTAIN. Yes and no.

LAURA. I believe you want to make out I'm guilty, so you can get rid of me and have absolute control of the child. But you won't catch me in any such trap.

CAPTAIN. Do you think, if I were convinced of your guilt, I should want to take on another man's child?

LAURA. No, I'm sure you wouldn't. So evidently you were lying when you said you'd forgive me in advance.

CAPTAIN (*rising*). Laura, save me and my reason! You can't have understood what I was saying. If the child's not mine, I have no rights over her, nor do I want any. And that's how you'd like it, isn't it? But that's not all. You want complete power over the child, don't you, with me still there to support you both?

LAURA. Power, that's it. What's this whole life and death struggle for if not power?

CAPTAIN. For me, as I don't believe in a life to come, this child was my life after death, my conception of immortality—the only one, perhaps, that's valid. If you take her away, you cut my life short.

LAURA. Why didn't we separate sooner?

CAPTAIN. Because the child bound us together, but the bond became a chain. How was that? I never thought of this before, but now memories return, accusing, perhaps condemning. After two years of marriage we were still childless—you know best why. Then I was ill and almost died. One day, between bouts of fever, I heard voices in the next room. You and the lawyer were discussing the property I still owned then. He was explaining that as there were no children, you could not inherit, and he asked if by any chance you were pregnant. I did not hear your reply. I recovered and we had a child. Who is the father?

LAURA. You are.

CAPTAIN. No, I am not. There's a crime buried here that's beginning to stink. And what a fiendish crime! You women, who were so tender-hearted about freeing black slaves, kept the white ones. I have slaved for you, your child, your mother, your servants. I have sacrificed career and promotion. Tortured, beaten, sleepless—my hair has gone grey through the agony of mind you have inflicted on me. All this I have suffered in order that you might enjoy a care-free life and, when you were old, relive it in your child. This is the lowest form of theft, the cruellest slavery. I have had seventeen years of penal servitude—and I was innocent. How can you make up to me for this?

LAURA. Now you really are mad.

CAPTAIN (*sitting*). So you hope. I have watched you trying to conceal your crime, but because I didn't understand I pitied you. I've soothed your conscience, thinking I was chasing away some nightmare. I've heard you crying out in your sleep without giving your words a second thought. But now . . . now! The other night—Bertha's birthday—comes back to me. I was still up in the early hours, reading, and you suddenly screamed as if someone were trying to strangle you. "Don't! Don't!" you cried. I knocked on the wall—I didn't want to hear any more. For a long time I have had vague suspicions. I did not want them confirmed. This is what I have suffered for you. What will you do for me?

LAURA. What can I do? Swear before God and all that I hold sacred that you are Bertha's father?

CAPTAIN. What good would that do? You have already said that a mother can and ought to commit any crime for her child. I implore you by the memory of the past, I implore you as a wounded man begs to be put out of his misery, tell me the truth. Can't you see I'm helpless as a child? Can't you hear me crying to my mother that I'm hurt? Forget I'm a man, a soldier whose word men—and even beasts—obey. I am nothing but a sick creature in need of pity. I renounce every vestige of power and only beg for mercy on my life.

LAURA (*laying her hand on his forehead*). What? You, a man, in tears?

CAPTAIN. Yes, a man in tears. Has not a man eyes? Has not a man hands, limbs, senses, opinions, passions? Is he not nourished by the same food as a woman, wounded by the same weapons, warmed and chilled by the same winter and summer? If you prick us, do we not bleed? If you tickle us, do we not laugh? If you poison us, do we not die? Why should a man suffer in silence or a soldier hide his tears? Because it's not manly? Why isn't it manly?

LAURA. Weep, then, my child, and you shall have your mother again. Remember, it was as your second mother that I came into your life. You were big and strong, yet not fully a man. You were a giant child who had come into the world too soon, or perhaps an unwanted child.

CAPTAIN. That's true. My father and mother had me against their will, and therefore I was born without a will. That is why, when you and I became one, I felt I was completing myself—and that is why you dominated. I—in the army the one to command—became at home the one to obey. I grew up at your side, looked up to you as a superior being and listened to you as if I were your foolish little boy.

LAURA. Yes, that's how it was, and I loved you as if you were my little boy. But didn't you see how, when your feelings changed and you came to me as a lover, I was ashamed? The joy I felt in your embraces was followed by such a sense of guilt my very blood seemed tainted. The mother became the mistress—horrible!

CAPTAIN. I saw, but I didn't understand. I thought you despised my lack of virility, so I tried to win you as a woman by proving myself as a man.

LAURA. That was your mistake. The mother was your friend, you see, but the woman was your enemy. Sexual love is conflict. And don't imagine I gave myself. I didn't give. I only took what I meant to take. Yet you did dominate me . . . I felt it and wanted you to feel it.

CAPTAIN. You always dominated me. You could hypnotise me when I was wide awake, so that I neither saw nor heard, but simply obeyed. You could give me a raw potato and make me think it was a peach; you could make me take your ridiculous ideas for flashes of genius. You could corrupt me—yes, make me do the shabbiest things. You never had any real intelligence, yet, instead of being guided by me, you would take the reins into your own hands. And when at last I woke to the realisation that I had lost my integrity, I wanted to blot out my humiliation by some heroic action—some feat, some discovery—even by committing *hara-kiri*. I wanted to go to war, but I couldn't. It was then that I gave all my energies to science. And now—now when I should be stretching out my hand to gather the fruit, you chop off my arm. I'm robbed of my laurels; I'm finished. A man cannot live without repute.

LAURA. Can a woman?

CAPTAIN. Yes—she has her children, but he has not . . . Yet you and I and everyone else went on living, unconscious as children, full of fancies and ideals and illusions, until we woke up. Right— but we woke topsy-turvy, and what's more, we'd been woken by someone who was talking in his own sleep. When women are old and stop being women, they grow beards on their chins. What do men grow, I wonder, when they are old and stop being men? In this false dawn, the birds that crowed weren't cocks, they were capons, and the hens that answered their call were sexless, too. So when the sun should have risen for us, we found ourselves back among the ruins in the full moonlight, just as in the good old times. Our light morning sleep had only been troubled by fantastic dreams—there had been no awakening.

LAURA. You should have been a writer, you know.

CAPTAIN. Perhaps.

LAURA. But I'm sleepy now, so if you have any more fantasies, keep them till to-morrow.

CAPTAIN. Just one thing more—a fact. Do you hate me?

LAURA. Sometimes—as a man.

CAPTAIN. It's like race-hatred. If it's true we are descended from the ape, it must have been from two different species. There's no likeness between us, is there?

LAURA. What are you getting at?

CAPTAIN. In this fight, one of us must go under.

LAURA. Which?

CAPTAIN. The weaker naturally.

LAURA. Then is the stronger in the right?

CAPTAIN. Bound to be as he has the power.

LAURA. Then I am in the right.

CAPTAIN. Why, what power have you?

LAURA. All I need. And it will be legal power to-morrow when I've put you under restraint.

CAPTAIN. Under restraint?

LAURA. Yes. Then I shall decide my child's future myself out of reach of your fantasies.

CAPTAIN. Who will pay for her if I'm not there?

LAURA. Your pension.

CAPTAIN (*moving towards her menacingly*). How can you have me put under restraint?

LAURA (*producing a letter*). By means of this letter, an attested copy of which is already in the hands of the authorities.

CAPTAIN. What letter?

LAURA (*retreating*). Your own. The one in which you told the doctor you were mad. (*He stares at her in silence.*) Now you have fulfilled the unfortunately necessary functions of father and breadwinner. You are no longer needed, and you must go. You must go, now that you realise my wits are as strong as my will—you won't want to stay and acknowledge my superiority.

(*The* CAPTAIN *goes to the table, picks up the lighted lamp and throws it at* LAURA, *who escapes backward through the door.*)

ACT THREE

The same. The following evening. A new lamp, lighted, is on the table. The wall-papered door is barricaded with a chair. From the room above comes the sound of pacing footsteps. The NURSE *stands listening, troubled. Enter* LAURA *from within.*

LAURA. Did he give you the keys?

NURSE. Give? No, God help us, I took them from the coat Nöjd had out to brush.

LAURA. Then it's Nöjd who's on duty?

NURSE. Aye, it's Nöjd.

LAURA. Give me the keys.

NURSE. Here you are, but it's no better than stealing. Hark at him up there! To and fro, to and fro.

LAURA. Are you sure the door's safely bolted?

NURSE. It's bolted safe enough. (*Weeps.*)

LAURA (*opening the bureau and sitting down at it*). Pull yourself together, Margaret. The only way we can protect ourselves is by keeping calm. (*A knock at the hall door.*) See who that is.

NURSE (*opening door*). It's Nöjd.

LAURA. Tell him to come in.

NÖJD (*entering*). Despatch from the Colonel.

LAURA. Give it to me. (*Reads.*) I see . . . Nöjd, have you removed the cartridges from all the guns and pouches?

NÖJD. Yes, Ma'am, just as you said.

LAURA. Wait outside while I write to the Colonel.

(*Exit* NÖJD. LAURA *writes. Sound of sawing above.*)

NURSE. Listen, Madam. Whatever is he doing now?

LAURA. Do be quiet. I'm writing.

NURSE (*muttering*). Lord have mercy on us! What will be the end of all this?

LAURA (*holding out the note*). Here you are. Give it to Nöjd. And, remember, my mother's to know nothing of all this.

(*Exit* NURSE *with note.* LAURA *opens the bureau drawers and takes out papers. Enter* PASTOR.)

PASTOR. My dear Laura! As you probably gathered, I have been out all day and only just got back. I hear you've been having a terrible time.

LAURA. Yes, brother, I've never been through such a night and day in all my life!

PASTOR. Well, I see you're looking none the worse for it.

LAURA. No, thank heaven, I wasn't hurt. But just think what might have happened!

PASTOR. Tell me all about it. I've only heard rumours. How did it begin?

LAURA. It began by him raving about not being Bertha's father, and ended by him throwing the lighted lamp in my face.

PASTOR. But this is appalling. He must be quite out of his mind. What in heaven's name are we to do?

LAURA. We must try to prevent further violence. The doctor has sent to the hospital for a strait-jacket. I have just written a note to the Colonel, and now I'm trying to get some idea of the state of our affairs, which Adolf has so shockingly mismanaged. (*Opens another drawer.*)

PASTOR. It's a miserable business altogether, but I always feared something of the kind might happen. When fire and water meet, there's bound to be an explosion. (*Looks in drawer.*) Whatever's all this?

LAURA. Look! This is where he's kept everything hidden.

PASTOR. Good heavens! Here's your old doll! And there's your christening cap . . . and Bertha's rattle . . . and your letters . . . and that locket . . . (*Wipes his eyes.*) He must have loved you very dearly, Laura. I never kept this kind of thing.

LAURA. I believe he did love me once, but time changes everything.

PASTOR. What's this imposing document? (*Examines it.*) The purchase of a grave! Well, better a grave than the asylum! Laura, be frank with me. Aren't you at all to blame?

LAURA. How can I be to blame because someone goes out of his mind?

PASTOR. We—ell! I will say no more. After all, blood's thicker than water.

LAURA. Meaning what, if I may ask?

PASTOR (*gazing at her*). Oh come now!

LAURA. What?

PASTOR. Come, come! You can scarcely deny that it would suit you down to the ground to have complete control of your daughter.

LAURA. I don't understand.

PASTOR. I can't help admiring you.

LAURA. Really?

PASTOR. And as for me—I shall be appointed guardian to that Freethinker whom, as you know, I always regarded as a tare among our wheat.

(LAURA *gives a quick laugh which she suppresses.*)

LAURA. You dare say that to me, his wife?

PASTOR. How strong-willed you are, Laura, how amazingly strong-willed! Like a fox in a trap that would gnaw off its own leg rather than be caught. Like a master-thief working alone, without even a conscience for accomplice. Look in the mirror! You daren't.

LAURA. I never use a mirror.

PASTOR. No. You daren't look at yourself. Let me see your hand. Not one tell-tale spot of blood, not a trace of that subtle poison. A little innocent murder that the law cannot touch. An unconscious crime. Unconscious? A stroke of genius that. Listen to him up there! Take care, Laura! If that man gets loose, he will saw you in pieces too.

LAURA. You must have a bad conscience to talk like that. Pin the guilt on me if you can.

PASTOR. I can't.

LAURA. You see? You can't, and so—I am innocent. And now, you look after your charge and I'll take care of mine. (*Enter* DOCTOR.) Ah, here is the Doctor! (*Rises.*) I'm so glad to see you, Doctor. I know I can count on you to help me, although I'm afraid not much can be done now. You hear him up there. Are you convinced at last?

DOCTOR. I am convinced there has been an act of violence. But the question is—should that act of violence be regarded as an outbreak of temper or insanity?

PASTOR. But apart from this actual outbreak, you must admit that he suffers from fixed ideas.

DOCTOR. I have a notion, Pastor, that *your* ideas are even more fixed.

PASTOR. My firmly rooted convictions of spiritual . . .

DOCTOR. Convictions apart, it rests with you, Madam, to decide if your husband is to be fined or imprisoned or sent to the asylum. How do you regard his conduct?

LAURA. I can't answer that now.

DOCTOR. Oh? Have you no—er—firmly rooted convictions of what would be best for the family? And you, Pastor?

PASTOR. There's bound to be a scandal either way. It's not easy to give an opinion.

LAURA. But if he were only fined for violence he could be violent again.

DOCTOR. And if he were sent to prison he would soon be out again. So it seems best for all parties that he should be treated as insane. Where is the nurse?

LAURA. Why?

DOCTOR. She must put the strait-jacket on the patient. Not at once, but after I have had a talk with him—and not then until I give the order. I have the—er—garment outside. (*Goes out to hall and returns with a large parcel.*) Kindly call the nurse.

(LAURA *rings. The* DOCTOR *begins to unpack the strait-jacket.*)

PASTOR. Dreadful! Dreadful!

(*Enter* NURSE.)

DOCTOR. Ah, Nurse! Now please pay attention. You see this jacket. When I give you the word I want you to slip it on the Captain from behind. So as to prevent any further violence, you understand. Now it has, you see, unusually long sleeves. That is to restrict his movements. These sleeves must be tied together behind his back. And now here are two straps with buckles, which afterwards you must fasten to the arm of a chair—or to whatever's easiest. Can you do this, do you think?

NURSE. No, Doctor, I can't. No, not that.

LAURA. Why not do it yourself, Doctor?

DOCTOR. Because the patient distrusts me. You, Madam, are the proper person, but I'm afraid he doesn't trust you either. (LAURA *grimaces*.) Perhaps you, Pastor . . .

PASTOR. I must beg to decline.

(*Enter* NÖJD.)

LAURA. Did you deliver my note?

NÖJD. Yes, Madam.

DOCTOR. Oh, it's you, Nöjd! You know the state of things here, don't you? You know the Captain has had a mental breakdown. You must help us look after the patient.

NÖJD. If there's aught I can do for Captain, he knows I'll do it.

DOCTOR. You are to put this jacket on him.

NURSE. He's not to touch him. Nöjd shan't hurt him. I'd rather do it myself, gently, gently. But Nöjd can wait outside and help me if need be—yes, that's what he'd best do.

(*A pounding on the paper-covered door.*)

DOCTOR. Here he is! (*To* NURSE.) Put the jacket on that chair under your shawl. And now go away, all of you, while the Pastor and I talk to him. That door won't hold long. Hurry!

NURSE (*going out*). Lord Jesus, help us!

(LAURA *shuts the bureau and follows the* NURSE. NÖJD *goes out to the hall. The paper-covered door bursts open, the lock broken and the chair hurled to the floor. The* CAPTAIN *comes out, carrying a pile of books.*)

CAPTAIN (*putting the books on the table*). Here it all is. You can read it in every one of these volumes. So I wasn't mad after all. (*Picks one up.*) Here it is in the Odyssey, Book I, page 6, line 215 in the Uppsala translation. Telemachus speaking to Athene: "My mother says I am Odysseus' son; but for myself I cannot tell. It's a wise child that knows its own father." And that's the suspicion Telemachus has about Penelope, the most virtuous of women. Fine state of affairs, eh? (*Takes up another book.*) And here we have the Prophet Ezekiel: "The fool saith, Lo, here is my father; but who can tell whose loins have engendered him?" That's clear enough. (*Picks up another.*) And what's this? A history of Russian literature by Merzlyakov. Alexander Pushkin, Russia's greatest poet, was mortally wounded—but more by the rumours of his wife's unfaithfulness than by the bullet he received in his breast at the duel. On his deathbed he swore she was innocent.

Jackass! How could he swear any such thing? I *do* read my books, you see! Hullo, Jonas, are you here? And the Doctor, of course. Did I ever tell you what I said to the English lady who was deploring the habit Irishmen have of throwing lighted lamps in their wives' faces? "God, what women!" I said. "Women?" she stammered. "Of course," I replied. "When things get to such a pass that a man who has loved, has worshipped a woman, picks up a lighted lamp and flings it in her face, then you may be sure . . ."

PASTOR. Sure of what?

CAPTAIN. Nothing. You can never be sure of anything—you can only believe. That's right, isn't it, Jonas? One believes and so one is saved. Saved, indeed! No. One can be damned through believing. That's what I've learnt.

DOCTOR. But, Captain . . .

CAPTAIN. Hold your tongue! I don't want any chat from you. I don't want to hear you relaying all the gossip from in there like a telephone. In there—you know what I mean. Listen to me, Jonas. Do you imagine you're the father of your children? I seem to remember you had a tutor in the house, a pretty boy about whom there was quite a bit of gossip.

PASTOR. Take care, Adolf!

CAPTAIN. Feel under your wig and see if you don't find two little nobs. Upon my soul, he's turning pale! Well, well! It was only talk, of course, but my God, how they talked! But we married men are all figures of fun, every man Jack of us. Isn't that right, Doctor? What about your own marriage bed? Didn't you have a certain lieutenant in your house, eh? Wait now, let me guess. He was called . . . (*Whispers in the* DOCTOR's *ear.*) By Jove, he's turned pale too! But don't worry. She's dead and buried, so what was done can't be done again. As a matter of fact, I knew him, and he's now—look at me, Doctor—no, straight in the eyes! He is now a major of Dragoons. Good Lord, I believe *he* has horns too!

DOCTOR (*angrily*). Be so good as to change the subject, Captain.

CAPTAIN. See! As soon as I mention horns he wants to change the subject.

PASTOR. I suppose you know, brother-in-law, that you're not in your right mind?

CAPTAIN. Yes, I do know. But if I had the handling of your decorated heads, I should soon have you shut up too. I am mad. But how did I become mad? Doesn't that interest you? No, it doesn't interest anyone. (*Takes the photograph album from the table.*)

Christ Jesus, there is my daughter! Mine? That's what we can
never know. Shall I tell you what we should have to do so as to
know? First marry, in order to be accepted by society, then immediately divorce; after that become lovers and finally adopt the
children. That way one could at least be sure they were one's own
adopted children. Eh? But what good's that to me? What good's
anything now you have robbed me of my immortality? What can
science or philosophy do for me when I have nothing left to live
for? How can I live without honour? I grafted my right arm and
half my brain and spinal cord on to another stem. I believed they
would unite and grow into a single, more perfect tree. Then
someone brought a knife and cut below the graft, so now I'm
only half a tree. The other part, with my arm and half my brain,
goes on growing. But I wither—I am dying, for it was the best
part of myself I gave away. Let me die. Do what you like with
me. I'm finished.

(*The* DOCTOR *and* PASTOR *whisper, then go out. The* CAPTAIN
sinks into a chair by the table. BERTHA *enters.*)

BERTHA (*going to him*). Are you ill, Father?

CAPTAIN (*looking up stupidly at word "Father"*). Me?

BERTHA. Do you know what you did? You threw a lamp at Mother.

CAPTAIN. Did I?

BERTHA. Yes. Supposing she'd been hurt!

CAPTAIN. Would that have mattered?

BERTHA. You're not my father if you talk like that.

CAPTAIN. What d'you say? Not your father? How d'you know? Who
told you? Who is your father, then? Who?

BERTHA. Not you, anyway.

CAPTAIN. Anyone but me! Who then? Who? You seem well informed.
Who told you? That I should live to hear my own child tell me to
my face I am not her father! Do you realise you're insulting your
mother by saying this? Don't you understand that, if it's true, *she*
is disgraced?

BERTHA. You're not to say anything against Mother, I tell you!

CAPTAIN. Yes, all in league against me, just as you've always been.

BERTHA. Father!

CAPTAIN. Don't call me that again!

BERTHA. Father, Father!

CAPTAIN (*drawing her to him*). Bertha, my beloved child, yes, you *are*
my child. Yes, yes, it must be so—it *is* so. All that was only a
sick fancy—it came on the wind like an infection or a fever.
Look at me! Let me see my soul in your eyes . . . But I see *her*

soul as well. You have two souls. You love me with one and hate me with the other. You must love me and only me. You must have only one soul or you'll have no peace—neither shall I. You must have only one mind, fruit of my mind. You must have only one will—mine!

BERTHA. No, no! I want to be myself.

CAPTAIN. Never! I am a cannibal, you see, and I'm going to eat you. Your mother wanted to eat me, but she didn't succeed. I am Saturn who devoured his children because it was foretold that otherwise they would devour him. To eat or to be eaten—that is the question. If I don't eat you, you will eat me—you've shown your teeth already. (*Goes to the rack.*) Don't be afraid, my darling child. I shan't hurt you. (*Takes down a revolver.*)

BERTHA (*dodging away from him*). Help! Mother, help! He wants to kill me!

NURSE (*hurrying in*). What in heaven's name are you doing, Mr. Adolf?

CAPTAIN (*examining the revolver*). Did you remove the cartridges?

NURSE. Well, I did just tidy them away, but sit down here and take it easy and I'll soon fetch them back. (*She takes the* CAPTAIN *by the arm and leads him to a chair. He slumps down. She picks up the strait-jacket and goes behind the chair.* BERTHA *creeps out.*) Mr. Adolf, do you remember when you were my dear little boy, and I used to tuck you up at night and say your prayers with you? And do you remember how I used to get up in the night to get you a drink when you were thirsty? And how, when you had bad dreams and couldn't go to sleep again, I'd light the candle and tell you pretty stories. Do you remember?

CAPTAIN. Go on talking, Margaret. It soothes my mind. Go on talking.

NURSE. Aye, that I will, but you listen carefully. D'you remember how once you took a great big kitchen knife to carve a boat with, and I came in and had to trick the knife away from you? You were such a silly little lad, one had to trick you, you never would believe what anyone did was for your own good . . . "Give me that snake," I said, "or else he'll bite you." And then, see, you let go of the knife. (*Takes the revolver from his hand.*) And then, too, when it was time for you to dress yourself, and you wouldn't. I had to coax you, and say you should have a golden coat and be dressed just like a prince. Then I took your little tunic, that was just made of green wool, and held it up in front of you and said: "In with your arms, now, both together." (*Gets the jacket on.*) And then I said: "Sit nice and still now, while I button it up behind." (*Ties the sleeves behind him.*) And then I said: "Up

with you, and walk across the floor like a good boy, so Nurse
can see how it fits." (*Leads him to the sofa.*) And then I said:
"Now you must go to bed."

CAPTAIN. What's that? Go to bed, when I'd just been dressed? My
God! What have you done to me? (*Tries to get free.*) Oh you
fiendish woman, what devilish cunning! Who would have thought
you had the brains for it? (*Lies down on the sofa.*) Bound, fleeced,
outwitted and unable to die!

NURSE. Forgive me, Mr. Adolf, forgive me! I had to stop you killing the
child.

CAPTAIN. Why didn't you let me kill her? If life's hell and death's
heaven, and children belong to heaven?

NURSE. What do you know of the hereafter?

CAPTAIN. It's the only thing one does know. Of life one knows nothing.
Oh, if one had known from the beginning!

NURSE. Humble your stubborn heart, Mr. Adolf, and cry to God for
mercy! Even now it's not too late. It wasn't too late for the thief
on the Cross, for Our Saviour said: "To-day shalt thou be with
me in paradise."

CAPTAIN. Croaking for a corpse already, old crow? (*She takes her
hymn-book from her pocket. He calls.*) Nöjd! Are you there,
Nöjd? (*Enter* NÖJD.) Throw this woman out of the house or
she'll choke me to death with her hymn-book. Throw her out of
the window, stuff her up the chimney, do what you like only get
rid of her!

NÖJD (*staring at the* NURSE). God save you, Captain—and that's from
the bottom of my heart—but I can't do that, I just can't. If it were
six men now, but a woman!

CAPTAIN. What? You can't manage one woman?

NÖJD. I could manage her all right, but there's something stops a man
laying hands on a woman.

CAPTAIN. What is this something? Haven't they laid hands on me?

NÖJD. Yes, but I just can't do it, Sir. Same as if you was to tell me to
hit Pastor. It's like religion, it's in your bones. I can't do it.
(*Enter* LAURA. *She signs to* NÖJD, *who goes out.*)

CAPTAIN. Omphale! Omphale! Playing with the club while Hercules
spins your wool.

LAURA (*approaching the sofa*). Adolf, look at me! Do you believe I'm
your enemy?

CAPTAIN. Yes, I do. I believe all you women are my enemies. My
mother did not want me to come into the world because my birth
would give her pain. She was my enemy. She robbed my embryo
of nourishment, so I was born incomplete. My sister was my

enemy when she made me knuckle under to her. The first woman I took in my arms was my enemy. She gave me ten years of sickness in return for the love I gave her. When my daughter had to choose between you and me, she became my enemy. And you, you, my wife, have been my mortal enemy, for you have not let go your hold until there is no life left in me.

LAURA. But I didn't mean this to happen. I never really thought it out. I may have had some vague desire to get rid of you—you were in my way—and perhaps, if you see some plan in my actions, there was one, but I was unconscious of it. I have never given a thought to my actions—they simply ran along the rails you laid down. My conscience is clear, and before God I feel innocent, even if I'm not. You weighed me down like a stone, pressing and pressing till my heart tried to shake off its intolerable burden. That's how it's been, and if without meaning to I have brought you to this, I ask your forgiveness.

CAPTAIN. Very plausible, but how does that help me? And whose fault is it? Perhaps our cerebral marriage is to blame. In the old days one married a wife. Now one goes into partnership with a business woman or sets up house with a friend. Then one rapes the partner or violates the friend. What becomes of love, the healthy love of the senses? It dies of neglect. And what happens to the dividends from those love shares, payable to holder, when there's no joint account? Who is the holder when the crash comes? Who is the bodily father of the cerebral child?

LAURA. Your suspicions about our daughter are entirely unfounded.

CAPTAIN. That's the horror of it. If they had some foundation, there would at least be something to catch hold of, to cling to. Now there are only shadows, lurking in the undergrowth, peering out with grinning faces. It's like fighting with air, a mock battle with blank cartridges. Reality, however deadly, puts one on one's mettle, nerves body and soul for action, but as it is . . . my thoughts dissolve in fog, my brain grinds a void till it catches fire . . . Put a pillow under my head. Lay something over me. I'm cold. I'm terribly cold.

(LAURA *takes off her shawl and spreads it over him. Exit* NURSE.)

LAURA. Give me your hand, my dear.

CAPTAIN. My hand! Which you have bound behind my back. Omphale, Omphale! But I can feel your shawl soft against my mouth. It's warm and gentle like your arms and smells of vanilla like your hair when you were young. When you were young, Laura, and we used to walk in the birch woods. There were primroses and thrushes—lovely, lovely! Think how beautiful life was then—

and what it has become! You did not want it to become like this,
neither did I. Yet it has. Who then rules our lives?

LAURA. God.

CAPTAIN. The God of strife then—or nowadays the Goddess! (*Enter
NURSE with a pillow.*) Take away this cat that's lying on me.
Take it away! (NURSE *removes the shawl and puts the pillow
under his head.*) Bring my uniform. Put my tunic over me. (*The
NURSE takes the tunic from a peg and spreads it over him. To
LAURA*) Ah, my tough lion's-skin that you would take from me!
Omphale! Omphale! You cunning woman, lover of peace and
contriver of disarmament. Wake, Hercules, before they take away
your club! You would trick us out of our armour, calling it tinsel.
It was iron, I tell you, before it became tinsel. In the old days
the smith forged the soldier's coat, now it is made by the needle-
woman. Omphale! Omphale! Rude strength has fallen before
treacherous weakness. Shame on you, woman of Satan, and a
curse on all your sex! (*He raises himself to spit at her, but sinks
back again.*) What sort of a pillow have you given me, Margaret?
How hard and cold it is! So cold! Come and sit beside me on this
chair. (*She does so.*) Yes, like that. Let me put my head on
your lap. Ah, that's warmer! Lean over me so I can feel your
breast. Oh how sweet it is to sleep upon a woman's breast, be
she mother or mistress! But sweetest of all a mother's.

LAURA. Adolf, tell me, do you want to see your child?

CAPTAIN. My child? A man has no children. Only women have children. So the future is theirs, while we die childless. O God, who
holds all children dear!

NURSE. Listen! He's praying to God.

CAPTAIN. No, to you, to put me to sleep. I'm tired, so tired. Goodnight, Margaret. "Blessed art thou among women." (*He raises
himself, then with a cry falls back on the NURSE'S knees.*)

LAURA (*at the door, calling*). Doctor! (*Enter DOCTOR and PASTOR.*)
Help him, Doctor—if it's not too late! Look, he has stopped
breathing!

DOCTOR (*feeling his pulse*). It is a stroke.

PASTOR. Is he dead?

DOCTOR. No, he might still wake—but to what, who can say?

PASTOR. ". . . once to die, but after this the judgment." *

DOCTOR. No judgment—and no recriminations. You who believe that
a God rules over human destiny must lay this to his charge.

NURSE. Ah Pastor, with his last breath he prayed to God!

PASTOR (*to LAURA*). Is this true?

* HEBREWS: ix, 27.

LAURA. It is true.

DOCTOR. If this be so, of which I am as poor a judge as of the cause of his illness, in any case my skill is at an end. Try yours now, Pastor.

LAURA. Is that all you have to say at this deathbed, Doctor?

DOCTOR. That is all. I know no more. Let him who knows more, speak.

(BERTHA *comes and runs to* LAURA.)

BERTHA. Mother! Mother!

LAURA. My child! My own child!

PASTOR. Amen.

End

THE CHERRY ORCHARD [1904]

by Anton Chekhov

translated by Constance Garnett

Characters

MADAME RANEVSKY (LYUBOV ANDREYEVNA), *the owner of the cherry orchard*

ANYA, *her daughter, aged seventeen*

VARYA, *her adopted daughter, aged twenty-four*

GAEV, LEONID ANDREYEVITCH, *brother of Madame Ranevsky*

LOPAHIN, YERMOLAY ALEXEYEVITCH, *a merchant*

TROFIMOV, PYOTR SERGEYEVITCH, *a student*

SEMYONOV-PISHTCHIK, *a landowner*

CHARLOTTA IVANOVNA, *a governess*

EPIHODOV, SEMYON PANTALEYEVITCH, *a clerk*

DUNYASHA, *a maid*

FIRS, *an old valet, aged eighty-seven*

YASHA, *a young valet*

A VAGRANT

THE STATION MASTER

A POST-OFFICE CLERK

VISITORS

SERVANTS

The action takes place on the estate of Madame Ranevsky.

The Cherry Orchard by Anton Chekhov, translated by Constance Garnett. Reprinted by permission of David Garnett and Chatto & Windus Ltd.

ACT ONE

Scene. A room, which has always been called the nursery. One of the doors leads into ANYA'S *room. Dawn, sun rises during the scene. May, the cherry trees in flower, but it is cold in the garden with the frost of early morning. Windows closed.*

(*Enter* DUNYASHA *with a candle and* LOPAHIN *with a book in his hand.*)

LOPAHIN. The train's in, thank God. What time is it?

DUNYASHA. Nearly two o'clock. (*Puts out the candle.*) It's daylight already.

LOPAHIN. The train's late! Two hours, at least. (*Yawns and stretches.*) I'm a pretty one; what a fool I've been. Came here on purpose to meet them at the station and dropped asleep. . . . Dozed off as I sat in the chair. It's annoying. . . . You might have waked me.

DUNYASHA. I thought you had gone. (*Listens.*) There, I do believe they're coming!

LOPAHIN. (*Listens.*) No, what with the luggage and one thing and another. (*A pause.*) Lyubov Andreyevna has been abroad five years; I don't know what she is like now. . . . She's a splendid woman. A good-natured, kind-hearted woman. I remember when I was a lad of fifteen, my poor father—he used to keep a little shop here in the village in those days—gave me a punch in the face with his fist and made my nose bleed. We were in the yard here, I forget what we'd come about—he had had a drop. Lyubov Andreyevna—I can see her now—she was a slim young girl then—took me to wash my face, and then brought me into this very room, into the nursery. "Don't cry, little peasant," says she, "it will be well in time for your wedding day." . . . (*A pause.*) Little peasant. . . . My father was a peasant, it's true, but here am I in a white waistcoat and brown shoes, like a pig in a bun shop. Yes, I'm a rich man, but for all my money, come to think, a peasant I was, and a peasant I am. (*Turns over the pages of the book.*) I've been reading this book and I can't make head or tail of it. I fell asleep over it. (*A pause.*)

DUNYASHA. The dogs have been awake all night, they feel that the mistress is coming.

LOPAHIN. Why, what's the matter with you, Dunyasha?

DUNYASHA. My hands are all of a tremble. I feel as though I should faint.

LOPAHIN. You're a spoilt soft creature, Dunyasha. And dressed like a lady too, and your hair done up. That's not the thing. One must know one's place.

(*Enter* EPIHODOV *with a nosegay; he wears a pea jacket and highly polished creaking topboots; he drops the nosegay as he comes in.*)

EPIHODOV (*picking up the nosegay*). Here! the gardener's sent this, says you're to put it in the dining room. (*Gives* DUNYASHA *the nosegay.*)

LOPAHIN. And bring me some kvass.

DUNYASHA. I will. (*Goes out.*)

EPIHODOV. It's chilly this morning, three degrees of frost, though the cherries are all in flower. I can't say much for our climate. (*Sighs.*) I can't. Our climate is not often propitious to the occasion. Yermolay Alexeyevitch, permit me to call your attention to the fact that I purchased myself a pair of boots the day before yesterday, and they creak, I venture to assure you, so that there's no tolerating them. What ought I to grease them with?

LOPAHIN. Oh, shut up! Don't bother me.

EPIHODOV. Every day some misfortune befalls me. I don't complain. I'm used to it, and I wear a smiling face. (DUNYASHA *comes in, hands* LOPAHIN *the kvass.*) I am going. (*Stumbles against a chair, which falls over.*) There! (*As though triumphant*) There you see now, excuse the expression, an accident like that among others. . . . It's positively remarkable. (*Goes out.*)

DUNYASHA. Do you know, Yermolay Alexeyevitch, I must confess, Epihodov has made me a proposal.

LOPAHIN. Ah!

DUNYASHA. I'm sure I don't know. . . . He's a harmless fellow, but sometimes when he begins talking, there's no making anything of it. It's all very fine and expressive, only there's no understanding it. I've a sort of liking for him too. He loves me to distraction. He's an unfortunate man; every day there's something. They tease him about it—two and twenty misfortunes they call him.

LOPAHIN (*listening*). There! I do believe they're coming.

DUNYASHA. They are coming! What's the matter with me? . . . I'm cold all over.

LOPAHIN. They really are coming. Let's go and meet them. Will she know me? It's five years since I saw her.

DUNYASHA (*in a flutter*). I shall drop this very minute. . . . Ah, I shall drop.

(*There is a sound of two carriages driving up to the house. LOPAHIN and DUNYASHA go out quickly. The stage is left empty. A noise is heard in the adjoining rooms. FIRS, who has driven to meet* MADAME RANEVSKY, *crosses the stage hurriedly leaning on a stick. He is wearing old-fashioned livery and a high hat. He says something to himself, but not a word can be distinguished. The noise behind the scenes goes on increasing. A voice: "Come, let's go in here." Enter* LYUBOV ANDREYEVNA, ANYA, *and* CHARLOTTA IVANOVNA *with a pet dog on a chain, all in travelling dresses.* VARYA *in an outdoor coat with a kerchief over her head,* GAEV, SEMYONOV-PISHTCHIK, LOPAHIN, DUNYASHA *with bag and parasol, servants with other articles. All walk across the room.*)

ANYA. Let's come in here. Do you remember what room this is, mamma?

LYUBOV (*joyfully, through her tears*). The nursery!

VARYA. How cold it is, my hands are numb. (*To* LYUBOV ANDREYEVNA) Your rooms, the white room and the lavender one, are just the same as ever, mamma.

LYUBOV. My nursery, dear delightful room. . . . I used to sleep here when I was little. . . . (*Cries.*) And here I am, like a little child. . . . (*Kisses her brother and* VARYA, *and then her brother again.*) Varya's just the same as ever, like a nun. And I knew Dunyasha. (*Kisses* DUNYASHA.)

GAEV. The train was two hours late. What do you think of that? Is that the way to do things?

CHARLOTTA (*to* PISHTCHIK). My dog eats nuts, too.

PISHTCHIK (*wonderingly*). Fancy that!

(*They all go out except* ANYA *and* DUNYASHA.)

DUNYASHA. We've been expecting you so long. (*Takes* ANYA'S *hat and coat.*)

ANYA. I haven't slept for four nights on the journey. I feel dreadfully cold.

DUNYASHA. You set out in Lent, there was snow and frost, and now? My darling! (*Laughs and kisses her.*) I *have* missed you, my precious, my joy. I must tell you . . . I can't put it off a minute. . . .

ANYA (*wearily*). What now?

DUNYASHA. Epihodov, the clerk, made me a proposal just after Easter.

ANYA. It's always the same thing with you. . . . (*Straightening her hair*) I've lost all my hairpins. . . . (*She is staggering from exhaustion.*)

DUNYASHA. I don't know what to think, really. He does love me, he does love me so!

ANYA (*looking towards her door, tenderly*). My own room, my windows just as though I had never gone away. I'm home! Tomorrow morning I shall get up and run into the garden. . . . Oh, if I

could get to sleep! I haven't slept all the journey, I was so anxious
and worried.

DUNYASHA. Pyotr Sergeyevitch came the day before yesterday.

ANYA (*joyfully*). Petya!

DUNYASHA. He's asleep in the bathhouse, he has settled in there. I'm
afraid of being in their way, says he. (*Glancing at her watch*) I
was to have waked him, but Varvara Mihalovna told me not to.
Don't you wake him, says she.

(*Enter* VARYA *with a bunch of keys at her waist.*)

VARYA. Dunyasha, coffee and make haste. . . . Mamma's asking for
coffee.

DUNYASHA. This very minute. (*Goes out.*)

VARYA. Well, thank God, you've come. You're home again (*petting
her*). My little darling has come back! My precious beauty has
come back again!

ANYA. I have had a time of it!

VARYA. I can fancy.

ANYA. We set off in Holy Week—it was so cold then, and all the way
Charlotta would talk and show off her tricks. What did you want
to burden me with Charlotta for?

VARYA. You couldn't have travelled all alone, darling. At seventeen!

ANYA. We got to Paris at last, it was cold there—snow. I speak French
shockingly. Mamma lives on the fifth floor, I went up to her and
there were a lot of French people, ladies, an old priest with a book.
The place smelt of tobacco and so comfortless. I felt sorry, oh! so
sorry for mamma all at once, I put my arms round her neck, and
hugged her and wouldn't let her go. Mamma was as kind as she
could be, and she cried. . . .

VARYA (*through her tears*). Don't speak of it, don't speak of it!

ANYA. She had sold her villa at Mentone, she had nothing left, nothing.
I hadn't a farthing left either, we only just had enough to get here.
And mamma doesn't understand! When we had dinner at the sta-
tions, she always ordered the most expensive things and gave the
waiters a whole rouble. Charlotta's just the same. Yasha too must
have the same as we do; it's simply awful. You know Yasha is
mamma's valet now, we brought him here with us.

VARYA. Yes, I've seen the young rascal.

ANYA. Well, tell me—have you paid the arrears on the mortgage?

VARYA. How could we get the money?

ANYA. Oh, dear! Oh, dear!

VARYA. In August the place will be sold.

ANYA. My goodness!

LOPAHIN. (*Peeps in at the door and moos like a cow.*) Moo! (*Disappears.*)

VARYA (*weeping*). There, that's what I could do to him (*shakes her fist*).

ANYA (*embracing* VARYA, *softly*). Varya, has he made you an offer? (VARYA *shakes her head.*) Why, but he loves you. Why is it you don't come to an understanding? What are you waiting for?

VARYA. I believe that there never will be anything between us. He has a lot to do, he has no time for me . . . and takes no notice of me. Bless the man, it makes me miserable to see him. . . . Everyone's talking of our being married, everyone's congratulating me, and all the while there's really nothing in it; it's all like a dream. (*In another tone*) You have a new brooch like a bee.

ANYA (*mournfully*). Mamma bought it. (*Goes into her own room and in a lighthearted childish tone*) And you know, in Paris I went up in a balloon!

VARYA. My darling's home again! My pretty is home again!

(DUNYASHA *returns with the coffee pot and is making the coffee.*)

VARYA (*standing at the door*). All day long, darling, as I go about looking after the house, I keep dreaming all the time. If only we could marry you to a rich man, then I should feel more at rest. Then I would go off by myself on a pilgrimage to Kiev, to Moscow . . . and so I would spend my life going from one holy place to another. . . . I would go on and on. . . . What bliss!

ANYA. The birds are singing in the garden. What time is it?

VARYA. It must be nearly three. It's time you were asleep, darling. (*Going into* ANYA'S *room*) What bliss!

(YASHA *enters with a rug and a travelling bag.*)

YASHA. (*Crosses the stage, mincingly.*) May one come in here, pray?

DUNYASHA. I shouldn't have known you, Yasha. How you have changed abroad.

YASHA. H'm! . . . And who are you?

DUNYASHA. When you went away, I was that high. (*Shows distance from floor.*) Dunyasha, Fyodor's daughter. . . . You don't remember me!

YASHA. H'm! . . . You're a peach! (*Looks round and embraces her: she shrieks and drops a saucer.* YASHA *goes out hastily.*)

VARYA (*in the doorway, in a tone of vexation*). What now?

DUNYASHA (*through her tears*). I have broken a saucer.

VARYA. Well, that brings good luck.

ANYA (*coming out of her room*). We ought to prepare mamma: Petya is here.

VARYA. I told them not to wake him.

ANYA (*dreamily*). It's six years since father died. Then only a month later little brother Grisha was drowned in the river, such a pretty boy he was, only seven. It was more than mamma could bear, so she went away, went away without looking back (*shuddering*). . . . How well I understand her, if only she knew! (*A pause.*) And Petya Trofimov was Grisha's tutor, he may remind her.

(*Enter* FIRS: *he is wearing a pea jacket and a white waistcoat.*)

FIRS. (*Goes up to the coffee pot, anxiously.*) The mistress will be served here. (*Puts on white gloves.*) Is the coffee ready? (*Sternly to* DUN-YASHA) Girl! Where's the cream?

DUNYASHA. Ah, mercy on us! (*Goes out quickly.*)

FIRS (*fussing round the coffee pot*). Ech! you good-for-nothing! (*Muttering to himself*) Come back from Paris. And the old master used to go to Paris too . . . horses all the way. (*Laughs.*)

VARYA. What is it, Firs?

FIRS. What is your pleasure? (*Gleefully*) My lady has come home! I have lived to see her again! Now I can die. (*Weeps with joy.*)

(*Enter* LYUBOV ANDREYEVNA, GAEV *and* SEMYONOV-PISHTCHIK; *the latter is in a short-waisted full coat of fine cloth, and full trousers.* GAEV, *as he comes in, makes a gesture with his arms and his whole body, as though he were playing billiards.*)

LYUBOV. How does it go? Let me remember. Cannon off the red!

GAEV. That's it—in off the white! Why, once, sister, we used to sleep together in this very room, and now I'm fifty-one, strange as it seems.

LOPAHIN. Yes, time flies.

GAEV. What do you say?

LOPAHIN. Time, I say, flies.

GAEV. What a smell of patchouli!

ANYA. I'm going to bed. Good night, mamma. (*Kisses her mother.*)

LYUBOV. My precious darling. (*Kisses her hands.*) Are you glad to be home? I can't believe it.

ANYA. Good night, uncle.

GAEV (*kissing her face and hands*). God bless you! How like you are to your mother! (*To his sister*) At her age you were just the same, Lyuba.

(*ANYA shakes hands with* LOPAHIN *and* PISHTCHIK, *then goes out, shutting the door after her.*)

LYUBOV. She's quite worn out.

PISHTCHIK. Aye, it's a long journey, to be sure.

VARYA (*to* LOPAHIN *and* PISHTCHIK). Well, gentlemen? It's three o'clock and time to say good-by.

LYUBOV. (*Laughs.*) You're just the same as ever, Varya. (*Draws her to her and kisses her.*) I'll just drink my coffee and then we will all go and rest. (FIRS *puts a cushion under her feet.*) Thanks, friend. I am so fond of coffee, I drink it day and night. Thanks, dear old man. (*Kisses* FIRS.)

VARYA. I'll just see whether all the things have been brought in. (*Goes out.*)

LYUBOV. Can it really be me sitting here? (*Laughs.*) I want to dance about and clap my hands. (*Covers her face with her hands.*) And I could drop asleep in a moment! God knows I love my country, I love it tenderly; I couldn't look out of the window in the train, I kept crying so. (*Through her tears*) But I must drink my coffee, though. Thank you, Firs, thanks, dear old man. I'm so glad to find you still alive.

FIRS. The day before yesterday.

GAEV. He's rather deaf.

LOPAHIN. I have to set off for Harkov directly, at five o'clock. . . . It is annoying! I wanted to have a look at you, and a little talk. . . . You are just as splendid as ever.

PISHTCHIK (*breathing heavily*). Handsomer, indeed. . . . Dressed in Parisian style . . . completely bowled me over.

LOPAHIN. Your brother, Leonid Andreyevitch here, is always saying that I'm a low-born knave, that I'm a money grubber, but I don't care one straw for that. Let him talk. Only I do want you to believe in me as you used to. I do want your wonderful tender eyes to look at me as they used to in the old days. Merciful God! My father was a serf of your father and of your grandfather, but you —you—did so much for me once, that I've forgotten all that; I love you as though you were my kin . . . more than my kin.

LYUBOV. I can't sit still, I simply can't. . . . (*Jumps up and walks about in violent agitation.*) This happiness is too much for me. . . . You may laugh at me, I know I'm silly. . . . My own bookcase. (*Kisses the bookcase.*) My little table.

GAEV. Nurse died while you were away.

LYUBOV. (*Sits down and drinks coffee.*) Yes, the Kingdom of Heaven be hers! You wrote me of her death.

GAEV. And Anastasy is dead. Squinting Petruchka has left me and is in service now with the police captain in the town. (*Takes a box of caramels out of his pocket and sucks one.*)

PISHTCHIK. My daughter, Dashenka, wishes to be remembered to you.

LOPAHIN. I want to tell you something very pleasant and cheering (*glancing at his watch*). I'm going directly . . . there's no time to say much . . . well, I can say it in a couple of words. I needn't tell you your cherry orchard is to be sold to pay your debts; the

22nd of August is the date fixed for the sale; but don't you worry, dearest lady, you may sleep in peace, there is a way of saving it. . . . This is what I propose. I beg your attention! Your estate is not twenty miles from the town, the railway runs close by it, and if the cherry orchard and the land along the river bank were cut up into building plots and then let on lease for summer villas, you would make an income of at least 25,000 roubles a year out of it.

GAEV. That's all rot, if you'll excuse me.

LYUBOV. I don't quite understand you, Yermolay Alexeyevitch.

LOPAHIN. You will get a rent of at least 25 roubles a year for a three-acre plot from summer visitors, and if you say the word now, I'll bet you what you like there won't be one square foot of ground vacant by the autumn, all the plots will be taken up. I congratulate you; in fact, you are saved. It's a perfect situation with that deep river. Only, of course, it must be cleared—all the old buildings, for example, must be removed, this house too, which is really good for nothing and the old cherry orchard must be cut down.

LYUBOV. Cut down? My dear fellow, forgive me, but you don't know what you are talking about. If there is one thing interesting—remarkable indeed—in the whole province, it's just our cherry orchard.

LOPAHIN. The only thing remarkable about the orchard is that it's a very large one. There's a crop of cherries every alternate year, and then there's nothing to be done with them, no one buys them.

GAEV. This orchard is mentioned in the "Encyclopædia."

LOPAHIN (*glancing at his watch*). If we don't decide on something and don't take some steps, on the 22nd of August the cherry orchard and the whole estate too will be sold by auction. Make up your minds! There is no other way of saving it, I'll take my oath on that. No, no!

FIRS. In old days, forty or fifty years ago, they used to dry the cherries, soak them, pickle them, make jam too, and they used——

GAEV. Be quiet, Firs.

FIRS. And they used to send the preserved cherries to Moscow and to Harkov by the wagon-load. That brought the money in! And the preserved cherries in those days were soft and juicy, sweet and fragrant. . . . They knew the way to do them then. . . .

LYUBOV. And where is the recipe now?

FIRS. It's forgotten. Nobody remembers it.

PISHTCHIK (*to* LYUBOV ANDREYEVNA). What's it like in Paris? Did you eat frogs there?

LYUBOV. Oh, I ate crocodiles.

PISHTCHIK. Fancy that now!

LOPAHIN. There used to be only the gentlefolks and the peasants in the country, but now there are these summer visitors. All the towns, even the small ones, are surrounded nowadays by these summer villas. And one may say for sure, that in another twenty years there'll be many more of these people and that they'll be everywhere. At present the summer visitor only drinks tea in his verandah, but maybe he'll take to working his bit of land too, and then your cherry orchard would become happy, rich and prosperous. . . .

GAEV (*indignant*). What rot!

(*Enter* VARYA *and* YASHA.)

VARYA. There are two telegrams for you, mamma. (*Takes out keys and opens an old-fashioned bookcase with a loud crack.*) Here they are.

LYUBOV. From Paris. (*Tears the telegrams, without reading them.*) I have done with Paris.

GAEV. Do you know, Lyuba, how old that bookcase is? Last week I pulled out the bottom drawer and there I found the date branded on it. The bookcase was made just a hundred years ago. What do you say to that? We might have celebrated its jubilee. Though it's an inanimate object, still it is a *book* case.

PISHTCHIK (*amazed*). A hundred years! Fancy that now.

GAEV. Yes. . . . It is a thing . . . (*feeling the bookcase*). Dear, honoured, bookcase! Hail to thee who for more than a hundred years hast served the pure ideals of good and justice; thy silent call to fruitful labour has never flagged in those hundred years, maintaining (*in tears*) in the generations of man, courage and faith in a brighter future and fostering in us ideals of good and social consciousness. (*A pause.*)

LOPAHIN. Yes. . . .

LYUBOV. You are just the same as ever, Leonid.

GAEV (*a little embarrassed*). Cannon off the right into the pocket!

LOPAHIN (*looking at his watch*). Well, it's time I was off.

YASHA (*handing* LYUBOV ANDREYEVNA *medicine*). Perhaps you will take your pills now.

PISHTCHIK. You shouldn't take medicines, my dear madam . . . they do no harm and no good. Give them here . . . honoured lady. (*Takes the pillbox, pours the pills into the hollow of his hand, blows on them, puts them in his mouth and drinks off some kvass.*) There!

LYUBOV (*in alarm*). Why, you must be out of your mind!

PISHTCHIK. I have taken all the pills.

LOPAHIN. What a glutton! (*All laugh.*)

FIRS. His honour stayed with us in Easter week, ate a gallon and a half of cucumbers. . . . (*Mutters.*)

LYUBOV. What is he saying?

VARYA. He has taken to muttering like that for the last three years. We are used to it.

YASHA. His declining years!

(CHARLOTTA IVANOVNA, *a very thin, lanky figure in a white dress with a lorgnette in her belt, walks across the stage.*)

LOPAHIN. I beg your pardon, Charlotta Ivanovna, I have not had time to greet you. (*Tries to kiss her hand.*)

CHARLOTTA (*pulling away her hand*). If I let you kiss my hand, you'll be wanting to kiss my elbow, and then my shoulder.

LOPAHIN. I've no luck today! (*All laugh.*) Charlotta Ivanovna, show us some tricks!

LYUBOV. Charlotta, do show us some tricks!

CHARLOTTA. I don't want to. I'm sleepy. (*Goes out.*)

LOPAHIN. In three weeks' time we shall meet again. (*Kisses* LYUBOV ANDREYEVNA'S *hand.*) Good-by till then—I must go. (*To* GAEV) Good-by (*Kisses* PISHTCHIK.) Good-by. (*Gives his hand to* VARYA, *then to* FIRS *and* YASHA.) I don't want to go. (*To* LYUBOV ANDRE-YEVNA) If you think over my plan for the villas and make up your mind, then let me know; I will lend you 50,000 roubles. Think of it seriously.

VARYA (*angrily*). Well, do go, for goodness sake.

LOPAHIN. I'm going, I'm going. (*Goes out.*)

GAEV. Low-born knave! I beg pardon, though . . . Varya is going to marry him, he's Varya's fiancé.

VARYA. Don't talk nonsense, uncle.

LYUBOV. Well, Varya, I shall be delighted. He's a good man.

PISHTCHIK. He is, one must acknowledge, a most worthy man. And my Dashenka . . . says too that . . . she says . . . various things. (*Snores, but at once wakes up.*) But all the same, honoured lady, could you oblige me . . . with a loan of 240 roubles . . . to pay the interest on my mortgage tomorrow?

VARYA (*dismayed*). No, no.

LYUBOV. I really haven't any money.

PISHTCHIK. It will turn up. (*Laughs.*) I never lose hope. I thought everything was over, I was a ruined man, and lo and behold— the railway passed through my land and . . . they paid me for it. And something else will turn up again, if not today, then tomor-row . . . Dashenka'll win two hundred thousand . . . she's got a lottery ticket.

LYUBOV. Well, we've finished our coffee, we can go to bed.

FIRS. (*Brushes* GAEV, *reprovingly.*) You have got on the wrong trousers again! What am I to do with you?

VARYA (*softly*). Anya's asleep. (*Softly opens the window.*) Now the sun's risen, it's not a bit cold. Look, mamma, what exquisite trees! My goodness! And the air! The starlings are singing!

GAEV. (*Opens another window.*) The orchard is all white. You've not forgotten it, Lyuba? That long avenue that runs straight, straight as an arrow, how it shines on a moonlight night. You remember? You've not forgotten?

LYUBOV (*looking out of the window into the garden*). Oh, my childhood, my innocence! It was in this nursery I used to sleep, from here I looked out into the orchard, happiness waked with me every morning and in those days the orchard was just the same, nothing has changed. (*Laughs with delight.*) All, all white! Oh, my orchard! After the dark gloomy autumn, and the cold winter; you are young again, and full of happiness, the heavenly angels have never left you. . . . If I could cast off the burden that weighs on my heart, if I could forget the past!

GAEV. H'm! and the orchard will be sold to pay our debts; it seems strange. . . .

LYUBOV. See, our mother walking . . . all in white, down the avenue! (*Laughs with delight.*) It is she!

GAEV. Where?

VARYA. Oh, don't, mamma!

LYUBOV. There is no one. It was my fancy. On the right there, by the path to the arbor, there is a white tree bending like a woman. . . . (*Enter* TROFIMOV *wearing a shabby student's uniform and spectacles.*)

LYUBOV. What a ravishing orchard! White masses of blossom, blue sky. . . .

TROFIMOV. Lyubov Andreyevna! (*She looks round at him.*) I will just pay my respects to you and then leave you at once. (*Kisses her hand warmly.*) I was told to wait until morning, but I hadn't the patience to wait any longer. . . .

(LYUBOV ANDREYEVNA *looks at him in perplexity.*)

VARYA (*through her tears*). This is Petya Trofimov.

TROFIMOV. Petya Trofimov, who was your Grisha's tutor. . . . Can I have changed so much?

(LYUBOV ANDREYEVNA *embraces him and weeps quietly.*)

GAEV (*in confusion*). There, there, Lyuba.

VARYA (*crying*). I told you, Petya, to wait till tomorrow.

LYUBOV. My Grisha . . . my boy . . . Grisha . . . my son!

VARYA. We can't help it, mamma, it is God's will.

TROFIMOV (*softly through his tears*). There . . . there.

LYUBOV (*weeping quietly*). My boy was lost . . . drowned. Why?
Oh, why, dear Petya? (*More quietly*) Anya is asleep in there, and
I'm talking loudly . . . making this noise. . . . But, Petya? Why
have you grown so ugly? Why do you look so old?

TROFIMOV. A peasant woman in the train called me a mangy-looking
gentleman.

LYUBOV. You were quite a boy then, a pretty little student, and now
your hair's thin—and spectacles. Are you really a student still?
(*Goes towards the door.*)

TROFIMOV. I seem likely to be a perpetual student.

LYUBOV. (*Kisses her brother, then* VARYA.) Well, go to bed. . . . You
are older too, Leonid.

PISHTCHIK. (*Follows her.*) I suppose it's time we were asleep. . . .
Ugh! my gout. I'm staying the night! Lyubov Andreyevna, my
dear soul, if you could . . . tomorrow morning . . . 240 roubles.

GAEV. That's always his story.

PISHTCHIK. 240 roubles . . . to pay the interest on my mortgage.

LYUBOV. My dear man, I have no money.

PISHTCHIK. I'll pay it back, my dear . . . a trifling sum.

LYUBOV. Oh, well. Leonid will give it you. . . . You give him the
money, Leonid.

GAEV. Me give it him! Let him wait till he gets it!

LYUBOV. It can't be helped, give it him. He needs it. He'll pay it back.
(LYUBOV ANDREYEVNA, TROFIMOV, PISHTCHIK *and* FIRS *go out.*
GAEV, VARYA *and* YASHA *remain.*)

GAEV. Sister hasn't got out of the habit of flinging away her money.
(*To* YASHA) Get away, my good fellow, you smell of the hen
house.

YASHA (*with a grin*). And you, Leonid Andreyevitch, are just the same
as ever.

GAEV. What's that? (*To* VARYA) What did he say?

VARYA (*to* YASHA). Your mother has come from the village; she has
been sitting in the servants' room since yesterday, waiting to see
you.

YASHA. Oh, bother her!

VARYA. For shame!

YASHA. What's the hurry? She might just as well have come tomorrow.
(*Goes out.*)

VARYA. Mamma's just the same as ever, she hasn't changed a bit. If
she had her own way, she'd give away everything.

GAEV. Yes. (*A pause.*) If a great many remedies are suggested for some disease, it means that the disease is incurable. I keep thinking and racking my brains; I have many schemes, a great many, and that really means none. If we could only come in for a legacy from somebody, or marry our Anya to a very rich man, or we might go to Yaroslavl and try our luck with our old aunt, the Countess. She's very, very rich, you know.

VARYA. (*Weeps.*) If God would help us.

GAEV. Don't blubber. Aunt's very rich, but she doesn't like us. First, sister married a lawyer instead of a nobleman. . . . (ANYA *appears in the doorway.*) And then her conduct, one can't call it virtuous. She is good, and kind, and nice, and I love her, but, however one allows for extenuating circumstances, there's no denying that she's an immoral woman. One feels it in her slightest gesture.

VARYA (*in a whisper*). Anya's in the doorway.

GAEV. What do you say? (*A pause.*) It's queer, there seems to be something wrong with my right eye. I don't see as well as I did. And on Thursday when I was in the district Court . . .

(*Enter* ANYA.)

VARYA. Why aren't you asleep, Anya?

ANYA. I can't get to sleep.

GAEV. My pet. (*Kisses* ANYA'S *face and hands.*) My child. (*Weeps.*) You are not my niece, you are my angel, you are everything to me. Believe me, believe . . .

ANYA. I believe you, uncle. Everyone loves you and respects you . . . but, uncle dear, you must be silent . . . simply be silent. What were you saying just now about my mother, about your own sister? What made you say that?

GAEV. Yes, yes . . . (*Puts his hand over his face.*) Really, that was awful! My God, save me! And today I made a speech to the bookcase . . . so stupid! And only when I had finished, I saw how stupid it was.

VARYA. It's true, uncle, you ought to keep quiet. Don't talk, that's all.

ANYA. If you could keep from talking, it would make things easier for you, too.

GAEV. I won't speak. (*Kisses* ANYA'S *and* VARYA'S *hands.*) I'll be silent. Only this is about business. On Thursday I was in the district Court; well, there was a large party of us there and we began talking of one thing and another, and this and that, and do you know, I believe that it will be possible to raise a loan on an I.O.U. to pay the arrears on the mortgage.

VARYA. If the Lord would help us!

GAEV. I'm going on Tuesday; I'll talk of it again. (*To* VARYA) Don't blubber. (*To* ANYA) Your mamma will talk to Lopahin; of course, he won't refuse her. And as soon as you're rested you shall go to Yaroslavl to the Countess, your great-aunt. So we shall all set to work in three directions at once, and the business is done. We shall pay off arrears, I'm convinced of it. (*Puts a caramel in his mouth.*) I swear on my honour, I swear by anything you like, the estate shan't be sold (*excitedly*). By my own happiness, I swear it! Here's my hand on it, call me the basest, vilest of men, if I let it come to an auction! Upon my soul I swear it!

ANYA. (*Her equanimity has returned, she is quite happy.*) How good you are, uncle, and how clever! (*Embraces her uncle.*) I'm at peace now! Quite at peace! I'm happy!

(*Enters* FIRS.)

FIRS (*reproachfully*). Leonid Andreyevitch, have you no fear of God? when are you going to bed?

GAEV. Directly, directly. You can go, Firs. I'll . . . yes, I will undress myself. Come, children, by-by. We'll go into details tomorrow, but now go to bed. (*Kisses* ANYA *and* VARYA.) I'm a man of the eighties. They run down that period, but still I can say I have had to suffer not a little for my convictions in my life. It's not for nothing that the peasant loves me. One must know the peasant! One must know how . . .

ANYA. At it again, uncle!

VARYA. Uncle dear, you'd better be quiet!

FIRS (*angrily*). Leonid Andreyevitch!

GAEV. I'm coming. I'm coming. Go to bed. Potted the shot—there's a shot for you! A beauty! (*Goes out,* FIRS *hobbling after him.*)

ANYA. My mind's at rest now. I don't want to go to Yaroslavl, I don't like my great-aunt, but still my mind's at rest. Thanks to uncle. (*Sits down.*)

VARYA. We must go to bed. I'm going. Something unpleasant happened while you were away. In the old servants' quarters there are only the old servants, as you know—Efimyushka, Polya and Yevstigney —and Karp too. They began letting stray people in to spend the night—I said nothing. But all at once I heard they had been spreading a report that I gave them nothing but pease pudding to eat. Out of stinginess, you know. . . . And it was all Yevstigney's doing. . . . Very well, I said to myself. . . . If that's how it is, I thought, wait a bit. I sent for Yevstigney. . . . (*Yawns.*) He comes. . . . "How's this, Yevstigney," I said, "you could be such a fool as to? . . ." (*Looking at* ANYA) Anitchka! (*A pause.*)

She's asleep. (*Puts her arm round* ANYA.) Come to bed . . . come along! (*Leads her.*) My darling has fallen asleep! Come . . . (*They go.*)

(*Far away beyond the orchard a shepherd plays on a pipe.* TROFIMOV *crosses the stage and, seeing* VARYA *and* ANYA, *stands still.*)

VARYA. 'Sh! asleep, asleep. Come, my own.

ANYA (*softly, half asleep*). I'm so tired. Still those bells. Uncle . . . dear . . . mamma and uncle. . . .

VARYA. Come, my own, come along.

(*They go into* ANYA'S *room.*)

TROFIMOV (*tenderly*). My sunshine! My spring.

ACT TWO

Scene. The open country. An old shrine, long abandoned and fallen out of the perpendicular; near it a well, large stones that have apparently once been tombstones, and an old garden seat. The road to GAEV'S *house is seen. On one side rise dark poplars; and there the cherry orchard begins. In the distance a row of telegraph poles and far, far away on the horizon there is faintly outlined a great town, only visible in very fine clear weather. It is near sunset.* CHARLOTTA, YASHA *and* DUNYASHA *are sitting on the seat.* EPIHODOV *is standing near, playing something mournful on a guitar. All sit plunged in thought.* CHARLOTTA *wears an old forage cap; she has taken a gun from her shoulder and is tightening the buckle on the strap.*

CHARLOTTA (*musingly*). I haven't a real passport of my own, and I don't know how old I am, and I always feel that I'm a young thing. When I was a little girl, my father and mother used to travel about to fairs and give performances—very good ones. And I used to dance *salto-mortale* and all sorts of things. And when papa and mamma died, a German lady took me and had me educated. And so I grew up and became a governess. But where I came from, and who I am, I don't know. . . . Who my parents were, very likely they weren't married . . . I don't know. (*Takes a cucumber out of her pocket and eats.*) I know nothing at all. (*A pause.*) One wants to talk and has no one to talk to . . . I have nobody.

EPIHODOV. (*Plays on the guitar and sings.*) "What care I for the noisy world! What care I for friends or foes!" How agreeable it is to play on the mandolin!

DUNYASHA. That's a guitar, not a mandolin. (*Looks in a hand mirror and powders herself.*)

EPIHODOV. To a man mad with love, it's a mandolin. (*Sings.*) "Were her heart but aglow with love's mutual flame." (YASHA *joins in.*)

CHARLOTTA. How shockingly these people sing! Foo! Like jackals!

DUNYASHA (*to* YASHA). What happiness, though, to visit foreign lands.

YASHA. Ah, yes! I rather agree with you there. (*Yawns, then lights a cigar.*)

EPIHODOV. That's comprehensible. In foreign lands everything has long since reached full complexion.

YASHA. That's so, of course.

EPIHODOV. I'm a cultivated man, I read remarkable books of all sorts, but I can never make out the tendency I am myself precisely inclined for, whether to live or to shoot myself, speaking precisely, but nevertheless I always carry a revolver. Here it is . . . (*Shows revolver.*)

CHARLOTTA. I've had enough, and now I'm going. (*Puts on the gun.*) Epihodov, you're a very clever fellow, and a very terrible one too, all the women must be wild about you. Br-r-r! (*Goes.*) These clever fellows are all so stupid; there's not a creature for me to speak to. . . . Always alone, alone, nobody belonging to me . . . and who I am, and why I'm on earth, I don't know. (*Walks away slowly.*)

EPIHODOV. Speaking precisely, not touching upon other subjects, I'm bound to admit about myself, that destiny behaves mercilessly to me, as a storm to a little boat. If, let us suppose, I am mistaken, then why did I wake up this morning, to quote an example, and look round, and there on my chest was a spider of fearful magnitude . . . like this. (*Shows with both hands.*) And then I take up a jug of kvass, to quench my thirst, and in it there is something in the highest degree unseemly of the nature of a cockroach. (*A pause.*) Have you read Buckle? (*A pause.*) I am desirous of troubling you, Dunyasha, with a couple of words.

DUNYASHA. Well, speak.

EPIHODOV. I should be desirous to speak with you alone. (*Sighs.*)

DUNYASHA (*embarrassed*). Well—only bring me my mantle first. It's by the cupboard. It's rather damp here.

EPIHODOV. Certainly. I will fetch it. Now I know what I must do with my revolver. (*Takes a guitar and goes off playing on it.*)

YASHA. Two and twenty misfortunes! Between ourselves, he's a fool. (*Yawns.*)

DUNYASHA. God grant he doesn't shoot himself! (*A pause.*) I am so nervous, I'm always in a flutter. I was a little girl when I was taken into our lady's house, and now I have quite grown out of peasant ways, and my hands are white, as white as a lady's. I'm such a delicate, sensitive creature, I'm afraid of everything. I'm so frightened. And if you deceive me, Yasha, I don't know what will become of my nerves.

YASHA. (*Kisses her.*) You're a peach! Of course a girl must never forget herself; what I dislike more than anything is a girl being flighty in her behaviour.

DUNYASHA. I'm passionately in love with you, Yasha; you are a man of culture—you can give your opinion about anything. (*A pause.*)

YASHA. (*Yawns.*) Yes, that's so. My opinion is this: if a girl loves anyone, that means that she has no principles. (*A pause.*) It's pleasant smoking a cigar in the open air. (*Listens.*) Someone's coming this way . . . it's the gentlefolk (DUNYASHA *embraces him impulsively.*) Go home, as though you had been to the river to bathe; go by that path, or else they'll meet you and suppose I have made an appointment with you here. That I can't endure.

DUNYASHA (*coughing softly*). The cigar has made my head ache. . . . (*Goes off.* YASHA *remains sitting near the shrine. Enter* LYUBOV ANDREYEVNA, GAEV *and* LOPAHIN.)

LOPAHIN. You must make up your mind once for all—there's no time to lose. It's quite a simple question, you know. Will you consent to letting the land for building or not? One word in answer: Yes or no? Only one word!

LYUBOV. Who is smoking such horrible cigars here? (*Sits down.*)

GAEV. Now the railway line has been brought near, it's made things very convenient. (*Sits down.*) Here we have been over and lunched in town. Cannon off the white! I should like to go home and have a game.

LYUBOV. You have plenty of time.

LOPAHIN. Only one word! (*Beseechingly*) Give me an answer!

GAEV (*yawning*). What do you say?

LYUBOV. (*Looks in her purse.*) I had quite a lot of money here yesterday, and there's scarcely any left today. My poor Varya feeds us all on milk soup for the sake of economy; the old folks in the kitchen get nothing but pease pudding, while I waste my money in a senseless way. (*Drops purse, scattering gold pieces.*) There, they have all fallen out (*annoyed*)!

YASHA. Allow me, I'll soon pick them up. (*Collects the coins.*)

LYUBOV. Pray do, Yasha. And what did I go off to the town to lunch for? Your restaurant's a wretched place with its music and the tablecloth smelling of soap. . . . Why drink so much, Leonid? And eat so much? And talk so much? Today you talked a great deal again in the restaurant, and all so inappropriately. About the era of the 'seventies, about the decadents. And to whom? Talking to waiters about decadents!

LOPAHIN. Yes.

GAEV (*waving his hand*). I'm incorrigible; that's evident. (*Irritably to* YASHA) Why is it you keep fidgeting about in front of us!

YASHA. (*Laughs.*) I can't help laughing when I hear your voice.

GAEV (*to his sister*). Either I or he . . .

LYUBOV. Get along! Go away, Yasha.

YASHA. (*Gives* LYUBOV ANDREYEVNA *her purse.*) Directly (*hardly able to suppress his laughter*). This minute. . . . (*Goes off.*)

LOPAHIN. Deriganov, the millionaire, means to buy your estate. They say he is coming to the sale himself.

LYUBOV. Where did you hear that?

LOPAHIN. That's what they say in town.

GAEV. Our aunt in Yaroslavl has promised to send help; but when, and how much she will send, we don't know.

LOPAHIN. How much will she send? A hundred thousand? Two hundred?

LYUBOV. Oh, well! . . . Ten or fifteen thousand, and we must be thankful to get that.

LOPAHIN. Forgive me, but such reckless people as you are—such queer, unbusinesslike people—I never met in my life. One tells you in plain Russian your estate is going to be sold, and you seem not to understand it.

LYUBOV. What are we to do? Tell us what to do.

LOPAHIN. I do tell you every day. Every day I say the same thing. You absolutely must let the cherry orchard and the land on building leases; and do it at once, as quick as may be—the auction's close upon us! Do understand! Once make up your mind to build villas, and you can raise as much money as you like, and then you are saved.

LYUBOV. Villas and summer visitors—forgive me saying so—it's so vulgar.

GAEV. There I perfectly agree with you.

LOPAHIN. I shall sob, or scream, or fall into a fit. I can't stand it! You drive me mad! (*To* GAEV) You're an old woman!

GAEV. What do you say?

LOPAHIN. An old woman! (*Gets up to go.*)

LYUBOV (*in dismay*). No, don't go! Do stay, my dear friend! Perhaps we shall think of something.

LOPAHIN. What is there to think of?

LYUBOV. Don't go, I entreat you! With you here it's more cheerful, anyway. (*A pause.*) I keep expecting something, as though the house were going to fall about our ears.

GAEV (*in profound dejection*). Potted the white! It fails—a kiss.

LYUBOV. We have been great sinners. . . .

LOPAHIN. You have no sins to repent of.

GAEV. (*Puts a caramel in his mouth.*) They say I've eaten up my property in caramels. (*Laughs.*)

LYUBOV. Oh, my sins! I've always thrown my money away recklessly like a lunatic. I married a man who made nothing but debts. My husband died of champagne—he drank dreadfully. To my misery I loved another man, and immediately—it was my first punishment—the blow fell upon me, here, in the river . . . my boy was drowned and I went abroad—went away for ever, never to return, not to see that river again . . . I shut my eyes, and fled, distracted, and *he* after me . . . pitilessly, brutally. I bought a villa at Mentone, for *he* fell ill there, and for three years I had no rest day or night. His illness wore me out, my soul was dried up. And last year, when my villa was sold to pay my debts, I went to Paris and there he robbed me of everything and abandoned me for another woman; and I tried to poison myself. . . . So stupid, so shameful! . . . And suddenly I felt a yearning for Russia, for my country, for my little girl. . . . (*Dries her tears.*) Lord, Lord, be merciful! Forgive my sins! Do not chastise me more! (*Takes a telegram out of her pocket.*) I got this today from Paris. He implores forgiveness, entreats me to return. (*Tears up the telegram.*) I fancy there is music somewhere. (*Listens.*)

GAEV. That's our famous Jewish orchestra. You remember, four violins, a flute and a double bass.

LYUBOV. That still in existence? We ought to send for them one evening, and give a dance.

LOPAHIN. (*Listens.*) I can't hear. . . . (*Hums softly.*) "For money the Germans will turn a Russian into a Frenchman." (*Laughs.*) I did see such a piece at the theatre yesterday! It was funny!

LYUBOV. And most likely there was nothing funny in it. You shouldn't look at plays, you should look at yourself a little oftener. How grey your lives are! How much nonsense you talk.

LOPAHIN. That's true. One may say honestly, we live a fool's life. (*Pause.*) My father was a peasant, an idiot; he knew nothing and taught me nothing, only beat me when he was drunk, and always with his stick. In reality I am just such another blockhead and idiot. I've learnt nothing properly. I write a wretched hand. I write so that I feel ashamed before folks, like a pig.

LYUBOV. You ought to get married, my dear fellow.

LOPAHIN. Yes . . . that's true.

LYUBOV. You should marry our Varya, she's a good girl.

LOPAHIN. Yes.

LYUBOV. She's a good-natured girl, she's busy all day long, and what's more, she loves you. And you have liked her for ever so long.

LOPAHIN. Well? I'm not against it. . . . She's a good girl. (*Pause.*)

GAEV. I've been offered a place in the bank: 6,000 roubles a year. Did you know?

LYUBOV. You would never do for that! You must stay as you are.

(*Enter* FIRS *with overcoat.*)

FIRS. Put it on, sir, it's damp.

GAEV (*putting it on*). You bother me, old fellow.

FIRS. You can't go on like this. You went away in the morning without leaving word. (*Looks him over.*)

LYUBOV. You look older, Firs!

FIRS. What is your pleasure?

LOPAHIN. You look older, she said.

FIRS. I've had a long life. They were arranging my wedding before your papa was born. . . . (*Laughs.*) I was the head footman before the emancipation came. I wouldn't consent to be set free then; I stayed on with the old master. . . . (*A pause.*) I remember what rejoicings they made and didn't know themselves what they were rejoicing over.

LOPAHIN. Those were fine old times. There was flogging anyway.

FIRS (*not hearing*). To be sure! The peasants knew their place, and the masters knew theirs; but now they're all at sixes and sevens, there's no making it out.

GAEV. Hold your tongue, Firs. I must go to town tomorrow. I have been promised an introduction to a general, who might let us have a loan.

LOPAHIN. You won't bring that off. And you won't pay your arrears, you may rest assured of that.

LYUBOV. That's all his nonsense. There is no such general.

(*Enter* TROFIMOV, ANYA *and* VARYA.)

GAEV. Here come our girls.

ANYA. There's mamma on the seat.

LYUBOV (*tenderly*). Come here, come along. My darlings! (*Embraces* ANYA *and* VARYA.) If you only knew how I love you both. Sit beside me, there, like that.

(*All sit down.*)

LOPAHIN. Our perpetual student is always with the young ladies.

TROFIMOV. That's not your business.

LOPAHIN. He'll soon be fifty, and he's still a student.

TROFIMOV. Drop your idiotic jokes.

LOPAHIN. Why are you so cross, you queer fish?

TROFIMOV. Oh, don't persist!

LOPAHIN. (*Laughs.*) Allow me to ask you what's your idea of me?

TROFIMOV. I'll tell you my idea of you, Yermolay Alexeyevitch: you are a rich man, you'll soon be a millionaire. Well, just as in the economy of nature a wild beast is of use, who devours everything that comes in his way, so you too have your use.

(*All laugh.*)

VARYA. Better tell us something about the planets, Petya.

LYUBOV. No, let us go on with the conversation we had yesterday.

TROFIMOV. What was it about?

GAEV. About pride.

TROFIMOV. We had a long conversation yesterday, but we came to no conclusion. In pride, in your sense of it, there is something mystical. Perhaps you are right from your point of view; but if one looks at it simply, without subtlety, what sort of pride can there be, what sense is here in it, if a man in his physiological formation is very imperfect, if in the immense majority of cases he is coarse, dull-witted, profoundly unhappy? One must give up glorification of self. One should work, and nothing else.

GAEV. One must die in any case.

TROFIMOV. Who knows? And what does it mean—dying? Perhaps man has a hundred senses, and only the five we know are lost at death, while the other ninety-five remain alive.

LYUBOV. How clever you are, Petya!

LOPAHIN (*ironically*). Fearfully clever!

TROFIMOV. Humanity progresses, perfecting its powers. Everything that is beyond its ken now will one day become familiar and comprehensible; only we must work, we must with all our powers aid the seeker after truth. Here among us in Russia the workers are few in number as yet. The vast majority of the intellectual people I know, seek nothing, do nothing, are not fit as yet for work of any kind. They call themselves intellectual, but they treat their servants as inferiors, behave to the peasants as though they were animals, learn little, read nothing seriously, do practically nothing, only talk about science and know very little about art. They are all serious people, they all have severe faces, they all talk of weighty matters and air their theories, and yet the vast majority of us—ninety-nine per cent.—live like savages, at the least thing fly to blows and abuse, eat piggishly, sleep in filth and stuffiness, bugs everywhere, stench and damp and moral impurity. And it's clear all our fine talk is only to divert our attention and other people's. Show me where to find the crèches there's so much talk about, and the reading rooms? They only exist in novels: in real life there are none of them. There is nothing but filth and vulgarity and Asiatic apathy. I fear and dislike very serious faces. I'm afraid of serious conversations. We should do better to be silent.

LOPAHIN. You know, I get up at five o'clock in the morning, and I work from morning to night; and I've money, my own and other people's, always passing through my hands, and I see what people are made of all round me. One has only to begin to do anything to see how few honest, decent people there are. Sometimes when I lie awake at night, I think: "Oh! Lord, thou hast given us immense forests, boundless plains, the widest horizons, and living here we ourselves ought really to be giants."

LYUBOV. You ask for giants! They are no good except in storybooks; in real life they frighten us.

(EPIHODOV *advances in the background, playing on the guitar.*)

LYUBOV (*dreamily*). There goes Epihodov.

ANYA (*dreamily*). There goes Epihodov.

GAEV. The sun has set, my friends.

TROFIMOV. Yes.

GAEV (*not loudly, but, as it were, declaiming*). O nature, divine nature, thou art bright with eternal luster, beautiful and indifferent! Thou, whom we call mother, thou dost unite within thee life and death! Thou dost give life and dost destroy!

VARYA (*in a tone of supplication*). Uncle!

ANYA. Uncle, you are at it again!

TROFIMOV. You'd much better be cannoning off the red!

GAEV. I'll hold my tongue, I will.

(*All sit plunged in thought. Perfect stillness. The only thing audible is the muttering of* FIRS. *Suddenly there is a sound in the distance, as it were from the sky—the sound of a breaking harp string, mournfully dying away.*)

LYUBOV. What is that?

LOPAHIN. I don't know. Somewhere far away a bucket fallen and broken in the pits. But somewhere very far away.

GAEV. It might be a bird of some sort—such as a heron.

TROFIMOV. Or an owl.

LYUBOV. (*Shudders.*) I don't know why, but it's horrid. (*A pause.*)

FIRS. It was the same before the calamity—the owl hooted and the samovar hissed all the time.

GAEV. Before what calamity?

FIRS. Before the emancipation. (*A pause.*)

LYUBOV. Come, my friends, let us be going; evening is falling. (*To* ANYA) There are tears in your eyes. What is it, darling? (*Embraces her.*)

ANYA. Nothing, mamma; it's nothing.

TROFIMOV. There is somebody coming.

(*The wayfarer appears in a shabby white forage cap and an overcoat; he is slightly drunk.*)

WAYFARER. Allow me to inquire, can I get to the station this way?

GAEV. Yes. Go along that road.

WAYFARER. I thank you most feelingly (*coughing*). The weather is superb. (*Declaims*) My brother, my suffering brother! . . . Come out to the Volga! Whose groan do you hear? . . . (*To* VARYA) Mademoisetlle, vouchsafe a hungry Russian thirty kopeks.

(VARYA *utters a shriek of alarm.*)

LOPAHIN (*angrily*). There's a right and a wrong way of doing everything!

LYUBOV (*hurriedly*). Here, take this. (*Looks in her purse.*) I've no silver. No matter—here's gold for you.

WAYFARER. I thank you most feelingly! (*Goes off.*)

(*Laughter.*)

VARYA (*frightened*). I'm going home—I'm going . . . Oh, mamma, the servants have nothing to eat, and you gave him gold!

LYUBOV. There's no doing anything with me. I'm so silly! When we get home, I'll give you all I possess. Yermolay Alexeyevitch, you will lend me some more . . . !

LOPAHIN. I will.

LYUBOV. Come, friends, it's time to be going. And Varya, we have made a match of it for you. I congratuate you.

VARYA (*through her tears*). Mamma, that's not a joking matter.

LOPAHIN. "Ophelia, get thee to a nunnery!"

GAEV. My hands are trembling; it's a long while since I had a game of billiards.

LOPAHIN. "Ophelia! Nymph, in thy orisons be all my sins remember'd."

LYUBOV. Come, it will soon be suppertime.

VARYA. How he frightened me! My heart's simply throbbing.

LOPAHIN. Let me remind you, ladies and gentlemen: on the 22nd of August the cherry orchard will be sold. Think about that! Think about it!

(*All go off, except* TROFIMOV *and* ANYA.)

ANYA (*laughing*). I'm grateful to the wayfarer! He frightened Varya and we are left alone.

TROFIMOV. Varya's afraid we shall fall in love with each other, and for days together she won't leave us. With her narrow brain she can't grasp that we are above love. To eliminate the petty and transitory which hinders us from being free and happy—that is the aim and meaning of our life. Forward! We go forward irresistibly towards the bright star that shines yonder in the distance. Forward! Do not lag behind, friends.

ANYA. (*Claps her hands.*) How well you speak! (*A pause.*) It is divine here today.

TROFIMOV. Yes, it's glorious weather.

ANYA. Somehow, Petya, you've made me so that I don't love the cherry orchard as I used to. I used to love it so dearly. I used to think that there was no spot on earth like our garden.

TROFIMOV. All Russia is our garden. The earth is great and beautiful —there are many beautiful places in it. (*A pause.*) Think only, Anya, your grandfather, and great-grandfather, and all your ancestors were slave owners—the owners of living souls—and from every cherry in the orchard, from every leaf, from every trunk there are human creatures looking at you. Cannot you hear their voices? Oh, it is awful! Your orchard is a fearful thing, and when in the evening or at night one walks about the orchard, the old bark on the trees glimmers dimly in the dusk, and the old cherry trees seem to be dreaming of centuries gone by and tortured by fearful visions. Yes! We are at least two hundred years behind, we have really gained nothing yet, we have no definite attitude to the past, we do nothing but theorize or complain of depression or drink vodka. It is clear that to begin to live in the present we must first expiate our past, we must break with it; and we can expiate it only by suffering, by extraordinary unceasing labour. Understand that, Anya.

ANYA. The house we live in has long ceased to be our own, and I shall leave it, I give you my word.

TROFIMOV. If you have the house keys, fling them into the well and go away. Be free as the wind.

ANYA (*in ecstasy*). How beautifully you said that!

TROFIMOV. Believe me, Anya, believe me! I am not thirty yet, I am young, I am still a student, but I have gone through so much already! As soon as winter comes I am hungry, sick, careworn, poor as a beggar, and what ups and downs of fortune have I not known! And my soul was always, every minute, day and night, full of inexplicable forebodings. I have a foreboding of happiness,. Anya. I see glimpses of it already.

ANYA (*pensively*). The moon is rising.

(EPIHODOV *is heard playing still the same mournful song on the guitar. The moon rises. Somewhere near the poplars* VARYA *is looking for* ANYA *and calling "Anya! where are you?"*)

TROFIMOV. Yes, the moon is rising. (*A pause.*) Here is happiness—here it comes! It is coming nearer and nearer; already I can hear its footsteps. And if we never see it—if we may never know it—what does it matter? Others will see it after us.

VARYA'S VOICE. Anya! Where are you?

TROFIMOV. That Varya again! (*Angrily*) It's revolting!

ANYA. Well, let's go down to the river. It's lovely there.

TROFIMOV. Yes, let's go.

(*They go.*)

VARYA'S VOICE. Anya! Anya!

ACT THREE

Scene. A drawing room divided by an arch from a larger drawing room. A chandelier burning. The Jewish orchestra, the same that was mentioned in Act II, is heard playing in the anteroom. It is evening. In the larger drawing room they are dancing the grand chain. The voice of SEMYONOV-PISHTCHIK: "Promenade à une paire!" *Then enter the drawing room in couples first* PISH-TCHIK *and* CHARLOTTA IVANOVNA, *then* TROFIMOV *and* LYUBOV ANDREYEVNA, *thirdly* ANYA *with the Post Office Clerk, fourthly* VARYA *with the Station Master, and other guests.* VARYA *is quietly weeping and wiping away her tears as she dances. In the last couple is* DUNYASHA. *They move across the drawing room.* PISH-TCHIK *shouts:* "Grand rond, balancez!" *and* "Les Cavaliers à genou et remerciez vos dames."

(FIRS *in a swallow-tail coat brings in seltzer water on a tray.* PISHTCHIK *and* TROFIMOV *enter the drawing room.*)

PISHTCHIK. I am a full-blooded man; I have already had two strokes. Dancing's hard work for me, but as they say, if you're in the pack, you must bark with the rest. I'm as strong, I may say, as a horse. My parent, who would have his joke—may the Kingdom of Heaven be his!—used to say about our origin that the ancient stock of the Semyonov-Pishtchiks was derived from the very horse that Caligula made a member of the senate. (*Sits down.*) But I've no money, that's where the mischief is. A hungry dog believes in nothing but meat. . . . (*Snores, but at once wakes up.*) That's like me . . . I can think of nothing but money.

TROFIMOV. There really is something horsy about your appearance.

PISHTCHIK. Well . . . a horse is a fine beast . . . a horse can be sold. (*There is the sound of billiards being played in an adjoining room.* VARYA *appears in the arch leading to the larger drawing room.*)

TROFIMOV (*teasing*). Madame Lopahin! Madame Lopahin!

VARYA (*angrily*). Mangy-looking gentleman!

TROFIMOV. Yes, I am a mangy-looking gentleman, and I'm proud of it!

VARYA (*pondering bitterly*). Here we have hired musicians and nothing to pay them! (*Goes out.*)

TROFIMOV (*to* PISHTCHIK). If the energy you have wasted during your lifetime in trying to find the money to pay your interest, had gone to something else, you might in the end have turned the world upside down.

PISHTCHIK. Nietzsche, the philosopher, a very great and celebrated man . . . of enormous intellect . . . says in his works, that one can make forged bank notes.

TROFIMOV. Why, have you read Nietzsche?

PISHTCHIK. What next . . . Dashenka told me. . . . And now I am in such a position, I might just as well forge bank notes. The day after tomorrow I must pay 310 roubles—130 I have procured. (*Feels in his pockets, in alarm.*) The money's gone! I have lost my money! (*Through his tears*) Where's the money? (*Gleefully*) Why, here it is behind the lining. . . . It has made me hot all over.

(*Enter* LYUBOV ANDREYEVNA *and* CHARLOTTA IVANOVNA.)

LYUBOV. (*Hums the Lezginka.*) Why is Leonid so long? What can he be doing in town? (*To* DUNYASHA) Offer the musicians some tea.

TROFIMOV. The sale hasn't taken place, most likely.

LYUBOV. It's the wrong time to have the orchestra, and the wrong time to give a dance. Well, never mind. (*Sits down and hums softly.*)

CHARLOTTA. (*Gives* PISHTCHIK *a pack of cards.*) Here's a pack of cards. Think of any card you like.

PISHTCHIK. I've thought of one.

CHARLOTTA. Shuffle the pack now. That's right. Give it here, my dear Mr. Pishtchik. Ein, zwei, drei—now look, it's in your breast pocket.

PISHTCHIK (*taking a card out of his breast pocket*). The eight of spades! Perfectly right! (*Wonderingly*) Fancy that now!

CHARLOTTA (*holding pack of cards in her hands, to* TROFIMOV). Tell me quickly which is the top card.

TROFIMOV. Well, the queen of spades.

CHARLOTTA. It is! (*To* PISHTCHIK) Well, which card is uppermost?

PISHTCHIK. The ace of hearts.

CHARLOTTA. It is! (*Claps her hands, pack of cards disappears.*) Ah! what lovely weather it is today!

(*A mysterious feminine voice which seems coming out of the floor answers her.* "Oh, yes, it's magnificent weather, madam.")

CHARLOTTA. You are my perfect ideal.

VOICE. And I greatly admire you too, madam.

STATION MASTER (*applauding*). The lady ventriloquist—bravo!

PISHTCHIK (*wonderingly*). Fancy that now! Most enchanting Charlotta Ivanovna. I'm simply in love with you.

CHARLOTTA. In love? (*Shrugging shoulders*) What do you know of love, guter Mensch, aber schlechter Musikant.

TROFIMOV. (*Pats* PISHTCHIK *on the shoulder.*) You dear old horse. . . .

CHARLOTTA. Attention, please! Another trick! (*Takes a travelling rug from a chair.*) Here's a very good rug; I want to sell it (*shaking it out*). Doesn't anyone want to buy it?

PISHTCHIK (*wonderingly*). Fancy that!

CHARLOTTA. Ein, zwei, drei! (*Quickly picks up rug she has dropped; behind the rug stands* ANYA; *she makes a curtsey, runs to her mother, embraces her and runs back into the larger drawing room amidst general enthusiasm.*)

LYUBOV. (*Applauds.*) Bravo! Bravo!

CHARLOTTA. Now again! Ein, zwei, drei! (*Lifts up the rug; behind the rug stands* VARYA, *bowing.*)

PISHTCHIK (*wonderingly*). Fancy that now!

CHARLOTTA. That's the end. (*Throws the rug at* PISHTCHIK, *makes a curtsey, runs into the larger drawing room.*)

PISHTCHIK. (*Hurries after her.*) Mischievous creature! Fancy! (*Goes out.*)

LYUBOV. And still Leonid doesn't come. I can't understand what he's doing in the town so long! Why, everything must be over by now. The estate is sold, or the sale has not taken place. Why keep us so long in suspense?

VARYA (*trying to console her*). Uncle's bought it. I feel sure of that.

TROFIMOV (*ironically*). Oh, yes!

VARYA. Great-aunt sent him an authorization to buy it in her name,

and transfer the debt. She's doing it for Anya's sake, and I'm
sure God will be merciful. Uncle will buy it.

LYUBOV. My aunt in Yaroslavl sent fifteen thousand to buy the estate
in her name, she doesn't trust us—but that's not enough even
to pay the arrears. (*Hides her face in her hands.*) My fate is
being sealed today, my fate . . .

TROFIMOV (*teasing* VARYA). Madame Lopahin.

VARYA (*angrily*). Perpetual student! Twice already you've been sent
down from the University.

LYUBOV. Why are you angry, Varya? He's teasing you about Lopahin.
Well, what of that? Marry Lopahin if you like, he's a good man,
and interesting; if you don't want to, don't! Nobody compels you,
darling.

VARYA. I must tell you plainly, mamma, I look at the matter seriously;
he's a good man, I like him.

LYUBOV. Well, marry him. I can't see what you're waiting for.

VARYA. Mamma. I can't make him an offer myself. For the last two
years, everyone's been talking to me about him. Everyone talks;
but he says nothing or else makes a joke. I see what it means.
He's growing rich, he's absorbed in business, he has no thoughts
for me. If I had money, were it ever so little, if I had only a
hundred roubles, I'd throw everything up and go far away. I
would go into a nunnery.

TROFIMOV. What bliss!

VARYA (*to* TROFIMOV). A student ought to have sense! (*In a soft tone
with tears*) How ugly you've grown, Petya! How old you look!
(*To* LYUBOV ANDREYEVNA, *no longer crying*) But I can't do without work, mamma; I must have something to do every minute.
(*Enter* YASHA.)

YASHA (*hardly restraining his laughter*). Epihodov has broken a billiard
cue! (*Goes out.*)

VARYA. What is Epihodov doing here? Who gave him leave to play
billiards? I can't make these people out. (*Goes out.*)

LYUBOV. Don't tease her, Petya. You see she has grief enough without
that.

TROFIMOV. She is so very officious, meddling in what's not her business. All the summer she's given Anya and me no peace. She's
afraid of a love affair between us. What's it to do with her? Besides, I have given no grounds for it. Such triviality is not in my
line. We are above love!

LYUBOV. And I suppose I am beneath love. (*Very uneasily*) Why is it
Leonid's not here? If only I could know whether the estate is

sold or not! It seems such an incredible calamity that I really don't know what to think. I am distracted . . . I shall scream in a minute . . . I shall do something stupid. Save me, Petya, tell me something, talk to me!

TROFIMOV. What does it matter whether the estate is sold today or not? That's all done with long ago. There's no turning back, the path is overgrown. Don't worry yourself, dear Lyubov Andreyevna. You mustn't deceive yourself; for once in your life you must face the truth!

LYUBOV. What truth? You see where the truth lies, but I seem to have lost my sight, I see nothing. You settle every great problem so boldly, but tell me, my dear boy, isn't it because you're young— because you haven't yet understood one of your problems through suffering? You look forward boldly, and isn't it that you don't see and don't expect anything dreadful because life is still hidden from your young eyes? You're bolder, more honest, deeper than we are, but think, be just a little magnanimous, have pity on me. I was born here, you know, my father and mother lived here, my grand-father lived here, I love this house. I can't conceive of life with-out the cherry orchard, and if it really must be sold, then sell me with the orchard. (*Embraces* TROFIMOV, *kisses him on the fore-head.*) My boy was drowned here. (*Weeps.*) Pity me, my dear kind fellow.

TROFIMOV. You know I feel for you with all my heart.

LYUBOV. But that should have been said differently, so differently. (*Takes out her handkerchief, telegram falls on the floor.*) My heart is so heavy today. It's so noisy here my soul is quivering at every sound, I'm shuddering all over, but I can't go away; I'm afraid to be quiet and alone. Don't be hard on me, Petya . . . I love you as though you were one of ourselves. I would gladly let you marry Anya—I swear I would—only, my dear boy, you must take your degree, you do nothing—you're simply tossed by fate from place to place. That's so strange. It is, isn't it? And you must do something with your beard to make it grow somehow. (*Laughs.*) You look so funny!

TROFIMOV. (*Picks up the telegram.*) I've no wish to be a beauty.

LYUBOV. That's a telegram from Paris. I get one every day. One yester-day and one today. That savage creature is ill again, he's in trouble again. He begs forgiveness, beseeches me to go, and really I ought to go to Paris to see him. You look shocked, Petya. What am I to do, my dear boy, what am I to do? He is ill, he is alone and un-happy, and who'll look after him, who'll keep him from doing the wrong thing, who'll give him his medicine at the right time?

And why hide it or be silent? I love him, that's clear. I love him! I love him! He's a millstone about my neck, I'm going to the bottom with him, but I love that stone and can't live without it. (*Presses* TROFIMOV'S *hand.*) Don't think ill of me, Petya, don't tell me anything, don't tell me . . .

TROFIMOV (*through his tears*). For God's sake forgive my frankness: why, he robbed you!

LYUBOV. No! No! No! You mustn't speak like that. (*Covers her ears.*)

TROFIMOV. He is a wretch! You're the only person that doesn't know it! He's a worthless creature! A despicable wretch!

LYUBOV (*getting angry, but speaking with restraint*). You're twenty-six or twenty-seven years old, but you're still a schoolboy.

TROFIMOV. Possibly.

LYUBOV. You should be a man at your age! You should understand what love means! And you ought to be in love yourself. You ought to fall in love! (*Angrily*) Yes, yes, and it's not purity in you, you're simply a prude, a comic fool, a freak.

TROFIMOV (*in horror*). The things she's saying!

LYUBOV. I am above love! You're not above love, but simply as our Firs here says, "You are a good-for-nothing." At your age not to have a mistress!

TROFIMOV (*in horror*). This is awful! The things she is saying! (*Goes rapidly into the larger drawing room clutching his head.*) This is awful! I can't stand it! I'm going. (*Goes off, but at once returns.*) All is over between us! (*Goes off into the anteroom.*)

LYUBOV. (*Shouts after him.*) Petya! Wait a minute! You funny creature! I was joking! Petya!

(*There is a sound of somebody running quickly downstairs and suddenly falling with a crash.* ANYA *and* VARYA *scream, but there is a sound of laughter at once.*)

LYUBOV. What has happened?

(ANYA *runs in.*)

ANYA (*laughing*). Petya's fallen downstairs! (*Runs out.*)

LYUBOV. What a queer fellow that Petya is!

(*The Station Master stands in the middle of the larger room and reads "The Magdalene," by Alexey Tolstoy. They listen to him, but before he has recited many lines strains of a waltz are heard from the anteroom and the reading is broken off. All dance.* TROFIMOV, ANYA, VARYA *and* LYUBOV ANDREYEVNA *come in from the anteroom.*)

LYUBOV. Come, Petya—come, pure heart! I beg your pardon. Let's have a dance! (*Dances with* PETYA.)

(ANYA *and* VARYA *dance.* FIRS *comes in, puts his stick down near the side door.* YASHA *also comes into the drawing room and looks on at the dancing.*)

YASHA. What is it, old man?

FIRS. I don't feel well. In old days we used to have generals, barons and admirals dancing at our balls, and now we send for the post office clerk and the station master and even they're not overanxious to come. I am getting feeble. The old master, the grandfather, used to give sealing wax for all complaints. I have been taking sealing wax for twenty years or more. Perhaps that's what's kept me alive.

YASHA. You bore me, old man! (*Yawns.*) It's time you were done with.

FIRS. Ach, you're a good-for-nothing! (*Mutters.*)

(TROFIMOV *and* LYUBOV ANDREYEVNA *dance in larger room and then on to the stage.*)

LYUBOV. *Merci.* I'll sit down a little. (*Sits down.*) I'm tired.

(*Enter* ANYA.)

ANYA (*excitedly*). There's a man in the kitchen has been saying that the cherry orchard's been sold today.

LYUBOV. Sold to whom?

ANYA. He didn't say to whom. He's gone away.

(*She dances with* TROFIMOV, *and they go off into the larger room.*)

YASHA. There was an old man gossiping there, a stranger.

FIRS. Leonid Andreyevitch isn't here yet, he hasn't come back. He has his light overcoat on, *demi-saison,* he'll catch cold for sure. Ach! Foolish young things!

LYUBOV. I feel as though I should die. Go, Yasha, find out to whom it has been sold.

YASHA. But he went away long ago, the old chap. (*Laughs.*)

LYUBOV (*with slight vexation*). What are you laughing at? What are you pleased at?

YASHA. Epihodov is so funny. He's a silly fellow, two and twenty misfortunes.

LYUBOV. Firs, if the estate is sold, where will you go?

FIRS. Where you bid me, there I'll go.

LYUBOV. Why do you look like that? Are you ill? You ought to be in bed.

FIRS. Yes (*ironically*). Me go to bed and who's to wait here? Who's to see to things without me? I'm the only one in all the house.

YASHA (*to* LYUBOV ANDREYEVNA). Lyubov Andreyevna, permit me to make a request of you; if you go back to Paris again, be so kind as to take me with you. It's positively impossible for me to stay here (*looking about him; in an undertone*). There's no need to say it, you see for yourself—an uncivilized country, the people have no morals, and then the dullness! The food in the kitchen's abominable, and then Firs runs after one muttering all sorts of unsuitable words. Take me with you, please do!

(*Enter* PISHTCHIK.)

PISHTCHIK. Allow me to ask you for a waltz, my dear lady. (LYUBOV ANDREYEVNA *goes with him.*) Enchanting lady, I really must borrow of you just 180 roubles (*dances*), only 180 roubles. (*They pass into the larger room.*)

YASHA. (*Hums softly.*) "Knowest thou my soul's emotion."

(*In the larger drawing room, a figure in a gray top hat and in check trousers is gesticulating and jumping about. Shouts of* "Bravo, Charlotta Ivanovna.")

DUNYASHA. (*She has stopped to powder herself.*) My young lady tells me to dance. There are plenty of gentlemen, and too few ladies, but dancing makes me giddy and makes my heart beat. Firs, the post office clerk said something to me just now that quite took my breath away.

(*Music becomes more subdued.*)

FIRS. What did he say to you?

DUNYASHA. He said I was like a flower.

YASHA. (*Yawns.*) What ignorance! (*Goes out.*)

DUNYASHA. Like a flower. I am a girl of such delicate feelings, I am awfully fond of soft speeches.

FIRS. Your head's being turned.

(*Enter* EPIHODOV.)

EPIHODOV. You have no desire to see me, Dunyasha. I might be an insect. (*Sighs.*) Ah! life!

DUNYASHA. What is it you want?

EPIHODOV. Undoubtedly you may be right. (*Sighs.*) But of course, if one looks at it from that point of view, if I may so express myself, you have, excuse my plain speaking, reduced me to a complete state of mind. I know my destiny. Every day some misfortune befalls me and I have long ago grown accustomed to it, so that I look upon my fate with a smile. You gave me your word, and though I——

DUNYASHA. Let us have a talk later, I entreat you, but now leave me in peace, for I am lost in reverie. (*Plays with her fan.*)

EPIHODOV. I have a misfortune every day, and if I may venture to express myself, I merely smile at it, I even laugh.

(VARYA *enters from the larger drawing room.*)

VARYA. You still have not gone, Epihodov. What a disrespectful creature you are, really! (*To* DUNYASHA) Go along, Dunyasha! (*To* EPIHODOV) First you play billiards and break the cue, then you go wandering about the drawing room like a visitor!

EPIHODOV. You really cannot, if I may so express myself, call me to account like this.

VARYA. I'm not calling you to account, I'm speaking to you. You do nothing but wander from place to place and don't do your work. We keep you as a counting-house clerk, but what use you are I can't say.

EPIHODOV (*offended*). Whether I work or whether I walk, whether I eat or whether I play billiards, is a matter to be judged by persons of understanding and my elders.

VARYA. You dare to tell me that! (*Firing up*) You dare! You mean to say I've no understanding. Begone from here! This minute!

EPIHODOV (*intimidated*). I beg you to express yourself with delicacy.

VARYA (*beside herself with anger*). This moment! get out! away! (*He goes towards the door, she following him.*) Two and twenty misfortunes! Take yourself off! Don't let me set eyes on you! (EPIHODOV *has gone out, behind the door his voice,* "I shall lodge a complaint against you.") What! You're coming back? (*Snatches up the stick* FIRS *has put down near the door.*) Come! Come! Come! I'll show you! What! You're coming? Then take that! (*She swings the stick, at the very moment that* LOPAHIN *comes in.*)

LOPAHIN. Very much obliged to you!

VARYA (*angrily and ironically*). I beg your pardon!

LOPAHIN. Not at all! I humbly thank you for your kind reception!

VARYA. No need of thanks for it. (*Moves away, then looks round and asks softly*) I haven't hurt you?

LOPAHIN. Oh, no! Not at all! There's an immense bump coming up, though!

VOICES FROM LARGER ROOM. Lopahin has come! Yermolay Alexeyevitch!

PISHTCHIK. What do I see and hear? (*Kisses* LOPAHIN.) There's a whiff of cognac about you, my dear soul, and we're making merry here too!

(*Enter* LYUBOV ANDREYEVNA.)

LYUBOV. Is it you, Yermolay Alexeyevitch? Why have you been so long? Where's Leonid?

LOPAHIN. Leonid Andreyevitch arrived with me. He is coming.

LYUBOV (*in agitation*). Well! Well! Was there a sale? Speak!

LOPAHIN (*embarrassed, afraid of betraying his joy*). The sale was over at four o'clock. We missed our train—had to wait till half-past nine. (*Sighing heavily*) Ugh! I feel a little giddy.

(*Enter* GAEV. *In his right hand he has purchases, with his left hand is wiping away his tears.*)

LYUBOV. Well, Leonid? What news? (*Impatiently, with tears*) Make haste, for God's sake!

GAEV. (*Makes her no answer, simply waves his hand. To* FIRS, *weeping*) Here, take them; there's anchovies, Kertch herrings. I have eaten nothing all day. What I have been through! (*Door into the billiard room is open. There is heard a knocking of balls and the voice of* YASHA *saying "Eighty-seven."* GAEV'S *expression changes, he leaves off weeping.*) I am fearfully tired. Firs, come and help me change my things. (*Goes to his own room across the larger drawing room.*)

PISHTCHIK. How about the sale? Tell us, do!

LYUBOV. Is the cherry orchard sold?

LOPAHIN. It is sold.

LYUBOV. Who has bought it?

LOPAHIN. I have bought it.

(*A pause.* LYUBOV *is crushed; she would fall down if she were not standing near a chair and table.* VARYA *takes keys from her waistband, flings them on the floor in middle of drawing room and goes out.*)

LOPAHIN. I have bought it! Wait a bit, ladies and gentlemen, pray. My head's a bit muddled, I can't speak. (*Laughs.*) We came to the auction. Deriganov was there already. Leonid Andreyevitch only had 15,000 and Deriganov bid 30,000, besides the arrears, straight off. I saw how the land lay. I bid against him. I bid 40,000, he bid 45,000, I said 55, and so he went on, adding 5 thousands and I adding 10. Well . . . So it ended. I bid 90, and it was knocked down to me. Now the cherry orchard's mine! Mine! (*Chuckles.*) My God, the cherry orchard's mine! Tell me that I'm drunk, that I'm out of my mind, that it's all a dream. (*Stamps with his feet.*) Don't laugh at me! If my father and my grandfather could rise from their graves and see all that has happened! How their Yermolay, ignorant, beaten Yermolay, who used to run about barefoot in winter, how that very Yermolay has bought the finest estate in the world! I have bought the estate where my father and grandfather were slaves, where they weren't even admitted into the kitchen. I am asleep, I am dreaming! It is all fancy, it is the work of your imagination plunged in the darkness of ignorance. (*Picks up keys, smiling fondly.*) She threw away the keys; she means to show she's not the housewife now. (*Jingles the keys.*) Well, no matter. (*The orchestra is heard tuning up.*) Hey, musicians! Play! I want to hear you. Come, all of you, and look how Yermolay Lopahin will take the axe to the cherry orchard, how the trees will fall to the ground! We will build houses on it and our grandsons and great-grandsons will see a new life springing up there. Music! Play up!

(*Music begins to play.* LYUBOV ANDREYEVNA *has sunk into a chair and is weeping bitterly.*)

LOPAHIN (*reproachfully*). Why, why didn't you listen to me? My poor friend! Dear lady, there's no turning back now. (*With tears*) Oh, if all this could be over, oh, if our miserable disjointed life could somehow soon be changed!

PISHTCHIK. (*Takes him by the arm, in an undertone.*) She's weeping, let us go and leave her alone. Come. (*Takes him by the arm and leads him into the larger drawing room.*)

LOPAHIN. What's that? Musicians, play up! All must be as I wish it. (*With irony*) Here comes the new master, the owner of the cherry orchard! (*Accidentally tips over a little table, almost upsetting the candelabra.*) I can pay for everything!

(*Goes out with* PISHTCHIK. *No one remains on the stage or in the larger drawing room except* LYUBOV, *who sits huddled up, weeping bitterly. The music plays softly.* ANYA *and* TROFIMOV *come in quickly.* ANYA *goes up to her mother and falls on her knees before her.* TROFIMOV *stands at the entrance to the larger drawing room.*)

ANYA. Mamma! Mamma, you're crying, dear, kind, good mamma! My precious! I love you! I bless you! The cherry orchard is sold, it is gone, that's true, that's true! But don't weep, mamma! Life is still before you, you have still your good, pure heart! Let us go, let us go, darling, away from here! We will make a new garden, more splendid that this one; you will see it, you will understand. And joy, quiet, deep joy, will sink into your soul like the sun at evening! And you will smile, mamma! Come, darling, let us go!

ACT FOUR

Scene. Same as in First Act. There are neither curtains on the windows nor pictures on the walls: only a little furniture remains piled up in a corner as if for sale. There is a sense of desolation; near the outer door and in the background of the scene are packed trunks, travelling bags, etc. On the left the door is open, and from here the voices of VARYA *and* ANYA *are audible.* LOPAHIN *is standing waiting.* YASHA *is holding a tray with glasses full of champagne. In front of the stage* EPIHODOV *is tying up a box. In the background behind the scene a hum of talk from the peasants who have come to say good-by. The voice of* GAEV: "Thanks, brothers, thanks!"

YASHA. The peasants have come to say good-by. In my opinion, Yermolay Alexeyevitch, the peasants are good-natured, but they don't know much about things.

(*The hum of talk dies away. Enter across front of stage* LYUBOV ANDREYEVNA *and* GAEV. *She is not weeping, but is pale; her face is quivering—she cannot speak.*)

GAEV. You gave them your purse, Lyuba. That won't do—that won't do!

LYUBOV. I couldn't help it! I couldn't help it!

(*Both go out.*)

LOPAHIN (*in the doorway, calls after them*). You will take a glass at parting? Please do. I didn't think to bring any from the town, and at the station I could only get one bottle. Please take a glass. (*A pause.*) What? You don't care for any? (*Comes away from the door.*) If I'd known, I wouldn't have bought it. Well, and I'm not going to drink it. (YASHA *carefully sets the tray down on a chair.*) You have a glass, Yasha, anyway.

YASHA. Good luck to the travellers, and luck to those that stay behind! (*Drinks.*) This champagne isn't the real thing, I can assure you.

LOPAHIN. It cost eight roubles the bottle. (*A pause.*) It's devilish cold here.

YASHA. They haven't heated the stove today—it's all the same since we're going. (*Laughs.*)

LOPAHIN. What are you laughing for?

YASHA. For pleasure.

LOPAHIN. Though it's October, it's as still and sunny as though it were summer. It's just right for building! (*Looks at his watch; says in doorway*) Take note, ladies and gentlemen, the train goes in forty-seven minutes; so you ought to start for the station in twenty minutes. You must hurry up!

(TROFIMOV *comes in from out of doors wearing a greatcoat.*)

TROFIMOV. I think it must be time to start, the horses are ready. The devil only knows what's become of my galoshes; they're lost. (*In the doorway*) Anya! My galoshes aren't here. I can't find them.

LOPAHIN. And I'm getting off to Harkov. I am going in the same train with you. I'm spending all the winter at Harkov. I've been wasting all my time gossiping with you and fretting with no work to do. I can't get on without work. I don't know what to do with my hands, they flap about so queerly, as if they didn't belong to me.

TROFIMOV. Well, we're just going away, and you will take up your profitable labours again.

LOPAHIN. Do take a glass.

TROFIMOV. No, thanks.

LOPAHIN. Then you're going to Moscow now?

TROFIMOV. Yes. I shall see them as far as the town, and tomorrow I shall go on to Moscow.

LOPAHIN. Yes, I daresay, the professors aren't giving any lectures, they're waiting for your arrival.

TROFIMOV. That's not your business.

LOPAHIN. How many years have you been at the University?

TROFIMOV. Do think of something newer than that—that's stale and flat. (*Hunts for galoshes.*) You know we shall most likely never see each other again, so let me give you one piece of advice at parting: don't wave your arms about—get out of the habit. And another thing, building villas, reckoning up that the summer visitors will in time become independent farmers—reckoning like that, that's not the thing to do either. After all, I am fond of you: you have fine delicate fingers like an artist, you've a fine delicate soul.

LOPAHIN. (*Embraces him.*) Good-by, my dear fellow. Thanks for everything. Let me give you money for the journey, if you need it.

TROFIMOV. What for? I don't need it.

LOPAHIN. Why, you haven't got a halfpenny.

TROFIMOV. Yes, I have, thank you. I got some money for a translation. Here it is in my pocket, (*anxiously*) but where can my galoshes be!

VARYA (*from the next room*). Take the nasty things! (*Flings a pair of galoshes onto the stage.*)

TROFIMOV. Why are you so cross, Varya? h'm! . . . but those aren't my galoshes.

LOPAHIN. I sowed three thousand acres with poppies in the spring, and now I have cleared forty thousand profit. And when my poppies were in flower, wasn't it a picture! So here, as I say, I made forty thousand, and I'm offering you a loan because I can afford to. Why turn up your nose? I am a peasant—I speak bluntly.

TROFIMOV. Your father was a peasant, mine was a chemist—and that proves absolutely nothing whatever. (LOPAHIN *takes out his pocketbook.*) Stop that—stop that. If you were to offer me two hundred thousand I wouldn't take it. I am an independent man, and everything that all of you, rich and poor alike, prize so highly and hold so dear, hasn't the slightest power over me—it's like so much fluff fluttering in the air. I can get on without you. I can pass by you. I am strong and proud. Humanity is advancing towards the highest truth, the highest happiness, which is possible on earth, and I am in the front ranks.

LOPAHIN. Will you get there?

TROFIMOV. I shall get there. (*A pause.*) I shall get there, or I shall show others the way to get there.

(*In the distance is heard the stroke of an axe on a tree.*)

LOPAHIN. Good-by, my dear fellow; it's time to be off. We turn up our noses at one another, but life is passing all the while. When I am working hard without resting, then my mind is more at ease, and it seems to me as though I too know what I exist for; but how many people there are in Russia, my dear boy, who exist, one doesn't know what for. Well, it doesn't matter. That's not what keeps things spinning. They tell me Leonid Andreyevitch has taken a situation. He is going to be a clerk at the bank—6,000 roubles a year. Only, of course, he won't stick to it—he's too lazy.

ANYA (*in the doorway*). Mamma begs you not to let them chop down the orchard until she's gone.

TROFIMOV. Yes, really, you might have the tact. (*Walks out across the front of the stage.*)

LOPAHIN. I'll see to it! I'll see to it! Stupid fellows! (*Goes out after him.*)

ANYA. Has Firs been taken to the hospital?

YASHA. I told them this morning. No doubt they have taken him.

ANYA (*to* EPIHODOV, *who passes across the drawing room*). Semyon Pantaleyevitch, inquire, please, if Firs has been taken to the hospital.

YASHA (*in a tone of offense*). I told Yegor this morning—why ask a dozen times?

EPIHODOV. Firs is advanced in years. It's my conclusive opinion no treatment would do him good; it's time he was gathered to his fathers. And I can only envy him. (*Puts a trunk down on a cardboard hatbox and crushes it.*) There, now, of course—I knew it would be so.

YASHA (*jeeringly*). Two and twenty misfortunes!

VARYA (*through the door*). Has Firs been taken to the hospital?

ANYA. Yes.

VARYA. Why wasn't the note for the doctor taken too?

ANYA (*from the adjoining room*). Where's Yasha? Tell him his mother's come to say good-by to him.

YASHA. (*Waves his hand.*) They put me out of all patience! (DUN-

YASHA *has all this time been busy about the luggage. Now, when*
YASHA *is left alone, she goes up to him.*)

DUNYASHA. You might just give me one look, Yasha. You're going
away. You're leaving me. (*Weeps and throws herself on his neck.*)

YASHA. What are you crying for? (*Drinks the champagne.*) In six days
I shall be in Paris again. Tomorrow we shall get into the express
train and roll away in a flash. I can scarcely believe it! *Vive la
France!* It doesn't suit me here—it's not the life for me; there's
no doing anything. I have seen enough of the ignorance here. I
have had enough of it. (*Drinks champagne.*) What are you crying for? Behave yourself properly, and then you won't cry.

DUNYASHA. (*Powders her face, looking in a pocket mirror.*) Do send
me a letter from Paris. You know how I loved you, Yasha—how
I loved you! I am a tender creature, Yasha.

YASHA. Here they are coming!

(*Busies himself about the trunks, humming softly. Enter* LYUBOV
ANDREYEVNA, GAEV, ANYA *and* CHARLOTTA IVANOVNA.)

GAEV. We ought to be off. There's not much time now (*looking at*
YASHA). What a smell of herrings!

LYUBOV. In ten minutes we must get into the carriage. (*Casts a look
about the room.*) Farewell, dear house, dear old home of our
fathers! Winter will pass and spring will come, and then you will
be no more; they will tear you down! How much those walls have
seen! (*Kisses her daughter passionately.*) My treasure, how bright
you look! Your eyes are sparkling like diamonds! Are you glad?
Very glad?

ANYA. Very glad! A new life is beginning, mamma.

GAEV. Yes, really, everything is all right now. Before the cherry orchard was sold, we were all worried and wretched, but afterwards,
when once the question was settled conclusively, irrevocably, we
all felt calm and even cheerful. I am a bank clerk now—I am a
financier—cannon off the red. And you, Lyuba, after all, you are
looking better; there's no question of that.

LYUBOV. Yes. My nerves are better, that's true. (*Her hat and coat are
handed to her.*) I'm sleeping well. Carry out my things, Yasha.
It's time. (*To* ANYA) My darling, we shall soon see each other
again. I am going to Paris. I can live there on the money your
Yaroslavl auntie sent us to buy the estate with—hurrah for auntie!
—but that money won't last long.

ANYA. You'll come back soon, mamma, won't you? I'll be working up
for my examination in the high school, and when I have passed
that, I shall set to work and be a help to you. We will read all
sorts of things together, mamma, won't we? (*Kisses her mother's*

hands.) We will read in the autumn evenings. We'll read lots of books, and a new wonderful world will open out before us (*dreamily*). Mamma, come soon.

LYUBOV. I shall come, my precious treasure. (*Embraces her.*)

(*Enter* LOPAHIN. CHARLOTTA *softly hums a song.*)

GAEV. Charlotta's happy; she's singing!

CHARLOTTA. (*Picks up a bundle like a swaddled baby.*) By, by, my baby. (*A baby is heard crying: "Ooah! ooah!"*) Hush, hush, my pretty boy! (*Ooah! ooah!*) Poor little thing! (*Throws the bundle back.*) You must please find me a situation. I can't go on like this.

LOPAHIN. We'll find you one, Charlotta Ivanovna. Don't you worry yourself.

GAEV. Everyone's leaving us. Varya's going away. We have become of no use all at once.

CHARLOTTA. There's nowhere for me to be in the town. I must go away. (*Hums.*) What care I . . .

(*Enter* PISHTCHIK.)

LOPAHIN. The freak of nature!

PISHTCHIK (*gasping*). Oh! . . . let me get my breath. . . . I'm worn out . . . my most honoured . . . Give me some water.

GAEV. Want some money, I suppose? Your humble servant! I'll go out of the way of temptation. (*Goes out.*)

PISHTCHIK. It's a long while since I have been to see you . . . dearest lady. (*To* LOPAHIN) You are here . . . glad to see you . . . a man of immense intellect . . . take . . . here (*gives* LOPAHIN) . . . 400 roubles. That leaves me owing 840.

LOPAHIN (*shrugging his shoulders in amazement*). It's like a dream. Where did you get it?

PISHTCHIK. Wait a bit . . . I'm hot . . . a most extraordinary occurrence! Some Englishmen came along and found in my land some sort of white clay. (*To* LYUBOV ANDREYEVNA) And 400 for you . . . most lovely . . . wonderful. (*Gives money.*) The rest later. (*Sips water.*) A young man in the train was telling me just now that a great philosopher advises jumping off a housetop. "Jump!" says he; "the whole gist of the problem lies in that." (*Wonderingly*) Fancy that, now! Water, please!

LOPAHIN. What Englishmen?

PISHTCHIK. I have made over to them the rights to dig the clay for twenty-four years . . . and now, excuse me . . . I can't stay . . . I must be trotting on. I'm going to Znoikovo . . . to Kardamanovo. . . . I'm in debt all round. (*Sips.*) . . . To your very good health! . . . I'll come in on Thursday.

LYUBOV. We are just off to the town, and tomorrow I start for abroad.

PISHTCHIK. What! (*In agitation*) Why to the town? Oh, I see the furniture . . . the boxes. No matter . . . (*through his tears*) . . . no matter . . . men of enormous intellect . . . these Englishmen. . . . Never mind . . . be happy. God will succor you . . . no matter . . . everything in this world must have an end. (*Kisses* LYUBOV ANDREYEVNA's *hand.*) If the rumour reaches you that my end has come, think of this . . . old horse, and say: "There once was such a man in the world . . . Semyonov-Pishtchik . . . the Kingdom of Heaven be his!" . . . most extraordinary weather . . . yes. (*Goes out in violent agitation, but at once returns and says in the doorway*) Dashenka wishes to be remembered to you. (*Goes out.*)

LYUBOV. Now we can start. I leave with two cares in my heart. The first is leaving Firs ill. (*Looking at her watch*) We have still five minutes.

ANYA. Mamma, Firs has been taken to the hospital. Yasha sent him off this morning.

LYUBOV. My other anxiety is Varya. She is used to getting up early and working; and now, without work, she's like a fish out of water. She is thin and pale, and she's crying, poor dear! (*A pause.*) You are well aware, Yermolay Alexeyevitch, I dreamed of marrying her to you, and everything seemed to show that you would get married. (*Whispers to* ANYA *and motions to* CHARLOTTA *and both go out.*) She loves you—she suits you. And I don't know—I don't know why it is you seem, as it were, to avoid each other. I can't understand it!

LOPAHIN. I don't understand it myself, I confess. It's queer somehow, altogether. If there's still time, I'm ready now at once. Let's settle it straight off, and go ahead; but without you, I feel I shan't make her an offer.

LYUBOV. That's excellent. Why, a single moment's all that's necessary. I'll call her at once.

LOPAHIN. And there's champagne all ready too (*looking into the glasses*). Empty! Someone's emptied them already. (YASHA *coughs.*) I call that greedy.

LYUBOV (*eagerly*). Capital! We will go out. Yasha, *allez!* I'll call her in. (*At the door*) Varya, leave all that; come here. Come along! (*Goes out with* YASHA.)

LOPAHIN (*looking at his watch*). Yes.

(*A pause. Behind the door, smothered laughter and whispering, and, at last, enter* VARYA.)

VARYA (*looking a long while over the things*). It is strange, I can't find it anywhere.

LOPAHIN. What are you looking for?

VARYA. I packed it myself, and I can't remember. (*A pause.*)

LOPAHIN. Where are you going now, Varvara Mihailova?

VARYA. I? To the Ragulins. I have arranged to go to them to look after the house—as a housekeeper.

LOPAHIN. That's in Yashnovo? It'll be seventy miles away. (*A pause.*) So this is the end of life in this house!

VARYA (*looking among the things*). Where is it? Perhaps I put it in the trunk. Yes, life in this house is over—there will be no more of it.

LOPAHIN. And I'm just off to Harkov—by this next train. I've a lot of business there. I'm leaving Epihodov here, and I've taken him on.

VARYA. Really!

LOPAHIN. This time last year we had snow already, if you remember; but now it's so fine and sunny. Though it's cold, to be sure—three degrees of frost.

VARYA. I haven't looked. (*A pause.*) And besides, our thermometer's broken.

(*A pause. Voice at the door from the yard:* "Yermolay Alexeyevitch!")

LOPAHIN (*as though he had long been expecting this summons*). This minute!

(LOPAHIN *goes out quickly.* VARYA *sitting on the floor and laying her head on a bag full of clothes, sobs quietly. The door opens.* LYUBOV ANDREYEVNA *comes in cautiously.*)

LYUBOV. Well? (*A pause.*) We must be going.

VARYA. (*Has wiped her eyes and is no longer crying.*) Yes, mamma, it's time to start. I shall have time to get to the Ragulins today, if only you're not late for the train.

LYUBOV (*in the doorway*). Anya, put your things on.

(*Enter* ANYA, *then* GAEV *and* CHARLOTTA IVANOVNA. GAEV *has on a warm coat with a hood. Servants and cabmen come in.* EPIHODOV *bustles about the luggage.*)

LYUBOV. Now we can start on our travels.

ANYA (*joyfully*). On our travels!

GAEV. My friends—my dear, my precious friends! Leaving this house forever, can I be silent? Can I refrain from giving utterance at leave-taking to those emotions which now flood all my being?

ANYA (*supplicatingly*). Uncle!

VARYA. Uncle, you mustn't!

GAEV (*dejectedly*). Cannon and into the pocket . . . I'll be quiet. . . .

(*Enter* TROFIMOV *and afterwards* LOPAHIN.)

TROFIMOV. Well, ladies and gentlemen, we must start.

LOPAHIN. Epihodov, my coat!

LYUBOV. I'll stay just one minute. It seems as though I have never seen before what the walls, what the ceilings in this house were like, and now I look at them with greediness, with such tender love.

GAEV. I remember when I was six years old sitting in that window on Trinity Day watching my father going to church.

LYUBOV. Have all the things been taken?

LOPAHIN. I think all. (*Putting on overcoat, to* EPIHODOV) You, Epihodov, mind you see everything is right.

EPIHODOV (*in a husky voice*). Don't you trouble, Yermolay Alexeyevitch.

LOPAHIN. Why, what's wrong with your voice?

EPIHODOV. I've just had a drink of water, and I choked over something.

YASHA (*contemptuously*). The ignorance!

LYUBOV. We are going—and not a soul will be left here.

LOPAHIN. Not till the spring.

VARYA. (*Pulls a parasol out of a bundle, as though about to hit someone with it.* LOPAHIN *makes a gesture as though alarmed.*) What is it? I didn't mean anything.

TROFIMOV. Ladies and gentlemen, let us get into the carriage. It's time. The train will be in directly.

VARYA. Petya, here they are, your galoshes, by that box. (*With tears*) And what dirty old things they are!

TROFIMOV (*putting on his galoshes*). Let us go, friends!

GAEV (*greatly agitated, afraid of weeping*). The train—the station! Double balk, ah!

LYUBOV. Let us go!

LOPAHIN. Are we all here? (*Locks the side door on left.*) The things are all here. We must lock up. Let us go!

ANYA. Good-by, home! Good-by to the old life!

TROFIMOV. Welcome to the new life!

(TROFIMOV *goes out with* ANYA. VARYA *looks round the room and goes out slowly.* YASHA *and* CHARLOTTA IVANOVNA, *with her dog, go out.*)

LOPAHIN. Till the spring, then! Come, friends, till we meet!

(*Goes out.* LYUBOV ANDREYEVNA *and* GAEV *remain alone. As though they had been waiting for this, they throw themselves on each other's necks, and break into subdued smothered sobbing, afraid of being overheard.*)

GAEV (*in despair*). Sister, my sister!

LYUBOV. Oh, my orchard!—my sweet, beautiful orchard! My life, my youth, my happiness, good-by! good-by!

VOICE OF ANYA (*calling gaily*). Mamma!

VOICE OF TROFIMOV (*gaily, excitedly*). Aa—oo!

LYUBOV. One last look at the walls, at the windows. My dear mother loved to walk about this room.

GAEV. Sister, sister!

VOICE OF ANYA. Mamma!

VOICE OF TROFIMOV. Aa—oo!

LYUBOV. We are coming.

(*They go out. The stage is empty. There is the sound of the doors being locked up, then of the carriages driving away. There is silence. In the stillness there is the dull stroke of an axe in a tree, clanging with a mournful lonely sound. Footsteps are heard.* FIRS *appears in the doorway on the right. He is dressed as always—in a pea jacket and white waistcoat with slippers on his feet. He is ill.*)

FIRS. (*Goes up to the doors, and tries the handles.*) Locked! They have gone. . . . (*Sits down on sofa.*) They have forgotten me. . . . Never mind . . . I'll sit here a bit. . . . I'll be bound Leonid Andreyevitch hasn't put his fur coat on and has gone off in his thin overcoat. (*Sighs anxiously.*) I didn't see after him. . . . These young people . . . (*Mutters something that can't be distinguished.*) Life has slipped by as though I hadn't lived. (*Lies down.*) I'll lie down a bit. . . . There's no strength in you, nothing left you—all gone! Ech! I'm good for nothing.

(*Lies motionless. A sound is heard that seems to come from the sky, like a breaking harp string, dying away mournfully. All is still again, and there is heard nothing but the strokes of the axe far away in the orchard.*)

ARMS AND THE MAN [1894]
A Pleasant Play

by George Bernard Shaw

Characters

CATHERINE PETKOFF, *a Bulgarian lady*
RAINA, *her daughter*
LOUKA, *the Petkoffs' maid*
BLUNTSCHLI, *a Swiss officer*
NICOLA, *the Petkoffs' butler*
PETKOFF, *a major in the Bulgarian Army*
SERGIUS, RAINA'S *fiancé, a captain in the Bulgarian Army*

ACT ONE

Night. A lady's bedchamber in Bulgaria, in a small town near the Dragoman Pass, late in November in the year 1885. Through an open window with a little balcony a peak of the Balkans, wonderfully white and beautiful in the starlit snow, seems quite close at hand, though it is really miles away. The interior of the room is not like anything to be seen in the west of Europe. It is half rich Bulgarian, half cheap Viennese. Above the head of the bed, which stands against a little wall cutting off the left hand corner of the room, is a painted wooden shrine, blue and gold, with an ivory image of Christ, and a light hanging before it in a pierced metal ball suspended by three chains. The principal seat, placed towards the other side of the room and opposite the window, is a Turkish ottoman. The counterpane and hangings of the bed, the window curtains, the little carpet, and all the ornamental textile fabrics in the room are oriental and gorgeous; the paper on the walls is occidental and paltry. The washstand, against the wall on the side nearest the ottoman and window, consists of an enamelled iron basin with a pail beneath it in a painted metal frame, and a single towel on the rail at the side. The dressing table, between the bed and the window, is a common pine table, covered with a cloth of many colours, with an expensive toilet mirror on it. The door is on the side nearest the bed; and there is a chest of drawers between. This chest of drawers is also covered by a variegated native cloth; and on it there is a pile of paper-backed novels, a box of chocolate creams, and a miniature easel with a large photograph of an extremely handsome officer, whose lofty bearing and magnetic glance can be felt even from the portrait. The room is lighted by a candle on the chest of drawers, and another on the dressing table with a box of matches beside it.

The window is hinged doorwise and stands wide open. Outside, a pair of wooden shutters, opening outwards, also stand open. On the balcony a young lady, intensely conscious of the romantic beauty of the night, and of the fact that her own youth and beauty are part of it, is gazing at the snowy Balkans. She is in her nightgown, well covered by a long mantle of furs, worth, on a moderate estimate, about three times the furniture of the room.

Her reverie is interrupted by her mother, CATHERINE PETKOFF, *a woman over forty, imperiously energetic, with magnificent black hair and eyes, who might be a very splendid specimen of the wife*

*of a mountain farmer, but is determined to be a Viennese lady,
and to that end wears a fashionable tea gown on all occasions.*

CATHERINE (*entering hastily, full of good news*). Raina! (*She pronounces it Rah-eena, with the stress on the ee.*) Raina! (*She goes
to the bed, expecting to find* RAINA *there.*) Why, where—? (RAINA
looks into the room.) Heavens, child! are you out in the night air
instead of in your bed? Youll catch your death. Louka told me
you were asleep.

RAINA (*dreamily*). I sent her away. I wanted to be alone. The stars are
so beautiful! What is the matter?

CATHERINE. Such news! There has been a battle.

RAINA (*her eyes dilating*). Ah! (*She comes eagerly to* CATHERINE.)

CATHERINE. A great battle at Slivnitza! A victory! And it was won by
Sergius.

RAINA (*with a cry of delight*). Ah! (*They embrace rapturously.*) Oh,
mother! (*Then, with sudden anxiety*) Is father safe?

CATHERINE. Of course! he sends me the news. Sergius is the hero of
the hour, the idol of the regiment.

RAINA. Tell me, tell me. How was it? (*Ecstatically*) Oh, mother!
mother! mother! (*She pulls her mother down on the ottoman; and
they kiss one another frantically.*)

CATHERINE (*with surging enthusiasm*). You cant guess how splendid it
is. A cavalry charge! think of that! He defied our Russian com-
manders—acted without orders—led a charge on his own responsibility—headed it himself—was the first man to sweep through
their guns. Cant you see it, Raina: our gallant splendid Bulgarians
with their swords and eyes flashing, thundering down like an ava-
lanche and scattering the wretched Serbs and their dandified Austrian officers like chaff. And you! you kept Sergius waiting a year
before you would be betrothed to him. Oh, if you have a drop of
Bulgarian blood in your veins, you will worship him when he
comes back.

RAINA. What will he care for my poor little worship after the acclama-
tions of a whole army of heroes? But no matter: I am so happy!
so proud! (*She rises and walks about excitedly.*) It proves that
all our ideas were real after all.

CATHERINE (*indignantly*). Our ideas real! What do you mean?

RAINA. Our ideas of what Sergius would do. Our patriotism. Our heroic
ideals. I sometimes used to doubt whether they were anything but
dreams. Oh, what faithless little creatures girls are! When I
buckled on Sergius's sword he looked so noble: it was treason to

think of disillusion or humiliation or failure. And yet—and yet—
(*She sits down again suddenly.*) Promise me youll never tell him.

CATHERINE. Dont ask me for promises until I know what I'm promising.

RAINA. Well, it came into my head just as he was holding me in his
arms and looking into my eyes, that perhaps we only had our
heroic ideas because we are so fond of reading Byron and Pushkin, and because we were so delighted with the opera that season
at Bucharest. Real life is so seldom like that! indeed never, as far
as I knew it then. (*Remorsefully*) Only think, mother: I doubted
him: I wondered whether all his heroic qualities and his soldier-
ship might not prove mere imagination when he went into a real
battle. I had an uneasy fear that he might cut a poor figure there
beside all those clever officers from the Tsar's court.

CATHERINE. A poor figure! Shame on you! The Serbs have Austrian
officers who are just as clever as the Russians; but we have beaten
them in every battle for all that.

RAINA (*laughing and snuggling against her mother*). Yes: I was only
a prosaic little coward. Oh, to think that it was all true! that
Sergius is just as splendid and noble as he looks! that the world
is really a glorious world for women who can see its glory and
men who can act its romance! What happiness! what unspeakable
fulfilment!

(*They are interrupted by the entry of* LOUKA, *a handsome proud
girl in a pretty Bulgarian peasant's dress with double apron, so
defiant that her servility to* RAINA *is almost insolent. She is afraid
of* CATHERINE, *but even with her goes as far as she dares.*)

LOUKA. If you please, madam, all the windows are to be closed and
the shutters made fast. They say there may be shooting in the
streets. (RAINA *and* CATHERINE *rise together, alarmed.*) The Serbs
are being chased right back through the pass; and they say they
may run into the town. Our cavalry will be after them; and our
people will be ready for them, you may be sure, now theyre running away. (*She goes out on the balcony, and pulls the outside
shutters to; then steps back into the room.*)

CATHERINE (*businesslike, housekeeping instincts aroused*). I must see
that everything is made safe downstairs.

RAINA. I wish our people were not so cruel. What glory is there in
killing wretched fugitives?

CATHERINE. Cruel! Do you suppose they would hesitate to kill you—
or worse?

RAINA (*to* LOUKA). Leave the shutters so that I can just close them if
I hear any noise.

CATHERINE (*authoritatively, turning on her way to the door*). Oh no, dear: you must keep them fastened. You would be sure to drop off to sleep and leave them open. Make them fast, Louka.

LOUKA. Yes, madam. (*She fastens them.*)

RAINA. Dont be anxious about me. The moment I hear a shot, I shall blow out the candles and roll myself up in bed with my ears well covered.

CATHERINE. Quite the wisest thing you can do, my love. Goodnight.

RAINA. Goodnight. (*Her emotion comes back for a moment.*) Wish me joy. (*They kiss.*) This is the happiest night of my life—if only there are no fugitives.

CATHERINE. Go to bed, dear; and dont think of them. (*She goes out.*)

LOUKA (*secretly to* RAINA). If you would like the shutters open, just give them a push like this. (*She pushes them: they open: she pulls them to again.*) One of them ought to be bolted at the bottom; but the bolt's gone.

RAINA (*with dignity, reproving her*). Thanks, Louka; but we must do what we are told. (LOUKA *makes a grimace.*) Goodnight.

LOUKA (*carelessly*). Goodnight. (*She goes out, swaggering.*)

(RAINA, *left alone, takes off her fur cloak and throws it on the ottoman. Then she goes to the chest of drawers, and adores the portrait there with feelings that are beyond all expression. She does not kiss it or press it to her breast, or show it any mark of bodily affection; but she takes it in her hands and elevates it, like a priestess.*)

RAINA (*looking up at the picture*). Oh, I shall never be unworthy of you any more, my soul's hero: never, never, never. (*She replaces it reverently. Then she selects a novel from the little pile of books. She turns over the leaves dreamily; finds her page; turns the book inside out at it; and, with a happy sigh, gets into bed and prepares to read herself to sleep. But before abandoning herself to fiction, she raises her eyes once more, thinking of the blessed reality, and murmurs*) My hero! my hero!

(*A distant shot breaks the quiet of the night. She starts, listening; and two more shots, much nearer, follow, startling her so that she scrambles out of bed, and hastily blows out the candle on the chest of drawers. Then, putting her fingers in her ears, she runs to the dressing table, blows out the light there, and hurries back to bed in the dark, nothing being visible but the glimmer of the light in the pierced ball before the image, and the starlight seen through the slits at the top of the shutters. The firing breaks out again: there is a startling fusillade quite close at hand. Whilst it is still echoing, the shutters disappear, pulled open from without;*

*and for an instant the rectangle of snowy starlight flashes out
with the figure of a man silhouetted in black upon it. The shutters
close immediately; and the room is dark again. But the silence is
now broken by the sound of panting. Then there is a scratch; and
the flame of a match is seen in the middle of the room.*)

RAINA (*crouching on the bed*). Who's there? (*The match is out instantly.*) Who's there? Who is that?

A MAN'S VOICE (*in the darkness, subduedly, but threateningly*). Sh—sh!
Dont call out; or youll be shot. Be good; and no harm will happen
to you. (*She is heard leaving her bed, and making for the door.*)
Take care: it's no use trying to run away.

RAINA. But who—

THE VOICE (*warning*). Remember: if you raise your voice my revolver
will go off. (*Commandingly*) Strike a light and let me see you.
Do you hear? (*Another moment of silence and darkness as she
retreats to the chest of drawers. Then she lights a candle; and the
mystery is at an end. He is a man of about 35, in a deplorable
plight, bespattered with mud and blood and snow, his belt and the
strap of his revolver case keeping together the torn ruins of the
blue tunic of a Serbian artillery officer. All that the candlelight
and his unwashed unkempt condition make it possible to discern
is that he is of middling stature and undistinguished appearance,
with strong neck and shoulders, roundish obstinate looking head
covered with short crisp bronze curls, clear quick eyes and good
brows and mouth, hopelessly prosaic nose like that of a strong-
minded baby, trim soldierlike carriage and energetic manner, and
with all his wits about him in spite of his desperate predicament:
even with a sense of the humor of it, without, however, the least
intention of trifling with it or throwing away a chance. Reckoning
up what he can guess about RAINA: her age, her social position,
her character, and the extent to which she is frightened, he continues, more politely but still most determinedly*) Excuse my disturbing you; but you recognize my uniform? Serb! If I'm caught
I shall be killed. (*Menacingly*) Do you understand that?

RAINA. Yes.

THE MAN. Well, I don't intend to get killed if I can help it. (*Still more
formidably*) Do you understand that? (*He locks the door quickly
but quietly.*)

RAINA (*disdainfully*). I suppose not. (*She draws herself up superbly,
and looks him straight in the face, adding, with cutting emphasis*)
Some soldiers, I know, are afraid to die.

THE MAN (*with grim good humor*). All of them, dear lady, all of them, believe me. It is our duty to live as long as we can. Now, if you raise an alarm—

RAINA (*cutting him short*). You will shoot me. How do you know that *I* am afraid to die?

THE MAN (*cunningly*). Ah; but suppose I dont shoot you, what will happen then? A lot of your cavalry will burst into this pretty room of yours and slaughter me here like a pig; for I'll fight like a demon: they shant get me into the street to amuse themselves with: I know what they are. Are you prepared to receive that sort of company in your present undress? (RAINA, *suddenly conscious of her nightgown, instinctively shrinks and gathers it more closely about her neck. He watches her and adds pitilessly*) Hardly presentable, eh? (*She turns to the ottoman. He raises his pistol instantly, and cries*) Stop! (*She stops.*) Where are you going?

RAINA (*with dignified patience*). Only to get my cloak.

THE MAN (*passing swiftly to the ottoman and snatching the cloak*). A good idea! I'll keep the cloak; and you'll take care that nobody comes in and sees you without it. This is a better weapon than the revolver: eh? (*He throws the pistol down on the ottoman.*)

RAINA (*revolted*). It is not the weapon of a gentleman!

THE MAN. It's good enough for a man with only you to stand between him and death. (*As they look at one another for a moment,* RAINA *hardly able to believe that even a Serbian officer can be so cynically and selfishly unchivalrous, they are startled by a sharp fusillade in the street. The chill of imminent death hushes the man's voice as he adds*) Do you hear? If you are going to bring those blackguards in on me you shall receive them as you are.

(*Clamor and disturbance. The pursuers in the street batter at the house door, shouting* Open the door! Open the door! Wake up, will you! *A man servant's voice calls to them angrily from within* This is Major Petkoff's house: you cant come in here; *but a renewal of the clamor, and a torrent of blows on the door, end with his letting a chain down with a clank, followed by a rush of heavy footsteps and a din of triumphant yells, dominated at last by the voice of* CATHERINE, *indignantly addressing an officer with* What does this mean, sir? Do you know where you are? *The noise subsides suddenly.*)

LOUKA (*outside, knocking at the bedroom door*). My lady! my lady! get up quick and open the door. If you dont they will break it down.

(*The fugitive throws up his head with the gesture of a man who sees that it is all over with him, and drops the manner he has been assuming to intimidate* RAINA.)

THE MAN (*sincerely and kindly*). No use, dear: I'm done for. (*Flinging the cloak to her*) Quick! wrap yourself up: theyre coming.

RAINA. Oh, thank you. (*She wraps herself up with intense relief.*)

THE MAN (*between his teeth*). Dont mention it.

RAINA (*anxiously*). What will you do?

THE MAN (*grimly*). The first man in will find out. Keep out of the way; and dont look. It wont last long; but it will not be nice. (*He draws his sabre and faces the door, waiting.*)

RAINA (*impulsively*). I'll help you. I'll save you.

THE MAN. You cant.

RAINA. I can. I'll hide you. (*She drags him towards the window.*) Here! behind the curtains.

THE MAN (*yielding to her*). Theres just half a chance, if you keep your head.

RAINA (*drawing the curtain before him*). S-sh! (*She makes for the ottoman.*)

THE MAN (*putting out his head*). Remember—

RAINA (*running back to him*). Yes?

THE MAN. —nine soldiers out of ten are born fools.

RAINA. Oh! (*She draws the curtain angrily before him.*)

THE MAN (*looking out at the other side*). If they find me, I promise you a fight: a devil of a fight.

(*She stamps at him. He disappears hastily. She takes off her cloak, and throws it across the foot of the bed. Then, with a sleepy, disturbed air, she opens the door.* LOUKA *enters excitedly.*)

LOUKA. One of those beasts of Serbs has been seen climbing up the waterpipe to your balcony. Our men want to search for him; and they are so wild and drunk and furious. (*She makes for the other side of the room to get as far from the door as possible.*) My lady says you are to dress at once and to—(*She sees the revolver lying on the ottoman, and stops, petrified.*)

RAINA (*as if annoyed at being disturbed*). They shall not search here. Why have they been let in?

CATHERINE (*coming in hastily*). Raina, darling, are you safe? Have you seen anyone or heard anything?

RAINA. I heard the shooting. Surely the soldiers will not dare come in here?

CATHERINE. I have found a Russian officer, thank Heaven: he knows Sergius. (*Speaking through the door to someone outside*) Sir: will you come in now. My daughter will receive you.

(*A young Russian officer, in Bulgarian uniform, enters, sword in hand.*)

OFFICER (*with soft feline politeness and stiff military carriage*). Good evening, gracious lady. I am sorry to intrude; but there is a Serb hiding on the balcony. Will you and the gracious lady your mother please to withdraw whilst we search?

RAINA (*petulantly*). Nonsense, sir: you can see that there is no one on the balcony.

(*She throws the shutters wide open and stands with her back to the curtain where the man is hidden, pointing to the moonlit balcony. A couple of shots are fired right under the window; and a bullet shatters the glass opposite* RAINA, *who winks and gasps, but stands her ground; whilst* CATHERINE *screams, and the officer, with a cry of* Take care! *rushes to the balcony.*)

THE OFFICER (*on the balcony, shouting savagely down to the street*). Cease firing, you fools: do you hear? Cease firing, damn you! (*He glares down for a moment; then turns to* RAINA, *trying to resume his polite manner.*) Could anyone have got in without your knowledge? Were you asleep?

RAINA. No: I have not been to bed.

THE OFFICER (*impatiently, coming back into the room*). Your neighbors have their heads so full of runaway Serbs that they see them everywhere. (*Politely*) Gracious lady: a thousand pardons. Goodnight.

(*Military bow, which* RAINA *returns coldly. Another to* CATHERINE, *who follows him out.* RAINA *closes the shutters. She turns and sees* LOUKA, *who has been watching the scene curiously.*)

RAINA. Dont leave my mother, Louka, until the soldiers go away.

(LOUKA *glances at* RAINA, *at the ottoman, at the curtain; then purses her lips secretively, laughs insolently, and goes out.* RAINA, *highly offended by this demonstration, follows her to the door, and shuts it behind her with a slam, locking it violently. The man immediately steps out from behind the curtain, sheathing his sabre. Then, dismissing the danger from his mind in a businesslike way, he comes affably to* RAINA.)

THE MAN. A narrow shave; but a miss is as good as a mile. Dear young lady: your servant to the death. I wish for your sake I had joined the Bulgarian army instead of the other one. I am not a native Serb.

RAINA (*haughtily*). No: you are one of the Austrians who set the Serbs on to rob us of our national liberty, and who officer their army for them. We hate them!

THE MAN. Austrian! not I. Dont hate me, dear young lady. I am a Swiss, fighting merely as a professional soldier. I joined the Serbs because they came first on the road from Switzerland. Be generous: youve beaten us hollow.

RAINA. Have I not been generous?

THE MAN. Noble! Heroic! But I'm not saved yet. This particular rush will soon pass through; but the pursuit will go on all night by fits and starts. I must take my chance to get off in a quiet interval. (*Pleasantly*) You don't mind my waiting just a minute or two, do you?

RAINA (*putting on her most genteel society manner*). Oh, not at all. Wont you sit down?

THE MAN. Thanks. (*He sits on the foot of the bed.*)

(RAINA *walks with studied elegance to the ottoman and sits down. Unfortunately she sits on the pistol, and jumps up with a shriek. The man, all nerves, shies like a frightened horse to the other side of the room.*)

THE MAN (*irritably*). Dont frighten me like that. What is it?

RAINA. Your revolver! It was staring that officer in the face all the time. What an escape!

THE MAN (*vexed at being unnecessarily terrified*). Oh, is that all?

RAINA (*staring at him rather superciliously as she conceives a poorer and poorer opinion of him, and feels proportionately more and more at her ease*). I am sorry I frightened you. (*She takes up the pistol and hands it to him.*) Pray take it to protect yourself against me.

THE MAN (*grinning wearily at the sarcasm as he takes the pistol*). No use, dear young lady: there's nothing in it. It's not loaded. (*He makes a grimace at it, and drops it disparagingly into his revolver case.*)

RAINA. Load it by all means.

THE MAN. Ive no ammunition. What use are cartridges in battle? I always carry chocolate instead; and I finished the last cake of that hours ago.

RAINA (*outraged in her most cherished ideals of manhood*). Chocolate! Do you stuff your pockets with sweets—like a schoolboy—even in the field?

THE MAN (*grinning*). Yes: isnt it contemptible? (*Hungrily*). I wish I had some now.

RAINA. Allow me. (*She sails away scornfully to the chest of drawers, and returns with the box of confectionery in her hand.*) I am sorry I have eaten them all except these. (*She offers him the box.*)

THE MAN (*ravenously*). Youre an angel! (*He gobbles the contents.*) Creams! Delicious! (*He looks anxiously to see whether there are any more. There are none: he can only scrape the box with his fingers and suck them. When that nourishment is exhausted he accepts the inevitable with pathetic good humor, and says, with grateful emotion*) Bless you, dear lady! You can always tell an old soldier by the inside of his holsters and cartridge boxes. The young ones carry pistols and cartridges: the old ones, grub. Thank you. (*He hands back the box. She snatches it contemptuously from him and throws it away. He shies again, as if she had meant to strike him.*) Ugh! Dont do things so suddenly, gracious lady. It's mean to revenge yourself because I frightened you just now.

RAINA (*loftily*). Frighten me! Do you know, sir, that though I am only a woman, I think I am at heart as brave as you.

THE MAN. I should think so. You havent been under fire for three days as I have. I can stand two days without showing it much; but no man can stand three days: I'm as nervous as a mouse. (*He sits down on the ottoman, and takes his head in his hands.*) Would you like to see me cry?

RAINA (*alarmed*). No.

THE MAN. If you would, all you have to do is to scold me just as if I were a little boy and you my nurse. If I were in camp now, theyd play all sorts of tricks on me.

RAINA (*a little moved*). I'm sorry. I wont scold you. (*Touched by the sympathy in her tone, he raises his head and looks gratefully at her: she immediately draws back and says stiffly*) You must excuse me: our soldiers are not like that. (*She moves away from the ottoman.*)

THE MAN. Oh yes they are. There are only two sorts of soldiers: old ones and young ones. Ive served fourteen years: half of your fellows never smelt powder before. Why, how is it that youve just beaten us? Sheer ignorance of the art of war, nothing else. (*Indignantly*) I never saw anything so unprofessional.

RAINA (*ironically*). Oh! was it unprofessional to beat you?

THE MAN. Well, come! is it professional to throw a regiment of cavalry on a battery of machine guns, with the dead certainty that if the guns go off not a horse or man will ever get within fifty yards of the fire? I couldn't believe my eyes when I saw it.

RAINA (*eagerly turning to him, as all her enthusiasm and her dreams of glory rush back on her*). Did you see the great cavalry charge? Oh, tell me about it. Describe it to me.

THE MAN. You never saw a cavalry charge, did you?

RAINA. How could I?

THE MAN. Ah, perhaps not. No: of course not! Well, it's a funny sight. It's like slinging a handful of peas against a window pane: first one comes; then two or three close behind him; and then all the rest in a lump.

RAINA (*her eyes dilating as she raises her clasped hands ecstatically*). Yes, first One! the bravest of the brave!

THE MAN (*prosaically*). Hm! you should see the poor devil pulling at his horse.

RAINA. Why should he pull at his horse?

THE MAN (*impatient of so stupid a question*). It's running away with him, of course; do you suppose the fellow wants to get there before the others and be killed? Then they all come. You can tell the young ones by their wildness and their slashing. The old ones come bunched up under the number one guard: they know that theyre mere projectiles, and that it's no use trying to fight. The wounds are mostly broken knees, from the horses cannoning together.

RAINA. Ugh! But I dont believe the first man is a coward. I know he is a hero!

THE MAN (*goodhumoredly*). Thats what youd have said if youd seen the first man in the charge today.

RAINA (*breathless, forgiving him everything*). Ah, I knew it! Tell me. Tell me about him.

THE MAN. He did it like an operatic tenor. A regular handsome fellow, with flashing eyes and lovely moustache, shouting his war-cry and charging like Don Quixote at the windmills. We did laugh.

RAINA. You dared to laugh!

THE MAN. Yes; but when the sergeant ran up as white as a sheet, and told us theyd sent us the wrong ammunition, and that we couldnt fire a round for the next ten minutes, we laughed at the other side of our mouths. I never felt so sick in my life; though Ive been in one or two very tight places. And I hadnt even a revolver cartridge: only chocolate. We'd no bayonets: nothing. Of course, they just cut us to bits. And there was Don Quixote flourishing like a drum major, thinking he'd done the cleverest thing ever known, whereas he ought to be courtmartialled for it. Of all the fools ever let loose on a field of battle, that man must be the very maddest. He and his regiment simply committed suicide; only the pistol missed fire: thats all.

RAINA (*deeply wounded, but steadfastly loyal to her ideals*). Indeed! Would you know him again if you saw him?

THE MAN. Shall I ever forget him!

(*She again goes to the chest of drawers. He watches her with a vague hope that she may have something more for him to eat. She takes the portrait from its stand and brings it to him.*)

RAINA. That is a photograph of the gentleman—the patriot and hero—to whom I am betrothed.

THE MAN (*recognizing it with a shock*). I'm really very sorry. (*Looking at her*) Was it fair to lead me on? (*He looks at the portrait again.*) Yes: thats Don Quixote: not a doubt of it. (*He stifles a laugh.*)

RAINA (*quickly*). Why do you laugh?

THE MAN (*apologetic, but still greatly tickled*). I didnt laugh, I assure you. At least I didnt mean to. But when I think of him charging the windmills and imagining he was doing the finest thing—(*He chokes with suppressed laughter.*)

RAINA (*sternly*). Give me back the portrait, sir.

THE MAN (*with sincere remorse*). Of course. Certainly. I'm really very sorry. (*He hands her the picture. She deliberately kisses it and looks him straight in the face before returning to the chest of drawers to replace it. He follows her, apologizing.*) Perhaps I'm quite wrong, you know: no doubt I am. Most likely he had got wind of the cartridge business somehow, and knew it was a safe job.

RAINA. That is to say, he was a pretender and a coward! You did not dare say that before.

THE MAN (*with a comic gesture of despair*). It's no use, dear lady: I cant make you see it from the professional point of view.

(*As he turns away to get back to the ottoman, a couple of distant shots threaten renewed trouble.*)

RAINA (*sternly, as she sees him listening to the shots*). So much the better for you!

THE MAN (*turning*). How?

RAINA. You are my enemy; and you are at my mercy. What would I do if I were a professional soldier?

THE MAN. Ah, true, dear young lady: youre always right. I know how good youve been to me: to my last hour I shall remember those three chocolate creams. It was unsoldierly; but it was angelic.

RAINA (*coldly*). Thank you. And now I will do a soldierly thing. You cannot stay here after what you have just said about my future husband; but I will go out on the balcony and see whether it is safe for you to climb down into the street. (*She turns to the window.*)

THE MAN (*changing countenance*). Down that waterpipe! Stop! Wait! I cant! I darent! The very thought of it makes me giddy. I came up it fast enough with death behind me. But to face it now in cold blood—! (*He sinks on the ottoman.*) It's no use: I give up: I'm beaten. Give the alarm. (*He drops his head on his hands in the deepest dejection.*)

RAINA (*disarmed by pity*). Come: dont be disheartened. (*She stoops over him almost maternally: he shakes his head.*) Oh, you are a

very poor soldier: a chocolate cream soldier! Come, cheer up! it
takes less courage to climb down than to face capture: remember
that.

THE MAN (*dreamily, lulled by her voice*). No: capture only means
death; and death is sleep: oh, sleep, sleep, sleep, undisturbed sleep!
Climbing down the pipe means doing something—exerting myself
—thinking! Death ten times over first.

RAINA (*softly and wonderingly, catching the rhythm of his weariness*).
Are you as sleepy as that?

THE MAN. Ive not had two hours undisturbed sleep since I joined. I
havent closed my eyes for forty-eight hours.

RAINA (*at her wit's end*). But what am I to do with you?

THE MAN (*staggering up, roused by her desperation*). Of course. I must
do something. (*He shakes himself; pulls himself together; and
speaks with rallied vigor and courage.*) You see, sleep or no sleep,
hunger or no hunger, tired or not tired, you can always do a
thing when you know it must be done. Well, that pipe must be
got down: (*he hits himself on the chest*) do you hear that, you
chocolate cream soldier? (*He turns to the window.*)

RAINA (*anxiously*). But if you fall?

THE MAN. I shall sleep as if the stones were a feather bed. Goodbye.
(*He makes boldly for the window; and his hand is on the shutter
when there is a terrible burst of firing in the street beneath.*)

RAINA (*rushing to him*). Stop! (*She seizes him recklessly, and pulls
him quite round.*) Theyll kill you.

THE MAN (*coolly, but attentively*). Never mind: this sort of thing is
all in my day's work. I'm bound to take my chance. (*Decisively*)
Now do what I tell you. Put out the candle; so that they shant
see the light when I open the shutters. And keep away from the
window, whatever you do. If they see me theyre sure to have a
shot at me.

RAINA (*clinging to him*). Theyre sure to see you: it's bright moonlight.
I'll save you. Oh, how can you be so indifferent! You want me
to save you, dont you?

THE MAN. I really dont want to be troublesome. (*She shakes him in
her impatience.*) I am not indifferent, dear young lady, I assure
you. But how is it to be done?

RAINA. Come away from the window. (*She takes him firmly back to
the middle of the room. The moment she releases him he turns
mechanically towards the window again. She seizes him and turns
him back, exclaiming*) Please! (*He becomes motionless, like a
hypnotized rabbit, his fatigue gaining fast on him. She releases
him, and addresses him patronizingly.*) Now listen. You must

trust to our hospitality. You do not yet know in whose house you are. I am a Petkoff.

THE MAN. A pet what?

RAINA (*rather indignantly*). I mean that I belong to the family of the Petkoffs, the richest and best known in our country.

THE MAN. Oh yes, of course. I beg your pardon. The Petkoffs, to be sure. How stupid of me!

RAINA. You know you never heard of them until this moment. How can you stoop to pretend!

THE MAN. Forgive me: I'm too tired to think; and the change of subject was too much for me. Dont scold me.

RAINA. I forgot. It might make you cry. (*He nods, quite seriously. She pouts and then resumes her patronizing tone.*) I must tell you that my father holds the highest command of any Bulgarian in our army. He is (*proudly*) a Major.

THE MAN (*pretending to be deeply impressed*). A Major! Bless me! Think of that!

RAINA. You showed great ignorance in thinking that it was necessary to climb up to the balcony because ours is the only private house that has two rows of windows. There is a flight of stairs inside to get up and down by.

THE MAN. Stairs! How grand! You live in great luxury indeed, dear young lady.

RAINA. Do you know what a library is?

THE MAN. A library? A roomful of books?

RAINA. Yes. We have one, the only one in Bulgaria.

THE MAN. Actually a real library! I should like to see that.

RAINA (*affectedly*). I tell you these things to show you that you are not in the house of ignorant country folk who would kill you the moment they saw your Serbian uniform, but among civilized people. We go to Bucharest every year for the opera season; and I have spent a whole month in Vienna.

THE MAN. I saw that, dear young lady. I saw at once that you knew the world.

RAINA. Have you ever seen the opera of Ernani?

THE MAN. Is that the one with the devil in it in red velvet, and a soldiers' chorus?

RAINA (*contemptuously*). No!

THE MAN (*stifling a heavy sigh of weariness*). Then I dont know it.

RAINA. I thought you might have remembered the great scene where Ernani, flying from his foes just as you are tonight, takes refuge in the castle of his bitterest enemy, an old Castilian noble. The noble refuses to give him up. His guest is sacred to him.

THE MAN (*quickly, waking up a little*). Have your people got that notion?

RAINA (*with dignity*). My mother and I can understand that notion, as you call it. And if instead of threatening me with your pistol as you did you had simply thrown yourself as a fugitive on our hospitality, you would have been as safe as in your father's house.

THE MAN. Quite sure?

RAINA (*turning her back on him in disgust*). Oh, it is useless to try to make you understand.

THE MAN. Dont be angry: you see how awkward it would be for me if there was any mistake. My father is a very hospitable man: he keeps six hotels; but I couldnt trust him as far as that. What about your father?

RAINA. He is away at Slivnitza fighting for his country. I answer for your safety. There is my hand in pledge of it. Will that reassure you? (*She offers him her hand.*)

THE MAN (*looking dubiously at his own hand*). Better not touch my hand, dear young lady. I must have a wash first.

RAINA (*touched*). That is very nice of you. I see that you are a gentleman.

THE MAN (*puzzled*). Eh?

RAINA. You must not think I am surprised. Bulgarians of really good standing—people in our position—wash their hands nearly every day. So you see I can appreciate your delicacy. You may take my hand. (*She offers it again.*)

THE MAN (*kissing it with his hands behind his back*). Thanks, gracious young lady: I feel safe at last. And now would you mind breaking the news to your mother? I had better not stay here secretly longer than is necessary.

RAINA. If you will be so good as to keep perfectly still whilst I am away.

THE MAN. Certainly.

(*He sits down on the ottoman.* RAINA *goes to the bed and wraps herself in the fur cloak. His eyes close. She goes to the door. Turning for a last look at him, she sees that he is dropping off to sleep.*)

RAINA (*at the door*). You are not going asleep, are you? (*He murmurs inarticulately: she runs to him and shakes him.*) Do you hear? Wake up: you are falling asleep.

THE MAN. Eh? Falling aslee—? Oh no: not the least in the world: I was only thinking. It's all right: I'm wide awake.

RAINA (*severely*). Will you please stand up while I am away. (*He rises reluctantly.*) All the time, mind.

THE MAN (*standing unsteadily*). Certainly. Certainly: you may depend on me.

(RAINA *looks doubtfully at him. He smiles weakly. She goes reluctantly, turning again at the door, and almost catching him in the act of yawning. She goes out.*)

THE MAN (*drowsily*). Sleep, sleep, sleep, sleep, slee—(*The words trail off into a murmur. He wakes again with a shock on the point of falling.*) Where am I? Thats what I want to know: where am I? Must keep awake. Nothing keeps me awake except danger: remember that: (*intently*) danger, danger, danger, dan—(*trailing off again: another shock*) Wheres danger? Mus' find it. (*He starts off vaguely round the room in search of it.*) What am I looking for? Sleep—danger—dont know. (*He stumbles against the bed.*) Ah yes: now I know. All right now. I'm to go to bed, but not to sleep. Be sure not to sleep, because of danger. Not to lie down either, only sit down. (*He sits on the bed. A blissful expression comes into his face.*) Ah!

(*With a happy sigh he sinks back at full length; lifts his boots into the bed with a final effort; and falls fast asleep instantly.* CATHERINE *comes in, followed by* RAINA.)

RAINA (*looking at the ottoman*). He's gone! I left him here.

CATHERINE. Here! Then he must have climbed down from the—

RAINA (*seeing him*). Oh! (*She points.*)

CATHERINE (*scandalized*). Well! (*She strides to the bed,* RAINA *following until she is opposite her on the other side.*) He's fast asleep. The brute!

RAINA (*anxiously*). Sh!

CATHERINE (*shaking him*). Sir! (*Shaking him again, harder*) Sir!! (*Vehemently, shaking very hard*) Sir!!!

RAINA (*catching her arm*). Dont, mamma; the poor darling is worn out. Let him sleep.

CATHERINE (*letting him go, and turning amazed to* RAINA). The poor darling! Raina!!!

(*She looks sternly at her daughter. The man sleeps profoundly.*)

ACT TWO

The sixth of March, 1886. In the garden of MAJOR PETKOFF'S *house. It is a fine spring morning: the garden looks fresh and pretty. Beyond the paling the tops of a couple of minarets can be seen, shewing that there is a valley there, with the little town in it. A few miles further the Balkan mountains rise and shut in the landscape. Looking towards them from within the garden, the side of the house is seen on the left, with a garden door reached by a little flight of steps. On the right the stable yard, with its gateway, encroaches on the garden. There are fruit bushes along the paling and house, covered with washing spread out to dry. A path runs by the house, and rises by two steps at the corner, where it turns out of sight. In the middle, a small table, with two bent wood chairs at it, is laid for breakfast with Turkish coffee pot, cups, rolls, etc.; but the cups have been used and the bread broken. There is a wooden garden seat against the wall on the right.*

LOUKA, smoking a cigaret, is standing between the table and the house, turning her back with angry disdain on a man servant who is lecturing her. He is a middle-aged man of cool temperament and low but clear and keen intelligence, with the complacency of the servant who values himself on his rank in servitude, and the imperturbability of the accurate calculator who has no illusions. He wears a white Bulgarian costume: jacket with embroidered border, sash, wide knickerbockers, and decorated gaiters. His head is shaved up to the crown, giving him a high Japanese forehead. His name is NICOLA.

NICOLA. Be warned in time, Louka: mend your manners. I know the mistress. She is so grand that she never dreams that any servant could dare be disrespectful to her; but if she once suspects that you are defying her, out you go.

LOUKA. I do defy her. I will defy her. What do I care for her?

NICOLA. If you quarrel with the family, I never can marry you. It's the same as if you quarrelled with me!

LOUKA. You take her part against me, do you?

NICOLA (*sedately*). I shall always be dependent on the good will of the family. When I leave their service and start a shop in Sofia, their custom will be half my capital: their bad word would ruin me.

LOUKA. You have no spirit. I should like to catch them saying a word against me!

NICOLA (*pityingly*). I should have expected more sense from you, Louka. But youre young: youre young!

LOUKA. Yes; and you like me the better for it, dont you? But I know some family secrets they wouldnt care to have told, young as I am. Let them quarrel with me if they dare!

NICOLA (*with compassionate superiority*). Do you know what they would do if they heard you talk like that?

LOUKA. What could they do?

NICOLA. Discharge you for untruthfulness. Who would believe any stories you told after that? Who would give you another situation? Who in this house would dare be seen speaking to you ever again? How long would your father be left on his little farm? (*She impatiently throws away the end of her cigaret, and stamps on it.*) Child: you dont know the power such high people have over the like of you and me when we try to rise out of our poverty against them. (*He goes close to her and lowers his voice.*) Look at me, ten years in their service. Do you think I know no secrets? I know things about the mistress that she wouldnt have the master know for a thousand levas. I know things about him that she wouldnt let him hear the last of for six months if I blabbed them to her. I know things about Raina that would break off her match with Sergius if—

LOUKA (*turning on him quickly*). How do you know? I never told you!

NICOLA (*opening his eyes cunningly*). So thats your little secret, is it? I thought it might be something like that. Well, you take my advice and be respectful; and make the mistress feel that no matter what you know or dont know, she can depend on you to hold your tongue and serve the family faithfully. Thats what they like; and thats how youll make most out of them.

LOUKA (*with searching scorn*). You have the soul of a servant, Nicola.

NICOLA (*complacently*). Yes: thats the secret of success in service.

(*A loud knocking with a whip handle on a wooden door is heard from the stable yard.*)

MALE VOICE OUTSIDE. Hollo! Hollo there! Nicola!

LOUKA. Master! back from the war!

NICOLA (*quickly*). My word for it, Louka, the war's over. Off with you and get some fresh coffee. (*He runs out into the stable yard.*)

LOUKA (*as she collects the coffee pot and cups on the tray, and carries it into the house*). Youll never put the soul of a servant into me. (MAJOR PETKOFF *comes from the stable yard, followed by* NICOLA. *He is a cheerful, excitable, insignificant, unpolished man of about 50, naturally unambitious except as to his income and his importance in local society, but just now greatly pleased with the military rank which the war has thrust on him as a man of consequence in his town. The fever of plucky patriotism which the Serbian attack roused in all the Bulgarians has pulled him through the war; but he is obviously glad to be home again.*)

PETKOFF (*pointing to the table with his whip*). Breakfast out here, eh?

NICOLA. Yes, sir. The mistress and Miss Raina have just gone in.

PETKOFF (*sitting down and taking a roll*). Go in and say Ive come; and get me some fresh coffee.

NICOLA. It's coming, sir. (*He goes to the house door.* LOUKA, *with fresh coffee, a clean cup, and a brandy bottle on her tray, meets him.*) Have you told the mistress?

LOUKA. Yes: she's coming.

(NICOLA *goes into the house.* LOUKA *brings the coffee to the table.*)

PETKOFF. Well: the Serbs havnt run away with you, have they?

LOUKA. No, sir.

PETKOFF. Thats right. Have you brought me some cognac?

LOUKA (*putting the bottle on the table*). Here, sir.

PETKOFF. Thats right.

(*He pours some into his coffee.* CATHERINE, *who, having at this early hour made only a very perfunctory toilet, wears a Bulgarian apron over a once brilliant but now half worn-out dressing gown, and a colored handkerchief tied over her thick black hair, comes from the house with Turkish slippers on her bare feet, looking astonishingly handsome and stately under all the circumstances.* LOUKA *goes into the house.*)

CATHERINE. My dear Paul: what a surprise for us! (*She stoops over the back of his chair to kiss him.*) Have they brought you fresh coffee?

PETKOFF. Yes: Louka's been looking after me. The war's over. The treaty was signed three days ago at Bucharest; and the decree for our army to demobilize was issued yesterday.

CATHERINE (*springing erect, with flashing eyes*). Paul: have you let the Austrians force you to make peace?

PETKOFF (*submissively*). My dear: they didnt consult me. What could I do? (*She sits down and turns away from him.*) But of course we saw to it that the treaty was an honorable one. It declares peace—

CATHERINE (*outraged*). Peace!

PETKOFF (*appeasing her*). —but not friendly relations: remember that. They wanted to put that in; but I insisted on its being struck out. What more could I do?

CATHERINE. You could have annexed Serbia and made Prince Alexander Emperor of the Balkans. Thats what I would have done.

PETKOFF. I dont doubt it in the least, my dear. But I should have had to subdue the whole Austrian Empire first; and that would have kept me too long away from you. I missed you greatly.

CATHERINE (*relenting*). Ah! (*She stretches her hand affectionately across the table to squeeze his.*)

PETKOFF. And how have you been, my dear?

CATHERINE. Oh, my usual sore throats: thats all.

PETKOFF (*with conviction*). That comes from washing your neck every day. Ive often told you so.

CATHERINE. Nonsense, Paul!

PETKOFF (*over his coffee and cigaret*). I dont believe in going too far with these modern customs. All this washing cant be good for the health: it's not natural. There was an Englishman at Philippopolis who used to wet himself all over with cold water every morning when he got up. Disgusting! It all comes from the English: their climate makes them so dirty that they have to be perpetually washing themselves. Look at my father! he never had a bath in his life; and he lived to be ninety-eight, the healthiest man in Bulgaria. I dont mind a good wash once a week to keep up my position; but once a day is carrying the thing to a ridiculous extreme.

CATHARINE. You are a barbarian at heart still, Paul. I hope you behaved yourself before all those Russian officers.

PETKOFF. I did my best. I took care to let them know that we have a library.

CATHERINE. Ah; but you didnt tell them that we have an electric bell in it? I have had one put up.

PETKOFF. Whats an electric bell?

CATHERINE. You touch a button; something tinkles in the kitchen; and then Nicola comes up.

PETKOFF. Why not shout for him?

CATHERINE. Civilized people never shout for their servants. Ive learnt that while you were away.

PETKOFF. Well, I'll tell you something Ive learnt too. Civilized people dont hang out their washing to dry where visitors can see it; so youd better have all that (*indicating the clothes on the bushes*) put somewhere else.

CATHERINE. Oh, thats absurd, Paul: I dont believe really refined people notice such things.

SERGIUS (*knocking at the stable gates*). Gate, Nicola!

PETKOFF. Theres Sergius. (*Shouting*) Hollo, Nicola!

CATHERINE. Oh, dont shout, Paul: it really isnt nice.

PETKOFF. Bosh! (*He shouts louder than before.*) Nicola!

NICOLA (*appearing at the house door*). Yes, sir.

PETKOFF. Are you deaf? Dont you hear Major Saranoff knocking?

Bring him round this way. (*He pronounces the name with the stress on the second syllable:* SARAHNOFF.)

NICOLA. Yes, Major. (*He goes into the stable yard.*)

PETKOFF. You must talk to him, my dear, until Raina takes him off our hands. He bores my life out about our not promoting him. Over my head, if you please.

CATHERINE. He certainly ought to be promoted when he marries Raina. Besides, the country should insist on having at least one native general.

PETKOFF. Yes; so that he could throw away whole brigades instead of regiments. It's no use, my dear: he hasnt the slightest chance of promotion until we're quite sure that the peace will be a lasting one.

NICOLA (*at the gate, announcing*). Major Sergius Saranoff!

(*He goes into the house and returns presently with a third chair, which he places at the table. He then withdraws.* MAJOR SERGIUS SARANOFF, *the original of the portrait in* RAINA'S *room, is a tall romantically handsome man, with the physical hardihood, the high spirit, and the susceptible imagination of an untamed mountaineer chieftain. But his remarkable personal distinction is of a characteristically civilized type. The ridges of his eyebrows, curving with an interrogative twist round the projections at the outer corners; his jealously observant eye; his nose, thin, keen, and apprehensive in spite of the pugnacious high bridge and large nostril; his assertive chin would not be out of place in a Parisian salon, showing that the clever imaginative barbarian has an acute critical faculty which has been thrown into intense activity by the arrival of western civilization in the Balkans. The result is precisely what the advent of nineteenth-century thought first produced in England: to wit, Byronism. By his brooding on the perpetual failure, not only of others, but of himself, to live up to his ideals; by his consequent cynical scorn for humanity; by his jejune credulity as to the absolute validity of his concepts and the unworthiness of the world in disregarding them; by his wincings and mockeries under the sting of the petty disillusions which every hour spent among men brings to his sensitive observation, he has acquired the half tragic, half ironic air, the mysterious moodiness, the suggestion of a strange and terrible history that has left nothing but undying remorse, by which Childe Harold fascinated the grandmothers of his English contemporaries. It is clear that here or nowhere is* RAINA'S *ideal hero.* CATHERINE *is hardly less enthusiastic about him than her daughter, and much less reserved in showing her enthusiasm. As he enters from the stable gate, she*) *rises effusively to greet him.* PETKOFF *is distinctly less disposed to make a fuss about him.*)

PETKOFF. Here already, Sergius! Glad to see you.

CATHERINE. My dear Sergius! (*She holds out both her hands.*)

SERGIUS (*kissing them with scrupulous gallantry*). My dear mother, if I may call you so.

PETKOFF (*drily*). Mother-in-law, Sergius: mother-in-law! Sit down; and have some coffee.

SERGIUS. Thank you: none for me. (*He gets away from the table with a certain distaste for* PETKOFF'S *enjoyment of it, and posts himself with conscious dignity against the rail of the steps leading to the house.*)

CATHERINE. You look superb. The campaign has improved you, Sergius. Everybody here is mad about you. We were all wild with enthusiasm about that magnificent cavalry charge.

SERGIUS (*with grave irony*). Madam: it was the cradle and the grave of my military reputation.

CATHERINE. How so?

SERGIUS. I won the battle the wrong way when our worthy Russian generals were losing it the right way. In short, I upset their plans, and wounded their self-esteem. Two Cossack colonels had their regiments routed on the most correct principles of scientific warfare. Two major-generals got killed strictly according to military etiquette. The two colonels are now major-generals; and I am still a simple major.

CATHERINE. You shall not remain so, Sergius. The women are on your side; and they will see that justice is done you.

SERGIUS. It is too late. I have only waited for the peace to send in my resignation.

PETKOFF (*dropping his cup in his amazement*). Your resignation!

CATHERINE. Oh, you must withdraw it!

SERGIUS (*with resolute measured emphasis, folding his arms*). I never withdraw.

PETKOFF (*vexed*). Now who could have supposed you were going to do such a thing?

SERGIUS (*with fire*). Everyone that knew me. But enough of myself and my affairs. How is Raina; and where is Raina?

RAINA (*suddenly coming round the corner of the house and standing at the top of the steps in the path*). Raina is here.

(*She makes a charming picture as they turn to look at her. She wears an underdress of pale green silk, draped with an overdress of thin ecru canvas embroidered with gold. She is crowned with a dainty eastern cap of gold tinsel.* SERGIUS *goes impulsively to*

*meet her. Posing regally, she presents her hand: he drops chival-
rously on one knee and kisses it.*)

PETKOFF (*aside to* CATHERINE, *beaming with parental pride*). Pretty,
isnt it? She always appears at the right moment.

CATHERINE (*impatiently*). Yes; she listens for it. It is an abominable
habit.

(SERGIUS *leads* RAINA *forward with splendid gallantry. When they
arrive at the table, she turns to him with a bend of the head: he
bows; and thus they separate, he coming to his place and she
going behind her father's chair.*)

RAINA (*stooping and kissing her father*). Dear father! Welcome home!

PETKOFF (*patting her cheek*). My little pet girl.

(*He kisses her. She goes to the chair left by* NICOLA *for* SERGIUS,
and sits down.)

CATHERINE. And so youre no longer a soldier, Sergius.

SERGIUS. I am no longer a soldier. Soldiering, my dear madam, is the
coward's art of attacking mercilessly when you are strong, and
keeping out of harm's way when you are weak. That is the whole
secret of successful fighting. Get your enemy at a disadvantage;
and never, on any account, fight him on equal terms.

PETKOFF. They wouldnt let us make a fair standup fight of it. However, I suppose soldiering has to be a trade like any other trade.

SERGIUS. Precisely. But I have no ambition to shine as a tradesman;
so I have taken the advice of that bagman of a captain that
settled the exchange of prisoners with us at Pirot, and given it up.

PETKOFF. What! that Swiss fellow? Sergius: Ive often thought of that
exchange since. He over-reached us about those horses.

SERGIUS. Of course he over-reached us. His father was a hotel and
livery stable keeper; and he owed his first step to his knowledge
of horse-dealing. (*With mock enthusiasm*) Ah, he was a soldier:
every inch a soldier! If only I had bought the horses for my
regiment instead of foolishly leading it into danger, I should have
been a field-marshal now!

CATHERINE. A Swiss? What was he doing in the Serbian army?

PETKOFF. A volunteer, of course: keen on picking up his profession.
(*Chuckling*) We shouldnt have been able to begin fighting if
these foreigners hadnt shown us how to do it: we knew nothing
about it; and neither did the Serbs. Egad, there'd have been no
war without them!

RAINA. Are there many Swiss officers in the Serbian army?

PETKOFF. No. All Austrians, just as our officers were all Russians.
This was the only Swiss I came across. I'll never trust a Swiss

again. He humbugged us into giving him fifty ablebodied men
for two hundred worn-out chargers. They werent even eatable!

SERGIUS. We were two children in the hands of that consummate
soldier, Major: simply two innocent little children.

RAINA. What was he like?

CATHERINE. Oh, Raina, what a silly question!

SERGIUS. He was like a commercial traveller in uniform. Bourgeois
to his boots!

PETKOFF (*grinning*). Sergius: tell Catherine that queer story his friend
told us about how he escaped after Slivnitza. You remember.
About his being hid by two women.

SERGIUS (*with bitter irony*). Oh yes: quite a romance! He was serving
in the very battery I so unprofessionally charged. Being a thor-
ough soldier, he ran away like the rest of them, with our cavalry
at his heels. To escape their sabres he climbed a waterpipe and
made his way into the bedroom of a young Bulgarian lady. The
young lady was enchanted by his persuasive commercial traveller's manners. She very modestly entertained him for an hour or
so, and then called in her mother lest her conduct should appear
unmaidenly. The old lady was equally fascinated; and the fugitive
was sent on his way in the morning, disguised in an old coat
belonging to the master of the house, who was away at the war.

RAINA (*rising with marked stateliness*). Your life in the camp has
made you coarse, Sergius. I did not think you would have repeated
such a story before me. (*She turns away coldly.*)

CATHERINE (*also rising*). She is right, Sergius. If such women exist,
we should be spared the knowledge of them.

PETKOFF. Pooh! nonsense! what does it matter?

SERGIUS (*ashamed*). No, Petkoff: I was wrong. (*To* RAINA, *with earnest humility*) I beg your pardon. I have behaved abominably.
Forgive me, Raina. (*She bows reservedly.*) And you too, madam.
(CATHERINE *bows graciously and sits down. He proceeds solemnly,
again addressing* RAINA.) The glimpses I have had of the seamy
side of life during the last few months have made me cynical; but
I should not have brought my cynicism here: least of all into your
presence, Raina. I—(*Here, turning to the others, he is evidently
going to begin a long speech when the* MAJOR *interrupts him.*)

PETKOFF. Stuff and nonsense, Sergius! Thats quite enough fuss about
nothing: a soldier's daughter should be able to stand up without
flinching to a little strong conversation. (*He rises.*) Come: it's
time for us to get to business. We have to make up our minds
how those three regiments are to get back to Philippopolis: theres

no forage for them on the Sofia route. (*He goes towards the
house.*) Come along. (SERGIUS *is about to follow him when*
CATHERINE *rises and intervenes.*)

CATHERINE. Oh, Paul, cant you spare Sergius for a few moments?
Raina has hardly seen him yet. Perhaps I can help you to settle
about the regiments.

SERGIUS (*protesting*). My dear madam, impossible: you—

CATHERINE (*stopping him playfully*). You stay here, my dear Sergius:
theres no hurry. I have a word or two to say to Paul. (SERGIUS
instantly bows and steps back.) Now, dear (*taking* PETKOFF'S
arm): come and see the electric bell.

PETKOFF. Oh, very well, very well.

(*They go into the house together affectionately.* SERGIUS, *left
alone with* RAINA, *looks anxiously at her, fearing that she is still
offended. She smiles, and stretches out her arms to him.*)

SERGIUS (*hastening to her*). Am I forgiven?

RAINA (*placing her arms on his shoulders as she looks up at him with
admiration and worship*). My hero! My king!

SERGIUS. My queen! (*He kisses her on the forehead.*)

RAINA. How I have envied you, Sergius! You have been out in the
world, on the field of battle, able to prove yourself there worthy
of any woman in the world; whilst I have had to sit at home inactive—dreaming—useless—doing nothing that could give me
the right to call myself worthy of any man.

SERGIUS. Dearest: all my deeds have been yours. You inspired me. I
have gone through the war like a knight in a tournament with
his lady looking down at him!

RAINA. And you have never been absent from my thoughts for a moment. (*Very solemnly*) Sergius: I think we two have found the
higher love. When I think of you, I feel that I could never do a
base deed, or think an ignoble thought.

SERGIUS. My lady and my saint! (*He clasps her reverently.*)

RAINA (*returning his embrace*). My lord and my—

SERGIUS. Sh-sh! Let me be the worshipper, dear. You little know how
unworthy even the best man is of a girl's pure passion!

RAINA. I trust you. I love you. You will never disappoint me, Sergius.
(LOUKA *is heard singing within the house. They quickly release
each other.*) I cant pretend to talk indifferently before her: my
heart is too full. (LOUKA *comes from the house with her tray. She
goes to the table, and begins to clear it, with her back turned to
them.*) I will get my hat; and then we can go out until lunch
time. Wouldnt you like that?

SERGIUS. Be quick. If you are away five minutes, it will seem five hours. (RAINA *runs to the top of the steps, and turns there to exchange looks with him and wave him a kiss with both hands. He looks after her with emotion for a moment; then turns slowly away, his face radiant with the loftiest exaltation. The movement shifts his field of vision, into the corner of which there now comes the tail of* LOUKA's *double apron. His attention is arrested at once. He takes a stealthy look at her, and begins to twirl his moustache mischievously, with his left hand akimbo on his hip. Finally, striking the ground with his heels in something of a cavalry swagger, he strolls over to the other side of the table, opposite her, and says*) Louka: do you know what the higher love is?

LOUKA (*astonished*). No, sir.

SERGIUS. Very fatiguing thing to keep up for any length of time, Louka. One feels the need of some relief after it.

LOUKA (*innocently*). Perhaps you would like some coffee, sir? (*She stretches her hand across the table for the coffee pot.*)

SERGIUS (*taking her hand*). Thank you, Louka.

LOUKA (*pretending to pull*). Oh, sir, you know I didnt mean that. I'm surprised at you!

SERGIUS (*coming clear of the table and drawing her with him*). I am surprised at myself, Louka. What would Sergius, the hero of Slivnitza, say if he saw me now? What would Sergius, the apostle of the higher love, say if he saw me now? What would the half dozen Sergiuses who keep popping in and out of this handsome figure of mine say if they caught us here? (*Letting go her hand and slipping his arm dexterously round her waist*) Do you consider my figure handsome, Louka?

LOUKA. Let me go, sir. I shall be disgraced. (*She struggles: he holds her inexorably.*) Oh, will you let go?

SERGIUS (*looking straight into her eyes*). No.

LOUKA. Then stand back where we cant be seen. Have you no common sense?

SERGIUS. Ah! thats reasonable. (*He takes her into the stable yard gateway, where they are hidden from the house.*)

LOUKA (*plaintively*). I may be seen from the windows: Miss Raina is sure to be spying about after you.

SERGIUS (*stung: letting her go*). Take care, Louka. I may be worthless enough to betray the higher love; but do not you insult it.

LOUKA (*demurely*). Not for the world, sir, I'm sure. May I go on with my work, please, now?

SERGIUS (*again putting his arm round her*). You are a provoking little witch, Louka. If you were in love with me, would you spy out of windows on me?

LOUKA. Well, you see, sir, since you say you are half a dozen different gentlemen all at once, I should have a great deal to look after.

SERGIUS (*charmed*). Witty as well as pretty. (*He tries to kiss her.*)

LOUKA (*avoiding him*). No: I dont want your kisses. Gentlefolk are all alike: you making love to me behind Miss Raina's back; and she doing the same behind yours.

SERGIUS (*recoiling a step*). Louka!

LOUKA. It shows how little you really care.

SERGIUS (*dropping his familiarity, and speaking with freezing politeness*). If our conversation is to continue, Louka, you will please remember that a gentleman does not discuss the conduct of the lady he is engaged to with her maid.

LOUKA. It's so hard to know what a gentleman considers right. I thought from your trying to kiss me that you had given up being so particular.

SERGIUS (*turning away from her and striking his forehead as he comes back into the garden from the gateway*). Devil! devil!

LOUKA. Ha! ha! I expect one of the six of you is very like me, sir; though I am only Miss Raina's maid. (*She goes back to her work at the table, taking no further notice of him.*)

SERGIUS (*speaking to himself*). Which of the six is the real man? thats the question that torments me. One of them is a hero, another a buffoon, another a humbug, another perhaps a bit of a blackguard. (*He pauses, and looks furtively at* LOUKA *as he adds, with deep bitterness*) And one, at least, is a coward: jealous, like all cowards. (*He goes to the table.*) Louka.

LOUKA. Yes?

SERGIUS. Who is my rival?

LOUKA. You shall never get that out of me, for love or money.

SERGIUS. Why?

LOUKA. Never mind why. Besides, you would tell that I told you; and I should lose my place.

SERGIUS (*holding out his right hand in affirmation*). No! on the honor of a—(*he checks himself; and his hand drops, nerveless, as he concludes sardonically*)—of a man capable of behaving as I have been behaving for the last five minutes. Who is he?

LOUKA. I dont know. I never saw him. I only heard his voice through the door of her room.

SERGIUS. Damnation! How dare you?

LOUKA (*retreating*). Oh, I mean no harm: youve no right to take up my words like that. The mistress knows all about it. And I tell you that if that gentleman ever comes here again, Miss Raina will marry him, whether he likes it or not. I know the difference between the sort of manner you and she put on before one another and the real manner.

(SERGIUS *shivers as if she had stabbed him. Then, setting his face like iron, he strides grimly to her, and grips her above the elbows with both hands.*)

SERGIUS. Now listen you to me.

LOUKA (*wincing*). Not so tight; youre hurting me.

SERGIUS. That doesnt matter. You have stained my honor by making me a party to your eavesdropping. And you have betrayed your mistress.

LOUKA (*writhing*). Please—

SERGIUS. That shows that you are an abominable little clod of common clay, with the soul of a servant. (*He lets her go as if she were an unclean thing, and turns away, dusting his hands of her, to the bench by the wall, where he sits down with averted head, meditating gloomily.*)

LOUKA (*whimpering angrily with her hands up her sleeves, feeling her bruised arms*). You know how to hurt with your tongue as well as with your hands. But I dont care, now Ive found out that whatever clay I'm made of, youre made of the same. As for her, she's a liar; and her fine airs are a cheat; and I'm worth six of her.

(*She shakes the pain off hardily; tosses her head; and sets to work to put the things on the tray. He looks doubtfully at her. She finishes packing the tray, and laps the cloth over the edges, so as to carry all out together. As she stoops to lift it, he rises.*)

SERGIUS. Louka! (*She stops and looks defiantly at him.*) A gentleman has no right to hurt a woman under any circumstances. (*With profound humility, uncovering his head*) I beg your pardon.

LOUKA. That sort of apology may satisfy a lady. Of what use is it to a servant?

SERGIUS (*rudely crossed in his chivalry, throws it off with a bitter laugh, and says slightingly*). Oh! you wish to be paid for the hurt! (*He puts on his shako, and takes some money from his pocket.*)

LOUKA (*her eyes filling with tears in spite of herself*). No: I want my hurt made well.

SERGIUS (*sobered by her tone*). How?

(*She rolls up her left sleeve; clasps her arm with the thumb and fingers of her right hand; and looks down at the bruise. Then she raises her head and looks straight at him. Finally, with a superb gesture, she presents her arm to be kissed. Amazed, he looks at her; at the arm; at her again; hesitates; and then, with shuddering*) *intensity, exclaims* Never! *and gets away as far as possible from her. Her arm drops. Without a word, and with unaffected dignity, she takes her tray, and is approaching the house when* RAINA *returns, wearing a hat and jacket in the height of the Vienna fashion of the previous year, 1885.* LOUKA *makes way proudly for her, and then goes into the house.*)

RAINA. I'm ready. Whats the matter? (*Gaily*) Have you been flirting with Louka?

SERGIUS (*hastily*). No, no. How can you think such a thing?

RAINA (*ashamed of herself*). Forgive me, dear: it was only a jest. I am so happy today.

(*He goes quickly to her, and kisses her hand remorsefully.* CATH-ERINE *comes out and calls to them from the top of the steps.*)

CATHERINE (*coming down to them*). I am sorry to disturb you, chil-dren; but Paul is distracted over those three regiments. He doesnt know how to send them to Philippopolis; and he objects to every suggestion of mine. You must go and help him, Sergius. He is in the library.

RAINA (*disappointed*). But we are just going out for a walk.

SERGIUS. I shall not be long. Wait for me just five minutes. (*He runs up the steps to the door.*)

RAINA (*following him to the foot of the steps and looking up at him with timid coquetry*). I shall go round and wait in full view of the library windows. Be sure you draw father's attention to me. If you are a moment longer than five minutes, I shall go in and fetch you, regiments or no regiments.

SERGIUS (*laughing*). Very well. (*He goes in.*)

(RAINA *watches him until he is out of her sight. Then, with a perceptible relaxation of manner, she begins to pace up and down the garden in a brown study.*)

CATHERINE. Imagine their meeting that Swiss and hearing the whole story! The very first thing your father asked for was the old coat we sent him off in. A nice mess you have got us into!

RAINA (*gazing thoughtfully at the gravel as she walks*). The little beast!

CATHERINE. Little beast! What little beast?

RAINA. To go and tell! Oh, if I had him here, I'd cram him with choco-late creams til he couldnt ever speak again!

CATHERINE. Dont talk such stuff. Tell me the truth, Raina. How long was he in your room before you came to me?

RAINA (*whisking round and recommencing her march in the opposite direction*). Oh, I forget.

CATHERINE. You cannot forget! Did he really climb up after the soldiers were gone; or was he there when that officer searched the room?

RAINA. No. Yes: I think he must have been there then.

CATHERINE. You think! Oh, Raina! Raina! Will anything ever make you straightforward? If Sergius finds out, it will be all over between you.

RAINA (*with cool impertinence*). Oh, I know Sergius is your pet. I sometimes wish you could marry him instead of me. You would just suit him. You would pet him, and spoil him, and mother him to perfection.

CATHERINE (*opening her eyes very widely indeed*). Well, upon my word!

RAINA (*capriciously: half to herself*). I always feel a longing to do or say something dreadful to him—to shock his propriety—to scandalize the five senses out of him. (*To* CATHERINE, *perversely*) I dont care whether he finds out about the chocolate cream soldier or not. I half hope he may. (*She again turns and strolls flippantly away up the path to the corner of the house.*)

CATHERINE. And what should I be able to say to your father, pray?

RAINA (*over her shoulder, from the top of the two steps*). Oh, poor father! As if he could help himself! (*She turns the corner and passes out of sight.*)

CATHERINE (*looking after her, her fingers itching*). Oh, if you were only ten years younger! (LOUKA *comes from the house with a salver, which she carries hanging down by her side.*) Well?

LOUKA. Theres a gentleman just called, madam. A Serbian officer.

CATHERINE (*flaming*). A Serb! And how dare he—(*Checking herself bitterly*) Oh, I forgot. We are at peace now. I suppose we shall have them calling every day to pay their compliments. Well: if he is an officer why dont you tell your master? He is in the library with Major Saranoff. Why do you come to me?

LOUKA. But he asks for you, madam. And I dont think he knows who you are: he said the lady of the house. He gave me this little ticket for you. (*She takes a card out of her bosom; puts it on the salver; and offers it to* CATHERINE.)

CATHERINE (*reading*). "Captain Bluntschli"? Thats a German name.

LOUKA. Swiss, madam, I think.

CATHERINE (*with a bound that makes* LOUKA *jump back*). Swiss! What is he like?

LOUKA (*timidly*). He has a big carpet bag, madam.

CATHERINE. Oh Heavens! he's come to return the coat. Send him away: say we're not at home: ask him to leave his address and I'll write to him. Oh stop: that will never do. Wait! (*She throws herself into a chair to think it out.* LOUKA *waits.*) The master and Major Saranoff are busy in the library, arnt they?

LOUKA. Yes, madam.

CATHERINE (*decisively*). Bring the gentleman out here at once. (*Peremptorily*) And be very polite to him. Dont delay. Here (*impatiently snatching the salver from her*): leave that here; and go straight back to him.

LOUKA. Yes, madam (*going*).

CATHERINE. Louka!

LOUKA (*stopping*). Yes, madam.

CATHERINE. Is the library door shut?

LOUKA. I think so, madam.

CATHERINE. If not, shut it as you pass through.

LOUKA. Yes, madam (*going*).

CATHERINE. Stop! (LOUKA *stops.*) He will have to go that way (*indicating the gate of the stable yard.*) Tell Nicola to bring his bag here after him. Dont forget.

LOUKA (*surprised*). His bag?

CATHERINE. Yes: here: as soon as possible. (*Vehemently*) Be quick! (LOUKA *runs into the house.* CATHERINE *snatches her apron off and throws it behind a bush. She then takes up the salver and uses it as a mirror, with the result that the handkerchief tied round her head follows the apron. A touch to her hair and a shake to her dressing gown make her presentable.*) Oh, how? how? how can a man be such a fool! Such a moment to select! (LOUKA *appears at the door of the house, announcing* Captain Bluntschli. *She stands aside at the top of the steps to let him pass before she goes in again. He is the man of the midnight adventure in* RAINA'S *room, clean, well brushed, smartly uniformed, and out of trouble, but still unmistakably the same man. The moment* LOUKA'S *back is turned,* CATHERINE *swoops on him with impetuous, urgent, coaxing appeal.*) Captain Bluntschli: I am very glad to see you; but you must leave this house at once. (*He raises his eyebrows.*) My husband has just returned with my future son-in-law; and they know nothing. If they did, the consequences would be terrible. You are a foreigner: you do not feel our national animosities as we do. We still hate the Serbs: the effect of the peace on my husband has been to make him feel like a lion baulked of his prey. If he discovers our secret, he will never forgive me; and my daughter's life will hardly be safe. Will you, like the chivalrous gentleman and soldier you are, leave at once before he finds you here?

BLUNTSCHLI (*disappointed, but philosophical*). At once, gracious lady. I only came to thank you and return the coat you lent me. If you will allow me to take it out of my bag and leave it with your servant as I pass out, I need detain you no further. (*He turns to go into the house.*)

CATHERINE (*catching him by the sleeve*). Oh, you must not think of going back that way. (*Coaxing him across to the stable gates*) This is the shortest way out. Many thanks. So glad to have been of service to you. Good-bye.

BLUNTSCHLI. But my bag?

CATHERINE. It shall be sent on. You will leave me your address.

BLUNTSCHLI. True. Allow me.

(*He takes out his cardcase, and stops to write his address, keeping* CATHERINE *in an agony of impatience. As he hands her the card,* PETKOFF, *hatless, rushes from the house in a fluster of hospitality, followed by* SERGIUS.)

PETKOFF (*as he hurries down the steps*). My dear Captain Bluntschli—

CATHERINE. Oh Heavens! (*She sinks on the seat against the wall.*)

PETKOFF (*too preoccupied to notice her as he shakes* BLUNTSCHLI'S *hand heartily*). Those stupid people of mine thought I was out here, instead of in the—haw!—library (*he cannot mention the library without betraying how proud he is of it*). I saw you through the window. I was wondering why you didnt come in. Saranoff is with me: you remember him, dont you?

SERGIUS (*saluting humorously, and then offering his hand with great charm of manner*). Welcome, our friend the enemy!

PETKOFF. No longer the enemy, happily. (*Rather anxiously*) I hope youve called as a friend, and not about horses or prisoners.

CATHERINE. Oh, quite as a friend, Paul. I was just asking Captain Bluntschli to stay to lunch; but he declares he must go at once.

SERGIUS (*sardonically*). Impossible, Bluntschli. We want you here badly. We have to send on three cavalry regiments to Philippopolis; and we dont in the least know how to do it.

BLUNTSCHLI (*suddenly attentive and businesslike*). Philippopolis? The forage is the trouble, I suppose.

PETKOFF (*eagerly*). Yes: thats it (*To* SERGIUS) He sees the whole thing at once.

BLUNTSCHLI. I think I can show you how to manage that.

SERGIUS. Invaluable man! Come along!

(*Towering over* BLUNTSCHLI, *he puts his hand on his shoulder and takes him to the steps,* PETKOFF *following.* RAINA *comes from the house as* BLUNTSCHLI *puts his foot on the first step.*)

RAINA. Oh! The chocolate cream soldier!

(BLUNTSCHLI *stands rigid.* SERGIUS, *amazed, looks at* RAINA, *then at* PETKOFF, *who looks back at him and then at his wife.*)

CATHERINE (*with commanding presence of mind*). My dear Raina, dont you see that we have a guest here? Captain Bluntschli: one of our new Serbian friends.

(RAINA *bows:* BLUNTSCHLI *bows.*)

RAINA. How silly of me! (*She comes down into the centre of the group, between* BLUNTSCHLI *and* PETKOFF.) I made a beautiful ornament this morning for the ice pudding; and that stupid Nicola has just put down a pile of plates on it and spoilt it. (*To* BLUNTSCHLI, *winningly*) I hope you didnt think that you were the chocolate cream soldier, Captain Bluntschli.

BLUNTSCHLI (*laughing*). I assure you I did. (*Stealing a whimsical glance at her*) Your explanation was a relief.

PETKOFF (*suspiciously, to* RAINA). And since when, pray, have you taken to cooking?

CATHERINE. Oh, whilst you were away. It is her latest fancy.

PETKOFF (*testily*). And has Nicola taken to drinking? He used to be careful enough. First he shows Captain Bluntschli out here when he knew quite well I was in the library; and then he goes downstairs and breaks Raina's chocolate soldier. He must—(NICOLA *appears at the top of the steps with the bag. He descends; places it respectfully before* BLUNTSCHLI; *and waits for further orders. General amazement.* NICOLA, *unconscious of the effect he is producing, looks perfectly satisfied with himself. When* PETKOFF *recovers his power of speech, he breaks out at him with*) Are you mad, Nicola?

NICOLA (*taken aback*). Sir?

PETKOFF. What have you brought that for?

NICOLA. My lady's orders, Major. Louka told me that—

CATHERINE (*interrupting him*). My orders! Why should I order you to bring Captain Bluntschli's luggage out here? What are you thinking of, Nicola?

NICOLA (*after a moment's bewilderment, picking up the bag as he addresses* BLUNTSCHLI *with the very perfection of servile discretion*). I beg your pardon, Captain, I am sure. (*To* CATHERINE) My fault, madame: I hope youll overlook it. (*He bows, and is going to the steps with the bag, when* PETKOFF *addresses him angrily.*)

PETKOFF. Youd better go and slam that bag, too, down on Miss Raina's ice pudding! (*This is too much for* NICOLA. *The bag drops from his hand almost on his master's toes, eliciting a roar of*) Begone, you butter-fingered donkey.

NICOLA (*snatching up the bag, and escaping into the house*). Yes, Major.

CATHERINE. Oh, never mind. Paul: dont be angry.

PETKOFF (*blustering*). Scoundrel! He's got out of hand while I was away. I'll teach him. Infernal blackguard! The sack next Saturday! I'll clear out the whole establishment—

(*He is stifled by the caresses of his wife and daughter, who hang round his neck, petting him.*)

CATHERINE		Now, now, now, it mustnt be angry. He meant no harm. Be good to please me, dear. Sh-sh-sh-sh!
	(*together*)	
RAINA		Wow, wow, wow: not on your first day at home. I'll make another ice pudding. Tch-ch-ch!

PETKOFF (*yielding*). Oh well, never mind. Come, Bluntschli: lets have no more nonsense about going away. You know very well youre not going back to Switzerland yet. Until you do go back youll stay with us.

RAINA. Oh, do, Captain Bluntschli.

PETKOFF (*to* CATHERINE). Now, Catherine: it's of you he's afraid. Press him: and he'll stay.

CATHERINE. Of course I shall be only too delighted if (*appealingly*) Captain Bluntschli really wishes to stay. He knows my wishes.

BLUNTSCHLI (*in his driest military manner*). I am at madam's orders.

SERGIUS (*cordially*). That settles it!

PETKOFF (*heartily*). Of course!

RAINA. You see you must stay.

BLUNTSCHLI (*smiling*). Well, if I must, I must.

(*Gesture of despair from* CATHERINE.)

ACT THREE

In the library after lunch. It is not much of a library. Its literary equipment consists of a single fixed shelf stocked with old paper-covered novels, broken-backed, coffee-stained, torn and thumbed; and a couple of little hanging shelves with a few gift books on them: the rest of the wall space being occupied by trophies of war and the chase. But it is a most comfortable sitting room. A row

*of three large windows shows a mountain panorama, just now
seen in one of its friendliest aspects in the mellowing afternoon
light. In the corner next the right hand window a square earthen-
ware stove, a perfect tower of glistening pottery, rises nearly to
the ceiling and guarantees plenty of warmth. The ottoman is like
that in* RAINA'S *room, and similarly placed; and the window seats
are luxurious with decorated cushions. There is one object, however, hopelessly out of keeping with its surroundings. This is a
small kitchen table, much the worse for wear, fitted as a writing
table with an old canister full of pens, an eggcup filled with ink,
and a deplorable scrap of heavily used pink blotting paper.*

*At the side of this table, which stands to the left of anyone fac-
ing the window,* BLUNTSCHLI *is hard at work with a couple of
maps before him, writing orders. At the head of it sits* SERGIUS,
*who is supposed to be also at work, but is actually gnawing the
feather of a pen, and contemplating* BLUNTSCHLI'S *quick, sure,
businesslike progress with a mixture of envious irritation at his
own incapacity and awestruck wonder at an ability which seems
to him almost miraculous, though its prosaic character forbids
him to esteem it. The* MAJOR *is comfortably established on the
ottoman, with a newspaper in his hand and the tube of his hookah
within easy reach.* CATHERINE *sits at the stove, with her back to
them, embroidering.* RAINA, *reclining on the divan, is gazing in a
daydream out at the Balkan landscape, with a neglected novel in
her lap.*

*The door is on the same side as the stove, farther from the
window. The button of the electric bell is at the opposite side,
behind* BLUNTSCHLI.

PETKOFF (*looking up from his paper to watch how they are getting on
at the table*). Are you sure I cant help in any way, Bluntschli?

BLUNTSCHLI (*without interrupting his writing or looking up*). Quite
sure, thank you. Saranoff and I will manage it.

SERGIUS (*grimly*). Yes: we'll manage it. He finds out what to do; draws
up the orders; and I sign em. Division of labor! (BLUNTSCHLI
passes him a paper.) Another one? Thank you. (*He plants the
paper squarely before him; sets his chair carefully parallel to it;
and signs with his cheek on his elbow and his protruded tongue
following the movements of his pen*). This hand is more accustomed to the sword than to the pen.

PETKOFF. It's very good of you, Bluntschli: it is indeed, to let yourself be put upon in this way. Now are you quite sure I can do
nothing?

CATHERINE (*in a low warning tone*). You can stop interrupting, Paul.

PETKOFF (*starting and looking round at her*). Eh? Oh! Quite right. (*He takes his newspaper up again, but presently lets it drop.*) Ah, you havnt been campaigning, Catherine: you dont know how pleasant it is for us to sit here, after a good lunch, with nothing to do but enjoy ourselves. Theres only one thing I want to make me thoroughly comfortable.

CATHERINE. What is that?

PETKOFF. My old coat. I'm not at home in this one: I feel as if I were on parade.

CATHERINE. My dear Paul, how absurd you are about that old coat! It must be hanging in the blue closet where you left it.

PETKOFF. My dear Catherine, I tell you Ive looked there. Am I to believe my own eyes or not? (CATHERINE *rises and crosses the room to press the button of the electric bell.*) What are you showing off that bell for? (*She looks at him majestically, and silently resumes her chair and her needlework.*) My dear: if you think the obstinacy of your sex can make a coat out of two old dressing gowns of Raina's, your waterproof, and my mackintosh, youre mistaken. Thats exactly what the blue closet contains at present. (NICOLA *presents himself.*)

CATHERINE. Nicola: go to the blue closet and bring your master's old coat here: the braided one he wears in the house.

NICOLA. Yes, madame. (*He goes out.*)

PETKOFF. Catherine.

CATHERINE. Yes, Paul.

PETKOFF. I bet you any piece of jewelry you like to order from Sofia against a week's housekeeping money that the coat isnt there.

CATHERINE. Done, Paul!

PETKOFF (*excited by the prospect of a gamble*). Come: heres an opportunity for some sport. Wholl bet on it? Bluntschli: I'll give you six to one.

BLUNTSCHLI (*imperturbably*). It would be robbing you, Major. Madame is sure to be right. (*Without looking up, he passes another batch of papers to* SERGIUS.)

SERGIUS (*also excited*). Bravo, Switzerland! Major: I bet my best charger against an Arab mare for Raina that Nicola finds the coat in the blue closet.

PETKOFF (*eagerly*). Your best char—

CATHERINE (*hastily interrupting him*). Dont be foolish, Paul. An Arabian mare will cost you 50,000 levas.

RAINA (*suddenly coming out of her picturesque revery*). Really, mother, if you are going to take the jewelry, I don't see why you should grudge me my Arab.

(NICOLA *comes back with the coat, and brings it to* PETKOFF, *who can hardly believe his eyes.*)

CATHERINE. Where was it, Nicola?

NICOLA. Hanging in the blue closet, madame.

PETKOFF. Well, I am d—

CATHERINE (*stopping him*). Paul!

PETKOFF. I could have sworn it wasnt there. Age is beginning to tell on me. I'm getting hallucinations. (*To* NICOLA) Here: help me to change. Excuse me, Bluntschli. (*He begins changing coats,* NICOLA *acting as valet.*) Remember: I didnt take that bet of yours, Sergius. Youd better give Raina that Arab steed yourself, since youve roused her expectations. Eh, Raina? (*He looks round at her; but she is again rapt in the landscape. With a little gush of parental affection and pride, he points her out to them, and says*) She's dreaming, as usual.

SERGIUS. Assuredly she shall not be the loser.

PETKOFF. So much the better for her. *I* shant come off so cheaply, I expect. (*The change is now complete.* NICOLA *goes out with the discarded coat.*) Ah, now I feel at home at last. (*He sits down and takes his newspaper with a grunt of relief.*)

BLUNTSCHLI (*to* SERGIUS, *handing a paper*). Thats the last order.

PETKOFF (*jumping up*). What! Finished?

BLUNTSCHLI. Finished.

PETKOFF (*with childlike envy*). Havnt you anything for me to sign?

BLUNTSCHLI. Not necessary. His signature will do.

PETKOFF (*inflating his chest and thumping it*). Ah well, I think weve done a thundering good day's work. Can I do anything more?

BLUNTSCHLI. You had better both see the fellows that are to take these. (SERGIUS *rises.*) Pack them off at once; and show them that Ive marked on the orders the time they should hand them in by. Tell them that if they stop to drink or tell stories—if theyre five minutes late, theyll have the skin taken off their backs.

SERGIUS (*stiffening indignantly*). I'll say so. (*He strides to the door.*) And if one of them is man enough to spit in my face for insulting him, I'll buy his discharge and give him a pension. (*He goes out.*)

BLUNTSCHLI (*confidentially*). Just see that he talks to them properly, Major, will you?

PETKOFF (*officiously*). Quite right, Bluntschli, quite right. I'll see to it. (*He goes to the door importantly, but hesitates on the threshold.*) By the bye, Catherine, you may as well come too. Theyll be far more frightened of you than of me.

CATHERINE (*putting down her embroidery*). I daresay I had better. You would only splutter at them. (*She goes out,* PETKOFF *holding the door for her and following her.*)

BLUNTSCHLI. What an army! They make cannons out of cherry trees; and the officers send for their wives to keep discipline!

(*He begins to fold and docket the papers.* RAINA, *who has risen from the divan, marches slowly down the room with her hands clasped behind her, and looks mischievously at him.*)

RAINA. You look ever so much nicer than when we last met. (*He looks up, surprised.*) What have you done to yourself?

BLUNTSCHLI. Washed; brushed; good night's sleep and breakfast. Thats all.

RAINA. Did you get back safely that morning?

BLUNTSCHLI. Quite, thanks.

RAINA. Were they angry with you for running away from Sergius's charge?

BLUNTSCHLI (*grinning*). No: they were glad; because theyd all just run away themselves.

RAINA (*going to the table, and leaning over it towards him*). It must have made a lovely story for them: all that about me and my room.

BLUNTSCHLI. Capital story. But I only told it to one of them: a particular friend.

RAINA. On whose discretion you could absolutely rely?

BLUNTSCHLI. Absolutely.

RAINA. Hm! He told it all to my father and Sergius the day you exchanged the prisoners. (*She turns away and strolls carelessly across to the other side of the room.*)

BLUNTSCHLI (*deeply concerned, and half incredulous*). No! You dont mean that, do you?

RAINA (*turning, with sudden earnestness*). I do indeed. But they dont know that it was in this house you took refuge. If Sergius knew, he would challenge you and kill you in a duel.

BLUNTSCHLI. Bless me! then dont tell him.

RAINA. Please be serious, Captain Bluntschli. Can you not realize what it is to me to deceive him? I want to be quite perfect with Sergius: no meanness, no smallness, no deceit. My relation to him is the one really beautiful and noble part of my life. I hope you can understand that.

BLUNTSCHLI (*sceptically*). You mean that you wouldnt like him to find out that the story about the ice pudding was a—a—a—You know.

RAINA (*wincing*). Ah, dont talk of it in that flippant way. I lied: I know it. But I did it to save your life. He would have killed you. That was the second time I ever uttered a falsehood. (BLUNTSCHLI *rises quickly and looks doubtfully and somewhat severely at her.*) Do you remember the first time?

BLUNTSCHLI. I! No. Was I present?

RAINA. Yes; and I told the officer who was searching for you that you were not present.

BLUNTSCHLI. True. I should have remembered it.

RAINA (*greatly encouraged*). Ah, it is natural that you should forget it first. It cost you nothing: it cost me a lie! A lie!

(*She sits down on the ottoman, looking straight before her with her hands clasped around her knee.* BLUNTSCHLI, *quite touched, goes to the ottoman with a particularly reassuring and considerate air, and sits down beside her.*)

BLUNTSCHLI. My dear young lady, dont let this worry you. Remember: I'm a soldier. Now what are the two things that happen to a soldier so often that he comes to think nothing of them? One is hearing people tell lies (RAINA *recoils.*) the other is getting his life saved in all sorts of ways by all sorts of people.

RAINA (*rising in indignant protest*). And so he becomes a creature incapable of faith and gratitude.

BLUNTSCHLI (*making a wry face*). Do you like gratitude? I dont. If pity is akin to love, gratitude is akin to the other thing.

RAINA. Gratitude! (*Turning on him*) If you are incapable of gratitude you are incapable of any noble sentiment. Even animals are grateful. Oh, I see now exactly what you think of me! You were not surprised to hear me lie. To you it was something I probably did every day! every hour! That is how men think of women. (*She paces the room tragically.*)

BLUNTSCHLI (*dubiously*). Theres reason in everything. You said youd told only two lies in your whole life. Dear young lady: isnt that rather a short allowance? I'm quite a straightforward man myself; but it wouldnt last me a whole morning.

RAINA (*staring haughtily at him*). Do you know, sir, that you are insulting me?

BLUNTSCHLI. I cant help it. When you strike that noble attitude and speak in that thrilling voice, I admire you; but I find it impossible to believe a single word you say.

RAINA (*superbly*). Captain Bluntschli!

BLUNTSCHLI (*unmoved*). Yes?

RAINA (*standing over him, as if she could not believe her senses*). Do you mean what you said just now? Do you know what you said just now?

BLUNTSCHLI. I do.

RAINA (*gasping*). I! I!!! (*She points to herself incredulously, meaning "I,* RAINA PETKOFF *tell lies!" He meets her gaze unflinchingly. She suddenly sits down beside him, and adds, with a complete change of manner from the heroic to a babyish familiarity*) How did you find me out?

BLUNTSCHLI (*promptly*). Instinct, dear young lady. Instinct, and experience of the world.

RAINA (*wonderingly*). Do you know, you are the first man I ever met who did not take me seriously?

BLUNTSCHLI. You mean, dont you, that I am the first man that has ever taken you quite seriously?

RAINA. Yes: I suppose I do mean that. (*Cosily, quite at her ease with him*) How strange it is to be talked to in such a way! You know, Ive always gone on like that.

BLUNTSCHLI. You mean the—?

RAINA. I mean the noble attitude and the thrilling voice. (*They laugh together.*) I did it when I was a tiny child to my nurse. She believed in it. I do it before my parents. They believe in it. I do it before Sergius. He believes in it.

BLUNTSCHLI. Yes; he's a little in that line himself, isnt he?

RAINA (*startled*). Oh! Do you think so?

BLUNTSCHLI. You know him better than I do.

RAINA. I wonder—I wonder is he? If I thought that—! (*Discouraged*) Ah, well; what does it matter? I suppose, now youve found me out, you despise me.

BLUNTSCHLI (*warmly, rising*). No, my dear young lady, no, no, no a thousand times. It's part of your youth: part of your charm. I'm like all the rest of them: the nurse, your parents, Sergius: I'm your infatuated admirer.

RAINA (*pleased*). Really?

BLUNTSCHLI (*slapping his breast smartly with his hand, German fashion*). Hand aufs Herz! Really and truly.

RAINA (*very happy*). But what did you think of me for giving you my portrait?

BLUNTSCHLI (*astonished*). Your portrait! You never gave me your portrait.

RAINA (*quickly*). Do you mean to say you never got it?

BLUNTSCHLI. No. (*He sits down beside her, with renewed interest, and says, with some complacency*) When did you send it to me?

RAINA (*indignantly*). I did not send it to you. (*She turns her head away, and adds, reluctantly*) It was in the pocket of that coat.

BLUNTSCHLI (*pursing his lips and rounding his eyes*). Oh-o-oh! I never found it. It must be there still.

RAINA (*springing up*). There still! for my father to find the first time he puts his hand in his pocket! Oh, how could you be so stupid?

BLUNTSCHLI (*rising also*). It doesnt matter: I suppose it's only a photograph: how can he tell who it was intended for? Tell him he put it there himself.

RAINA (*bitterly*). Yes: that is so clever! isnt it? (*Distractedly*) Oh! what shall I do?

BLUNTSCHLI. Ah, I see. You wrote something on it. That was rash.

RAINA (*vexed almost to tears*). Oh, to have done such a thing for you, who care no more—except to laugh at me—oh! Are you sure nobody has touched it?

BLUNTSCHLI. Well, I cant be quite sure. You see, I couldnt carry it about with me all the time: one cant take much luggage on active service.

RAINA. What did you do with it?

BLUNTSCHLI. When I got through to Pirot I had to put it in safe keeping somehow. I thought of the railway cloak room; but thats the surest place to get looted in modern warfare. So I pawned it.

RAINA. Pawned it!!!

BLUNTSCHLI. I know it doesnt sound nice: but it was much the safest plan. I redeemed it the day before yesterday. Heaven only knows whether the pawnbroker cleared out the pockets or not.

RAINA (*furious: throwing the words right into his face*). You have a low shopkeeping mind. You think of things that would never come into a gentleman's head.

BLUNTSCHLI (*phlegmatically*). Thats the Swiss national character, dear lady. (*He returns to the table.*)

RAINA. Oh, I wish I had never met you. (*She flounces away, and sits at the window fuming.* LOUKA *comes in with a heap of letters and telegrams on her salver, and crosses, with her bold free gait, to the table. Her left sleeve is looped up to the shoulder with a brooch, shewing her naked arm, with a broad gilt bracelet covering the bruise.*)

LOUKA (*to* BLUNTSCHLI). For you. (*She empties the salver with a fling on to the table.*) The messenger is waiting. (*She is determined not to be civil to an enemy, even if she must bring him his letters.*)

BLUNTSCHLI (*to* RAINA). Will you excuse me: the last postal delivery that reached me was three weeks ago. These are the subsequent accumulations. Four telegrams: a week old. (*He opens one.*) Oho! Bad news!

RAINA (*rising and advancing a little remorsefully*). Bad news?

BLUNTSCHLI. My father's dead. (*He looks at the telegram with his lips*

pursed, musing on the unexpected change in his arrangements.
LOUKA *crosses herself hastily.*)

RAINA. Oh, how very sad!

BLUNTSCHLI. Yes: I shall have to start for home in an hour. He has
left a lot of big hotels behind him to be looked after. (*He takes
up a fat letter in a long blue envelope.*) Here's a whacking letter
from the family solicitor. (*He puts out the enclosures and glances
over them.*) Great Heavens! Seventy! Two hundred! (*In a cre-
scendo of dismay*) Four hundred! Four thousand!! Nine thousand six hundred!!! What on earth am I to do with them all?

RAINA (*timidly*). Nine thousand hotels?

BLUNTSCHLI. Hotels! nonsense. If you only knew! Oh, it's too ridiculous! Excuse me: I must give my fellow orders about starting. (*He
leaves the room hastily, with the documents in his hand.*)

LOUKA (*knowing instinctively that she can annoy* RAINA *by disparag-
ing* BLUNTSCHLI). He has not much heart, that Swiss. He has not
a word of grief for his poor father.

RAINA (*bitterly*). Grief! A man who has been doing nothing but killing
people for years! What does he care? What does any soldier care?
(*She goes to the door, restraining her tears with difficulty.*)

LOUKA. Major Saranoff has been fighting too; and he has plenty of
heart left. (RAINA, *at the door, draws herself up haughtily and
goes out.*) Aha! I thought you wouldnt get much feeling out of
your soldier.

(*She is following* RAINA *when* NICOLA *enters with an armful of
logs for the stove.*)

NICOLA (*grinning amorously at her*). Ive been trying all the afternoon
to get a minute alone with you, my girl. (*His countenance changes
as he notices her arm.*) Why, what fashion is that of wearing your
sleeve, child?

LOUKA (*proudly*). My own fashion.

NICOLA. Indeed! If the mistress catches you, she'll talk to you. (*He
puts the logs down, and seats himself comfortably on the ottoman.*)

LOUKA. Is that any reason why you should take it on yourself to talk
to me?

NICOLA. Come! dont be so contrary with me. Ive some good news for
you. (*She sits down beside him. He takes out some paper money.*
LOUKA, *with an eager gleam in her eyes, tries to snatch it; but he
shifts it quickly to his left hand, out of her reach.*) See! a twenty
leva bill! Sergius gave me that, out of pure swagger. A fool and
his money are soon parted. Theres ten levas more. The Swiss gave

me that for backing up the mistress' and Raina's lies about him. He's no fool, he isnt. You should have heard old Catherine downstairs as polite as you please to me, telling me not to mind the Major being a little impatient; for they knew what a good servant I was—after making a fool and a liar of me before them all! The twenty will go to our savings; and you shall have the ten to spend if youll only talk to me so as to remind me I'm a human being. I get tired of being a servant occasionally.

LOUKA. Yes: sell your manhood for 30 levas and buy me for 10! (*Rising scornfully*) Keep your money. You were born to be a servant. I was not. When you set up your shop you will only be everybody's servant instead of somebody's servant. (*She goes moodily to the table and seats herself regally in* SERGIUS'S *chair.*)

NICOLA (*picking up his logs, and going to the stove*). Ah, wait til you see. We shall have our evenings to ourselves; and I shall be master in my own house, I promise you. (*He throws the logs down and kneels at the stove.*)

LOUKA. You shall never be master in mine.

NICOLA (*turning, still on his knees, and squatting down rather forlornly on his calves, daunted by her implacable disdain*). You have a great ambition in you, Louka. Remember if any luck comes to you, it was I that made a woman of you.

LOUKA. You!

NICOLA (*scrambling up and going to her*). Yes, me. Who was it made you give up wearing a couple of pounds of false black hair on your head and reddening your lips and cheeks like any other Bulgarian girl! I did. Who taught you to trim your nails, and keep your hands clean, and be dainty about yourself, like a fine Russian lady! Me: do you hear that? me! (*She tosses her head defiantly; and he turns away, adding more coolly*) Ive often thought that if Raina were out of the way, and you just a little less of a fool and Sergius just a little more of one, you might come to be one of my grandest customers, instead of only being my wife and costing me money.

LOUKA. I believe you would rather be my servant than my husband. You would make more out of me. Oh, I know that soul of yours.

NICOLA (*going closer to her for greater emphasis*). Never you mind my soul; but just listen to my advice. If you want to be a lady, your present behavior to me wont do at all, unless when we're alone. It's too sharp and impudent; and impudence is a sort of familiarity: it shows affection for me. And dont you try being high and mighty with me, either. Youre like all country girls: you think it's genteel to treat a servant the way I treat a stableboy.

Thats only your ignorance; and dont you forget it. And dont be so ready to defy everybody. Act as if you expected to have your own way, not as if you expected to be ordered about. The way to get on as a lady is the same as the way to get on as a servant: youve got to know your place: thats the secret of it. And you may depend on me to know my place if you get promoted. Think over it, my girl. I'll stand by you: one servant should always stand by another.

LOUKA (*rising impatiently*). Oh, I must behave in my own way. You take all the courage out of me with your cold-blooded wisdom. Go and put those logs in the fire: thats the sort of thing you understand.

(*Before* NICOLA *can retort,* SERGIUS *comes in. He checks himself a moment on seeing* LOUKA; *then goes to the stove.*)

SERGIUS (*to* NICOLA). I am not in the way of your work, I hope.

NICOLA (*in a smooth, elderly manner*). Oh no, sir: thank you kindly. I was only speaking to this foolish girl about her habit of running up here to the library whenever she gets a chance, to look at the books. Thats the worst of her education, sir: it gives her habits above her station. (*To* LOUKA) Make that table tidy, Louka, for the Major. (*He goes out sedately.* LOUKA, *without looking at* SERGIUS, *pretends to arrange the papers on the table. He crosses slowly to her, and studies the arrangement of her sleeve reflectively.*)

SERGIUS. Let me see: is there a mark there? (*He turns up the bracelet and sees the bruise made by his grasp. She stands motionless, not looking at him: fascinated, but on her guard.*) Ffff! Does it hurt?

LOUKA. Yes.

SERGIUS. Shall I cure it?

LOUKA (*instantly withdrawing herself proudly, but still not looking at him*). No. You cannot cure it now.

SERGIUS (*masterfully*). Quite sure? (*He makes a movement as if to take her in his arms.*)

LOUKA. Dont trifle with me, please. An officer should not trifle with a servant.

SERGIUS (*indicating the bruise with a merciless stroke of his forefinger*). That was no trifle, Louka.

LOUKA (*flinching; then looking at him for the first time*). Are you sorry?

SERGIUS (*with measured emphasis, folding his arms*). I am never sorry.

LOUKA (*wistfully*). I wish I could believe a man could be as unlike a woman as that. I wonder are you really a brave man?

SERGIUS (*unaffectedly, relaxing his attitude*). Yes: I am a brave man. My heart jumped like a woman's at the first shot; but in the charge I found that I was brave. Yes: that at least is real about me.

LOUKA. Did you find in the charge that the men whose fathers are poor like mine were any less brave than the men who are rich like you?

SERGIUS (*with bitter levity*). Not a bit. They all slashed and cursed and yelled like heroes. Psha! the courage to rage and kill is cheap. I have an English bull terrier who has as much of that sort of courage as the whole Bulgarian nation, and the whole Russian nation at its back. But he lets my groom thrash him, all the same. Thats your soldier all over! No, Louka: your poor men can cut throats; but they are afraid of their officers; they put up with insults and blows; they stand by and see one another punished like children: aye, and help to do it when they are ordered. And the officers!!! Well (*with a short harsh laugh*), I am an officer. Oh (*fervently*), give me the man who will defy to the death any power on earth or in heaven that sets itself up against his own will and conscience: he alone is the brave man.

LOUKA. How easy it is to talk! Men never seem to me to grow up: they all have schoolboy's ideas. You dont know what true courage is.

SERGIUS (*ironically*). Indeed! I am willing to be instructed. (*He sits on the ottoman, sprawling magnificently.*)

LOUKA. Look at me! How much am I allowed to have my own will? I have to get your room ready for you: to sweep and dust, to fetch and carry. How could that degrade me if it did not degrade you to have it done for you? But (*with subdued passion*) if I were Empress of Russia, above everyone in the world, then!! Ah then, though according to you I could show no courage at all, you should see, you should see.

SERGIUS. What would you do, most noble Empress?

LOUKA. I would marry the man I loved, which no other queen in Europe has the courage to do. If I loved you, though you would be as far beneath me as I am beneath you, I would dare to be the equal of my inferior. Would you dare as much if you loved me? No: if you felt the beginnings of love for me you would not let it grow. You would not dare: you would marry a rich man's daughter because you would be afraid of what other people would say of you.

SERGIUS (*bounding up*). You lie: it is not so, by all the stars! If I loved you, and I were the Czar himself, I would set you on the

throne by my side. You know that I love another woman, a
woman as high above you as heaven is above earth. And you
are jealous of her.

LOUKA. I have no reason to be. She will never marry you now. The
man I told you of has come back. She will marry the Swiss.

SERGIUS (*recoiling*). The Swiss!

LOUKA. A man worth ten of you. Then you can come to me; and I
will refuse you. You are not good enough for me. (*She turns to
the door.*)

SERGIUS (*springing after her and catching her fiercely in his arms*).
I will kill the Swiss; and afterwards I will do as I please with you.

LOUKA (*in his arms, passive and steadfast*). The Swiss will kill you,
perhaps. He has beaten you in love. He may beat you in war.

SERGIUS (*tormentedly*). Do you think I believe that she—she! whose
worst thoughts are higher than your best ones, is capable of
trifling with another man behind my back?

LOUKA. Do you think she would believe the Swiss if he told her now
that I am in your arms?

SERGIUS (*releasing her in despair*). Damnation! Oh, damnation! Mockery! mockery everywhere! everything I think is mocked by everything I do. (*He strikes himself frantically on the breast.*) Coward! liar! fool! Shall I kill myself like a man, or live and pretend to laugh at myself? (*She again turns to go.*) Louka! (*She
stops near the door.*) Remember: you belong to me.

LOUKA (*turning*). What does that mean? An insult?

SERGIUS (*commandingly*). It means that you love me, and that I
have had you here in my arms, and will perhaps have you there
again. Whether that is an insult I neither know nor care: take
it as you please. But (*vehemently*) I will not be a coward and
a trifler. If I choose to love you, I dare marry you, in spite of
all Bulgaria. If these hands ever touch you again, they shall
touch my affianced bride.

LOUKA. We shall see whether you dare keep your word. And take care.
I will not wait long.

SERGIUS (*again folding his arms and standing motionless in the middle of the room*). Yes: we shall see. And you shall wait my pleasure. (BLUNTSCHLI, *much preoccupied, with his papers still in his
hand, enters, leaving the door open for* LOUKA *to go out. He goes
across to the table, glancing at her as he passes.* SERGIUS, *without
altering his resolute attitude, watches him steadily.* LOUKA *goes
out, leaving the door open.*)

BLUNTSCHLI (*absently, sitting at the table as before, and putting down
his papers*). Thats a remarkable looking young woman.

SERGIUS (*gravely, without moving*). Captain Bluntschli.

BLUNTSCHLI. Eh?

SERGIUS. You have deceived me. You are my rival. I brook no rivals. At six o'clock I shall be in the drilling-ground on the Klissoura road, alone, on horseback, with my sabre. Do you understand?

BLUNTSCHLI (*staring, but sitting quite at his ease*). Oh, thank you: thats a cavalry man's proposal. I'm in the artillery; and I have the choice of weapons. If I go, I shall take a machine gun. And there shall be no mistake about the cartridges this time.

SERGIUS (*flushing, but with deadly coldness*). Take care, sir. It is not our custom in Bulgaria to allow invitations of that kind to be trifled with.

BLUNTSCHLI (*warmly*). Pooh! dont talk to me about Bulgaria. You dont know what fighting is. But have it your own way. Bring your sabre along. I'll meet you.

SERGIUS (*fiercely delighted to find his opponent a man of spirit*). Well said, Switzer. Shall I lend you my best horse?

BLUNTSCHLI. No; damn your horse! thank you all the same, my dear fellow. (RAINA *comes in, and hears the next sentence.*) I shall fight you on foot. Horseback's too dangerous; I dont want to kill you if I can help it.

RAINA (*hurrying forward anxiously*). I have heard what Captain Bluntschli said, Sergius. You are going to fight. Why? (SERGIUS *turns away in silence, and goes to the stove, where he stands watching her as she continues, to* BLUNTSCHLI.) What about?

BLUNTSCHLI. I dont know: he hasnt told me. Better not interfere, dear young lady. No harm will be done: Ive often acted as sword instructor. He wont be able to touch me; and I'll not hurt him. It will save explanations. In the morning I shall be off home; and youll never see me or hear of me again. You and he will then make it up and live happily ever after.

RAINA (*turning away deeply hurt, almost with a sob in her voice*). I never said I wanted to see you again.

SERGIUS (*striding forward*). Ha! That is a confession.

RAINA (*haughtily*). What do you mean?

SERGIUS. You love that man!

RAINA (*scandalized*). Sergius!

SERGIUS. You allow him to make love to you behind my back, just as you treat me as your affianced husband behind his. Bluntschli: you knew our relations; and you deceived me. It is for that that I call you to account, not for having received favors *I* never enjoyed.

BLUNTSCHLI (*jumping up indignantly*). Stuff! Rubbish! I have received no favors. Why, the young lady doesnt even know whether I'm married or not.

RAINA (*forgetting herself*). Oh! (*Collapsing on the ottoman*) Are you?

SERGIUS. You see the young lady's concern, Captain Bluntschli. Denial is useless. You have enjoyed the privilege of being received in her own room, late at night—

BLUNTSCHLI (*interrupting him pepperily*). Yes, you blockhead! she received me with a pistol at her head. Your cavalry were at my heels. I'd have blown out her brains if she'd uttered a cry.

SERGIUS (*taken aback*). Bluntschli! Raina: is this truc?

RAINA (*rising in wrathful majesty*). Oh, how dare you, how dare you?

BLUNTSCHLI. Apologize, man: apologize. (*He resumes his seat at the table.*)

SERGIUS (*with the old measured emphasis, folding his arms*). I never apologize!

RAINA (*passionately*). This is the doing of that friend of yours, Captain Bluntschli. It is he who is spreading this horrible story about me. (*She walks about excitedly.*)

BLUNTSCHLI. No: he's dead. Burnt alive.

RAINA (*stopping, shocked*). Burnt alive!

BLUNTSCHLI. Shot in the hip in a woodyard. Couldnt drag himself out. Your fellows' shells set the timber on fire and burnt him, with half a dozen other poor devils in the same predicament.

RAINA. How horrible!

SERGIUS. And how ridiculous! Oh, war! war! the dream of patriots and heroes! A fraud, Bluntschli. A hollow sham, like love.

RAINA (*outraged*). Likc lovc! You say that before me!

BLUNTSCHLI. Come, Saranoff: that matter is explained.

SERGIUS. A hollow sham, I say. Would you have come back here if nothing had passed between you except at the muzzle of your pistol? Raina is mistaken about your friend who was burnt. He was not my informant.

RAINA. Who then? (*Suddenly guessing the truth*) Ah, Louka! my maid! my servant! You were with her this morning all that time after—after—Oh, what sort of god is this I have been worshipping! (*He meets her gaze with sardonic enjoyment of her disenchantment. Angered all the more, she goes closer to him, and says, in a lower, intenser tone*) Do you know that I looked out of the window as I went upstairs, to have another sight of my hero; and I saw something I did not understand then. I know now that you were making love to her.

SERGIUS (*with grim humor*). You saw that?

RAINA. Only too well. (*She turns away, and throws herself on the divan under the centre window, quite overcome.*)

SERGIUS (*cynically*). Raina: our romance is shattered. Life's a farce.

BLUNTSCHLI (*to* RAINA, *whimsically*). You see: he's found himself out now.

SERGIUS (*going to him*). Bluntschli: I have allowed you to call me a blockhead. You may now call me a coward as well. I refuse to fight you. Do you know why?

BLUNTSCHLI. No; but it doesn't matter. I didnt ask the reason when you cried on; and I dont ask the reason now that you cry off. I'm a professional soldier! I fight when I have to, and am very glad to get out of it when I havnt to. Youre only an amateur: you think fighting's an amusement.

SERGIUS (*sitting down at the table, nose to nose with him*). You shall hear the reason all the same, my professional. The reason is that it takes two men—real men—men of heart, blood and honor— to make a genuine combat. I could no more fight with you than I could make love to an ugly woman. Youve no magnetism: youre not a man: youre a machine.

BLUNTSCHLI (*apologetically*). Quite true, quite true. I always was that sort of chap. I'm very sorry.

SERGIUS. Psha!

BLUNTSCHLI. But now that youve found that life isnt a farce, but something quite sensible and serious, what further obstacle is there to your happiness?

RAINA (*rising*). You are very solicitous about my happiness and his. Do you forget his new love—Louka? It is not you that he must fight now, but his rival, Nicola.

SERGIUS. Rival!! (*Bounding half across the room.*)

RAINA. Dont you know that theyre engaged?

SERGIUS. Nicola! Are fresh abysses opening? Nicola!

RAINA (*sarcastically*). A shocking sacrifice, isnt it? Such beauty! such intellect! such modesty! wasted on a middle-aged servant man. Really, Sergius, you cannot stand by and allow such a thing. It would be unworthy of your chivalry.

SERGIUS (*losing all self-control*). Viper! Viper! (*He rushes to and fro, raging.*)

BLUNTSCHLI. Look here, Saranoff: youre getting the worst of this.

RAINA (*getting angrier*). Do you realize what he has done, Captain Bluntschli? He has set this girl as a spy on us; and her reward is that he makes love to her.

SERGIUS. False! Monstrous!

RAINA. Monstrous! (*Confronting him*) Do you deny that she told you about Captain Bluntschli being in my room?

SERGIUS. No; but—

RAINA (*interrupting*). Do you deny that you were making love to her when she told you?

SERGIUS. No; but I tell you—

RAINA (*cutting him short contemptuously*). It is unnecessary to tell us anything more. That is quite enough for us. (*She turns away from him and sweeps majestically back to the window.*)

BLUNTSCHLI (*quietly, as* SERGIUS, *in an agony of mortification, sinks on the ottoman, clutching his averted head between his fists*). I told you you were getting the worst of it, Saranoff.

SERGIUS. Tiger cat!

RAINA (*running excitedly to* BLUNTSCHLI). You hear this man calling me names, Captain Bluntschli?

BLUNTSCHLI. What else can he do, dear lady? He must defend himself somehow. Come (*very persuasively*): dont quarrel. What good does it do?

(RAINA, *with a gasp, sits down on the ottoman, and after a vain effort to look vexedly at* BLUNTSCHLI, *falls a victim to her sense of humor, and actually leans back babyishly against the writhing shoulder of* SERGIUS.)

SERGIUS. Engaged to Nicola! Ha! ha! Ah well, Bluntschli, you are right to take this huge imposture of a world coolly.

RAINA (*quaintly to* BLUNTSCHLI, *with an intuitive guess at his state of mind*). I daresay you think us a couple of grown-up babies, don't you?

SERGIUS (*grinning savagely*). He does: he does. Swiss civilization nurse-tending Bulgarian barbarism, eh?

BLUNTSCHLI (*blushing*). Not at all, I assure you. I'm only very glad to get you two quieted. There! there! let's be pleasant and talk it over in a friendly way. Where is this other young lady?

RAINA. Listening at the door, probably.

SERGIUS (*shivering as if a bullet had struck him, and speaking with quiet but deep indignation*). I will prove that that, at least, is a calumny. (*He goes with dignity to the door and opens it. A yell of fury bursts from him as he looks out. He darts into the passage, and returns dragging in* LOUKA, *whom he flings violently against the table, exclaiming*) Judge her, Bluntschli. You, the cool impartial man: judge the eavesdropper.

(LOUKA *stands her ground, proud and silent.*)

BLUNTSCHLI (*shaking his head*). I mustnt judge her. I once listened myself outside a tent when there was a mutiny brewing. It's all a question of the degree of provocation. My life was at stake.

LOUKA. My love was at stake. I am not ashamed.

RAINA (*contemptuously*). Your love! Your curiosity, you mean.

LOUKA (*facing her and returning her contempt with interest*). My love, stronger than anything you can feel, even for your chocolate cream soldier.

SERGIUS (*with quick suspicion, to* LOUKA). What does that mean?

LOUKA (*fiercely*). I mean—

SERGIUS (*interrupting her slightingly*). Oh, I remember: the ice pudding. A paltry taunt, girl!

(MAJOR PETKOFF *enters, in his shirtsleeves.*)

PETKOFF. Excuse my shirtsleeves, gentlemen. Raina: somebody has been wearing that coat of mine: I'll swear it. Somebody with a differently shaped back. It's all burst open at the sleeve. Your mother is mending it. I wish she'd make haste: I shall catch cold. (*He looks more attentively at them.*) Is anything the matter?

RAINA. No. (*She sits down at the stove, with a tranquil air.*)

SERGIUS. Oh no. (*He sits down at the end of the table, as at first.*)

BLUNTSCHLI (*who is already seated*). Nothing. Nothing.

PETKOFF (*sitting down on the ottoman in his old place*). Thats all right. (*He notices* LOUKA.) Anything the matter, Louka?

LOUKA. No, sir.

PETKOFF (*genially*). Thats all right. (*He sneezes*) Go and ask your mistress for my coat, like a good girl, will you?

(NICOLA *enters with the coat.* LOUKA *makes a pretense of having business in the room by taking the little table with the hookah away to the wall near the windows.*)

RAINA (*rising quickly as she sees the coat on* NICOLA'S *arm*). Here it is, papa. Give it to me, Nicola; and do you put some more wood on the fire.

(*She takes the coat, and brings it to the* MAJOR, *who stands up to put it on.* NICOLA *attends to the fire.*)

PETKOFF (*to* RAINA, *teasing her affectionately*). Aha! Going to be very good to poor old papa just for one day after his return from the wars, eh?

RAINA (*with solemn reproach*). Ah, how can you say that to me, father?

PETKOFF. Well, well, only a joke, little one. Come: give me a kiss. (*She kisses him.*) Now give me the coat.

RAINA. No: I am going to put it on for you. Turn your back. (*He turns his back and feels behind him with his arms for the sleeves. She dexterously takes the photograph from the pocket and throws it on the table before* BLUNTSCHLI, *who covers it with a sheet of paper under the very nose of* SERGIUS, *who looks on amazed, with his suspicions roused in the highest degree. She then helps* PETKOFF *on with his coat.*) There, dear! Now are you comfort‑ able?

PETKOFF. Quite, little love. Thanks. (*He sits down; and* RAINA *returns to her seat near the stove.*) Oh, by the bye, Ive found something funny. Whats the meaning of this? (*He puts his hand into the picked pocket.*) Eh? Hallo! (*He tries the other pocket.*) Well, I could have sworn—! (*Much puzzled, he tries the breast pocket.*) I wonder—(*trying the original pocket*). Where can it—? (*He rises, exclaiming*) Your mother's taken it!

RAINA (*very red*). Taken what?

PETKOFF. Your photograph, with the inscription "Raina, to her Choco‑ late Cream Soldier: a Souvenir." Now you know theres some‑ thing more in this than meets the eye; and I'm going to find it out. (*Shouting*) Nicola!

NICOLA (*coming to him*). Sir!

PETKOFF. Did you spoil any pastry of Miss Raina's this morning?

NICOLA. You heard Miss Raina say that I did, sir.

PETKOFF. I know that, you idiot. Was it true?

NICOLA. I am sure Miss Raina is incapable of saying anything that is not true, sir.

PETKOFF. Are you? Then I'm not. (*Turning to the others*) Come: do you think I dont see it all? (*He goes to* SERGIUS, *and slaps him on the shoulder.*) Sergius: youre the chocolate cream soldier, arnt you?

SERGIUS (*starting up*). I! A chocolate cream soldier! Certainly not.

PETKOFF. Not! (*He looks at them. They are all very serious and very conscious.*) Do you mean to tell me that Raina sends things like that to other men?

SERGIUS (*enigmatically*). The world is not such an innocent place as we used to think, Petkoff.

BLUNTSCHLI (*rising*). It's all right, Major. I'm the chocolate cream soldier. (PETKOFF *and* SERGIUS *are equally astonished.*) The gracious young lady saved my life by giving me chocolate creams when I was starving: shall I ever forget their flavor! My late friend Stolz told you the story of Pirot. I was the fugitive.

PETKOFF. You! (*He gasps.*) Sergius: do you remember how those two women went on this morning when we mentioned it? (SERGIUS *smiles cynically.* PETKOFF *confronts* RAINA *severely.*) Youre a nice young woman, arnt you?

RAINA (*bitterly*). Major Saranoff has changed his mind. And when I

wrote that on the photograph, I did not know that Captain
Bluntschli was married.

BLUNTSCHLI (*startled into vehement protest*). I'm not married.

RAINA (*with deep reproach*). You said you were.

BLUNTSCHLI. I did not. I positively did not. I never was married in
my life.

PETKOFF (*exasperated*). Raina: will you kindly inform me, if I am
not asking too much, which of these gentlemen you are engaged
to?

RAINA. To neither of them. This young lady (*introducing* LOUKA,
who faces them all proudly) is the object of Major Saranoff's
affections at present.

PETKOFF. Louka! Are you mad, Sergius? Why, this girl's engaged to
Nicola.

NICOLA. I beg your pardon, sir. There is a mistake. Louka is not engaged to me.

PETKOFF. Not engaged to you, you scoundrel! Why, you had twenty-
five levas from me on the day of your betrothal; and she had
that gilt bracelet from Miss Raina.

NICOLA (*with cool unction*). We gave it out so, sir. But it was only
to give Louka protection. She had a soul above her station; and
I have been no more than her confidential servant. I intend, as
you know, sir, to set up a shop later on in Sofia; and I look
forward to her custom and recommendation should she marry
into the nobility. (*He goes out with impressive discretion, leaving them all staring after him.*)

PETKOFF (*breaking the silence*). Well, I am—hm!

SERGIUS. This is either the finest heroism or the most crawling baseness. Which is it, Bluntschli?

BLUNTSCHLI. Never mind whether it's heroism or baseness. Nicola's
the ablest man Ive met in Bulgaria. I'll make him manager of a
hotel if he can speak French and German.

LOUKA (*suddenly breaking out at* SERGIUS). I have been insulted by
everyone here. You set them the example. You owe me an
apology.

(SERGIUS, *like a repeating clock of which the spring has been
touched, immediately begins to fold his arms.*)

BLUNTSCHLI (*before he can speak*). It's no use. He never apologizes.

LOUKA. Not to you, his equal and his enemy. To me his poor servant,
he will not refuse to apologize.

SERGIUS (*approvingly*). You are right. (*He bends his knee in his
grandest manner.*) Forgive me.

LOUKA. I forgive you. (*She timidly gives him her hand, which he kisses.*) That touch makes me your affianced wife.

SERGIUS (*springing up*). Ah! I forgot that.

LOUKA (*coldly*). You can withdraw if you like.

SERGIUS. Withdraw! Never! You belong to me.

(*He puts his arm about her.* CATHERINE *comes in and finds* LOUKA *in* SERGIUS'S *arms, with all the rest gazing at them in bewildered astonishment.*)

CATHERINE. What does this mean?

(SERGIUS *releases* LOUKA.)

PETKOFF. Well, my dear, it appears that Sergius is going to marry Louka instead of Raina. (*She is about to break out indignantly at him: he stops her by exclaiming testily*) Dont blame me: Ive nothing to do with it. (*He retreats to the stove.*)

CATHERINE. Marry Louka! Sergius: you are bound by your word to us!

SERGIUS (*folding his arms*). Nothing binds me.

BLUNTSCHLI (*much pleased by this piece of common sense*). Saranoff: your hand. My congratulations. These heroics of yours have their practical side after all. (*To* LOUKA) Gracious young lady: the best wishes of a good Republican! (*He kisses her hand, to* RAINA'S *great disgust, and returns to his seat.*)

CATHERINE. Louka: you have been telling stories.

LOUKA. I have done Raina no harm.

CATHERINE (*haughtily*) Raina!

(RAINA, *equally indignant, almost snorts at the liberty.*)

LOUKA. I have a right to call her Raina: she calls me Louka. I told Major Saranoff she would never marry him if the Swiss gentleman came back.

BLUNTSCHLI (*rising, much surprised*). Hallo!

LOUKA (*turning to* RAINA). I thought you were fonder of him than of Sergius. You know best whether I was right.

BLUNTSCHLI. What nonsense! I assure you, my dear Major, my dear Madame, the gracious young lady simply saved my life, nothing else. She never cared two straws for me. Why, bless my heart and soul, look at the young lady and look at me. She, rich, young, beautiful, with her imagination full of fairy princes and noble natures and cavalry charges and goodness knows what! And I, a commonplace Swiss soldier who hardly knows what a decent life is after fifteen years of barracks and battles: a vagabond, a man who has spoiled all his chances in life through an incurably romantic disposition, a man—

SERGIUS (*starting as if a needle had pricked him and interrupting* BLUNTSCHLI *in incredulous amazement*). Excuse me, Bluntschli: what did you say had spoiled your chances in life?

BLUNTSCHLI (*promptly*). An incurably romantic disposition. I ran away from home twice when I was a boy. I went into the army instead of into my father's business. I climbed the balcony of this house when a man of sense would have dived into the nearest cellar. I came sneaking back here to have another look at the young lady when any other man of my age would have sent the coat back—

PETKOFF. My coat!

BLUNTSCHLI. —yes: thats the coat I mean—would have sent it back and gone quietly home. Do you suppose I am the sort of fellow a young girl falls in love with? Why, look at our ages! I'm thirty-four: I dont suppose the young lady is much over seventeen. (*This estimate produces a marked sensation, all the rest turning and staring at one another. He proceeds innocently.*) All that adventure which was life or death to me, was only a schoolgirl's game to her—chocolate creams and hide and seek. Heres the proof! (*He takes the photograph from the table.*) Now, I ask you, would a woman who took the affair seriously have sent me this and written on it "Raina, to her Chocolate Cream Soldier: a Souvenir"? (*He exhibits the photograph triumphantly, as if it settled the matter beyond all possibility of refutation.*)

PETKOFF. Thats what I was looking for. How the deuce did it get there? (*He comes from the stove to look at it, and sits down on the ottoman.*)

BLUNTSCHLI (*to* RAINA, *complacently*). I have put everything right, I hope, gracious young lady.

RAINA (*going to the table to face him*). I quite agree with your account of yourself. You are a romantic idiot. (BLUNTSCHLI *is unspeakably taken aback.*) Next time, I hope you will know the difference between a schoolgirl of seventeen and a woman of twenty-three.

BLUNTSCHLI (*stupefied*). Twenty-three!

(RAINA *snaps the photograph contemptuously from his hand; tears it up; throws the pieces in his face; and sweeps back to her former place.*)

SERGIUS (*with grim enjoyment of his rival's discomfiture*). Bluntschli: my one last belief is gone. Your sagacity is a fraud, like everything else. You have less sense than even I!

BLUNTSCHLI (*overwhelmed*). Twenty-three! Twenty-three!! (*He con-*

siders.) Hm. (*Swiftly making up his mind and coming to his host*) In that case, Major Petkoff, I beg to propose formally to become a suitor for your daughter's hand, in place of Major Saranoff retired.

RAINA. You dare!

BLUNTSCHLI. If you were twenty-three when you said those things to me this afternoon, I shall take them seriously.

CATHERINE (*loftily polite*). I doubt, sir, whether you quite realize either my daughter's position or that of Major Sergius Saranoff, whose place you propose to take. The Petkoffs and the Saranoffs are known as the richest and most important families in the country. Our position is almost historical: we can go back for twenty years.

PETKOFF. Oh, never mind that, Catherine. (*To* BLUNTSCHLI) We should be most happy, Bluntschli, if it were only a question of your position; but hang it, you know, Raina is accustomed to a very comfortable establishment. Sergius keeps twenty horses.

BLUNTSCHLI. But who wants twenty horses? We're not going to keep a circus.

CATHERINE (*severely*). My daughter, sir, is accustomed to a first-rate stable.

RAINA. Hush, mother: youre making me ridiculous.

BLUNTSCHLI. Oh well, if it comes to a question of an establishment, here goes! (*He darts impetuously to the table; seizes the papers in the blue envelope; and turns to* SERGIUS.) How many horses did you say?

SERGIUS. Twenty, noble Switzer.

BLUNTSCHLI. I have two hundred horses. (*They are amazed.*) How many carriages?

SERGIUS. Three.

BLUNTSCHLI. I have seventy. Twenty-four of them will hold twelve inside, besides two on the box, without counting the driver and conductor. How many tablecloths have you?

SERGIUS. How the deuce do I know?

BLUNTSCHLI. Have you four thousand?

SERGIUS. No.

BLUNTSCHLI. I have. I have nine thousand six hundred pairs of sheets and blankets, with two thousand four hundred eider-down quilts. I have ten thousand knives and forks, and the same quantity of dessert spoons. I have three hundred servants. I have six palatial establishments, besides two livery stables, a tea garden, and a private house. I have four medals for distinguished services;

I have the rank of an officer and the standing of a gentleman; and I have three native languages. Show me any man in Bulgaria that can offer as much!

PETKOFF (*with childish awe*). Are you Emperor of Switzerland?

BLUNTSCHLI. My rank is the highest known in Switzerland: I am a free citizen.

CATHERINE. Then, Captain Bluntschli, since you are my daughter's choice—

RAINA (*mutinously*). He's not.

CATHERINE (*ignoring her*). —I shall not stand in the way of her happiness. (PETKOFF *is about to speak*.) That is Major Petkoff's feeling also.

PETKOFF. Oh, I shall be only too glad. Two hundred horses! Whew!

SERGIUS. What says the lady?

RAINA (*pretending to sulk*). The lady says that he can keep his tablecloths and his omnibuses. I am not here to be sold to the highest bidder. (*She turns her back on him*.)

BLUNTSCHLI. I wont take that answer. I appealed to you as a fugitive, a beggar, and a starving man. You accepted me. You gave me your hand to kiss, your bed to sleep in, and your roof to shelter me.

RAINA. I did not give them to the Emperor of Switzerland.

BLUNTSCHLI. Thats just what I say. (*He catches her by the shoulders and turns her face-to-face with him*.) Now tell us whom you did give them to.

RAINA (*succumbing with a shy smile*). To my chocolate cream soldier.

BLUNTSCHLI (*with a boyish laugh of delight*). Thatll do. Thank you. (*He looks at his watch and suddenly becomes businesslike*.) Time's up, Major. Youve managed those regiments so well that youre sure to be asked to get rid of some of the infantry of the Timok division. Send them home by way of Lom Palanka. Saranoff: dont get married until I come back: I shall be here punctually at five in the evening on Tuesday fortnight. Gracious ladies (*his heels click*) good evening. (*He makes them a military bow, and goes*.)

SERGIUS. What a man! Is he a man!

SIX CHARACTERS IN SEARCH OF
AN AUTHOR [1921]

A Comedy in the Making

by Luigi Pirandello

translated by Edward Storer

Characters of the comedy in the making

THE FATHER	MADAME PACE
THE MOTHER	THE BOY
THE STEP-DAUGHTER	THE CHILD
THE SON	(*The last two do not speak.*)

Actors of the company

THE MANAGER	OTHER ACTORS AND ACTRESSES
LEADING LADY	PROPERTY MAN
LEADING MAN	PROMPTER
SECOND LADY	MACHINIST
LEAD	MANAGER'S SECRETARY
L'INGÉNUE	DOOR-KEEPER
JUVENILE LEAD	SCENE-SHIFTERS

Daytime. The stage of a theatre.

N. B. The Comedy is without acts or scenes. The performance is interrupted once, without the curtain being lowered, when the manager and the chief characters withdraw to arrange the scenario. A second interruption of the action takes place when, by mistake, the stage hands let the curtain down.

Six Characters in Search of an Author, from Naked Masks: Five Plays by Luigi Pirandello. Copyright, 1922, 1952 by E. P. Dutton & Co., Inc. Renewal, 1950, in the names of Stefano, Fausto and Lietta Pirandello. Reprinted by permission of the publishers.

ACT ONE

The spectators will find the curtain raised and the stage as it usually is during the day time. It will be half dark, and empty, so that from the beginning the public may have the impression of an impromptu performance.

Prompter's box and a small table and chair for the manager.

Two other small tables and several chairs scattered about as during rehearsals.

The ACTORS *and* ACTRESSES *of the company enter from the back of the stage:*

first one, then another, then two together; nine or ten in all. They are about to rehearse a Pirandello play: Mixing It Up.* *Some of the company move off towards their dressing rooms. The* PROMPTER *who has the "book" under his arm, is waiting for the manager in order to begin the rehearsal.*

The ACTORS *and* ACTRESSES, *some standing, some sitting, chat and smoke. One perhaps reads a paper; another cons his part.*

Finally, the MANAGER *enters and goes to the table prepared for him. His* SECRETARY *brings him his mail, through which he glances. The* PROMPTER *takes his seat, turns on a light, and opens the "book."*

THE MANAGER (*throwing a letter down on the table*). I can't see (*To* PROPERTY MAN) Let's have a little light, please!

PROPERTY MAN. Yes sir, yes, at once. (*A light comes down onto the stage.*)

THE MANAGER (*clapping his hands*). Come along! Come along! Second act of "Mixing It Up." (*Sits down. The* ACTORS *and* ACTRESSES *go from the front of the stage to the wings, all except the three who are to begin the rehearsal.*)

THE PROMPTER (*reading the "book"*). "Leo Gala's house. A curious room serving as dining-room and study."

THE MANAGER (*to* PROPERTY MAN). Fix up the old red room.

PROPERTY MAN (*noting it down*). Red set. All right!

THE PROMPTER (*continuing to read from the "book"*). "Table already laid and writing desk with books and papers. Book-shelves. Exit rear to Leo's bedroom. Exit left to kitchen. Principal exit to right."

THE MANAGER (*energetically*). Well, you understand: The principal exit over there; here, the kitchen. (*Turning to actor who is to play the part of* SOCRATES) You make your entrances and exits here.

* I.e., *Il giuoco delle parti.*

(*To* PROPERTY MAN) The baize doors at the rear, and curtains.

PROPERTY MAN (*noting it down*). Right!

PROMPTER (*reading as before*). "When the curtain rises, Leo Gala, dressed in cook's cap and apron is busy beating an egg in a cup. Philip, also dressed as a cook, is beating another egg. Guido Venanzi is seated and listening."

LEADING MAN (*to* MANAGER). Excuse me, but must I absolutely wear a cook's cap?

THE MANAGER (*annoyed*). I imagine so. It says so there anyway (*pointing to the "book"*).

LEADING MAN. But it's ridiculous!

THE MANAGER (*jumping up in a rage*). Ridiculous? Ridiculous? Is it my fault if France won't send us any more good comedies, and we are reduced to putting on Pirandello's works, where nobody understands anything, and where the author plays the fool with us all? (*The* ACTORS *grin. The* MANAGER *goes to* LEADING MAN *and shouts.*) Yes sir, you put on the cook's cap and beat eggs. Do you suppose that with all this egg-beating business you are on an ordinary stage? Get that out of your head. You represent the shell of the eggs you are beating! (*Laughter and comments among the* ACTORS.) Silence! and listen to my explanations, please! (*To* LEADING MAN) "The empty form of reason without the fullness of instinct, which is blind."—You stand for reason, your wife is instinct. It's a mixing up of the parts, according to which you who act your own part become the puppet of yourself. Do you understand?

LEADING MAN. I'm hanged if I do.

THE MANAGER. Neither do I. But let's get on with it. It's sure to be a glorious failure anyway. (*Confidentially*) But I say, please face three-quarters. Otherwise, what with the abstruseness of the dialogue, and the public that won't be able to hear you, the whole thing will go to hell. Come on! come on!

PROMPTER. Pardon sir, may I get into my box? There's a bit of a draught.

THE MANAGER. Yes, yes, of course!

At this point, the DOOR-KEEPER *has entered from the stage door and advances towards the manager's table, taking off his braided cap. During this manoeuvre, the* SIX CHARACTERS *enter, and stop by the door at back of stage, so that when the* DOOR-KEEPER *is about to announce their coming to the* MANAGER, *they are already on the stage. A tenuous light surrounds them, almost as if irradiated by them—the faint breath of their fantastic reality.*

This light will disappear when they come forward towards the actors. They preserve, however, something of the dream lightness in which they seem almost suspended; but this does not detract from the essential reality of their forms and expressions.

He who is known as the FATHER *is a man of about 50: hair, reddish in colour, thin at the temples; he is not bald, however; thick moustaches, falling over his still fresh mouth, which often opens in an empty and uncertain smile. He is fattish, pale; with an especially wide forehead. He has blue, oval-shaped eyes, very clear and piercing. Wears light trousers and a dark jacket. He is alternatively mellifluous and violent in his manner.*

The MOTHER *seems crushed and terrified as if by an intolerable weight of shame and abasement. She is dressed in modest black and wears a thick widow's veil of crêpe. When she lifts this, she reveals a wax-like face. She always keeps her eyes downcast.*

The STEP-DAUGHTER, *is dashing, almost impudent, beautiful. She wears mourning too, but with great elegance. She shows contempt for the timid half-frightened manner of the wretched* BOY (*14 years old, and also dressed in black*); *on the other hand, she displays a lively tenderness for her little sister, the* CHILD (*about four*), *who is dressed in white, with a black silk sash at the waist.*

The SON (*22*) *tall, severe in his attitude of contempt for the* FATHER, *supercilious and indifferent to the* MOTHER. *He looks as if he had come on the stage against his will.*

DOOR-KEEPER (*cap in hand*). Excuse me, sir . . .

THE MANAGER (*rudely*). Eh? What is it?

DOOR-KEEPER (*timidly*). These people are asking for you, sir.

THE MANAGER (*furious*). I am rehearsing, and you know perfectly well no one's allowed to come in during rehearsals! (*Turning to the* CHARACTERS) Who are you, please? What do you want?

THE FATHER (*coming forward a little, followed by the others who seem embarrassed*). As a matter of fact . . . we have come here in search of an author . . .

THE MANAGER (*half angry, half amazed*). An author? What author?

THE FATHER. Any author, sir.

THE MANAGER. But there's no author here. We are not rehearsing a new piece.

THE STEP-DAUGHTER (*vivaciously*). So much the better, so much the better! We can be your new piece.

AN ACTOR (*coming forward from the others*). Oh, do you hear that?

THE FATHER (*to* STEP-DAUGHTER). Yes, but if the author isn't here . . . (*To* MANAGER) unless you would be willing . . .

THE MANAGER. You are trying to be funny.

THE FATHER. No, for Heaven's sake, what are you saying? We bring you a drama, sir.

THE STEP-DAUGHTER. We may be your fortune.

THE MANAGER. Will you oblige me by going away? We haven't time to waste with mad people.

THE FATHER (*mellifluously*). Oh sir, you know well that life is full of infinite absurdities, which, strangely enough, do not even need to appear plausible, since they are true.

THE MANAGER. What the devil is he talking about?

THE FATHER. I say that to reverse the ordinary process may well be considered a madness: that is, to create credible situations, in order that they may appear true. But permit me to observe that if this be madness, it is the sole *raison d'être* of your profession, gentlemen. (*The* ACTORS *look hurt and perplexed.*)

THE MANAGER (*getting up and looking at him*). So our profession seems to you one worthy of madmen then?

THE FATHER. Well, to make seem true that which isn't true . . . without any need . . . for a joke as it were . . . Isn't that your mission, gentlemen: to give life to fantastic characters on the stage?

THE MANAGER (*interpreting the rising anger of the* COMPANY). But I would beg you to believe, my dear sir, that the profession of the comedian is a noble one. If today, as things go, the playwrights give us stupid comedies to play and puppets to represent instead of men, remember we are proud to have given life to immortal works here on these very boards! (*The* ACTORS, *satisfied, applaud their* MANAGER.)

THE FATHER (*interrupting furiously*). Exactly, perfectly, to living beings more alive than those who breathe and wear clothes: beings less real perhaps, but truer! I agree with you entirely. (*The* ACTORS *look at one another in amazement.*)

THE MANAGER. But what do you mean? Before, you said . . .

THE FATHER. No, excuse me, I meant it for you, sir, who were crying out that you had no time to lose with madmen, while no one better than yourself knows that nature uses the instrument of human fantasy in order to pursue her high creative purpose.

THE MANAGER. Very well,—but where does all this take us?

THE FATHER. Nowhere! It is merely to show you that one is born to life in many forms, in many shapes, as tree, or as stone, as water, as butterfly, or as woman. So one may also be born a character in a play.

THE MANAGER (*with feigned comic dismay*). So you and these other friends of yours have been born characters?

THE FATHER. Exactly, and alive as you see! (MANAGER *and* ACTORS *burst out laughing.*)

THE FATHER (*hurt*). I am sorry you laugh, because we carry in us a drama, as you can guess from this woman here veiled in black.

THE MANAGER (*losing patience at last and almost indignant*). Oh, chuck it! Get away please! Clear out of here! (*To* PROPERTY MAN) For Heaven's sake, turn them out!

THE FATHER (*resisting*). No, no, look here, we . . .

THE MANAGER (*roaring*). We come here to work, you know.

LEADING ACTOR. One cannot let oneself be made such a fool of.

THE FATHER (*determined, coming forward*). I marvel at your incredulity, gentlemen. Are you not accustomed to see the characters created by an author spring to life in yourselves and face each other? Just because there is no "book" (*pointing to the* PROMPTER'S *box*) which contains us, you refuse to believe . . .

THE STEP-DAUGHTER. (*Advances towards* MANAGER, *smiling and coquettish.*) Believe me, we are really six most interesting characters, sir; side-tracked however.

THE FATHER. Yes, that is the word! (*To* MANAGER *all at once*) In the sense, that is, that the author who created us alive no longer wished, or was no longer able, materially to put us into a work of art. And this was a real crime, sir; because he who has had the luck to be born a character can laugh even at death. He cannot die. The man, the writer, the instrument of the creation will die, but his creation does not die. And to live for ever, it does not need to have extraordinary gifts or to be able to work wonders. Who was Sancho Panza? Who was Don Abbondio? Yet they live eternally because—live germs as they were—they had the fortune to find a fecundating matrix, a fantasy which could raise and nourish them: make them live for ever!

THE MANAGER. That is quite all right. But what do you want here, all of you?

THE FATHER. We want to live.

THE MANAGER (*ironically*). For Eternity?

THE FATHER. No, sir, only for a moment . . . in you.

AN ACTOR. Just listen to him!

LEADING LADY. They want to live, in us . . . !

JUVENILE LEAD (*pointing to the* STEP-DAUGHTER). I've no objection, as far as that one is concerned!

THE FATHER. Look here! look here! The comedy has to be made. (*To the* MANAGER) But if you and your actors are willing, we can soon concert it among ourselves.

THE MANAGER (*annoyed*). But what do you want to concert? We don't go in for concerts here. Here we play dramas and comedies!

THE FATHER. Exactly! That is just why we have come to you.

THE MANAGER. And where is the "book"?

THE FATHER. It is in us! (*The* ACTORS *laugh.*) The drama is in us, and we are the drama. We are impatient to play it. Our inner passion drives us on to this.

THE STEP-DAUGHTER (*disdainful, alluring, treacherous, full of impudence*). My passion, sir! Ah, if you only knew! My passion for him! (*Points to the* FATHER *and makes a pretence of embracing him. Then she breaks out into a loud laugh.*)

THE FATHER (*angrily*). Behave yourself! And please don't laugh in that fashion.

THE STEP-DAUGHTER. With your permission, gentlemen, I, who am a two months' orphan, will show you how I can dance and sing. (*Sings and then dances "Prenez garde à Tchou-Tchin-Tchou."*)
Les chinois sont un peuple malin,
De Shangaî à Pekin,
Ils ont mis des écriteaux partout:
Prenez garde à Tchou-Tchin-Tchou.

ACTORS AND ACTRESSES. Bravo! Well done! Tip-top!

THE MANAGER. Silence! This isn't a café concert, you know! (*Turning to the* FATHER *in consternation*) Is she mad?

THE FATHER. Mad? No, she's worse than mad.

THE STEP-DAUGHTER (*to* MANAGER). Worse? Worse? Listen! Stage this drama for us at once! Then you will see that at a certain moment I . . . when this little darling here . . . (*Takes the* CHILD *by the hand and leads her to the* MANAGER.) Isn't she a dear? (*Takes her up and kisses her.*) Darling! Darling! (*Puts her down again and adds feelingly*) Well, when God suddenly takes this dear little child away from that poor mother there; and this imbecile here (*seizing hold of the* BOY *roughly and pushing him forward*) does the stupidest things, like the fool he is, you will see me run away. Yes, gentlemen, I shall be off. But the moment hasn't arrived yet. After what has taken place between him and me. (*Indicates the* FATHER *with a horrible wink.*) I can't remain any longer in this society, to have to witness the anguish of this mother here for that fool . . . (*Indicates the* SON.) Look at him! Look at him! See how indifferent, how frigid he is, because he is the legitimate son. He despises me, despises him (*pointing to the* BOY), despises this baby here; because . . . we are bastards. (*Goes to the* MOTHER *and embraces her.*) And he doesn't want to recognize her as his mother—she who is the common mother of us all. He looks down upon her as if she were only the mother of us three bastards. Wretch! (*She says all this very rapidly, excitedly. At the word "bastards" she raises her voice, and almost spits out the final "Wretch!"*)

THE MOTHER (*to the* MANAGER, *in anguish*). In the name of these two little children, I beg you . . . (*She grows faint and is about to fall.*) Oh God!

THE FATHER (*coming forward to support her as do some of the* ACTORS). Quick, a chair, a chair for this poor widow!

THE ACTORS. Is it true? Has she really fainted?

THE MANAGER. Quick, a chair! Here!

(*One of the* ACTORS *brings a chair, the* OTHERS *proffer assistance. The* MOTHER *tries to prevent the* FATHER *from lifting the veil which covers her face.*)

THE FATHER. Look at her! Look at her!

THE MOTHER. No, no; stop it please!

THE FATHER (*raising her veil*). Let them see you!

THE MOTHER (*rising and covering her face with her hands, in desperation*). I beg you, sir, to prevent this man from carrying out his plan which is loathsome to me.

THE MANAGER (*dumbfounded*). I don't understand at all. What is the situation? (*To the* FATHER) Is this lady your wife?

THE FATHER. Yes, gentlemen: my wife!

THE MANAGER. But how can she be a widow if you are alive?

(*The* ACTORS *find relief for their astonishment in a loud laugh.*)

THE FATHER. Don't laugh! Don't laugh like that, for Heaven's sake. Her drama lies just here in this: she has had a lover, a man who ought to be here.

THE MOTHER (*with a cry*). No! No!

THE STEP-DAUGHTER. Fortunately for her, he is dead. Two months ago as I said. We are in mourning, as you see.

THE FATHER. He isn't here you see, not because he is dead. He isn't here—look at her a moment and you will understand—because her drama isn't a drama of the love of two men for whom she was incapable of feeling anything except possibly a little gratitude—gratitude not for me but for the other. She isn't a woman, she is a mother, and her drama—powerful sir, I assure you—lies, as a matter of fact, all in these four children she has had by two men.

THE MOTHER. I had them? Have you got the courage to say that I wanted them? (*To the* COMPANY) It was his doing. It was he who gave me that other man, who forced me to go away with him.

THE STEP-DAUGHTER. It isn't true.

THE MOTHER (*startled*). Not true, isn't it?

THE STEP-DAUGHTER. No, it isn't true, it just isn't true.

THE MOTHER. And what can you know about it?

THE STEP-DAUGHTER. It isn't true. Don't believe it. (*To* MANAGER) Do you know why she says so? For that fellow there. (*Indicates the* SON.) She tortures herself, destroys herself on account of the neglect of that son there; and she wants him to believe that if she abandoned him when he was only two years old, it was because he (*indicates the* FATHER) made her do so.

THE MOTHER (*vigorously*). He forced me to it, and I call God to witness it. (*To the* MANAGER) Ask him (*indicates* HUSBAND) if it isn't true. Let him speak. You (*to* DAUGHTER) are not in a position to know anything about it.

THE STEP-DAUGHTER. I know you lived in peace and happiness with my father while he lived. Can you deny it?

THE MOTHER. No, I don't deny it . . .

THE STEP-DAUGHTER. He was always full of affection and kindness for you. (*To the* BOY, *angrily*) It's true, isn't it? Tell them! Why don't you speak, you little fool?

THE MOTHER. Leave the poor boy alone. Why do you want to make me appear ungrateful, daughter? I don't want to offend your father. I have answered him that I didn't abandon my house and my son through any fault of mine, nor from any wilful passion.

THE FATHER. It is true. It was my doing.

LEADING MAN (*to the* COMPANY). What a spectacle!

LEADING LADY. We are the audience this time.

JUVENILE LEAD. For once, in a way.

THE MANAGER (*beginning to get really interested*). Let's hear them out. Listen!

THE SON. Oh yes, you're going to hear a fine bit now. He will talk to you of the Demon of Experiment.

THE FATHER. You are a cynical imbecile. I've told you so already a hundred times. (*To the* MANAGER) He tries to make fun of me on account of this expression which I have found to excuse myself with.

THE SON (*with disgust*). Yes, phrases! phrases!

THE FATHER. Phrases! Isn't everyone consoled when faced with a trouble or fact he doesn't understand, by a word, some simple word, which tells us nothing and yet calms us?

THE STEP-DAUGHTER. Even in the case of remorse. In fact, especially then.

THE FATHER. Remorse? No, that isn't true. I've done more than use words to quieten the remorse in me.

THE STEP-DAUGHTER. Yes, there was a bit of money too. Yes, yes, a bit of money. There were the hundred lire he was about to offer me in payment, gentlemen. . . .

(*Sensation of horror among the* ACTORS.)

THE SON (*to the* STEP-DAUGHTER). This is vile.

THE STEP-DAUGHTER. Vile? There they were in a pale blue envelope on a little mahogany table in the back of Madame Pace's shop. You know Madame Pace—one of those ladies who attract poor girls of good family into their ateliers, under the pretext of their selling *robes et manteaux.*

THE SON. And he thinks he has bought the right to tyrannize over us all with those hundred lire he was going to pay; but which, fortunately—note this, gentlemen—he had no chance of paying.

THE STEP-DAUGHTER. It was a near thing, though, you know! (*Laughs ironically.*)

THE MOTHER (*protesting*). Shame, my daughter, shame!

THE STEP-DAUGHTER. Shame indeed! This is my revenge! I am dying to live that scene . . . The room . . . I see it . . . Here is the window with the mantles exposed, there the divan, the looking-glass, a screen, there in front of the window the little mahogany table with the blue envelope containing one hundred lire. I see it. I see it. I could take hold of it . . . But you, gentlemen, you ought to turn your backs now: I am almost nude, you know. But I don't blush: I leave that to him (*indicating* FATHER).

THE MANAGER. I don't understand this at all.

THE FATHER. Naturally enough. I would ask you, sir, to exercise your authority a little here, and let me speak before you believe all she is trying to blame me with. Let me explain.

THE STEP-DAUGHTER. Ah yes, explain it in your own way.

THE FATHER. But don't you see that the whole trouble lies here. In words, words. Each one of us has within him a whole world of things, each man of us his own special world. And how can we ever come to an understanding if I put in the words I utter the sense and value of things as I see them; while you who listen to me must inevitably translate them according to the conception of things each one of you has within himself. We think we understand each other, but we never really do. Look here! This woman (*indicating the* MOTHER) takes all my pity for her as a specially ferocious form of cruelty.

THE MOTHER. But you drove me away.

THE FATHER. Do you hear her? I drove her away! She believes I really sent her away.

THE MOTHER. You know how to talk, and I don't; but, believe me, sir (*to* MANAGER), after he had married me . . . who knows why? . . . I was a poor insignificant woman . . .

THE FATHER. But, good Heavens! it was just for your humility that I married you. I loved this simplicity in you. (*He stops when he sees she makes signs to contradict him, opens his arms wide in sign of desperation, seeing how hopeless it is to make himself understood.*) You see she denies it. Her mental deafness, believe me, is phenomenal, the limit: (*touches his forehead*) deaf, deaf, mentally deaf! She has plenty of feeling. Oh yes, a good heart for the children; but the brain—deaf, to the point of desperation——!

THE STEP-DAUGHTER. Yes, but ask him how his intelligence has helped us.

THE FATHER. If we could see all the evil that may spring from good, what should we do?

(*At this point the* LEADING LADY *who is biting her lips with rage at seeing the* LEADING MAN *flirting with the* STEP-DAUGHTER, *comes forward and says to the* MANAGER)

LEADING LADY. Excuse me, but are we going to rehearse today?

MANAGER. Of course, of course; but let's hear them out.

JUVENILE LEAD. This is something quite new.

L'INGÉNUE. Most interesting!

LEADING LADY. Yes, for the people who like that kind of thing. (*Casts a glance at* LEADING MAN.)

THE MANAGER (*to* FATHER). You must please explain yourself quite clearly. (*Sits down.*)

THE FATHER. Very well then: listen! I had in my service a poor man, a clerk, a secretary of mine, full of devotion, who became friends with her (*indicating the* MOTHER). They understood one another, were kindred souls in fact, without, however, the least suspicion of any evil existing. They were incapable even of thinking of it.

THE STEP-DAUGHTER. So he thought of it—for them!

THE FATHER. That's not true. I meant to do good to them—and to myself, I confess, at the same time. Things had come to the point that I could not say a word to either of them without their making a mute appeal, one to the other, with their eyes. I could see them silently asking each other how I was to be kept in countenance, how I was to be kept quiet. And this, believe me, was just about enough of itself to keep me in a constant rage, to exasperate me beyond measure.

THE MANAGER. And why didn't you send him away then—this secretary of yours?

THE FATHER. Precisely what I did, sir. And then I had to watch this poor woman drifting forlornly about the house like an animal without a master, like an animal one has taken in out of pity.

THE MOTHER. Ah yes . . . !

THE FATHER (*suddenly turning to the* MOTHER). It's true about the son anyway, isn't it?

THE MOTHER. He took my son away from me first of all.

THE FATHER. But not from cruelty. I did it so that he should grow up healthy and strong by living in the country.

THE STEP-DAUGHTER (*pointing to him ironically*). As one can see.

THE FATHER (*quickly*). Is it my fault if he has grown up like this? I sent him to a wet nurse in the country, a peasant, as *she* did not seem to me strong enough, though she is of humble origin. That was, anyway, the reason I married her. Unpleasant all this may be, but how can it be helped? My mistake possibly, but there we are! All my life I have had these confounded aspirations towards a certain moral sanity. (*At this point the* STEP-DAUGHTER *bursts into a noisy laugh.*) Oh, stop it! Stop it! I can't stand it.

THE MANAGER. Yes, please stop it, for Heaven's sake.

THE STEP-DAUGHTER. But imagine moral sanity from him, if you please —the client of certain ateliers like that of Madame Pace!

THE FATHER. Fool! That is the proof that I am a man! This seeming contradiction, gentlemen, is the strongest proof that I stand here a live man before you. Why, it is just for this very incongruity in my nature that I have had to suffer what I have. I could not live by the side of that woman (*indicating the* MOTHER) any longer; but not so much for the boredom she inspired me with as for the pity I felt for her.

THE MOTHER. And so he turned me out—.

THE FATHER. —well provided for! Yes, I sent her to that man, gentlemen . . . to let her go free of me.

THE MOTHER. And to free himself.

THE FATHER. Yes, I admit it. It was also a liberation for me. But great evil has come of it. I meant well when I did it; and I did it more for her sake than mine. I swear it. (*Crosses his arms on his chest; then turns suddenly to the* MOTHER.) Did I ever lose sight of you until that other man carried you off to another town, like the angry fool he was? And on account of my pure interest in you . . . my pure interest, I repeat, that had no base motive in it . . . I watched with the tenderest concern the new family that grew up around her. She can bear witness to this. (*Points to the* STEP-DAUGHTER.)

THE STEP-DAUGHTER. Oh yes, that's true enough. When I was a kiddie, so so high, you know, with plaits over my shoulders and knickers longer than my skirts, I used to see him waiting outside the school for me to come out. He came to see how I was growing up.

THE FATHER. This is infamous, shameful!

THE STEP-DAUGHTER. No. Why?

THE FATHER. Infamous! infamous! (*Then excitedly to* MANAGER *explaining*) After she (*indicating* MOTHER) went away, my house seemed suddenly empty. She was my incubus, but she filled my house. I was like a dazed fly alone in the empty rooms. This boy here (*indicating the* SON) was educated away from home, and when he came back, he seemed to me to be no more mine. With no mother to stand between him and me, he grew up entirely for himself, on his own, apart, with no tie of intellect or affection binding him to me. And then—strange but true—I was driven, by curiosity at first and then by some tender sentiment, towards her family, which had come into being through my will. The thought of her began gradually to fill up the emptiness I felt all around me. I wanted to know if she were happy in living out the simple daily duties of life. I wanted to think of her as fortunate and happy because far away from the complicated torments of my spirit. And so, to have proof of this, I used to watch that child coming out of school.

THE STEP-DAUGHTER. Yes, yes. True. He used to follow me in the street and smiled at me, waved his hand, like this. I would look at him with interest, wondering who he might be. I told my mother, who guessed at once. (*The* MOTHER *agrees with a nod.*) Then she didn't want to send me to school for some days; and when I finally went back, there he was again—looking so ridiculous—with a paper parcel in his hands. He came close to me, caressed me, and drew out a fine straw hat from the parcel, with a bouquet of flowers—all for me!

THE MANAGER. A bit discursive this, you know!

THE SON (*contemptuously*). Literature! Literature!

THE FATHER. Literature indeed! This is life, this is passion!

THE MANAGER. It may be, but it won't act.

THE FATHER. I agree. This is only the part leading up. I don't suggest this should be staged. She (*pointing to the* STEP-DAUGHTER), as you see, is no longer the flapper with plaits down her back—.

THE STEP-DAUGHTER. —and the knickers showing below the skirt!

THE FATHER. The drama is coming now, sir; something new, complex, most interesting.

THE STEP-DAUGHTER. As soon as my father died . . .

THE FATHER. —there was absolute misery for them. They came back here, unknown to me. Through her stupidity! (*pointing to the* MOTHER) It is true she can barely write her own name; but she could anyhow have got her daughter to write to me that they were in need . . .

THE MOTHER. And how was I to divine all this sentiment in him?

THE FATHER. That is exactly your mistake, never to have guessed any of my sentiments.

THE MOTHER. After so many years apart, and all that had happened . . .

THE FATHER. Was it my fault if that fellow carried you away? It happened quite suddenly; for after he had obtained some job or other, I could find no trace of them; and so, not unnaturally, my interest in them dwindled. But the drama culminated unforeseen and violent on their return, when I was impelled by my miserable flesh that still lives . . . Ah! what misery, what wretchedness is that of the man who is alone and disdains debasing *liaisons*! Not old enough to do without women, and not young enough to go and look for one without shame. Misery? It's worse than misery; it's a horror; for no woman can any longer give him love; and when a man feels this . . . One ought to do without, you say? Yes, yes, I know. Each of us when he appears before his fellows is clothed in a certain dignity. But every man knows what unconfessable things pass within the secrecy of his own heart. One gives way to the temptation, only to rise from it again, afterwards, with a great eagerness to re-establish one's dignity, as if it were a tombstone to place on the grave of one's shame, and a monument to hide and sign the memory of our weaknesses. Everybody's in the same case. Some folks haven't the courage to say certain things, that's all!

THE STEP-DAUGHTER. All appear to have the courage to do them though.

THE FATHER. Yes, but in secret. Therefore, you want more courage to say these things. Let a man but speak these things out, and folks at once label him a cynic. But it isn't true. He is like all the others, better indeed, because he isn't afraid to reveal with the light of the intelligence the red shame of human bestiality on which most men close their eyes so as not to see it. Woman —for example, look at her case! She turns tantalizing inviting glances on you. You seize her. No sooner does she feel herself in your grasp than she closes her eyes. It is the sign of her mission, the sign by which she says to man: "Blind yourself, for I am blind."

THE STEP-DAUGHTER. Sometimes she can close them no more: when she no longer feels the need of hiding her shame to herself, but dry-eyed and dispassionately, sees only that of the man who has blinded himself without love. Oh, all these intellectual complications make me sick, disgust me—all this philosophy that uncovers the beast in man, and then seeks to save him, excuse him . . . I can't stand it, sir. When a man seeks to "simplify" life bestially, throwing aside every relic of humanity, every chaste aspiration, every pure feeling, all sense of ideality, duty, modesty, shame . . . then nothing is more revolting and nauseous than a certain kind of remorse—crocodiles' tears, that's what it is.

THE MANAGER. Let's come to the point. This is only discussion.

THE FATHER. Very good, sir! But a fact is like a sack which won't stand up when it is empty. In order that it may stand up, one has to put into it the reason and sentiment which have caused it to exist. I couldn't possibly know that after the death of that man, they had decided to return here, that they were in misery, and that she (*pointing to the* MOTHER) had gone to work as a modiste, and at a shop of the type of that of Madame Pace.

THE STEP-DAUGHTER. A real high-class modiste, you must know, gentlemen. In appearance, she works for the leaders of the best society; but she arranges matters so that these elegant ladies serve her purpose . . . without prejudice to other ladies who are . . . well . . . only so so.

THE MOTHER. You will believe me, gentlemen, that it never entered my mind that the old hag offered me work because she had her eye on my daughter.

THE STEP-DAUGHTER. Poor mamma! Do you know, sir, what that woman did when I brought her back the work my mother had finished? She would point out to me that I had torn one of my frocks, and she would give it back to my mother to mend. It was I who paid for it, always I; while this poor creature here believed she was sacrificing herself for me and these two children here, sitting up at night sewing Madame Pace's robes.

THE MANAGER. And one day you met there . . .

THE STEP-DAUGHTER. Him, him. Yes sir, an old client. There's a scene for you to play! Superb!

THE FATHER. She, the Mother arrived just then . . .

THE STEP-DAUGHTER (*treacherously*). Almost in time!

THE FATHER (*crying out*). No, in time! in time! Fortunately I recognized her . . . in time. And I took them back home with me to my house. You can imagine now her position and mine; she, as you see her; and I who cannot look her in the face.

THE STEP-DAUGHTER. Absurd! How can I possibly be expected—after that—to be a modest young miss, a fit person to go with his confounded aspirations for "a solid moral sanity"?

THE FATHER. For the drama lies all in this—in the conscience that I have, that each one of us has. We believe this conscience to be a single thing, but it is many-sided. There is one for this person, and another for that. Diverse consciences. So we have this illusion of being one person for all, of having a personality that is unique in all our acts. But it isn't true. We perceive this when, tragically perhaps, in something we do, we are as it were, suspended, caught up in the air on a kind of hook. Then we perceive that all of us was not in that act, and that it would be an atrocious injustice to judge us by that action alone, as if all our existence were summed up in that one deed. Now do you understand the perfidy of this girl? She surprised me in a place, where she ought not to have known me, just as I could not exist for her; and she now seeks to attach to me a reality such as I could never suppose I should have to assume for her in a shameful and fleeting moment of my life. I feel this above all else. And the drama, you will see, acquires a tremendous value from this point. Then there is the position of the others . . . his . . . (*indicating the* SON).

THE SON (*shrugging his shoulders scornfully*). Leave me alone! I don't come into this.

THE FATHER. What? You don't come into this?

THE SON. I've got nothing to do with it, and don't want to have; because you know well enough I wasn't made to be mixed up in all this with the rest of you.

THE STEP-DAUGHTER. We are only vulgar folk! He is the fine gentleman. You may have noticed, Mr. Manager, that I fix him now and again with a look of scorn while he lowers his eyes—for he knows the evil he has done me.

THE SON (*scarcely looking at her*). I?

THE STEP-DAUGHTER. You! you! I owe my life on the streets to you. Did you or did you not deny us, with your behaviour, I won't say the intimacy of home, but even that mere hospitality which makes guests feel at their ease? We were intruders who had come to disturb the kingdom of your legitimacy. I should like to have you witness, Mr. Manager, certain scenes between him and me. He says I have tyrannized over everyone. But it was just his behaviour which made me insist on the reason for which I had come into the house,—this reason he calls "vile"—into his house, with my mother who is his mother too. And I came as mistress of the house.

THE SON. It's easy for them to put me always in the wrong. But imagine, gentlemen, the position of a son, whose fate it is to see arrive one day at his home a young woman of impudent bearing, a young woman who inquires for his father, with whom who knows what business she has. This young man has then to witness her return bolder than ever, accompanied by that child there. He is obliged to watch her treat his father in an equivocal and confidential manner. She asks money of him in a way that lets one suppose he must give it her, *must,* do you understand, because he has every obligation to do so.

THE FATHER. But I have, as a matter of fact, this obligation. I owe it to your mother.

THE SON. How should I know? When had I ever seen or heard of her? One day there arrive with her (*indicating* STEP-DAUGHTER) that lad and this baby here. I am told: "This is *your* mother too, you know." I divine from her manner (*indicating* STEP-DAUGHTER *again*) why it is they have come home. I had rather not say what I feel and think about it. I shouldn't even care to confess to myself. No action can therefore be hoped for from me in this affair. Believe me, Mr. Manager, I am an "unrealized" character, dramatically speaking; and I find myself not at all at ease in their company. Leave me out of it, I beg you.

THE FATHER. What? It is just because you are so that . . .

THE SON. How do you know what I am like? When did you ever bother your head about me?

THE FATHER. I admit it. I admit it. But isn't that a situation in itself? This aloofness of yours which is so cruel to me and to your mother, who returns home and sees you almost for the first time grown up, who doesn't recognize you but knows you are her son . . . (*Pointing out the* MOTHER *to the* MANAGER) See, she's crying!

THE STEP-DAUGHTER (*angrily, stamping her foot*). Like a fool!

THE FATHER (*indicating* STEP-DAUGHTER). She can't stand him you know. (*Then referring again to the* SON) He says he doesn't come into the affair, whereas he is really the hinge of the whole action. Look at that lad who is always clinging to his mother, frightened and humiliated. It is on account of this fellow here. Possibly his situation is the most painful of all. He feels himself a stranger more than the others. The poor little chap feels mortified, humiliated at being brought into a home out of charity as it were. (*In confidence*) He is the image of his father. Hardly talks at all. Humble and quiet.

THE MANAGER. Oh, we'll cut him out. You've no notion what a nuisance boys are on the stage . . .

THE FATHER. He disappears soon, you know. And the baby too. She is the first to vanish from the scene. The drama consists finally in this: when that mother re-enters my house, her family born outside of it, and shall we say superimposed on the original, ends with the death of the little girl, the tragedy of the boy and the flight of the elder daughter. It cannot go on, because it is foreign to its surroundings. So after much torment, we three remain: I, the mother, that son. Then, owing to the disappearance of that extraneous family, we too find ourselves strange to one another. We find we are living in an atmosphere of mortal desolation which is the revenge, as he (*indicating* SON) scornfully said of the Demon of Experiment, that unfortunately hides in me. Thus, sir, you see when faith is lacking, it becomes impossible to create certain states of happiness, for we lack the necessary humility. Vaingloriously, we try to substitute ourselves for this faith, creating thus for the rest of the world a reality which we believe after their fashion, while, actually, it doesn't exist. For each one of us has his own reality to be respected before God, even when it is harmful to one's very self.

THE MANAGER. There is something in what you say. I assure you all this interests me very much. I begin to think there's the stuff for a drama in all this, and not a bad drama either.

THE STEP-DAUGHTER (*coming forward*). When you've got a character like me.

THE FATHER (*shutting her up, all excited to learn the decision of the* MANAGER). You be quiet!

THE MANAGER (*reflecting, heedless of interruption*). It's new . . . hem . . . yes . . .

THE FATHER. Absolutely new!

THE MANAGER. You've got a nerve though, I must say, to come here and fling it at me like this . . .

THE FATHER. You will understand, sir, born as we are for the stage . . .

THE MANAGER. Are you amateur actors then?

THE FATHER. No. I say born for the stage, because . . .

THE MANAGER. Oh, nonsense. You're an old hand, you know.

THE FATHER. No, sir, no. We act that rôle for which we have been cast, that rôle which we are given in life. And in my own case, passion itself, as usually happens, becomes a trifle theatrical when it is exalted.

THE MANAGER. Well, well, that will do. But you see, without an author . . . I could give you the address of an author if you like . . .

THE FATHER. No, no. Look here! You must be the author.

THE MANAGER. I? What are you talking about?

THE FATHER. Yes, you, you! Why not?

THE MANAGER. Because I have never been an author: that's why.

THE FATHER. Then why not turn author now? Everybody does it. You don't want any special qualities. Your task is made much easier by the fact that we are all here alive before you . . .

THE MANAGER. It won't do.

THE FATHER. What? When you see us live our drama . . .

THE MANAGER. Yes, that's all right. But you want someone to write it.

THE FATHER. No, no. Someone to take it down, possibly, while we play it, scene by scene! It will be enough to sketch it out at first, and then try it over.

THE MANAGER. Well . . . I am almost tempted. It's a bit of an idea. One might have a shot at it.

THE FATHER. Of course. You'll see what scenes will come out of it. I can give you one, at once . . .

THE MANAGER. By Jove, it tempts me. I'd like to have a go at it. Let's try it out. Come with me to my office. (*Turning to the* ACTORS) You are at liberty for a bit, but don't step out of the theatre for long. In a quarter of an hour, twenty minutes, all back here again! (*To the* FATHER) We'll see what can be done. Who knows if we don't get something really extraordinary out of it?

THE FATHER. There's no doubt about it. They (*indicating the* CHARACTERS) had better come with us too, hadn't they?

THE MANAGER. Yes, yes. Come on! come on! (*Moves away and then turning to the* ACTORS) *Be punctual, please!*

(MANAGER *and the* SIX CHARACTERS *cross the stage and go off. The other* ACTORS *remain, looking at one another in astonishment.*)

LEADING MAN. Is he serious? What the devil does he want to do?

JUVENILE LEAD. This is rank madness.

THIRD ACTOR. Does he expect to knock up a drama in five minutes?

JUVENILE LEAD. Like the improvisers!

LEADING LADY. If he thinks I'm going to take part in a joke like this . . .

JUVENILE LEAD. I'm out of it anyway.

FOURTH ACTOR. I should like to know who they are. (*Alludes to* CHARACTERS.)

THIRD ACTOR. What do you suppose? Madmen or rascals!

JUVENILE LEAD. And he takes them seriously!

L'INGÉNUE. Vanity! He fancies himself as an author now.

LEADING MAN. It's absolutely unheard of. If the stage has come to this
. . . well I'm . . .

FIFTH ACTOR. It's rather a joke.

THIRD ACTOR. Well, we'll see what's going to happen next.

(*Thus talking, the* ACTORS *leave the stage; some going out by the
little door at the back; others retiring to their dressing-rooms.*)

*The curtain remains up. The action of the play is suspended for
twenty minutes.*

ACT TWO

*The stage call-bells ring to warn the company that the play is
about to begin again.*

THE STEP-DAUGHTER. (*Comes out of the* MANAGER'S *office along with
the* CHILD *and the* BOY. *As she comes out of the office, she cries*)
Nonsense! nonsense! Do it yourselves! I'm not going to mix myself up in this mess. (*Turning to the* CHILD *and coming quickly
with her on to the stage.*) Come on, Rosetta, let's run!
(*The* BOY *follows them slowly, remaining a little behind and seeming perplexed.*)

THE STEP-DAUGHTER. (*Stops, bends over the* CHILD *and takes the latter's
face between her hands.*) My little darling! You're frightened,
aren't you? You don't know where we are, do you? (*Pretending to
reply to a question of the* CHILD) What is the stage? It's a place,
baby, you know, where people play at being serious, a place where
they act comedies. We've got to act a comedy now, dead serious,
you know; and you're in it also, little one. (*Embraces her, pressing
the little head to her breast, and rocking the* CHILD *for a moment.*)
Oh darling, darling, what a horrid comedy you've got to play!
What a wretched part they've found for you! A garden . . . a
fountain . . . look . . . just suppose, kiddie, it's here. Where,
you say? Why, right here in the middle. It's all pretence you
know. That's the trouble, my pet: it's all make-believe here. It's
better to imagine it though, because if they fix it up for you, it'll
only be painted cardboard, painted cardboard for the rockery,
the water, the plants . . . Ah, but I think a baby like this one

would sooner have a make-believe fountain than a real one, so she could play with it. What a joke it'll be for the others! But for you, alas! not quite such a joke: you who are real, baby dear, and really play by a real fountain that is big and green and beautiful, with ever so many bamboos around it that are reflected in the water, and a whole lot of little ducks swimming about . . . No, Rosetta, no, your mother doesn't bother about you on account of that wretch of a son there. I'm in the devil of a temper, and as for that lad . . . (*Seizes* BOY *by the arm to force him to take one of his hands out of his pockets.*) What have you got there? What are you hiding? (*Pulls his hand out of his pocket, looks into it and catches the glint of a revolver.*) Ah! where did you get this? (*The* BOY, *very pale in the face, looks at her, but does not answer.*) Idiot! If I'd been in your place, instead of killing myself, I'd have shot one of those two, or both of them: father and son. (*The* FATHER *enters from the office, all excited from his work. The* MANAGER *follows him.*)

THE FATHER. Come on, come on dear! Come here for a minute! We've arranged everything. It's all fixed up.

THE MANAGER (*also excited*). If you please, young lady, there are one or two points to settle still. Will you come along?

THE STEP-DAUGHTER (*following him towards the office*). Ouff! what's the good, if you've arranged everything.

(*The* FATHER, MANAGER *and* STEP-DAUGHTER *go back into the office again [off] for a moment. At the same time, the* SON *followed by the* MOTHER, *comes out.*)

THE SON (*looking at the three entering office*). Oh this is fine, fine! And to think I can't even get away!

(*The* MOTHER *attempts to look at him, but lowers her eyes immediately when he turns away from her. She then sits down. The* BOY *and the* CHILD *approach her. She casts a glance again at the* SON, *and speaks with humble tones, trying to draw him into conversation.*)

THE MOTHER. And isn't my punishment the worst of all? (*Then seeing from the* SON'S *manner that he will not bother himself about her*) My God! Why are you so cruel? Isn't it enough for one person to support all this torment? Must you then insist on others seeing it also?

THE SON (*half to himself, meaning the* MOTHER *to hear, however*). And they want to put it on the stage! If there was at least a reason for it! He thinks he has got at the meaning of it all. Just as if each one of us in every circumstance of life couldn't find his own explanation of it! (*Pauses.*) He complains he was discovered in a place where he ought not to have been seen, in a moment of his life which ought to have remained hidden and kept out of the reach of that convention which he has to maintain for other people. And what about my case? Haven't I had to reveal what no son ought ever to reveal: how father and mother live and are man and wife for themselves quite apart from that idea of father and mother which we give them? When this idea is revealed, our life is then linked at one point only to that man and that woman; and as such it should shame them, shouldn't it?

(*The* MOTHER *hides her face in her hands. From the dressing-rooms and the little door at the back of the stage the* ACTORS *and* STAGE MANAGER *return, followed by the* PROPERTY MAN, *and the* PROMPTER. *At the same moment, the* MANAGER *comes out of his office, accompanied by the* FATHER *and the* STEP-DAUGHTER.)

THE MANAGER. Come on, come on, ladies and gentlemen! Heh! you there, machinist!

MACHINIST. Yes sir?

THE MANAGER. Fix up the white parlor with the floral decorations. Two wings and a drop with a door will do. Hurry up!

(*The* MACHINIST *runs off at once to prepare the scene, and arranges it while the* MANAGER *talks with the* STAGE MANAGER, *the* PROPERTY MAN, *and the* PROMPTER *on matters of detail.*)

THE MANAGER (*to* PROPERTY MAN). Just have a look, and see if there isn't a sofa or divan in the wardrobe . . .

PROPERTY MAN. There's the green one.

THE STEP-DAUGHTER. No no! Green won't do. It was yellow, ornamented with flowers—very large! and most comfortable!

PROPERTY MAN. There isn't one like that.

THE MANAGER. It doesn't matter. Use the one we've got.

THE STEP-DAUGHTER. Doesn't matter? It's most important!

THE MANAGER. We're only trying it now. Please don't interfere. (*To* PROPERTY MAN) See if we've got a shop window—long and narrowish.

THE STEP-DAUGHTER. And the little table! The little mahogany table for the pale blue envelope!

PROPERTY MAN (*to* MANAGER). There's that little gilt one.

THE MANAGER. That'll do fine.

THE FATHER. A mirror.

THE STEP-DAUGHTER. And the screen! We must have a screen. Otherwise how can I manage?

PROPERTY MAN. That's all right, Miss. We've got any amount of them.

THE MANAGER (*to the* STEP-DAUGHTER). We want some clothes pegs too, don't we?

THE STEP-DAUGHTER. Yes, several, several!

THE MANAGER. See how many we've got and bring them all.

PROPERTY MAN. All right!

(*The* PROPERTY MAN *hurries off to obey his orders. While he is putting the things in their places, the* MANAGER *talks to the* PROMPTER *and then with the* CHARACTERS *and the* ACTORS.)

THE MANAGER (*to* PROMPTER). Take your seat. Look here: this is the outline of the scenes, act by act. (*Hands him some sheets of paper.*) And now I'm going to ask you to do something out of the ordinary.

PROMPTER. Take it down in shorthand?

THE MANAGER (*pleasantly surprised*). Exactly! Can you do shorthand?

PROMPTER. Yes, a little.

THE MANAGER. Good! (*Turning to a* STAGE HAND) Go and get some paper from my office, plenty, as much as you can find.

(*The* STAGE HAND *goes off, and soon returns with a handful of paper which he gives to the* PROMPTER.)

THE MANAGER (*to* PROMPTER). You follow the scenes as we play them, and try and get the points down, at any rate the most important ones. (*Then addressing the* ACTORS) Clear the stage, ladies and gentlemen! Come over here (*pointing to the left*) and listen attentively.

LEADING LADY. But, excuse me, we . . .

THE MANAGER (*guessing her thought*). Don't worry! You won't have to improvise.

LEADING MAN. What have we to do then?

THE MANAGER. Nothing. For the moment you just watch and listen. Everybody will get his part written out afterwards. At present we're going to try the thing as best we can. They're going to act now.

THE FATHER (*as if fallen from the clouds into the confusion of the stage*). We? What do you mean, if you please, by a rehearsal?

THE MANAGER. A rehearsal for them. (*Points to the* ACTORS.)

THE FATHER. But since we are the characters . . .

THE MANAGER. All right: "characters" then, if you insist on calling yourselves such. But here, my dear sir, the characters don't act. Here the actors do the acting. The characters are there, in the "book" (*pointing towards* PROMPTER'S *box*)—when there is a "book"!

THE FATHER. I won't contradict you; but excuse me, the actors aren't the characters. They want to be, they pretend to be, don't they? Now if these gentlemen here are fortunate enough to have us alive before them . . .

THE MANAGER. Oh this is grand! You want to come before the public yourselves then?

THE FATHER. As we are . . .

THE MANAGER. I can assure you it would be a magnificent spectacle!

LEADING MAN. What's the use of us here anyway then?

THE MANAGER. You're not going to pretend that you can act? It makes me laugh! (*The* ACTORS *laugh.*) There, you see, they are laughing at the notion. But, by the way, I must cast the parts. That won't be difficult. They cast themselves. (*To the* SECOND LADY LEAD) You play the Mother. (*To the* FATHER) We must find her a name.

THE FATHER. Amalia, sir.

THE MANAGER. But that is the real name of your wife. We don't want to call her by her real name.

THE FATHER. Why ever not, if it is her name? . . . Still, perhaps, if that lady must . . . (*Makes a slight motion of the hand to indicate the* SECOND LADY LEAD.) I see this woman here (*means the* MOTHER) as Amalia. But do as you like. (*Gets more and more confused.*) I don't know what to say to you. Already, I begin to hear my own words ring false, as if they had another sound . . .

THE MANAGER. Don't you worry about it. It'll be our job to find the right tones. And as for her name, if you want her Amalia, Amalia it shall be; and if you don't like it, we'll find another! For the moment though, we'll call the characters in this way: (*To* JUVENILE LEAD) You are the Son. (*To the* LEADING LADY) You naturally are the Step-Daughter . . .

THE STEP-DAUGHTER (*excitedly*). What? what? I, that woman there? (*Bursts out laughing.*)

THE MANAGER (*angry*). What is there to laugh at?

LEADING LADY (*indignant*). Nobody has ever dared to laugh at me. I insist on being treated with respect; otherwise I go away.

THE STEP-DAUGHTER. No, no, excuse me . . . I am not laughing at you . . .

THE MANAGER (*to* STEP-DAUGHTER). You ought to feel honored to be played by . . .

LEADING LADY (*at once, contemptuously*). "That woman there" . . .

THE STEP-DAUGHTER. But I wasn't speaking of you, you know. I was speaking of myself—whom I can't see at all in you! That is all. I don't know . . . but . . . you . . . aren't in the least like me . . .

THE FATHER. True. Here's the point. Look here, sir, our temperaments, our souls . . .

THE MANAGER. Temperament, soul, be hanged! Do you suppose the spirit of the piece is in you? Nothing of the kind!

THE FATHER. What, haven't we our own temperaments, our own souls?

THE MANAGER. Not at all. Your soul or whatever you like to call it takes shape here. The actors give body and form to it, voice and gesture. And my actors—I may tell you—have given expression to much more lofty material than this little drama of yours, which may or may not hold up on the stage. But if it does, the merit of it, believe me, will be due to my actors.

THE FATHER. I don't dare contradict you, sir; but, believe me, it is a terrible suffering for us who are as we are, with these bodies of ours, these features to see . . .

THE MANAGER (*cutting him short and out of patience*). Good heavens! The make-up will remedy all that, man, the make-up . . .

THE FATHER. Maybe. But the voice, the gestures . . .

THE MANAGER. Now, look here! On the stage, you as yourself, cannot exist. The actor here acts you, and that's an end to it!

THE FATHER. I understand. And now I think I see why our author who conceived us as we are, all alive, didn't want to put us on the stage after all. I haven't the least desire to offend your actors. Far from it! But when I think that I am to be acted by . . . I don't know by whom . . .

LEADING MAN (*on his dignity*). By me, if you've no objection!

THE FATHER (*humbly, mellifluously*). Honored, I assure you, sir. (*Bows.*) Still, I must say that try as this gentleman may, with all his good will and wonderful art, to absorb me into himself . . .

LEADING MAN. Oh chuck it! "Wonderful art!" Withdraw that, please!

THE FATHER. The performance he will give, even doing his best with make-up to look like me . . .

LEADING MAN. It will certainly be a bit difficult! (*The* ACTORS *laugh.*)

THE FATHER. Exactly! It will be difficult to act me as I really am. The effect will be rather—apart from the make-up—according as to how he supposes I am, as he senses me—if he does sense me—and not as I inside of myself feel myself to be. It seems to me then that account should be taken of this by everyone whose duty it may become to criticize us . . .

THE MANAGER. Heavens! The man's starting to think about the critics now! Let them say what they like. It's up to us to put on the play if we can. (*Looking around*) Come on! come on! Is the stage set? (*To the* ACTORS *and* CHARACTERS) Stand back—stand back! Let me see, and don't let's lose any more time! (*To the* STEP-DAUGHTER) Is it all right as it is now?

THE STEP-DAUGHTER. Well, to tell the truth, I don't recognize the scene.

THE MANAGER. My dear lady, you can't possibly suppose that we can construct that shop of Madame Pace piece by piece here? (*To the*

FATHER) You said a white room with flowered wall paper, didn't you?

THE FATHER. Yes.

THE MANAGER. Well then. We've got the furniture right more or less. Bring that little table a bit further forward. (*The* STAGE HANDS *obey the order. To* PROPERTY MAN) You go and find an envelope, if possible, a pale blue one; and give it to that gentleman. (*Indicates* FATHER.)

PROPERTY MAN. An ordinary envelope?

MANAGER AND FATHER. Yes, yes, an ordinary envelope.

PROPERTY MAN. At once, sir. (*Exit.*)

THE MANAGER. Ready, everyone! First scene—the Young Lady. (*The* LEADING LADY *comes forward.*) No, no, you must wait. I meant her (*indicating the* STEP-DAUGHTER). You just watch—

THE STEP-DAUGHTER (*adding at once*). How I shall play it, how I shall live it! . . .

LEADING LADY (*offended*). I shall live it also, you may be sure, as soon as I begin!

THE MANAGER (*with his hands to his head*). Ladies and gentlemen, if you please! No more useless discussions! Scene I: the young lady with Madame Pace: Oh! (*Looks around as if lost.*) And this Madame Pace, where is she?

THE FATHER. She isn't with us, sir.

THE MANAGER. Then what the devil's to be done?

THE FATHER. But she is alive too.

THE MANAGER. Yes, but where is she?

THE FATHER. One minute. Let me speak! (*Turning to the* ACTRESSES) If these ladies would be so good as to give me their hats for a moment . . .

THE ACTRESSES (*half surprised, half laughing, in chorus*). What?
Why?
Our hats?
What does he say?

THE MANAGER. What are you going to do with the ladies' hats? (*The* ACTORS *laugh.*)

THE FATHER. Oh nothing. I just want to put them on these pegs for a moment. And one of the ladies will be so kind as to take off her mantle . . .

THE ACTORS. Oh, what d'you think of that?
Only the mantle?
He must be mad.

SOME ACTRESSES. But why?
Mantles as well?

THE FATHER. To hang them up here for a moment. Please be so kind, will you?

THE ACTRESSES (*taking off their hats, one or two also their cloaks, and going to hang them on the racks*). After all, why not?

There you are!

This is really funny.

We've got to put them on show.

THE FATHER. Exactly; just like that, on show.

THE MANAGER. May we know why?

THE FATHER. I'll tell you. Who knows if, by arranging the stage for her, she does not come here herself, attracted by the very articles of her trade? (*Inviting the* ACTORS *to look towards the exit at back of stage*) Look! Look!

(*The door at the back of stage opens and* MADAME PACE *enters and takes a few steps forward. She is a fat, oldish woman with puffy oxygenated hair. She is rouged and powdered, dressed with a comical elegance in black silk. Round her waist is a long silver chain from which hangs a pair of scissors. The* STEP-DAUGHTER *runs over to her at once amid the stupor of the actors.*)

THE STEP-DAUGHTER (*turning towards her*). There she is! There she is!

THE FATHER (*radiant*). It's she! I said so, didn't I? There she is!

THE MANAGER (*conquering his surprise, and then becoming indignant*). What sort of a trick is this?

LEADING MAN (*almost at the same time*). What's going to happen next?

JUVENILE LEAD. Where does *she* come from?

L'INGÉNUE. They've been holding her in reserve, I guess.

LEADING LADY. A vulgar trick!

THE FATHER (*dominating the protests*). Excuse me, all of you! Why are you so anxious to destroy in the name of a vulgar, common-place sense of truth, this reality which comes to birth attracted and formed by the magic of the stage itself, which has indeed more right to live here than you, since it is much truer than you you who is to play Madame Pace? Well, here is Madame Pace —if you don't mind my saying so? Which is the actress among herself. And you will allow, I fancy, that the actress who acts her will be less true than this woman here, who is herself in person. You see my daughter recognized her and went over to her at once. Now you're going to witness the scene!

(*But the scene between the* STEP-DAUGHTER *and* MADAME PACE *has already begun despite the protest of the actors and the reply of the* FATHER. *It has begun quietly, naturally, in a manner impossible for the stage. So when the actors, called to attention by the* FATHER, *turn round and see* MADAME PACE, *who has placed*

one hand under the STEP-DAUGHTER'S *chin to raise her head, they*
observe her at first with great attention, but hearing her speak in
an unintelligible manner their interest begins to wane.)

THE MANAGER. Well? well?

LEADING MAN. What does she say?

LEADING LADY. One can't hear a word.

JUVENILE LEAD. Louder! Louder please!

THE STEP-DAUGHTER (*leaving* MADAME PACE, *who smiles a Sphinx-like*
smile, and advancing towards the actors). Louder? Louder? What
are you talking about? These aren't matters which can be shouted
at the top of one's voice. If I have spoken them out loud, it was
to shame him and have my revenge. (*Indicates* FATHER) But for
Madame it's quite a different matter.

THE MANAGER. Indeed? Indeed? But here, you know, people have got
to make themselves heard, my dear. Even we who are on the
stage can't hear you. What will it be when the public's in the
theatre? And anyway, you can very well speak up now among
yourselves, since we shan't be present to listen to you as we are
now. You've got to pretend to be alone in a room at the back
of a shop where no one can hear you.

(*The* STEP-DAUGHTER *coquettishly and with a touch of malice*
makes a sign of disagreement two or three times with her finger.)

THE MANAGER. What do you mean by no?

THE STEP-DAUGHTER (*sotto voce, mysteriously*). There's someone who
will hear us if she (*indicating* MADAME PACE) speaks out loud.

THE MANAGER (*in consternation*). What? Have you got someone else
to spring on us now? (*The* ACTORS *burst out laughing.*)

THE FATHER. No, no sir. She is alluding to me. I've got to be here—
there behind that door, in waiting; and Madame Pace knows it.
In fact, if you will allow me, I'll go there at once, so I can be
quite ready. (*Moves away.*)

THE MANAGER (*stopping him*). No! Wait! wait! We must observe the
conventions of the theatre. Before you are ready . . .

THE STEP-DAUGHTER (*interrupting him*). No, get on with it at once!
I'm just dying, I tell you, to act this scene. If he's ready, I'm more
than ready.

THE MANAGER (*shouting*). But, my dear young lady, first of all, we
must have the scene between you and this lady . . . (*Indicates*
MADAME PACE.) Do you understand? . . .

THE STEP-DAUGHTER. Good Heavens! She's been telling me what you
know already: that mamma's work is badly done again, that the
material's ruined; and that if I want her to continue to help us
in our misery I must be patient . . .

MADAME PACE (*coming forward with an air of great importance*). Yes indeed, sir, I no wanta take advantage of her, I no wanta be hard . . . (*Note:* MADAME PACE *is supposed to talk in a jargon half Italian, half English.*)

THE MANAGER (*alarmed*). What? What? She talks like that?

(*The* ACTORS *burst out laughing again.*)

THE STEP-DAUGHTER (*also laughing*). Yes yes, that's the way she talks, half English, half Italian! Most comical it is!

MADAME PACE. Itta seem not verra polite gentlemen laugha atta me eef I trya best speaka English.

THE MANAGER. *Diamine!* Of course! Of course! Let her talk like that! Just what we want. Talk just like that, Madame, if you please! The effect will be certain. Exactly what was wanted to put a little comic relief into the crudity of the situation. Of course she talks like that! Magnificent!

THE STEP-DAUGHTER. Magnificent? Certainly! When certain suggestions are made to one in language of that kind, the effect is certain, since it seems almost a joke. One feels inclined to laugh when one hears her talk about an "old signore" "who wanta talka nicely with you." Nice old signore, eh, Madame?

MADAME PACE. Not so old my dear, not so old! And even if you no lika him, he won't make any scandal!

THE MOTHER (*jumping up amid the amazement and consternation of the actors who had not been noticing her. They move to restrain her.*) You old devil! You murderess!

THE STEP-DAUGHTER (*running over to calm her* MOTHER). Calm yourself, Mother, calm yourself! Please don't . . .

THE FATHER (*going to her also at the same time*). Calm yourself! Don't get excited! Sit down now!

THE MOTHER. Well then, take that woman away out of my sight!

THE STEP-DAUGHTER (*to* MANAGER). It is impossible for my mother to remain here.

THE FATHER (*to* MANAGER). They can't be here together. And for this reason, you see: that woman there was not with us when we came . . . If they are on together, the whole thing is given away inevitably, as you see.

THE MANAGER. It doesn't matter. This is only a first rough sketch—just to get an idea of the various points of the scene, even confusedly . . . (*Turning to the* MOTHER *and leading her to her chair*) Come along, my dear lady, sit down now, and let's get on with the scene . . .

(*Meanwhile, the* STEP-DAUGHTER, *coming forward again, turns to* MADAME PACE.)

THE STEP-DAUGHTER. Come on, Madame, come on!

MADAME PACE (*offended*). No, no, *grazie*. I not do anything witha your mother present.

THE STEP-DAUGHTER. Nonsense! Introduce this "old signore" who wants to talk nicely to me. (*Addressing the* COMPANY *imperiously*) We've got to do this scene one way or another, haven't we? Come on! (*To* MADAME PACE) You can go!

MADAME PACE. Ah yes! I go'way! I go'way! Certainly! (*Exits furious.*)

THE STEP-DAUGHTER (*to the* FATHER). Now you make your entry. No, you needn't go over here. Come here. Let's suppose you've already come in. Like that, yes! I'm here with bowed head, modest like. Come on! Out with your voice! Say "Good morning, Miss" in that peculiar tone, that special tone . . .

THE MANAGER. Excuse me, but are you the Manager, or am I? (*To the* FATHER, *who looks undecided and perplexed*) Get on with it, man! Go down there to the back of the stage. You needn't go off. Then come right forward here.

(*The* FATHER *does as he is told, looking troubled and perplexed at first. But as soon as he begins to move, the reality of the action affects him, and he begins to smile and to be more natural. The* ACTORS *watch intently.*)

THE MANAGER (*sotto voce, quickly to the* PROMPTER *in his box*). Ready! ready? Get ready to write now.

THE FATHER (*coming forward and speaking in a different tone*). Good afternoon, Miss!

THE STEP-DAUGHTER (*head bowed down slightly, with restrained disgust*). Good afternoon!

THE FATHER. (*Looks under her hat which partly covers her face. Perceiving she is very young, he makes an exclamation, partly of surprise, partly of fear lest he compromise himself in a risky adventure.*) Ah . . . but . . . ah . . . I say . . . this is not the first time you have come here is it?

THE STEP-DAUGHTER (*modestly*). No sir.

THE FATHER. You've been here before, eh? (*Then seeing her nod agreement*) More than once? (*Waits for her to answer, looks under her hat, smiles, and then says.*) Well then, there's no need to be so shy, is there? May I take off your hat?

THE STEP-DAUGHTER (*anticipating him and with veiled disgust*). No sir . . . I'll do it myself. (*Takes it off quickly.*)

(*The* MOTHER, *who watches the progress of the scene with the* SON *and the other two children who cling to her, is on thorns; and follows with varying expressions of sorrow, indignation, anx-*

iety, and horror the words and actions of the other two. From time to time she hides her face in her hands and sobs.)

THE MOTHER. Oh, my God, my God!

THE FATHER (*playing his part with a touch of gallantry*). Give it to me! I'll put it down. (*Takes hat from her hands.*) But a dear little head like yours ought to have a smarter hat. Come and help me choose one from the stock, won't you?

L'INGÉNUE (*interrupting*). I say . . . those are our hats you know.

THE MANAGER (*furious*). Silence! silence! Don't try and be funny, if you please . . . We're playing the scene now I'd have you notice. (*To the* STEP-DAUGHTER) Begin again, please!

THE STEP-DAUGHTER (*continuing*). No thank you, sir.

THE FATHER. Oh, come now. Don't talk like that. You must take it. I shall be upset if you don't. There are some lovely little hats here; and then—Madame will be pleased. She expects it, anyway, you know.

THE STEP-DAUGHTER. No, no! I couldn't wear it!

THE FATHER. Oh, you're thinking about what they'd say at home if they saw you come in with a new hat? My dear girl, there's always a way round these little matters, you know.

THE STEP-DAUGHTER (*all keyed up*). No, it's not that. I couldn't wear it because I am . . . as you see . . . you might have noticed . . . (*showing her black dress*).

THE FATHER. . . . in mourning! Of course: I beg your pardon: I'm frightfully sorry . . .

THE STEP-DAUGHTER (*forcing herself to conquer her indignation and nausea*). Stop! Stop! It's I who must thank you. There's no need for you to feel mortified or specially sorry. Don't think any more of what I've said. (*Tries to smile.*) I must forget that I am dressed so . . .

THE MANAGER (*interrupting and turning to the* PROMPTER). Stop a minute! Stop! Don't write that down. Cut out that last bit. (*Then to the* FATHER *and* STEP-DAUGHTER) Fine! it's going fine! (*To the* FATHER *only*) And now you can go on as we arranged. (*To the* ACTORS) Pretty good that scene, where he offers her the hat, eh?

THE STEP-DAUGHTER. The best's coming now. Why can't we go on?

THE MANAGER. Have a little patience! (*To the* ACTORS) Of course, it must be treated rather lightly.

LEADING MAN. Still, with a bit of go in it!

LEADING LADY. Of course! It's easy enough! (*To* LEADING MAN) Shall you and I try it now?

LEADING MAN. Why, yes! I'll prepare my entrance. (*Exit in order to make his entrance.*)

THE MANAGER (*to* LEADING LADY). See here! The scene between you and Madame Pace is finished. I'll have it written out properly after. You remain here . . . oh, where are you going?

LEADING LADY. One minute. I want to put my hat on again. (*Goes over to hat-rack and puts her hat on her head.*)

THE MANAGER. Good! You stay here with your head bowed down a bit.

THE STEP-DAUGHTER. But she isn't dressed in black.

LEADING LADY. But I shall be, and much more effectively than you.

THE MANAGER (*to* STEP-DAUGHTER). Be quiet please, and watch! You'll be able to learn something. (*Clapping his hands*) Come on! come on! Entrance, please!

(*The door at rear of stage opens, and the* LEADING MAN *enters with the lively manner of an old gallant. The rendering of the scene by the* ACTORS *from the very first words is seen to be quite a different thing, though it has not in any way the air of a parody. Naturally, the* STEP-DAUGHTER *and the* FATHER, *not being able to recognize themselves in the* LEADING LADY *and the* LEADING MAN, *who deliver their words in different tones and with a different psychology, express, sometimes with smiles, sometimes with gestures, the impression they receive.*)

LEADING MAN. Good afternoon, Miss . . .

THE FATHER (*at once unable to contain himself*). No! no!

(*The* STEP-DAUGHTER *noticing the way the* LEADING MAN *enters, bursts out laughing.*)

THE MANAGER (*furious*). Silence! And you please just stop that laughing. If we go on like this, we shall never finish.

THE STEP-DAUGHTER. Forgive me, sir, but it's natural enough. This lady (*indicating* LEADING LADY) stands there still; but if she is supposed to be me, I can assure you that if I heard anyone say "Good afternoon" in that manner and in that tone, I should burst out laughing as I did.

THE FATHER. Yes, yes, the manner, the tone . . .

THE MANAGER. Nonsense! Rubbish! Stand aside and let me see the action.

LEADING MAN. If I've got to represent an old fellow who's coming into a house of an equivocal character . . .

THE MANAGER. Don't listen to them, for Heaven's sake! Do it again! It goes fine. (*Waiting for the* ACTORS *to begin again*) Well?

LEADING MAN. Good afternoon, Miss.

LEADING LADY. Good afternoon.

LEADING MAN (*imitating the gesture of the* FATHER *when he looked under the hat, and then expressing quite clearly first satisfaction and then fear).* Ah, but . . . I say . . . this is not the first time that you have come here, is it?

THE MANAGER. Good, but not quite so heavily. Like this. (*Acts himself.*) "This isn't the first time that you have come here" . . . (*To* LEADING LADY) And you say: "No, sir."

LEADING LADY. No, sir.

LEADING MAN. You've been here before, more than once.

THE MANAGER. No, no, stop! Let her nod "yes" first. "You've been here before, eh?" (*The* LEADING LADY *lifts up her head slightly and closes her eyes as though in disgust. Then she inclines her head twice.*)

THE STEP-DAUGHTER (*unable to contain herself*). Oh my God! (*Puts a hand to her mouth to prevent herself from laughing.*)

THE MANAGER (*turning round*). What's the matter?

THE STEP-DAUGHTER. Nothing, nothing!

THE MANAGER (*to* LEADING MAN). Go on!

LEADING MAN. You've been here before, eh? Well then, there's no need to be so shy, is there? May I take off your hat?
(*The* LEADING MAN *says this last speech in such a tone and with such gestures that the* STEP-DAUGHTER, *though she has her hand to her mouth, cannot keep from laughing.*)

LEADING LADY (*indignant*). I'm not going to stop here to be made a fool of by that woman there.

LEADING MAN. Neither am I! I'm through with it!

THE MANAGER (*shouting to* STEP-DAUGHTER). Silence! for once and all, I tell you!

THE STEP-DAUGHTER. Forgive me! forgive me!

THE MANAGER. You haven't any manners: that's what it is! You go too far.

THE FATHER (*endeavouring to intervene*). Yes, it's true, but excuse her . . .

THE MANAGER. Excuse what? It's absolutely disgusting.

THE FATHER. Yes, sir, but believe me, it has such a strange effect when . . .

THE MANAGER. Strange? Why strange? Where is it strange?

THE FATHER. No, sir; I admire your actors—this gentleman here, this lady; but they are certainly not us!

THE MANAGER. I should hope not. Evidently they cannot be you, if they are actors.

THE FATHER. Just so: actors! Both of them act our parts exceedingly well. But, believe me, it produces quite a different effect on us. They want to be us, but they aren't, all the same.

THE MANAGER. What is it then anyway?

THE FATHER. Something that is . . . that is theirs—and no longer ours . . .

THE MANAGER. But naturally, inevitably. I've told you so already.

THE FATHER. Yes, I understand . . . I understand . . .

THE MANAGER. Well then, let's have no more of it! (*Turning to the* ACTORS) We'll have the rehearsals by ourselves, afterwards, in the ordinary way. I never could stand rehearsing with the author present. He's never satisfied! (*Turning to* FATHER *and* STEP-DAUGHTER) Come on! Let's get on with it again; and try and see if you can't keep from laughing.

THE STEP-DAUGHTER. Oh, I shan't laugh any more. There's a nice little bit coming for me now: you'll see.

THE MANAGER. Well then: when she says "Don't think any more of what I've said. I must forget, etc.," you (*addressing the* FATHER) come in sharp with "I understand, I understand"; and then you ask her . . .

THE STEP-DAUGHTER (*interrupting*). What?

THE MANAGER. Why she is in mourning.

THE STEP-DAUGHTER. Not at all! See here: when I told him that it was useless for me to be thinking about my wearing mourning, do you know how he answered me? "Ah well," he said, "then let's take off this little frock."

THE MANAGER. Great! Just what we want, to make a riot in the theatre!

THE STEP-DAUGHTER. But it's the truth!

THE MANAGER. What does that matter? Acting is our business here. Truth up to a certain point, but no further.

THE STEP-DAUGHTER. What do you want to do then?

THE MANAGER. You'll see, you'll see! Leave it to me.

THE STEP-DAUGHTER. No sir! What you want to do is to piece together a little romantic sentimental scene out of my disgust, out of all the reasons, each more cruel and viler than the other, why I am what I am. He is to ask me why I'm in mourning; and I'm to answer with tears in my eyes, that it is just two months since papa died. No sir, no! He's got to say to me; as he did say: "Well, let's take off this little dress at once." And I, with my two months' mourning in my heart, went there behind that screen, and with these fingers tingling with shame . . .

THE MANAGER (*running his hands through his hair*). For Heaven's sake! What are you saying?

THE STEP-DAUGHTER (*crying out excitedly*). The truth! The truth!

THE MANAGER. It may be. I don't deny it, and I can understand all your horror; but you must surely see that you can't have this kind of thing on the stage. It won't go.

THE STEP-DAUGHTER. Not possible, eh? Very well! I'm much obliged to you—but I'm off!

THE MANAGER. Now be reasonable! Don't lose your temper!

THE STEP-DAUGHTER. I won't stop here! I won't! I can see you've fixed it all up with him in your office. All this talk about what is possible for the stage . . . I understand! He wants to get at his complicated "cerebral drama," to have his famous remorses and torments acted; but I want to act my part, *my part!*

THE MANAGER (*annoyed, shaking his shoulders*). Ah! Just *your* part! But, if you will pardon me, there are other parts than yours: His (*indicating the* FATHER) and hers (*indicating the* MOTHER)! On the stage you can't have a character becoming too prominent and overshadowing all the others. The thing is to pack them all into a neat little framework and then act what is actable. I am aware of the fact that everyone has his own interior life which he wants very much to put forward. But the difficulty lies in this fact: to set out just so much as is necessary for the stage, taking the other characters into consideration, and at the same time hint at the unrevealed interior life of each. I am willing to admit, my dear young lady, that from your point of view it would be a fine idea if each character could tell the public all his troubles in a nice monologue or a regular one hour lecture. (*Good humoredly*) You must restrain yourself, my dear, and in your own interest, too; because this fury of yours, this exaggerated disgust you show, may make a bad impression, you know. After you have confessed to me that there were others before him at Madame Pace's and more than once . . .

THE STEP-DAUGHTER (*bowing her head, impressed*). It's true. But remember those others mean him for me all the same.

THE MANAGER (*not understanding*). What? The others? What do you mean?

THE STEP-DAUGHTER. For one who has gone wrong, sir, he who was responsible for the first fault is responsible for all that follow. He is responsible for my faults, was, even before I was born. Look at him, and see if it isn't true!

THE MANAGER. Well, well! And does the weight of so much responsibility seem nothing to you? Give him a chance to act it, to get it over!

THE STEP-DAUGHTER. How? How can he act all his "noble remorses," all his "moral torments," if you want to spare him the horror of being discovered one day—after he had asked her what he did ask her—in the arms of her, that already fallen woman, that child, sir, that child he used to watch come out of school? (*She is moved. The* MOTHER *at this point is overcome with emotion, and breaks out into a fit of crying. All are touched. A long pause.*)

THE STEP-DAUGHTER (*as soon as the* MOTHER *becomes a little quieter, adds resolutely and gravely*). At present, we are unknown to the public. Tomorrow, you will act us as you wish, treating us in your own manner. But do you really want to see drama, do you want to see it flash out as it really did?

THE MANAGER. Of course! That's just what I do want, so I can use as much of it as is possible.

THE STEP-DAUGHTER. Well then, ask that Mother there to leave us.

THE MOTHER (*changing her low plaint into a sharp cry*). No! No! Don't permit it, sir, don't permit it!

THE MANAGER. But it's only to try it.

THE MOTHER. I can't bear it. I can't.

THE MANAGER. But since it has happened already . . . I don't understand!

THE MOTHER. It's taking place now. It happens all the time. My torment isn't a pretended one. I live and feel every minute of my torture. Those two children there—have you heard them speak? They can't speak any more. They cling to me to keep up my torment actual and vivid for me. But for themselves, they do not exist, they aren't any more. And she (*indicating the* STEP-DAUGHTER) has run away, she has left me, and is lost. If I now see her here before me, it is only to renew for me the tortures I have suffered for her too.

THE FATHER. The eternal moment! She (*indicating the* STEP-DAUGHTER) is here to catch me, fix me, and hold me eternally in the stocks for that one fleeting and shameful moment of my life. She can't give it up! And you sir, cannot either fairly spare me it.

THE MANAGER. I never said I didn't want to act it. It will form, as a matter of fact, the nucleus of the whole first act right up to her surprise. (*Indicates the* MOTHER.)

THE FATHER. Just so! This is my punishment: the passion in all of us that must culminate in her final cry.

THE STEP-DAUGHTER. I can hear it still in my ears. It's driven me mad, that cry!—You can put me on as you like; it doesn't matter. Fully dressed, if you like—provided I have at least the arm bare; because standing like this (*She goes close to the* FATHER *and leans her head on his breast.*) with my head so, and my arms round his neck, I saw a vein pulsing in my arm here; and then, as if that live vein had awakened disgust in me, I closed my eyes like this, and let my head sink on his breast. (*Turning to the* MOTHER) Cry out mother! Cry out! (*Buries head in* FATHER's *breast, and with her shoulders raised as if to prevent her hearing the cry, adds in tones of intense emotion*) Cry out as you did then!

THE MOTHER (*coming forward to separate them*). No! My daughter, my daughter! (*And after having pulled her away from him*) You brute! you brute! She is my daughter! Don't you see she's my daughter?

THE MANAGER (*walking backwards towards footlights*). Fine! fine! Damned good! And then, of course—curtain!

THE FATHER (*going towards him excitedly*). Yes, of course, because that's the way it really happened.

THE MANAGER (*convinced and pleased*). Oh, yes, no doubt about it. Curtain here, curtain!

(*At the reiterated cry of the* MANAGER, *the* MACHINIST *lets the curtain down, leaving the* MANAGER *and the* FATHER *in front of it before the footlights.*)

THE MANAGER. The darned idiot! I said "curtain" to show the act should end there, and he goes and lets it down in earnest. (*To the* FATHER, *while he pulls the curtain back to go on to the stage again*) Yes, yes, it's all right. Effect certain! That's the right ending. I'll guarantee the first act at any rate.

ACT THREE

When the curtain goes up again, it is seen that the stage hands have shifted the bit of scenery used in the last part, and have rigged up instead at the back of the stage a drop, with some trees, and one or two wings. A portion of a fountain basin is visible. The MOTHER *is sitting on the right with the two children by her side. The* SON *is on the same side, but away from the others. He seems bored, angry, and full of shame. The* FATHER *and the* STEP-DAUGHTER *are also seated towards the right front. On the other side* (*left*) *are the* ACTORS, *much in the positions they occupied before the curtain was lowered. Only the* MANAGER *is standing up in the middle of the stage, with his hand closed over his mouth in the act of meditating.*

THE MANAGER (*shaking his shoulders after a brief pause*). Ah yes: the second act! Leave it to me, leave it all to me as we arranged, and you'll see! It'll go fine!

THE STEP-DAUGHTER. Our entry into his house (*indicates* FATHER) in spite of him. . . . (*Indicates the* SON.)

THE MANAGER (*out of patience*). Leave it to me, I tell you!

THE STEP-DAUGHTER. Do let it be clear, at any rate, that it is in spite of my wishes.

THE MOTHER (*from her corner, shaking her head*). For all the good that's come of it . . .

THE STEP-DAUGHTER (*turning towards her quickly*). It doesn't matter. The more harm done us, the more remorse for him.

THE MANAGER (*impatiently*). I understand! Good Heavens! I understand! I'm taking it into account.

THE MOTHER (*supplicatingly*). I beg you, sir, to let it appear quite plain that for conscience' sake I did try in every way . . .

THE STEP-DAUGHTER (*interrupting indignantly and continuing for the* MOTHER). . . . to pacify me, to dissuade me from spiting him. (*To* MANAGER) Do as she wants: satisfy her, because it is true! I enjoy it immensely. Anyhow, as you can see, the meeker she is, the more she tries to get at his heart, the more distant and aloof does he become.

THE MANAGER. Are we going to begin this second act or not?

THE STEP-DAUGHTER. I'm not going to talk any more now. But I must tell you this: you can't have the whole action take place in the garden, as you suggest. It isn't possible!

THE MANAGER. Why not?

THE STEP-DAUGHTER. Because he (*indicates the* SON *again*) is always shut up alone in his room. And then there's all the part of that poor dazed-looking boy there which takes place indoors.

THE MANAGER. Maybe! On the other hand, you will understand—we can't change scenes three or four times in one act.

THE LEADING MAN. They used to once.

THE MANAGER. Yes, when the public was up to the level of that child there.

THE LEADING LADY. It makes the illusion easier.

THE FATHER (*irritated*). The illusion! For Heaven's sake, don't say illusion. Please don't use that word, which is particularly painful for us.

THE MANAGER (*astounded*). And why, if you please?

THE FATHER. It's painful, cruel, really cruel; and you ought to understand that.

THE MANAGER. But why? What ought we to say then? The illusion, I tell you, sir, which we've got to create for the audience . . .

THE LEADING MAN. With our acting.

THE MANAGER. The illusion of a reality.

THE FATHER. I understand; but you, perhaps, do not understand us. Forgive me! You see . . . here for you and your actors, the thing is only—and rightly so . . . a kind of game . . .

THE LEADING LADY (*interrupting indignantly*). A game! We're not children here, if you please! We are serious actors.

THE FATHER. I don't deny it. What I mean is the game, or play, of your art, which has to give, as the gentleman says, a perfect illusion of reality.

THE MANAGER. Precisely—!

THE FATHER. Now, if you consider the fact that we (*indicates himself and the other five* CHARACTERS), as we are, have no other reality outside of this illusion . . .

THE MANAGER (*astonished, looking at his* ACTORS, *who are also amazed*). And what does that mean?

THE FATHER (*after watching them for a moment with a wan smile*). As I say, sir, that which is a game of art for you is our sole reality. (*Brief pause. He goes a step or two nearer the* MANAGER *and adds*) But not only for us, you know, by the way. Just you think it over well. (*Looks him in the eyes.*) Can you tell me who you are?

THE MANAGER (*perplexed, half smiling*). What? Who am I? I am myself.

THE FATHER. And if I were to tell you that that isn't true, because you and I . . . ?

THE MANAGER. I should say you were mad—! (*The* ACTORS *laugh.*)

THE FATHER. You're quite right to laugh: because we are all making believe here. (*To* MANAGER) And you can therefore object that it's only for a joke that that gentleman there (*indicates the* LEADING MAN), who naturally is himself, has to be me, who am on the contrary myself—this thing you see here. You see I've caught you in a trap! (*The* ACTORS *laugh.*)

THE MANAGER (*annoyed*). But we've had all this over once before. Do you want to begin again?

THE FATHER. No, no! That wasn't my meaning! In fact, I should like to request you to abandon this game of art (*looking at the* LEADING LADY *as if anticipating her*) which you are accustomed to play here with your actors, and to ask you seriously once again: who are you?

THE MANAGER (*astonished and irritated, turning to his* ACTORS). If this fellow here hasn't got a nerve! A man who calls himself a character comes and asks me who I am!

THE FATHER (*with dignity, but not offended*). A character, sir, may always ask a man who he is. Because a character has really a life of his own, marked with his especial characteristics; for which reason he is always "somebody." But a man—I'm not speaking of you now—may very well be "nobody."

THE MANAGER. Yes, but you are asking these questions of me, the boss, the manager! Do you understand?

THE FATHER. But only in order to know if you, as you really are now, see yourself as you once were with all the illusions that were yours then, with all the things both inside and outside of you as they seemed to you—as they were then indeed for you. Well, sir, if you think of all those illusions that mean nothing to you now, of all those things which don't even *seem* to you to exist any more, while once they *were* for you, don't you feel that—I won't say these boards—but the very earth under your feet is sinking away from you when you reflect that in the same way this *you* as you feel it today—all this present reality of yours—is fated to seem a mere illusion to you tomorrow?

THE MANAGER (*without having understood much, but astonished by the specious argument*). Well, well! And where does all this take us anyway?

THE FATHER. Oh, nowhere! It's only to show you that if we (*indicating the* CHARACTERS) have no other reality beyond the illusion, you too must not count overmuch on your reality as you feel it today, since, like that of yesterday, it may prove an illusion for you tomorrow.

THE MANAGER (*determining to make fun of him*). Ah, excellent! Then you'll be saying next that you, with this comedy of yours that you brought here to act, are truer and more real than I am.

THE FATHER (*with the greatest seriousness*). But of course; without doubt!

THE MANAGER. Ah, really?

THE FATHER. Why, I thought you'd understand that from the beginning.

THE MANAGER. More real than I?

THE FATHER. If your reality can change from one day to another . . .

THE MANAGER. But everyone knows it can change. It is always changing, the same as anyone else's.

THE FATHER (*with a cry*). No, sir, not ours! Look here! That is the very difference! Our reality doesn't change: it can't change! It can't be other than what it is, because it is already fixed for ever. It's terrible. Ours is an immutable reality which should make you shudder when you approach us if you are really conscious of the fact that your reality is a mere transitory and fleeting illusion, taking this form today and that tomorrow, according to the conditions, according to your will, your sentiments, which in turn are controlled by an intellect that shows them to you today in one manner and tomorrow . . . who knows how? . . . Illusions of reality represented in this fatuous comedy of life that never ends, nor can ever end! Because if tomorrow it were to end . . . then why, all would be finished.

THE MANAGER. Oh for God's sake, will you *at least* finish with this philosophizing and let us try and shape this comedy which you yourself have brought me here? You argue and philosophize a bit too much, my dear sir. You know you seem to me almost, almost . . . (*Stops and looks him over from head to foot.*) Ah, by the way, I think you introduced yourself to me as a—what shall . . . we say—a "character," created by an author who did not afterward care to make a drama of his own creations.

THE FATHER. It is the simple truth, sir.

THE MANAGER. Nonsense! Cut that out, please! None of us believes it, because it isn't a thing, as you must recognize yourself, which one can believe seriously. If you want to know, it seems to me you are trying to imitate the manner of a certain author whom I heartily detest—I warn you—although I have unfortunately bound myself to put on one of his works. As a matter of fact, I was just starting to rehearse it, when you arrived. (*Turning to the* ACTORS) And this is what we've gained—out of the frying-pan into the fire!

THE FATHER. I don't know to what author you may be alluding, but believe me I feel what I think; and I seem to be philosophizing only for those who do not think what they feel, because they blind themselves with their own sentiment. I know that for many people this self-blinding seems much more "human"; but the contrary is really true. For man never reasons so much and becomes so introspective as when he suffers; since he is anxious to get at the cause of his sufferings, to learn who has produced them, and whether it is just or unjust that he should have to bear them. On the other hand, when he is happy, he takes his happiness as it comes and doesn't analyze it, just as if happiness were his right. The animals suffer without reasoning about their sufferings. But take the case of a man who suffers and begins to reason about it. Oh no! it can't be allowed! Let him suffer like an animal, and then—ah yet, he is "human"!

THE MANAGER. Look here! Look here! You're off again, philosophizing worse than ever.

THE FATHER. Because I suffer, sir! I'm not philosophizing: I'm crying aloud the reason of my sufferings.

THE MANAGER. (*Makes brusque movement as he is taken with a new idea.*) I should like to know if anyone has ever heard of a character who gets right out of his part and perorates and speechifies as you do. Have you ever heard of a case? I haven't.

THE FATHER. You have never met such a case, sir, because authors, as a rule, hide the labour of their creations. When the characters are really alive before their author, the latter does nothing but follow them in their action, in their words, in the situations which they suggest to him; and he has to will them the way they will themselves—for there's trouble if he doesn't. When a character is born, he acquires at once such an independence, even of his own author, that he can be imagined by everybody even in many other situations where the author never dreamed of placing him; and so he acquires for himself a meaning which the author never thought of giving him.

THE MANAGER. Yes, yes, I know this.

THE FATHER. What is there then to marvel at in us? Imagine such a misfortune for characters as I have described to you: to be born of an author's fantasy, and be denied life by him; and then answer me if these characters left alive, and yet without life, weren't right in doing what they did do and are doing now, after they have attempted everything in their power to persuade him to give them their stage life. We've all tried him in turn, I, she (*indicating the* STEP-DAUGHTER) and she (*indicating the* MOTHER).

THE STEP-DAUGHTER. It's true. I too have sought to tempt him, many, many times, when he has been sitting at his writing table, feeling a bit melancholy, at the twilight hour. He would sit in his armchair too lazy to switch on the light, and all the shadows that crept into his room were full of our presence coming to tempt him. (*As if she saw herself still there by the writing table, and was annoyed by the presence of the* ACTORS.) Oh, if you would only go away, go away and leave us alone—mother here with that son of hers—I with that Child—that Boy there always alone—and then I with him (*just hints at the* FATHER)—and then I alone, alone . . . in those shadows! (*Makes a sudden movement as if in the vision she has of herself illuminating those shadows she wanted to seize hold of herself.*) Ah! my life! my life! Oh, what scenes we proposed to him—and I tempted him more than any of the others!

THE FATHER. Maybe. But perhaps it was your fault that he refused to give us life: because you were too insistent, too troublesome.

THE STEP-DAUGHTER. Nonsense! Didn't he make me so himself? (*Goes close to the* MANAGER *to tell him as if in confidence*) In my opinion he abandoned us in a fit of depression, of disgust for the ordinary theatre as the public knows it and likes it.

THE SON. Exactly what it was, sir; exactly that!

THE FATHER. Not at all! Don't believe it for a minute. Listen to me! You'll be doing quite right to modify, as you suggest, the excesses both of this girl here, who wants to do too much, and of this young man, who won't do anything at all.

THE SON. No, nothing!

THE MANAGER. You too get over the mark occasionally, my dear sir, if I may say so.

THE FATHER. I? When? Where?

THE MANAGER. Always! Continuously! Then there's this insistence of yours in trying to make us believe you are a character. And then too, you must really argue and philosophize less, you know, much less.

THE FATHER. Well, if you want to take away from me the possibility of representing the torment of my spirit which never gives me peace, you will be suppressing me: that's all. Every true man, sir, who is a little above the level of the beasts and plants does not live for the sake of living, without knowing how to live; but he lives so as to give a meaning and a value of his own to life. For me this is *everything*. I cannot give up this, just to represent a mere fact as she (*indicating the* STEP-DAUGHTER) wants. It's all very well for her, since her "vendetta" lies in the "fact." I'm not going to do it. It destroys my *raison d'être*.

THE MANAGER. Your *raison d'être*! Oh, we're going ahead fine! First she starts off, and then you jump in. At this rate, we'll never finish.

THE FATHER. Now, don't be offended! Have it your own way—provided, however, that within the limits of the parts you assign us each one's sacrifice isn't too great.

THE MANAGER. You've got to understand that you can't go on arguing at your own pleasure. Drama is action, sir, action and not confounded philosophy.

THE FATHER. All right. I'll do just as much arguing and philosophizing as everybody does when he is considering his own torments.

THE MANAGER. If the drama permits! But for Heaven's sake, man, let's get along and come to the scene.

THE STEP-DAUGHTER. It seems to me we've got too much action with our coming into his house. (*Indicating* FATHER) You said, before, you couldn't change the scene every five minutes.

THE MANAGER. Of course not. What we've got to do is to combine and

group up all the facts in one simultaneous, close-knit, action. We
can't have it as you want, with your little brother wandering like
a ghost from room to room, hiding behind doors and meditating
a project which—what did you say it did to him?

THE STEP-DAUGHTER. Consumes him, sir, wastes him away!

THE MANAGER. Well, it may be. And then at the same time, you want
the little girl there to be playing in the garden . . . one in the
house, and the other in the garden: isn't that it?

THE STEP-DAUGHTER. Yes, in the sun, in the sun! That is my only
pleasure: to see her happy and careless in the garden after the
misery and squalor of the horrible room where we all four slept
together. And I had to sleep with her—I, do you understand?—
with my vile contaminated body next to hers; with her folding me
fast in her loving little arms. In the garden, whenever she spied
me, she would run to take me by the hand. She didn't care for
the big flowers, only the little ones; and she loved to show me
them and pet me.

THE MANAGER. Well then, we'll have it in the garden. Everything shall
happen in the garden; and we'll group the other scenes there.
(*Calls a* STAGE HAND.) Here, a backcloth with trees and something to do as a fountain basin. (*Turning round to look at the
back of the stage*) Ah, you've fixed it up. Good! (*To* STEP-DAUGH-
TER) This is just to give an idea, of course. The Boy, instead of
hiding behind the doors, will wander about here in the garden,
hiding behind the trees. But it's going to be rather difficult to find
a child to do that scene with you where she shows you the flowers.
(*Turning to the* BOY) Come forward a little, will you please? Let's
try it now! Come along! come along! (*Then seeing him come
shyly forward, full of fear and looking lost*) It's a nice business,
this lad here. What's the matter with him? We'll have to give him
a word or two to say. (*Goes close to him, puts a hand on his
shoulders, and leads him behind one of the trees.*) Come on! come
on! Let me see you a little! Hide here . . . yes, like that. Try and
show your head just a little as if you were looking for someone . . . (*Goes back to observe the effect, when the* BOY *at once
goes through the action.*) Excellent! fine! (*Turning to* STEP-
DAUGHTER) Suppose the little girl there were to surprise him as
he looks round, and run over to him, so we could give him a
word or two to say?

THE STEP-DAUGHTER. It's useless to hope he will speak, as long as that
fellow there is here . . . . (*Indicates the* SON.) You must send
him away first.

THE SON (*jumping up*). Delighted! Delighted! I don't ask for anything better. (*Begins to move away.*)

THE MANAGER (*at once stopping him*). No! No! Where are you going? Wait a bit!

(*The* MOTHER *gets up alarmed and terrified at the thought that he is really about to go away. Instinctively she lifts her arms to prevent him, without, however, leaving her seat.*)

THE SON (*to* MANAGER *who stops him*). I've got nothing to do with this affair. Let me go please! Let me go!

THE MANAGER. What do you mean by saying you've got nothing to do with this?

THE STEP-DAUGHTER (*calmly, with irony*). Don't bother to stop him: he won't go away.

THE FATHER. He has to act the terrible scene in the garden with his mother.

THE SON (*suddenly resolute and with dignity*). I shall act nothing at all. I've said so from the very beginning. (*To the* MANAGER) Let me go!

THE STEP-DAUGHTER (*going over to the* MANAGER). Allow me? (*Puts down the* MANAGER'S *arm which is restraining the* SON.) Well, go away then, if you want to! (*The* SON *looks at her with contempt and hatred. She laughs and says*) You see, he can't, he can't go away! He is obliged to stay here, indissolubly bound to the chain. If I, who fly off when that happens which has to happen, because I can't bear him—if I am still here and support that face and expression of his, you can well imagine that he is unable to move. He has to remain here, has to stop with that nice father of his, and that mother whose only son he is. (*Turning to the* MOTHER) Come on, mother, come along! (*Turning to* MANAGER *to indicate her*) You see, she was getting up to keep him back. (*To the* MOTHER, *beckoning her with her hand*) Come on! come on! (*Then to* MANAGER) You can imagine how little she wants to show these actors of yours what she really feels; but so eager is she to get near him that . . . There, you see? She is willing to act her part. (*And in fact, the* MOTHER *approaches him; and as soon as the* STEP-DAUGHTER *has finished speaking, opens her arms to signify that she consents.*)

THE SON (*suddenly*). No! no! If I can't go away, then I'll stop here; but I repeat: I act nothing!

THE FATHER (*to* MANAGER *excitedly*). You can force him, sir.

THE SON. Nobody can force me.

THE FATHER. I can.

THE STEP-DAUGHTER. Wait a minute, wait . . . First of all, the baby has to go to the fountain . . . (*Runs to take the* CHILD *and leads her to the fountain.*)

THE MANAGER. Yes, yes of course; that's it. Both at the same time.
(*The* SECOND LADY LEAD *and the* JUVENILE LEAD *at this point separate themselves from the group of* ACTORS. *One watches the* MOTHER *attentively; the other moves about studying the movements and manner of the* SON *whom he will have to act.*)

THE SON (*to* MANAGER). What do you mean by both at the same time? It isn't right. There was no scene between me and her. (*Indicates the* MOTHER.) Ask her how it was!

THE MOTHER. Yes, it's true. I had come into his room . . .

THE SON. Into my room, do you understand? Nothing to do with the garden.

THE MANAGER. It doesn't matter. Haven't I told you we've got to group the action?

THE SON (*observing the* JUVENILE LEAD *studying him*). What do you want?

THE JUVENILE LEAD. Nothing! I was just looking at you.

THE SON (*turning towards the* SECOND LADY LEAD). Ah! she's at it too: to re-act her part (*indicating the* MOTHER)!

THE MANAGER. Exactly! And it seems to me that you ought to be grateful to them for their interest.

THE SON. Yes, but haven't you yet perceived that it isn't possible to live in front of a mirror which not only freezes us with the image of ourselves, but throws our likeness back at us with a horrible grimace?

THE FATHER. That is true, absolutely true. You must see that.

THE MANAGER (*to* SECOND LADY LEAD *and* JUVENILE LEAD). He's right! Move away from them!

THE SON. Do as you like. I'm out of this!

THE MANAGER. Be quiet, you, will you? And let me hear your mother! (*To* MOTHER) You were saying you had entered . . .

THE MOTHER. Yes, into his room, because I couldn't stand it any longer. I went to empty my heart to him of all the anguish that tortures me . . . But as soon as he saw me come in . . .

THE SON. Nothing happened! There was no scene. I went away, that's all! I don't care for scenes!

THE MOTHER. It's true, true. That's how it was.

THE MANAGER. Well now, we've got to do this bit between you and him. It's indispensable.

THE MOTHER. I'm ready . . . when you are ready. If you could only find a chance for me to tell him what I feel here in my heart.

THE FATHER (*going to* SON *in a great rage*). You'll do this for your
mother, for your mother, do you understand?

THE SON (*quite determined*). I do nothing!

THE FATHER (*taking hold of him and shaking him*). For God's sake,
do as I tell you! Don't you hear your mother asking you for a
favor? Haven't you even got the guts to be a son?

THE SON (*taking hold of the* FATHER). No! No! And for God's sake
stop it, or else . . .
(*General agitation. The* MOTHER, *frightened, tries to separate
them.*)

THE MOTHER (*pleading*). Please! please!

THE FATHER (*not leaving hold of the* SON). You've got to obey, do you
hear?

THE SON (*almost crying from rage*). What does it mean, this madness
you've got? (*They separate.*) Have you no decency, that you insist on showing everyone our shame? I won't do it! I won't! And
I stand for the will of our author in this. He didn't want to put
us on the stage, after all!

THE MANAGER. Man alive! You came here . . .

THE SON (*indicating* FATHER). *He* did! I didn't!

THE MANAGER. Aren't you here now?

THE SON. It was his wish, and he dragged us along with him. He's told
you not only the things that did happen, but also things that have
never happened at all.

THE MANAGER. Well, tell me then what did happen. You went out of
your room without saying a word?

THE SON. Without a word, so as to avoid a scene!

THE MANAGER. And then what did you do?

THE SON. Nothing . . . walking in the garden . . . (*Hesitates for a
moment with expression of gloom.*)

THE MANAGER (*coming closer to him, interested by his extraordinary
reserve*). Well, well . . . walking in the garden . . .

THE SON (*exasperated*). Why on earth do you insist? It's horrible! (*The
MOTHER trembles, sobs, and looks towards the fountain.*)

THE MANAGER (*slowly observing the glance and turning towards the
SON with increasing apprehension*). The baby?

THE SON. There in the fountain . . .

THE FATHER (*pointing with tender pity to the* MOTHER). She was following him at the moment . . .

THE MANAGER (*to the* SON *anxiously*). And then you . . .

THE SON. I ran over to her; I was jumping in to drag her out when I
saw something that froze my blood . . . the boy standing stock
still, with eyes like a madman's, watching his little drowned sister,

in the fountain! (*The* STEP-DAUGHTER *bends over the fountain to hide the* CHILD. *She sobs.*) Then . . . (*A revolver shot rings out behind the trees where the* BOY *is hidden.*)

THE MOTHER (*with a cry of terror runs over in that direction together with several of the* ACTORS *amid general confusion*). My son! My son! (*Then amid the cries and exclamations one hears her voice.*) Help! Help!

THE MANAGER (*pushing the* ACTORS *aside while they lift up the* BOY *and carry him off*). Is he really wounded?

SOME ACTORS. He's dead! dead!

OTHER ACTORS. No, no, it's only make believe, it's only pretence!

THE FATHER (*with a terrible cry*). Pretence? Reality, sir, reality!

THE MANAGER. Pretence? Reality? To hell with it all! Never in my life has such a thing happened to me. I've lost a whole day over these people, a whole day!

Curtain

THE GHOST SONATA [1907]

by *August Strindberg*

translated by Elizabeth Sprigge

Characters

THE OLD MAN, *Hummel, a company director*
THE STUDENT, *Arkenholtz*
THE MILKMAID, *an apparition*
THE CARETAKER'S WIFE
THE CARETAKER
THE LADY IN BLACK, *the daughter of the* CARETAKER'S WIFE *and the dead man. Also referred to as the* DARK LADY
THE COLONEL
THE MUMMY, *the* COLONEL'S *wife*
THE GIRL, *the* COLONEL'S *daughter, actually the daughter of the* OLD MAN
THE ARISTOCRAT, *Baron Skanskorg. Engaged to the* LADY IN BLACK
JOHANSSON, *the* OLD MAN'S *servant*
BENGTSSON, *the* COLONEL'S *servant*
THE FIANCÉE, *a white-haired old woman, once betrothed to the* OLD MAN
THE COOK
A MAIDSERVANT
BEGGARS
DEAD MAN

The Ghost Sonata, reprinted by permission of Willis Kingsley Wing. Copyright © 1951 by Prentice-Hall, Inc. All rights whatsoever in this play are strictly reserved and applications for performances, etc. should be made to Willis Kingsley Wing, 24 East 38th Street, New York, N.Y. 10016.

Scene One

Outside the house. The corner of the façade of a modern house, showing the ground floor above, and the street in front. The ground floor terminates on the right in the Round Room, above which, on the first floor, is a balcony with a flagstaff. The windows of the Round Room face the street in front of the house, and at the corner look on to the suggestion of a side-street running towards the back. At the beginning of the scene the blinds of the Round Room are down. When, later, they are raised, the white marble statue of a young woman can be seen, surrounded with palms and brightly lighted by rays of sunshine.

To the left of the Round Room is the Hyacinth Room; its window filled with pots of hyacinths, blue, white and pink. Further left, at the back, is an imposing double front door with laurels in tubs on either side of it. The doors are wide open, showing a staircase of white marble with a banister of mahogany and brass. To the left of the front door is another ground-floor window, with a window-mirror.* On the balcony rail in the corner above the Round Room are a blue silk quilt and two white pillows. The windows to the left of this are hung with white sheets.†

In the foreground, in front of the house, is a green bench; to the right a street drinking-fountain, to the left an advertisement column.

It is a bright Sunday morning, and as the curtain rises the bells of several churches, some near, some far away, are ringing.

On the staircase the LADY IN BLACK *stands motionless.*

The CARETAKER'S WIFE *sweeps the doorstep, then polishes the brass on the door and waters the laurels.*

In a wheel-chair by the advertisement column sits the OLD MAN, *reading a newspaper. His hair and beard are white and he wears spectacles.*

The MILKMAID *comes round the corner on the right, carrying milk bottles in a wire basket. She is wearing a summer dress with brown shoes, black stockings and a white cap. She takes off her cap and hangs it on the fountain, wipes the perspiration from her forehead, washes her hands and arranges her hair, using the water as a mirror.*

A steamship bell is heard, and now and then the silence is broken by the deep notes of an organ in a nearby church.

---

* Set at an angle inside the window, so as to show what is going on in the street.

† Sign of mourning.

After a few moments, when all is silent and the MILKMAID *has finished her toilet, the* STUDENT *enters from the left. He has had a sleepless night and is unshaven. He goes straight up to the fountain. There is a pause before he speaks.*

STUDENT. May I have the cup? (*The* MILKMAID *clutches the cup to her.*) Haven't you finished yet?
(*The* MILKMAID *looks at him with horror.*)
OLD MAN (*to himself*). Who's he talking to? I don't see anybody. Is he crazy?
(*He goes on watching them in great astonishment.*)
STUDENT (*to the* MILKMAID). What are you staring at? Do I look so terrible? Well, I've had no sleep, and of course you think I've been making a night of it . . . (*The* MILKMAID *stays just as she is.*) You think I've been drinking, eh? Do I smell of liquor? (*The* MILKMAID *does not change.*) I haven't shaved, I know. Give me a drink of water, girl. I've earned it. (*Pause.*) Oh well, I suppose I'll have to tell you. I spent the whole night dressing wounds and looking after the injured. You see, I was there when that house collapsed last night. Now you know. (*The* MILKMAID *rinses the cup and gives him a drink.*) Thanks. (*The* MILKMAID *stands motionless. Slowly*) Will you do me a great favor? (*Pause.*) The thing is, my eyes, as you can see, are inflamed, but my hands have been touching wounds and corpses, so it would be dangerous to put them near my eyes. Will you take my handkerchief—it's quite clean—and dip it in the fresh water and bathe my eyes? Will you do this? Will you play the good Samaritan? (*The* MILKMAID *hesitates, but does as he bids.*) Thank you, my dear. (*He takes out his purse. She makes a gesture of refusal.*) Forgive my stupidity, but I'm only half-awake. . . .
(*The* MILKMAID *disappears.*)
OLD MAN (*to the* STUDENT). Excuse me speaking to you, but I heard you say you were at the scene of the accident last night. I was just reading about it in the paper.
STUDENT. Is it in the paper already?
OLD MAN. The whole thing, including your portrait. But they regret that they have been unable to find out the name of the splendid young student. . . .
STUDENT. Really? (*Glances at the paper.*) Yes, that's me. Well I never!
OLD MAN. Who was it you were talking to just now?
STUDENT. Didn't you see? (*Pause.*)
OLD MAN. Would it be impertinent to inquire—what in fact your name is?

STUDENT. What would be the point? I don't care for publicity. If you get any praise, there's always disapproval too. The art of running people down has been developed to such a pitch. . . . Besides, I don't want any reward.

OLD MAN. You're well off, perhaps.

STUDENT. No, indeed. On the contrary, I'm very poor.

OLD MAN. Do you know, it seems to me I've heard your voice before. When I was young I had a friend who pronounced certain words just as you do. I've never met anyone else with quite that pronunciation. Only him—and you. Are you by any chance related to Mr. Arkenholtz, the merchant?

STUDENT. He was my father.

OLD MAN. Strange are the paths of fate. I saw you when you were an infant, under very painful circumstances.

STUDENT. Yes, I understand I came into the world in the middle of a bankruptcy.

OLD MAN. Just that.

STUDENT. Perhaps I might ask your name.

OLD MAN. I am Mr. Hummel.

STUDENT. Are you the . . . ? I remember that . . .

OLD MAN. Have you often heard my name mentioned in your family?

STUDENT. Yes.

OLD MAN. And mentioned perhaps with a certain aversion? (*The* STUDENT *is silent.*) Yes, I can imagine it. You were told, I suppose, that I was the man who ruined your father? All who ruin themselves through foolish speculations consider they were ruined by those they couldn't fool. (*Pause.*) Now these are the facts. Your father robbed me of seventeen thousand crowns—the whole of my savings at that time.

STUDENT. It's queer that the same story can be told in two such different ways.

OLD MAN. You surely don't believe I'm telling you what isn't true?

STUDENT. What am I to believe? My father didn't lie.

OLD MAN. That is so true. A father never lies. But I too am a father, and so it follows . . .

STUDENT. What are you driving at?

OLD MAN. I saved your father from disaster, and he repaid me with all the frightful hatred that is born of an obligation to be grateful. He taught his family to speak ill of me.

STUDENT. Perhaps you made him ungrateful by poisoning your help with unnecessary humiliation.

OLD MAN. All help is humiliating, sir.

STUDENT. What do you want from me?

OLD MAN. I'm not asking for the money, but if you will render me a few small services, I shall consider myself well paid. You see that I am a cripple. Some say it is my own fault; others lay the blame on my parents. I prefer to blame life itself, with it pitfalls. For if you escape one snare, you fall headlong into another. In any case, I am unable to climb stairs or ring doorbells, and that is why I am asking you to help me.

STUDENT. What can I do?

OLD MAN. To begin with, push my chair so that I can read those play-bills. I want to see what is on tonight.

STUDENT (*pushing the chair*). Haven't you got an attendant?

OLD MAN. Yes, but he has gone on an errand. He'll be back soon. Are you a medical student?

STUDENT. No, I am studying languages, but I don't know at all what I'm going to do.

OLD MAN. Aha! Are you good at mathematics?

STUDENT. Yes, fairly.

OLD MAN. Good. Perhaps you would like a job.

STUDENT. Yes, why not?

OLD MAN. Splendid. (*He studies the playbills.*) They are doing *The Valkyrie* for the matinée. That means the Colonel will be there with his daughter, and as he always sits at the end of the sixth row, I'll put you next to him. Go to that telephone kiosk please and order a ticket for seat eighty-two in the sixth row.

STUDENT. Am I to go to the Opera in the middle of the day?

OLD MAN. Yes. Do as I tell you and things will go well with you. I want to see you happy, rich and honored. Your début last night as the brave rescuer will make you famous by tomorrow and then your name will be worth something.

STUDENT (*going to the telephone kiosk*). What an odd adventure!

OLD MAN. Are you a gambler?

STUDENT. Yes, unfortunately.

OLD MAN. We'll make it fortunately. Go on now, telephone. (*The* STUDENT *goes. The* OLD MAN *reads his paper. The* LADY IN BLACK *comes out on to the pavement and talks to the* CARETAKER'S WIFE. *The* OLD MAN *listens, but the audience hears nothing. The* STU-DENT *returns.*) Did you fix it up?

STUDENT. It's done.

OLD MAN. You see that house?

STUDENT. Yes, I've been looking at it a lot. I passed it yesterday when the sun was shining on the windowpanes, and I imagined all the beauty and elegance there must be inside. I said to my companion: "Think of living up there in the top flat, with a beautiful young wife, two pretty little children and an income of twenty thousand crowns a year."

OLD MAN. So that's what you said. That's what you said. Well, well! I too am very fond of this house.

STUDENT. Do you speculate in houses?

OLD MAN. Mm—yes. But not in the way you mean.

STUDENT. Do you know the people who live here?

OLD MAN. Every one of them. At my age one knows everybody, and their parents and grandparents too, and one's always related to them in some way or other. I am just eighty, but no one knows me—not really. I take an interest in human destiny. (*The blinds of the Round Room are drawn up. The* COLONEL *is seen, wearing mufti. He looks at the thermometer outside one of the windows, then turns back into the room and stands in front of the marble statue.*) Look, that's the Colonel, whom you will sit next to this afternoon.

STUDENT. Is he—the Colonel? I don't understand any of this, but it's like a fairy story.

OLD MAN. My whole life's like a book of fairy stories, sir. And although the stories are different, they are held together by one thread, and the main theme constantly recurs.

STUDENT. Who is that marble statue of?

OLD MAN. That, naturally, is his wife.

STUDENT. Was she such a wonderful person?

OLD MAN. Er . . . yes.

STUDENT. Tell me.

OLD MAN. We can't judge people, young man. If I were to tell you that she left him, that he beat her, that she returned to him and married him a second time, and that now she is sitting inside there like a mummy, worshipping her own statue—then you would think me crazy.

STUDENT. I don't understand.

OLD MAN. I didn't think you would. Well, then we have the window with the hyacinths. His daughter lives there. She has gone out for a ride, but she will be home soon.

STUDENT. And who is the dark lady talking to the caretaker?

OLD MAN. Well, that's a bit complicated, but it is connected with the dead man, up there where you see the white sheets.

STUDENT. Why, who was he?

OLD MAN. A human being like you or me, but the most conspicuous thing about him was his vanity. If you were a Sunday child, you would see him presently come out of that door to look at the Consulate flag flying at half-mast. He was, you understand, a

Consul, and he reveled in coronets and lions and plumed hats
and colored ribbons.

STUDENT. Sunday child, you say? I'm told I was born on a Sunday.

OLD MAN. No, were you really? I might have known it. I saw it from
the color of your eyes. Then you can see what others can't. Have
you noticed that?

STUDENT. I don't know what others do see, but at times. . . . Oh, but
one doesn't talk of such things!

OLD MAN. I was almost sure of it. But you can talk to me, because I
understand such things.

STUDENT. Yesterday, for instance . . . I was drawn to that obscure
little street where later on the house collapsed. I went there and
stopped in front of that building which I had never seen before.
Then I noticed a crack in the wall. . . . I heard the floor boards
snapping. . . . I dashed over and picked up a child that was
passing under the wall. . . . The next moment the house collapsed. I was saved, but in my arms, which I thought held the
child, was nothing at all.

OLD MAN. Yes, yes, just as I thought. Tell me something. Why were
you gesticulating that way just now by the fountain? And why
were you talking to yourself?

STUDENT. Didn't you see the milkmaid I was talking to?

OLD MAN (*in horror*). Milkmaid?

STUDENT. Surely. The girl who handed me the cup.

OLD MAN. Really? So that's what was going on. Ah well, I haven't
second sight, but there are things I can do. (*The* FIANCÉE *is now
seen to sit down by the window which has the window-mirror.*)
Look at that old woman in the window. Do you see her? Well,
she was my fiancée once, sixty years ago. I was twenty. Don't be
alarmed. She doesn't recognize me. We see one another every
day, and it makes no impression on me, although once we vowed
to love one another eternally. Eternally!

STUDENT. How foolish you were in those days! We never talk to our
girls like that.

OLD MAN. Forgive us, young man. We didn't know any better. But
can you see that that old woman was once young and beautiful?

STUDENT. It doesn't show. And yet there's some charm in her looks. I
can't see her eyes.

(*The* CARETAKER'S WIFE *comes out with a basket of chopped fir
branches.**)

OLD MAN. Ah, the caretaker's wife! That dark lady is her daughter
by the dead man. That's why her husband was given the job of

---

* It was customary in Sweden to strew the ground with these for a funeral.

caretaker. But the dark lady has a suitor, who is an aristocrat with great expectations. He is in the process of getting a divorce—from his present wife, you understand. She's presenting him with a stone mansion in order to be rid of him. This aristocratic suitor is the son-in-law of the dead man, and you can see his bedclothes being aired on the balcony upstairs. It is complicated, I must say.

STUDENT. It's fearfully complicated.

OLD MAN. Yes, that it is, internally and externally, although it looks quite simple.

STUDENT. But then who was the dead man?

OLD MAN. You asked me that just now, and I answered. If you were to look round the corner, where the tradesmen's entrance is, you would see a lot of poor people whom he used to help—when it suited him.

STUDENT. He was a kind man then.

OLD MAN. Yes—sometimes.

STUDENT. Not always?

OLD MAN. No-o. That's the way of people. Now, sir, will you push my chair a little, so that it gets into the sun. I'm horribly cold. When you're never able to move about, the blood congeals. I'm going to die soon, I know that, but I have a few things to do first. Take my hand and feel how cold I am.

STUDENT (*taking it*). Yes, inconceivably. (*He shrinks back, trying in vain to free his hand.*)

OLD MAN. Don't leave me. I am tired now and lonely, but I haven't always been like this, you know. I have an enormously long life behind me, enormously long. I have made people unhappy and people have made me unhappy—the one cancels out the other—but before I die I want to see you happy. Our fates are entwined through your father—and other things.

STUDENT. Let go of my hand. You are taking all my strength. You are freezing me. What do you want with me?

OLD MAN (*letting go*). Be patient and you shall see and understand. Here comes the young lady.

(*They watch the* GIRL *approaching, though the audience cannot yet see her.*)

STUDENT. The Colonel's daughter?

OLD MAN. His daughter—yes. Look at her. Have you ever seen such a masterpiece?

STUDENT. She is like the marble statue in there.

OLD MAN. That's her mother, you know.

STUDENT. You are right. Never have I seen such a woman of woman born. Happy the man who may lead her to the altar and his home.

OLD MAN. You can see it. Not everyone recognizes her beauty. So, then, it is written.

(*The* GIRL *enters, wearing an English riding habit. Without noticing anyone she walks slowly to the door, where she stops to say a few words to the* CARETAKER'S WIFE. *Then she goes into the house. The* STUDENT *covers his eyes with his hand.*)

OLD MAN. Are you weeping?

STUDENT. In the face of what's hopeless there can be nothing but despair.

OLD MAN. I can open doors and hearts, if only I find an arm to do my will. Serve me and you shall have power.

STUDENT. Is it a bargain? Am I to sell my soul?

OLD MAN. Sell nothing. Listen. All my life I have *taken*. Now I have a craving to give—give. But no one will accept. I am rich, very rich, but I have no heirs, except for a good-for-nothing who torments the life out of me. Become my son. Inherit me while I am still alive. Enjoy life so that I can watch, at least from a distance.

STUDENT. What am I to do?

OLD MAN. First go to *The Valkyrie*.

STUDENT. That's settled. What else?

OLD MAN. This evening you must be in there—in the Round Room.

STUDENT. How am I to get there?

OLD MAN. By way of *The Valkyrie*.

STUDENT. Why have you chosen me as your medium? Did you know me before?

OLD MAN. Yes, of course. I have had my eye on you for a long time. But now look up there at the balcony. The maid is hoisting the flag to half-mast for the Consul. And now she is turning the bedclothes. Do you see that blue quilt? It was made for two to sleep under, but now it covers only one. (*The* GIRL, *having changed her dress, appears in the window and waters the hyacinths.*) There is my little girl. Look at her, look! She is talking to the flowers. Is she not like that blue hyacinth herself? She gives them drink —nothing but pure water, and they transform the water into color and fragrance. Now here comes the Colonel with the newspaper. He is showing her the bit about the house that collapsed. Now he's pointing to your portrait. She's not indifferent. She's reading of your brave deed. . . .

I believe it's clouding over. If it turns to rain I shall be in a pretty fix, unless Johansson comes back soon. (*It grows cloudy and dark. The* FIANCÉE *at the window-mirror closes her window.*) Now my fiancée is closing the window. Seventy-nine years old. The window-mirror is the only mirror she uses, because in it

she sees not herself, but the world outside—in two directions.
But the world can see her; she hasn't thought of that. Anyhow
she's a handsome old woman.

(*Now the* DEAD MAN, *wrapped in a winding sheet, comes out of
the door.*)

STUDENT. Good God, what do I see?

OLD MAN. What do you see?

STUDENT. Don't *you* see? There, in the doorway, the dead man?

OLD MAN. I see nothing, but I expected this. Tell me.

STUDENT. He is coming out into the street. (*Pause.*) Now he is turning
his head and looking up at the flag.

OLD MAN. What did I tell you? You may be sure he'll count the wreaths
and read the visiting cards. Woe to him who's missing.

STUDENT. Now he's turning the corner.

OLD MAN. He's gone to count the poor at the back door. The poor are
in the nature of a decoration, you see. "Followed by the blessings
of many." Well, he's not going to have my blessing. Between
ourselves he was a great scoundrel.

STUDENT. But charitable.

OLD MAN. A charitable scoundrel, always thinking of his grand funeral.
When he knew his end was near, he cheated the State out of
fifty thousand crowns. Now his daughter has relations with another woman's husband and is wondering about the Will. Yes,
the scoundrel can hear every word we're saying, and he's welcome
to it. Ah, here comes Johansson! (JOHANSSON *enters.*) Report!
(JOHANSSON *speaks, but the audience does not hear.*) Not at home,
eh? You are an ass. And the telegram? Nothing? Go on. . . . At
six this evening? That's good. Special edition, you say? With his
name in full. Arkenholtz, a student, born . . . parents . . .
That's splendid. . . . I think it's beginning to rain. . . . What
did he say about it? So—so. He wouldn't? Well, he must. Here
comes the aristocrat. Push me round the corner, Johansson, so
I can hear what the poor are saying. And, Arkenholtz, you wait
for me here. Understand? (*To* JOHANSSON) Hurry up now, hurry
up.

(JOHANSSON *wheels the chair round the corner. The* STUDENT
remains watching the GIRL, *who is now loosening the earth round
the hyacinths. The* ARISTOCRAT, *wearing mourning, comes in and
speaks to the* DARK LADY, *who has been walking to and fro on the
pavement.*)

ARISTOCRAT. But what can we do about it? We shall have to wait.

LADY. I can't wait.

ARISTOCRAT. You can't? Well then, go into the country.

LADY. I don't want to do that.

ARISTOCRAT. Come over here or they will hear what we are saying. (*They move towards the advertisement column and continue their conversation inaudibly.* JOHANSSON *returns.*)

JOHANSSON (*to the* STUDENT). My master asks you not to forget that other thing, sir.

STUDENT (*hesitating*). Look here . . . first of all tell me . . . who is your master?

JOHANSSON. Well, he's so many things, and he has been everything.

STUDENT. Is he a wise man?

JOHANSSON. Depends what that is. He says all his life he's been looking for a Sunday child, but that may not be true.

STUDENT. What does he want? He's grasping, isn't he?

JOHANSSON. It's power he wants. The whole day long he rides round in his chariot like the god Thor himself. He looks at houses, pulls them down, opens up new streets, builds squares. . . . But he breaks into houses too, sneaks through windows, play havoc with human destinies, kills his enemies—and never forgives. Can you imagine it, sir? This miserable cripple was once a Don Juan—although he always lost his women.

STUDENT. How do you account for that?

JOHANSSON. You see he's so cunning he makes the women leave him when he's tired of them. But what he's most like now is a horse-thief in the human market. He steals human beings in all sorts of different ways. He literally stole me out of the hands of the law. Well, as a matter of fact I'd made a slip—hm, yes—and only he knew about it. Instead of getting me put in gaol, he turned me into a slave. I slave—for my food alone, and that's none of the best.

STUDENT. Then what is it he means to do in this house?

JOHANSSON. I'm not going to talk about that. It's too complicated.

STUDENT. I think I'd better get away from it all.

(*The* GIRL *drops a bracelet out the window.*)

JOHANSSON. Look! The young lady has dropped her bracelet out of the window. (*The* STUDENT *goes slowly over, picks up the bracelet and returns it to the* GIRL, *who thanks him stiffly. The* STUDENT *goes back to* JOHANSSON.) So you mean to get away. That's not so easy as you think, once he's got you in his net. And he's afraid of nothing between heaven and earth—yes, of one thing he is— of one person rather. . . .

STUDENT. Don't tell me. I think perhaps I know.

JOHANSSON. How can you know?

STUDENT. I'm guessing. Is it a little milkmaid he's afraid of?

JOHANSSON. He turns his head the other way whenever he meets a milk cart. Besides, he talks in his sleep. It seems he was once in Hamburg. . . .

STUDENT. Can one trust this man?

JOHANSSON. You can trust him—to do anything.

STUDENT. What's he doing now round the corner?

JOHANSSON. Listening to the poor. Sowing a little word, loosening one stone at a time, till the house falls down—metaphorically speaking. You see I'm an educated man. I was once a book-seller. . . . Do you still mean to go away?

STUDENT. I don't like to be ungrateful. He saved my father once, and now he only asks a small service in return.

JOHANSSON. What is that?

STUDENT. I am to go to *The Valkyrie*.

JOHANSSON. That's beyond me. But he's always up to new tricks. Look at him now, talking to that policeman. He is always thick with the police. He uses them, gets them involved in his interests, holds them with false promises and expectations, while all the time he's pumping them. You'll see that before the day is over he'll be received in the Round Room.

STUDENT. What does he want there? What connection has he with the Colonel?

JOHANSSON. I think I can guess, but I'm not sure. You'll see for yourself once you're in there.

STUDENT. I shall never be in there.

JOHANSSON. That depends on yourself. Go to *The Valkyrie*.

STUDENT. Is that the way?

JOHANSSON. Yes, if he said so. Look. Look at him in his war chariot, drawn in triumph by the beggars, who get nothing for their pains but the hint of a treat at his funeral.

(*The* OLD MAN *appears standing up in his wheel-chair, drawn by one of the beggars and followed by the rest.*)

OLD MAN. Hail the noble youth who, at the risk of his own life, saved so many others in yesterday's accident. Three cheers for Arkenholtz! (*The* BEGGARS *bare their heads but do not cheer. The* GIRL *at the window waves her handkerchief. The* COLONEL *gazes from the window of the Round Room. The* OLD WOMAN *rises at her window. The* MAID *on the balcony hoists the flag to the top.*) Clap your hands, citizens. True, it is Sunday, but the ass in the pit and the ear in the corn field will absolve us. And although I am not a Sunday child, I have the gift of prophecy and also that of healing. Once I brought a drowned person back to life. That was in Hamburg on a Sunday morning just like this. . . .

(*The* MILKMAID *enters, seen only by the* STUDENT *and the* OLD
MAN. *She raises her arms like one who is drowning and gazes
fixedly at the* OLD MAN. *He sits down, then crumples up, stricken
with horror.*)
Johansson! Take me away! Quick! . . . Arkenholtz, don't forget
The Valkyrie.
STUDENT. What is all this?
JOHANSSON. We shall see. We shall see.

Scene Two

*Inside the Round Room. At the back is a white porcelain stove.
On either side of it are a mirror, a pendulum clock and candelabra.
On the right of the stove is the entrance to the hall beyond which
is a glimpse of a room furnished in green and mahogany. On the
left of the stove is the door to a cupboard, papered like the wall.
The statue, shaded by palms has a curtain which can be drawn to
conceal it.*

A door on the left leads into the Hyacinth Room, where the
GIRL *sits reading.*

The back of the COLONEL *can be seen, as he sits in the Green
Room, writing.*

BENGTSSON, *the Colonel's servant, comes in from the hall. He
is wearing livery, and is followed by* JOHANSSON, *dressed as a
waiter.*

BENGTSSON. Now you'll have to serve the tea, Johansson, while I take
the coats. Have you ever done it before?
JOHANSSON. It's true I push a war chariot in the daytime, as you know,
but in the evenings I go as a waiter to receptions and so forth.
It's always been my dream to get into this house. They're queer
people here, aren't they?
BENGTSSON. Ye-es. A bit out of the ordinary anyhow.
JOHANSSON. Is it to be a musical party or what?
BENGTSSON. The usual ghost supper, as we call it. They drink tea and
don't say a word—or else the Colonel does all the talking. And
they crunch their biscuits, all at the same time. It sounds like
rats in an attic.
JOHANSSON. Why do you call it the ghost supper?
BENGTSSON. They look like ghosts. And they've kept this up for twenty
years, always the same people saying the same things or saying
nothing at all for fear of being found out.

JOHANSSON. Isn't there a mistress of the house?

BENGTSSON. Oh yes, but she's crazy. She sits in a cupboard because her eyes can't bear the light. (*He points to the papered door.*) She sits in there.

JOHANSSON. In there?

BENGTSSON. Well, I told you they were a bit out of the ordinary.

JOHANSSON. But then—what does she look like?

BENGTSSON. Like a mummy. Do you want to have a look at her? (*He opens the door.*) There she is.

(*The figure of the Colonel's wife is seen, white and shrivelled into a* MUMMY.)

JOHANSSON. Oh my God!

MUMMY (*babbling*). Why do you open the door? Haven't I told you to keep it closed?

BENGTSSON (*in a wheedling tone*). Ta, ta, ta, ta. Be a good girl now, then you'll get something nice. Pretty Polly.

MUMMY (*parrot-like*). Pretty Polly. Are you there, Jacob? Currrrr!

BENGTSSON. She thinks she's a parrot, and maybe she's right. (*To the* MUMMY) Whistle for us, Polly.

(*The* MUMMY *whistles.*)

JOHANSSON. Well, I've seen a few things in my day, but this beats everything.

BENGTSSON. You see, when a house gets old, it grows moldy, and when people stay a long time together and torment each other they go mad. The mistress of the house—shut up, Polly!—that mummy there, has been living here for forty years—same husband, same furniture, same relatives, same friends. (*He closes the papered door.*) And the goings-on in this house—well, they're beyond me. Look at that statue—that's her when she was young.

JOHANSSON. Good Lord! Is that the mummy?

BENGTSSON. Yes. It's enough to make you weep. And somehow, carried away by her own imagination or something, she's got to be a bit like a parrot—the way she talks and the way she can't stand cripples or sick people. She can't stand the sight of her own daughter, because she's sick.

JOHANSSON. Is the young lady sick?

BENGTSSON. Didn't you know that?

JOHANSSON. No. And the Colonel, who is he?

BENGTSSON. You'll see.

JOHANSSON (*looking at the statue*). It's horrible to think that . . . How old is she now?

BENGTSSON. Nobody knows. But it's said that when she was thirty-five she looked nineteen, and that's what she made the Colonel believe she was—here in this very house. Do you know what that black Japanese screen by the couch is for? They call it the death-screen, and when someone's going to die, they put it round—same as in a hospital.

JOHANSSON. What a horrible house! And the student was longing to get in, as if it were paradise.

BENGTSSON. What student? Oh, I know. The one who's coming here this evening. The Colonel and the young lady happened to meet him at the Opera, and both of them took a fancy to him. Hm. Now it's my turn to ask questions. Who is your master—the man in the wheelchair?

JOHANSSON. Well, he er . . . Is he coming here too?

BENGTSSON. He hasn't been invited.

JOHANSSON. He'll come uninvited—if need be.

(*The* OLD MAN *appears in the hall on crutches, wearing a frock-coat and top-hat. He steals forward and listens.*)

BENGTSSON. He's a regular old devil, isn't he?

JOHANSSON. Up to the ears.

BENGTSSON. He looks like old Nick himself.

JOHANSSON. And he must be a wizard too, for he goes through locked doors.

(*The* OLD MAN *comes forward and takes hold of* JOHANSSON *by the ear.*)

OLD MAN. Rascal—take care! (*To* BENGTSSON) Tell the Colonel I am here.

BENGTSSON. But we are expecting guests.

OLD MAN. I know. But my visit is as good as expected, if not exactly looked forward to.

BENGTSSON. I see. What name shall I say? Mr. Hummel?

OLD MAN. Exactly. Yes. (BENGTSSON *crosses the hall to the Green Room, the door of which he closes behind him. To* JOHANSSON) Get out! (JOHANSSON *hesitates.*) Get out! (JOHANSSON *disappears into the hall. The* OLD MAN *inspects the room and stops in front of the statue in much astonishment.*) Amelia! It is she—she!

MUMMY (*from the cupboard*). Prrr-etty Polly.

(*The* OLD MAN *starts.*)

OLD MAN. What was that? Is there a parrot in the room? I don't see it.

MUMMY. Are you there, Jacob?

OLD MAN. The house is haunted.

MUMMY. Jacob!

OLD MAN. I'm scared. So these are the kind of secrets they guard in this house. (*With his back turned to the cupboard he stands looking at a portrait.*) There he is—he!

(*The* MUMMY *comes out behind the* OLD MAN *and gives a pull at his wig.*)

MUMMY. Currrrr! Is it . . . ? Currrrr!

OLD MAN (*jumping out of his skin*). God in heaven! Who is it?

MUMMY (*in a natural voice*). Is it Jacob?

OLD MAN. Yes, my name is Jacob.

MUMMY (*with emotion*). And my name is Amelia.

OLD MAN. No, no, no . . . Oh my God!

MUMMY. That's how I look. Yes. (*Pointing to the statue*) And that's how I *did* look. Life opens one's eyes, does it not? I live mostly in the cupboard to avoid seeing and being seen. . . . But, Jacob, what do you want here?

OLD MAN. My child. Our child.

MUMMY. There she is.

OLD MAN. Where?

MUMMY. There—in the Hyacinth Room.

OLD MAN (*looking at the* GIRL). Yes, that is she. (*Pause.*) And what about her father—the Colonel, I mean—your husband?

MUMMY. Once, when I was angry with him, I told him everything.

OLD MAN. Well . . . ?

MUMMY. He didn't believe me. He just said: "That's what all wives say when they want to murder their husbands." It was a terrible crime none the less. It has falsified his whole life—his family tree too. Sometimes I take a look in the Peerage, and then I say to myself: Here she is, going about with a false birth certificate like some servant girl, and for such things people are sent to the reformatory.

OLD MAN. Many do it. I seem to remember your own date of birth was given incorrectly.

MUMMY. My mother made me do that. I was not to blame. And in our crime, *you* played the biggest part.

OLD MAN. No. Your husband caused that crime, when he took my fiancée from me. I was born one who cannot forgive until he has punished. That was to me an imperative duty—and is so still.

MUMMY. What are you expecting to find in this house? What do you want? How did you get in? Is it to do with my daughter? If you touch her, you shall die.

OLD MAN. I mean well by her.

MUMMY. Then you must spare her father.

OLD MAN. No.

MUMMY. Then you shall die. In this room, behind that screen.

OLD MAN. That may be. But I can't let go once I've got my teeth into a thing.

MUMMY. You want to marry her to that student. Why? He is nothing and has nothing.

OLD MAN. He will be rich, through me.

MUMMY. Have you been invited here tonight?

OLD MAN. No, but I propose to get myself an invitation to this ghost supper.

MUMMY. Do you know who is coming?

OLD MAN. Not exactly.

MUMMY. The Baron. The man who lives up above—whose father-in-law was buried this afternoon.

OLD MAN. The man who is getting a divorce in order to marry the daughter of the Caretaker's wife . . . The man who used to be —your lover.

MUMMY. Another guest will be your former fiancée, who was seduced by my husband.

OLD MAN. A select gathering.

MUMMY. Oh God, if only we might die, might die!

OLD MAN. Then why have you stayed together?

MUMMY. Crime and secrets and guilt bind us together. We have broken our bonds and gone our own ways, times without number, but we are always drawn together again.

OLD MAN. I think the Colonel is coming.

MUMMY. Then I will go in to Adèle. (*Pause.*) Jacob, mind what you do. Spare him. (*Pause. She goes into the Hyacinth Room and disappears.*)

(*The* COLONEL *enters, cold and reserved, with a letter in his hand.*)

COLONEL. Be seated, please. (*Slowly the* OLD MAN *sits down. Pause. The* COLONEL *stares at him.*) You wrote this letter, sir?

OLD MAN. I did.

COLONEL. Your name is Hummel?

OLD MAN. It is. (*Pause.*)

COLONEL. As I understand, you have bought in all my unpaid promissory notes. I can only conclude that I am in your hands. What do you want?

OLD MAN. I want payment, in one way or another.

COLONEL. In what way?

OLD MAN. A very simple one. Let us not mention the money. Just bear with me in your house as a guest.

COLONEL. If so little will satisfy you . . .

OLD MAN. Thank you.

COLONEL. What else?

OLD MAN. Dismiss Bengtsson.

COLONEL. Why should I do that? My devoted servant, who has been with me a lifetime, who has the national medal for long and faithful service—why should I do that?

OLD MAN. That's how you see him—full of excellent qualities. He is not the man he appears to be.

COLONEL. Who is?

OLD MAN (*taken aback*). True. But Bengtsson must go.

COLONEL. Are you going to run my house?

OLD MAN. Yes. Since everything here belongs to me—furniture, curtains, dinner service, linen . . . and more too.

COLONEL. How do you mean—more?

OLD MAN. Everything. I own everything here. It is mine.

COLONEL. Very well, it is yours. But my family escutcheon and my good name remain my own.

OLD MAN. No, not even those. (*Pause.*) You are not a nobleman.

COLONEL. How dare you!

OLD MAN (*producing a document*). If you read this extract from *The Armorial Gazette*, you will see the family whose name you are using has been extinct for a hundred years.

COLONEL. I have heard rumors to this effect, but I inherited the name from my father. (*Reads.*) It is true. You are right. I am not a nobleman. Then I must take off my signet ring. It is true, it belongs to you. (*Gives it to him.*) There you are.

OLD MAN (*pocketing the ring*). Now we will continue. You are not a Colonel either.

COLONEL. I am not . . . ?

OLD MAN. No. You once held the temporary rank of Colonel in the American Volunteer Force, but after the war in Cuba and the reorganization of the Army, all such titles were abolished.

COLONEL. Is this true?

OLD MAN (*indicating his pocket*). Do you want to read it?

COLONEL. No, that's not necessary. Who are you, and what right have you to sit there stripping me in this fashion?

OLD MAN. You will see. But as far as stripping you goes . . . do you know who you are?

COLONEL. How dare you?

OLD MAN. Take off that wig and have a look at yourself in the mirror. But take your teeth out at the same time and shave off your moustache. Let Bengtsson unlace your metal stays and perhaps a certain X.Y.Z., a lackey, will recognize himself. The fellow who was a cupboard lover in a certain kitchen . . . (*The COLONEL reaches for the bell on the table, but HUMMEL checks him.*) Don't touch that bell, and don't call Bengtsson. If you do, I'll have him arrested. (*Pause.*) And now the guests are beginning to arrive.

Keep your composure and we will continue to play our old parts for a while.

COLONEL. Who are you? I recognize your voice and eyes.

OLD MAN. Don't try to find out. Keep silent and obey.

(*The* STUDENT *enters and bows to the* COLONEL.)

STUDENT. How do you do, sir.

COLONEL. Welcome to my house, young man. Your splendid behavior at that great disaster has brought your name to everybody's lips, and I count it an honor to receive you in my home.

STUDENT. My humble descent, sir . . . Your illustrious name and noble birth. . . .

COLONEL. May I introduce Mr. Arkenholtz—Mr. Hummel. If you will join the ladies in here, Mr. Arkenholtz—I must conclude my conversation with Mr. Hummel. (*He shows the* STUDENT *into the Hyacinth Room, where he remains visible, talking shyly to the* GIRL.) A splendid young man, musical, sings, writes poetry. If he only had blue blood in him, if he were of the same station, I don't think I should object . . .

OLD MAN. To what?

COLONEL. To my daughter . . .

OLD MAN. *Your* daughter! But apropos of that, why does she spend all her time in there?

COLONEL. She insists on being in the Hyacinth Room except when she is out-of-doors. It's a peculiarity of hers. Ah, here comes Miss Beatrice von Holsteinkrona—a charming woman, a pillar of the Church, with just enough money of her own to suit her birth and position.

OLD MAN (*to himself*). My fiancée.

(*The* FIANCÉE *enters, looking a little crazy.*)

COLONEL. Miss Holsteinkrona—Mr. Hummel. (*The* FIANCÉE *curtseys and takes a seat. The* ARISTOCRAT *enters and seats himself. He wears mourning and looks mysterious.*) Baron Skanskorg . . .

OLD MAN (*aside, without rising*). That's the jewel-thief, I think. (*To the* COLONEL) If you bring in the Mummy, the party will be complete.

COLONEL (*at the door of the Hyacinth Room*). Polly!

MUMMY (*entering*). Currrrr . . . !

COLONEL. Are the young people to come in too?

OLD MAN. No, not the young people. They shall be spared.

(*They all sit silent in a circle.*)

COLONEL. Shall we have the tea brought in?

OLD MAN. What's the use? No one wants tea. Why should we pretend about it?

COLONEL. Then shall we talk?

OLD MAN. Talk of the weather, which we know? Inquire about each other's health, which we know just as well? I prefer silence— then one can hear thoughts and see the past. Silence cannot hide anything—but words can. I read the other day that differences of language originated among savages for the purpose of keeping one tribe's secrets hidden from another. Every language therefore is a code, and he who finds the key can understand every language in the world. But this does not prevent secrets from being exposed without a key, specially when there is a question of paternity to be proved. Proof in a Court of Law is another matter. Two false witnesses suffice to prove anything about which they are agreed, but one does not take witnesses along on the kind of explorations I have in mind. Nature herself has instilled in human beings a sense of modesty which tries to hide what should be hidden, but we slip into situations unintentionally, and by chance sometimes the deepest secret is divulged—the mask torn from the impostor, the villain exposed. . . . (*Pause. All look at each other in silence.*) What a silence there is now! (*Long silence.*) Here, for instance, in this honorable house, in this elegant home, where beauty, wealth and culture are united. . . . (*Long silence.*) All of us now sitting here know who we are—do we not? There's no need for me to tell you. And you know me, although you pretend ignorance. (*He indicates the Hyacinth Room.*) In there is my daughter. *Mine*—you know that too. She had lost the desire to live, without knowing why. The fact is she was withering away in this air charged with crime and deceit and falseness of every kind. That is why I looked for a friend for her in whose company she might enjoy the light and warmth of noble deeds. (*Long silence.*) That was my mission in this house: to pull up the weeds, to expose the crimes, to settle all accounts, so that those young people might start afresh in this home, which is my gift to them. (*Long silence.*) Now I am going to grant safe-conduct, to each of you in his and her proper time and turn. Whoever stays I shall have arrested. (*Long silence.*) Do you hear the clock ticking like a death-watch beetle in the wall? Do you hear what it says? "It's time, it's time, it's time." When it strikes, in a few moments, your time will be up. Then you can go, but not before. It's raising its arm against you before it strikes. Listen! It is warning you. "The clock can strike." And I can strike too. (*He strikes the table with one of his crutches.*) Do you hear?

(*Silence. The MUMMY goes up to the clock and stops it, then speaks in a normal and serious voice.*)

MUMMY. But I can stop time in its course. I can wipe out the past and undo what is done. But not with bribes, not with threats—only through suffering and repentance. (*She goes up to the* OLD MAN.) We are miserable human beings, that we know. We have erred and we have sinned, we like all the rest. We are not what we seem, because at bottom we are better than ourselves, since we detest our sins. But when you, Jacob Hummel, with your false name, choose to sit in judgment over us, you prove yourself worse than us miserable sinners. For you are not the one you appear to be. You are a thief of human souls. You stole me once with false promises. You murdered the Consul who was buried today; you strangled him with debts. You have stolen the student, binding him by the pretence of a claim on his father, who never owed you a farthing. (*Having tried to rise and speak, the* OLD MAN *sinks back in his chair and crumples up more and more as she goes on.*) But there is one dark spot in your life which I am not quite sure about, although I have my suspicions. I think Bengtsson knows. (*She rings the bell on the table.*)

OLD MAN. No, not Bengtsson, not him.

MUMMY. So he does know. (*She rings again. The* MILKMAID *appears in the hallway door, unseen by all but the* OLD MAN, *who shrinks back in horror. The* MILKMAID *vanishes as* BENGTSSON *enters.*) Do you know this man, Bengtsson?

BENGTSSON. Yes, I know him and he knows me. Life, as you are aware, has its ups and downs. I have been in his service; another time he was in mine. For two whole years he was a sponger in my kitchen. As he had to be away by three, the dinner was got ready at two, and the family had to eat the warmed-up leavings of that brute. He drank the soup stock, which the cook then filled up with water. He sat out there like a vampire, sucking the marrow out of the house, so that we became like skeletons. And he nearly got us put in prison when we called the cook a thief. Later I met this man in Hamburg under another name. He was a usurer then, a blood-sucker. But while he was there he was charged with having lured a young girl out on to the ice so as to drown her, because she had seen him commit a crime he was afraid would be discovered. . . .

(*The* MUMMY *passes her hand over the* OLD MAN'S *face.*)

MUMMY. *This* is you. Now give up the notes and the Will. (JOHANSSON *appears in the hallway door and watches the scene with great interest, knowing he is now to be freed from slavery. The* OLD MAN *produces a bundle of papers and throws it on the table. The*

MUMMY *goes over and strokes his back.*) Parrot. Are you there, Jacob?

OLD MAN (*like a parrot*). Jacob is here. Pretty Polly. Currrrr!

MUMMY. May the clock strike?

OLD MAN (*with a clucking sound*). The clock may strike. (*Imitating a cuckoo clock.*) Cuckoo, cuckoo, cuckoo. . . .

(*The* MUMMY *opens the cupboard door.*)

MUMMY. Now the clock has struck. Rise, and enter the cupboard where I have spent twenty years repenting our crime. A rope is hanging there, which you can take as the one with which you strangled the Consul, and with which you meant to strangle your benefactor. . . . Go! (*The* OLD MAN *goes in to the cupboard. The* MUMMY *closes the door.*) Bengtsson! Put up the screen—the death-screen. (BENGTSSON *places the screen in front of the door.*) It is finished. God have mercy on his soul.

ALL. Amen.

(*Long silence. The* GIRL *and the* STUDENT *appear in the Hyacinth Room. She has a harp, on which he plays a prelude, and then accompanies the* STUDENT'S *recitation.*)

STUDENT.

I saw the sun. To me it seemed
that I beheld the Hidden.
Men must reap what they have sown;
blest is he whose deeds are good.
Deeds which you have wrought in fury,
cannot in evil find redress.
Comfort him you have distressed
with loving-kindness—this will heal.
No fear has he who does no ill.
Sweet is innocence.

Scene Three

Inside the Hyacinth Room. The general effect of the room is exotic and oriental. There are hyacinths everywhere, of every color, some in pots, some with the bulbs in glass vases and the roots going down into the water.

On top of the tiled stove is a large seated Buddha, in whose lap rests a bulb from which rises the stem of a shallot (Allium ascalonicum), bearing its globular cluster of white, starlike flowers.

On the right is an open door, leading into the Round Room, where the COLONEL *and the* MUMMY *are seated, inactive and silent. A part of the death-screen is also visible.*

On the left is a door to the pantry and kitchen.
The STUDENT *and the* GIRL *(Adèle) are beside the table; he standing, she seated with her harp.*

GIRL. Now sing to my flowers.

STUDENT. Is this the flower of your soul?

GIRL. The one and only. Do you too love the hyacinth?

STUDENT. I love it above all other flowers—its virginal shape rising straight and slender out of the bulb, resting on the water and sending its pure white roots down into the colorless fluid. I love its colors: the snow-white, pure as innocence, the yellow honey-sweet, the youthful pink, the ripe red, but best of all the blue —the dewy blue, deep-eyed and full of faith. I love them all, more than gold or pearls. I have loved them ever since I was a child, have worshipped them because they have all the fine qualities I lack. . . . And yet . . .

GIRL. Go on.

STUDENT. My love is not returned, for these beautiful blossoms hate me.

GIRL. How do you mean?

STUDENT. Their fragrance, strong and pure as the early winds of spring which have passed over melting snows, confuses my senses, deafens me, blinds me, thrusts me out of the room, bombards me with poisoned arrows that wound my heart and set my head on fire. Do you know the legend of that flower?

GIRL. Tell it to me.

STUDENT. First its meaning. The bulb is the earth, resting on the water or buried in the soil. Then the stalk rises, straight as the axis of the world, and at the top are the six-pointed star-flowers.

GIRL. Above the earth—the stars. Oh, that is wonderful! Where did you learn this? How did you find it out?

STUDENT. Let me think . . . In your eyes. And so, you see, it is an image of the Cosmos. This is why Buddha sits holding the earth-bulb, his eyes brooding as he watches it grow, outward and up-ward, transforming itself into a heaven. This poor earth will be-come a heaven. It is for this that Buddha waits.

GIRL. I see it now. Is not the snowflake six-pointed too like the hyacinth flower?

STUDENT. You are right. The snowflakes must be falling stars.

GIRL. And the snowdrop is a snow-star, grown out of snow.

STUDENT. But the largest and most beautiful of all the stars in the firmament, the golden-red Sirius, is the narcissus with its gold and red chalice and its six white rays.

GIRL. Have you seen the shallot in bloom?

STUDENT. Indeed I have. It bears its blossoms within a ball, a globe like the celestial one, strewn with white stars.

GIRL. Oh how glorious! Whose thought was that?

STUDENT. Yours.

GIRL. Yours.

STUDENT. Ours. We have given birth to it together. We are wedded.

GIRL. Not yet.

STUDENT. What's still to do?

GIRL. Waiting, ordeals, patience.

STUDENT. Very well. Put me to the test. (*Pause.*) Tell me. Why do your parents sit in there so silently, not saying a single word?

GIRL. Because they have nothing to say to each other, and because neither believes what the other says. This is how my father puts it: What's the point of talking, when neither of us can fool the other?

STUDENT. What a horrible thing to hear!

GIRL. Here comes the Cook. Look at her, how big and fat she is. (*They watch the* COOK, *although the audience cannot yet see her.*)

STUDENT. What does she want?

GIRL. To ask me about the dinner. I have to do the housekeeping as my mother's ill.

STUDENT. What have we to do with the kitchen?

GIRL. Me must eat. Look at the Cook. I can't bear the sight of her.

STUDENT. Who is that ogress?

GIRL. She belongs to the Hummel family of vampires. She is eating us.

STUDENT. Why don't you dismiss her?

GIRL. She won't go. We have no control over her. We've got her for our sins. Can't you see that we are pining and wasting away?

STUDENT. Don't you get enough to eat?

GIRL. Yes, we get many dishes, but all the strength has gone. She boils the nourishment out of the meat and gives us the fibre and water, while she drinks the stock herself. And when there's a roast, she first boils out the marrow, eats the gravy and drinks the juices herself. Everything she touches loses its savor. It's as if she sucked with her eyes. We get the grounds when she has drunk the coffee. She drinks the wine and fills the bottles up with water.

STUDENT. Send her packing.

GIRL. We can't.

STUDENT. Why not?

GIRL. We don't know. She won't go. No one has any control over her. She has taken all our strength from us.

STUDENT. May I get rid of her?

GIRL. No. It must be as it is. Here she is. She will ask me what is to be for dinner. I shall tell her. She will make objections and get her own way.

STUDENT. Let her do the ordering herself then.

GIRL. She won't do that.

STUDENT. What an extraordinary house! It is bewitched.

GIRL. Yes. But now she is turning back, because she has seen you.

THE COOK (*in the doorway*). No, that wasn't the reason. (*She grins, showing all her teeth.*)

STUDENT. Get out!

COOK. When it suits me. (*Pause.*) It does suit me now. (*She disappears.*)

GIRL. Don't lose your temper. Practise patience. She is one of the ordeals we have to go through in this house. You see, we have a housemaid too, whom we have to clean up after.

STUDENT. I am done for. *Cor in œthere.* Music!

GIRL. Wait.

STUDENT. Music!

GIRL. Patience. This room is called the room of ordeals. It looks beautiful, but it is full of defects.

STUDENT. Really? Well, such things must be seen too. It is very beautiful, but a little cold. Why don't you have a fire?

GIRL. Because it smokes.

STUDENT. Can't you have the chimney swept?

GIRL. It doesn't help. You see that writing-desk there?

STUDENT. An unusually fine piece.

GIRL. But it wobbles. Every day I put a piece of cork under that leg, and every day the housemaid takes it away when she sweeps and I have to cut a new piece. The penholder is covered with ink every morning and so is the inkstand. I have to clean them up every morning after that woman, as sure as the sun rises. (*Pause.*) What's the worst job you can think of?

STUDENT. To count the washing. Ugh!

GIRL. That I have to do. Ugh!

STUDENT. What else?

GIRL. To be waked in the middle of the night and have to get up and see to the window, which the housemaid has left banging.

STUDENT. What else?

GIRL. To get up on a ladder and tie the cord on the damper* which the housemaid has torn off.

STUDENT. What else?

GIRL. To sweep after her, to dust after her, to light the fire in the stove

* Damper to the big stove.

when all she's done is throw in some wood. To see to the damper, to wipe the glasses, to lay the table over again, to open the bottles, to see that the rooms are aired, to remake my bed, to rinse the water-bottle when it's green with sediment, to buy matches and soap which are always lacking, to wipe the chimneys and trim the wicks to keep the lamps from smoking—and so that they don't go out when we have company, I have to fill them myself. . . .

STUDENT. Music!

GIRL. Wait. The labor comes first. The labor of keeping the dirt of life at a distance.

STUDENT. But you are wealthy and have two servants.

GIRL. It doesn't help. Even if we had three. Living is hard work, and sometimes I grow tired. (*Pause.*) Think then if there were a nursery as well.

STUDENT. The greatest of joys.

GIRL. And the costliest. Is life worth so much hardship?

STUDENT. That must depend on the reward you expect for your labors. I would not shrink from anything to win your hand.

GIRL. Don't say that. You can never have me.

STUDENT. Why not?

GIRL. You mustn't ask. (*Pause.*)

STUDENT. You dropped your bracelet out of the window. . . .

GIRL. Because my hand has grown so thin. (*Pause. The* COOK *appears with a Japanese bottle in her hand.*) There she is—the one who devours me and all of us.

STUDENT. What has she in her hand?

GIRL. It is the bottle of coloring matter that has letters like scorpions on it. It is the soy which turns water into soup and takes the place of gravy. She makes cabbage soup with it—and mock-turtle soup too.

STUDENT (*to* COOK). Get out!

COOK. You drain us of sap, and we drain you. We take the blood and leave you the water, but colored . . . colored. I am going now, but all the same I shall stay, as long as I please. (*She goes out.*)

STUDENT. Why did Bengtsson get a medal?

GIRL. For his great merits.

STUDENT. Has he no defects?

GIRL. Yes, great ones. But you don't get a medal for them. (*They smile.*)

STUDENT. You have many secrets in this house.

GIRL. As in all others. Permit us to keep ours.

STUDENT. Don't you approve of candor?

GIRL. Yes—within reason.

STUDENT. Sometimes I'm seized with a raging desire to say all I think. But I know the world would go to pieces if one were completely candid. (*Pause.*) I went to a funeral the other day . . . in church. It was very solemn and beautiful.

GIRL. Was it Mr. Hummel's?

STUDENT. My false benefactor's—yes. At the head of the coffin stood an old friend of the deceased. He carried the mace. I was deeply impressed by the dignified manner and moving words of the clergyman. I cried. We all cried. Afterwards we went to a tavern, and there I learned that the man with the mace had been in love with the dead man's son. . . . (*The* GIRL *stares at him, trying to understand.*) And that the dead man had borrowed money from his son's admirer. (*Pause.*) Next day the clergyman was arrested for embezzling the church funds. A pretty story.

GIRL. Oh . . . ! (*Pause.*)

STUDENT. Do you know how I am thinking about you now?

GIRL. Don't tell me, or I shall die.

STUDENT. I must, or I shall die.

GIRL. It is in asylums that people say everything they think.

STUDENT. Exactly. My father finished up in an asylum.

GIRL. Was he ill?

STUDENT. No, he was well, but he was mad. You see, he broke out once—in these circumstances. Like all of us, he was surrounded with a circle of acquaintances; he called them friends for short. They were a lot of rotters, of course, as most people are, but he had to have some society—he couldn't get on all alone. Well, as you know, in everyday life no one tells people what he thinks of them, and he didn't either. He knew perfectly well what frauds they were—he'd sounded the depths of their deceit—but as he was a wise and well-bred man, he was always courteous to them. Then one day he gave a big party. It was in the evening and he was tired by the day's work and by the strain of holding his tongue and at the same time talking rubbish with his guests. . . . (*The* GIRL *is frightened.*) Well, at the dinner table he rapped for silence, raised his glass, and began to speak. Then something loosed the trigger. He made an enormous speech in which he stripped the whole company naked, one after the other, and told them of all their treachery. Then, tired out, he sat down on the table and told them all to go to hell.

GIRL. Oh!

STUDENT. I was there, and I shall never forget what happened then. Father and Mother came to blows, the guests rushed for the door . . . and my father was taken to a madhouse, where he died.

(*Pause.*) Water that is still too long stagnates, and so it is in this
house too. There is something stagnating here. And yet I thought
it was paradise itself that first time I saw you coming in here.
There I stood that Sunday morning, gazing in. I saw a Colonel
who was no Colonel. I had a benefactor who was a thief and
had to hang himself. I saw a mummy who was not a mummy and
an old maid—what of the maidenhood, by the way? Where is
beauty to be found? In nature, and in my own mind, when it is
in its Sunday clothes. Where are honor and faith? In fairy-tales
and children's fancies. Where is anything that fulfills its promise?
In my imagination. Now your flowers have poisoned me and I
have given the poison back to you. I asked you to become my
wife in a home full of poetry and song and music. Then the Cook
came. . . . *Sursum Corda!* Try once more to strike fire and
glory out of the golden harp. Try, I beg you, I implore you on
my knees. (*Pause.*) Then I will do it myself. (*He picks up the
harp, but the strings give no sound.*) It is dumb and deaf. To think
that the most beautiful flowers are so poisonous, are the most
poisonous. The curse lies over the whole of creation, over life
itself. Why will you not be my bride? Because the very life-spring
within you is sick . . . now I can feel that vampire in the kitchen
beginning to suck me. I believe she is a Lamia, one of those that
suck the blood of children. It is always in the kitchen quarters
that the seed-leaves of the children are nipped, if it has not already
happened in the bedroom. There are poisons that destroy the
sight and poisons that open the eyes. I seem to have been born
with the latter kind, for I cannot see what is ugly as beautiful, nor
call evil good. I cannot. Jesus Christ descended into hell. That
was His pilgrimage on earth—to this madhouse, this prison, this
charnel-house, this earth. And the madmen killed Him when He
wanted to set them free; but the robber they let go. The robber
always gets the sympathy. Woe! Woe to us all. Saviour of the
world, save us! We perish.

(*And now the* GIRL *has drooped, and it is seen that she is dying.
She rings.* BENGTSSON *enters.*)

GIRL. Bring the screen. Quick. I am dying.

(BENGTSSON *comes back with the screen, opens it and arranges it
in front of the* GIRL.)

STUDENT. The Liberator is coming. Welcome, pale and gentle one.
Sleep, you lovely, innocent, doomed creature, suffering for no
fault of your own. Sleep without dreaming, and when you wake
again . . . may you be greeted by a sun that does not burn, in
a home without dust, by friends without stain, by a love without

flaw. You wise and gentle Buddha, sitting there waiting for a Heaven to sprout from the earth, grant us patience in our ordeal and purity of will, so that this hope may not be confounded. (*The strings of the harp hum softly and a white light fills the room.*)

I saw the sun. To me it seemed
that I beheld the Hidden.
Men must reap what they have sown,
blest is he whose deeds are good.
Deeds which you have wrought in fury,
cannot in evil find redress.
Comfort him you have distressed
with loving-kindness—this will heal.
No fear has he who does no ill.
Sweet is innocence.

(*A faint moaning is heard behind the screen.*) You poor little child, child of this world of illusion, guilt, suffering and death, this world of endless change, disappointment, and pain. May the Lord of Heaven be merciful to you upon your journey.

(*The room disappears. Böcklin's picture* The Island of the Dead *is seen in the distance, and from the island comes music, soft, sweet, and melancholy.*)

BLOOD WEDDING [1933]

Tragedy in Three Acts and Seven Scenes

by Federico García Lorca

translated by James Graham-Luján *and*
Richard L. O'Connell

Characters

THE MOTHER	LEONARDO
THE BRIDE	THE BRIDEGROOM
THE MOTHER-IN-LAW	THE BRIDE'S FATHER
LEONARDO'S WIFE	THE MOON
THE SERVANT WOMAN	BEGGAR WOMAN, *Death*
THE NEIGHBOR WOMAN	WOODCUTTERS
YOUNG GIRLS	YOUNG MEN

Blood Wedding, from *Three Tragedies of Federico García Lorca.* Translated by James Graham-Luján and Richard L. O'Connell. Copyright 1945 by James Graham-Luján and Richard L. O'Connell. Reprinted by permission of New Directions, Publishers.

ACT ONE

Scene One

A room painted yellow.

BRIDEGROOM (*entering*). Mother.
MOTHER. What?
BRIDEGROOM. I'm going.
MOTHER. Where?
BRIDEGROOM. To the vineyard.
  (*He starts to go.*)
MOTHER. Wait.
BRIDEGROOM. You want something?
MOTHER. Your breakfast, son.
BRIDEGROOM. Forget it. I'll eat grapes. Give me the knife.
MOTHER. What for?
BRIDEGROOM (*laughing*). To cut the grapes with.
MOTHER (*muttering as she looks for the knife*). Knives, knives. Cursed
  be all knives, and the scoundrel who invented them.
BRIDEGROOM. Let's talk about something else.
MOTHER. And guns and pistols and the smallest little knife—and even
  hoes and pitchforks.
BRIDEGROOM. All right.
MOTHER. Everything that can slice a man's body. A handsome man,
  full of young life, who goes out to the vineyards or to his own
  olive groves—his own because he's inherited them . . .
BRIDEGROOM (*lowering his head*). Be quiet.
MOTHER. . . . and then that man doesn't come back. Or if he does
  come back it's only for someone to cover him over with a palm
  leaf or a plate of rock salt so he won't bloat. I don't know how
  you dare carry a knife on your body—or how I let this serpent
  (*she takes a knife from a kitchen chest*) stay in the chest.
BRIDEGROOM. Have you had your say?
MOTHER. If I lived to be a hundred I'd talk of nothing else. First your
  father; to me he smelled like a carnation and I had him for barely
  three years. Then your brother. Oh, is it right—how can it be—
  that a small thing like a knife or a pistol can finish off a man—
  a bull of a man? No, I'll never be quiet. The months pass and the
  hopelessness of it stings in my eyes and even to the roots of my
  hair.
BRIDEGROOM (*forcefully*). Let's quit this talk!
MOTHER. No. No. Let's not quit this talk. Can anyone bring me your

father back? Or your brother? Then there's the jail. What do they mean, jail? They eat there, smoke there, play music there! My dead men choking with weeds, silent, turning to dust. Two men like two beautiful flowers. The killers in jail, carefree, looking at the mountains.

BRIDEGROOM. Do you want me to go kill them?

MOTHER. No . . . If I talk about it it's because . . . Oh, how can I help talking about it, seeing you go out that door? It's . . . I don't like you to carry a knife. It's just that . . . that I wish you wouldn't go out to the fields.

BRIDEGROOM (*laughing*). Oh, come now!

MOTHER. I'd like it if you were a woman. Then you wouldn't be going out to the arroyo now and we'd both of us embroider flounces and little woolly dogs.

BRIDEGROOM. (*He puts his arm around his mother and laughs.*) Mother, what if I should take you with me to the vineyards?

MOTHER. What would an old lady do in the vineyards? Were you going to put me down under the young vines?

BRIDEGROOM (*lifting her in his arms*). Old lady, old lady—you little old, little old lady!

MOTHER. Your father, he used to take me. That's the way with men of good stock; good blood. Your grandfather left a son on every corner. That's what I like. Men, men; wheat, wheat.

BRIDEGROOM. And I, Mother?

MOTHER. You, what?

BRIDEGROOM. Do I need to tell you again?

MOTHER (*seriously*). Oh!

BRIDEGROOM. Do you think it's bad?

MOTHER. No.

BRIDEGROOM. Well, then?

MOTHER. I don't really know. Like this, suddenly, it always surprises me. I know the girl is good. Isn't she? Well behaved. Hard working. Kneads her bread, sews her skirts, but even so when I say her name I feel as though someone had hit me on the forehead with a rock.

BRIDEGROOM. Foolishness.

MOTHER. More than foolishness. I'll be left alone. Now only you are left me—I hate to see you go.

BRIDEGROOM. But you'll come with us.

MOTHER. No. I can't leave your father and brother here alone. I have to go to them every morning and if I go away it's possible one of the Félix family, one of the killers, might die—and they'd bury him next to ours. And that'll never happen! Oh, no! That'll never

happen! Because I'd dig them out with my nails and, all by myself crush them against the wall.

BRIDEGROOM (*sternly*). There you go again.

MOTHER. Forgive me.

(*Pause.*)

How long have you known her?

BRIDEGROOM. Three years. I've been able to buy the vineyard.

MOTHER. Three years. She used to have another sweetheart, didn't she?

BRIDEGROOM. I don't know. I don't think so. Girls have to look at what
they'll marry.

MOTHER. Yes. I looked at nobody. I looked at your father, and when
they killed him I looked at the wall in front of me. One woman
with one man, and that's all.

BRIDEGROOM. You know my girl's good.

MOTHER. I don't doubt it. All the same, I'm sorry not to have known
what her mother was like.

BRIDEGROOM. What difference does it make now?

MOTHER (*looking at him*). Son.

BRIDEGROOM. What is it?

MOTHER. That's true! You're right! When do you want me to ask for
her?

BRIDEGROOM (*happily*). Does Sunday seem all right to you?

MOTHER (*seriously*). I'll take her the bronze earrings, they're very old
—and you buy her . . .

BRIDEGROOM. You know more about that . . .

MOTHER. . . . you buy her some open-work stockings—and for you,
two suits—three! I have no one but you now!

BRIDEGROOM. I'm going. Tomorrow I'll go see her.

MOTHER. Yes, yes—and see if you can make me happy with six grandchildren—or as many as you want, since your father didn't live to
give them to me.

BRIDEGROOM. The first-born for you!

MOTHER. Yes, but have some girls. I want to embroider and make lace,
and be at peace.

BRIDEGROOM. I'm sure you'll love my wife.

MOTHER. I'll love her. (*She starts to kiss him but changes her mind.*)
Go on. You're too big now for kisses. Give them to your wife.
(*Pause. To herself*) When she is your wife.

BRIDEGROOM. I'm going.

MOTHER. And that land around the little mill—work it over. You've
not taken good care of it.

BRIDEGROOM. You're right. I will.

MOTHER. God keep you. (*The* SON *goes out. The* MOTHER *remains seated—her back to the door. A* NEIGHBOR WOMAN *with a 'kerchief on her head appears in the door.*) Come in.

NEIGHBOR. How are you?

MOTHER. Just as you see me.

NEIGHBOR. I came down to the store and stopped in to see you. We live so far away!

MOTHER. It's twenty years since I've been up to the top of the street.

NEIGHBOR. You're looking well.

MOTHER. You think so?

NEIGHBOR. Things happen. Two days ago they brought in my neighbor's son with both arms sliced off by the machine. (*She sits down.*)

MOTHER. Rafael?

NEIGHBOR. Yes. And there you have him. Many times I've thought your son and mine are better off where they are—sleeping, resting—not running the risk of being left helpless.

MOTHER. Hush. That's all just something thought up—but no consolation.

NEIGHBOR (*sighing*). Ay!

MOTHER (*sighing*). Ay!

(*Pause.*)

NEIGHBOR (*sadly*). Where's your son?

MOTHER. He went out.

NEIGHBOR. He finally bought the vineyard!

MOTHER. He was lucky.

NEIGHBOR. Now he'll get married.

MOTHER. (*As though reminded of something, she draws her chair near the* NEIGHBOR.) Listen.

NEIGHBOR (*in a confidential manner*). Yes. What is it?

MOTHER. You know my son's sweetheart?

NEIGHBOR. A good girl!

MOTHER. Yes, but . . .

NEIGHBOR. But who knows her really well? There's nobody. She lives out there alone with her father—so far away—fifteen miles from the nearest house. But she's a good girl. Used to being alone.

MOTHER. And her mother?

NEIGHBOR. Her mother I *did* know. Beautiful. Her face glowed like a saint's—but *I* never liked her. She didn't love her husband.

MOTHER (*sternly*). Well, what a lot of things certain people know!

NEIGHBOR. I'm sorry. I didn't mean to offend—but it's true. Now, whether she was decent or not nobody said. That wasn't discussed. She was haughty.

MOTHER. There you go again!

NEIGHBOR. You asked me.

MOTHER. I wish no one knew anything about them—either the live one or the dead one—that they were like two thistles no one even names but cuts off at the right moment.

NEIGHBOR. You're right. Your son is worth a lot.

MOTHER. Yes—a lot. That's why I look after him. They told me the girl had a sweetheart some time ago.

NEIGHBOR. She was about fifteen. He's been married two years now—to a cousin of hers, as a matter of fact. But nobody remembers about their engagement.

MOTHER. How do you remember it?

NEIGHBOR. Oh, what questions you ask!

MOTHER. We like to know all about the things that hurt us. Who was the boy?

NEIGHBOR. Leonardo.

MOTHER. What Leonardo?

NEIGHBOR. Leonardo Félix.

MOTHER. Félix!

NEIGHBOR. Yes, but—how is Leonardo to blame for anything? He was eight years old when those things happened.

MOTHER. That's true. But I hear that name—Félix—and it's all the same. (*Muttering*) Félix, a slimy mouthful. (*She spits.*) It makes me spit—spit so I won't kill!

NEIGHBOR. Control yourself. What good will it do?

MOTHER. No good. But you see how it is.

NEIGHBOR. Don't get in the way of your son's happiness. Don't say anything to him. You're old. So am I. It's time for you and me to keep quiet.

MOTHER. I'll say nothing to him.

NEIGHBOR (*kissing her*). Nothing.

MOTHER (*calmly*). Such things . . . !

NEIGHBOR. I'm going. My men will soon be coming in from the fields.

MOTHER. Have you ever known such a hot sun?

NEIGHBOR. The children carrying water out to the reapers are black with it. Goodbye, woman.

MOTHER. Goodbye. (*The* MOTHER *starts toward the door at the left. Halfway there she stops and slowly crosses herself.*)

Curtain

Scene Two

A room painted rose with copperware and wreaths of common flowers. In the center of the room is a table with a tablecloth. It is morning.

    LEONARDO'S MOTHER-IN-LAW *sits in one corner holding a child in her arms and rocking it. His* WIFE *is in the other corner mending stockings.*

MOTHER-IN-LAW.

    Lullaby, my baby
    once there was a big horse
    who didn't like water.
    The water was black there
    under the branches.
    When it reached the bridge
    it stopped and it sang.
    Who can say, my baby,
    what the stream holds
    with its long tail
    in its green parlor?

WIFE (*softly*).

    Carnation, sleep and dream,
    the horse won't drink from the stream.

MOTHER-IN-LAW.

    My rose, asleep now lie,
    the horse is starting to cry.
    His poor hooves were bleeding,
    his long mane was frozen,
    and deep in his eyes
    stuck a silvery dagger.
    Down he went to the river,
    Oh, down he went down!
    And his blood was running,
    Oh, more than the water.

WIFE.

    Carnation, sleep and dream,
    the horse won't drink from the stream.

MOTHER-IN-LAW.

    My rose, asleep now lie,
    the horse is starting to cry.

WIFE.

    He never did touch
    the dank river shore

though his muzzle was warm
and with silvery flies.
So, to the hard mountains
he could only whinny
just when the dead stream
covered his throat.
Ay-y-y, for the big horse
who didn't like water!
Ay-y-y, for the snow-wound
big horse of the dawn!

MOTHER-IN-LAW.

Don't come in! Stop him
and close up the window
with branches of dreams
and a dream of branches.

WIFE.

My baby is sleeping.

MOTHER-IN-LAW.

My baby is quiet.

WIFE.

Look, horse, my baby
has him a pillow.

MOTHER-IN-LAW.

His cradle is metal.

WIFE.

His quilt a fine fabric.

MOTHER-IN-LAW.

Lullaby, my baby.

WIFE.

Ay-y-y, for the big horse
who didn't like water!

MOTHER-IN-LAW.

Don't come near, don't come in!
Go away to the mountains
and through the grey valleys,
that's where your mare is.

WIFE (*looking at the baby*).

My baby is sleeping.

MOTHER-IN-LAW.

My baby is resting.

WIFE (*softly*).

Carnation, sleep and dream,
the horse won't drink from the stream.

MOTHER-IN-LAW (*getting up, very softly*).
My rose, asleep now lie
for the horse is starting to cry.
(*She carries the child out.* LEONARDO *enters.*)

LEONARDO. Where's the baby?

WIFE. He's sleeping.

LEONARDO. Yesterday he wasn't well. He cried during the night.

WIFE. Today he's like a dahlia. And you? Were you at the black-smith's?

LEONARDO. I've just come from there. Would you believe it? For more than two months he's been putting new shoes on the horse and they're always coming off. As far as I can see he pulls them off on the stones.

WIFE. Couldn't it just be that you use him so much?

LEONARDO. No. I almost never use him.

WIFE. Yesterday the neighbors told me they'd seen you on the far side of the plains.

LEONARDO. Who said that?

WIFE. The women who gather capers. It certainly surprised me. Was it you?

LEONARDO. No. What would I be doing there, in that wasteland?

WIFE. That's what I said. But the horse was streaming sweat.

LEONARDO. Did you see him?

WIFE. No. Mother did.

LEONARDO. Is she with the baby?

WIFE. Yes. Do you want some lemonade?

LEONARDO. With good cold water.

WIFE. And then you didn't come to eat!

LEONARDO. I was with the wheat weighers. They always hold me up.

WIFE (*very tenderly, while she makes the lemonade*). Did they pay you a good price?

LEONARDO. Fair.

WIFE. I need a new dress and the baby a bonnet with ribbons.

LEONARDO (*getting up*). I'm going to take a look at him.

WIFE. Be careful. He's asleep.

MOTHER-IN-LAW (*coming in*). Well! Who's been racing the horse that way? He's down there, worn out, his eyes popping from their sockets as though he'd come from the ends of the earth.

LEONARDO (*acidly*). I have.

MOTHER-IN-LAW. Oh, excuse me! He's your horse.

WIFE (*timidly*). He was at the wheat buyers.

MOTHER-IN-LAW. He can burst for all of me!
(*She sits down. Pause.*)

WIFE. Your drink. Is it cold?

LEONARDO. Yes.

WIFE. Did you hear they're going to ask for my cousin?

LEONARDO. When?

WIFE. Tomorrow. The wedding will be within a month. I hope they're going to invite us.

LEONARDO (*gravely*). I don't know.

MOTHER-IN-LAW. His mother, I think, wasn't very happy about the match.

LEONARDO. Well, she may be right. She's a girl to be careful with.

WIFE. I don't like to have you thinking bad things about a good girl.

MOTHER-IN-LAW (*meaningfully*). If he does, it's because he knows her. Didn't you know he courted her for three years?

LEONARDO. But I left her. (*To his* WIFE) Are you going to cry now? Quit that! (*He brusquely pulls her hands away from her face.*) Let's go see the baby.

(*They go in with their arms around each other. A* GIRL *appears. She is happy. She enters running.*)

GIRL. Señora.

MOTHER-IN-LAW. What is it?

GIRL. The groom came to the store and he's bought the best of everything they had.

MOTHER-IN-LAW. Was he alone?

GIRL. No. With his mother. Stern, tall. (*She imitates her.*) And such extravagance!

MOTHER-IN-LAW. They have money.

GIRL. And they bought some open-work stockings! Oh, such stockings! A woman's dream of stockings! Look: a swallow here (*she points to her ankle*), a ship here (*she points to her calf*), and here, (*she points to her thigh*) a rose!

MOTHER-IN-LAW. Child!

GIRL. A rose with the seeds and the stem! Oh! All in silk.

MOTHER-IN-LAW. Two rich families are being brought together.

(LEONARDO *and his* WIFE *appear.*)

GIRL. I came to tell you what they're buying.

LEONARDO (*loudly*). We don't care.

WIFE. Leave her alone.

MOTHER-IN-LAW. Leonardo, it's not that important.

GIRL. Please excuse me. (*She leaves, weeping.*)

MOTHER-IN-LAW. Why do you always have to make trouble with people?

LEONARDO. I didn't ask for your opinion. (*He sits down.*)

MOTHER-IN-LAW. Very well.

(*Pause.*)

WIFE (*to* LEONARDO). What's the matter with you? What idea've you
  got boiling there inside your head? Don't leave me like this, not
  knowing anything.

LEONARDO. Stop that.

WIFE. No. I want you to look at me and tell me.

LEONARDO. Let me alone. (*He rises.*)

WIFE. Where are you going, love?

LEONARDO (*sharply*). Can't you shut up?

MOTHER-IN-LAW (*energetically, to her daughter*). Be quiet! (LEONARDO
  goes out.) The baby! (*She goes into the bedroom and comes out
  again with the baby in her arms. The* WIFE *has remained standing,
  unmoving.*)
  His poor hooves were bleeding,
  his long mane was frozen,
  and deep in his eyes
  stuck a silvery dagger.
  Down he went to the river,
  Oh, down he went down!
  And his blood was running,
  Oh, more than the water.

WIFE (*turning slowly, as though dreaming*).
  Carnation, sleep and dream,
  the horse is drinking from the stream.

MOTHER-IN-LAW.
  My rose, asleep now lie
  the horse is starting to cry.

WIFE.
  Lullaby, my baby.

MOTHER-IN-LAW.
  Ay-y-y, for the big horse
  who didn't like water!

WIFE (*dramatically*).
  Don't come near, don't come in!
  Go away to the mountains!
  Ay-y-y, for the snow-wound,
  big horse of the dawn!

MOTHER-IN-LAW (*weeping*).
  My baby is sleeping . . .

WIFE (*weeping, as she slowly moves closer*).
  My baby is resting . . .

MOTHER-IN-LAW.
  Carnation, sleep and dream,

the horse won't drink from the stream.

WIFE (*weeping, and leaning on the table*).
    My rose, asleep now lie,
    the horse is starting to cry.

Curtain

Scene Three

Interior of the cave where the BRIDE *lives. At the back is a cross
of large rose colored flowers. The round doors have lace curtains
with rose colored ties. Around the walls, which are of a white and
hard material, are round fans, blue jars, and little mirrors.*

SERVANT. Come right in . . . (*She is very affable, full of humble hy-
    pocrisy. The* BRIDEGROOM *and his* MOTHER *enter. The* MOTHER
    is dressed in black satin and wears a lace mantilla; the BRIDEGROOM
    in black corduroy with a great golden chain.) Won't you sit
    down? They'll be right here.
    (*She leaves. The* MOTHER *and* SON *are left sitting motionless as
    statues. Long pause.*)
MOTHER. Did you wear the watch?
BRIDEGROOM. Yes. (*He takes it out and looks at it.*)
MOTHER. We have to be back on time. How far away these people live!
BRIDEGROOM. But this is good land.
MOTHER. Good; but much too lonesome. A four hour trip and not
    one house, not one tree.
BRIDEGROOM. This is the wasteland.
MOTHER. Your father would have covered it with trees.
BRIDEGROOM. Without water?
MOTHER. He would have found some. In the three years we were
    married he planted ten cherry trees (*remembering*), those three
    walnut trees by the mill, a whole vineyard and a plant called
    Jupiter which had scarlet flowers—but it dried up.
    (*Pause.*)
BRIDEGROOM (*referring to the* BRIDE). She must be dressing.
    (*The* BRIDE'S FATHER *enters. He is very old, with shining white
    hair. His head is bowed. The* MOTHER *and the* BRIDEGROOM *rise.
    They shake hands in silence.*)
FATHER. Was it a long trip?
MOTHER. Four hours.
    (*They sit down.*)

FATHER. You must have come the longest way.

MOTHER. I'm too old to come along the cliffs by the river.

BRIDEGROOM. She gets dizzy.

(*Pause.*)

FATHER. A good hemp harvest.

BRIDEGROOM. A really good one.

FATHER. When I was young this land didn't even grow hemp. We've had to punish it, even weep over it, to make it give us anything useful.

MOTHER. But now it does. Don't complain. I'm not here to ask you for anything.

FATHER (*smiling*). You're richer than I. Your vineyards are worth a fortune. Each young vine a silver coin. But—do you know?— what bothers me is that our lands are separated. I like to have everything together. One thorn I have in my heart, and that's the little orchard there, stuck in between my fields—and they won't sell it to me for all the gold in the world.

BRIDEGROOM. That's the way it always is.

FATHER. If we could just take twenty teams of oxen and move your vineyards over here, and put them down on that hillside, how happy I'd be!

MOTHER. But why?

FATHER. What's mine is hers and what's yours is his. That's why. Just to see it all together. How beautiful it is to bring things together!

BRIDEGROOM. And it would be less work.

MOTHER. When I die, you could sell ours and buy here, right alongside.

FATHER. Sell, sell? Bah! Buy, my friend, buy everything. If I had had sons I would have bought all this mountainside right up to the part with the stream. It's not good land, but strong arms can make it good, and since no people pass by, they don't steal your fruit and you can sleep in peace.

(*Pause.*)

MOTHER. You know what I'm here for.

FATHER. Yes.

MOTHER. And?

FATHER. It seems all right to me. They have talked it over.

MOTHER. My son has money and knows how to manage it.

FATHER. My daughter too.

MOTHER. My son is handsome. He's never known a woman. His good name cleaner than a sheet spread out in the sun.

FATHER. No need to tell you about my daughter. At three, when the morning star shines, she prepares the bread. She never talks: soft as wool, she embroiders all kinds of fancy work and she can cut a strong cord with her teeth.

MOTHER. God bless her house.

FATHER. May God bless it.

(*The* SERVANT *appears with two trays. One with drinks and the other with sweets.*)

MOTHER (*to the* SON). When would you like the wedding?

BRIDEGROOM. Next Thursday.

FATHER. The day on which she'll be exactly twenty-two years old.

MOTHER. Twenty-two! My oldest son would be that age if he were alive. Warm and manly as he was, he'd be living now if men hadn't invented knives.

FATHER. One mustn't think about that.

MOTHER. Every minute. Always a hand on your breast.

FATHER. Thursday, then? Is that right?

BRIDEGROOM. That's right.

FATHER. You and I and the bridal couple will go in a carriage to the church which is very far from here; the wedding party on the carts and horses they'll bring with them.

MOTHER. Agreed.

(*The* SERVANT *passes through.*)

FATHER. Tell her she may come in now. (*To the* MOTHER) I shall be much pleased if you like her.

(*The* BRIDE *appears. Her hands fall in a modest pose and her head is bowed.*)

MOTHER. Come here. Are you happy?

BRIDE. Yes, señora.

FATHER. You shouldn't be so solemn. After all, she's going to be your mother.

BRIDE. I'm happy. I've said "yes" because I wanted to.

MOTHER. Naturally. (*She takes her by the chin.*) Look at me.

FATHER. She resembles my wife in every way.

MOTHER. Yes? What a beautiful glance! Do you know what it is to be married, child?

BRIDE (*seriously*). I do.

MOTHER. A man, some children and a wall two yards thick for everything else.

BRIDEGROOM. Is anything else needed?

MOTHER. No. Just that you all live—that's it! Live long!

BRIDE. I'll know how to keep my word.

MOTHER. Here are some gifts for you.

BRIDE. Thank you.

FATHER. Shall we have something?

MOTHER. Nothing for me. (*To the* SON) But you?

BRIDEGROOM. Yes, thank you.

(*He takes one sweet, the* BRIDE *another.*)

FATHER (*to the* BRIDEGROOM). Wine?

MOTHER. He doesn't touch it.

FATHER. All the better.

(*Pause. All are standing.*)

BRIDEGROOM (*to the* BRIDE). I'll come tomorrow.

BRIDE. What time?

BRIDEGROOM. Five.

BRIDE. I'll be waiting for you.

BRIDEGROOM. When I leave your side I feel a great emptiness, and something like a knot in my throat.

BRIDE. When you are my husband you won't have it any more.

BRIDEGROOM. That's what I tell myself.

MOTHER. Come. The sun doesn't wait. (*To the* FATHER) Are we agreed on everything?

FATHER. Agreed.

MOTHER (*to the* SERVANT). Goodbye, woman.

SERVANT. God go with you!

(*The* MOTHER *kisses the* BRIDE *and they begin to leave in silence.*)

MOTHER (*at the door*). Goodbye, daughter.

(*The* BRIDE *answers with her hand.*)

FATHER. I'll go out with you.

(*They leave.*)

SERVANT. I'm bursting to see the presents.

BRIDE (*sharply*). Stop that!

SERVANT. Oh, child, show them to me.

BRIDE. I don't want to.

SERVANT. At least the stockings. They say they're all open work. Please!

BRIDE. I said no.

SERVANT. Well, my Lord. All right then. It looks as if you didn't want to get married.

BRIDE (*biting her hand in anger*). Ay-y-y!

SERVANT. Child, child! What's the matter with you? Are you sorry to give up your queen's life? Don't think of bitter things. Have you any reason to? None. Let's look at the presents.

(*She takes the box.*)

BRIDE (*holding her by the wrists*). Let go.

SERVANT. Ay-y-y, girl!

BRIDE. Let go, I said.

SERVANT. You're stronger than a man.

BRIDE. Haven't I done a man's work? I wish I were.

SERVANT. Don't talk like that.

BRIDE. Quiet, I said. Let's talk about something else.

(*The light is fading from the stage. Long pause.*)

SERVANT. Did you hear a horse last night?

BRIDE. What time?

SERVANT. Three.

BRIDE. It might have been a stray horse—from the herd.

SERVANT. No. It carried a rider.

BRIDE. How do you know?

SERVANT. Because I saw him. He was standing by your window. It shocked me greatly.

BRIDE. Maybe it was my fiancé. Sometimes he comes by at that time.

SERVANT. No.

BRIDE. You saw him?

SERVANT. Yes.

BRIDE. Who was it?

SERVANT. It was Leonardo.

BRIDE (*strongly*). Liar! You liar! Why should he come here?

SERVANT. He came.

BRIDE. Shut up! Shut your cursed mouth.

(*The sound of a horse is heard.*)

SERVANT (*at the window*). Look. Lean out. Was it Leonardo?

BRIDE. It was!

Quick curtain

ACT TWO

Scene One

The entrance hall of the BRIDE'S *house. A large door in the back. It is night. The* BRIDE *enters wearing ruffled white petticoats full of laces and embroidered bands, and a sleeveless white bodice. The* SERVANT *is dressed the same way.*

SERVANT. I'll finish combing your hair out here.

BRIDE. It's too warm to stay in there.

SERVANT. In this country it doesn't even cool off at dawn.

(*The* BRIDE *sits on a low chair and looks into a little hand mirror. The* SERVANT *combs her hair.*)

BRIDE. My mother came from a place with lots of trees—from a fertile country.

SERVANT. And she was so happy!

BRIDE. But she wasted away here.

SERVANT. Fate.

BRIDE. As we're all wasting away here. The very walls give off heat. Ay-y-y! Don't pull so hard.

SERVANT. I'm only trying to fix this wave better. I want it to fall over your forehead. (*The* BRIDE *looks at herself in the mirror.*) How beautiful you are! Ay-y-y! (*She kisses her passionately.*)

BRIDE (*seriously*). Keep right on combing.

SERVANT (*combing*). Oh, lucky you—going to put your arms around a man; and kiss him; and feel his weight.

BRIDE. Hush.

SERVANT. And the best part will be when you'll wake up and you'll feel him at your side and when he caresses your shoulders with his breath, like a little nightingale's feather.

BRIDE (*sternly*). Will you be quiet.

SERVANT. But, child! What *is* a wedding? A wedding is just that and nothing more. Is it the sweets—or the bouquets of flowers? No. It's a shining bed and a man and a woman.

BRIDE. But you shouldn't talk about it.

SERVANT. Oh, *that's* something else again. But fun enough too.

BRIDE. Or bitter enough.

SERVANT. I'm going to put the orange blossoms on from here to here, so the wreath will shine out on top of your hair. (*She tries on the sprigs of orange blossom.*)

BRIDE (*looking at herself in the mirror*). Give it to me. (*She takes the wreath, looks at it and lets her head fall in discouragement.*)

SERVANT. Now what's the matter?

BRIDE. Leave me alone.

SERVANT. This is no time for you to start feeling sad. (*Encouragingly*) Give me the wreath. (*The* BRIDE *takes the wreath and hurls it away.*) Child! You're just asking God to punish you, throwing the wreath on the floor like that. Raise your head! Don't you want to get married? Say it. You can still withdraw.
(*The* BRIDE *rises.*)

BRIDE. Storm clouds. A chill wind that cuts through my heart. Who hasn't felt it?

SERVANT. You love your sweetheart, don't you?

BRIDE. I love him.

SERVANT. Yes, yes. I'm sure you do.

BRIDE. But this is a very serious step.

SERVANT. You've got to take it.

BRIDE. I've already given my word.

SERVANT. I'll put on the wreath.

BRIDE. (*She sits down.*) Hurry. They should be arriving by now.

SERVANT. They've already been at least two hours on the way.

BRIDE. How far is it from here to the church?

SERVANT. Five leagues by the stream, but twice that by the road. (*The
BRIDE rises and the SERVANT grows excited as she looks at her.*)
Awake, O Bride, awaken,
On your wedding morning waken!
The world's rivers may all
Bear along your bridal Crown!

BRIDE (*smiling*). Come now.

SERVANT (*enthusiastically kissing her and dancing around her*).
Awake,
with the fresh bouquet
of flowering laurel.
Awake,
by the trunk and branch
of the laurels!
(*The banging of the front door latch is heard.*)

BRIDE. Open the door! That must be the first guests.
(*She leaves. The SERVANT opens the door.*)

SERVANT (*in astonishment*). You!

LEONARDO. Yes, me. Good morning.

SERVANT. The first one!

LEONARDO. Wasn't I invited?

SERVANT. Yes.

LEONARDO. That's why I'm here.

SERVANT. Where's your wife?

LEONARDO. I came on my horse. She's coming by the road.

SERVANT. Didn't you meet anyone?

LEONARDO. I *passed* them on my horse.

SERVANT. You're going to kill that horse with so much racing.

LEONARDO. When he dies, he's dead!
(*Pause.*)

SERVANT. Sit down. Nobody's up yet.

LEONARDO. Where's the bride?

SERVANT. I'm just on my way to dress her.

LEONARDO. The bride! She ought to be happy!

SERVANT (*changing the subject*). How's the baby?

LEONARDO. What baby?

SERVANT. Your son.

LEONARDO (*remembering, as though in a dream*). Ah!

SERVANT. Are they bringing him?

LEONARDO. No.
(*Pause. Voices sing distantly.*)

VOICES.

> Awake, O Bride, awaken,
> On your wedding morning waken!

LEONARDO.

> Awake, O Bride, awaken,
> On your wedding morning waken!

SERVANT. It's the guests. They're still quite a way off.

LEONARDO. The bride's going to wear a big wreath, isn't she? But it ought not to be so large. One a little smaller would look better on her. Has the groom already brought her the orange blossom that must be worn on the breast?

BRIDE (*appearing, still in petticoats and wearing the wreath*). He brought it.

SERVANT (*sternly*). Don't come out like that.

BRIDE. What does it matter? (*Seriously*) Why do you ask if they brought the orange blossom? Do you have something in mind?

LEONARDO. Nothing. What would I have in mind? (*Drawing near her*) You, you know me; you know I don't. Tell me so. What have I ever meant to you? Open your memory, refresh it. But two oxen and an ugly little hut are almost nothing. That's the thorn.

BRIDE. What have you come here to do?

LEONARDO. To see your wedding.

BRIDE. Just as I saw yours!

LEONARDO. Tied up by you, done with your two hands. Oh, they can kill me but they can't spit on me. But even money, which shines so much, spits sometimes.

BRIDE. Liar!

LEONARDO. I don't want to talk. I'm hot-blooded and I don't want to shout so all these hills will hear me.

BRIDE. My shouts would be louder.

SERVANT. You'll have to stop talking like this. (*To the* BRIDE) You don't have to talk about what's past.

(*The* SERVANT *looks around uneasily at the doors.*)

BRIDE. She's right. I shouldn't even talk to you. But it offends me to the soul that you come here to watch me, and spy on my wedding, and ask about the orange blossom with something on your mind. Go and wait for your wife at the door.

LEONARDO. But, can't you and I even talk?

SERVANT (*with rage*). No! No, you can't talk.

LEONARDO. Ever since I got married I've been thinking night and day about whose fault it was, and every time I think about it, out comes a new fault to eat up the old one; but always there's a fault left!

BRIDE. A man with a horse knows a lot of things and can do a lot to ride roughshod over a girl stuck out in the desert. But I have my pride. And that's why I'm getting married. I'll lock myself in with my husband and then I'll have to love him above everyone else.

LEONARDO. Pride won't help you a bit. (*He draws near to her.*)

BRIDE. Don't come near me!

LEONARDO. To burn with desire and keep quiet about it is the greatest punishment we can bring on ourselves. What good was pride to me—and not seeing you, and letting you lie awake night after night? No good! It only served to bring the fire down on me! You think that time heals and walls hide things, but it isn't true, it isn't true! When things get that deep inside you there isn't anybody can change them.

BRIDE (*trembling*). I can't listen to you. I can't listen to your voice. It's as though I'd drunk a bottle of anise and fallen asleep wrapped in a quilt of roses. It pulls me along, and I know I'm drowning—but I go on down.

SERVANT (*seizing* LEONARDO *by the lapels*). You've got to go right now!

LEONARDO. This is the last time I'll ever talk to her. Don't you be afraid of anything.

BRIDE. And I know I'm crazy and I know my breast rots with longing; but here I am—calmed by hearing him, by just seeing him move his arms.

LEONARDO. I'd never be at peace if I didn't tell you these things. I got married. Now you get married.

SERVANT. But she *is* getting married!

(*Voices are heard singing, nearer.*)

VOICES.
>   Awake, O Bride, awaken,
>   On your wedding morning waken!

BRIDE.
>   Awake, O Bride, awaken.

(*She goes out, running toward her room.*)

SERVANT. The people are here now. (*To* LEONARDO) Don't you come near her again.

LEONARDO. Don't worry. (*He goes out to the left. Day begins to break.*)

FIRST GIRL (*entering*).
>   Awake, O Bride, awaken,
>   the morning you're to marry;
>   sing round and dance round;
>   balconies a wreath must carry.

VOICES.
>   Bride, awaken!

SERVANT (*creating enthusiasm*).

>Awake,
>with the green bouquet
>of love in flower.
>Awake,
>by the trunk and the branch
>of the laurels!

SECOND GIRL (*entering*).

>Awake,
>with her long hair,
>snowy sleeping gown,
>patent leather boots with silver—
>her forehead jasmines crown.

SERVANT.

>Oh, shepherdess,
>the moon begins to shine!

FIRST GIRL.

>Oh, gallant,
>leave your hat beneath the vine!

FIRST YOUNG MAN (*entering, holding his hat on high*).

>Bride, awaken,
>for over the fields
>the wedding draws nigh
>with trays heaped with dahlias
>and cakes piled high.

VOICES.

>Bride, awaken!

SECOND GIRL.

>The bride
>has set her white wreath in place
>and the groom
>ties it on with a golden lace.

SERVANT.

>By the orange tree,
>sleepless the bride will be.

THIRD GIRL (*entering*).

>By the citron vine,
>gifts from the groom will shine.
>(*Three* GUESTS *come in.*)

FIRST YOUTH.

>Dove, awaken!
>In the dawn
>shadowy bells are shaken.

GUEST.

>The bride, the white bride
>today a maiden,
>tomorrow a wife.

FIRST GIRL.

>Dark one, come down
>trailing the train of your silken gown.

GUEST.

>Little dark one, come down,
>cold morning wears a dewy crown.

FIRST GUEST.

>Awaken, wife, awake,
>orange blossoms the breezes shake.

SERVANT.

>A tree I would embroider her
>with garnet sashes wound,
>And on each sash a cupid,
>with "Long Live" all around.

VOICES.

>Bride, awaken.

FIRST YOUTH.

>The morning you're to marry!

GUEST.

>The morning you're to marry
>how elegant you'll seem;
>worthy, mountain flower,
>of a captain's dream.

FATHER (*entering*).

>A captain's wife
>the groom will marry.
>He comes with his oxen the treasure to carry!

THIRD GIRL.

>The groom
>is like a flower of gold.
>When he walks,
>blossoms at his feet unfold.

SERVANT.

>Oh, my lucky girl!

SECOND YOUTH.

>Bride, awaken.

SERVANT.

>Oh, my elegant girl!

FIRST GIRL.
Through the windows
hear the wedding shout.
SECOND GIRL.
Let the bride come out.
FIRST GIRL.
Come out, come out!
SERVANT.
Let the bells
ring and ring out clear!
FIRST YOUTH.
For here she comes!
For now she's near!
SERVANT.
Like a bull, the wedding
is arising here!

(*The* BRIDE *appears. She wears a black dress in the style of 1900, with a bustle and large train covered with pleated gauzes and heavy laces. Upon her hair, brushed in a wave over her forehead, she wears an orange blossom wreath. Guitars sound. The* GIRLS *kiss the* BRIDE.)

THIRD GIRL. What scent did you put on your hair?
BRIDE (*laughing*). None at all.
SECOND GIRL (*looking at her dress*). This cloth is what you can't get.
FIRST YOUTH. Here's the groom!
BRIDEGROOM. Salud!
FIRST GIRL (*putting a flower behind his ear*).
The groom
is like a flower of gold.
SECOND GIRL.
Quiet breezes
from his eyes unfold.

(*The* GROOM *goes to the* BRIDE.)

BRIDE. Why did you put on those shoes?
BRIDEGROOM. They're gayer than the black ones.
LEONARDO'S WIFE (*entering and kissing the* BRIDE). Salud!
(*They all speak excitedly.*)
LEONARDO (*entering as one who performs a duty*).
The morning you're to marry
We give you a wreath to wear.
LEONARDO'S WIFE.
So the fields may be made happy

with the dew dropped from your hair!

MOTHER (*to the* FATHER). Are those people here, too?

FATHER. They're part of the family. Today is a day of forgiveness!

MOTHER. I'll put up with it, but I don't forgive.

BRIDEGROOM. With your wreath, it's a joy to look at you!

BRIDE. Let's go to the church quickly.

BRIDEGROOM. Are you in a hurry?

BRIDE. Yes. I want to be your wife right now so that I can be with you alone, not hearing any voice but yours.

BRIDEGROOM. That's what I want!

BRIDE. And not seeing any eyes but yours. And for you to hug me so hard, that even though my dead mother should call me, I wouldn't be able to draw away from you.

BRIDEGROOM. My arms are strong. I'll hug you for forty years without stopping.

BRIDE (*taking his arm, dramatically*). Forever!

FATHER. Quick now! Round up the teams and carts! The sun's already out.

MOTHER. And go along carefully! Let's hope nothing goes wrong.
(*The great door in the background opens.*)

SERVANT (*weeping*).
    As you set out from your house,
    oh, maiden white,
    remember you leave shining
    with a star's light.

FIRST GIRL.
    Clean of body, clean of clothes
    from her home to church she goes
    (*They start leaving.*)

SECOND GIRL.
    Now you leave your home
    for the church!

SERVANT.
    The wind sets flowers
    on the sands.

THIRD GIRL.
    Ah, the white maid!

SERVANT.
    Dark winds are the lace
    of her mantilla.
    (*They leave. Guitars, castanets and tambourines are heard.* LEO-NARDO *and his* WIFE *are left alone.*)

WIFE. Let's go.

LEONARDO. Where?

WIFE. To the church. But not on your horse. You're coming with me.

LEONARDO. In the cart?

WIFE. Is there anything else?

LEONARDO. I'm not the kind of man to ride in a cart.

WIFE. Nor I the wife to go to a wedding without her husband. I can't stand any more of this!

LEONARDO. Neither can I!

WIFE. And why do you look at me that way? With a thorn in each eye.

LEONARDO. Let's go!

WIFE. I don't know what's happening. But I think, and I don't want to think. One thing I do know. I'm already cast off by you. But I have a son. And another coming. And so it goes. My mother's fate was the same. Well, I'm not moving from here.

(VOICES *outside*.)

VOICES.

As you set out from your home
and to the church go
remember you leave shining
with a star's glow.

WIFE (*weeping*).

Remember you leave shining
with a star's glow!
I left my house like that too. They could have stuffed the whole countryside in my mouth. I was that trusting.

LEONARDO (*rising*). Let's go!

WIFE. But you with me!

LEONARDO. Yes. (*Pause*.) Start moving! (*They leave*.)

VOICES.

As you set out from your home
and to the church go,
remember you leave shining
with a star's glow.

Slow curtain

Scene Two

The exterior of the BRIDE'S *cave home, in white gray and cold blue tones. Large cactus trees. Shadowy and silver tones. Panoramas of light tan tablelands, everything hard like a landscape in popular ceramics.*

SERVANT (*arranging glasses and trays on a table*).
  A-turning,
  the wheel was a-turning
  and the water was flowing,
  for the wedding night comes.
  May the branches part
  and the moon be arrayed
  at her white balcony rail.
  (*In a loud voice*) Set out the tablecloths!
  (*In a pathetic voice*)
  A-singing,
  bride and groom were singing
  and the water was flowing
  for their wedding night comes.
  Oh, rime frost, flash! —
  and almonds bitter
  fill with honey!
  (*In a loud voice*) Get the wine ready!
  (*In a poetic tone*)
  Elegant girl,
  most elegant in the world,
  see the way the water is flowing,
  for your wedding night comes.
  Hold your skirts close in
  under the bridegroom's wing
  and never leave your house,
  for the Bridegroom is a dove
  with his breast a firebrand
  and the fields wait for the whisper
  of spurting blood.
  A-turning
  the wheel was a-turning
  and the water was flowing
  and your wedding night comes.
  Oh, water, sparkle!
MOTHER (*entering*). At last!
FATHER. Are we the first ones?
SERVANT. No. Leonardo and his wife arrived a while ago. They drove
    like demons. His wife got here dead with fright. They made the
    trip as though they'd come on horseback.
FATHER. That one's looking for trouble. He's not of good blood.
MOTHER. What blood would you expect him to have? His whole
    family's blood. It comes down from his great grandfather, who

started in killing, and it goes on down through the whole evil breed of knife-wielding and false-smiling men.

FATHER. Let's leave it at that!

SERVANT. But how can she leave it at that?

MOTHER. It hurts me to the tips of my veins. On the forehead of all of them I see only the hand with which they killed what was mine. Can you really see me? Don't I seem mad to you? Well, it's the madness of not having shrieked out all my breast needs to. Always in my breast there's a shriek standing tiptoe that I have to beat down and hold in under my shawls. But the dead are carried off and one has to keep still. And then, people find fault. (*She removes her shawl.*)

FATHER. Today's not the day for you to be remembering these things.

MOTHER. When the talk turns on it, I have to speak. And more so today. Because today I'm left alone in my house.

FATHER. But with the expectation of having someone with you.

MOTHER. That's my hope: grandchildren.

(*They sit down.*)

FATHER. I want them to have a lot of them. This land needs hands that aren't hired. There's a battle to be waged against weeds, the thistles, the big rocks that come from one doesn't know where. And those hands have to be the owner's, who chastises and dominates, who makes the seeds grow. Lots of sons are needed.

MOTHER. And some daughters! Men are like the wind! They're forced to handle weapons. Girls never go out into the street.

FATHER (*happily*). I think they'll have both.

MOTHER. My son will cover her well. He's of good seed. His father could have had many sons with me.

FATHER. What I'd like is to have all this happen in a day. So that right away they'd have two or three boys.

MOTHER. But it's not like that. It takes a long time. That's why it's so terrible to see one's own blood spilled out on the ground. A fountain that spurts for a minute, but costs us years. When I got to my son, he lay fallen in the middle of the street. I wet my hands with his blood and licked them with my tongue—because it was my blood. You don't know what that's like. In a glass and topaze shrine I'd put the earth moistened by his blood.

FATHER. Now you must hope. My daughter is wide-hipped and your son is strong.

MOTHER. That's why I'm hoping.

(*They rise.*)

FATHER. Get the wheat trays ready!

SERVANT. They're all ready.

LEONARDO'S WIFE (*entering*). May it be for the best!

MOTHER. Thank you.

LEONARDO. Is there going to be a celebration?

FATHER. A small one. People can't stay long.

SERVANT. Here they are!

> (GUESTS *begin entering in gay groups. The* BRIDE *and* GROOM *come in arm-in-arm.* LEONARDO *leaves.*)

BRIDEGROOM. There's never been a wedding with so many people!

BRIDE (*sullen*). Never.

FATHER. It was brilliant.

MOTHER. Whole branches of families came.

BRIDEGROOM. People who never went out of the house.

MOTHER. Your father sowed well, and now you're reaping it.

BRIDEGROOM. There were cousins of mine whom I no longer knew.

MOTHER. All the people from the seacoast.

BRIDEGROOM (*happily*). They were frightened of the horses.

> (*They talk.*)

MOTHER (*to the* BRIDE). What are you thinking about?

BRIDE. I'm not thinking about anything.

MOTHER. Your blessings weigh heavily.

> (*Guitars are heard.*)

BRIDE. Like lead.

MOTHER (*stern*). But they shouldn't weigh so. Happy as a dove you ought to be.

BRIDE. Are you staying here tonight?

MOTHER. No. My house is empty.

BRIDE. You ought to stay!

FATHER (*to the* MOTHER). Look at the dance they're forming. Dances of the far away seashore.

> (LEONARDO *enters and sits down. His* WIFE *stands rigidly behind him.*)

MOTHER. They're my husband's cousins. Stiff as stones at dancing.

FATHER. It makes me happy to watch them. What a change for this house! (*He leaves.*)

BRIDEGROOM (*to the* BRIDE). Did you like the orange blossom?

BRIDE (*looking at him fixedly*). Yes.

BRIDEGROOM. It's all of wax. It will last forever. I'd like you to have had them all over your dress.

BRIDE. No need of that.

> (LEONARDO *goes off to the right.*)

FIRST GIRL. Let's go and take out your pins.

BRIDE (*to the* GROOM). I'll be right back.

LEONARDO'S WIFE. I hope you'll be happy with my cousin!

BRIDEGROOM. I'm sure I will.

LEONARDO'S WIFE. The two of you here; never going out; building a home. I wish I could live far away like this, too!

BRIDEGROOM. Why don't you buy land? The mountainside is cheap and children grow up better.

LEONARDO'S WIFE. We don't have any money. And at the rate we're going . . . !

BRIDEGROOM. Your husband is a good worker.

LEONARDO'S WIFE. Yes, but he likes to fly around too much; from one thing to another. He's not a patient man.

SERVANT. Aren't you having anything? I'm going to wrap up some wine cakes for your mother. She likes them so much.

BRIDEGROOM. Put up three dozen for her.

LEONARDO'S WIFE. No, no. A half-dozen's enough for her!

BRIDEGROOM. But today's a day!

LEONARDO'S WIFE (*to the* SERVANT). Where's Leonardo?

BRIDEGROOM. He must be with the guests.

LEONARDO'S WIFE. I'm going to go see. (*She leaves.*)

SERVANT (*looking off at the dance*). That's beautiful there.

BRIDEGROOM. Aren't you dancing?

SERVANT. No one will ask me.

(TWO GIRLS *pass across the back of the stage; during this whole scene the background should be an animated crossing of figures.*)

BRIDEGROOM (*happily*). They just don't know anything. Lively old girls like you dance better than the young ones.

SERVANT. Well! Are you tossing me a compliment, boy? What a family yours is! Men among men! As a little girl I saw your grandfather's wedding. What a figure! It seemed as if a mountain were getting married.

BRIDEGROOM. I'm not as tall.

SERVANT. But there's the same twinkle in your eye. Where's the girl?

BRIDEGROOM. Taking off her wreath.

SERVANT. Ah! Look. For midnight, since you won't be sleeping, I have prepared ham for you, and some large glasses of old wine. On the lower shelf of the cupboard. In case you need it.

BRIDEGROOM (*smiling*). I won't be eating at midnight.

SERVANT (*slyly*). If not you, maybe the bride. (*She leaves.*)

FIRST YOUTH (*entering*). You've got to come have a drink with us!

BRIDEGROOM. I'm waiting for the bride.

SECOND YOUTH. You'll have her at dawn!

FIRST YOUTH. That's when it's best!

SECOND YOUTH. Just for a minute.

BRIDEGROOM. Let's go.

(*They leave. Great excitement is heard. The* BRIDE *enters. From the opposite side* TWO GIRLS *come running to meet her.*)

FIRST GIRL. To whom did you give the first pin; me or this one?

BRIDE. I don't remember.

FIRST GIRL. To me, you gave it to me here.

SECOND GIRL. To me, in front of the altar.

BRIDE (*uneasily, with a great inner struggle*). I don't know anything about it.

FIRST GIRL. It's just that I wish you'd . . .

BRIDE (*interrupting*). Nor do I care. I have a lot to think about.

SECOND GIRL. Your pardon.

(LEONARDO *crosses at the rear of the stage.*)

BRIDE. (*She sees* LEONARDO.) And this is an upsetting time.

FIRST GIRL. We wouldn't know anything about that!

BRIDE. You'll know about it when your time comes. This step is a very hard one to take.

FIRST GIRL. Has she offended you?

BRIDE. No. You must pardon me.

SECOND GIRL. What for? But *both* the pins are good for getting married, aren't they?

BRIDE. Both of them.

FIRST GIRL. Maybe now one will get married before the other.

BRIDE. Are you so eager?

SECOND GIRL (*shyly*). Yes.

BRIDE. Why?

FIRST GIRL. Well . . .

(*She embraces the* SECOND GIRL. *Both go running off. The* GROOM *comes in very slowly and embraces the* BRIDE *from behind.*)

BRIDE (*in sudden fright*). Let go of me!

BRIDEGROOM. Are you frightened of me?

BRIDE. Ay-y-y! It's you?

BRIDEGROOM. Who else would it be? (*Pause.*) Your father or me.

BRIDE. That's true!

BRIDEGROOM. Of course, your father would have hugged you more gently.

BRIDE (*darkly*). Of course!

BRIDEGROOM (*embracing her strongly and a little bit brusquely*). Because he's old.

BRIDE (*curtly*). Let me go!

BRIDEGROOM. Why? (*He lets her go.*)

BRIDE. Well . . . the people. They can see us.

(*The* SERVANT *crosses at the back of the stage again without looking at the* BRIDE *and* BRIDEGROOM.)

BRIDEGROOM. What of it? It's consecrated now.

BRIDE. Yes, but let me be . . . Later.

BRIDEGROOM. What's the matter with you? You look frightened!

BRIDE. I'm all right. Don't go.

(LEONARDO'S WIFE *enters.*)

LEONARDO'S WIFE. I don't mean to intrude . . .

BRIDEGROOM. What is it?

LEONARDO'S WIFE. Did my husband come through here?

BRIDEGROOM. No.

LEONARDO'S WIFE. Because I can't find him, and his horse isn't in the stable either.

BRIDEGROOM (*happily*). He must be out racing it.

(*The* WIFE *leaves, troubled. The* SERVANT *enters.*)

SERVANT. Aren't you two proud and happy with so many good wishes?

BRIDEGROOM. I wish it were over with. The bride is a little tired.

SERVANT. That's no way to act, child.

BRIDE. It's as though I'd been struck on the head.

SERVANT. A bride from these mountains must be strong. (*To the* GROOM) You're the only one who can cure her, because she's yours. (*She goes running off.*)

BRIDEGROOM (*embracing the* BRIDE). Let's go dance a little. (*He kisses her.*)

BRIDE (*worried*). No. I'd like to stretch out on my bed a little.

BRIDEGROOM. I'll keep you company.

BRIDE. Never! With all these people here? What would they say? Let me be quiet for a moment.

BRIDEGROOM. Whatever you say! But don't be like that tonight!

BRIDE (*at the door*). I'll be better tonight.

BRIDEGROOM. That's what I want.

(*The* MOTHER *appears.*)

MOTHER. Son.

BRIDEGROOM. Where've you been?

MOTHER. Out there—in all that noise. Are you happy?

BRIDEGROOM. Yes.

MOTHER. Where's your wife?

BRIDEGROOM. Resting a little. It's a bad day for brides!

MOTHER. A bad day? The only good one. To me it was like coming into my own. (*The* SERVANT *enters and goes toward the* BRIDE'S *room.*) Like the breaking of new ground; the planting of new trees.

BRIDEGROOM. Are you going to leave?

MOTHER. Yes. I ought to be at home.

BRIDEGROOM. Alone.

MOTHER. Not alone. For my head is full of things: of men, and fights.

BRIDEGROOM. But now the fights are no longer fights.

(*The* SERVANT *enters quickly; she disappears at the rear of the stage, running.*)

MOTHER. While you live, you have to fight.

BRIDEGROOM. I'll always obey you!

MOTHER. Try to be loving with your wife, and if you see she's acting foolish or touchy, caress her in a way that will hurt her a little: a strong hug, a bite and then a soft kiss. Not so she'll be angry, but just so she'll feel you're the man, the boss, the one who gives orders. I learned that from your father. And since you don't have him, I have to be the one to tell you about these strong defenses.

BRIDEGROOM. I'll always do as you say.

FATHER (*entering*). Where's my daughter?

BRIDEGROOM. She's inside.

(*The* FATHER *goes to look for her.*)

FIRST GIRL. Get the bride and groom! We're going to dance a round!

FIRST YOUTH (*to the* BRIDEGROOM). You're going to lead it.

FATHER (*entering*). She's not there.

BRIDEGROOM. No?

FATHER. She must have gone up to the railing.

BRIDEGROOM. I'll go see!

(*He leaves. A hubbub of excitement and guitars is heard.*)

FIRST GIRL. They've started it already! (*She leaves.*)

BRIDEGROOM (*entering*). She isn't there.

MOTHER (*uneasily*). Isn't she?

FATHER. But where could she have gone?

SERVANT (*entering*). But where's the girl, where is she?

MOTHER (*seriously*). That we don't know.

(*The* BRIDEGROOM *leaves. Three guests enter.*)

FATHER (*dramatically*). But, isn't she in the dance?

SERVANT. She's not in the dance.

FATHER (*with a start*). There are a lot of people. Go look!

SERVANT. I've already looked.

FATHER (*tragically*). Then where is she?

BRIDEGROOM (*entering*). Nowhere. Not anywhere.

MOTHER (*to the* FATHER). What does this mean? Where is your daughter?

(LEONARDO'S WIFE *enters.*)

LEONARDO'S WIFE. They've run away! They've run away! She and Leonardo. On the horse. With their arms around each other, they rode off like a shooting star!

FATHER. That's not true! Not my daughter!

MOTHER. Yes, your daughter! Spawn of a wicked mother, and he, he too. But now she's my son's wife!

BRIDEGROOM (*entering*). Let's go after them! Who has a horse?

MOTHER. Who has a horse? Right away! Who has a horse? I'll give him all I have—my eyes, my tongue even. . . .

VOICE. Here's one.

MOTHER (*to the* SON). Go! After them! (*He leaves with two young men.*) No. Don't go. Those people kill quickly and well . . . but yes, run, and I'll follow!

FATHER. It couldn't be my daughter. Perhaps she's thrown herself in the well.

MOTHER. Decent women throw themselves in water; not that one! But now she's my son's wife. Two groups. There are two groups here. (*They all enter.*) My family and yours. Everyone set out from here. Shake the dust from your heels! We'll go help my son. (*The people separate into two groups.*) For he has his family: his cousins from the sea, and all who came from inland. Out of here! On all roads. The hour of blood has come again. Two groups! You with yours and I with mine. After them! After them!

Curtain

ACT THREE

Scene One

A forest. It is nighttime. Great moist tree trunks. A dark atmosphere. Two violins are heard. THREE WOODCUTTERS *enter.*

FIRST WOODCUTTER. And have they found them?

SECOND WOOCUTTER. No. But they're looking for them everywhere.

THIRD WOODCUTTER. They'll find them.

SECOND WOODCUTTER. Sh-h-h!

THIRD WOODCUTTER. What?

SECOND WOODCUTTER. They seem to be coming closer on all the roads at once.

FIRST WOODCUTTER. When the moon comes out they'll see them.

SECOND WOODCUTTER. They ought to let them go.

FIRST WOODCUTTER. The world is wide. Everybody can live in it.

THIRD WOODCUTTER. But they'll kill them.

SECOND WOODCUTTER. You have to follow your passion. They did right to run away.

FIRST WOODCUTTER. They were deceiving themselves but at the last blood was stronger.

THIRD WOODCUTTER. Blood!

FIRST WOODCUTTER. You have to follow the path of your blood.

SECOND WOODCUTTER. But blood that sees the light of day is drunk up by the earth.

FIRST WOODCUTTER. What of it? Better dead with the blood drained away than alive with it rotting.

THIRD WOODCUTTER. Hush!

FIRST WOODCUTTER. What? Do you hear something?

THIRD WOODCUTTER. I hear the crickets, the frogs, the night's ambush.

FIRST WOODCUTTER. But not the horse.

THIRD WOODCUTTER. No.

FIRST WOODCUTTER. By now he must be loving her.

SECOND WOODCUTTER. Her body for him; his body for her.

THIRD WOODCUTTER. They'll find them and they'll kill them.

FIRST WOODCUTTER. But by then they'll have mingled their bloods. They'll be like two empty jars, like two dry arroyos.

SECOND WOODCUTTER. There are many clouds and it would be easy for the moon not to come out.

THIRD WOODCUTTER. The bridegroom will find them with or without the moon. I saw him set out. Like a raging star. His face the color of ashes. He looked the fate of all his clan.

FIRST WOODCUTTER. His clan of dead men lying in the middle of the street.

SECOND WOODCUTTER. There you have it!

THIRD WOODCUTTER. You think they'll be able to break through the circle?

SECOND WOODCUTTER. It's hard to. There are knives and guns for ten leagues 'round.

THIRD WOODCUTTER. He's riding a good horse.

SECOND WOODCUTTER. But he's carrying a woman.

FIRST WOODCUTTER. We're close by now.

SECOND WOODCUTTER. A tree with forty branches. We'll soon cut it down.

THIRD WOODCUTTER. The moon's coming out now. Let's hurry.

(*From the left shines a brightness.*)

FIRST WOODCUTTER.

O rising moon!
Moon among the great leaves.

SECOND WOODCUTTER.

Cover the blood with jasmines!

FIRST WOODCUTTER.
> O lonely moon!
> Moon among the great leaves.

SECOND WOODCUTTER.
> Silver on the bride's face.

THIRD WOODCUTTER.
> O evil moon!
> Leave for their love a branch in shadow.

FIRST WOODCUTTER.
> O sorrowing moon!
> Leave for their love a branch in shadow.
> (*They go out. The* MOON *appears through the shining brightness at the left. The* MOON *is a young woodcutter with a white face. The stage takes on an intense blue radiance.*)

MOON.
> Round swan in the river
> and a cathedral's eye,
> false dawn on the leaves,
> they'll not escape; these things am I!
> Who is hiding? And who sobs
> in the thornbrakes of the valley?
> The moon sets a knife
> abandoned in the air
> which being a leaden threat
> yearns to be blood's pain.
> Let me in! I come freezing
> down to walls and windows!
> Open roofs, open breasts
> where I may warm myself!
> I'm cold! My ashes
> of somnolent metals
> seek the fire's crest
> on mountains and streets.
> But the snow carries me
> upon its mottled back
> and pools soak me
> in their water, hard and cold.
> But this night there will be
> red blood for my cheeks,
> and for the reeds that cluster
> at the wide feet of the wind.
> Let there be neither shadow nor bower,
> and then they can't get away!

O let me enter a breast
where I may get warm!
A heart for me!
Warm! That will spurt
over the mountains of my chest;
let me come in, oh let me!
(*To the branches*)
I want no shadows. My rays
must get in everywhere,
even among the dark trunks I want
the whisper of gleaming lights,
so that this night there will be
sweet blood for my cheeks,
and for the reeds that cluster
at the wide feet of the wind.
Who is hiding? Out, I say!
No! They will not get away!
I will light up the horse
with a fever bright as diamonds.

(*He disappears among the trunks, and the stage goes back to its
dark lighting. An old woman comes out completely covered by
thin green cloth. She is barefooted. Her face can barely be seen
among the folds.*)

BEGGAR WOMAN.

That moon's going away, just when they's near.
They won't get past here. The river's whisper
and the whispering tree trunks will muffle
the torn flight of their shrieks.
It has to be here, and soon. I'm worn out.
The coffins are ready, and white sheets
wait on the floor of the bedroom
for heavy bodies with torn throats.
Let not one bird awake, let the breeze,
gathering their moans in her skirt,
fly with them over black tree tops
or bury them in soft mud.
(*Impatiently*)
Oh, that moon! That moon!

(*The* MOON *appears. The intense blue light returns.*)

MOON. They're coming. One band through the ravine and the other
along the river. I'm going to light up the boulders. What do you
need?

BEGGAR WOMAN. Nothing.

MOON. The wind blows hard now, with a double edge.

BEGGAR WOMAN. Light up the waistcoat and open the buttons; the knives will know the path after that.

MOON.

But let them be a long time a-dying. So the blood
will slide its delicate hissing between my fingers.
Look how my ashen valleys already are waking
in longing for this fountain of shuddering gushes!

BEGGAR WOMAN. Let's not let them get past the arroyo. Silence!

MOON. There they come! (*He goes. The stage is left dark.*)

BEGGAR WOMAN. Quick! Lots of light! Do you hear me? They can't get away!

(*The* BRIDEGROOM *and the* FIRST YOUTH *enter. The* BEGGAR WOMAN *sits down and covers herself with her cloak.*)

BRIDEGROOM. This way.

FIRST YOUTH. You won't find them.

BRIDEGROOM (*angrily*). Yes, I'll find them.

FIRST YOUTH. I think they've taken another path.

BRIDEGROOM. No. Just a moment ago I felt the galloping.

FIRST YOUTH. It could have been another horse.

BRIDEGROOM (*intensely*). Listen to me. There's only one horse in the whole world, and this one's it. Can't you understand that? If you're going to follow me, follow me without talking.

FIRST YOUTH. It's only that I want to . . .

BRIDEGROOM. Be quiet. I'm sure of meeting them there. Do you see this arm? Well, it's not my arm. It's my brother's arm, and my father's, and that of all the dead ones in my family. And it has so much strength that it can pull this tree up by the roots, if it wants to. And let's move one, because here I feel the clenched teeth of all my people in me so that I can't breathe easily.

BEGGAR WOMAN (*whining*). Ay-y-y!

FIRST YOUTH. Did you hear that?

BRIDEGROOM. You go that way and then circle back.

FIRST YOUTH. This is a hunt.

BRIDEGROOM. A hunt. The greatest hunt there is.

(*The* YOUTH *goes off. The* BRIDEGROOM *goes rapidly to the left and stumbles over the* BEGGAR WOMAN, *Death.*)

BEGGAR WOMAN. Ay-y-y!

BRIDEGROOM. What do you want?

BEGGAR WOMAN. I'm cold.

BRIDEGROOM. Which way are you going?

BEGGAR WOMAN (*always whining like a beggar*). Over there, far away . . .

BRIDEGROOM. Where are you from?

BEGGAR WOMAN. Over there . . . very far away.

BRIDEGROOM. Have you seen a man and a woman running away on a horse?

BEGGAR WOMAN (*awakening*). Wait a minute. . . . (*She looks at him.*) Handsome young man. (*She rises.*) But you'd be much handsomer sleeping.

BRIDEGROOM. Tell me; answer me. Did you see them?

BEGGAR WOMAN. Wait a minute . . . What broad shoulders! How would you like to be laid out on them and not have to walk on the soles of your feet which are so small?

BRIDEGROOM (*shaking her*). I asked you if you saw them! Have they passed through here?

BEGGAR WOMAN (*energetically*). No. They haven't passed; but they're coming from the hill. Don't you hear them?

BRIDEGROOM. No.

BEGGAR WOMAN. Do you know the road?

BRIDEGROOM. I'll go, whatever it's like!

BEGGAR WOMAN. I'll go along with you. I know this country.

BRIDEGROOM (*impatiently*). Well, let's go! Which way?

BEGGAR WOMAN (*dramatically*). This way!

(*They go rapidly out. Two violins, which represent the forest, are heard distantly. The* WOODCUTTERS *return. They have their axes on their shoulders. They move slowly among the tree trunks.*)

FIRST WOODCUTTER.

O rising death!

Death among the great leaves.

SECOND WOODCUTTER.

Don't open the gush of blood!

FIRST WOODCUTTER.

O lonely death!

Death among the dried leaves.

THIRD WOODCUTTER.

Don't lay flowers over the wedding!

SECOND WOODCUTTER.

O sad death!

Leave for their love a green branch.

FIRST WOODCUTTER.

O evil death!

Leave for their love a branch of green!

(*They go out while they are talking.* LEONARDO *and the* BRIDE *appear.*)

LEONARDO.
> Hush!

BRIDE.
> From here I'll go on alone.
> You go now! I want you to turn back.

LEONARDO.
> Hush, I said!

BRIDE.
> With your teeth, with your hands, anyway
>   you can,
> take from my clean throat
> the metal of this chain,
> and let me live forgotten
> back there in my house in the ground.
> And if you don't want to kill me
> as you would kill a tiny snake,
> set in my hands, a bride's hands,
> the barrel of your shotgun.
> Oh, what lamenting, what fire,
> sweeps upward through my head!
> What glass splinters are stuck in my tongue!

LEONARDO.
> We've taken the step now; hush!
> because they're close behind us,
> and I must take you with me.

BRIDE.
> Then it must be by force!

LEONARDO.
> By force? Who was it first
> went down the stairway?

BRIDE.
> I went down it.

LEONARDO.
> And who was it put
> a new bridle on the horse?

BRIDE.
> I myself did it. It's true.

LEONARDO.
> And whose were the hands
> strapped spurs to my boots?

BRIDE.
> The same hands, these that are yours,

but which when they see you would like
to break the blue branches
and sunder the purl of your veins.
I love you! I love you! But leave me!
For if I were able to kill you
I'd wrap you 'round in a shroud
with the edges bordered in violets.
Oh, what lamenting, what fire,
sweeps upward through my head!

LEONARDO.

What glass splinters are stuck in my tongue!
Because I tried to forget you
and put a wall of stone
between your house and mine.
It's true. You remember?
And when I saw you in the distance
I threw sand in my eyes.
But I was riding a horse
and the horse went straight to your door.
And the silver pins of your wedding
turned my red blood black.
And in me our dream was choking
my flesh with its poisoned weeds.
Oh, it isn't my fault—
the fault is the earth's—
and this fragrance that you exhale
from your breasts and your braids.

BRIDE.

Oh, how untrue! I want
from you neither bed nor food,
yet there's not a minute each day
that I don't want to be with you,
because you drag me, and I come,
then you tell me to go back
and I follow you,
like chaff blown on the breeze.
I have left a good, honest man,
and all his people,
with the wedding feast half over
and wearing my bridal wreath.
But you are the one will be punished
and that I don't want to happen.
Leave me alone now! You run away!

There is no one who will defend you.

LEONARDO.

> The birds of early morning
> are calling among the trees.
> The night is dying
> on the stone's ridge.
> Let's go to a hidden corner
> where I may love you forever,
> for to me the people don't matter,
> nor the venom they throw on us.
> (*He embraces her strongly.*)

BRIDE.

> And I'll sleep at your feet,
> to watch over your dreams.
> Naked, looking over the fields,
> as though I were a bitch.
> Because that's what I am! Oh, I look at **you**
> and your beauty sears me.

LEONARDO.

> Fire is stirred by fire.
> The same tiny flame
> will kill two wheat heads together.
> Let's go!

BRIDE.

> Where are you taking me?

LEONARDO.

> Where they cannot come,
> these men who surround us.
> Where I can look at you!

BRIDE (*sarcastically*).

> Carry me with you from fair to fair,
> a shame to clean women,
> so that people will see me
> with my wedding sheets
> on the breeze like banners.

LEONARDO.

> I, too, would want to leave you
> if I thought as men should.
> But wherever you go, I go.
> You're the same. Take a step. Try.
> Nails of moonlight have fused
> my waist and your thighs.
> (*This whole scene is violent, full of great sensuality.*)

BRIDE.

> Listen!

LEONARDO.

> > They're coming.

BRIDE.

> > > Run!
> It's fitting that I should die here,
> with water over my feet,
> with thorns upon my head.
> And fitting the leaves should mourn me,
> a woman lost and virgin.

LEONARDO.

> Be quiet. Now they're appearing.

BRIDE.

> > > > Go now!

LEONARDO.

> Quiet. Don't let them hear us.
> (*The* BRIDE *hesitates.*)

BRIDE.

> Both of us!

LEONARDO (*embracing her*).

> > > Any way you want!
> If they separate us, it will be
> because I am dead.

BRIDE.

> > > And I dead too.

(*They go out in each other's arms. The* MOON *appears very slowly. The stage takes on a strong blue light. The two violins are heard. Suddenly two long, ear-splitting shrieks are heard, and the music of the two violins is cut short. At the second shriek the* BEGGAR WOMAN *appears and stands with her back to the audience. She opens her cape and stands in the center of the stage like a great bird with immense wings. The* MOON *halts. The curtain comes down in absolute silence.*)

Curtain

Scene Two

The Final Scene. A white dwelling with arches and thick walls. To the right and left, are white stairs. At the back, a great arch and a wall of the same color. The floor also should be shining white. This simple dwelling should have the monumental feeling

of a church. There should not be a single gray nor any shadow,
not even what is necessary for perspective. TWO GIRLS *dressed in*
dark blue are winding a red skein.

FIRST GIRL.

Wool, red wool,
what would you make?

SECOND GIRL.

Oh, jasmine for dresses,
fine wool like glass.
At four o'clock born,
at ten o'clock dead.
A thread from this wool yarn,
a chain 'round your feet
a knot that will tighten
the bitter white wreath.

LITTLE GIRL (*singing*).

Were you at the wedding?

FIRST GIRL.

No.

LITTLE GIRL.

Well, neither was I!
What could have happened
'midst the shoots of the vineyards?
What could have happened
'neath the branch of the olive?
What really happened
that no one came back?
Were you at the wedding?

SECOND GIRL.

We told you once, no.

LITTLE GIRL (*leaving*).

Well, neither was I!

SECOND GIRL.

Wool, red wool,
what would you sing?

FIRST GIRL.

Their wounds turning waxen
balm-myrtle for pain.
Asleep in the morning,
and watching at night.

LITTLE GIRL (*in the doorway*).

And then, the thread stumbled
on the flinty stones,

but mountains, blue mountains,
are letting it pass.
Running, running, running,
and finally to come
to stick in a knife blade,
to take back the bread.
(*She goes out.*)

SECOND GIRL.

Wool, red wool,
what would you tell?

FIRST GIRL.

The lover is silent,
crimson the groom,
at the still shoreline
I saw them laid out.
(*She stops and looks at the skein.*)

LITTLE GIRL (*appearing in the doorway*).

Running, running, running,
the thread runs to here.
All covered with clay
I feel them draw near.
Bodies stretched stiffly
in ivory sheets!
(*The* WIFE *and* MOTHER-IN-LAW *of* LEONARDO *appear. They are anguished.*)

FIRST GIRL. Are they coming yet?

MOTHER-IN-LAW (*harshly*). We don't know.

SECOND GIRL. What can you tell us about the wedding?

FIRST GIRL. Yes, tell me.

MOTHER-IN-LAW (*curtly*). Nothing.

LEONARDO'S WIFE. I want to go back and find out all about it.

MOTHER-IN-LAW (*sternly*).

You, back to your house.
Brave and alone in your house.
To grow old and to weep.
But behind closed doors.
Never again. Neither dead nor alive.
We'll nail up our windows
and let rains and nights
fall on the bitter weeds.

LEONARDO'S WIFE. What could have happened?

MOTHER-IN-LAW.

It doesn't matter what.

Put a veil over your face.
Your children are yours,
that's all. On the bed
put a cross of ashes
where his pillow was.
(*They go out.*)

BEGGAR WOMAN (*at the door*). A crust of bread, little girls.

LITTLE GIRL. Go away!
(*The* GIRLS *huddle close together.*)

BEGGAR WOMAN. Why?

LITTLE GIRL. Because you whine; go away!

FIRST GIRL. Child!

BEGGAR WOMAN.
I might have asked for your eyes! A cloud
of birds is following me. Will you have one?

LITTLE GIRL. I want to get away from here!

SECOND GIRL (*to the* BEGGAR WOMAN). Don't mind her!

FIRST GIRL. Did you come by the road through the arroyo?

BEGGAR WOMAN. I came that way!

FIRST GIRL (*timidly*). Can I ask you something?

BEGGAR WOMAN.
I saw them: they'll be here soon; two torrents
still at last, among the great boulders,
two men at the horse's feet.
Two dead men in the night's splendor.
(*With pleasure.*)
Dead, yes, dead.

FIRST GIRL. Hush, old woman, hush!

BEGGAR WOMAN.
Crushed flowers for eyes, and their teeth
two fistfuls of hard-frozen snow.
Both of them fell, and the Bride returns
with bloodstains on her skirt and hair.
And they come covered with two sheets
carried on the shoulders of two tall boys.
That's how it was; nothing more. What was fitting.
Over the golden flower, dirty sand.
(*She goes. The* GIRLS *bow their heads and start going out rhythmically.*)

FIRST GIRL.
Dirty sand.

SECOND GIRL.
Over the golden flower.

LITTLE GIRL.
　　Over the golden flower
　　they're bringing the dead from the arroyo.
　　Dark the one,
　　dark the other.
　　What shadowy nightingale flies and weeps
　　over the golden flower!
　　(*She goes. The stage is left empty. The* MOTHER *and a* NEIGHBOR
　　WOMAN *appear. The* NEIGHBOR *is weeping.*)
MOTHER. Hush.
NEIGHBOR. I can't.
MOTHER. Hush, I said.
　　(*At the door*) Is there anybody here? (*She puts her hands to her
　　forehead.*) My son ought to answer me. But now my son is an
　　armful of shrivelled flowers. My son is a fading voice beyond the
　　mountains now. (*With rage, to the* NEIGHBOR) Will you shut
　　up? I want no wailing in this house. Your tears are only tears
　　from your eyes, but when I'm alone mine will come—from the
　　soles of my feet, from my roots—burning more than blood.
NEIGHBOR. You come to my house; don't you stay here.
MOTHER. I want to be here. Here. In peace. They're all dead now: and
　　at midnight I'll sleep, sleep without terror of guns or knives.
　　Other mothers will go to their windows, lashed by rain, to watch
　　for their sons' faces. But not I. And of my dreams I'll make a
　　cold ivory dove that will carry camellias of white frost to the
　　graveyard. But no; not graveyard, not graveyard: the couch of
　　earth, the bed that shelters them and rocks them in the sky.
　　(*A woman dressed in black enters, goes toward the right, and
　　there kneels. To the* NEIGHBOR.) Take your hands from your
　　face. We have terrible days ahead. I want to see no one. The
　　earth and I. My grief and I. And these four walls. Ay-y-y! Ay-y-y!
　　(*She sits down, overcome.*)
NEIGHBOR. Take pity on yourself!
MOTHER (*pushing back her hair*). I must be calm. (*She sits down.*)
　　Because the neighbor women will come and I don't want them
　　to see me so poor. So poor! A woman without even one son to
　　hold to her lips.
　　(*The* BRIDE *appears. She is without her wreath and wears a black
　　shawl.*)
NEIGHBOR (*with rage, seeing the* BRIDE). Where are you going?
BRIDE. I'm coming here.
MOTHER (*to the* NEIGHBOR). Who is it?

NEIGHBOR. Don't you recognize her?

MOTHER. That's why I asked who it was. Because I don't want to recognize her, so I won't sink my teeth in her throat. You snake! (*She moves wrathfully on the* BRIDE, *then stops. To the* NEIGHBOR) Look at her! There she is, and she's crying, while I stand here calmly and don't tear her eyes out. I don't understand myself. Can it be I didn't love my son? But, where's his good name? Where is it now? Where is it? (*She beats the* BRIDE *who drops to the floor.*)

NEIGHBOR. For God's sake! (*She tries to separate them.*)

BRIDE (*to the* NEIGHBOR). Let her; I came here so she'd kill me and they'd take me away with them. (*To the* MOTHER) But not with her hands; with grappling hooks, with a sickle—and with force —until they break on my bones. Let her! I want her to know I'm clean, that I may be crazy, but that they can bury me without a single man ever having seen himself in the whiteness of my breasts.

MOTHER. Shut up, shut up; what do I care about that?

BRIDE. Because I ran away with the other one; I ran away! (*With anguish*) You would have gone, too. I was a woman burning with desire, full of sores inside and out, and your son was a little bit of water from which I hoped for children, land, health; but the other one was a dark river, choked with brush, that brought near me the undertone of its rushes and its whispered song. And I went along with your son who was like a little boy of cold water—and the other sent against me hundreds of birds who got in my way and left white frost on my wounds, my wounds of a poor withered woman, of a girl caressed by fire. I didn't want to; remember that! I didn't want to. Your son was my destiny and I have not betrayed him, but the other one's arm dragged me along like the pull of the sea, like the head toss of a mule, and he would have dragged me always, always, always—even if I were an old woman and all your son's sons held me by the hair!

(*A* NEIGHBOR *enters.*)

MOTHER. She is not to blame; nor am I! (*Sarcastically*) Who is, then? It's a delicate, lazy, sleepless woman who throws away an orange blossom wreath and goes looking for a piece of bed warmed by another woman!

BRIDE. Be still! Be still! Take your revenge on me; here I am! See how soft my throat is; it would be less work for you than cutting a dahlia in your garden. But never that! Clean, clean as a new-

born little girl. And strong enough to prove it to you. Light the
fire. Let's stick our hands in; you, for your son, I, for my body.
You'll draw yours out first.

(*Another* NEIGHBOR *enters.*)

MOTHER. But what does your good name matter to me? What does
your death matter to me? What does anything about anything
matter to me? Blesséd be the wheat stalks, because my sons are
under them; blesséd be the rain, because it wets the face of the
dead. Blesséd be God, who stretches us out together to rest.

(*Another* NEIGHBOR *enters.*)

BRIDE. Let me weep with you.

MOTHER. Weep. But at the door.

(*The* GIRL *enters, the* BRIDE *stays at the door. The* MOTHER *is at
the center of the stage.*)

LEONARDO'S WIFE (*entering and going to the left*).
    He was a beautiful horseman,
    now he's a heap of snow.
    He rode to fairs and mountains
    and women's arms.
    Now, the night's dark moss
    crowns his forehead.

MOTHER.
    A sunflower to your mother,
    a mirror of the earth.
    Let them put on your breast
    the cross of bitter rosebay;
    and over you a sheet
    of shining silk;
    between your quiet hands
    let water form its lament.

WIFE.
    Ay-y-y, four gallant boys
    come with tired shoulders!

BRIDE.
    Ay-y-y, four gallant boys
    carry death on high!

MOTHER.
    Neighbors.

LITTLE GIRL (*at the door*).
    They're bringing them now.

MOTHER.
    It's the same thing.
    Always the cross, the cross.

WOMEN.
> Sweet nails.
> cross adored,
> sweet name
> of Christ our Lord.

BRIDE. May the cross protect both the quick and the dead.

MOTHER.
> Neighbors: with a knife,
> with a little knife,
> on their appointed day, between two and three,
> these two men killed each other for love.
> With a knife,
> with a tiny knife
> that barely fits the hand,
> but that slides in clean
> through the astonished flesh
> and stops at the place
> where trembles, enmeshed,
> the dark root of a scream.

BRIDE.
> And this is a knife,
> a tiny knife
> that barely fits the hand;
> fish without scales, without river,
> so that on their appointed day, between two and three,
> with this knife,
> two men are left stiff,
> with their lips turning yellow.

MOTHER.
> And it barely fits the hand
> but it slides in clean
> through the astonished flesh
> and stops there, at the place
> where trembles enmeshed
> the dark root of a scream.
>
> (*The* NEIGHBORS, *kneeling on the floor, sob.*)

Curtain

MOTHER COURAGE AND HER CHILDREN [1939]

by Bertolt Brecht

English version by Eric Bentley

Characters

COLONEL

SCRIVENER

OLDER SOLDIER

YOUNGER SOLDIER

FIRST SOLDIER

OLD PEASANT

SECOND SOLDIER

PEASANT WOMAN

SOLDIER, *singing*

OLD WOMAN

VOICES, *two*

YOUNG MAN

VOICE, *girl singing*

LIEUTENANT

YOUNG PEASANT

(ONE SUPER)

(TWO EXTRAS)

The time: 1624-1636
The place: Sweden, Poland, Germany

*Mother Courage and Her Children: A Chronicle of the Thirty Years'
War* by Bertolt Brecht. English version by Eric Bentley. Copyright ©
1955, 1959, 1961, 1962, 1963 by Eric Bentley. Published by Grove
Press, Inc. Reprinted by permission of Grove Press, Inc., Methuen &
Co., Ltd., and Suhrkamp.

Scene One

Spring, 1624. In Dalarna, the Swedish Commander Oxenstierna is recruiting for the campaign in Poland. The canteen woman Anna Fierling, commonly known as MOTHER COURAGE, *loses a son.*

(Highway outside a town. A SERGEANT *and a* RECRUITING OFFICER *stand shivering.)*

RECRUITING OFFICER. How the hell can you line up a company in a place like this? You know what I keep thinking about, Sergeant? Suicide. I'm supposed to knock four platoons together by the twelfth—four platoons the Chief's asking for! And they're so friendly around here, I'm scared to go to sleep at night. Suppose I do get my hands on some character and squint at him so I don't notice he's pigeon-chested and has varicose veins. I get him drunk and relaxed, he signs on the dotted line. I pay for the drinks, he steps outside for a minute. I have a hunch I should follow him to the door, and am I right? Away he's gone like a louse from a scratch. You can't take a man's word any more, Sergeant. There's no loyalty left in the world, no trust, no faith, no sense of honour. I'm losing my confidence in mankind, Sergeant.

SERGEANT. What they could do with around here is a good war. What else can you expect with peace running wild all over the place? You know what the trouble with peace is? No organization. And when do you get organization? In a war. Peace is one big waste of equipment. Anything goes, no one gives a damn. See the way they eat? Cheese on pumpernickel, bacon on the cheese? Disgusting! How many horses have they got in this town? How many young men? Nobody knows! They haven't bothered to count 'em! That's peace for you! I've been in places where they haven't had a war for seventy years and you know what? The people haven't even been given names! They don't know who they are! It takes a war to fix that. In a war, everyone registers, everyone's name's on a list. Their shoes are stacked, their corn's in the bag, you count it all up—cattle, men, *et cetera*—and you take it away! That's the story: no organization, no war!

RECRUITING OFFICER. It's God's truth, you know.

SERGEANT. Of course, a war's like any good deal: hard to get going. But when it does get moving, it's a winner, and they're all scared of peace, like a dice player who daren't stop—'cause when peace comes they have to pay up. Of course, *until* it gets going, they're just as scared of war, it's such a novelty!

RECRUITING OFFICER. Hey, look, here's a canteen wagon. Two women and a couple of young lads. Stop the old lady, Sergeant. And if there's nothing doing this time, you won't catch me freezing my arse in the April wind a minute longer.

(*A harmonica is heard. A canteen wagon rolls on, drawn by two young fellows.* MOTHER COURAGE *is sitting on it with her dumb daughter,* KATTRIN.)

MOTHER COURAGE. A good day to you, Sergeant!

SERGEANT (*barring the way*). Good day to *you!* Who d'you think you are?

MOTHER COURAGE. Tradespeople. (*She sings.*)
Here's Mother Courage and her wagon!
   Hey, Captain, let them come and buy!
Beer by the keg! Wine by the flagon!
   Let your men drink before they die!
Sabres and swords are hard to swallow:
   First you must give them beer to drink.
Then they can face what is to follow—
   But let 'em swim before they sink!
     Christians, awake! The winter's gone!
     The snows depart, the dead sleep on.
     And though you may not long survive,
     Get out of bed and look alive!

Your men will march till they are dead, sir.
   But cannot fight unless they eat.
The blood they spill for you is red, sir,
   What fires that blood is my red meat.
For meat and soup and jam and jelly
   In this old cart of mine are found:
So fill the hole up in your belly
   Before you fill one underground.
     Christians, awake! The winter's gone!
     The snows depart, the dead sleep on.
     And though you may not long survive,
     Get out of bed and look alive!

(*She prepares to go.*)

SERGEANT. Halt! Where are you from, riffraff?

EILIF. Second Finnish Regiment!

SERGEANT. Where are your papers?

MOTHER COURAGE. Papers?

SWISS CHEESE. But this is Mother Courage!

SERGEANT. Never heard of her. Where'd she get a name like that?

MOTHER COURAGE. They call me Mother Courage 'cause I was afraid I'd be ruined. So I drove through the bombardment of Riga like a madwoman, with fifty loaves of bread in my cart. They were going moldly, I couldn't please myself.

SERGEANT. No funny business! Where are your papers?

(MOTHER COURAGE *rummages among papers in a tin box and clambers down from her wagon.*)

MOTHER COURAGE. Here, Sergeant! Here's a Bible—I got it in Altötting to wrap my cucumbers in. Here's a map of Moravia—God knows if I'll ever get there—the birds can have it. And here's a document saying my horse hasn't got foot and mouth disease—pity he died on us, he cost fifteen gilders, thank God I didn't pay it. Is that enough paper?

SERGEANT. Are you making a pass at me? Well, you've got another guess coming. You need a license and you know it.

MOTHER COURAGE. Show a little respect for a lady and don't go telling these half-grown children of mine I'm making a pass at you. What would I want with you? My license in the Second Protestant Regiment is an honest face. If *you* wouldn't know how to read it, that's not my fault, I want no rubber stamp on it anyhow.

RECRUITING OFFICER. Sergeant, we have a case of insubordination on our hands. Do you know what we need in the army? Discipline!

MOTHER COURAGE. I was going to say sausages.

SERGEANT. Name?

MOTHER COURAGE. Anna Fierling.

SERGEANT. So you're all Fierlings.

MOTHER COURAGE. I was talking about me.

SERGEANT. And I was talking about your children.

MOTHER COURAGE. Must they all have the same name? (*Pointing to the elder son*) This fellow, for instance, I call him Eilif Noyocki—he got the name from his father who told me he was called Koyocki. Or was it Moyocki? Anyhow, the lad remembers him to this day. Only the man he remembers is someone else, a Frenchman with a pointed beard. But he certainly has his father's brains—that man could whip the breeches off a farmer's backside before he could turn around. So we all have our own names.

SERGEANT. You're all called something different?

MOTHER COURAGE. Are you trying to make out you don't understand?

SERGEANT (*pointing at the younger son*). He's a Chinese, I suppose.

MOTHER COURAGE. Wrong again. A Swiss.

SERGEANT. After the Frenchman?

MOTHER COURAGE. Frenchman? What Frenchman? Don't confuse the issue, Sergeant, or we'll be here all day. He's a Swiss, but he happens to be called Feyos, a name that has nothing to do with his father, who was called something else—a military engineer, if you please, and a drunkard.

(SWISS CHEESE *nods, beaming; even* KATTRIN *smiles.*)

SERGEANT. Then how is it his name's Feyos?

MOTHER COURAGE. Oh, Sergeant, you have no imagination. *Of course* he's called Feyos: When he came, I was with a Hungarian. He didn't mind. He had a floating kidney, though he never touched a drop. He was a very *honest* man. The boy takes after him.

SERGEANT. But that wasn't his father!

MOTHER COURAGE. I said: he took after him. I call him Swiss Cheese. Why? Because he's good at pulling wagons. (*Pointing to her daughter*) And that is Kattrin Haupt, she's half German.

SERGEANT. A nice family, I must say!

MOTHER COURAGE. And we've seen the whole wide world together— this wagonload and me.

SERGEANT. We'll need all that in writing. (*He writes.*) You're from Bamberg in Bavaria. What are you doing here?

MOTHER COURAGE. I can't wait till the war is good enough to come to Bamberg.

RECRUITING OFFICER. And you two oxen pull the cart. Jacob Ox and Esau Ox! D'you ever get out of harness?

EILIF. Mother! May I smack him in the kisser?

MOTHER COURAGE. You stay where you are. And now, gentlemen, what about a brace of pistols? Or a belt? Sergeant? Yours is worn clean through.

SERGEANT. It's something else *I'm* looking for. These lads of yours are straight as birch trees, strong limbs, massive chests . . . What are such fine specimens doing out of the army?

MOTHER COURAGE (*quickly*). A soldier's life is not for sons of mine.

RECRUITING OFFICER. Why not? It means money. It means fame. Peddling shoes is woman's work. (*To* EILIF) Step this way and let's see if that's muscle or chicken fat.

MOTHER COURAGE. It's chicken fat. Give him a good hard look, and he'll fall right over.

RECRUITING OFFICER. Yes, and kill a calf in the falling! (*He tries to hustle* EILIF *away.*)

MOTHER COURAGE. Let him alone! He's not for you!

RECRUITING OFFICER. He called my face a kisser. That is an insult. The two of us will now go and settle the affair on the field of honor.

EILIF. Don't worry, Mother, I can handle him.

MOTHER COURAGE. Stay here. You're never happy till you're in a fight. He has a knife in his boot and he knows how to use it.

RECRUITING OFFICER. I'll draw it out of him like a milk tooth. Come on, young fellow-me-lad!

MOTHER COURAGE. Officer, I'll report you to the Colonel, and he'll throw you in jail. His lieutenant is courting my daughter.

SERGEANT (*to* OFFICER). Go easy. (*To* MOTHER COURAGE) What have you got against the service, wasn't his own father a soldier? Didn't you say he died a soldier's death?

MOTHER COURAGE. This one's just a baby. You'll lead him like a lamb to the slaughter. I know you. You'll get five gilders for him.

RECRUITING OFFICER (*to* EILIF). First thing you know, you'll have a lovely cap and high boots, how about it?

EILIF. Not from you.

MOTHER COURAGE. "Let's you and me go fishing," said the angler to the worm. (*To* SWISS CHEESE) Run and tell everybody they're trying to steal your brother! (*She draws a knife.*) Yes, just you try, and I'll cut you down like dogs! We sell cloth, we sell ham, we are peaceful people!

SERGEANT. You're peaceful all right: your knife proves that. Why, you should be ashamed of yourself. Give me that knife, you hag! You admit you live off the war, what else *could* you live off? Now tell me, how can we have a war without soldiers?

MOTHER COURAGE. Do they have to be mine?

SERGEANT. So that's the trouble. The war should swallow the peach-stone and spit out the peach, hm? Your brood should get fat off the war, but the poor war must ask nothing in return, it can look after itself, can it? Call yourself Mother Courage and then get scared of the war, your breadwinner? Your sons aren't scared, I know that much.

EILIF. Takes more than a war to scare me.

SERGEANT. Correct! Take me. The soldier's life hasn't done *me* any harm, has it? I enlisted at seventeen.

MOTHER COURAGE. You haven't reached seventy.

SERGEANT. I will, though.

MOTHER COURAGE. Above ground?

SERGEANT. Are you trying to rile me, telling me I'll die?

MOTHER COURAGE. Suppose it's the truth? Suppose I see it's your fate? Suppose I *know* you're just a corpse on furlough?

SWISS CHEESE. She can look into the future. Everyone says so.

RECRUITING OFFICER. Then by all means look into the sergeant's future. It might amuse him.

SERGEANT. I don't believe in that stuff.

MOTHER COURAGE. Helmet!

(SERGEANT *gives her his helmet.*)

SERGEANT. It means less than a shit in the grass. Anything for a laugh.

(MOTHER COURAGE *takes a sheet of parchment and tears it in two.*)

MOTHER COURAGE. Eilif, Swiss Cheese, Kattrin! So shall we all be torn in two if we let ourselves get too deep into this war! (*To the* SERGEANT) I'll give you the bargain rate, and do it free. Watch! Death is black, so I draw a black cross.

SWISS CHEESE. And the other she leaves blank, see?

MOTHER COURAGE. I fold them, put them in the helmet, and mix 'em up, the way all of us are mixed from our mother's womb on. Now draw!

(*The* SERGEANT *hesitates.*)

RECRUITING OFFICER (*to* EILIF). I don't take just anybody. I'm choosy. And you've got guts, I like that.

SERGEANT. It's silly. Means as much as blowing your nose.

SWISS CHEESE. The black cross! Oh, his number's up!

RECRUITING OFFICER. Don't let them get under your skin. There aren't enough bullets to go round.

SERGEANT (*hoarsely*). You cheated me!

MOTHER COURAGE. You cheated yourself the day you enlisted. And now we must drive on. There isn't a war every day in the week, we must get to work.

SERGEANT. Hell, you're not getting away with this! We're taking that bastard of yours with *us!*

EILIF. I'd like that, Mother.

MOTHER COURAGE. Quiet—you Finnish devil, you!

EILIF. And Swiss Cheese wants to be a soldier, too.

MOTHER COURAGE. That's news to me. I see I'll have to draw lots for all three of you. (*She goes to the back to draw the crosses on bits of paper.*)

RECRUITING OFFICER (*to* EILIF). People've been saying the Swedish soldier is religious. That kind of loose talk has hurt us a lot. One verse of a hymn every Sunday—and then only if you have a voice . . .

(MOTHER COURAGE *returns with the slips and puts them in the* SERGEANT'S *helmet.*)

MOTHER COURAGE. So they'd desert their old mother, would they, the rascals? They take to war like a cat to cream. But I'll consult these slips, and they'll see the world's no promised land, with a "Join up, son, you're officer material!" Sergeant, I'm afraid for them, very afraid they won't get through this war. They have terrible

qualities, all three. (*She holds the helmet out to* EILIF.) There.
Draw your lot. (EILIF *fishes in the helmet, unfolds a slip. She
snatches it from him.*) There you have it: a cross. Unhappy
mother that I am, rich only in a mother's sorrows! He dies. In
the springtime of his life, he must go. If he's a soldier, he must
bite the dust, that's clear. He's too brave, like his father. And if
he doesn't use his head, he'll go the way of all flesh, the slip proves
it. (*Hectoring him*) Will you use your head?

EILIF. Why not?

MOTHER COURAGE. It's using your head to stay with your mother. And
when they make fun of you and call you a chicken, just laugh.

RECRUITING OFFICER. If you're going to wet your pants, I'll try your
brother.

MOTHER COURAGE. I told you to laugh. Laugh! Now it's your turn,
Swiss Cheese. You should be a better bet, you're honest. (*He
fishes in the helmet.*) Oh, dear, why are you giving that slip such
a funny look? You've drawn a blank for sure. It can't be there's
a cross on it. It can't be I'm going to lose *you*. (*She takes the
slip.*) A cross? Him too! Could it be 'cause he's so simple-minded?
Oh, Swiss Cheese, you'll be a goner too, if you aren't honest,
honest, honest the whole time, the way I always brought you up
to be, the way you always bring me all the change when you buy
me a loaf. It's the only way you can save yourself. Look, Sergeant,
if it isn't a black cross!

SERGEANT. It's a cross! I don't understand how *I* got one. I always
stay well in the rear. (*To the* OFFICER) But it can't be a trick: it
gets *her* children too.

SWISS CHEESE. It gets me too. But I don't accept it!

MOTHER COURAGE (*to* KATTRIN). And now all I have left for certain
is you, you're a cross in yourself, you have a good heart. (*She
holds the helmet up high toward the wagon but takes the slip
out herself.*) Oh, I could give up in despair! There must be some
mistake, I didn't mix them right. Don't be too kind, Kattrin, just
don't, there's a cross in your path too. Always be very quiet, it
can't be hard since you're dumb. Well, so now you know, all
of you: be careful, you'll need to be. Now let's climb on the
wagon and move on. (*She returns the helmet to the* SERGEANT
and climbs on the wagon.)

RECRUITING OFFICER (*to the* SERGEANT). Do something!

SERGEANT. I don't feel very well.

RECRUITING OFFICER. Maybe you caught a chill when you handed over
your helmet in all this wind. Get her involved in a business trans-
action! (*Aloud*) That belt, Sergeant, you could at least take a look

at it. These good people live by trade, don't they? Hey, all of you, the Sergeant wants to buy the belt!

MOTHER COURAGE. Half a gilder. A belt like that is worth two gilders. (*She clambers down again from the wagon.*)

SERGEANT. It isn't new. But there's too much wind here. I'll go and look at it behind the wagon. (*He does so.*)

MOTHER COURAGE. I don't find it windy.

SERGEANT. Maybe it's worth half a gilder at that. There's silver on it.

MOTHER COURAGE (*following him behind the wagon*). A solid six ounces worth!

RECRUITING OFFICER (*to* EILIF). And we can have a drink, just us men. I'll advance you some money to cover it. Let's go.

(EILIF *stands undecided.*)

MOTHER COURAGE. Half a gilder, then.

SERGEANT. I don't understand it. I always stay in the rear. There's no safer spot for a sergeant to be. You can send the others on ahead in quest of fame. My appetite is ruined. I can tell you right now: I won't be able to get anything down.

MOTHER COURAGE. You shouldn't take on so, just because you can't eat. Just stay in the rear. Here, take a slug of brandy, man. (*She gives him brandy.*)

RECRUITING OFFICER (*who has taken* EILIF *by the arm and is making off toward the back*). Ten gilders in advance and you're a soldier of the king and a stout fellow and the women will be mad about you. And you can give me a smack in the kisser for insulting you. (*Both leave. Dumb* KATTRIN *jumps down from the wagon and lets out harsh cries.*)

MOTHER COURAGE. Coming, Kattrin, coming! The sergeant's just paying up. (*She bites the half gilder.*) I'm suspicious of all money, I've been badly burned, Sergeant. But this money's good. And now we'll be going. Where's Eilif?

SWISS CHEESE. Gone with the recruiting officer.

MOTHER COURAGE (*stands quite still, then*). Oh, you simpleton! (*To* KATTRIN) You *can't* speak, I know. You are innocent.

SERGEANT. That's life, Mother Courage. Take a slug yourself, Mother. Being a soldier isn't the worst that could happen. You want to live off war and keep you and yours out of it, do you?

MOTHER COURAGE. You must help your brother now, Kattrin.

(BROTHER *and* SISTER *get into harness together and pull the wagon.* MOTHER COURAGE *walks at their side. The wagon gets under way.*)

SERGEANT (*looking after them*).

When a war gives you all you earn
One day it may claim something in return!

Scene Two

In the years 1625 and 1626 MOTHER COURAGE *journeys through Poland in the baggage train of the Swedish army. She meets her son again before Wallhof castle. Of the successful sale of a capon and great days for the brave son.*

(*Tent of the Swedish Commander. Kitchen next to it. Thunder of cannon. The* COOK *is quarreling with* MOTHER COURAGE, *who is trying to sell him a capon.*)

COOK. Sixty hellers for that paltry piece of poultry?

MOTHER COURAGE. Paltry poultry? Why, he's the fattest fowl you ever saw! I see no reason why I shouldn't get sixty hellers for him—this Commander can eat till the cows come home—and woe betide you when there's nothing in your pantry . . .

COOK. They're ten hellers a dozen on every street corner.

MOTHER COURAGE. A capon like this on every street corner! With a siege going on and people all skin and bones? Maybe you can get a field rat! I said maybe. Because we're all out of *them* too. Didn't you see the soldiers running five deep after one hungry little field rat? All right then, in a siege, my price for a giant capon is fifty hellers.

COOK. But we're not "in a siege," we're doing the besieging, it's the other side that's "in a siege," when will you get this into your head?

MOTHER COURAGE. A fat lot of difference that makes, *we* haven't got a thing to eat either. They took everything in the town with them before all this started, and now they've nothing to do but eat and drink, I hear. It's us I'm worried about. Look at the farmers round here, they haven't a thing.

COOK. Certainly they have. They hide it.

MOTHER COURAGE (*triumphant*). They have not! They're ruined, that's what. They're so hungry I've seen 'em digging up roots to eat. I could boil your leather belt and make their mouths water with it. That's how things are round here. And I'm expected to let a capon go for forty hellers!

COOK. Thirty. Not forty. I said thirty hellers.

MOTHER COURAGE. I say this is no ordinary capon. It was a talented animal, so I hear. It would only feed to music—one march in particular was its favorite. It was so intelligent it could count. Forty hellers is too much for all this? I know *your* problem: if you don't find something to eat and quick, the Chief will—cut—your—fat—head—off!

COOK. All right, just watch. (*He takes a piece of beef and lays his knife on it.*) Here's a piece of beef, I'm going to roast it. I give you one more chance.

MOTHER COURAGE. Roast it, go ahead, it's only one year old.

COOK. One *day* old! Yesterday it was a cow. I saw it running around.

MOTHER COURAGE. In that case it must have started stinking before it died.

COOK. I don't care if I have to cook it five hours: I *must* know if it'll still be hard. (*He cuts into it.*)

MOTHER COURAGE. Put plenty of pepper in, so the Commander won't smell the smell.

(*The* SWEDISH COMMANDER, *a* CHAPLAIN, *and* EILIF *enter the tent.*)

COMMANDER (*clapping* EILIF *on the shoulder*). In the Commander's tent with you, my son! Sit at my right hand, you happy warrior! You've played a hero's part, you've served the Lord in his own Holy War, *that's* the thing! And you'll get a gold bracelet out of it when we take the town if *I* have any say in the matter! We come to save their souls and what do they do, the filthy, irreligious sons of bitches? Drive their cattle away from us, while they stuff their priests with beef at both ends! But you showed 'em. So here's a can of red wine for you, we'll drink together! (*They do so.*) The chaplain gets the dregs, he's pious. Now what would you like for dinner, my hearty?

EILIF. How about a slice of meat?

COMMANDER. Cook, meat!

COOK. Nothing to eat, so he brings company to eat it!

(MOTHER COURAGE *makes him stop talking, she wants to listen.*)

EILIF. Tires you out, skinning peasants. Gives you an appetite.

MOTHER COURAGE. Dear God, it's my Eilif!

COOK. Who?

MOTHER COURAGE. My eldest. It's two years since I saw him, he was stolen from me right off the street. He must be in high favor if the Commander's invited him to dinner. And what do you have to eat? Nothing. You hear what the Commander's guest wants? Meat! Better take my advice, buy the capon. The price is one gilder.

COMMANDER (*who has sat down with* EILIF *and the* CHAPLAIN, *roaring*). Cook! Dinner, you pig, or I'll have your head!

COOK. This is blackmail. Give me the damn thing!

MOTHER COURAGE. Paltry poultry like this?

COOK. You were right. Give it here. It's highway robbery, fifty hellers.

MOTHER COURAGE. I said one gilder. Nothing's too high for my eldest, the Commander's guest of honor.

COOK (*giving her the money*). Well, you might at least pluck it till I have a fire going.

MOTHER COURAGE (*sitting down to pluck the capon*). I can't wait to see his face when he sees me. This is my brave and clever son. I also have a stupid one but he's honest. The daughter is nothing. At least, she doesn't talk: we must be thankful for small mercies.

COMMANDER. Have another glass, my son, it's my favorite Falernian. There's only one cask left—two at the most—but it's worth it to meet a soldier that still believes in God! The shepherd of our flock here just looks on, he only preaches, he hasn't a clue how anything gets done. So now, Eilif, my son, give us the details: tell us how you fixed the peasants and grabbed the twenty bullocks. And let's hope they'll soon be here.

EILIF. In one day's time. Two at most.

MOTHER COURAGE. Now that's considerate of Eilif—to bring the oxen tomorrow—otherwise my capon wouldn't have been so welcome today.

EILIF. Well, it was like this. I found out that the peasants had hidden their oxen and—on the sly and chiefly at night—had driven them into a certain wood. The people from the town were to pick them up there. I let them get their oxen in peace—they ought to know better than me where they are, I said to myself. Meanwhile I made my men crazy for meat. Their rations were short and I made sure they got shorter. Their mouths'd water at the sound of any word beginning with M, like mother.

COMMANDER. Smart fella.

EILIF. Not bad. The rest was a walkover. Only the peasants had clubs and outnumbered us three to one and made a murderous attack on us. Four of them drove me into a clump of trees, knocked my good sword from my hand, and yelled, "Surrender!" What now, I said to myself, they'll make mincemeat of me.

COMMANDER. What did you do?

EILIF. I laughed.

COMMANDER. You what?

EILIF. I laughed. And so we got to talking. I came right down to business and said: "Twenty gilders an ox is too much, I bid fifteen." Like I wanted to buy. That foxed 'em. So while they were scratching their heads, I reached for my good sword and cut 'em to pieces. Necessity knows no law, huh?

COMMANDER. What do *you* say, shepherd of the flock?

CHAPLAIN. Strictly speaking, that saying is not in the Bible. Our Lord made five hundred loaves out of five so that no such necessity would arise. When he told men to love their neighbors, their bellies were full. Nowadays things are different.

COMMANDER (*laughing*). Quite different. A swallow of wine for those wise words, you pharisee! (*To* EILIF) You cut 'em to pieces in a good cause, our chaps were hungry and you gave 'em to eat. Doesn't it say in the Bible "Whatsoever thou doest to the least of these my children, thou doest unto me"? And what *did* you do to 'em? You got 'em the best steak dinner they ever tasted. Moldy bread is not what they're used to. They always ate white bread, and drank wine in their helmets, before going out to fight for God.

EILIF. I reached for my good sword and cut 'em to pieces.

COMMANDER. You have the makings of a Julius Caesar, why, you should be presented to the King!

EILIF. I've seen him—from a distance of course. He seemed to shed a light all around. I must try to be like him!

COMMANDER. I think you're succeeding, my boy! Oh, Eilif, you don't know how I value a brave soldier like you! I treat such a chap as my very own son. (*He takes him to the map.*) Take a look at our position, Eilif, it isn't all it might be, is it?

MOTHER COURAGE (*who has been listening and is now plucking angrily at her capon*). He must be a very bad commander.

COOK. Just a greedy one. Why bad?

MOTHER COURAGE. Because he needs *brave* soldiers, that's why. If his plan of campaign was any good, why would he need *brave* soldiers, wouldn't plain, ordinary soldiers do? Whenever there are great virtues, it's a sure sign something's wrong.

COOK. You mean, it's a sure sign something's right.

MOTHER COURAGE. I mean what I say. Listen. When a general or a king is stupid and leads his soldiers into a trap, they need this virtue of courage. When he's tightfisted and hasn't enough soldiers, the few he does have need the heroism of Hercules—another virtue. And if he's a sloven and doesn't give a damn about anything, they have to be wise as serpents or they're finished. Loyalty's another virtue and you need plenty of it if the king's always asking too much of you. All virtues which a well-regulated country with a good king or a good general wouldn't need. In a good country virtues wouldn't be necessary. Everybody could be quite ordinary, middling, and, for all I care, cowards.

COMMANDER. I bet your father was a soldier.

EILIF. I've heard he was a great soldier. My mother warned me. I know a song about that.

COMMANDER. Sing it to us. (*Roaring*) Bring that meat!

EILIF. It's called "The Song of the Fishwife and the Soldier." (*He sings and at the same time does a war dance with his sabre.*)
>   To a soldier lad comes an old fishwife
>   And this old fishwife, says she:
>   A gun will shoot, a knife will knife,
>   You will drown if you fall in the sea.
>   Keep away from the ice if you want my advice,
>   Says the old fishwife, says she.
>   The soldier laughs and loads his gun
>   Then grabs his knife and starts to run:
>   It's the life of a hero for me!
>   From the north to the south I shall march through the land
>   With a knife at my side and a gun in my hand!
>   Says the soldier lad, says he.
>
>   When the lad defies the fishwife's cries
>   The old fishwife, says she:
>   The young are young, the old are wise,
>   You will drown if you fall in the sea.
>   Don't ignore what I say or you'll rue it one day!
>   Says the old fishwife, says she.
>   But gun in hand and knife at side
>   The soldier steps into the tide:
>   It's the life of a hero for me!
>   When the new moon is shining on shingle roofs white
>   We are all coming back, go and pray for that night!
>   Says the soldier lad, says he.

(MOTHER COURAGE *continues the song from her kitchen, beating on a pan with a spoon.*)
>   And the fishwife old does what she's told:
>   Down upon her knees drops she.
>   When the smoke is gone, the air is cold,
>   Your heroic deeds won't warm me!
>   See the smoke, how it goes! May God scatter his foes!
>   Down upon her knees drops she.

EILIF. What's that?

MOTHER COURAGE (*singing on*).
>   But gun in hand and knife at side
>   The lad is swept out by the tide:
>   He floats with the ice to the sea.
>   And the new moon is shining on shingle roofs white
>   But the lad and his laughter are lost in the night:

He floats with the ice to the sea.

COMMANDER. What a kitchen I've got! There's no end to the liberties they take!

EILIF. (*Has entered the kitchen and embraced his mother.*) To see you again! Where are the others?

MOTHER COURAGE (*in his arms*). Happy as ducks in a pond. Swiss Cheese is paymaster with the Second Regiment, so at least he isn't in the fighting. I couldn't keep him out altogether.

EILIF. Are your feet holding up?

MOTHER COURAGE. I've a bit of trouble getting my shoes on in the morning.

COMMANDER (*who has come over*). So, you're his mother! I hope you have more sons for me like this chap.

EILIF. If I'm not the lucky one: you sit there in the kitchen and hear your son being feasted!

MOTHER COURAGE. Yes. I heard all right. (*Gives him a box on the ear.*)

EILIF (*his hand to his cheek*). Because I took the oxen?

MOTHER COURAGE. No. Because you didn't surrender when the four peasants let fly at you and tried to make mincemeat of you! Didn't I teach you to take care of yourself? You Finnish devil, you!

(*The* COMMANDER *and the* CHAPLAIN *stand laughing in the doorway.*)

Scene Three

Three years pass and MOTHER COURAGE, *with parts of a Finnish regiment, is taken prisoner. Her daughter is saved, her wagon likewise, but her honest son dies.*

(*A camp. The regimental flag is flying from a pole. Afternoon. All sorts of wares hanging on the wagon.* MOTHER COURAGE'S *clothes line is tied to the wagon at one end, to a cannon at the other. She and* KATTRIN *are folding the washing on the cannon. At the same time she is bargaining with an* ORDNANCE OFFICER *over a bag of bullets.* SWISS CHEESE, *in paymaster's uniform now, looks on.* YVETTE POTTER, *a very good-looking young person, is sewing at a colored hat, a glass of brandy before her. She is in stocking feet. Her red boots are near by.*)

OFFICER. I'm letting you have the bullets for two gilders. Dirt cheap. 'Cause I need the money. The Colonel's been drinking with the officers for three days and we've run out of liquor.

MOTHER COURAGE. They're army property. If they find 'em on me, I'll be courtmartialed. You sell your bullets, you bastards, and send your men out to fight with nothing to shoot with.

OFFICER. Oh, come on, if you scratch my back, I'll scratch yours.

MOTHER COURAGE. I won't take army stuff. Not at *that* price.

OFFICER. You can resell 'em for five gilders, maybe eight, to the Ordnance Officer of the Fourth Regiment. All you have to do is give him a receipt for twelve. He hasn't a bullet left.

MOTHER COURAGE. Why don't you do it yourself?

OFFICER. I don't trust him. We're friends.

MOTHER COURAGE (*takes the bag*). Give it here. (*To* KATTRIN) Take it round the back and pay him a gilder and a half. (*As the* OFFICER *protests*) I said a gilder and a half!

(KATTRIN *drags the bag away. The* OFFICER *follows.* MOTHER COURAGE *speaks to* SWISS CHEESE.)

Here's your underwear back, take care of it; it's October now, autumn may come at any time; I purposely don't say it must come, I've learnt from experience there's nothing that must come, not even the seasons. But your books *must* balance now you're the regimental paymaster. *Do* they balance?

SWISS CHEESE. Yes, Mother.

MOTHER COURAGE. Don't forget they made you paymaster because you're honest and so simple you'd never think of running off with the cash. Don't lose that underwear.

SWISS CHEESE. No, Mother. I'll put it under the mattress. (*He starts to go.*)

OFFICER. I'll go with you, paymaster.

MOTHER COURAGE. Don't teach him any hanky-panky.

(*Without a good-bye the* OFFICER *leaves with* SWISS CHEESE.)

YVETTE (*waving to him*). You might at least say good-bye!

MOTHER COURAGE (*to* YVETTE). I don't like that. *He's* no sort of company for my Swiss Cheese. But the war's not making a bad start. Before all the different countries get into it, four or five years'll have gone by like nothing. If I look ahead and make no mistakes, business will be good. Don't you know you shouldn't drink in the morning with your illness?

YVETTE. Who says I'm ill? That's libel!

MOTHER COURAGE. They all say so.

YVETTE. They're all liars. I'm desperate, Mother Courage. They all avoid me like a stinking fish. Because of those lies. So what am I fixing my hat for? (*She throws it down.*) That's why I drink in the morning. I never used to, it gives you crow's feet. But now it's all one, every man in the regiment knows me. I should have stayed home when my first was unfaithful. But pride isn't for the likes of us, you eat dirt or down you go.

MOTHER COURAGE. Now don't you start again with your friend Peter and how it all happened—in front of my innocent daughter.

YVETTE. She's the one that should hear it. So she'll get hardened against love.

MOTHER COURAGE. That's something no one ever gets hardened against.

YVETTE. I'll tell you about it, and get it off my chest. I grew up in Flanders' fields, that's where it starts, or I'd never even have caught sight of him and I wouldn't be here in Poland today. He was an army cook, blond, a Dutchman, but thin. Kattrin, beware of thin men! I didn't. I didn't even know he'd had another girl before me and she called him Peter Piper because he never took his pipe out of his mouth the whole time, it meant so little to him. (*She sings "The Fraternization Song."*)

Scarce seventeen was I when
   The foe came to our land
And laid aside his sabre
   And took me by the hand.
     And we performed by day
     The sacred rite of May
     And we performed by night
     Another sacred rite.
     The regiment, well exercised,
     Presented arms, then stood at ease,
     Then took us off behind the trees
     Where we fraternized.

Each of us had her foe and
   A cook fell to my lot.
I hated him by daylight
   But in the dark did not.
     So we perform by day
     The sacred rite of May
     And we perform by night
     That other sacred rite.
     The regiment, well exercised,
     Presents its arms, then stands at ease,
     Then takes us off behind the trees
     Where we fraternize.

Ecstasy filled my heart, O
   My love seemed heaven-born!

But why were people saying
  It was not love but scorn?
    The springtime's soft amour
    Through summer may endure
    But swiftly comes the fall
    And winter ends it all.
    December came. All of the men
    Filed past the trees where once we hid
    Then quickly marched away and did
    Not come back again.

I made the mistake of running after him, I never found him. It's ten years ago now. (*With swaying gait she goes behind the wagon.*)

MOTHER COURAGE. You're leaving your hat.

YVETTE. For the birds.

MOTHER COURAGE. Let this be a lesson to you, Kattrin, never start anything with a soldier. Love does seem heaven-born, so watch out! Even with those who're not in the army life's no honey pot. He tells you he'd like to kiss the ground under your feet—did you wash 'em yesterday, while we're on the subject? And then if you don't look out, your number's up, you're his slave for life. Be glad you're dumb, Kattrin: you'll never contradict yourself, you'll never want to bite your tongue off because you spoke out of turn. Dumbness is a gift from God. Here comes the Commander's Cook, what's bothering *him*?

(*Enter the* COOK *and the* CHAPLAIN.)

CHAPLAIN. I bring a message from your son Eilif. The Cook came with me. You've made, ahem, an impression on him.

COOK. I thought I'd get a little whiff of the balmy breeze.

MOTHER COURAGE. You're always welcome to that if you behave yourself and, even if you don't, I think I can handle you. But what does Eilif want? I've no money to spare.

CHAPLAIN. Actually, I have something to tell his brother, the paymaster.

MOTHER COURAGE. He isn't here. And he isn't anywhere else either. He's not his brother's paymaster, and I won't have him led into temptation. Let Eilif try it on with someone else! (*She takes money from the purse at her belt.*) Give him this. It's a sin. He's speculating in mother love, he ought to be ashamed of himself.

COOK. Not for long. He has to go with his regiment now—to his death maybe. Send some more money, or you'll be sorry. You women are hard—and sorry afterwards. A glass of brandy wouldn't cost

very much, but you refuse to provide it, and six feet under goes
your man and you can't dig him up again.

CHAPLAIN. All very touching, my dear Cook, but to fall in this war is
not a misfortune, it's a blessing. This is a war of religion. Not
just any old war but a special one, a religious one, and therefore
pleasing unto God.

COOK. Correct. In one sense it's a war because there's fleecing, bribing,
plundering, not to mention a little raping, but it's different from
all other wars because it's a war of religion. That's clear. All the
same, it makes you thirsty.

CHAPLAIN (*to* MOTHER COURAGE, *pointing at the* COOK). I tried to hold
him off but he said you'd bewitched him. He dreams about you.

COOK (*lighting a clay pipe*). Brandy from the fair hand of a lady, that's
for me. And don't embarrass me any more: the stories the chaplain was telling on the way over still have me blushing.

MOTHER COURAGE. A man of his cloth! I must get you both something
to drink or you'll be making improper advances out of sheer
boredom.

CHAPLAIN. That is indeed a temptation, said the Court Chaplain, and
gave way to it. (*Turning toward* KATTRIN *as he walks*) And who
is this captivating young person?

MOTHER COURAGE. She's not a captivating young person, she's a respectable young person.

(*The* CHAPLAIN *and the* COOK *go with* MOTHER COURAGE *behind
the cart, and one hears them talk politics.*)

MOTHER COURAGE. The trouble here in Poland is that the Poles *would*
keep meddling. It's true our King moved in on them with man,
beast, and wagon, but instead of keeping the peace the Poles were
always meddling in their own affairs. They attacked the Swedish
King when he was in the act of peacefully withdrawing. So they
were guilty of a breach of the peace and their blood is on their
own heads.

CHAPLAIN. Anyway, our King was thinking of nothing but freedom.
The Kaiser enslaved them all, Poles and Germans alike, so our
King *had* to liberate them.

COOK. Just what *I* think. Your health! Your brandy is first rate, I'm
never mistaken in a face. (KATTRIN *looks after them, leaves the
washing, and goes to the hat, picks it up, sits down, and takes up
the red boots.*) And the war is a war of religion. (*Singing while*
KATTRIN *puts the boots on*) "A mighty fortress is our God . . ."
(*He sings a verse or so of Luther's hymn.*) And talking of King
Gustavus, this freedom he tried to bring to Germany cost him a
pretty penny. Back in Sweden he had to levy a salt tax, the poorer

folks didn't like it a bit. Then, too, he had to lock up the Germans and even cut their heads off, they clung so to slavery and their Kaiser. Of course, if no one had *wanted* to be free, the King wouldn't have had any fun. First it was just Poland he tried to protect from bad men, specially the Kaiser, then his appetite grew with eating, and he ended up protecting Germany too. Now Germany put up a pretty decent fight. So the good King had nothing but worries in return for his outlay and his goodness, and of course he had to get his money back with taxes, which made bad blood, but he didn't shrink even from that. For he had one thing in his favor anyway, God's Holy Word, which was all to the good, because otherwise they could have said he did it for himself or for profit. That's how he kept his conscience clear. He always put conscience first.

MOTHER COURAGE. It's plain you're no Swede, or you'd speak differently of the Hero King.

CHAPLAIN. What's more, you eat his bread.

COOK. I don't eat his bread. I bake his bread.

MOTHER COURAGE. He can never be conquered, and I'll tell you why: his men believe in him. (*Earnestly*) To hear the big chaps talk, they wage the war from fear of God and for all things bright and beautiful, but just look into it, and you'll see they're not so silly: they want a good profit out of it, or else the little chaps like you and me wouldn't back 'em up.

COOK. That's right.

CHAPLAIN. And as a Dutchman you'd do well to see which flag's flying here before you express an opinion!

MOTHER COURAGE. All good Protestants for ever!

COOK. A health!

(KATTRIN *has begun to strut around with* YVETTE'S *hat on, copying* YVETTE'S *sexy walk. Suddenly cannon and shots. Drums.* MOTHER COURAGE, *the* COOK, *and the* CHAPLAIN *rush round to the front of the cart, the two last with glasses in their hands. The* ORDNANCE OFFICER *and a* SOLDIER *come running to the cannon and try to push it along.*)

MOTHER COURAGE. What's the matter? Let me get my washing off that gun, you slobs! (*She tries to do so.*)

OFFICER. The Catholics! Surprise attack! We don't know if we can get away! (*To the* SOLDIER) Get that gun! (*Runs off.*)

COOK. For heaven's sake! I must go to the Commander. Mother Courage, I'll be back in a day or two—for a short conversation. (*Rushes off.*)

MOTHER COURAGE. Hey, you've left your pipe!

COOK (*off*). Keep it for me, I'll need it!

MOTHER COURAGE. This *would* happen when we were just making money.

CHAPLAIN. Well, I must be going too. Yes, if the enemy's so close, it can be dangerous. "Blessed are the peacemakers," a good slogan in wartime! If only I had a cloak.

MOTHER COURAGE. I'm lending no cloaks. Not even to save a life I'm not. I've had experience in that line.

CHAPLAIN. But I'm in special danger. Because of my religion!

MOTHER COURAGE (*brings him a cloak*). It's against my better judgment. Now run!

CHAPLAIN. I thank you, you're very generous, but maybe I'd better stay and sit here. If I run, I might attract the enemy's attention. I might arouse suspicion.

MOTHER COURAGE (*to the* SOLDIER). Let it alone, you dolt, who's going to pay you for this? It'll cost you your life, let me hold it for you.

SOLDIER (*running away*). You're my witness: I tried!

MOTHER COURAGE. I'll swear to it! (*Seeing* KATTRIN *with the hat*) What on earth are you up to—with a whore's hat! Take it off this minute! Are you crazy? With the enemy coming? (*She tears the hat off her head.*) Do you want them to find you and make a whore of you? And she has the boots on too, straight from Babylon. I'll soon fix that. (*She tries to get them off.*) Oh God, Chaplain, help me with these boots, I'll be back straightaway. (*She runs to the wagon.*)

YVETTE (*entering and powdering her face*). What's that you say: the Catholics are coming? Where's my hat? Who's been trampling on it? I can't run around in that, what will they think of me? And I've no mirror either. (*To the* CHAPLAIN) How do I look—too much powder?

CHAPLAIN. Just, er, right.

YVETTE. And where are my red boots? (*She can't find them because* KATTRIN *is hiding her feet under her skirt.*) I left them here! Now I've got to go barefoot to my tent, it's a scandal! (*Exit.* SWISS CHEESE *comes running in carrying a cashbox.* MOTHER COURAGE *enters with her hands full of ashes. To* KATTRIN) Ashes! (*To* SWISS CHEESE) What have you got there?

SWISS CHEESE. The regimental cashbox.

MOTHER COURAGE. Throw it away! Your paymastering days are over!

SWISS CHEESE. It's a trust! (*He goes to the back.*)

MOTHER COURAGE (*to the* CHAPLAIN). Off with your pastor's coat, Chaplain, or they'll recognize you, cloak or no cloak. (*She is rubbing ashes into* KATTRIN's *face.*) Keep still. A little dirt, and you're safe. A calamity! The sentries were drunk. Well, one must hide one's light under a bushel, as they say. When a soldier sees a clean face, there's one more whore in the world. Specially a Catholic soldier. For weeks on end, no grub. Then, when they get some by way of plunder, they jump on top of the womenfolk. That should do. Let me look at you. Not bad. Looks like you've been rolling in muck. Don't tremble. Nothing can happen to you now. (*To* SWISS CHEESE) Where've you left the cashbox?

SWISS CHEESE. I thought I'd just put it in the wagon.

MOTHER COURAGE (*horrified*). What!? In my wagon? God punish you for a prize idiot! If I just look away for a moment! They'll hang all three of us!

SWISS CHEESE. Then I'll put it somewhere else. Or escape with it.

MOTHER COURAGE. You'll stay where you are. It's too late.

CHAPLAIN (*still changing his clothes*). For Heaven's sake: the flag!

MOTHER COURAGE (*taking down the flag*). God in Heaven! I don't notice it any more. I've had it twenty-five years.

(*The thunder of cannon grows.*)

(*Three days later. Morning. The cannon is gone.* MOTHER COURAGE, KATTRIN, *the* CHAPLAIN *and* SWISS CHEESE *sit anxiously eating.*)

SWISS CHEESE. This is the third day I've been sitting here doing nothing, and the Sergeant, who's always been patient with me, may be slowly beginning to ask, "Where on earth is Swiss Cheese with that cashbox?"

MOTHER COURAGE. Be glad they're not on the scent.

CHAPLAIN. What about me? I can't hold service here or I'll be in hot water. It is written, "Out of the abundance of the heart, the tongue speaketh." But woe is me if *my* tongue speaketh!

MOTHER COURAGE. That's how it is. Here you sit—one with his religion, the other with his cashbox, I don't know which is more dangerous.

CHAPLAIN. We're in God's hands now!

MOTHER COURAGE. I hope we're not as desperate as *that,* but it *is* hard to sleep at night. 'Course it'd be easier if *you* weren't here, Swiss Cheese, all the same I've not done badly. I told them I was against the Antichrist, who's a Swede with horns on his head. I told them I noticed his left horn's a bit threadbare. When they cross-questioned me, I always asked where I could buy holy candles a bit cheaper. I know these things because Swiss Cheese's father was a Catholic and made jokes about it. They didn't quite believe me but they needed a canteen, so they turned a blind eye. Maybe it's all for the best. We're prisoners. But so are lice in fur.

CHAPLAIN. The milk is good. As far as quantity goes, we may have to reduce our Swedish appetites somewhat. We are defeated.

MOTHER COURAGE. Who's defeated? The defeats and victories of the chaps at the top aren't always defeats and victories for the chaps at the bottom. Not at all. There've been cases where a defeat is a victory for the chaps at the bottom, it's only their honor that's lost, nothing serious. In Livonia once, our Chief took such a knock from the enemy, in the confusion I got a fine gray mare out of the baggage train, it pulled my wagon seven months—till we won and inventory was taken. But in general both defeat and victory are a costly business for us that haven't got much. The best thing is for politics to kind of get stuck in the mud. (*To* SWISS CHEESE.) Eat!

SWISS CHEESE. I don't like it. How will the Sergeant pay his men?

MOTHER COURAGE. Soldiers in flight don't get paid.

SWISS CHEESE. Well, they could claim to be. No pay, no flight. They can refuse to budge.

MOTHER COURAGE. Swiss Cheese, your sense of duty worries me. I've brought you up to be honest because you're not very bright. But don't go too far! And now I'm going with the Chaplain to buy a Catholic flag and some meat. There's no one can hunt out meat like him, sure as a sleepwalker. He can tell a good piece of meat from the way his mouth waters. A good thing they let me stay in the business. In business you ask what price, not what religion. And Protestant trousers keep you just as warm.

CHAPLAIN. As the mendicant monk said when there was talk of the Lutherans standing everything on its head in town and country: Beggars will *always* be needed. (MOTHER COURAGE *disappears into the wagon*.) She's worried about the cashbox. Up to now they've ignored us—as if we were part of the wagon—but can it last?

SWISS CHEESE. I can get rid of it.

CHAPLAIN. That's almost *more* dangerous. Suppose you're seen. They have spies. Yesterday morning one jumped out of the very hole I was relieving myself in. I was so off guard I almost broke out in prayer—*that* would have given me away all right! I believe their favorite way of finding a Protestant is smelling his, um, excrement. The spy was a little brute with a bandage over one eye.

MOTHER COURAGE (*clambering out of the wagon with a basket*). I've found you out, you shameless hussy! (*She holds up* YVETTE'S *red boots in triumph*.) Yvette's red boots! She just swiped them— because you went and told her she was a captivating person. (*She lays them in the basket*.) Stealing Yvette's boots! But *she* disgraces herself for money, *you* do it for nothng—for pleasure!

I told you, you must wait for the peace. No soldiers! Save your
proud, peacock ways for peacetime!

CHAPLAIN. I don't find her proud.

MOTHER COURAGE. Prouder than she can afford to be. I like her when
people say "I never noticed the poor thing." I like her when she's
a stone in Dalarna where there's nothing but stones. (*To* SWISS
CHEESE) Leave the cashbox where it is, do you hear? And pay
attention to your sister, she needs it. Between the two of you,
you'll be the death of me yet. I'd rather take care of a bag of fleas.
(*She leaves with the* CHAPLAIN. KATTRIN *clears the dishes away.*)

SWISS CHEESE. Not many days more when you can sit in the sun in
your shirt sleeves. (KATTRIN *points to a tree.*) Yes, the leaves are
yellow already. (*With gestures,* KATTRIN *asks if he wants a drink.*)
I'm not drinking, I'm thinking. (*Pause.*) She says she can't sleep.
So I *should* take the cashbox away. I've found a place for it. I'll
keep it in the mole hole by the river till the time comes. I might
get it tonight before sunrise and take it to the regiment. How far
can they have fled in three days? The Sergeant's eyes'll pop out
of his head. "You've disappointed me most pleasantly, Swiss
Cheese," he'll say, "*I* trust you with the cashbox and *you* bring it
back!" Yes, Kattrin, I *will* have a glass now!

(*When* KATTRIN *reappears behind the wagon two men confront
her. One of them is a sergeant. The other doffs his hat and
flourishes it in a showy greeting. He has a bandage over one eye.*)

THE MAN WITH THE BANDAGE. Good morning, young lady. Have you
seen a man from the Second Protestant Regiment?

(*Terrified,* KATTRIN *runs away, spilling her brandy. The two men
look at each other and then withdraw after seeing* SWISS CHEESE.)

SWISS CHEESE (*starting up from his reflection*). You're spilling it!
What's the matter with you, can't you see where you're going? I
don't understand you. Anyway, I must be off, I've decided it's the
thing to do. (*He stands up. She does all she can to make him
aware of the danger he is in. He only pushes her away.*) I'd like
to know what you mean. I know you mean well, poor thing, you
just can't get it out. And don't trouble yourself about the brandy,
I'll live to drink so much of it, what's one glass? (*He takes the
cashbox out of the wagon and puts it under his coat.*) I'll be back
straightaway. But don't hold me up or I'll have to scold you. Yes,
I know you mean well. If you could only speak!

(*When she tries to hold him back he kisses her and pulls himself
free. Exit. She is desperate and runs up and down, emitting little
sounds.* MOTHER COURAGE *and the* CHAPLAIN *return.* KATTRIN
rushes at her mother.)

MOTHER COURAGE. What *is* it, what *is* it, Kattrin! Control yourself! Has someone done something to you? Where is Swiss Cheese? (*To the* CHAPLAIN) Don't stand around, get that Catholic flag up! (*She takes a Catholic flag out of her basket and the* CHAPLAIN *runs it up the pole.*)

CHAPLAIN (*bitterly*). All good Catholics forever!

MOTHER COURAGE. Now, Kattrin, calm down and tell me all about it, your mother understands. What, that little bastard of mine's taken the cashbox away? I'll box his ears for him, the rascal! Now take your time and don't try to talk, use your hands. I don't like it when you howl like a dog, what'll the Chaplain think of you? See how shocked he looks. A man with one eye was here?

CHAPLAIN. That fellow with one eye is an informer! Have they caught Swiss Cheese? (KATTRIN *shakes her head, shrugs her shoulders.*) This is the end. (*Voices off. The two men bring in* SWISS CHEESE.)

SWISS CHEESE. Let me go. I've nothing on me. You're breaking my shoulder! I am innocent.

SERGEANT. This is where he comes from. These are his friends.

MOTHER COURAGE. Us? Since when?

SWISS CHEESE. I don't even know 'em. I was just getting my lunch here. Ten hellers it cost me. Maybe you saw me sitting on that bench. It was too salty.

SERGEANT. Who *are* you people, anyway?

MOTHER COURAGE. Law-abiding citizens! It's true what he says. He bought his lunch here. And it was too salty.

SERGEANT. Are you pretending you don't know him?

MOTHER COURAGE. I can't know all of them, can I? *I don't ask,* "What's your name and are you a heathen?" If they pay up, they're not heathens to me. Are you a heathen?

SWISS CHEESE. Oh, no!

CHAPLAIN. He sat there like a law-abiding chap and never once opened his mouth. Except to eat. Which is necessary.

SERGEANT. Who do you think *you* are?

MOTHER COURAGE. Oh, he's my barman. And you're thirsty, I'll bring you a glass of brandy. You must be footsore and weary!

SERGEANT. No brandy on duty. (*To* SWISS CHEESE) You were carrying something. You must have hidden it by the river. We saw the bulge in your shirt.

MOTHER COURAGE. Sure it was him?

SWISS CHEESE. I think you mean another fellow. There *was* a fellow with something under his shirt, I saw him. I'm the wrong man.

MOTHER COURAGE. I think so too. It's a misunderstanding. Could happen to anyone. Oh, I know what people are like, I'm Mother Courage, you've heard of me, everyone knows about me, and I can tell you this: he looks honest.

SERGEANT. We're after the regimental cashbox. And we know what the man looks like who's been keeping it. We've been looking for him two days. It's you.

SWISS CHEESE. No, it's not!

SERGEANT. And if you don't shell out, you're dead, see? Where is it?

MOTHER COURAGE (*urgently*). 'Course he'd give it to you to save his life. He'd up and say, I do have it, here it is, you're stronger than me. He's not *that* stupid. Speak, little stupid, the Sergeant's giving you a chance!

SWISS CHEESE. What if I haven't got it?

SERGEANT. Come with us. We'll get it out of you. (*They take him off.*)

MOTHER COURAGE (*shouting after them*). He'd tell you! He's not *that* stupid! And don't you break his shoulder blade! (*She runs after them.*)

(*The same evening. The* CHAPLAIN *and* KATTRIN *are rinsing glasses and polishing knives.*)

CHAPLAIN. Cases of people getting caught like this are by no means unknown in the history of religion. I am reminded of the Passion of Our Lord and Saviour. There's an old song about it. (*He sings.*)

THE SONG OF THE HOURS

In the first hour of the day
Simple Jesus Christ was
Presented as a murderer
To the heathen Pilate.

Pilate found no fault in him
No cause to condemn him
So he sent the Lord away.
Let King Herod see him!

Hour the third: the Son of God
Was with scourges beaten
And they set a crown of thorns
On the head of Jesus.

And they dressed him as a king
Joked and jested at him

And the cross to die upon
He himself must carry.

Six: they stripped Lord Jesus bare.
To the cross they nailed him.
When the blood came gushing, he
Prayed and loud lamented.

From their neighbour crosses, thieves
Mocked him like the others.
And the bright sun crept away
Not to see such doings.

Nine: Lord Jesus cried aloud
That he was forsaken!
In a sponge upon a pole
Vinegar was fed him.

Then the Lord gave up the ghost
And the earth did tremble.
Temple curtain split in twain.
Rocks fell in the ocean.

Evening: they broke the bones
Of the malefactors.
They they took a spear and pierced
The side of gentle Jesus.

And the blood and water ran
And they laughed at Jesus.
Of this simple son of man
Such and more they tell us.

MOTHER COURAGE (*entering, excited*). It's life and death. But the
Sergeant will still listen to us. The only thing is, he mustn't
know it's our Swiss Cheese, or they'll say we helped him. It's
only a matter of money, but where can *we* get money? Wasn't
Yvette here? I met her on the way over. She's picked up a
Colonel! Maybe he'll buy her a canteen business!

CHAPLAIN. You'd sell the wagon, everything?

MOTHER COURAGE. Where else would I get the money for the Sergeant?

CHAPLAIN. What are you to live off?

MOTHER COURAGE. That's just it.

(*Enter* YVETTE POTTIER *with a hoary old* COLONEL.)

YVETTE (*embracing* MOTHER COURAGE). *Dear* Mistress Courage, we meet again! (*Whispering*) He didn't say no. (*Aloud*) This is my friend, my, um, business adviser. I happened to hear you might like to sell your wagon. Due to special circumstances, I'd like to think about it.

MOTHER COURAGE. I want to pawn it, not sell it. And nothing hasty. In war time you don't find another wagon like that so easy.

YVETTE (*disappointed*). Only pawn it? I thought you wanted to sell, I don't know if I'm interested. (*To the* COLONEL) What do *you* think, my dear?

COLONEL. I quite agree with you, ducky.

MOTHER COURAGE. It's only for pawn.

YVETTE. I thought you *had* to have the money.

MOTHER COURAGE (*firmly*). I do have to have it. But I'd rather wear my feet off looking for an offer than just sell. We live off the wagon. It's an opportunity for you, Yvette. Who knows when you'll have another such? Who knows when you'll find another . . . business adviser?

COLONEL. Take it, take it!

YVETTE. My friend thinks I should go ahead, but I'm not sure, if it's only for pawn. You think we should buy it outright, don't you?

COLONEL. I do, ducky, I do!

MOTHER COURAGE. Then you must hunt up something that's for sale. Maybe you'll find it—if you have the time, and your friend goes with you, let's say in about a week, or two weeks, you may find the right thing.

YVETTE. Yes, we can certainly look around for something. I love going around looking, I love going around with you, Poldy . . .

COLONEL. Really? Do you?

YVETTE. Oh, it's lovely! I could take two weeks of it!

COLONEL. Really, could you?

YVETTE. If you get the money, when are you thinking of paying it back?

MOTHER COURAGE. In two weeks. Maybe one.

YVETTE. I can't make up my mind. Poldy, advise me, *chéri!* (*She takes the* COLONEL *to one side.*) She'll *have* to sell, don't worry. That lieutenant—the blond one—you know the one I mean—he'll lend me the money. He's *mad* about me, he says I remind him of someone. What do you advise?

COLONEL. Oh, I have to warn you against *him*. He's no good. He'll exploit the situation. I told you, ducky, I told you *I'd* buy you something, didn't I tell you that?

YVETTE. I simply can't let you!

COLONEL. Oh, please, please!

YVETTE. Well, if you think the lieutenant might exploit the situation I *will* let you!

COLONEL. I do think so.

YVETTE. So you advise me to?

COLONEL. I do, ducky, I do!

YVETTE (*returning to* MOTHER COURAGE). My friend says all right. Write me out a receipt saying the wagon's mine when the two weeks are up—with everything in it. I'll just run through it all now, the two hundred gilders can wait. (*To the* COLONEL) You go on ahead to the camp, I'll follow, I must go over all this so nothing'll be missing later from *my* wagon!

COLONEL. Wait, I'll help you up! (*He does so.*) Come soon, ducky-wucky! (*Exit.*)

MOTHER COURAGE. Yvette, Yvette!

YVETTE. There aren't many boots left!

MOTHER COURAGE. Yvette, this is no time to go through the wagon, yours or not yours. You promised you'd talk to the Sergeant about Swiss Cheese. There isn't a minute to lose. He's up before the court martial one hour from now.

YVETTE. I just want to check through these shirts.

MOTHER COURAGE (*dragging her down the steps by the skirt*). You hyena, Swiss Cheese's life's at stake! And don't say who the money comes from. Pretend he's your sweetheart, for heaven's sake, or we'll all get it for helping him.

YVETTE. I've arranged to meet One Eye in the bushes. He must be there by now.

CHAPLAIN. And don't hand over all two hundred, a hundred and fifty's sure to be enough.

MOTHER COURAGE. Is it your money? I'll thank you to keep your nose out of this, I'm not doing *you* out of your porridge. Now run, and no haggling, remember his life's at stake. (*She pushes* YVETTE *off.*)

CHAPLAIN. I didn't want to talk you into anything, but what are we going to live on? You have an unmarriageable daughter round your neck.

MOTHER COURAGE. I'm counting on that cashbox, smart alec. They'll pay his expenses out of it.

CHAPLAIN. You think she can work it?

MOTHER COURAGE. It's to her interest: I pay the two hundred and she gets the wagon. She knows what she's doing, she won't have her colonel on the string forever. Kattrin, go and clean the knives, use pumice stone. And don't *you* stand around like Jesus in Gethsemane. Get a move on, wash those glasses. There'll be over fifty cavalrymen here tonight, and you'll be saying you're not used to running around, "oh my poor feet, in church I never had to run around like this!" I think they'll let us have him. Thanks be to God they're corruptible. They're not wolves, they're human and after money. God is merciful, and men are bribable, that's how His will is done on earth as it is in Heaven. Corruption is our only hope. As long as there's corruption, there'll be merciful judges and even the innocent may get off.

YVETTE (*comes panting in*). They'll do it for two hundred if you make it snappy, these things change from one minute to the next. I'd better take One Eye to my colonel at once. He confessed he had the cashbox, they put the thumb screws on him. But he threw it in the river when he noticed them coming up behind him. So it's gone. Shall I run and get the money from my colonel?

MOTHER COURAGE. The cashbox gone? How'll I ever get my two hundred back?

YVETTE. So you thought you could get it from the cashbox? I *would* have been sunk. Not a hope, Mother Courage. If you want your Swiss Cheese, you'll have to pay. Or should I let the whole thing drop, so you can keep your wagon?

MOTHER COURAGE. I wasn't reckoning on this. But you needn't hound me, you'll get the wagon, it's yours already, and it's been mine seventeen years. I need a minute to think it over, it's all so sudden. What can I do? I *can't* pay two hundred. I *should* have haggled with them. I must hold on to something, or any passer-by can kick me in the ditch. Go and say I'll pay a hundred and twenty or the deal's off. Even then I lose the wagon.

YVETTE. I won't do it. And anyway, One Eye's in a hurry. He keeps looking over his shoulder all the time, he's so worked up. Hadn't I better give them the whole two hundred?

MOTHER COURAGE (*desperate*). I can't pay it! I've been working thirty years. She's twenty-five and still no husband. I have her to think of. So leave me alone, I know what I'm doing. A hundred and twenty or no deal.

YVETTE. You know best.

(*Runs off.* MOTHER COURAGE *turns away and slowly walks a few paces to the rear. Then she turns round, looks neither at the* CHAPLAIN *nor her daughter, and sits down to help* KATTRIN *polish the knives.*)

MOTHER COURAGE. Don't break the glasses, they're not ours. Watch what you're doing, you're cutting yourself. Swiss Cheese will be back, I'll give two hundred, if it's necessary. You'll get your brother back. With eighty gilders we could pack a hamper with goods and begin again. It wouldn't be the end of the world.

CHAPLAIN. The Bible says: the Lord will provide.

MOTHER COURAGE. You should rub them dry, I said!

(*They clean the knives in silence. Suddenly* KATTRIN *runs sobbing behind the wagon.*)

YVETTE (*comes running in*). They won't do it. I warned you. One Eye was going to drop it then and there. There's no point, he said. He said the drums would roll any second now and that's the sign a verdict has been pronounced. I offered a hundred and fifty, he didn't even shrug his shoulders. I could hardly get him to stay there while I came to you.

MOTHER COURAGE. Tell him I'll pay two hundred. Run! (YVETTE *runs.* MOTHER COURAGE *sits, silent. The* CHAPLAIN *has stopped doing the glasses.*) I believe—I've haggled too long. (*In the distance, a roll of drums. The* CHAPLAIN *stands up and walks toward the rear.* MOTHER COURAGE *remains seated. It grows dark. It gets light again.* MOTHER COURAGE *has not moved.*)

YVETTE. (*Appears, pale.*) Now you've done it—with your haggling. You can keep the wagon now. He got eleven bullets, that's what. I don't know why I still bother about you, you don't deserve it, but I just happened to learn they don't think the cashbox is really in the river. They suspect it's here, they think you have something to do with him. I think they mean to bring him here to see if you'll give yourself away when you see him. You'd better not know him or we're in for it. And I'd better tell you straight, they're just behind me. Shall I keep Kattrin away? (MOTHER COURAGE *shakes her head.*) Does she know? Maybe she never heard the drums or didn't understand.

MOTHER COURAGE. She knows. Bring her.

(YVETTE *brings* KATTRIN, *who walks over to her mother and stands by her.* MOTHER COURAGE *takes her hand. Two men come on with a stretcher; there is a sheet on it and something underneath. Beside them, the* SERGEANT. *They put the stretcher down.*)

SERGEANT. Here's a man we don't know the name of. But he has to be registered to keep the records straight. He bought a meal from you. Look at him, see if you know him. (*He pulls back the sheet.*) Do you know him? (MOTHER COURAGE *shakes her head.*) What? You never saw him before he took that meal? (MOTHER COURAGE *shakes her head.*) Lift him up. Throw him on the junk heap. He has no one that knows him.

(*They carry him off.*)

Scene Four

MOTHER COURAGE *sings "The Song of the Great Capitulation."*

(Outside an officer's tent, MOTHER COURAGE *waits. A* SCRIVENER *looks out of the tent.)*

SCRIVENER. I know you. You had a Protestant paymaster with you, he was hiding with you. Better make no complaint.

MOTHER COURAGE. I will too! I'm innocent and if I give up it'll look like I have a bad conscience. They cut everything in my wagon to ribbons with their sabres and then claimed a fine of five thalers for nothing and less than nothing.

SCRIVENER. For your own good, keep your trap shut. We haven't many canteens, so we let you stay in business, especially if you've a bad conscience and have to pay a fine now and then.

MOTHER COURAGE. I'm going to lodge a complaint.

SCRIVENER. As you wish. Wait here till the captain has time. (*Withdraws into the tent.*)

YOUNG SOLDIER (*comes storming in*). Bugger the captain! Where *is* the son of a bitch? Swiping my reward, spending it on brandy for his whores, I'll rip his belly open!

OLDER SOLDIER (*coming after him*). Shut your hole, you'll wind up in the stocks.

YOUNG SOLDIER. Come out, you thief, I'll make lamb chops out of you! I was the only one in the squad who swam the river and *he* grabs my money, I can't even buy myself a beer. Come on out! And let me slice you up!

OLDER SOLDIER. Holy Christ, he'll destroy himself!

YOUNG SOLDIER. Let me go or I'll run *you* down too. This thing has got to be settled!

OLDER SOLDIER. Saved the colonel's horse and didn't get the reward. He's young, he hasn't been at it long.

MOTHER COURAGE. Let him go. He doesn't have to be chained, he's not a dog. Very reasonable to want a reward. Why else should he want to shine?

YOUNG SOLDIER. He's in there pouring it down! You're all chickens. I've done something special, I want the reward!

MOTHER COURAGE. Young man, don't scream at *me,* I have my own troubles. And go easy on your voice, you may need it when the Captain comes. The Captain'll come and you'll be hoarse and can't make a sound, so he'll have to deny himself the pleasure of sticking you in the stocks till you pass out. The screamers don't scream long, only half an hour, after which they have to be sung to sleep, they're all in.

YOUNG SOLDIER. I'm not all in, and sleep's out of the question. I'm hungry. They're making their bread out of acorns and hemp-seed, and not even much of that. He's whoring on my money, and I'm hungry. I'll murder him!

MOTHER COURAGE. I understand: you're hungry. Last year your Commander ordered you people out of the streets and into the fields. So the crops got trampled down. I could have got ten gilders for boots, if anyone'd had ten gilders, and if I'd had any boots. He didn't expect to be around this year, but he is, and there's famine. I understand: you're angry.

YOUNG SOLDIER. It's no use you talking. I won't stand for injustice!

MOTHER COURAGE. You're quite right. But how long? How long won't you stand for injustice? One hour? Or two? You haven't asked yourself that, have you? And yet it's the main thing. It's pure misery to sit in the stocks. Especially if you leave it till then to decide you do stand for injustice.

YOUNG SOLDIER. I don't know why I listen to you. Bugger that captain! Where is he?

MOTHER COURAGE. You listen because you know I'm right. Your rage has calmed down already. It was a short one and you'd need a long one. But where would you find it?

YOUNG SOLDIER. Are you trying to say it's not right to ask for the money?

MOTHER COURAGE. Just the opposite. I only say, your rage won't last. You'll get nowhere with it, it's a pity. If your rage was a long one, I'd urge you on. Slice him up, I'd advise you. But what's the use if you *don't* slice him up because you can feel your tail between your legs? You stand there and the captain lets you have it.

OLDER SOLDIER. You're quite right, he's mad.

YOUNG SOLDIER. All right, we'll see whether I slice him up or not. (*Draws his sword.*) When he comes out, I slice him up!

SCRIVENER (*looking out*). The captain will be out in a minute. (*In the tone of military command.*) Be seated! (*The* YOUNG SOLDIER *sits.*)

MOTHER COURAGE. And he *is* seated. What did I tell you? You are seated. They know us through and through. They know how they must work it. Be seated! And we sit. And in sitting there's no revolt. Better not stand up again—not the way you did before— don't stand up again. And don't be embarrassed in front of me, I'm no better, not a scrap. We don't stick our necks out, do we, and why not? It wouldn't be good for business. Let me tell you about the great capitulation. (*She sings "The Song of the Great Capitulation."*)

Long, long ago, a green beginner
  I thought myself a special case.
(None of your ordinary, run of the mill girls, with my looks and
    my talent and my love of the higher things!)
I picked a hair out of my dinner
  And put the waiter in his place.
(All or nothing. Anyway, never the second best. I am the master
    of my fate. I'll take no orders from no one.)
Then a little bird whispers!
  The bird says: "Wait a year or so
  And marching with the band you'll go
  Keeping in step, now fast, now slow,
  And piping out your little spiel.
  Then one day the battalions wheel
  And you go down upon your knees
  To God Almighty if you please!"

My friend, before that year was over
  I'd learned to drink their cup of tea.
(Two children round your neck and the price of bread and what
    all!)
When they were through with me, moreover,
  They had me where they wanted me.
(You must get well in with people. If you scratch my back, I'll
    scratch yours. Never stick your neck out!)
Then a little bird whispered!
  The bird says: "Scarce a year or so
  And marching with the band she'd go
  Keeping in step, now fast, now slow,
  And piping out her little spiel.
  Then one day the battalions wheel
  And she goes down upon her knees
  To God Almighty if you please!"

Our plans are big, our hopes colossal.
  We hitch our wagon to a star.
(Where there's a will, there's a way. You can't hold a good man
    down.)
"We can lift mountains," says the apostle.
  And yet: how heavy one cigar!
(You must cut your coat according to your cloth.)
That little bird whispers!
  The bird says: "Wait a year or so

And marching with the band we go
Keeping in step, now fast, now slow,
And piping out our little spiel.
Then one day the battalions wheel
And we go down upon our knees
To God Almighty if you please!"
And so I think you should stay here with your sword drawn if
you're set on it and your anger is big enough. You have good
cause, I admit. But if your anger is a short one, you'd better go.

YOUNG SOLDIER. Oh, shove it up! (*He stumbles off, the other soldier
following him.*)

SCRIVENER. (*Sticks his head out.*) The captain is here. You can lodge
your complaint.

MOTHER COURAGE. I've thought better of it. I'm not complaining.
(*Exit. The* SCRIVENER *looks after her, shaking his head.*)

Scene Five

*Two years have passed. The war covers wider and wider territory.
Forever on the move the little wagon crosses Poland, Moravia,
Bavaria, Italy, and again Bavaria. 1631. Tilly's victory at Magde-
burg costs* MOTHER COURAGE *four officer shirts.*

(*The wagon stands in a war-ruined village. Faint military music
from the distance. Two soldiers are being served at a counter by*
KATTRIN *and* MOTHER COURAGE. *One of them has a woman's fur
coat about his shoulders.*)

MOTHER COURAGE. What, you can't pay? No money, no brandy! They
can play victory marches, they should pay their men.

FIRST SOLDIER. I want my brandy! I arrived too late for plunder. The
Chief allowed one hour to plunder the town, it's a swindle. He's
not inhuman, he says. So I suppose they bought him off.

CHAPLAIN (*staggering in*). There are more in the farmhouse. A family
of peasants. Help me someone. I need linen!
(*The* SECOND SOLDIER *goes with him.* KATTRIN *is getting very excited. She tries to get her mother to bring linen out.*)

MOTHER COURAGE. I have none. I sold all my bandages to the regiment.
I'm not tearing up my officer's shirts for these people.

CHAPLAIN (*calling over his shoulder*). I said I need linen!

MOTHER COURAGE (*stopping* KATTRIN *from entering the wagon*). Not a
thing! They have nothing and they pay nothing!

CHAPLAIN (*to a woman he is carrying in*). Why did you stay out there
in the line of fire?

WOMAN. Our farm—

MOTHER COURAGE. Think they'd ever let go of *anything?* And now I'm supposed to pay. Well, I won't!

FIRST SOLDIER. They're Protestants, why should they be Protestants?

MOTHER COURAGE. Protestant, Catholic, what do *they* care? Their farm's gone, that's what.

SECOND SOLDIER. They're not Protestants anyway, they're Catholics.

FIRST SOLDIER. In a bombardment we can't pick and choose.

PEASANT (*brought on by* CHAPLAIN). My arm's gone.

CHAPLAIN. Where's that linen?

(*All look at* MOTHER COURAGE, *who doesn't budge.*)

MOTHER COURAGE. I can't give you any. With all I have to pay out— taxes, duties, bribes . . . (KATTRIN *takes up a board and threatens her mother with it, emitting gurgling sounds.*) Are you out of your mind? Put that board down or I'll fetch you one, you lunatic! I'm giving nothing, I daren't, I have myself to think of. (*The* CHAPLAIN *lifts her bodily off the steps of the wagon and sets her down on the ground. He takes out shirts from the wagon and tears them in strips.*) My shirts, my officer's shirts!

(*From the house comes the cry of a child in pain.*)

PEASANT. The child's still in there!

(KATTRIN *runs in.*)

CHAPLAIN (*to the woman*). Stay where you are. She's getting it for you.

MOTHER COURAGE. Hold her back, the roof may fall in!

CHAPLAIN. I'm not going back in there!

MOTHER COURAGE (*pulled in both directions at once*). Go easy on my expensive linen.

(*The* SECOND SOLDIER *holds her back.* KATTRIN *brings a baby out of the ruins.*)

MOTHER COURAGE. Another baby to drag around, you must be pleased with yourself. Give it to its mother this minute! Or do I have to fight you again for hours till I get it from you? Are you deaf (*To the* SECOND SOLDIER) Don't stand around gawking, go back there and tell 'em to stop that music, I can see their victory without it. I have nothing but losses from your victory!

CHAPLAIN (*bandaging*). The blood's coming through.

(KATTRIN *is rocking the child and half-humming a lullaby.*)

MOTHER COURAGE. There she sits, happy as a lark in all this misery. Give the baby back, the mother is coming to!

(*She sees the* FIRST SOLDIER. *He had been handling the drinks, and is now trying to make off with the bottle.*) God's blood! You beast! You want another victory, do you? Then pay for it!

FIRST SOLDIER. I have nothing.

MOTHER COURAGE (*snatching the fur coat back*). Then leave this coat, it's stolen goods anyhow.

CHAPLAIN. There's still someone in there.

Scene Six

Before the City of Ingolstadt in Bavaria MOTHER COURAGE *is present at the funeral of the fallen commander, Tilly. Conversations take place about war heroes and the duration of the war. The* CHAPLAIN *complains that his talents are lying fallow and* KATTRIN *gets the red boots. The year is 1632.*

(*The inside of a canteen tent. The inner side of a counter at the rear. Rain. In the distance, drums and funeral music. The* CHAPLAIN *and the* REGIMENTAL CLERK *are playing checkers.* MOTHER COURAGE *and her daughter are taking inventory.*)

CHAPLAIN. The funeral procession is just starting out.

MOTHER COURAGE. Pity about the Chief—twenty-two pairs of socks—getting killed that way. They say it was an accident. There was a fog over the fields that morning, and the fog was to blame. The Chief called up another regiment, told 'em to fight to the death, rode back again, missed his way in the fog, went forward instead of back, and ran smack into a bullet in the thick of the battle—only four lanterns left. (*A whistle from the rear. She goes to the counter. To a soldier*) It's a disgrace the way you're all skipping your Commander's funeral! (*She pours a drink.*)

SCRIVENER. They shouldn't have handed the money out before the funeral. Now the men are all getting drunk instead of going to it.

CHAPLAIN (*to the* SCRIVENER). Don't you have to be there?

SCRIVENER. I stayed away because of the rain.

MOTHER COURAGE. It's different for you, the rain might spoil your uniform. I hear they wanted to ring the bells for his funeral, which is natural, but it came out that the churches had been shot up by his orders, so the poor Commander won't be hearing any bells when they lower him in his grave. Instead, they will fire off three shots so the occasion won't be *too* sober—sixteen leather belts.

VOICE FROM THE COUNTER. Service! One brandy!

MOTHER COURAGE. Your money first. No, you *can't* come inside the tent, not with those boots on. You can drink outside, rain or no rain. I only let officers in here. (*To* SCRIVENER) The Chief had his

troubles lately, I hear. There was unrest in the Second Regiment
because he didn't pay 'em but said it was a war of religion and
they must fight it free of charge.

(*Funeral March. All look towards the rear.*)

CHAPLAIN. Now they're filing past the body.

MOTHER COURAGE. I feel sorry for a commander or an emperor like
that—when he might have had something special in mind, something they'd talk about in times to come, something they'd raise a
statue to him for. The conquest of the world now, *that's* a goal for
a commander, he couldn't do better than *that*, could he? . . .
Lord, worms have got into the biscuits. . . . In short he works
his hands to the bone and then it's all spoiled by the common
riffraff that only wants a jug of beer or a bit of company, not the
higher things in life. The finest plans have always been spoiled by
the littleness of them that should carry them out. Even emperors
can't do it all by themselves. They count on support from their
soldiers and the people round about. Am I right?

CHAPLAIN (*laughing*). You're right, Mother Courage, till you come to
the soldiers. They do what they can. Those chaps outside, for
example, drinking their brandy in the rain, I'd trust 'em to fight a
hundred years, one war after another, two at a time if necessary.
And I wasn't trained as a Commander.

MOTHER COURAGE. . . . Seventeen leather belts . . . Then you don't
think the war might end?

CHAPLAIN. Because a Commander's dead? Don't be childish, they're
sixpence a dozen. There are always heroes.

MOTHER COURAGE. Well, I wasn't asking just for the sake of argument.
I was wondering if I should buy up a lot of supplies. They happen
to be cheap just now. But if the war ended, I might just as well
throw them away.

CHAPLAIN. I realize you are serious, Mother Courage. Well, there's always been people going around saying someday the war will end.
I say, you can't be sure the war will *ever* end. Of course it may
have to pause occasionally—for breath, as it were—it can even
meet with an accident—nothing on this earth is perfect—a war of
which we could say it left nothing to be desired will probably
never exist. A war can come to a sudden halt—from unforeseen
causes—you can't think of everything—a little oversight, and the
war's in the hole, and someone's got to pull it out again! The
someone is the Emperor or the King or the Pope. They're such
friends in need, the war has really nothing to worry about, it can
look forward to a prosperous future.

(*A* SOLDIER *sings at the counter.*)

SOLDIER.

> One schnapps, mine host, be quick, make haste!
> A soldier's got no time to waste:
> He must be shooting, shooting, shooting,
> His Kaiser's enemies unrooting!
> Make it a double. This is a holiday.

MOTHER COURAGE. If I was sure you're right . . .

CHAPLAIN. Think it out for yourself: how *could* the war end?

SOLDIER.

> Two breasts, my girl, be quick, make haste!
> A soldier's got no time to waste:
> He must be hating, hating, hating,
> He cannot keep his Kaiser waiting!

SCRIVENER (*suddenly*). What about peace? Yes, peace. I'm from Bohemia. I'd like to get home once in a while.

CHAPLAIN. Oh, you would, would you? Dear old peace! What happens to the hole when the cheese is gone?

SOLDIER (*off stage*).

> Your blessing, priest, be quick, make haste!
> A soldier's got no time to waste:
> He must be dying, dying, dying,
> His Kaiser's greatness glorifying!

SCRIVENER. In the long run you can't live without peace!

CHAPLAIN. Well, I'd say there's peace even in war, war has its islands of peace. For war satisfies *all* needs, even those of peace, yes, they're provided for, or the war couldn't keep going. In war—as in the very thick of peace—you can empty your bowels, and between one battle and the next there's always a beer, and even on the march you can take a nap—on your elbow maybe, in a gutter—something can always be managed. Of course you can't play cards during an attack, but neither can you while plowing the fields in peacetime; it's when the victory's won that there are possibilities. You have your leg shot off, and at first you raise quite an outcry as if it *was* something, but soon you calm down or take a swig of brandy, and you end up hopping around, and the war is none the worse for your little misadventure. And can't you be fruitful and multiply in the thick of slaughter—behind a barn or somewhere? Nothing can keep you from it very long in any event. And so the war has your offspring and can carry on. War is like love, it always finds a way. Why *should* it end?

(KATTRIN *has stopped working. She stares at the* CHAPLAIN.)

MOTHER COURAGE. Then I *will* buy those supplies, I'll rely on you.

(KATTRIN *suddenly bangs a basket of glasses down on the ground and runs out.* MOTHER COURAGE *laughs.*) Kattrin! Lord, Kattrin's still going to wait for peace. I promised her she'll get a husband —when it's peace. (*Runs after her.*)

SCRIVENER (*standing up*). I win. You were talking. You pay.

MOTHER COURAGE (*returning with* KATTRIN). Be sensible, the war'll go on a bit longer, and we'll make a bit more money, then peace'll be all the nicer. Now you go into the town, it's not ten minutes' walk, and bring the things from the Golden Lion, just the dearer ones, we can get the rest later in the wagon. It's all arranged, the clerk will go with you, most of the soldiers are at the Commander's funeral, nothing can happen to you. Do a good job, don't lose anything, Kattrin, think of your trousseau!

(KATTRIN *ties a cloth round her head and leaves with the* SCRIVENER.)

CHAPLAIN. You don't mind her going with Scrivener?

MOTHER COURAGE. She's not so pretty anyone would want to ruin her.

CHAPLAIN. The way you run your business and always come through is highly commendable, Mother Courage—I see how you got your name.

MOTHER COURAGE. The poor need courage. They're lost, that's why. That they even get up in the morning is something—in *their* plight. Or that they plow a field—in wartime. Even their bringing children into the world shows they have courage, for they have no prospects. They have to hang each other one by one and slaughter each other in the lump, so if they want to look each other in the face once in a while, well, it takes courage. That they put up with an Emperor and a Pope, that takes an unnatural amount of courage, for *they* cost you your life. (*She sits, takes a small pipe from her pocket and smokes it.*) You might chop me a bit of firewood.

CHAPLAIN (*reluctantly taking his coat off and preparing to chop wood*). Properly speaking, I'm a pastor of souls, not a woodcutter.

MOTHER COURAGE. But I don't have a soul. And I do need wood.

CHAPLAIN. What's that little pipe you've got there?

MOTHER COURAGE. Just a pipe.

CHAPLAIN. I think it's a very particular pipe.

MOTHER COURAGE. Oh?

CHAPLAIN. The cook's pipe in fact. The cook from the Oxenstiern Regiment.

MOTHER COURAGE. If you know, why beat about the bush?

CHAPLAIN. Because I don't know if you've been *aware* that's what you've been smoking. It was possible you just rummaged among

your belongings and your fingers just lit on a pipe and you just
took it. In pure absentmindedness.

MOTHER COURAGE. How do you know that's not it?

CHAPLAIN. It isn't. You *are* aware of it. (*He brings the ax down on
the block with a crash.*)

MOTHER COURAGE. What if I was?

CHAPLAIN. I must give you a warning, Mother Courage, it's my duty.
You are unlikely ever again to see the gentleman but that's no pity,
you're in luck. Mother Courage, he did not impress me as trust-
worthy. On the contrary.

MOTHER COURAGE. Really? He was such a nice man.

CHAPLAIN. Well! So that's what you call a nice man. I do not. (*The
ax falls again.*) Far be it from me to wish him ill, but I cannot—
cannot—describe him as nice. No, no, he's a Don Juan, a cunning
Don Juan. Just look at that pipe if you don't believe me. You
must admit it tells all.

MOTHER COURAGE. I see nothing special in it. It's been, um, used.

CHAPLAIN. It's bitten half-way through! He's a man of great violence!
It is the pipe of a man of great violence, you can see *that* if you've
any judgment left! (*He deals the block a tremendous blow.*)

MOTHER COURAGE. Don't bite my chopping block halfway through!

CHAPLAIN. I told you I had no training as a woodcutter. The care of
souls was my field. Around here my gifts and capabilities are
grossly misused. In physical labor my god-given talents find no—
um—adequate expression—which is a sin. You haven't heard me
preach. Why, I can put such spirit into a regiment with a single
sermon that the enemy's a mere flock of sheep to them and their
own lives no more than smelly old shoes to be thrown away at
the thought of final victory! God has given me the gift of tongues.
I can preach you out of your senses!

MOTHER COURAGE. I need my senses, what would I do without them?

CHAPLAIN. Mother Courage, I have often thought that—under a veil
of plain speech—you conceal a heart. You are human, you need
warmth.

MOTHER COURAGE. The best way of warming this tent is to chop plenty
of firewood.

CHAPLAIN. You're changing the subject. Seriously, my dear Courage, I
sometimes ask myself how it would be if our relationship should
be somewhat more firmly cemented. I mean, now the wind of war
has whirled us so strangely together.

MOTHER COURAGE. The cement's pretty firm already. I cook your meals.
And you lend a hand—at chopping firewood, for instance.

CHAPLAIN (*going over to her, gesturing with the ax*). You know what I mean by a close relationship. It has nothing to do with eating and woodcutting and such base necessities. Let your heart speak!

MOTHER COURAGE. Don't come at me like that with your ax, that'd be *too* close a relationship!

CHAPLAIN. This is no laughing matter, I am in earnest. I've thought it all over.

MOTHER COURAGE. Dear Chaplain, be a sensible fellow. I like you, and I don't want to heap coals of fire on your head. All I'm after is to bring me and my children through in that wagon. It isn't just mine, the wagon, and anyway I've no mind to start having a private life. At the moment I'm taking quite a risk buying these things when the Commander's fallen and there's all this talk of peace. Where would you go, if I was ruined? See? You don't even know. Now chop some firewood and it'll be warm of an evening, which is quite a lot in times like these. What was that?

(*She stands up.* KATTRIN *enters, breathless, with a wound across the eye and forehead. She is dragging all sorts of articles, parcels, leather goods, a drum, etc.*)

MOTHER COURAGE. What is it, were you attacked? On the way back? She was attacked on the way back! I'll bet it was that soldier who got drunk on my liquor. I should never have let you go. Dump all that stuff! It's not bad, the wound is only a flesh wound. I'll bandage it for you, it'll be all healed up in a week. They're worse than animals. (*She bandages the wound.*)

CHAPLAIN. I reproach them with nothing. At home they never did these shameful things. The men who start the wars are responsible, they bring out the worst in people.

MOTHER COURAGE. Didn't the Scrivener walk you back home? That's because you're a respectable girl, he thought they'd leave you alone. The wound's not at all deep, it will never show. There: all bandaged up. Now, I've got something for you, rest easy. A secret. I've been holding it, you'll see. (*She digs* YVETTE's *red boots out of a bag.*) Well, what do you see? You always wanted them. Now you have them. Put them on quick, before I'm sorry I let you have them. (*She helps her to put the boots on.*) It will never show, though it wouldn't bother *me* if it did. The fate of the ones they like is the worst. They drag them around with them till they're through. A girl they don't care for they leave alone. I've seen so many girls, pretty as they come in the beginning, then all of a sudden they looked a fright—enough to scare a wolf. They can't even go behind a tree on the street without having something to fear from it. They lead a frightful life. Like with trees: the tall, straight ones are cut down for roof timber, and the crooked ones can enjoy life. So this wound here is really a piece of luck. The boots have kept well, I cleaned them good before I put them away.

(KATTRIN *leaves the boots and creeps into the wagon.*)

CHAPLAIN (*when she's gone*). I hope she won't be disfigured?

MOTHER COURAGE. There'll be a scar. She needn't wait for peace now.

CHAPLAIN. She didn't let them get any of the stuff away from her.

MOTHER COURAGE. Maybe I shouldn't have made such a point of it. If only I ever knew what went on inside her head. One time she stayed out all night, once in all the years. I could never get out of her what happened, I racked my brains for quite a while. (*She picks up the things* KATTRIN *spilled and sorts them angrily.*) This is war. A nice source of income, I must say!

(*Cannon shots.*)

CHAPLAIN. Now they're lowering the Commander in his grave! A historic moment.

MOTHER COURAGE. It's a historic moment to me when they hit my daughter over the eye. She's all but finished now, she'll never get a husband, and she's so mad about children! Even her dumbness comes from the war. A soldier stuck something in her mouth when she was little. I'll not see Swiss Cheese again, and where my Eilif is the Good Lord knows. Curse the war!

Scene Seven

MOTHER COURAGE *at the height of her business career.*

(*A highway. The* CHAPLAIN, MOTHER COURAGE, *and her daughter* KATTRIN *pull the wagon, and new wares are hanging from it.* MOTHER COURAGE *wears a necklace: a chain of silver coins.*)

MOTHER COURAGE. I won't let you spoil my war for me. Destroys the weak, does it? Well, what does peace do for 'em, huh? War feeds its people better. (*She sings.*)

If war don't suit your disposition
When victory comes you will be dead.
War is a business proposition:
Not with cream-cheese but steel and lead.

And staying in one place won't help either. Those who stay home are the first to go. (*She sings.*)

Too many seek a bed to sleep in:
Each ditch is taken, and each cave,
And he who digs a hole to creep in

Finds he has dug an early grave.
And many a man spends many a minute
In hurrying toward some resting place.
You wonder, when at last he's in it,
Just why the fellow forced the pace.
(*The wagon proceeds.*)

Scene Eight

1632. In this same year Gustavus Adolphus fell in the battle of Lützen. The peace threatens MOTHER COURAGE *with ruin. Her brave son performs one heroic deed too many and comes to a shameful end.*

(*A camp. A summer morning. In front of the wagon, an old woman and her son. The son is dragging a large bag of bedding.*)

MOTHER COURAGE (*from inside the wagon*). Must you come at the crack of dawn?

YOUNG MAN. We've been walking all night, twenty miles it was, we have to be back today.

MOTHER COURAGE (*still inside*). What do I want with bed feathers? People don't even have houses.

YOUNG MAN. At least wait till you see 'em.

OLD WOMAN. Nothing doing here either, let's go.

YOUNG MAN. And let 'em sign away the roof over our heads for taxes? Maybe she'll pay three gilders if you throw in that bracelet. (*Bells start ringing.*) You hear, mother?

VOICES (*from the rear*). It's peace! The King of Sweden's been killed!

MOTHER COURAGE. (*Sticking her head out of the wagon. She hasn't done her hair yet.*) Bells! What are the bells for, middle of the week?

CHAPLAIN (*crawling out from under the wagon*). What's that they're shouting?

YOUNG MAN. It's peace.

CHAPLAIN. Peace?

MOTHER COURAGE. Don't tell me peace has broken out—when I've just gone and bought all these supplies!

CHAPLAIN (*calling, toward the rear*). Is it peace?

VOICE (*from a distance*). They say the war stopped three weeks ago, I've only just heard.

CHAPLAIN (*to* MOTHER COURAGE). Or why would they ring the bells?

VOICE. A great crowd of Lutherans have just arrived with wagons— they brought the news.

YOUNG MAN. It's peace, mother. (*The* OLD WOMAN *collapses.*) What's the matter?

MOTHER COURAGE (*back in the wagon*). Kattrin, it's peace! Put on your black dress, we're going to church, we owe it to Swiss Cheese! Can it be true?

YOUNG MAN. The people here say so too, the war's over. Can you stand up? (*The* OLD WOMAN *stands up, dazed.*) I'll get the harness shop going again now, I promise you. Everything'll be all right, father will get his bed back. . . . Can you walk? (*To the* CHAPLAIN) She felt sick, it was the news. She didn't believe there'd ever be peace again. Father always said there would. We're going home. (*They leave.*)

MOTHER COURAGE (*off*). Give her some brandy.

CHAPLAIN. They've left already.

MOTHER COURAGE (*still off*). What's going on in the camp over there?

CHAPLAIN. They're all getting together, I think I'll go over. Shall I put my pastor's clothes on again?

MOTHER COURAGE. Better get the exact news first, and not risk being taken for the Antichrist. I'm glad about the peace even though I'm ruined. At least I've got two of my children through the war. Now I'll see my Eilif again.

CHAPLAIN. And who may this be coming down from the camp? Well, if it isn't our Swedish Commander's cook!

COOK (*somewhat bedraggled, carrying a bundle*). Who's here? The Chaplain!

CHAPLAIN. Mother Courage, a visitor!

(MOTHER COURAGE *clambers out.*)

COOK. Well, I promised I'd come over for a brief conversation as soon as I had time. I didn't forget your brandy, Mrs. Fierling.

MOTHER COURAGE. Jesus, the Commander's cook! After all these years! Where is Eilif, my eldest?

COOK. Isn't he here yet? He went on ahead yesterday, he was on his way over.

CHAPLAIN. I *will* put my pastor's clothes on. I'll be back. (*He goes behind the wagon.*)

MOTHER COURAGE. He may be here any minute then. (*Calls toward the wagon.*) Kattrin, Eilif's coming! Bring a glass of brandy for the cook, Kattrin! (KATTRIN *doesn't come.*) Pull your hair over it and have done. Mr. Lamb is no stranger. (*She gets the brandy herself.*) She won't come out. Peace is nothing to her, it was too long coming. They hit her right over the eye. You can hardly see it now. But she thinks people stare at her.

COOK. Ah yes, war! (*He and* MOTHER COURAGE *sit.*)

MOTHER COURAGE. Cook, you come at a bad time: I'm ruined.

COOK. What? That's terrible!

MOTHER COURAGE. The peace has broken my neck. On the Chaplain's advice I've gone and bought a lot of supplies. Now everybody's leaving and I'm holding the baby.

COOK. How could you listen to the Chaplain? If I'd had time—but the Catholics were too quick for me—I'd have warned you against him. He's a windbag. Well, so now he's the big man round here!

MOTHER COURAGE. He's been doing the dishes for me and helping with the wagon.

COOK. With the wagon—him! And I'll bet he's told you a few of his jokes. He has a most unhealthy attitude to women. I tried to influence him but it was no good. He isn't sound.

MOTHER COURAGE. Are you sound?

COOK. If I'm nothing else, I'm sound. Your health!

MOTHER COURAGE. Sound! Only one person around here was ever sound, and I never had to slave as I did then. He sold the blankets off the children's beds in the spring, and he found my harmonica unchristian. You aren't recommending yourself if you *admit* you're sound.

COOK. You fight tooth and nail, don't you? I like that.

MOTHER COURAGE. Don't tell me you've been dreaming of my teeth and nails.

COOK. Well, here we sit, while the bells of peace do ring, and you pouring your famous brandy as only you know how!

MOTHER COURAGE. I don't think much of the bells of peace at the moment. I don't see how they can hand out all this pay that's in arrears. And then where shall I be with my famous brandy? Have you all been paid?

COOK (*hesitating*). Not exactly. That's why we disbanded. In the circumstances, I thought, why stay? For the time being, I'll look up a couple of friends. So here I sit—with you.

MOTHER COURAGE. In other words, you're broke.

COOK (*annoyed by the bells*). It's about time they stopped that racket! I'd like to set myself up in some business. I'm fed up with being their cook. I'm supposed to make do with tree roots and shoe leather, and then they throw the hot soup in my face. Being a cook nowadays is a dog's life. I'd sooner do war service, but of course it's peace now. (*As the* CHAPLAIN *turns up, wearing his old costume*) We'll talk it over later.

CHAPLAIN. The coat's pretty good. Just a few moth holes.

COOK. I don't know why you take the trouble. You won't find another job. Who could you incite now to earn an honorable wage or risk his life for a cause? Besides I have a bone to pick with you.

CHAPLAIN. Have you?

COOK. I have. You advised a lady to buy superfluous goods on the pretext that the war would never end.

CHAPLAIN (*hotly*). I'd like to know what business it is of yours?

COOK. It's unprincipled behavior! How can you give unwanted advice? And interfere with the conduct of other people's businesses?

CHAPLAIN. Who's interfering now, I'd like to know? (*To* MOTHER COURAGE) I had no idea you were such a close friend of this gentleman and had to account to him for everything.

MOTHER COURAGE. Now don't get excited. The Cook's giving his personal opinion. You can't deny your war was a frost.

CHAPLAIN. You mustn't take the name of peace in vain, Courage. Remember, you're a hyena of the battlefield!

MOTHER COURAGE. A what?

COOK. If you insult my girl friend, you'll have to reckon with me!

CHAPLAIN. I am *not* speaking to you, your intentions are only too transparent! (*To* MOTHER COURAGE) But when I see *you* take take peace between finger and thumb like a snotty old hanky, my humanity rebels! It shows that you want war, not peace, for what you get out of it. But don't forget the proverb: he who sups with the devil must use a long spoon!

MOTHER COURAGE. Remember what one fox said to another that was caught in a trap? "If you stay there, you're just asking for trouble!" There isn't much love lost between me and the war. And when it comes to calling me a hyena, you and I part company.

CHAPLAIN. Then why all this grumbling about the peace just as everyone's heaving a sigh of relief? Is it just for the junk in your wagon?

MOTHER COURAGE. My goods are not junk. I live off them. *You've* been living off them.

CHAPLAIN. You live off war. Exactly.

COOK (*to the* CHAPLAIN). As a grown man, you should know better than to go around advising people. (*To* MOTHER COURAGE) Now, in your situation you'd be wise to get rid of certain goods at once —before the prices sink to nothing. Get ready and get going, there isn't a moment to lose!

MOTHER COURAGE. That's sensible advice, I think I'll take it.

CHAPLAIN. Because the Cooks says so.

MOTHER COURAGE. Why didn't *you* say so? He's right, I must get to the market. (*She climbs into the wagon.*)

COOK. One up for me, Chaplain. You have no presence of mind. You should have said, "*I* gave you advice? Why, I was just talking politics!" And you shouldn't take me on as a rival. Cockfights are not becoming to your cloth.

CHAPLAIN. If you don't shut your trap, I'll murder you, cloth or no cloth!

COOK (*taking his boots off and unwinding the wrappings on his feet*). If you hadn't degenerated into a godless tramp, you could easily get yourself a parsonage, now it's peace. Cooks won't be needed, there's nothing to cook, but there's still plenty to believe, and people are prepared to go right on believing it.

CHAPLAIN. Mr. Lamb, please don't drive me out! Since I became a tramp, I'm a somewhat better man. I couldn't preach to 'em any more.

(YVETTE POTTIER *enters, decked out in black, with a stick. She is much older, fatter, and heavily powdered. Behind her, a servant.*)

YVETTE. Hullo, everybody! Is this Mother Courage's establishment?

CHAPLAIN. Quite right. And with whom have we the pleasure?

YVETTE. I am Madame Colonel Starhemberg, good people. Where's Mother Courage?

CHAPLAIN (*calling to the wagon*). Madame Colonel Starhemberg wants to speak with you!

MOTHER COURAGE (*from inside*). Coming!

YVETTE (*calling*). It's Yvette!

MOTHER COURAGE (*inside*). Yvette!

YVETTE. Just to see how you're getting on! (*As the* COOK *turns round in horror*) Peter!

COOK. Yvette!

YVETTE. Of all things! How did *you* get here?

COOK. On a cart.

CHAPLAIN. Well! You know each other? Intimately?

YVETTE. Not half. (*Scrutinizing the* COOK) You're fat.

COOK. For that matter, *you're* no beanpole.

YVETTE. Anyway, nice meeting you, tramp. Now I can tell you what I think of you.

CHAPLAIN. Do so, tell him all, but wait till Mother Courage comes out.

COOK. Now don't make a scene . . .

MOTHER COURAGE (*comes out, laden with goods*). Yvette! (*They embrace.*) But why are you in mourning?

YVETTE. Doesn't it suit me? My husband, the colonel, died several years ago.

MOTHER COURAGE. The old fellow that nearly bought my wagon?

YVETTE. His older brother.

MOTHER COURAGE. So you're not doing badly. Good to see one person who got somewhere in the war.

YVETTE. I've had my ups and downs.

MOTHER COURAGE. Don't let's speak ill of Colonels. They make money like hay.

CHAPLAIN (*to the* COOK). If I were you, I'd put my shoes on again. (*To* YVETTE) You promised to give us your opinion of this gentleman.

COOK. Now, Yvette, don't make a stink!

MOTHER COURAGE. He's a friend of mine, Yvette.

YVETTE. He's—Peter Piper, that's who.

MOTHER COURAGE. What!?

COOK. Cut the nicknames. My name's Lamb.

MOTHER COURAGE (*laughing*). Peter Piper? Who turned the women's heads? And I've been keeping your pipe for you.

CHAPLAIN. And smoking it.

YVETTE. Lucky I can warn you against him. He's a bad lot. You won't find a worse on the whole coast of Flanders. He got more girls in trouble than . . .

COOK. That's a long time ago, it isn't true any more.

YVETTE. Stand up when you talk to a lady! Oh, how I loved that man! And all the time he was having a little bowlegged brunette. He got *her* in trouble too, of course.

COOK. I seem to have brought *you* luck!

YVETTE. Shut your trap, you hoary ruin! And you take care, Mother Courage, this type is still dangerous even in decay!

MOTHER COURAGE (*to* YVETTE). Come with me, I must get rid of this stuff before the prices fall.

YVETTE (*concentrating on* COOK). Miserable cur!

MOTHER COURAGE. Maybe you can help me at army headquarters, you have contacts.

YVETTE. Damnable whore hunter!

MOTHER COURAGE (*shouting into the wagon*). Kattrin, church is all off, I'm going to market!

YVETTE. Inveterate seducer!

MOTHER COURAGE (*still to* KATTRIN). When Eilif comes, give him something to drink!

YVETTE. That a man of *his* ilk should have been able to turn me from the straight and narrow! I have only my own star to thank that I rose nonetheless to the heights! But I've put an end to your tricks, Peter Piper, and one day—in a better life than this—the Lord God will reward me! Come, Mother Courage! (*Leaves with* MOTHER COURAGE.)

CHAPLAIN. As our text this morning let us take the saying, the mills of God grind slowly. And you complain of my jokes!

COOK. I never have any luck. I'll be frank, I was hoping for a good hot dinner, I'm starving. And now they'll be talking about me, and she'll get a completely wrong picture. I think I should go before she comes back.

CHAPLAIN. I think so too.

COOK. Chaplain, peace makes me sick. Mankind must perish by fire and sword, we're born and bred in sin! Oh, how I wish I was roasting a great fat capon for the Commander—God knows where *he's* got to—with mustard sauce and those little yellow carrots . . .

CHAPLAIN. Red cabbage—with capon, red cabbage.

COOK. You're right. But he always wanted yellow carrots.

CHAPLAIN. He never understood a thing.

COOK. You always put plenty away.

CHAPLAIN. Under protest.

COOK. Anyway, you must admit, those were the days.

CHAPLAIN. Yes, that I might admit.

COOK. Now you've called her a hyena, there's not much future for you here either. What are you staring at?

CHAPLAIN. It's Eilif! (*Followed by two soldiers with halberds,* EILIF *enters. His hands are fettered. He is white as chalk.*) What's happened to you?

EILIF. Where's mother?

CHAPLAIN. Gone to town.

EILIF. They said she was here. I was allowed a last visit.

COOK (*to the soldiers*). Where are you taking him?

SOLDIER. For a ride.

(*The other soldier makes the gesture of throat cutting.*)

CHAPLAIN. What has he done?

SOLDIER. He broke in on a peasant. The wife is dead.

CHAPLAIN. Eilif, how could you?

EILIF. It's no different. It's what I did before.

COOK. That was in wartime.

EILIF. Shut your hole. Can I sit down till she comes?

SOLDIER. No.

CHAPLAIN. It's true. In wartime they honored him for it. He sat at the Commander's right hand. It was bravery. Couldn't we speak with the provost?

SOLDIER. What's the use? Stealing cattle from a peasant, what's brave about that?

COOK. It was just stupid.

EILIF. If I'd been stupid, I'd have starved, clever dick.

COOK. So you were bright and paid for it.

CHAPLAIN. At least we must bring Kattrin out.

EILIF. Let her alone. Just give me some brandy.

SOLDIER. No.

CHAPLAIN. What shall we tell your mother?

EILIF. Tell her it was no different. Tell her it was the same. Oh, tell her nothing.

(*The soldiers take him away.*)

CHAPLAIN. I'll come with you, I'll . . .

EILIF. I don't need a priest!

CHAPLAIN. You don't know—yet. (*Follows him.*)

COOK (*calling after him*). I'll have to tell her, she'll want to see him!

CHAPLAIN. Better tell her nothing. Or maybe just that he was here, and he'll return, maybe tomorrow. Meantime I'll be back and can break the news.

(*Leaves quickly. The* COOK *looks after him, shakes his head, then walks uneasily around. Finally, he approaches the wagon.*)

COOK. Hi! Won't you come out? You want to sneak away from the peace, don't you? Well, so do I! I'm the Swedish Commander's cook, remember me? I was wondering if you've got anything to eat in there—while we're waiting for your mother. I wouldn't mind a bit of bacon—or even bread—just to pass the time. (*He looks in.*) She's got a blanket over her head.

(*The thunder of cannon.*)

MOTHER COURAGE (*running, out of breath, still carrying the goods*). Cook, the peace is over, the war's on again, has been for three days! I didn't get rid of this stuff after all, thank God! There's a shooting match in the town already—with the Lutherans. We must get away with the wagon. Pack, Kattrin! What's on *your* mind? Something the matter?

COOK. Nothing.

MOTHER COURAGE. But there is. I see it in your face.

COOK. Because the war's on again, most likely. May it last till tomorrow evening, so I can get something in my belly!

MOTHER COURAGE. You're not telling me.

COOK. Eilif was here. Only he had to go away again.

MOTHER COURAGE. He was here? Then we'll see him on the march. I'll be with our side this time. How'd he look?

COOK. The same.

MOTHER COURAGE. He'll *never* change. And the war couldn't get *him*,

he's bright. Help me with the packing. (*She starts it.*) Did he tell
you anything? Is he well in with the captain? Did he tell you about
his heroic deeds?

COOK (*darkly*). He's done one of them again.

MOTHER COURAGE. Tell me about it later. (KATTRIN *appears.*) Kattrin,
the peace is all through, we're on the move again. (*To the* COOK)
What *is* biting you?

COOK. I'll enlist.

MOTHER COURAGE. A good idea. Where's the Chaplain?

COOK. In the town. With Eilif.

MOTHER COURAGE. Stay with us a while, Lamb, I need a bit of help.

COOK. This matter of Yvette . . .

MOTHER COURAGE. Hasn't done you any harm at all in my eyes. Just
the opposite. Where there's smoke, there's fire, they say. You'll
come?

COOK. I may as well.

MOTHER COURAGE. The twelfth regiment's under way. Into harness
with you! Maybe I'll see Eilif before the day is out, just think!
That's what I like best. Well, it wasn't such a long peace, we can't
grumble. Let's go! (*The* COOK *and* KATTRIN *are in harness.* MOTHER
COURAGE *sings.*)

Up hill, down dale, past dome and steeple,
     My wagon always moves ahead.
The war can care for all its people
     So long as there is steel and lead.
Though steel and lead are stout supporters
     A war needs human beings too.
Report today to your headquarters!
     If it's to last, this war needs you!
          Christians, awake! The winter's gone!
          The snows depart, the dead sleep on.
          And though you may not long survive
          Get out of bed and look alive!

Scene Nine

*The great war of religion has lasted sixteen years and Germany
has lost half its inhabitants. Those who are spared in battle die
by plague. Over once blooming countryside hunger rages. Towns
are burned down. Wolves prowl the empty streets. In the autumn
of 1634 we find* MOTHER COURAGE *in the Fichtelgebirge not far
far from the road the Swedish army is taking. Winter has come*

early and is hard. Business is bad. Only begging remains. The
COOK *receives a letter from Utrecht and is sent packing.*

(*In front of a half-ruined parsonage. Early winter. A grey morning. Gusts of wind.* MOTHER COURAGE *and the* COOK *at the wagon
in shabby clothes.*)

COOK. There are no lights on. No one's up.

MOTHER COURAGE. But it's a parsonage. The parson'll have to leave
his feather bed and ring the bells. Then he'll have some hot soup.

COOK. Where'll he get it from? The whole village is starving.

MOTHER COURAGE. The house is lived in. There was a dog barking.

COOK. If the parson has anything, he'll stick to it.

MOTHER COURAGE. Maybe if we sang him something . . .

COOK. I've had enough. (*Suddenly*) I didn't tell you, a letter came from
Utrecht. My mother's died of cholera, the inn is mine. There's the
letter, if you don't believe me. I'll show it to you, though my aunt's
railing about me and my ups and downs is none of your business.

MOTHER COURAGE (*reading*). Lamb, I'm tired of wandering, too. I feel
like a butcher's dog taking meat to my customers and getting none
myself. I've nothing more to sell and people have nothing to pay
with. In Saxony someone tried to saddle me with a chestful of
books in return for two eggs. And in Württemberg they would
have let me have their plough for a bag of salt. Nothing grows any
more, only thorn bushes. I hear that in Pomerania the villagers
have been eating their younger children. Nuns have been caught
committing robbery.

COOK. The world's dying out.

MOTHER COURAGE. Sometimes I see myself driving through hell with
this wagon and selling brimstone. And sometimes I'm driving
through heaven handing out provisions to wandering souls! If only
we could find a place where there's no shooting, me and my children—what's left of 'em—we might rest a while.

COOK. We could open this inn together. Think about it, Courage. *My*
mind's made up. With or without you, I'm leaving for Utrecht.
And today too.

MOTHER COURAGE. I must talk to Kattrin, it's a little bit sudden, and
I don't like to make my decisions in the cold on an empty stomach.
(KATTRIN *emerges from the wagon.*) Kattrin, I've something to
tell you. The cook and I want to go to Utrecht, he's been left an
inn. You'd be able to stay put and get to know some people. Many
a man'd be prepared to take on a girl with a position. Looks aren't
everything. I wouldn't mind it. I get on well with the Cook. I'll
say this for him: he's has a head for business. We'd be sure of our

dinner, that would be all right, wouldn't it? You'd have your own bed, what do you think of *that?* In the long run, this is no life, on the road. You might be killed any time. You're already lousy. And we must decide now, because otherwise we go north with the Swedes. They must be over there somewhere. (*She points to the left.*) I think we'll decide to go, Kattrin.

COOK. Anna, I must have a word with you alone.

MOTHER COURAGE. Go back inside, Kattrin.

(KATTRIN *does so.*)

COOK. I'm interrupting because there's a misunderstanding, Anna. I thought I wouldn't have to say it right out, but I see I must. If you're bringing *her,* it's all off. Do we understand each other?

(KATTRIN *has her head out of the back of the wagon and is listening.*)

MOTHER COURAGE. You mean I leave Kattrin behind?

COOK. What do you think? There's no room in the inn, it isn't one of those places with three counters. If the two of us look lively we can earn a living, but three's too many. Let Kattrin keep your wagon.

MOTHER COURAGE. I was thinking we might find her a husband in Utrecht.

COOK. Don't make me laugh. With that scar? And old as she is? And dumb?

MOTHER COURAGE. Not so loud!

COOK. Loud or soft, what is, is. That's another reason I can't have her in the inn. Customers don't like having something like that always before their eyes. You can't blame them.

MOTHER COURAGE. Shut up. I told you not to talk so loud.

COOK. There's a light in the parsonage, we can sing now!

MOTHER COURAGE. Cook, how could she pull the wagon by herself? The war frightens her. She can't bear it. She has terrible dreams. I hear her groan at night, especially after battles. What she sees in her dreams I don't know. She suffers from pity. The other day I found a hedgehog with her that we'd run over.

COOK. The inn's too small. (*Calling*) Worthy Sir, menials, and all within! We now present the song of Solomon, Julius Caesar, and other great souls who came to no good, so you can see we're law-abiding folk too, and have a hard time getting by, especially in winter. (*He sings "The Song of the Great Souls of This Earth."*)
　　You've heard of wise old Solomon
　　　　You know his history.
　　He thought so little of this earth
　　He cursed the hour of his birth

Declaring: all is vanity.
How very wise was Solomon!
But ere night came and day did go
This fact was clear to everyone:
It was his wisdom that had brought him low.
Better for you if you have none.
For the virtues are dangerous in this world, as our fine song tells.
You're better off without, you have a nice life, breakfast included
—some good hot soup maybe . . . I'm an example of a man
who's not had any, and I'd like some, I'm a soldier, but what good
did my bravery do me in all those battles? None at all. I might
just as well have wet my pants like a poltroon and stayed home.
For why?
And Julius Caesar, who was brave,
You saw what came of him.
He sat like God on an altar-piece
And yet they tore him limb from limb
While his prestige did still increase!
"Et tu, Brute, I am undone!"
And ere night came and day did go
This fact was clear to everyone:
It was his bravery that brought him low
Better for you if you have none.
(*Under his breath*) They don't even look out. (*Aloud*) Worthy
Sir, menials, and all within! You should say, no, courage isn't the
thing to fill a man's belly, try honesty, that should be worth a
dinner, at any rate it must have *some* effect. Let's see.
You all know honest Socrates
Who always spoke the truth.
They owed him thanks for that, you'd think,
Yet they put hemlock in his drink
And swore that he was bad for youth.
How honest was the people's son!
But ere night came and day did go
This fact was clear to everyone:
It was his honesty that brought him low.
Better for you if you have none.
Yes, we're told to be unselfish and share what we have, but what
if we have nothing? And those who do share it don't have an easy
time either, for what's left when you've finished sharing? Un-
selfishness is a very rare virtue—it doesn't pay.
Unselfish Martin could not bear
His fellow creature's woes.

He met a beggar in the snows
And gave him half his cloak to wear:
　So both of them fell down and froze.
What an unselfish paragon!
　But ere night came and day did go
This fact was clear to everyone:
　It was unselfishness that brought him low.
Better for you if you have none.

That's how it is with us. We're law-abiding folk, we keep to ourselves, don't steal, don't kill, don't burn the place down. And in
this way we sink lower and lower and the song proves true and
there's no soup going. And if we were different, if we were thieves
and killers, maybe we could eat our fill! For virtues bring no reward, only vices. Such is the world, need it be so?

God's Ten Commandments we have kept
　And acted as we should.
　It has not done us any good.
O you who sit beside a fire
Please help us now: our need is dire!
Strict godliness we've always shown
　But ere night came and day did go
This fact was clear to everyone:
　It was our godliness that brought us low.
Better for you if you have none!

VOICES (*from above*). You there! Come up! There's some soup here
　for you!

MOTHER COURAGE. Lamb, I couldn't swallow a thing. I don't say what
　you said is unreasonable, but was it your last word? We've always
　understood each other.

COOK. Yes, Anna. Think it over.

MOTHER COURAGE. There's nothing to think over. I'm not leaving her
　here.

COOK. You're going to be silly, but what can I do? I'm not inhuman,
　it's just that the inn's a small one. And now we must go up, or
　it'll be nothing doing here too, and we've been singing in the cold
　to no avail.

MOTHER COURAGE. I'll fetch Kattrin.

COOK. Better stick something in your pocket for her. If there are three
　of us, they'll get a shock.

　(*Exeunt.* KATTRIN *clambers out of the wagon with a bundle. She
　makes sure they're both gone. Then, on a wagon wheel, she lays
　out a skirt of her mother's and a pair of the* COOK'S *trousers side*

*by side and easy to see. She has just finished, and has picked up
her bundle, when* MOTHER COURAGE *returns.*)
MOTHER COURAGE (*with a plate of soup*). Kattrin! Stay where you are,
Kattrin! Where do you think you're going with that bundle? (*She
examines the bundle.*) She's packed her things. Were you listening? I told him there was nothing doing, he can *have* Utrecht
and his lousy inn, what would we want with a lousy inn? (*She sees
the skirt and trousers.*) Oh, you're a stupid girl, Kattrin, what if
I'd seen that and you gone? (*She takes hold of* KATTRIN, *who's
trying to leave.*) And don't think I've sent him packing on your
account. It was the wagon. You can't part us, I'm too used to it,
you didn't come into it, it was the wagon. Now we're leaving, and
we'll put the cook's things here where he'll find 'em, the stupid
man. (*She clambers up and throws a couple of things down to go
with the trousers.*) There! He's sacked! The last man I'll take into
this business! Now let's be going, you and me. Get into harness.
This winter'll pass—like all the others.
(*They harness themselves to the wagon, turn it around, and start
out. A gust of wind. Enter the* COOK, *still chewing. He sees his
things.*)

Scene Ten

During the whole of 1635 MOTHER COURAGE *and* KATTRIN *pull the
wagon along the roads of central Germany in the wake of the
ever more ragged armies.*

(*On the highway,* MOTHER COURAGE *and* KATTRIN *are pulling the
wagon. They come to a prosperous farmhouse. Someone inside is
singing "The Song of Shelter."*
THE VOICE.
  In March a tree we planted
    To make the garden gay.
  In June we were enchanted:
  A lovely rose was blooming
  The balmy air perfuming!
    Blest of the gods are they
    Who have a garden gay!
  In June we were enchanted.

  When snow falls helter-skelter
    And loudly blows the storm

Our farmhouse gives us shelter.
The winter's in a hurry
But we've no cause to worry.
   Cosy are we and warm
   Though loudly blows the storm
Our farmhouse gives us shelter.

(MOTHER COURAGE *and* KATTRIN *have stopped to listen. Then they start out again.*)

Scene Eleven

January, 1636. Catholic troops threaten the Protestant town of Halle. The stone begins to speak. MOTHER COURAGE *loses her daughter and journeys onwards alone. The war is not yet near its end.*

(*The wagon, very far gone now, stands near a farmhouse with a straw roof. It is night. Out of the wood come a* LIEUTENANT *and* THREE SOLDIERS *in full armor.*)

LIEUTENANT. And there mustn't be a sound. If anyone yells, cut him down.

FIRST SOLDIER. But we'll have to knock—if we want a guide.

LIEUTENANT. Knocking's a natural noise, it's all right, could be a cow hitting the wall of the cowshed.

(*The* SOLDIERS *knock at the farmhouse door. An old* PEASANT WOMAN *opens. A hand is clapped over her mouth.* TWO SOLDIERS *enter.*)

MAN'S VOICE. What is it?

(*The* SOLDIERS *bring out an old* PEASANT *and his* SON.)

LIEUTENANT (*pointing to the wagon on which* KATTRIN *has appeared*). There's one. (A SOLDIER *pulls her out.*) Is this everybody that lives here?

PEASANTS (*alternating*). That's our son. And that's a girl that can't talk. Her mother's in town buying up stocks because the shopkeepers are running away and selling cheap. They're canteen people.

LIEUTENANT. I'm warning you. Keep quiet. One sound and we'll crack you one with a pike. And I need someone to show us the path to the town. (*Points to the* YOUNG PEASANT.) You! Come here!

YOUNG PEASANT. I don't know any path!

SECOND SOLDIER (*grinning*). He don't know any path!

YOUNG PEASANT. I don't help Catholics.

LIEUTENANT (*to* SECOND SOLDIER). Let him feel your pike in his side.

YOUNG PEASANT (*forced to his knees, the pike at his throat*). I'd rather die!

SECOND SOLDIER (*again mimicking*). He'd rather die!

FIRST SOLDIER. I know how to change his mind. (*Walks over to the cowshed.*) Two cows and a bull. Listen, you. If you aren't going to be reasonable, I'll sabre your cattle.

YOUNG PEASANT. Not the cattle!

PEASANT WOMAN (*weeping*). Spare the cattle, captain, or we'll starve!

LIEUTENANT. If he must be pigheaded!

FIRST SOLDIER. I think I'll start with the bull.

YOUNG PEASANT (*to the old one*). Do I have to? (*The* OLDER ONE *nods.*) I'll do it.

PEASANT WOMAN. Thank you, thank you, captain, for sparing us, for ever and ever. Amen.

(*The* OLD MAN *stops her going on thanking him.*)

FIRST SOLDIER. I knew the bull came first all right!

(*Led by the* YOUNG PEASANT, *the* LIEUTENANT *and the* SOLDIERS *go on their way.*)

OLD PEASANT. I wish we knew what it was. Nothing good, I suppose.

PEASANT WOMAN. Maybe they're just scouts. What are you doing?

OLD PEASANT (*setting a ladder against the roof and climbing up*). I'm seeing if they're alone. (*On the roof*) Things are moving—all over. I can see armor. And a cannon. There must be more than a regiment. God have mercy on the town and all within!

PEASANT WOMAN. Are there lights in the town?

OLD PEASANT. No, they're all asleep. (*He climbs down.*) There'll be an attack, and they'll all be slaughtered in their beds.

PEASANT WOMAN. The watchman'll give warning.

OLD PEASANT. They must have killed the watchman in the tower on the hill or he'd have sounded his horn before this.

PEASANT WOMAN. If there were more of us . . .

OLD PEASANT. But being that we're alone with that cripple . . .

PEASANT WOMAN. There's nothing we can do, is there?

OLD PEASANT. Nothing.

PEASANT WOMAN. We can't get down there. In the dark.

OLD PEASANT. The whole hillside's swarming with 'em.

PEASANT WOMAN. We could give a sign?

OLD PEASANT. And be cut down for it?

PEASANT WOMAN. No, there's nothing we can do. (*To* KATTRIN) Pray, poor thing, pray! There's nothing we can do to stop this bloodshed, so even if you can't talk, at least pray! He hears, if no one else does. I'll help you. (*All kneel,* KATTRIN *behind.*) Our Father, which art in Heaven, hear our prayer, let not the town perish with all that lie therein asleep and fearing nothing. Wake them, that they rise and go to the walls and see the foe that comes with fire and sword in the night down the hill and across the fields. (*Back to* KATTRIN) God protect our mother and make the watchman not sleep but wake ere it's too late. And save our son-in-law too, O God, he's there with his four children, let them not perish, they're innocent, they know nothing (*to* KATTRIN, *who groans*), one of them's not two years old, the eldest is seven. (KATTRIN *rises, troubled.*) Heavenly Father, hear us, only Thou canst help us or we die, for we are weak and have no sword nor nothing; we cannot thrust our own strength but only Thine, O Lord; we are in Thy hands, our cattle, our farm, and the town too, we're all in Thy hands, and the foe is nigh unto the walls with all his power. (KATTRIN *unperceived, has crept off to the wagon, has taken something out of it, put it under her apron, and has climbed up the ladder to the roof.*) Be mindful of the children in danger, especially the little ones, be mindful of the old folk who cannot move, and of all Christian souls, O Lord.

OLD PEASANT. And forgive us our trespasses as we forgive them that trespass against us. Amen.

(*Sitting on the roof,* KATTRIN *takes a drum from under her apron, and starts to beat it.*)

PEASANT WOMAN. Heavens, what's she doing?

OLD PEASANT. She's out of her mind!

PEASANT WOMAN. Bring her down, quick! (*The* OLD PEASANT *runs to the ladder but* KATTRIN *pulls it up on the roof.*) She'll get us in trouble.

OLD PEASANT. Stop it this minute, you silly cripple!

PEASANT WOMAN. The soldiers'll come!

OLD PEASANT (*looking for stones*). I'll stone you!

PEASANT WOMAN. Have you no pity, have you no heart? We have relations there too, four grandchildren, but there's nothing we can do. If they find us now, it's the end, they'll stab us to death! (KATTRIN *is staring into the far distance, toward the town. She goes on drumming.*)

PEASANT WOMAN (*to the* PEASANT). I told you not to let that riffraff in your farm. What do *they* care if we lose our cattle?

LIEUTENANT (*running back with* SOLDIERS *and* YOUNG PEASANT). I'll cut you all to bits!

PEASANT WOMAN. We're innocent, sir, there's nothing we can do. She did it, a stranger!

LIEUTENANT. Where's the ladder?

OLD PEASANT. On the roof.

LIEUTENANT (*calling*). Throw down the drum. I order you! (KATTRIN *goes on drumming.*) You're all in this, but you won't live to tell the tale.

OLD PEASANT. They've been cutting down fir trees around here. If we bring a tall enough trunk we can knock her off the roof . . .

FIRST SOLDIER (*to the* LIEUTENANT). I beg leave to make a suggestion. (*He whispers something to the* LIEUTENANT, *who nods.*) Listen, you! We have an idea—for your own good. Come down and go with us to the town. Show us your mother and we'll spare her. (KATTRIN *replies and goes on drumming.*)

LIEUTENANT (*pushing him away*). She doesn't trust you, no wonder with your face. (*He calls up to* KATTRIN.) Hey, you! Suppose I give you my word? I'm an officer, my word's my bond! (KATTRIN *drums louder.*) Nothing is sacred to her.

YOUNG PEASANT. Sir, it's not just because of her mother!

FIRST SOLDIER. This can't go on, they'll hear it in the town as sure as hell.

LIEUTENANT. We must make another noise with something. Louder than that drum. What can we make a noise with?

FIRST SOLDIER. But we mustn't make a noise!

LIEUTENANT. A harmless noise, fool, a peacetime noise!

OLD PEASANT. I could start chopping wood.

LIEUTENANT. That's it! (*The* PEASANT *brings his ax and chops away.*) Chop! Chop harder! Chop for your life! (KATTRIN *has been listening, beating her drum less hard. Very upset, and peering around, she now goes on drumming.*) It's not enough. (*To* FIRST SOLDIER) You chop too!

OLD PEASANT. I've only one ax. (*He stops chopping.*)

LIEUTENANT. We must set fire to the farm. Smoke her out.

OLD PEASANT. That's no good, Captain, when they see fire from the town, they'll know everything.

(*During the drumming* KATTRIN *has been listening again. Now she laughs.*)

LIEUTENANT. She's laughing at us, that's too much, I'll have her guts if it's the last thing I do. Bring a musket!

(*Two* SOLDIERS *go off.* KATTRIN *goes on drumming.*)

PEASANT WOMAN. I have it, Captain. That's their wagon over there, Captain. If we smash that, she'll stop. It's all they have, Captain.

LIEUTENANT (*to the* YOUNG PEASANT). Smash it! (*Calling.*) If you don't stop that noise, we'll smash your wagon!

(*The* YOUNG PEASANT *deals the wagon a couple of feeble blows with a board.*)

PEASANT WOMAN (*to* KATTRIN). Stop, you little beast!

(KATTRIN *stares at the wagon and pauses. Noises of distress come out of her. But she goes on drumming.*)

LIEUTENANT. Where are those sons of bitches with that gun?

FIRST SOLDIER. They can't have heard anything in the town or we'd hear their cannon.

LIEUTENANT (*calling*). They don't hear you. And now we're going to shoot you. I'll give you one more chance: throw down that drum!

YOUNG PEASANT (*dropping the board, screaming to* KATTRIN). Don't stop now! Or they're all done for. Go on, go on, go on . . .

(*The* SOLDIER *knocks him down and beats him with his pike.* KATTRIN *starts crying but goes on drumming.*)

PEASANT WOMAN. Not in the back, you're killing him!

(*The* SOLDIERS *arrive with the musket.*)

SECOND SOLDIER. The Colonel's foaming at the mouth. We'll be court-martialed.

LIEUTENANT. Set it up! Set it up! (*Calling while the musket is set up on forks.*) Once for all: stop that drumming!

(*Still crying,* KATTRIN *is drumming as hard as she can. The* SOLDIERS *fire.* KATTRIN *is hit. She gives the drum another feeble beat or two, then slowly collapses.*)

LIEUTENANT. That's an end to the noise.

(*But the last beats of the drum are lost in the din of cannon from the town. Mingled with the thunder of cannon, alarm bells are heard in the distance.*)

FIRST SOLDIER. She did it.

Scene Twelve

(*Toward morning. The drums and pipes of troops on the march, receding. In front of the wagon* MOTHER COURAGE *sits by* KATTRIN's *body. The* PEASANTS *of the last scene are standing near.*)

PEASANTS. You must leave, ma'am. There's only one regiment to go. You can never get away by yourself.

MOTHER COURAGE. Maybe she's fallen asleep. (*She sings.*)
Lullay, lullay, what's that in the hay?
The neighbor's babes cry but mine are gay.
The neighbor's babes are dressed in dirt:
Your silks were cut from an angel's skirt.
They are all starving: you have a cake;
If it's too stale, you need but speak.
Lullay, lullay, what's rustling there?
One lad fell in Poland. The other is where?

You shouldn't have told her about the children.

PEASANTS. If you hadn't gone off to the town to get your cut, maybe it wouldn't have happened.

MOTHER COURAGE. She's asleep now.

PEASANTS. She's not asleep, it's time you realized. She's through. You must get away. There are wolves in these parts. And the bandits are worse.

MOTHER COURAGE. That's right. (*She goes and fetches a piece of cloth from the wagon to cover the body.*)

PEASANTS. Have you no one now? Someone you can go to?

MOTHER COURAGE. There's one. My Eilif.

PEASANTS (*while* COURAGE *covers the body*). Leave *her* to us. We'll give her a proper burial. You needn't worry.

MOTHER COURAGE. Here's money for the expenses.

(*She pays the* PEASANT. *The* PEASANT *and his* SON *shake her hand and carry* KATTRIN *away.*)

PEASANT WOMAN (*also taking her hand, and bowing, as she goes away*). Hurry!

MOTHER COURAGE (*harnessing herself to the wagon*). I hope I can pull the wagon by myself. Yes, I'll manage, there's not much in it now. I must start up again in business.

(*Another regiment passes at the rear with pipe and drum.*)

MOTHER COURAGE. Hey! Take me with you! (*She starts pulling the wagon. Soldiers are heard singing.*)

Dangers, surprises, devastations—
    The war takes hold and will not quit.
But though it last three generations
    We shall get nothing out of it.
Starvation, filth, and cold enslave us.
    The army robs us of our pay.
Only a miracle can save us
    And miracles have had their day.
        Christians, awake! The winter's gone!
        The snows depart. The dead sleep on.
        And though you may not long survive
        Get out of bed and look alive!

TRANSLATOR'S NOTES TO MOTHER COURAGE

When I first translated *Mother Courage,* I worked from a copy of the play as printed in the *Versuche* series. It was marked up by a member of the staff of the Berlin Ensemble: I made the cuts indicated and put in the penciled additions. The translation appeared in *The Modern Theatre,* Volume 2, 1955, Doubleday Anchor Books.

Next I made a somewhat shorter stage version with new lyrics, which Darius Milhaud set to music. This version was published in *Seven Plays* by Bertolt Brecht, 1961.

The present text, commissioned by Methuen & Co. for their collected Brecht, is the only one of my three versions which is complete. The basis of this version is, in general, the text in the *Versuche,* but I have frequently consulted the text in the *Stücke* too.

The few words in my translation for which no equivalent will be found in either the *Versuche* or the *Stücke* I took from the Berlin Ensemble copy mentioned above; and Brecht has recorded them permanently in the Notes to the special Modell edition published by Henschel in East Berlin, 1958.

To the list of helpers acknowledged in former editions of the English *Mother Courage,* I should like to add the names of two who helped with this new effort: Miss Jill Booty and Dr. Hugo Schmidt.

The music for the lyrics here printed, which is by Darius Milhaud, has not yet (early 1962) been made available to producers. A score by Paul Dessau has been used in all authorized English-language productions. A piano reduction of Dessau's songs will be found in the Doubleday Anchor edition of *Mother Courage* with English words to fit. Some of these songs are to be found, sung by Germaine Montero, on a 12-inch disc (VKS-9022) distributed in the United States by Vanguard Records. The East-German records of some of the *Mother Courage* songs, performed by the original Berlin Ensemble cast, have usually been available from Deutsche Schallplatten, Deutscher Buch Export, Leninstrasse 16, Leipzig C.1, Germany. There is an East-German movie of the play which has not yet been generally released, and there is a British TV-film of the Bentley version which has not been shown outside Britain.

Mother Courage was first produced in 1941 in Zurich and since the Berlin Ensemble production (1949) has been performed in many countries. The Bentley version alone has been professionally produced in Dublin, London (TV only), Cleveland, and San Francisco. Pictures of each scene in the Berlin Ensemble production are provided in *Courage-Modell 1949,* published by the Henschel Verlag in East Berlin, along with Brecht's own scene-by-scene analysis of the play.

Eric Bentley

CORRUPTION IN THE PALACE OF JUSTICE [1949]
A Play in Three Acts

by Ugo Betti

translated by Henry Reed

People in the Play

VANAN, *president of the court*
ELENA, *his daughter*
ERZI, *investigating counsellor*
CROZ, *chief justice*
CUST, *a judge*
BATA, *a judge*
MAVERI, *a judge*
PERSIUS, *a judge*
MALGAI, *a record clerk*
A NURSE
STRANGER
and a number of officials, porters, bystanders

The time is the present.

The action takes place in a foreign city. The scene is the same throughout: a large severe room in the Palace of Justice.

Corruption in the Palace of Justice, printed by permission of Ninon Tallon Karlweis, exclusive agent for the Betti Estate. Caution: Professionals and amateurs are hereby warned that *Corruption in the Palace of Justice* being fully protected by copyright, is subject to a royalty. All applications for permission to perform the play, including readings, should be made to: Ninon Tallon Karlweis, 57 West 58th Street, New York 19, N.Y., as agent for the Betti Estate. Anyone presenting this play without a written permission will be liable to the penalties by law provided.

ACT ONE

The room is empty. MALGAI, *the record clerk, enters, pushing a wheeled basket. He goes round the tables, which are piled high with documents; some of these he selects and throws into the basket, after checking their dates against certain papers in his hand. He hums to himself.*

(*A* STRANGER *appears in the doorway.*)

STRANGER. I wonder if you could tell me where I can find Chief Justice Croz's office?

MALGAI. Will you ask the porter, sir? There's a porter for that purpose.

STRANGER. I'm sorry but I haven't been able to find any porters.

MALGAI. Well, you can't expect them to be here before they have to clock in, can you? Oh, it's no good looking at me; I'm one of the old brigade. What do you want to see Chief Justice Croz for?

STRANGER. I have to speak to him.

MALGAI. Well, that would be fine, sir, only unfortunately poor Mr. Croz is dying. Has been for months. He doesn't come to the office any more. It has to be something very special to bring Mr. Croz here, and even then they almost have to carry him.

STRANGER. All the same I think he will come this morning.

MALGAI (*glancing at him*). Ah. (*Cautiously*) Is there a judges' meeting perhaps?

STRANGER. I fancy we shall see them all here.

MALGAI. Ah. (*His tone has changed slightly.*) Well . . . If you want to get to Chief Justice Croz's office, you go down the corridor to the end, then to the right, then to the right again. . . . But if you don't mind my saying so, I think you'd do best to wait for him in here.

STRANGER. In here?

MALGAI. Yes, you'll hear his cane. You can always hear him when he comes up the corridor: he has to use a cane nowadays. If there *is* a sitting, they'll all have to come in here: this is the council chamber for the division. (*He points to a seat near the door.*) You can sit down if you wish.

STRANGER. Thank you. (*He sits.*)

MALGAI (*throwing another glance at the visitor, as he goes on with his work*). A huge building, this, isn't it? The place is just one great maze. We even get tourists in looking at it. In admiration. (*He drops his voice slightly.*) At the moment, unfortunately, the smell about the place isn't quite as sweet as it might be. I suppose it must be a dead rat or something, under one of the floorboards. What do you think about it all, sir? I don't know if you saw last night's papers?

STRANGER. Yes.

MALGAI. Well, it's no business of mine, of course, but I think there's something of a storm blowing up. There's thunder in the air.

STRANGER. Are you one of the clerks?

MALGAI. No, sir. I'm what you might call the gravedigger. This (*he smacks the side of the trolley*) is the hearse; and these (*he waves the papers in his hand*) are the death certificates; and these (*he taps the bundles of documents*) are the bodies.

STRANGER. And the graveyard?

MALGAI (*pointing to a door*). Through there. The Archives. A quiet, shady little spot; I take all this stuff in there and see it gets decent burial.

STRANGER. Are you one of the record clerks?

MALGAI. The undertaker I always call myself. When I think of all the sweat, and all the money and tears, that have gone into even the silliest little bundle of these things here! Well, well . . . (*He drops a bundle into the trolley, and takes up another one.*) I stick a great big number on them, and register them in a great big book, so that people can pretend to believe they'll go on being important per secula et seculorum, and they can always take the thing up again . . .

STRANGER. While actually the only things really concerned about your graveyard are the mice and the grubs?

MALGAI. No, it's not the mice and the grubs, sir. It's the interested parties themselves: they get bored after a time, and turn their minds to other things. It's surprising how easily people *do* get bored and turn to other things.

(*A newcomer has entered, looking very worried.* MALGAI *turns to him solicitously.*)

MALGAI. Oh, good morning, Judge Bata.

BATA (*as he enters*). Good morning, my dear fellow, good morning. (*Taking him aside, and whispering*) Have you heard?

MALGAI (*anxiously*). What?

BATA. You didn't come past the secretary's office this morning?

MALGAI. No, I never go round that way.

BATA (*cautiously*). I came past the door a few moments ago; there's an official posted outside it: rather important-looking.

MALGAI. An official?

BATA. Yes, a sort of policeman. He politely told us we couldn't go in.

MALGAI. Not even the judges?

BATA. He was stopping everyone.

MALGAI. What . . . what for?

BATA. Well, I was wondering if *you* . . .

MALGAI. No, sir, I haven't the foggiest.

BATA. You've no idea . . . what it's all about . . . ?

MALGAI. Good gracious, no! They'd never tell *me*. I expect it's just some new piece of nonsense they've—.

BATA (*trying to pooh-pooh the matter*). Oh yes, yes, of course it is, but I do think they might have mentioned it to the magistrates.

MALGAI. Of course, sir! Naturally. I hear there's a special meeting of the division today.

BATA. Yes, it's all very odd. It's taken us all by surprise rather.

(*The other judges are entering:* PERSIUS, MAVERI, *and, shortly after,* CUST.)

PERSIUS (*as he approaches*). Well, what is it all about?

BATA (*pointing to the archivist, who backs respectfully away*). He doesn't seem to know either.

MAVERI (*cautiously*). I think it's just a mistake; some order must have been misunderstood.

PERSIUS (*unconvinced*). Yes, quite. A mistake.

MAVERI. A misunderstanding. (*A brief silence.*)

BATA (*to* PERSIUS, *suddenly*). My dear Persius, you yourself can bear me out, can't you? I've been saying it for months; there are a lot of things need clearing up in here, we need more light and air in the place. The air in these courts is becoming too thick to breathe. I've said that again and again, haven't I? Haven't I?

PERSIUS. My dear fellow, you don't think you're the only one, do you?

MAVERI. Lots of people have been saying so.

CUST. We've said so, too: all of us.

MAVERI. A man with a clear conscience has nothing to fear from the light; nothing at all.

BATA. It's important to realize of course that it may have all just blown up out of nothing. People thrive on scandal. The law courts are always a hive of discontented murmuring. Someone starts spreading scandal about the place, someone else joins in, and by the next day there are ten or twenty of them, buzz- buzz- buzzing their heads off. It's like gangrene spreading.

MAVERI. And the newspapers too: you can't trust any of them.

PERSIUS. And the politicians: party intrigues the whole time. I can't help feeling the whole thing is a deliberate plot.

BATA. But it's the city itself, more than anything, surely? This filthy, diseased city. I never thought people could be so evil, so nasty.

PERSIUS. Yes, just listen to them talking: there isn't a word of truth in anything they say.

MAVERI. Not to mention the women.

BATA. Yes, the place is just a dungheap. The odd thing is to find them screaming with indignation because right in the middle of their own stink there should be a building where the atmosphere isn't (shall I say?) quite as fragrant as it might be. In fact, the magistrates' crime . . . is simply that they're a little too like the man in the street.

PERSIUS (*acidly*). My dear friend and colleague, I never think one ought to generalize too readily. I don't think I personally bear the remotest resemblance to a dungheap.

BATA. Neither do I; the very idea.

PERSIUS. As far as I personally am concerned, I'm in the fortunate position of being able to say that I've never even *met* this man called Ludvi-Pol, never. I've never even seen him.

BATA. You sound rather as if your colleagues were less fortunate—what? As if some of us were in danger of being compromised in some way.

PERSIUS (*diplomatically*). *Did* I say that? Nonesense. I always aim at saying precisely what I mean. And if any of our colleagues *have* been off their feed lately, and *have* been having bad nights, well, I'm not one of them, that's all. There are times when every man has to look out for himself. This is one of them. Don't *you* think so, Cust?

BATA (*spitefully*). We all know that, my dear friend, we all know that. Some of our colleagues seem to have been very busy pulling strings and turning wheels these last few weeks. There seems to have been a good deal of angry fist-shaking about the place.

PERSIUS (*sarcastically*). Maybe, but the impression I have is that a lot of people in danger are trying to cling to one another as hard as they can. One notices that certain of one's colleagues have become very friendly all of a sudden. They keep trying to get into conversation with one the whole time. You find them waiting behind for you, so that you can leave the place together. They are all clutching at each other. Unfortunately, I'm always in a hurry. I'm always going in a different direction. I never know anything. I'm made of stone, dear friend. Oh, incidentally, Cust, I wanted to ask you something . . . (*Rather ostentatiously, he draws* CUST *apart.*)

BATA (*to* MAVERI). Did you hear that? In any case, I don't quite see why it's suddenly become so very important whether people have

or haven't known Ludvi-Pol. It rather looks—it rather *looks* now
as if Ludvi-Pol had been put out of business. Though up to yesterday . . .

MAVERI. He was better respected than a cabinet minister!

BATA. One knows of course that these men are just like spiders; what
keeps them going is precisely the web of relationships they so skil-
fully spin all round them. It stands to reason that a lot of people
come into contact with them. It may be perfectly true that our
dear friend Persius there has never met Ludvi-Pol; he still may
have met one of his agents. (*He drops his voice.*) And considering what went on just before Persius was last promoted, he'd better not try being too self-righteous.

MAVERI (*dropping his voice*). Persius feels he's in a strong position.

BATA. Oh, does he? Why?

MAVERI. Important contacts.

BATA. Very likely; he's a born toady.

MAVERI. And now he's trying to suck up to Cust; as one might expect.

BATA. Oh. Why?

MAVERI. Cust! Our rising star.

BATA. Cust?

MAVERI. Cust. A very able man; and not overburdened with scruples, I
imagine.

BATA. But what about the great Vanan?

MAVERI. Done for. A corpse.

BATA. Are you sure? Oh dear, it's very difficult trying to steer one's
way, isn't it? One person's up and another's down, the whole
time. You can never be sure what's going on. (*Looking thoughtfully at* CUST) I've always been on very good terms with Cust, myself, of course.

MAVERI. Really? I thought he seemed rather offhand with you, just
now.

BATA (*disturbed*). Cust? With me?

MAVERI. I expect it's only his way.

BATA. I've always said that he was really one of the best people in this
place . . . (*Seeing that* MAVERI *is also about to join* CUST *and*
PERSIUS) Look, my dear Maveri, there's something I've been
wanting to say to you for a long time. You *are* related to President Tomisco, aren't you?

MAVERI (*warily*). Well, it's a . . . very *distant* relationship. Why?

BATA (*beaming sunnily*). I was with President Tomisco for a time, you
know, just when I was starting my career. A most admirable person. Influential. I'd so much like to meet him again sometime.

Perhaps you'll be so good as to give him my kind regards, when next you . . .

MAVERI (*evasively*). I hardly ever see him, you know, hardly ever.

BATA (*amiably*). Dear colleague, please don't think that I'm trying to steal a march on you; please don't think that. On the contrary. If there's any way in which *I* can help *you*. . . . I have the greatest admiration for you, as you know.

MAVERI. So have I. For you, I mean.

BATA. Thank you. Sometimes . . . if two people are willing to stick together, they can . . . well, back each other up, stand by each other, as it were. It would be dreadful to have enemies at a time like this!

MAVERI (*cautiously*). Dreadful! But I hope . . .

BATA. One never knows, dear colleague. One can sometimes be betrayed by the very last person one expects it from. Well, of course, it's not for me to say.

MAVERI. What do you mean . . . ?

BATA. Well, you know how it is: one's colleagues . . . sometimes talk rather inconsiderately; I don't say they mean any harm, but . . .

MAVERI. Have you . . . heard anyone say anything about me?

BATA. Oh no, no. But the other night . . . Oh, it was just nonsense of course. But old Hill was in here, you know . . . (*He breaks off and listens.*) Croz is coming.

(*A cane is heard in the corridor. This sound produces a rapid change in everyone present. The groups break up. Expressions change. CROZ enters, leaning heavily on one side on his cane, and on the other on a manservant. His appearance reveals extreme physical prostration and at the same time a malignant energy: a quiver of the head gives him the appearance of continuously approving or disapproving of something. He advances half way across the room; here he halts for a few moments in order to draw breath, his eyes closed. He turns to the manservant without looking at him.*)

CROZ. Come back and fetch me later. That is, unless I die in the meantime. (*The manservant bows slightly and goes out. CROZ takes a few more steps forward.*) Is the great Vanan here yet?

BATA. No.

CROZ. Do any of you know if the old fool intends to come?

BATA. I don't really see why we should know any more than you do. With the wind blowing the way it is, I should think it's pretty unlikely.

CROZ. In that case, since the President is absent, it is my duty, as senior

judge of the division, to deputize for him. (*Half-turning to* MAL-
GAI) You: get out. What are you doing here?

MALGAI. I'm just going, sir. (*He points to the* STRANGER, *who has just
risen.*) I only wanted to tell your worship that there was a gentleman here waiting to see you. (*He goes out.*)

CROZ (*turning to observe the newcomer*). You wanted . . . to speak
to me?

STRANGER. Yes, Justice Croz. I have a private communication for you.

CROZ (*to the other judges*). He said private. (*The other judges, half-
curious, half-worried, withdraw to the other half of the room.*
CROZ *walks a few steps towards the back. The* STRANGER *follows,
speaking to him in a very low voice.* CROZ *listens, asking questions
from time to time: finally he leads the* STRANGER *with great def-
erence to an imposing armchair; then he once more approaches
his colleagues.*) Dear colleagues. (*He pauses and thinks.*) I have
to tell you . . . . (*Breaking off*) Damn it, Persius, you *have* gone
green in the face! You look scared to death.

PERSIUS. You can spare me your little jests, Croz. You'd do much better to think about yourself.

CROZ. You mean if anyone ought to be scared to death, it's me, eh?
But, my dear Persius, I'm already dying in any case, am I not?
Moribundus. So obviously—

PERSIUS. *Moribundus,* yes, you've been *moribundus* for a long time. It's
an old trick, Croz; we're used to it, by now.

CROZ (*grinning*). Oh, such unkindness! Come, come. Well, dear colleagues, it appears that the Minister and the Lord High President
are both very disturbed, very upset, poor dear things. Because of
the lawcourts. The city is full of gossip. (*Satirically*) Justice! Justice! *Justitia fondamentum regni* (*He breaks off, coughing and
gasping heavily.*)

BATA. Quite, my dear Croz, quite; the city is full, etc. etc. I don't quite
see the point in coming here to tell *us* that; *we* can't shut the
mouths of several million scandal-mongers. The only thing to do
is to wait till they are tired of this subject and have found another. I don't see . . . (*He breaks off, under* CROZ's *stare.*)

CROZ. You very rarely do see. Anything. The Minister and the High
President have issued orders for an inquiry.

(*A silence.*)

BATA (*faintly*). An inquiry?

CROZ. I think that's what I said. (*Teasing*) But come, come, bless my
soul, we mustn't let it frighten us.

MAVERI. We are not frightened, as a matter of fact.

CROZ. Good, good. It's nothing very serious, just a little something among ourselves. A little look round, that's all, a few inquiries, clear things up . . . That's all.

BATA (*warmly*). And naturally we all agree very heartily. We shall all be very glad to put our modest talents at the public disposal in order to . . . to investigate the matter and find out what's wrong. (*Murmurs of assent.*)

CROZ. Perhaps I didn't make myself clear. It is not ourselves who have to do the investigating.

BATA. No?

CROZ. No. Others will be doing the investigating.

BATA. But what about us?

CROZ. Well, we, if I might so put it, are the ones who have to be investigated. Which is slightly different.

(*A silence.*)

PERSIUS (*bitterly*). I would like to know why respectable magistrates, after years and years of irreproachable service—I myself have been on the bench for twenty years—I'd like to know why we have to submit to—

CROZ. You are an ass, Persius! What about me? I'm on the eve of promotion. I've set great store by the thought of being buried with a President's cap on my head—always supposing of course that dear old brother Cust doesn't pop in ahead of me—eh, Cust? What do *you* think about all this nonsense? It *would* have to happen just now, of course, and endanger my promotion . . . My dear Persius, we are *all* respectable and irreproachable. I thought I'd made it quite, quite clear: all we have to do is to look into the matter, among ourselves. The magistrate who will carry out the inquiry is a friendly colleague of ours . . . (*He points to the* STRANGER, *who has risen.*) Councillor Erzi, from the Upper House; he himself was saying to me only a moment ago . . .

ERZI (*with great courtesy*). Yes, all we need is a certain amount of discussion, in strict confidence, as between friends. My only reason for coming was to exchange a few preliminary words with you . . . and to shake hands with you all.

BATA (*advancing with hand outstretched*). But of course, of course. My dear Erzi, I am so glad to meet you.

PERSIUS (*following suit, together with the others*). Welcome into our midst!

MAVERI. My dear Erzi! I've heard a good deal about you. Surely we've met before somewhere?

BATA. Yes, you can understand, my dear friend, that we're the first people, the very first, to want to see the whole thing . . .

PERSIUS. . . . floodlit!

BATA. In strict confidence—that was your own expression—would you like to know my own humble opinion?

ERZI. That is what I'm here for.

BATA (*pompously, to the others*). We have to be quite frank about all this. The time for circumlocution is over. My dear Erzi, we're far from trying to pretend that there hasn't been a considerable amount of confusion piling up in these courts.

CUST. It's slackness, more than anything else; people have been a bit too easy-going.

PERSIUS. A bit too casual, too broad-minded perhaps. One can be too broad-minded, you know.

BATA. One might go even further, I think, and admit that there's been a certain lack of moral earnestness, a certain tolerance towards rogues.

CUST. The law courts have become almost a rogues' paradise.

MAVERI. There are certain forms of tolerance I'm afraid I've always disapproved of.

PERSIUS. Oh, we all have. We've all disapproved of them.

BATA. One might put it like this, I think: it is as if in this immense ramification of corridors and offices and stairs and—and so forth —it's as if there were odd nooks and corners here and there which have never been properly lit; and piles of dirt and dust and whatnot have accumulated in them. But who are the people scratching about in the middle of it all? Doormen, clerks, pen-pushers and other fusty old rubbish—

PERSIUS. The main trouble about this place is that out of every hole—

MAVERI. —an army of gnawing rats comes tumbling . . .

BATA. I'd be inclined to say myself that the whole thing has nothing to do with the magistrates at all.

ERZI. The Minister's opinion is that the staleness and poisonous air you speak of have actually produced something rather more: it might be called a poisonous plant.

(*A silence.*)

BATA. I see. But think of ourselves for a moment: there are many hundreds of us here, all flapping our black gowns about the place and groaning out our prayers. It would be a little unnatural if so vast a monastery didn't harbor at least one or two wicked or negligent brethren.

ERZI. It is not about negligent brethren that the Minister is concerned. He is convinced that under one of the flapping gowns you speak of, securely hidden away, there must be somewhere a little red pustule of leprosy. Corruption.

BATA. Corruption?

ERZI. It is a leper we're looking for.

BATA. And why . . . why do you begin looking for your lepers in here, pray?

ERZI. You must regard that as an honor. Isn't this the division reserved for Major Causes?

CROZ. Hahaha! It's been a real pleasure to listen to you. What elegant conceits, what metaphors! I'm crazy about that sort of thing; I even try my hand at it myself sometimes. But the one you should really hear is Cust, he's an absolute artist. He's being very quiet today for some reason. I always think eloquence of expression adds so much to a magistrate—it's the sign of a highly developed brain, I think one can say. Well, perhaps you'll listen to a few of my own little similes? Do you know, my dear Erzi, what we poor devils really are?—we judges, in this division—yes, yes, I know, the division for Major Causes. But each of us, every single one, is a little, lonely, insecure rock on which from every direction tremendous waves keep breaking; frightful; great foaming mountains. And those waves are the implacable interests, the boundless wealth, the iron blocks manipulated by dreadfully powerful men: genuine wild forces, whose blows—unhappily for us—are something savage, irresistible, ferocious . . .

ERZI (*completing*). . . . a species of telluric phenomenon.

CROZ. Telluric: exactly. Telluric.

ERZI. And it's very difficult to teach that phenomenon good manners.

CROZ. You take the words right out of my mouth. I'd like to see how the Minister would get on in our place.

ERZI. The pity of it is that amidst these iron blocks a fair number of very fragile shells are also tossed about on the waters; and they very easily get dashed to pieces. Take the case, for example, the day before yesterday, of that prostitute in Panama Street: a little smoke and burnt paper were sufficient to send her to her Maker. Was it not this division that had decided in complete secrecy to raid the house in Panama Street and confiscate certain documents?

CROZ. Yes.

ERZI. But when the police arrived, the place had been blazing for a good ten minutes; so had the documents, and so, unfortunately, had a harmless caretaker. The papers are still screaming about it.

CROZ. Do you mean—?

ERZI. I mean that someone from here had warned the interested parties. (*Pause.*) That is only one case among many: but it sums up the situation.

(*A silence.*)

CROZ. Someone from here? One of us?

ERZI. One of you.

CROZ (*laughing loudly*). My dear friends. Just let's all take a close look at each other, shall we? You, for example, Bata: you have a look at me, while I of course have a look at you, eh? Can it be possible that not a tiny bead of sweat, not a single movement of the Adam's apple, not the slightest, smallest sign . . . should betray our ailing comrade? Our leper I mean. It could be myself; it could be you, Maveri; you've gone quite white. Or you, Cust.

CUST. No, no, Croz. That's not quite the way things work. There's an error in psychology there. If it were anybody, it would be the innocent man—if he had any imagination: he'd be the one who started to sweat, etc. Feel. (*He holds out his hand.*)

CROZ (*touching it*). Cold and clammy.

CUST. Yes. Once when I was a boy staying with friends, someone came and said a watch was missing. I . . . fainted.

CROZ. So you're the one with the imagination?

CUST. Obviously. And quite apart from that, I'd like to point out— simply in the interests of accuracy—that it isn't quite exact to say: one of us. It isn't true that *all* the men who took part in the decision you mentioned are here at this moment. Now, I don't want this to be taken as an insinuation, mind you. I am, after all, a referendary judge, and because of that I am always in very close contact with President Vanan; and no one knows better than I how completely above suspicion he is. I'm only saying this in order that we may maintain a certain precision, a certain strictness of method: President Vanan also took part in that decision. And he is not here at the moment.

CROZ (*pointing to* CUST *and speaking to* ERZI). Cust. A very fine brain. My great enemy, my rival as successor to Vanan. A most worthy character; and gnawed by the most infernal ambition. We've hated each other from the minute we met.

CUST. That isn't true as far as I am concerned.

CROZ. Old humbug. He's like one of those iron safes. Absolutely impregnable.

BATA. Well, since Vanan's name's been mentioned—and as colleague Erzi has invited us to make a full and friendly disclosure . . . and also . . . out of a real wish for sincerity, mind you, and since all this will remain strictly among ourselves . . .

PERSIUS (*slightly hysterical*). Get *on!* Don't you see we've all got to defend ourselves!

BATA. I consider it my duty to state . . . at all events, it seems to me an affectation to deny that the responsibility for the disorder here,

the . . . uneasiness we were talking of earlier, does, unfortunately, lie largely—well, not largely perhaps but partly—with the
great Vanan himself.

CROZ (*to* ERZI). You don't know the great Vanan?

ERZI. No.

CROZ. He has been a great man in his time; a very handsome one too.
Very fond of the women. Well, well. It's horrible to grow old.

BATA. Like Cust, I would be very ashamed indeed to suggest that the
great Vanan . . . had let himself be corrupted or bought up by
Ludvi-Pol, or by anyone else for that matter. But he has great
weaknesses: that I'm bound to say.

MAVERI. There are certain jobs he is no longer fitted for. He seems
somehow . . .

BATA. . . . finished. That's the word, if the truth must be told.

MAVERI. One of those old wooden beams that if you go like that to
them, your finger goes in.

BATA. Rotten.

CROZ. And terrific with the women, you understand? He himself must
know where his strength's gone to, at any rate.

MAVERI. And it's still the same. Even now! One gathers that's the reason for his rapid disintegration, as you might call it. Poor old
thing, it's very sad and terrible. He's been seen in the most frightful places.

BATA. In fact, when you talk to President Vanan, it's difficult to be sure
if he really knows what he's saying and doing any longer. A thousand pities. A thousand pities.

MAVERI. These last few months, I almost think you could tell from the
way he talks and moves about . . . well, he's in the final stages.
It's become pathological by now.

CROZ (*to* MAVERI). It's simply this, my dear fellow: he keeps himself
going with drink. (*He laughs and coughs.*)

BATA. Naturally, I must repeat that I'm not saying I . . . believe that
Vanan himself is the one . . . the man . . .

PERSIUS (*suddenly and brutally*). My dear colleagues, does this really
seem to you the moment for delicacy? Do you understand or don't
you, what a hell of a position we're in?

MAVERI (*supporting him*). The whole city's waiting. It wants somebody's head.

PERSIUS. It's a matter of life and death. Do we want to ruin ourselves,
just for Vanan's sweet sake? Don't you think it's about time we
all spoke out?

ERZI. Well?

PERSIUS. Look: if there was one man in this place who was absolutely *made* to be swallowed up by Ludvi-Pol, it was Vanan. If there was one man . . .

CUST (*interrupting*). One man. And why only one man? There's not the slightest evidence to show that our leper stands alone. We might all be infected. We might all have sold our souls to the devil, that is, to Ludvi-Pol.

CROZ. Perfect. Clever old Cust. (*To* ERZI) Logic goes to old Cust's head at times, like drink. He's gleaming with sweat!

(*He breaks off. Some one has knocked on the door leading to the corridor. They all turn. A gloomy-looking stranger, possibly a POLICE OFFICER, comes in, and goes and speaks privately to ERZI. ERZI listen to him, then signs to him to wait, and stands for a moment, lost in thought.*)

ERZI. It's very unfortunate Vanan isn't here. Do you know where he could be found?

CUST. As a matter of fact, it's been rather difficult lately to know where you will or won't find Vanan. His habits have become rather uncertain.

ERZI. You've been very close to him?

CUST. Yes.

ERZI. Would you say that what we've heard about Vanan in here this morning is more or less the truth?

CUST (*after a silence*). You put me in rather an embarrassing position; Vanan and I were fond of each other. There has perhaps been a certain amount of exaggeration.

ERZI. Go on.

CUST. The scale of human duties has become a little confused in Vanan's mind. He's been sentencing people far too long. That can be rather dangerous after a time.

ERZI. Is there anything else?

CUST (*after a silence, looking down*). Yes.

ERZI. Go on.

CUST. Vanan did know Ludvi-Pol. They had dealings. (*A silence.*) It's painful, for me, to speak of it. I think . . . I had the impression that Ludvi-Pol had passed a certain sum of money to President Vanan. (*His voice is low and calm.*) But look, Erzi, if what you said is true, surely Ludvi-Pol himself is the one who could give you the name you're after—or names, as the case may be. Don't you think he'd talk?

ERZI. No. I don't.

BATA. Yes, but surely Ludvi-Pol's papers would talk!

CROZ (*laughing*). Do you think he's such a fool as to have put these things down on paper?

CUST. No, but perhaps under prolonged expert interrogation—

ERZI. No. We shan't get anything out of Ludvi-Pol.

CUST. Why not?

ERZI. Because he's dead. (*A silence.*) His body was discovered by accident in the early hours of this morning; do any of you know where?

CROZ. Where?

ERZI. Here. In this building, in a place where Ludvi-Pol had no reason whatever to be, least of all at night. He's lying there now.

CUST. So he was another fragile shell.

ERZI. It was suicide.

CUST. Are they sure of that?

ERZI. Yes.

CUST (*almost imperceptibly excited*). Forgive me, but that too could be a put-up job. The person you're looking for had a great interest in seeing that Ludvi-Pol kept his mouth shut, hadn't he? That person must be feeling very relieved at this moment. In any case, this Ludvi-Pol was a very contemptible creature, his death sentence is hardly likely to arouse much protest in the tribunal of any human soul I can think of. Or . . . look: the very things put there purposely to suggest murder, even those could be the results of a put-up job. For what purpose? To put you off the trail. To implicate some innocent person. There are so many possibilities, one can go on multiplying them as one chooses . . . always supposing we attribute a certain amount of subtlety to the man you're looking for. I advise you not to disregard any of those threads.

ERZI. Suicide. (*Pause.*) Are there many people in the building at night?

CUST. Oh, you can see quite a number of windows lit up till a very late hour. Industrious officials, all anxious to get on, losing their sleep over their papers. I myself, as a matter of fact, was here very late last night. (*As though recalling something*) In fact . . . (*He breaks off.*)

ERZI. Go on.

CUST (*lower*). When I leave, I always have to go along the corridor that goes past the great Vanan's door. I may as well tell you the truth. As the corridor was in darkness . . . I saw a line of light under the door. I heard—(*He breaks off.*)

(MALGAI *enters excitedly: he clearly realizes what the situation is.*)

MALGAI. President Vanan.

(MALGAI *withdraws immediately. After a few moments* VANAN *appears; he is an old man, very tall and erect; his face is angry and inflamed, his hair like a mop of white cotton-wool; his tones are slightly stentorian. Sometimes he mutters to himself. He comes in, and looks round him.*)

VANAN. Quite. Quite . . . of course. Good morning to you all, my dear . . . friends. Here we are. (*To* BATA, *who is the nearest to him*) Good morning, Bata; of course, yes . . . Give me a what-is-it, a match. (*His words drop into a great silence; everyone has risen.*)

BATA (*backing away*). I don't think I have any.

VANAN. What's the matter? What's the matter? Sit down. You could . . . surely, surely have waited for me too. Eh? Eh? Cust, I'm talking to you. Absolutely. Good morning, Erzi, I'm glad to see you. (*Shouting*) Sit down! I'm perfectly aware of what's going on. You are here too, my clever Croz.

CROZ (*shrugging his shoulders*). Of course. What do you expect?

VANAN. Good. All of us. Absolutely. . . .

(*They are now all seated; only* VANAN *is standing.*)

ERZI (*with great courtesy*). Mr. President, we were just waiting for you. There is a little information we need, if you would be so very kind as to give it to us.

VANAN. Absolutely. I know perfectly well what's going on. Fantastic, isn't it? Absolutely disgraceful.

ERZI. Mr. President, I have no doubt that you are acquainted with a person who has in recent years been at the center of the biggest concerns in the city, and who has consequently also been involved here in a number of very important law suits. I mean Ludvi-Pol. (*A silence.*)

VANAN (*muttering*). No . . . not that man . . . no, certainly not. Never. Listen, Erzi; I never knew him.

ERZI. You have, however, judged many cases in which he was involved.

VANAN. But . . . my dear Erzi, how . . . how can you possibly ask . . . (*Suddenly roaring*) me, *me,* questions like this. It's fantastic . . . absolutely fantastic.

ERZI (*with extreme politeness*). There was nothing in my question that could possibly offend you.

VANAN. Eh? What? That man . . .

ERZI. Yes. It would appear that you know him. That has been confirmed by several people here. (*A silence.*)

VANAN. Private. Private. An absolutely private matter. Absolutely. (*Dropping his voice slightly*) In the lift. In the lift, Erzi, that's all! (*He laughs.*) In the lift in this building, that's all. What happens? A gentleman recognizes me and speaks to me. An acquaintance from long long ago, lost sight of. Boys . . . boys together, the family . . . ages ago, ages ago. In the lift. Ridiculous that I should have to . . . talk about that.

ERZI (*gently*). You received a sum of money from Ludvi-Pol?
(*A silence.*)

VANAN. (*His voice seems to diminish and he looks round him uncertainly.*) Croz . . . but why . . . why am I being asked all this? What's going on? Cust, you, say something. And the rest of you, you all know me, what do you think you're doing?
(*A silence.*)

ERZI (*quietly*). Certainly, we all know you, Mr. President. You can speak with perfect frankness.

VANAN. Quite, quite, my dear Erzi, quite. There's no reason for me to hide anything . . . it's simple. The whole thing is absolutely . . . simple. It seems that Ludvi-Pol was slightly in debt to us, to my family I mean . . . nothing important, old liabilities, I'd quite forgotten them. But he . . . he remembered. Perfectly. He was very determined . . . to pay them back. That's the truth, that's the truth, Erzi. Absolutely . . . ridiculous, isn't it? He remembered it all perfectly.

ERZI. And did you remember?

VANAN. Well, actually I . . . yes, vaguely.

ERZI. Was it a large amount? Was it at a time when you happened to be in need?

VANAN (*overcome with a kind of anguish*). I don't . . . I don't . . . why . . . Cust! It's all so unexpected, so sudden. Ludvi-Pol himself will surely explain all this to you, won't he? You'll only have to ask him, won't you? He will tell you everything.

ERZI. Were you in this building last night?

VANAN. I? In this building? (*Roaring*) But whatever do you . . . what does this mean . . . ?

ERZI. In your office, Mr. President: last night: were you alone?

VANAN. Absolutely. Absolutely. Alone. Absolutely.

ERZI. Cust.

CUST (*slowly approaching*). Yes. (*Affectionately, with regret*) I had to tell him, Vanan. Last night . . . possibly you don't remember now . . .

VANAN (*with some fury*). I? I don't remember? Shameful! Ridiculous! Absolutely grotesque! I don't remember, don't I? (*He breaks off; there is a moment of absolute silence; suddenly shouting and almost weeping*) Do you think I don't understand what . . . what

you're all trying to do? You're trying to drag me down . . . trying to accuse me . . . aren't you? I understand perfectly! You
blackguards! You filthy little pigmies! I'll crush you! I'll show
you! I'll bring . . . I'll bring the whole court down! I'll tell them
who's the guilty man, I'll tell them in the minutest detail! They
don't know me yet. They don't know who Vanan is! I'll tear them
to pieces, the whole lot of them. And after that . . . after . . .
(*He stands there for a moment with his arm raised, breathing
heavily: and then, as though his memory had suddenly given way,
he drops slowly across the table, his face in his hands. A silence.*)

ERZI (*politely, rising*). Gentlemen, thank you all very much; I shan't
need to take up any more of your time today. Though I shall
have to ask for a little of yours, Croz, in a short while; and
I also hope that you will all help me in the course of this inquiry.
At the moment I am being waited for elsewhere. (*Thoughtfully,
he turns to the police official who is still waiting.*) You. It's
about time they removed Ludvi-Pol's body. I don't suppose they
will be able to get it out of the building unnoticed. It's probably
too late for that now. All the same, try to keep it covered up, if
you possibly can, so that we shan't have to see his face in all the
newspapers tomorrow, streaked with blood, with his eyes closed.
He was a greatly respected man in his time. The city has all the
rest of him to trample on now; let's leave his body for the worms
alone—to whom all faces are the same. (*To the others*) Good
morning.

(*He goes out, followed by the official.* BATA, MAVERI, *and* PERSIUS,
*one after another, go out cautiously and almost on tiptoe, so as
not to attract the attention of* VANAN. CROZ *and* CUST *are standing at some distance from him.*)

CROZ (*observing his colleague*). What's the matter, Cust?

CUST (*looking at him before speaking*). This is going to require a certain amount of courage.

CROZ. What do you mean?

CUST (*drawing him away from* VANAN, *with a wan smile, and whispering*). Croz, have you ever been out hunting?

CROZ. No.

CUST. Neither have I, but I've often been told about it. Do you know
what it is the hunter always dreads most?

CROZ. No.

CUST. Finishing off the wounded quarry. Dying animals go on struggling; you have to take pity on them. Everyone'd be so very
obliged to them, if only they'd die by themselves. But no, they
struggle and fight for life; it's almost a point of honor with them.

They almost make the hunter feel angry with them, because they actually in the end force one to . . . (*Dropping his voice still lower*) smash their skulls in. It's horrible, isn't it? But it's something that has to be faced.

CROZ (*looking at* VANAN). Yes, yes, of course. The fool is going to ruin himself completely if he goes on like this. All those infantile lies! We shall have to . . . use a little persuasion.

CUST. It may not be difficult. A man who's just had a heavy blow on the head often behaves strangely docile. We are all of us fragile, but old men are like glass.

VANAN. (*Has risen: his words are threatening, but his voice has completely changed.*) Croz, Cust. Eh? What do you say about all this? Why don't you say something, you filthy traitors! (CUST and CROZ *look at him in silence.*) What are you thinking? Tell me what to do . . . don't stand there loking at me . . .

CUST (*quietly*). My dear Vanan, do you know who it is *you* must talk to, now? Yourself.

VANAN. Myself?

CUST. Yes. You must explain to yourself the reason for all the lies you've been telling.

VANAN. Lies?

CUST. Lies, Vanan. What was the reason for them?

VANAN. Because . . . my God, actually . . . Cust, I was so confused . . .

CUST. Why were you confused? M'm? Reflect on that, my dear Vanan, and then you'll see for yourself the best way to go about things. Reflect on it, at great length.

VANAN. But oh, my God, I'm . . . an old man now.

CUST. Why ever did you deny that you talked to Ludvi-Pol last night?

VANAN. Cust, I swear to you . . . that man had come simply to plead with me . . . he thought I could still save him . . . he was a fool, a madman . . .

CUST. But why did he come to you? First he asked something from you; and then he asked something else, from death. You were the last door but one he knocked at. Why?

VANAN (*shouting*). I don't know, Cust! I don't know!

CUST. And why are you so frightened, even now? (*Very quietly*) Oh no, Vanan, it's all too evident that your conscience is not untroubled. There is a doubt, in your conscience. They're saying that in this fine building of ours there is something rotten. But if you reflect on what you have been doing in here, yesterday, and every other day of your life, are you certain, quite certain, that you will be saved? What I advise you to do, my dear Vanan, is to make a long and minute examination of your conscience. Explore yourself, scrutinize yourself, go to bed with your doubt, carry it about with you by day. And only when one of the two, either you or it, has won, only then, and not before, must you come back here.

VANAN. Cust, what do you mean?

CUST. But of course, Vanan. You wouldn't want to insist on remaining here, in the courts, struggling, threatening, telling more bungling lies.

VANAN. You mean I ought to go away? Now?

CUST. For a few days.

VANAN. Never, never, never. I won't move from here, I'll defy them.

CUST. Good. And let them be even more vindictive against you in their inquiries, and lay more traps for you to fall into.

VANAN. No, Cust, I can't do it. To go away now would be . . .

CUST. . . . to put the matter in the hands of a very great doctor: time. Besides, would you really have the strength to face, day after day, the looks of contempt, the rudeness, the innuendoes? The very porters, the very walls are cruel to anyone who has fallen.

VANAN. My God.

CUST. Just be clever; let your enemies have a little rope. The important thing is simply to get through these next few days of suspicion and anger, and noise. Admit to some little thing or other, so as to give the fools, who are shouting so loudly, the illusion of victory. Throw a piece of flesh to the wolves who are following you . . .

VANAN. My God.

CUST. And very soon they'll all be thinking of something else; what you should do now is . . . (*He pauses.*)

VANAN. What?

CUST. My belief is that you ought to send the Investigating Councillor a note today; without saying too much, without giving your hand away; just telling him simply that in view of what has happened you don't feel that you ought, for the present—for the present— to remain in the building. For the present. Instead . . . (*He pauses again.*)

VANAN. . . . instead . . .

CUST. Very quietly, very very quietly, just stay at home and think. Reflect. And in the meantime do you know what you can do as well? On your own account, silently. You can write.

VANAN. Write what?

CUST. A full statement, in which you explain everything. Just pass the time doing that. For the present.

VANAN. For the present. . . .

CUST. The important thing is the little note; and you must hurry: the note must arrive before they can decide anything disagreeable. It will restrain them. Write it now, straight away. (*Pointing to a desk*) There.

VANAN. Cust, I don't want . . . Croz, what do you think?

CUST. Listen, Vanan, I've given you a piece of advice. I've probably gone too far in doing so.

VANAN (*suddenly pleading*). But, of course, I know, I am grateful, you must forgive me. And you too, Croz. Actually . . . you must understand my . . . (*He is gradually approaching the desk.*) Yes, Cust, there's a good deal of sense in what you say. A full . . . precise statement, absolutely! Absolutely. And now, a note: yes, I must write it now. You know, Cust: you've been the only . . . (*Almost weeping*) I've no friends: I've always been too proud. And now they'll all . . . be delighted, they all want to humiliate me. They've all become suddenly . . . wicked, treacherous. . . . (*He is fumbling at the desk; suddenly he breaks off, and listens intently; runs to the door, listens; and turns back to the other two men, his eyes widening in real fear.*) She's talking to the porter! My God! Look; the only person I have in the world will be here in a minute! I beg you by whatever you hold most dear . . . (*Trying to control himself*) Listen: it's my daughter. You don't know her. There's always been just the two of us; her mother died. She thinks I'm almost a king in here, she wouldn't understand anything of what's happened. I beg you, I beseech you not to let her suspect anything: pretend nothing has happened. It's a great favor. (*Changing his tone, speaking towards the door, which has just opened*) Yes, Elena. Come in, my dear. I'm glad you stopped in, we can go home together. (*A radiant young girl, and at the moment looking rather surprised, is in the doorway. She comes shyly into the room. Breathlessly, to his two colleagues*) This is my daughter. Elena. Fancy, she's never been here before. (ELENA *smiles at the two judges. Stammering, and fumbling about on the desk*) Elena, these are two very clever . . . friends of mine who . . . are very fond of me, in spite of the fact that your father is the most exacting president there could possibly be. Yes, certainly . . . I'm an absolute . . . tyrant. Absolutely, quite, quite. (*Fumbling confusedly on the desk*) Forgive me, Elena, I'm coming at once, I just have to finish a . . . a note; I'll finish it at once, my dear Cust. Tell me, Elena: I wonder whether you heard me in the corridor? I'm always shouting, I get angry over nothing, because . . . because everything falls

on my shoulders, do you understand? The President. I'm the
President. It's an honor, but it's also . . . a terrible responsibility.
(*He is already scribbling; there is a silence.* ELENA, *like someone
in very great awe, smiles again at the two judges, who look at
her attentively.* VANAN *has finished. He goes over in silence to*
CUST, *and places the letter in his hand, and then goes over to
his daughter and lifts his hand, vaguely touching her hair, as if
he wished to smoothe it.* ELENA *takes his hand and kisses it.*
VANAN *looks at the two judges with a flicker of sudden pride;
slips his daughter's arm beneath his own, nods good-by, and
goes out, very upright, in silence.* CROZ *and* CUST *stand there for
a moment as though lost in thought.* CROZ *gives a long glance at
his companion, and then goes out, leaning heavily on his cane,
without speaking.* CUST, *after his departure, goes slowly across to
a desk, sits at it, and suddenly seems overcome by a genuine
prostration; he remains for a little while thus: with his head in his
hands.* MALGAI *enters and begins to put the room in order.*)

MALGAI (*at the door*). Please sir, may I . . . ?

CUST (*without raising his head*). Yes.

MALGAI (*as he tidies up*). That was the President's daughter, wasn't it,
sir?

CUST (*as before*). Yes.

MALGAI. A pretty girl. She's quite grown up . . . quite a young lady.

CUST (*as before*). Yes. (*He looks up.*) She reminded me of something.

MALGAI. Sir, you're not looking very well.

CUST. I'm just tired, that's all. I feel rather upset. (*He pretends to
unfold a roll of documents, and begins to hum to himself; thinking, quietly.*) My God, how horrible everything is. What a wasted
life. Judge Cust. (*He hums again, and thinks idly.*) Yes, the girl
reminded me of something. There was something about her. (*Lost
in thought, as he goes on*) Attilio, do you know who Vanan's
daughter looked like? She looked like the figure on a box, a tin
box we once had at home when I was a boy; a woman with
flowing hair . . . and a crown . . . She was lifting a glass, it
was an advertisement for something. I used to be tremendously
fond of her. Tremendously. She looked like Vanan's daughter.

MALGAI (*as he goes out*). Ah, Mr. Cust, sir . . . When I was a boy,
I used to . . . (*He smiles.*) Oh, dear, the things that went through
one's mind! Well, well . . . (*He goes.*)

CUST (*almost singing the word*). Tremendously. Tremendously. (*He
begins to hum again; then, thinking*) I might very well have had
a daughter like that. "Elena, let's go out for a little shall we? Dear
Elena." Judge Cust and his daughter . . . (*Hums.*) Or else my

wife. "Come on, Elena, let's go home, shall we?" Judge Cust and his wife . . . (*Hums.*) Or my mother perhaps. I am a tiny little frog. She gives me milk. A young beloved mother, very young. (*He rises slowly to his feet.* ERZI *and* CROZ *have come in, and are walking across the room.* CUST *stares at them fixedly; just as they are about to go out, he calls*) Councillor Erzi!
(ERZI *and* CROZ *stop.*)

CUST. How's it going?

ERZI. What?

CUST. The inquiry.

ERZI. Are you interested in it?

CUST. Can't stop thinking about it.

ERZI (*dropping his voice a little*). Cust, was there something you wanted to say to me?

CUST. I? I only wanted to tell you that . . . if I can help you at all . . . in any humble way . . . I'd of course be very pleased.

ERZI. Have you had any ideas?

CUST. Any ideas? Any ideas. (*He looks at* ERZI *for a moment, and then hands* VANAN'S *letter to him.*) All the same, it would be a good thing, wouldn't it, if President Vanan were innocent, and the leper was somebody else.

ERZI. (*Has glanced at the letter, and now turns and stares at* CUST.) Do you think so?

CUST (*sighs*). I'm just thinking. I wonder if it wouldn't after all be a good thing to abandon the inquiry . . .

ERZI. And who's suggested that we intend to abandon it? No. It will be pursued. Right to the end. And you will help me.
(*He shakes* CUST'S *hand warmly, and goes out with* CROZ. CUST *stands looking after him.*)

Curtain

ACT TWO

Several days have passed. On one side of the stage, bored and impersonal, stands the gloomy POLICE OFFICER. BATA *and* PERSIUS, *wearing hats and overcoats, are wandering furtively about, rather as if they were spying. They meet, rapidly whisper something together, and part again with assumed indifference, as the door from the corridor opens.*

CUST *enters slowly.* BATA *and* PERSIUS, *torn between curiosity and*

*the fear of compromising themselves by starting a conversation,
make cautious nods of greeting towards him: prudence prevails
however; and nodding once more to* CUST, *they both slip towards
the door; here they throw a further long glance at him; and
disappear.*

CUST *has followed them with his eyes. He hesitates; at last he
removes his hat and overcoat, and approaches the* POLICE OFFICER.

CUST. I am Judge Cust. Councillor Erzi has sent for me. I don't know
what he wants. Would you mind telling him I'm here?
(*The officer nods and goes out. After a few moments a door opens
and* ERZI *enters.*)

ERZI. Ah thank you, my dear Cust, thank you; how good of you to
come. Sit down. Well, now. It's always a pleasure to talk with a
colleague like yourself. You've no idea, I suppose, why I asked
you if you'd mind coming?

CUST. No.

ERZI (*after a pause*). Did it really never occur to you to wonder?

CUST. No.

ERZI. Well . . . you did, after all, make me a promise. Yes, I asked
you to help me in my investigation. I was greatly impressed by
the acuteness of some of your observations. So I've always been
expecting to see you. But you've been in very seldom, and then
only fleetingly. I've been rather surprised at that.

CUST. I never thought you'd seriously need me.

ERZI. I needed someone who'd been breathing the air of this place for
a long time. Besides, you're expecting a promotion which will
be almost the goal of your whole career. It is in your own interest
that this mess should be cleared up.

CUST. I'm not the only one with such an interest.

ERZI. Quite so. But Judge Croz will also be here in a short time. So
will some of the others. (*A short pause; he smiles.*) My dear Cust,
this evening I am expected to present my conclusions. The whole
city is holding its breath. But before I go, as I shall do shortly, up
to the office of the Lord High Chancellor, I wanted to call a
few friends together again in here, and test the evidence once more.

CUST. I thought that the inquiry had already uncovered a great many
facts and implicated a great number of people.

ERZI. Yes. But in the end everything must center on one particular fact.
There must have been a beginning somewhere.

CUST. Has the inquiry broken down on that point?

ERZI. I'm not at all satisfied in my mind.

CUST. You had your eye on Vanan, or so I thought?

ERZI. Yes. Everything would seem to point to Vanan . . . if it were not that one authoritative voice had spoken in his favor.
(CUST *does not break the silence.*)

ERZI. Yours. It was you who told me that Vanan might in fact be innocent. Your observation showed me two things: first, that you had your own opinions, and secondly, that I must regard you yourself as above suspicion. Though in theory I might have suspected you also.

CUST. Yes.

ERZI. But I rather imagine that a guilty person would take great care not to call an investigator back off a false trail . . . and run the risk of having him at his own heels.

CUST. Unless he did so in order to *make* himself above suspicion.

ERZI. Quite so.

CUST (*slowly*). You have in fact sent for me in order to know what I really think of this matter.

ERZI. Precisely.

CUST. I think that if your leper really exists, and if it's not Vanan, then you're going to find it difficult to catch him.

ERZI. Not impossible, however. And why should it be difficult?

CUST. Because the thread of facts, which might have led you to him, has been snapped. Ludvi-Pol is dead: the mouth that could have talked has been shut.

ERZI. Then you think that, at this very moment, somewhere in one of the many rooms in this vast building, there is a person in whom, by now, all fear has ceased.

CUST (*thoughtfully*). The rooms in this place are very quiet ones. Unhealthy-looking men sit in them; they have the faces of men who rarely see the sun. Over a period of many years, they have listened in silence to thousands of lies; they have examined human actions of the most extraordinary subtlety and wickedness. Their experience is immense. The people who have faced them across the table have seen merely a few polite, rather tired gentlemen. But in reality, especially among those who achieve very high office, there are wrestlers, dear colleague; despite the fact that their hardened veins burst so easily. As a rule they find it difficult to sleep at night. And as a result of that . . . (*He breaks off.*)

ERZI. Well?

CUST. As a result they have a great deal of time to brood over their thoughts. They're capable of listening very attentively; they're tough; and they are extremely careful.

ERZI. It would be difficult to catch them out, in that case.

CUST. Yes. And one of them is the man you're looking for.

ERZI. The leper.

CUST. Today that man is on the heights. The day you succeed in un-
masking him, he will stand for a moment dumbfounded; millions
of eyes will be on him; and then he will hurtle down into an abyss
of darkness.

ERZI. And then?

CUST. Then he will begin to defend himself, dear colleague. I believe
that his situation must give him a strange intoxicating feeling of
liberty.

ERZI (*looking hard at him*). I imagine that one evening, at a very
late hour, this man, this judge we're looking for, lifted his gaze
from his desk. The person who had come in was very polite, the
visit was a perfectly legitimate one. Then the conversation drifted,
important friendships, secret powers, attractive enticements flick-
ered about it . . . (CROZ *appears at the door of the clerk's office
and stands listening, unseen by the others. Continuing without
interruption*) . . . The cautious visitor was trying to grope his
way towards something already waiting there in the judge's mind:
something called ambition; or greed perhaps; or envy; or hate.
And at what exact point did that perfectly legitimate cordiality,
those vague promises, become something more? When did that
subtle bond between them become a leash, held in a master's
hand?

CUST (*sweating slightly*). Yes: I think it's a very likely reconstruction.

ERZI (*with a barely perceptible increase of urgency*). That is how this
judge of ours came to place an acute and powerful intelligence
at the disposal of a master, and in the service of injustice. He
falsified decisions, he betrayed secrets, and he changed human
destinies. He spread in here a trouble which rapidly defiled the
entire Courts of Justice; he drove the iron wheel of the law over
many innocent men and women. Even a murderer can sometimes
regard himself as an executioner. But our man was well aware
that he was falsifying the sacred scales of justice. For the sake
of what? Why?

CROZ (*from the back, interrupting unexpectedly*). Probably because
he'd begun to have his doubts.

ERZI (*turning*). About what?

CROZ. Oh, about the sacred scales and so forth. (*He laughs, coughs, and
goes on.*) The devil—Ludvi-Pol I mean—had come to get him
that night, but that was probably just what our man had wanted,
wasn't it, Cust! A judge is just like a priest in these matters:
after officiating all his life in front of the holy altar, he conceives

a terrible hatred of it and a great wish to see the devil himself appear in front of him for a change.

ERZI (*staring now at* CROZ). But hadn't so many years of being there made him wise, so many years of being outside the game?

CROZ (*bursts out laughing*). Outside the game? But one's never outside the game, my dear Erzi! My dear good fellow, just think for a minute of one of those nasty black insects, that sting. You excite one of them: and it stings. You cripple it: and it stings. You cut it in two: and it stings. You transfix it and smash its head in: and its sting goes on stinging, stinging, stinging. Just for nothing. That's what life is.

CUST (*pointing a finger towards* CROZ). A spite which amuses even the dying quarry. Doesn't it Croz?

ERZI (*suddenly turning to* CUST). But then, Cust, if the thread of facts is broken off, and if the person is so sure of himself, and so determined and cautious, why do you only say it will be *difficult* to find him, and not impossible? After all, that's what you said. What can possibly betray him?

CUST (*speaking first with his eyes lowered, and eventually lifting them towards his questioner*). This: that men are rather fragile; the very things that they themselves construct, their thoughts . . . their laws . . . their crimes . . . lie too heavy on their backs.

ERZI (*slightly urging him on*). You mean that the man who was guilty of this crime doesn't sleep very easily.

CUST. Yes.

ERZI. Why?

CUST. Because he thinks about it too much.

ERZI. Guilt?

CUST. No; he's beyond that.

ERZI. Why then?

CUST (*smiling and staring at him*). Because he doesn't want his little red spot to be discovered.

ERZI. Well?

CUST (*a little uneasily*). Well, with extraordinary subtlety and patience, he calculates; he imagines that the slightest break in his voice, the quickest glance, may have left here and there traces, imperceptible signs . . .

ERZI. . . . which someone may find, and follow up . . .

CUST. Yes, and which he, with supreme caution, takes care to baffle and disperse.

ERZI. In what way?

CUST. He hastens to meet every tiny possible suspicion, even before it's born; sometimes indeed he even prompts the suspicion; and then he stares hard at it, and baffles it, makes it unsure of itself, dazed, destroyed by its own vagueness.

CROZ (*with a loud laugh*). It's a big job, isn't it, Cust?

CUST. It is. If one's to discover the man, the secret is to *be* him.

ERZI. What do you mean?

CUST. . . . to feel that one *is* the man. (*His breathing thickens slightly.*) To feel the same chill here on the scalp, the same heavy pounding, not quite in the heart, but lower, almost in the belly. Boom . . . boom . . . boom . . . the same trembling at the knees . . . the same weariness. I hope you see what I mean?

ERZI. Perfectly. (*Very quietly*) Then what exactly are his feelings, when he hears that we are at his heels? Fear, wouldn't you say?

CUST. You're wrong.

ERZI. Doesn't he know he's being pursued?

CUST. He's not a fool.

ERZI. You mean it doesn't alarm him?

CUST. Certainly not.

ERZI. Well?

CUST. He manages to control himself.

ERZI. What does he do?

CUST. We pretend to be him; he pretends to be us. He assumes we have a quite supernatural foresight. He dare not make a mistake.

CROZ (*satirically*). It really is a big job.

CUST (*pointing a finger at* CROZ, *harshly and aggressively*). Above all, he has to keep beginning over and over again.

ERZI. Why?

CROZ (*staring at* CUST *in his turn*). Because our eyes are always on him, our suspicions are always pursuing him . . .

CUST (*counterattacking*). . . . and he goes on arranging and constructing defenses ever more subtle and ingenious. (*Laughing, rather harshly*) Today, for example, his hand . . . It occurred to me, watching your hand, Croz, lying idly there on the table . . . What I mean is that his hand, or even one finger of his hand, at the precise moment that someone utters the name of Ludvi-Pol . . . at that moment one finger of his hand . . . (*He is still pointing at* CROZ's *hand.*) causes a tiny slacking of control; he is affected: for barely a second . . .

CROZ (*nervously and jestingly moving his hand*). Like that?

CUST. Like that. And what a mistake to make. Just because someone was staring at it . . . as we are staring at yours. And suppose someone had noticed that coincidence? And had thought about it? Was that imperceptible movement a confession? Yes, it's *that*

that the guilty man thinks about all night long. And by daybreak:
he has made up his mind.

ERZI. What to do?

CUST. An experiment. He will go back and face the other person . . .
and name Ludvi-Pol again! And he'll put his hand there again,
in the same position . . just as Croz has done! And he'll repeat
that imperceptible movement! But what matters this time is that
the color of his cheeks, the sweat of his forehead, the sound of
his voice, everything shall be beyond question. His hand will feel
itself scorched by our look. He'd love to withdraw it . . .

CROZ. You describe it with great accuracy.

CUST. But he has to hold on. The moment has come . . . his heart
turns to marble . . . Like this . . . (*He holds his breath for a
moment, and then shakes himself and laughs.*) And then everything's all right, he can breathe again!

CROZ. A bit tired?

CUST (*with a wan smile*). Almost exhausted.

CROZ. Can I move my hand, now? These moments are rather over-
powering.

ERZI (*pointing his finger at* CUST). But it would be incautious of him
to rest for a moment, you said so yourself. . . .

CROZ (*also urgently*). There's not a moment that may not bring him
some fresh danger . . .

CUST (*suddenly, hoarsely, looking down*). I believe the real dangers
are inside himself.

ERZI. How?

CUST (*painfully, and as though bewildered*). He is at the end of his
tether. He longs to run away . . . To run away . . . To be dead
and buried. That's the most complete flight of all. But then . . .

ERZI. Go on.

CUST (*almost to himself*). Who would be left, to keep the thing snug
and warm, the crime I mean, the danger, who would watch over
it . . . ? Who would *live* it?

CROZ (*bending over him*). Do you know what I think, Cust, really? I
believe his real wish, his most terrible need, is to talk about it.
The whole thing. To talk about it. Am I right?

CUST (*bewildered and lost in thought*). Perhaps. He is alone. Everyone is a long way away from him. Alone. And so . . .

ERZI (*returning to a previous question, almost cruelly*). Guilt!

CUST (*as before*). No. Astonishment. He is amazed. Amazed to see
himself so busy, thinking and doing such strange, wild, ridiculous
things . . . but he's forced on to them by the chain of consequences.

ERZI. And doesn't he feel a certain alarm?

CUST (*whispering*). Yes . . . he has the feeling one sometimes has in dreams: when one whispers to oneself: "But this isn't true! It's not true! It's not true! . . . I shall wake up in a minute." (*He breaks off. Someone has knocked at the door leading to the corridor. They all turn. The door opens. The* POLICE OFFICER *appears in the doorway; he looks at* ERZI *with a slight lift of the eyebrows and immediately withdraws. Coming up to the surface again, and laughing cheerfully to* ERZI.) There are times when I even fear you suspect him. (*He points to* CROZ.) . . . or me!

ERZI (*also laughing*). Oh please, please! I'm just looking for help. Well, Cust, since you've penetrated so well into the psychology of our criminal, what would you say, now, are the moves which he expects us to make? What is the point that worries him, in the circle of his defense.

CUST. (*Is still looking at the doorway where the* OFFICIAL *appeared; he thinks for a moment; then he turns and points to the archives; almost shouting.*) The papers! That's where I advise you to attack him!

ERZI. Explain what you mean exactly.

CUST (*almost mildly*). We're dealing with a judge, aren't we? Very well then; think of the vast number of words he uses to sustain the arguments in his statements, in pronouncing sentence, in discussions. All those words are now slumbering in there. The archives. Every one of them was a weight thrown into the scales you spoke of: but a weight that had been falsified. The records in there, taken singly, page by page, would tell you nothing. But if you were to consider them all together, however tough and clever he had been, don't you feel there must be something there that is bound to betray him? The insistent recurrence of such and such an ambiguity or quibble: the flavor of corruption. That will be the flavor that will distinguish that judge's words from those of all the others. That is the one single thread. (*He points once more.*) The papers.

ERZI. My dear Cust, did you know that the record clerk was already outside in the corridor? It's just as though you'd been reading my thoughts. But you have gone deep down into them, thrown light on them. We are here to obey you, in a sense. But not only because of that, Cust. Your guilty man hasn't thought of everything.

CROZ (*raising his voice slightly*). Are you there, Malgai? Come in.

(*The door from the corridor opens and* MALGAI *appears. He crosses and opens the door of the archives, and goes inside.*)

ERZI. He calls it his graveyard. Well, we shall exhume from it whatever may be needed to put our man into our hands. (*Confidentially*) It seems, among other things, that Ludvi-Pol himself was in the habit of suggesting certain specific and characteristic arguments in his own favor. We shall discover them all in there, shan't we? But with another signature attached to them. Eh? What do you think, Cust?

CROZ. Do you think our leper will be able to escape us?

CUST. It won't be easy. (*Suddenly, almost frightened, pointing towards the corridor*) But who's that who's come as well? There was someone else besides the record clerk . . . I thought I heard . . .

ERZI. It's another of the people I needed to have here. (*Turning towards the corridor*) Come in, come in, Vanan. We were expecting you. (VANAN *enters. They look at him in surprise. He is extraordinarily wasted, and even shrunk in size. His daughter accompanies him, and almost pushes him forward as though he were a naughty child. She makes him advance to the middle of the room.*)

CROZ. Compassionate Antigone, gentle Cordelia, your father is among friends now, and doesn't need you any more. (ELENA *is about to speak.*)

ERZI (*preventing her*). You may leave us. You would not be of any help to him. (ELENA *strokes her father's arm, and goes out.*)

CROZ (*with cruel gaiety as soon as the door is shut*). By God, Vanan, I believe you've actually shrunk. What's happened to you? I never thought you were so soft.

VANAN. Eh . . .

CROZ. You've crumpled right up, Vanan. It would be damned funny if you went before I did, wouldn't it? Now, you've got to listen to something. Our colleague Erzi, as you no doubt know, has a number of things to say to you.

ERZI (*in severe tones*). Mr. President Vanan! The High Council had allowed you a deferment; that deferment is up today. You have been summoned here today to make your final statement. You promised to prepare your defense.

VANAN (*uncertainly*). I . . . yes . . . yes, sir.

ERZI. Have you done so? (*A silence.*)

CROZ (*mutters*). You even seem to have lost the power of speech.

ERZI. A number of very grave charges are being made against you. You declared that you could disprove and demolish them. How? (*A silence.*)

CROZ. He's lost his tongue.

ERZI (*his voice becoming steadily more stern as he speaks*). Above all, you declared that if you were to reconsider certain remarks made by Ludvi-Pol, you would find yourself in a position to reveal the real criminal. Well? Vanan, who is it? (*A silence.*) Tell us the name, Vanan! (*A silence; he turns away and resumes his seat.*) Either from you, or in some other way, we shall know that name today. (*To the others*) But perhaps this silence is itself an answer. Vanan, am I to assume that you are acknowledging yourself guilty? Is it true then? Is it you who are responsible for the fraud that has poisoned this bench, this whole building, and the city itself?

CUST (*hoarsely*). Do speak, Vanan; speak out.

VANAN (*stammering, pleading, and oddly false in tone*). I must . . . express my thanks.

ERZI (*surprised*). What?

VANAN (*as before*). I have to say . . . that actually . . . the Administration has treated me . . . with very great kindness . . . (*agitated*) so that I have nothing to complain of.

ERZI (*surprised*). What are you talking about, Vanan?

VANAN (*as before*). As an old . . . magistrate, I feel . . . it's my duty to express my . . . to kiss . . . the generous hand . . .

ERZI (*suddenly shouting*). What do you mean, Vanan!

VANAN (*rather frightened*). No, don't do that . . . Of course . . . I'm very old, and . . . sick now, as you know.

ERZI (*quickly*). Vanan, are you admitting that you are guilty?

VANAN. (*Looks at him suspiciously; suddenly in a false oratorical voice*) I am innocent, sir! Innocent and falsely accused. Nailed to the cross . . . like our innocent Savior . . . Gentlemen, these gray hairs have been . . . trampled on . . .

ERZI. Vanan, who is the guilty man?

VANAN (*as before*). Oh, yes, sir, yes. There is, there *is* a guilty man. I swear before . . . before God's throne that someone is guilty! And I . . . and I can unmask him . . . The wicked shall be hurled to the dust . . . (*Suddenly becoming once more pitiful and pleading*) I am innocent, sir, innocent. . . .

ERZI (*sadly*). Vanan, what has happened to you? You don't seem like the same man.

VANAN (*in the tones of a beggar*). Sir . . . you must intercede . . . for this poor unfortunate judge . . . I don't deserve such . . . severity. (*With sincerity, almost whispering*) I only want . . . a little quiet. Nothing else.

(*A silence.*)

ERZI (*thoughtfully*). My dear Croz, although the whole thing is really quite clear, it is rather disturbing when one thinks how fragile and delicate the human organism is. Man is far more perishable than even the most trivial object shaped by his own hands. Our colleague is indeed much changed.

CROZ (*giggling*). He'll be even more changed before long.

ERZI. But those cunning papers which he—and the others—blackened with their hurrying pens, those, we shall now find, though they're dead and buried, will be more alive than he is. (*Raising his voice, to* VANAN) They will tell us the things which you wouldn't or couldn't tell us. You will wait for us here. (*To the others*) Shall we go?

(ERZI *goes across to the archives and enters.* CROZ *follows him.* CUST *and* VANAN *remain behind.*)

VANAN (*uneasily, his voice and attitude changing somewhat*). What are they going to do? Why . . . did they tell me to wait for them? I hate those two, I don't trust them. Cust . . . (*He sees* CUST'S *face.*) Cust! For God's sake, what's the matter with you?

CUST (*approaching him*). Listen, Vanan. I am here to help you, I want you to trust me! It rather looks to me as if you're not being sincere in all this. Or am I wrong? Eh? (*He wipes his brow.*) Listen, Vanan, is it really true that you . . . have been reconsidering . . . certain remarks made by poor Ludvi-Pol . . . Is it true that you have actually discovered the man . . . we're looking for?

VANAN (*moans*). I don't remember anything any more . . .

CUST (*dropping his voice*). But I remember advising you to write a detailed, exact statement. . . .

VANAN. I . . . I . . . what?

CUST (*harshly*). A statement.

VANAN (*moans*). No, no . . .

CUST (*urgently*). Where is it?

VANAN. But I . . .

CUST. Have you written it?

VANAN. No . . . No . . . I couldn't do it. I only want . . . I don't want them to hurt me.

(*A silence.*)

CUST (*with sudden fierceness*). My God, it's almost comic to think you can let yourself be buried so willingly. It's unnatural. (*Urgently and whispering*) What's happened, Vanan? What is it? Tell me.

VANAN (*suddenly whispering*). Cust, I'll tell you the truth. I'm tired.

CUST. What of?

VANAN. The whole thing. You told me to think about it.

CUST. Well?

VANAN. People were cross with me, because I always kept saying the same things.

CUST. Well?

VANAN. Well, actually . . . I began to think about it by myself, at night.

CUST. Good. Well?

VANAN. The trouble was that I was alone; everyone believed that things had happened . . . that other way; and so—Cust, have you ever been bathing in a river, and suddenly seen the water all running the other way? You stand there, still, alone, by yourself, in the middle of the flowing water . . . and you feel a sort of giddiness . . . It was like that; I began to . . .

CUST. Yes?

VANAN. I began to feel weighed down, Cust, disheartened. There were times when I spoke out loud, all by myself, boldly, saying I was innocent . . . but even my own voice hadn't any conviction in it any longer . . . (*Suddenly*) Do you know what it was? (*Whispering*) I almost stopped believing in it myself.

CUST. In what?

VANAN. I stopped believing in it. I admit there may have been some little things, when I've been taking evidence, that I may have modified a little . . . Perhaps I've been responsible for a certain amount of confusion . . . I don't know: I may even have been a bit at fault myself; they all say so . . . (*Suddenly pointing towards the corridor*) You know, Cust. *She's* my principal torment.

CUST. Who?

VANAN (*still pointing*). My daughter. It's she who drives me on.

CUST. What do you mean?

VANAN. Oh, yes, yes. She's become so naughty. She never leaves me in peace. Sometimes I pretend to be asleep, or feel unwell. But she has no pity, none at all.

CUST. Your daughter?

VANAN. Yes, yes.

CUST. What does she want you to do?

VANAN. She wants me . . . to . . . to write . . . to accuse somebody. She knows I'm innocent, so she wants me to make them listen to me . . . But I'm old, Cust, I'm tired . . . And now everyone here is so rude and insolent to me the whole time. She can't understand that. She can't see that to insist on speaking out only means getting into worse trouble!

CUST. Was it she who brought you here?

VANAN. It was, yes. (*He laughs.*) You can't think how furious she must have been when they sent her away. She's out there now, waiting for me. But do you know what I'm going to do? I shall go out that way, through the clerk's office. (*Suddenly pushing* CUST *aside, with a loud cry and a strange unexpected energy*) I hate all this! I hate you too, Cust. I could kill you. (*Moving almost solemnly towards the office door*) Let me go away. I don't want to think about these things any more. (ELENA *slips in through the corridor door. She makes a sign to* CUST *not to say anything. In a completely different voice, stopping*) Listen, Cust, I know I keep going about shouting that I am innocent, like Our Lord on the Cross; but suppose that was just a bit of hypocrisy? and suppose the Lord chastised me? (*Vaguely*) A man needs peace, he can't stand against the whole world . . . sometimes I tell my daughter that I'm coming to the courts, but I actually go to a little public garden I know in the town, and just sit there a little. That's where I go. Goodbye, my dear Cust. Goodbye.

(*He moves towards the door of the clerk's office: there he nods goodbye to* CUST, *and disappears;* CUST *and* ELENA *remain alone.*)

ELENA. I'm his daughter.

CUST. I know.

ELENA (*in distress*). He hasn't anyone else in the world. Neither have I. Don't you think it's sad he should run away from me like that? And silly that I should run after him?

CUST. It's never easy to understand what goes on inside us.

ELENA. Are you in charge of the inquiry?

CUST. Is there something you want to say?

ELENA. Yes, I came specially.

CUST. Well, you can speak. Is it about the inquiry?

ELENA. Yes. It's important, and private.

CUST. You'll have to be quick then. A decision has to be reached this evening.

ELENA. Sir, what my father told you wasn't the truth. I know he wasn't being sincere.

CUST (*cautiously*). When is a man being truly sincere? It's always difficult to be quite sure.

ELENA. Forgive me, sir. The earliest thing I can remember is when I used to sit on my father's knee. His hair wasn't gray in those days. He used to sit with his eyes closed, and I used to pretend I was drawing his face; I used to touch his eyes with my finger, like that, his nose, his mouth . . . it was one of our games; but we had so many games. I can't describe the happiness and delight we both had in those days! When I hear anyone talking of the people they love, I know that no one can ever be as we were,

father and I. Whenever anyone said I looked like him I used to
feel my cheeks go scarlet with pride. I would have refused to go
to heaven, if my father wasn't to be there too. (*She is silent for a
moment; then, without saying anything, she takes from her bag
an envelope and shows it to him.*)

CUST. What is that?

ELENA. It's his defense, sir. The statement. They've only to read it, and
I know my father will be acquitted.

(*A silence.*)

CUST. But only a few moments ago your father said . . .

ELENA. I know. He refuses to present it. I brought it myself, without
telling him.

CUST. But he's definitely denied having written it.

ELENA. But he's spent night after night on it . . . I helped him.

CUST. Then why should he deny it now?

ELENA (*sadly and anxiously*). Because he's so bewildered and frightened. Someone has put the most dreadful doubts and fears into
him; it's almost like an illness . . . He's like someone who has
fallen down . . . and doesn't want to get up again; he just wants
to shut his eyes.

CUST. Do you know the contents of this statement?

ELENA. Yes, of course. Father has remembered a thousand details . . .
his innocence is quite plain. It throws light on everything.

CUST. And does this light help us to find who the other man is? The
real culprit, I mean.

ELENA. Yes, sir, of course it does. As you read it, page by page, bit
by bit, you can see who the real culprit is, you can guess.

CUST. Can you recall the name? Is it someone called Croz?

ELENA (*uncertainly*). No, that isn't the name. (*She puts the statement
into* CUST'S *hand.*)

CUST. Good. (*He fingers the statement for a moment: suddenly he
hums for a moment to himself.*) My dear child. Elena your name
is, isn't it? Sit down. The friendship that binds me to your father
. . . and also something that really shines in you yourself and
. . . genuinely moves me . . . (*He breaks off.*) When I first
saw you, I said to myself: this is true innocence; the radiance of
justice herself entering into this sad place . . . (*Resuming*) Well,
all that, I was saying, compels me to make a request of you.
You don't imagine, do you, that what you feel is really anything
more than a mere hope? Or that the investigating magistrate
(*holding up the document*) is likely to find anything more than
that in here?

ELENA. I am certain, sir.

CUST. You will admit that the opinion of a judge may differ from that of a daughter?

ELENA. When you have read it you will run to my father and embrace him. You'll punish everyone who doubted him. You'll be so indignant; there's not a soul on earth who could be indifferent.

CUST. But your father, who is after all not inexperienced in these matters, must have had a reason for keeping silent about this document.

ELENA. But I've explained . . .

CUST. Yes, but you are probably not aware of all he said in here just now. He expressed a fear that any further light thrown on the facts might damage himself.

ELENA. Yes, exactly, he doesn't understand, it's what I was telling you.

CUST. He declares that the treatment given him by the Administration has been extremely indulgent; and that to insist might provoke great severity. Your father expressed his gratitude to us all.

ELENA. Sir, I have read that even people condemned to death—even when they've been innocent—at the last moment, they've begged forgiveness just as though they were guilty. I know that can happen. My father is a very tired man; but he is innocent.

CUST. Very well. (*He hums for a moment between his teeth, throws the statement down on the table, and goes on.*) Very well. You force me to this, my dear child. You are being very stubborn. Just now, while I was listening to you . . . (*He casts a glance towards the archives.*) I know time is very short and we haven't time to dawdle over all this . . . nevertheless, while I was listening to you, there were a lot of things I couldn't help thinking: rather silly things. For example: I'm old enough to be your father. Everything desirable that passes near us we would like in some way to make our own. (*Suddenly, in an almost anguished outburst*) And I made you my daughter, I stole you from Vanan! I would have held my breath so as not to sully you in any way. I tell you that in a way I have known you ever since I was a boy, but that's too long to tell about now. There is a very simple word which to me expresses what you seem like: loyal. Loyal. But everyone of us runs on, tied to the indifferent ribbon of time; and that produces an infinite number of mistaken meetings, wrong relationships. One could have been father, brother, husband, son, receiving and giving . . . something. Instead . . . you don't even realize how absurd it is that I, at such a moment, should waste so much time telling you this. However. I wanted to tell you . . .

(*With exaggerated anger, to force himself to stop talking*) . . .
a few moments ago, in here, your father explicitly confessed himself guilty.

(*A silence.*)

ELENA (*almost to herself*). I can't believe it.

CUST. You mean you don't want to believe it. Didn't you say your
father avoided you? What does that mean? It means that it's you
in particular he wants to hide something from.

ELENA (*lost in her own thoughts*). There will have been a reason. I
will believe anything, but not that he could have disgraced himself.

(*A silence.*)

CUST (*rather harshly*). What a cruel word. Disgraced. Sad that you
should use it, since it's your own father we're talking about. An
inhuman word. (*Almost pleading*) Can't you believe that one may
make mistakes . . . which one only notices . . . after one's
made them, and it's too late to turn back? One mistake is enough:
the first one.

ELENA (*after reflecting for a moment*). If I were to think that at some
given moment—and that moment must come sooner or later,
mustn't it, to people who commit these evil things—if I were to
think of my father, at some given moment, doing something
furtive, and secret, and looking round to see that no one was
watching; or sitting there listening to a man whispering secret,
wicked orders to him, and my father whispering back, hurriedly
consenting . . . My father! My father, doing that! My father!
(*She almost laughs.*)

CUST (*agitated, pleading*). Don't you think that everyone in the world,
even your father, may at some time or other, need a little pity?

ELENA. But my father couldn't, couldn't possibly do anything he'd
have to be ashamed or embarrassed about! You should see
my father when he's really angry and outraged! There is nothing
in my father but nobility and goodness and pride. People who disgrace themselves in such filthy ways have to be made of very
different stuff from my father. You can tell at a glance when
people are capable of such treachery: you feel a kind of contempt
for them the minute you see them.

CUST. Yes, hideous toads leap from their mouths, and go hopping about
these rooms. (*He hums for a moment.*) How cruel you are, my
little angel. But it's only your age. The blank blue snow of childhood, smitten by the first incandescent ray of youth. (*With a gust
of anger*) Intoxicating dazzle of light! It leaves one melancholy,
humiliated; oh, it's not your fault; you shine, literally, in the

midst of this hell of ours. You remind one of the pure crystals of which, as you've perhaps been taught at school, inorganic matter is composed. Do you mean to hand in this statement?

ELENA (*a little disturbed*). Yes.

CUST. Good. (*With a touch of harshness in his voice*) I was saying that we were all crystals like you, once, my dear child; that's why it makes one sad to look at you. It seems that life comes into existence at a later stage, born on the icy geometric forms of the inorganic, like a kind of rash, a malignant growth . . . yes, a leprosy indeed. And on that day your voice will have lost this resonant light, and you won't talk any more about disgrace.

ELENA. My father . . .

CUST (*interrupting*). Your father. Why not let us be quite frank about him? He's a successful man, he's one of those who have got a great deal out of life. Are we to believe that life simply *gave* him what he got? Did he get it for nothing? Was it a gift from life? A birthday present? Did it cost him nothing? Not even cleverness? Cleverness: a name by which many kinds of villainy get past. It is unlikely that the statement refers to those.

ELENA. But my father . . .

CUST. Is after all rather like the unfortunate rest of us, isn't he? The only consolation is we're all made of the same stuff, my dear. Haven't you ever noticed . . . how shall I put it, haven't you ever caught a look on your father's face . . . something in his voice—yes, his voice would be enough to show you—something that worried you a little? That voice, so familiar to you, so dear to you: but did you never hear that voice talking to one of your father's superiors, someone high up: the Minister perhaps; and being very polite, and excited, and eager? And then suddenly did you never hear the same voice, sharp and impatient, speaking to a beggar? Well? Did that never happen? It happens with all of us. And then again . . . didn't you ever hear him pretending to be kind and gentle, from above, with the old man at the gate . . . well? Look at me: of course you remember. You're already a little tarnished, my fair crystal. Such a daily heap of hypocrisy and wickedness in the inflections of one single voice! After all that, shall we really be so very surprised if these pages (*he waves the document in the air*) turn out to be a skillful selection of things which are true in themselves, but have been cunningly prised out of the whole. But if you really want to present it—

ELENA (*at a loss*). I'd like . . .

CUST. And we haven't even got to the real thing yet, have we? We haven't mentioned the words, have we?—only the voice! Do

you believe that these actions, just because no law book condemns
them, are any less vile than those that you've called vile? Evil
actions, hypocrisies, betrayals. Everywhere! Even here, in our
own thoughts, which we falsify—yes, even, those! As we formulate
them inside us . . . not as they first tremble in our conscience,
but as soon as certain cunning poisonous calculations occur to
us; even in some of our highest impulses whose mysterious purity
we contrive to cheat and twist and sully. (*Greatly agitated, but still
with an attempt at sarcasm*) Think, my dear, of the housewife
who has carefully stored away her beautiful jars of jam for the
winter: it's like that; one day we also decide to open our nice little
boxes of fine ideas, and what do we find inside . . . (*He throws
the statement onto the table.*) A swarming heap of maggots! And
I can think of nothing, nothing on earth, that escapes that fate!
(*He breaks off and turns round, us* MALGAI *enters.*) Have you
found anything, Malgai?

MALGAI. Not yet; we're still working. (*He takes up a paper from the
table and returns to the archives.*)

CUST (*between his teeth*). Good, so am I. (*He wipes his brow and
goes on.*) No, my dear. I know of nothing that escapes. A single
opaque mess asking one thing alone: to live. To live.

ELENA. But my father . . .

CUST (*shouting*). Your father was a man, and he was a man here
in this ditch! And let me tell you that there was nothing on earth
a man could do that he didn't know of!

ELENA (*impetuously*). But I am sure—

CUST. Of what? Sure of what?

ELENA. Whenever there's been any sort of injustice or mistake I've
always thought of my father; I used to think of him here, in this
building, in his ermine gown, looking very stern; and I used to
feel calm again at once.

CUST. Well, you were wrong, my dear! Look at me! You know I'm not
lying!

ELENA (*with a cry, and moving forward as though to retrieve the statement*). You don't know my father! You're not his friend!

CUST (*violently, breathing heavily, and seizing the statement again*).
My God! How stubborn you are! You only want to create havoc
here! I want to tell you something. Perhaps it's not even connected with all this; I don't know. But once when I was only a boy,
I remember an afternoon of atrocious, suffocating heat. It was
during the siesta; everyone was asleep, soaked in sweat, naked.
I must have heard a whisper somewhere in the house, perhaps that
was it; or perhaps it was some vicious instinct calling me. I got

up, and crept barefoot, furtively, through the shadowy house, towards that whisper, and at last, through a half-open door . . . What a silly disgusting commonplace story! Through the half-open door, that white-faced child saw a man and a woman . . . a man and a woman turned into animals by the stifling heat . . . unrecognizable faces, horrible gestures, choking, appalling words . . . It was my father and mother. My father, and my mother. Quite obvious, after all; what of it? Silly to make a tragedy of it; a door not closed properly, a nervous boy. (*Suddenly*) But no, they weren't my father and mother any more! They were something confused, black, blind, insane! Before that moment I'd never really known them, never known my father and mother; nor myself; nor anyone else. I was horribly shocked. There always comes a day when a door opens a little way and we look through. And that day has come for you too, now, my dear. Look! Look at your father, for God's sake, look at him for the first time; and look at yourself too, my dear child! What do you think, do you think that this sweet flower of your body will never be sullied, that it too won't one day be filled with desire and frenzy, do you think that you'll never damage it, never contaminate it, your beautiful little body—and your voice as well, your angel's breath, your very mind? (*Still excited, but suddenly quiet*) And did you really not know that the great Vanan was sick? Sick, sick, poor devil, that was what was making such a farcical muddle of everything he said. Life is very long, you know, it's very rare that towards the end a venerable white head is much more than to cover over a heap of nastiness; and nasty filthy sicknesses too, those are the things that make age weigh so heavily upon us. That wasn't written in the statement, I'm sure of it. Sad matters, aren't they? You know that I'm telling you the truth, the absolute truth, don't you? As a rule you blush very quickly. I've noticed. But now your color is slowly draining away from your cheeks. You are saying goodbye to the enchantment of youth. You are becoming a woman; it's a small disturbance, it has to come; like the first cigarette, we feel discomfort here. Yes, so it was I who didn't know the great Vanan! If you only realized how little *you* knew about him! And about the others! And about yourself. That is why you were unjust. You never even knew . . . (*with a sudden cry*) that your father hates you! He hates you, yes, he said so in here! (*With a change of tone*) You didn't even know about the slimy love affairs in which poor Vanan has got himself mixed up. The court itself, this very office, has had to look into it. No, that wasn't in the statement either. Slimy intrigues: the loves of old men. It's a sad and terrible thing, my poor angel; the loves of old men, horrible, unspeakable, tormenting! We all come to it. That's how we're made. They are things he never spoke to you about, aren't they? The man you used to kiss when he came back home at night! Suppose *you* look through the open door as well; it's a thing you have to get used to. You know it's the truth I'm telling you, don't you? Very well: you didn't even know that on the day when they first accused him, the great Vanan wrote a letter! And confessed! Yes, he confessed, my dear. He confessed right from the start. Do you want me to repeat the exact words of that letter! (*Striking his forehead*) They're engraved here. (*Beginning*) "My dear Lord Chief Justice . . . an aged magistrate writes to beg of you your extreme kindness . . ."

ELENA (*signing to him not to go on*). No. (*After a few moments, in a whisper*) Poor father. (*A pause.*) And poor me.
(*A silence.*)

CUST. Do you want your statement back? (*He holds it out to her.*)

ELENA (*shaking her head*). It won't be any use now. (*She goes towards the door; and stops.*)

CUST. You'd better be quick, and go; no one has seen you.

ELENA. (*Takes a few steps forward; whispers.*) I'm embarrassed, because now when I meet my father . . . I shan't know what to say to him. I'm afraid that when he looks at me, he'll see that I know. Poor father. I don't want to meet him. (*She moves still nearer to the door; and repeats, almost to herself*) I don't want to meet him.
(*She goes out. Perturbed, CUST stands looking at the door through which she has departed; suddenly, he begins feverishly unwrapping the statement; a few pages fall to the floor, quickly he picks them up. He breaks off in order to listen for any noise from the archives. He looks once more at the door through which the girl has disappeared.*)

CUST. After all, she was no more than a child. Her gentleness will be enough to . . . She is too gentle almost . . . Tomorrow the color will have returned to her cheeks; and she will have forgotten. (*A pause.*) But I . . . Oh God, how tired I am! Tired to death. (*He covers his face with his hands; suddenly he hears steps approaching; he throws the statement down on the table, turns, and waits. The door of the archives opens, and ERZI comes out, followed by CROZ. Loudly, almost shouting*) Well, dear friends, has any good come of your labors?

CROZ (*with a loud laugh*). Haha. You're very cheerful, Cust. You've already guessed.

CUST (*as before*). Haven't you found anything?

ERZI (*casually laying a hand upon the statement*). We find that in none of the suits have the documents survived.

CROZ (*grinning*). Cust! One of us has removed them.

CUST (*excited and suspicious*). Removed them? And then what?

ERZI (*removing his hand, and moving away*). Destroyed them.

CUST. Destroyed them? How? (*He laughs and almost shouts, excitedly, harshly.*) How! How! (*He gradually gets nearer the statement, takes it up, gesticulates with it, and then without disguising what he is doing, drops it into a basket.*) But, my dear friends, would it really have been as easy as all that? Do you think the criminal would have found it easy, or even possible, to burn or destroy, here, such a great number of documents?

ERZI. He could have . . .

CUST. . . . taken them away bit by bit, hidden about himself, do you think? That man, who doesn't want, (*almost shouting*) DOES NOT WANT to be found out, do you imagine he'd have gambled his whole position here, with the risk, however remote and theoretical, of being found with the papers on him in some accident or other, a fall, or a faint . . . ! My dear friends, you can't have the slightest idea what he must be really like! Why the very thought of it would have given him a fit!

ERZI (*interrupting him almost with a cry*). Cust. Where are those papers?

CUST (*calmly, pointing to the archives*). Still in there, in my opinion. But hidden away under mountains and mountains of other documents and papers. The man had patience, so we must have patience too . . . (*He breaks off.*) Did you hear that?

ERZI. What?

CUST. A noise. Not a noise exactly. Down there, somewhere in the building. It sounded to me like . . . (*Breaking off again*) Yes, there must be something wrong. There's someone running up the corridor.

MALGAI. (*Comes running out of the archives and hurries out of the door to the corridor.*) They say there's been an accident. (*He disappears.*)

BATA. (*Comes running in from the corridor, crosses the room towards the clerk's office.*) There's been an accident! Why are people always so careless? They go up and down, up and down, God knows what they're looking for. The gate up at the top must have been opened. Didn't you hear the shout? Yes, as she fell. A loud scream. (*He disappears.* ERZI *runs out into the corridor.*)

CROZ (*following him*). This building: horrible things happening the

whole time, blood on the ground, accidents. And it's no worse than
they deserve, most of the people who come here. If you ask me
. . . (*He disappears.* CUST *is alone; he has stood perfectly still
throughout; hurried footsteps and voices are heard outside.*)

A VOICE (*outside the room*). Let's have some light! Put the lights on!

ANOTHER. Call somebody! Tell somebody to come!

ANOTHER. Where's the porter? Porter!

MALGAI (*re-entering, breathless*). It was there, down at the bottom of
the elevator shaft. It's so dark everywhere in this damned place,
especially the stairs, and the passages. (*He is hastily clearing a
divan of the documents on it.*)

CUST (*without turning, almost tonelessly*). Is she dead?

MALGAI. They don't think so, not yet. They say it's the daughter—

CUST. (*Interrupts him with a gesture, turning round in sudden terror.*)
What are you doing?

MALGAI. I'm getting this couch ready . . .

CUST (*horrified*). Here? Why . . . No. No. (*He childishly points
towards the clerk's office.*) In there . . .

ERZI (*rushing back in: to* MALGAI). Yes, in there, that'll be better. We'll
take her in there. Call somebody! Do call somebody! Telephone.
(*He runs out again.*)

MALGAI. But who am I to call? There's no one there at this hour; everything's shut up. I ought to be at home too . . .

CUST (*stopping him*). Malgai, did you hear her cry out . . . ?

MALGAI. Yes, a loud cry—

CUST (*his teeth almost chattering*). What . . . what do you think?

MALGAI. About what?

CUST. Do you think it's . . . an accident?

MALGAI. I think she must have tripped, people never look where they're
going. She tried to dart back, but it was too late. (*He breaks off,
and turns toward the corridor.*) Here she is.
(*A low murmur of voices is heard, and the scrape of footsteps
approaching: finally the door on the corridor is thrown open wide.
A big man enters carrying the girl in his arms, apparently un-
harmed and as though asleep, her hair flowing over her shoulders.
A number of people follow. The man crosses the room, and disappears into the clerk's office: the door remains open. The others,
except for* CUST, *follow him, talking in low tones, as though in
church.*)

A VOICE. . . . yes, some strands of hair . . . in the iron work . . .

ANOTHER. . . . there was oil . . . there were traces of oil from the
elevator shaft . . . They ought to . . .

ANOTHER. . . . clean it, of course, clean it . . .

ERZI (*crossing the room with* MALGAI). Anyway, send for somebody
. . . send for a woman. Warn them . . . that they must send a
car. And her father. Send for him . . . Make some excuse . . .
Don't tell him . . .

CUST. (*They have all gone into the clerk's office.* CUST *remains alone;
he approaches the door of the office; stares at it: suddenly in a
hushed voice, with an extraordinary note of pleading*) Elena. (*A
pause.*) Elena. Don't die. Try to live. (*A silence.*) Elena . . .
(*He breaks off, as* MALGAI *hurries back in.*)

CUST. How is she, Malgai?

MALGAI. I don't think there's very much hope for her.

CUST (*with terror, almost with fury*). Do you mean this girl is going to
die?

MALGAI. It's a terrible accident, sir.

CUST (*stammering*). But that girl . . . she was in here a few moments
ago . . . blushing, at a mere nothing . . . she was so young
. . . I want to tell her . . . (*He breaks off.*)

MALGAI (*alarmed*). What's the matter, sir?

CUST. (*Stands looking at one of his hands in real terror; suddenly with
a suffocated cry*) Malgai! I have her blood here on my hands!
I've not touched her, Malgai! I've not touched her! (*He rubs his
hand hysterically.*)

MALGAI. But . . . but there's nothing odd about that, sir. I touched
her myself. You might easily have touched me, you might have
brushed by me. Or you might have touched the others, there's
nothing strange about that. (*He breaks off.*)

CROZ. (*Rushes in from the corridor, in great distress.*) Oh my God,
Cust; her father's here! They sent for him. Who's going to tell
him, what shall we do? Oh how dreadful it is, what a terrible
mess, the whole thing is . . .

CUST. (*With a fierce wild movement, runs to the door, throws it open
and cries*) Come in, Vanan! Come in. Quickly!

VANAN (*letting himself be dragged in, suspicious and whimpering*).
But what more do you want of me? What is it? Leave me alone!
Leave me in peace, why can't you?

CUST (*shouting*). You'll never be at peace any more, Vanan! (*Louder
still*) Never, never at peace, Vanan! You must do something!
Something terrible! Your daughter. Your beautiful . . . dear
Elena. (*Almost to himself alone*) She's dead. She's dead.

Curtain

ACT THREE

Late in the evening; a single lamp is burning. MALGAI *is just coming from out of the archives. He puts on his hat and overcoat in preparation for leaving.* CUST *appears at the corridor door.*

MALGAI (*noticing him*). Good evening, sir. Did you want something? (CUST *does not reply.*)

MALGAI. I'm really off duty now, but . . . never mind. We are always here when anybody wants us.

CUST (*absently*). No, you go along, Malgai. There's something I want to do, I shall be staying for a little while.

MALGAI. Ah yes, sir. You're another one who wears himself out, sir, working after hours!

CUST. Yes, I'm another. Are the archives open?

MALGAI. Yes sir, they're open. Mr. Justice Croz wanted to—

CUST. I'll see that they're locked up afterwards. Goodnight.

MALGAI (*surprised*). Then what shall I . . . very well, sir, very well. (*He goes out, hesitatingly.* CUST *waits until* MALGAI'S *footsteps have died away; then he goes to the door on tiptoe and turns the key; immediately afterwards he goes into the archives, and returns with an armful of documents which he throws on a table and begins to examine; very soon, however, something seems to distract him, and he stands there lost in thought; suddenly he starts: all the lamps have gone on.* CROZ *has risen slowly from a large armchair whose back has hidden him from sight; he has switched on the lights; now he gives way to a long burst of laughter mingled with coughing.* CUST *has turned round quickly; then he slowly returns to his previous attitude.*)

CROZ (*frequently pausing for breath*). Once upon a time there was a little mouse. And there was a trap. Instead of cheese, there were certain well-known papers hidden under mountains and mountains of other papers . . .

CUST (*absently*). What do you mean?

CROZ. You're losing your grip, Cust! For example, you just turned the key in the door there: excellent, but what about the other doors? A bit of a surprise, wasn't it, Cust, to find old Croz here?

CUST (*as before*). We heard bad news about your health.

CROZ. Yes, I hardly managed to get up here, as a matter of fact. But if I've got to die, I wanted to die here. Besides, I know that spite is almost as good as oxygen. (*With a change of tone*) Cust, it's all fixed for tonight, isn't it? The sentence on the guilty man; and the naming of the new president. (*He points towards the ceiling.*) The old men are already taking their seats up there. Cust, which of us two is going to walk off with it?

CUST (*as before*). Do you think the Upper Council will definitely eliminate Vanan?

CROZ. Self-possessed, aren't you? You even indulge in the luxury of thinking about Vanan! . . . (*Sarcastically*) Oh, he'll be sentenced all right . . . (*he pauses for breath*) . . . and you or I will get the nomination. But you're not looking very well either, Cust. In fact, quite the opposite.

CUST (*in a monotone*). It's just that my thoughts keep going over and over things which are already beyond the possibility of being changed.

CROZ. You must look after yourself.

CUST. I shall have to. Look at my hand: it costs me a great effort to stop trying to wipe it, though it's perfectly clean already. Like that, you see? (*He wipes his hand.*) I have done that so often that just here the skin has changed. I don't do it quite so much now.

CROZ. Cust, you've always interested me, you know. You've given me the creeps before now, often. You are very tough, aren't you? Stubborn. But now we're on the last lap.

CUST (*in a staccato monotone*). Yes, I'm very stubborn. And Vanan's daughter showed that she too was pretty stubborn. She hasn't spoken since that day. They say she won't last until tomorrow morning.

CROZ. Cust, what are you doing in here?

CUST. Most of all, it was the cry she uttered as she fell which shocked me. I have tried to analyze it, these last few days; tried to reconstruct it.

CROZ (*louder*). Cust, what are you doing here?

CUST (*quietly, and as though lost in thought*). You can see; I am looking for something. It wasn't so much a fall into an elevator shaft—I keep getting the idea of her being sucked down into a funnel. Slowly at first, then quickly, then down, vertically, swallowed up. I think that cry expressed other things, besides fear. But what other things? A kind of reproach. But most of all—incredulity; surprise.

CROZ. Cust, you keep on talking to me about that girl. Has she some connection with our problem?

CUST (*as before*). No real connection. What annoys me most of all is the fact of the interruption. That girl still had little round cheeks, almost like a baby's; and in fact she was very young: when you looked at her, it was like looking at a beautiful fresh leaf moving

gently on the branch: one caught a hint of seasons, enchanting
hours yet to come, long, long days drenched in sun . . . And
where is all that now? Broken off. It's very strange. I don't think
any logic in the whole world can explain that.

CROZ. Cust, I don't know if you've understood. This is the epilogue,
Cust, the auditing. You've waited for the right moment to take
me into your confidence.

CUST. Perhaps I've never really talked to anyone. Sometimes one begins to need to. Perhaps you'd understand me better than anyone
else.

CROZ. Undoubtedly. I've always understood you. In a way, you've kept
me company. I should have been bored without you. Cust, today
you've made your first mistake.

CUST (*still in the same indifferent, slightly surprised tones*). Possibly.
What was it?

CROZ. You were wrong to come here tonight! Those famous papers, eh?
A feeling of fright lest they should still exist in there, subtle, slight,
evil: they've drawn you here, like a rope. Right at the last moment, when everything was over, when the old men up aloft were
actually dipping their pens into the ink, you had to stumble over
this little pebble. (*Shouting*) Cust, what are you doing here?
What are you looking for?

CUST (*almost wearily*). The criminal.

CROZ. Well, help me then, because I'm looking for him too. And what
is it that drives you on?

CUST. The idea that from tonight onwards he may begin to be calm
again, that his footstep from tonight onwards may once more begin to be assured and authoritative in this place; as may his voice.
I feel a sort of revulsion and stupefaction at the thought. It's like
that girl's cry: I can't find a place for it anywhere in the world.

CROZ. Cust, you're a liar! You've sent the record clerk away by a trick!
You've come here at this time of night, in secret! You've fallen
into the trap; I have found you out!

CUST (*in a monotone*). Croz. You too are here in secret. It's I who've
found you out.

CROZ. Oh, is it really? Well, tell me then, (*pointing to the documents*)
have you found nothing in those things there?

CUST. Nothing.

CROZ. (*Gives a long laugh, and finds difficulty in getting his breath
back.*) Nothing! Nothing! A fine result after all the risks you've
taken. (*Mockingly*) Do you know what I'm afraid of? That it's
useless to go on looking any more; and that even in there
(*pointing to the archives*) everything's vanished.

CUST. Nothing left. That too is strange.

CROZ. Why is it strange? Suppose the papers kept on going in through that door there, and never came out; suppose all the scoundrels in the city had to sign a piece of paper for every penny they ever stole, every lie they ever told; and suppose all the papers stayed in there: by this time there'd be nothing else left on the surface of the earth but papers; and the sea of papers would go on growing and growing till it reached the moon. Haha. Fortunately (*pointing towards the door of the archives*) so much goes in, and so much comes out. As in everything else. Here's a graveyard that's even more of a graveyard than that: it's called the pulping-mill. (*In satirically mysterious tones*) Our friend has taken advantage of that. There's nothing left.

CUST (*in a monotone*). Not a single trace. At this moment that girl too is perhaps gone without trace. Nothing. It's that that's strange.

CROZ. Nothing? No trace? (*He taps himself on the forehead.*) What about this? You don't count what's inside here? The papers have gone to the pulping-mill, but Croz will have to be sent there as well, because Croz knows who the criminal is. (*Shouting*) He knows, he knows! Stay where you are, Cust. Don't you dare come near me. I know you're not a man of action, but you've good cause to send me to the pulping-mill too, haven't you? (*He goes over and unlocks the door.*) We don't quite know yet how this interview is going to finish. (*He pauses for breath.*) What a comfort it would be, wouldn't it, with me here, *moribundus,* almost at death's door, how very nice, when you come to think of it, if just one little vein, here inside me somewhere, were to burst and take your trouble away, now, here, at once, before Old Croz could get out of here and begin to chatter, eh?

CUST (*in a monotone*). It's you whose real interest is that *I* don't get out of here; because the criminal, and I've known it for some time, is you, Croz. Possibly some of the others as well. But you, quite certainly. Not me.

CROZ. Cust, I've always admired you. That was really why I always hated you: and you have quite seriously shortened my life, did you know? You're made of steel. Good God, you're not tired yet: what are you still frightened of? It's done now; there's nothing left inside there. Even if I wanted to accuse you, now, my words would be no more than words. A rival's spite, to try and undermine you. Your words against me would be the same. You needn't hold your breath, Cust. You can speak. I know how much you want to; you're dying to.

CUST (*rubbing his hand*). But I'm not guilty. It's you.

CROZ (*shouting*). Yes! Yes! I too! I've also been a cheat! Bah. I've never even taken much trouble to hide it. I'd go on being one. Yes, it would have been worth it, wouldn't it, being honest among our dear fellow-citizens—a lot of filthy traitors in exactly the same way, but above all stupid, and villainous, all of them. And how they multiply! Not a drop of cleanliness in one of them; how disgusting! You too: you were quite right, Cust. They must be stamped out underfoot. Cust! I've spoken! You speak too!

CUST (*in a monotone*). But I am not the criminal.

CROZ. Bah. (*He spits towards him: and stands there panting.*) What a swine you are. And you're a fool as well. It's stupid to care so much. (*He breathes heavily again.*) Who can tell how many men, century after century, must have stood . . . like us two, glaring at each other, quarrelling . . . their foreheads covered in sweat . . . and what a silly fuss to make of anything. It was all a lot of nonsense . . . because . . . (*He grips the table and sits down slowly in a strange way; and mutters.*) Damnation. (*He stays there gasping for breath.*)

CUST (*without moving*). Do you feel bad?

CROZ (*almost speechless*). Yes.

CUST. You've upset yourself. Do you want a drink of water?

CROZ. (*Does not answer; after a moment*) That'd be very nice. (*He gasps.*) Cust. You've always had the most outrageous luck. (*He slips to the floor.*)

CUST (*without moving*). Croz! (*Silence.*) Croz! (*Silence.*) Come on! (*Seeing that the other is trying to speak*) What is it, do you want to tell me something?

CROZ (*in a whisper*). I'm going, Cust.

CUST. Going? (*Calmly*) Ah, one can never tell that.

CROZ (*as before*). It's all over. (*He collapses onto the floor.*)

CUST (*after observing him for a moment*). By God, Croz, I'm almost afraid you're right. Croz! Can you hear me? Where are you in pain? (*A silence.*) It's been the same with me these last few days: did you know? I've felt as if there were something at my back, I've felt like a boy going along a dark corridor and whistling. Mustn't turn round, must go straight on, Croz, stick it out. (*A silence.*) Is it your heart? I don't want to frighten you, but this time it does really look like it, doesn't it? These have been hard days for me too, Croz. I've tried to sleep as much as I possibly could. Even a man condemned to death is like a free man, when he's asleep. Sleep is the same for everyone. And let us hope death will be the same, Croz. You are going to sleep for

a very long time now, I think. (*A silence.*) Listen, if it's really
true that you're going, that it's all over, and there's no more
danger, then . . . I may tell you . . . it's true, I *have* been a
lucky man. Yes, Croz, I was the man we were all looking for, and
I really needed, *needed,* to say so to somebody. I couldn't bear
it any longer. *I* was the leper. You were looking for me, weren't
you? But I'm still hopeful. I think I'm quite safe still. It's been a
big job. I'd been frightened that I might not be able to carry it
through, frightened I might suddenly begin to shout. We take far
too much upon ourselves. Do you know, Croz, I've kept having
the same dream over and over again, all these nights. I dreamt
about a child, a boy. I've never had any children. And what an
ugly child this was of mine! Naked, with an enormous belly, an evil
face, and horrible, quick, crooked little legs, leaping about like a
frog, yes, just like a frog; I would see it hiding in the record
clerk's trolley, or disappearing among the bookshelves and the
papers, in the most ridiculous places, and I would be after it . . .
always after it . . . trying to grab hold of it; sometimes I managed to cut it, with a knife . . . cut it up in a hundred pieces
. . . but every piece began to grow again with those little legs
. . . and to leap about with me after it, I couldn't catch it. I was
soaked in sweat, I had too many things to look out for, here, there,
everywhere; it was too much, yes, it was too much! Nobody else
could have borne it, I'm sure of that. (*In wild desperation*) That
girl's cry, Croz! I *studied* it! I pored over it! It's difficult to understand what she meant, one can make all sorts of guesses.
"Aaaaah!" Like that, she cried! "Aaaaah!" The idea I've formed
of it . . . is that it had somehow scratched something, made a
scratch on a piece of glass. No, not quite, not on a glass . . . it
was one of those scratches from which small drops of blood issue.
Every now and then, a little drop. It all seems finished; but you
look again; and there is another drop of blood. Yes, a scratch.
Blood. They all believe it was an accident . . . But I . . . I'm
mystified. I can't see . . . (*He breaks off.*)

CROZ. (*Raises his head, gets up slowly from the ground; in an ordinary voice, quietly*) To see ourselves clearly is a great privilege,
Cust. You want to set too many things in order. (*Suddenly,
wildly, and harshly, he begins to shout*) Help! I'm dying! Help
me, help me! Porter, porter! Hurry! (*He gasps for a moment.*)
Quickly someone! Porter! Porter! (*He begins to beat his stick on
the table.*) Help, help, help, help!

MALGAI (*running in*). What's the matter?

CROZ. It's me, I'm feeling bad, I am dying. Send for the Investigator, first . . . Councillor Erzi . . . tell him to come here at once. Then call the judges. All of them. Fetch as many people as you can, and Vanan as well, of course. Warn them . . . that I'm here, at the point of death, in the company of . . . him, my colleague Cust, look at him; tell them to hurry if they want . . . to find me alive. Hurry up, you fool. (MALGAI *runs out. Worn out by his efforts, speaks more slowly, breathing with difficulty.*) My poor Cust, I wish I could say that all this had only been . . . a charade for your benefit. Unfortunately . . . it's only too true . . . that I'm about to die; what a bloody disgrace. (*He pants slightly.*) My dear friend, the popular superstition about the words of the dying, strengthens . . . my credit. Strengthens it a great deal. I shall tell the truth; they will believe me; and you, at the very last minute, will have slipped up. You've spoken, you've told me. I could save you too, my dear fellow, I've always . . . liked a good joke . . . in that case I'd be the one who nominated you as president, I'd be the one who put the ermine gown on the back of the great leper; this filthy shell would have a snail inside worthy of it. A juicy sight! But I could never bring myself to help *you*, Cust. I don't like you. You're conceited. I want to punish you. (*He gasps for breath.*) The point of death makes me very powerful. I don't believe I have any duties. (*He gasps.*) I believe that things develop . . . according to a purely vegetable law. And it's not without . . . its comic side. I believe that if we . . . decided to think it was disgraceful to wear gray . . . (*He laughs.*) ha-ha, to wear gray stocking . . . anyone who actually had worn gray stockings . . . ha-ha-ha, would feel terrible guilt and shame. That's all it is. I don't believe that anything remains of us. We'd be in a real mess if . . . if anything could really be distilled from such a load of nonsense.

(BATA *arrives, in haste, accompanied by* MAVERI.)

BATA. Croz, how are you?

CROZ. Much as you'd expect a man to be, who knows he'll be dead . . . in about ten minutes. Just stay over there, my dear fellow, there's something I have to say . . . to my colleague. (*To* CUST, *privately*) All these judges . . . they've always turned my stomach. A lot of them are very upright and very worthy . . . and they'll live for a long time . . . They are made of wood. As for the rest . . . come a bit closer, Cust. They administer justice! Ha-ha-ha. (*He laughs.*) Which means they express their opinion that certain actions are just, and certain others are not. Just as one sausage is hung on to another sausage, this opinion is hung

on to the law books . . . beautifully bound of course . . . and
these law books are hung on to other law books—and statutes and
tables . . . older still. The trouble is, my dear fellow . . . (*He
breaks off, and says to* PERSIUS, *who has just arrived.*) What's
he doing?

PERSIUS. Who?

CROZ. Erzi. Silly old tortoise.

PERSIUS. They've sent for him. Everybody's on their way here.

CROZ (*turning to* CUST). . . . the trouble is that the main hook is
missing, the original clasp . . . and without that . . . the whole
string of sausages falls to the ground! But where, and how, and
when! Who was it who decided one thing was right and another
wasn't? We know perfectly well that things . . . are what they
are, all equal. That's why we judges are all hypocrites, all of us
stuffed with stale rancid sausage-meat. That's what the real corruption in these courts is, the whole place stinks terribly of it; I
can't wait to be free of it. (*He breathes with difficulty: he points
to the group of judges and winks.*) They all pretend. They don't
really believe it, those chaps, they don't really believe in the
resurrection after death, nor even in Lord Free-will; don't you see?
(*He emits a soft scandalized whistle; suddenly thoughtful.*) And
as a matter of fact, what reason on earth is there to expect that
at some point in this chain, something autonomous will break out?
The soul, I mean. I am speaking of the soul. But anyway, all that
. . . is rapidly ceasing . . . to concern me. Naturally. (*He remains for a moment with drooping head.*) What about Erzi?

MALGAI (*coming in*). He's coming up from the offices.

CROZ. Good. Come here, Malgai. And you, Persius. (*The two men
obey.*) Take hold of me firmly. You on that side, like that. You
on this. That's right. (*He has made the two men take him firmly
by the arms and lift him up.*) Now let's go and meet him. I've a
number of disclosures to make to him. (*With a touch of pride*)
I don't want . . . to wait for him and death . . . in here . . .
bent double . . . like a rat that . . . somebody's trampled on.
(*Supported by the two men, indeed almost carried by them,* CROZ
slowly crosses the room and goes out. CUST, BATA *and* MAVERI
stand looking at each other.)

BATA (*excitedly to* CUST). Poor Croz, the whole of his life, he's been
nothing but an old tin of poison. What does he want to talk to
Erzi about? Revelations at the point of death! What sort? Against
whom?

MAVERI (*distressed*). Do you know anything about it, Cust? What
was he saying to you just now?

CUST (*in a monotone*). I ought in duty to warn everyone that our poor friend is no longer himself; I'm afraid he's raving . . . (*He breaks off.*)

MALGAI (*appearing at the door, excited and jubilant*). Croz is talking to Erzi! Big things! He has said—and he is dictating to the secretary also—that he, Croz, in solemn declaration, testifies that President Vanan . . .

BATA (*taking the words out of his mouth*). . . . is innocent!

MALGAI. . . . and that if he manages to live another five minutes, he intends to reveal . . .

BATA. . . . the name of the real criminal!

MALGAI. Exactly! (*He rushes out again.*)

CUST (*as before*). Unfortunately the trust we can put in Croz's words is only relative. This crisis has produced a genuine disorder in him, and . . . (*He turns.*)

(VANAN *is entering, bent and terrified: a* NURSE *leads him in.* BATA *rushes up to him, making an overwhelming fuss of him.*)

BATA. Vanan! Vanan! Please allow someone who has never had a moment's doubt of you and your . . .

MAVERI (*in competition with* BATA). . . . your absolute integrity, which now shines again in such a sudden, unexpected, even marvellous . . .

NURSE (*stepping between the two judges and* VANAN, *who has timidly drawn back*). Forgive me, he has to be treated and spoken to very gently. I always have to be with him.

CUST (*who has stood staring at the* NURSE, *quietly, but in a voice slightly louder than necessary, almost solemnly*). You have left Elena? (*Something in his voice makes the others turn and look at him.*)

NURSE. Didn't you know, sir? The poor child has no need of me or anyone else now.

CUST (*in the same tones*). Is she dead?

NURSE. Two days ago, sir. What am I saying? Three. Her sufferings are over.

(*A silence.*)

CUST (*as before*). What a very small coffin, she will have needed. They told me she was much changed.

NURSE. Just like a tiny little bird, sir. She weighed nothing at all.

CUST. She didn't say anything further?

NURSE. Nor even heard anything. Nor even looked at anything.

CUST. Did she complain at all?

NURSE. No, poor little thing. Only towards the end, she kept doing

this with her poor little hand: as though to try and push something from her, or drive it away, a fly or something.

CUST. Was anyone at her side, when that gesture ceased?

NURSE (*dropping her voice*). You will hardly believe it, sir, but poor
Mr. Vanan refused to go and see her again. He made the excuse
that he was suffering too much. (*She shakes her head.*) At the
end he made even stranger and more childish excuses. It isn't
his fault.

CUST (*thoughtfully, while they all look at him in some amazement*).
So no one will ever again meet the young girl I saw at that door.
She stood there a little out of breath, as though after a race . . .
No one ever said anything more to her, she never listened to
anyone. (*To the woman almost threateningly*) You: why didn't
you make her listen to you, while there was time? Now no one
will ever be able to do that. (*Almost to himself*) I talked to her,
I passed long nights with her, begging her not to die, all night
through; but she didn't believe in me anymore.

NURSE. But that's not true, sir; you never once came.

CUST (*in a monotone, quietly turning to* VANAN). Vanan, I fear your
daughter did not attribute enough importance to her own life.
She ought to have been persuaded that in her there was . . . (*He
pauses with his arm upraised.*)

PERSIUS (*bursting in, greatly agitated*). At this very moment Croz is
revealing the criminal's name! They even sent *me* away. It appears
it really is one of us!

CUST (*who has listened without turning, goes on after a moment, in
a louder voice*). . . . that in her there was something which does
not exist and will never again exist at any other point of eternity . . . (*Suddenly, almost with fury*) Something immenser
than the immensest star . . .

VANAN (*retreating a little, to the woman*). Take me away, I don't want
to see that man.

CUST (*in amazed tones*). Vanan, her cry split the crystal of the heavens
in two, and was heard far, far away. You cannot have forgotten,
for you were her father. It is your duty . . .

VANAN (*in a distant, almost childish voice*). But it was all so long ago,
and our Lord knows what He does. (*Fervently*) I hope, hope,
hope for heaven, and I don't want to know anything more. (*He
makes the sign of the cross several times.*) Our Lord be praised
forever. (*He mumbles a prayer; suddenly with a strange obstinacy
and almost overbearingly*) My daughter died when she was a
little girl. It was years ago.

CUST (*bewildered*). What do you mean, Vanan?

VANAN (*with the same childish obstinacy and distrust*). Yes, yes, my daughter died when she was a little girl. The Lord willed it so . . .

CUST. Vanan . . . (*He breaks off; they have all turned to the door.*)

MALGAI. (*Has entered in haste, breathlessly.*) We know the criminal's name!

BATA. Come on, out with it, Malgai!

MALGAI (*excitedly, enjoying the delay*). I can imagine the outcry there's going to be!

MAVERI. Come on!

PERSIUS. What about Croz?

BATA. Is he dead?

MALGAI. No one will ever hear that fiendish old voice again. Even *I* couldn't tell you the impudent things the old devil invented before he was willing to give the real name of the criminal! He kept coughing, and winking the whole time. He kept letting out the most dreadful curses; he even pretended in the end to make Councillor Erzi play at guess-who, trying the names of this man and that! And suddenly Croz said: (*imitating him*) "No. It isn't any of them. The criminal's name is . . ."

ERZI (*who has already entered*). His name *was* . . . Croz. (*Advancing with a certain detachment*) Yes, gentlemen, your colleague Croz has disclosed at the point of death that the person responsible for the corruption in these courts was himself, and no one else; that Vanan is innocent; and that all the other judges are likewise innocent, mainly, he observed, because they hadn't the brains to be anything else; and that the best of the lot and the most deserving of being nominated for the Presidency . . . was you, Cust. He spoke of you in very respectful terms . . . though also, of course, satirically and sharply, as is his wont. He asked me to say to you . . . Wait a moment . . . (*He tries to remember.*) "That every man has to scratch his own scabs by himself."

BATA. Very fine. Anything else?

ERZI. He coughed, he blew a little, and he said (*imitating him*): "Well, well, you've been a hell of a bore, Erzi." And died.

BATA (*violently*). And that filthy blackguard dared to pass judgment on his own colleagues!

MAVERI. Not only that, he still contrived to be smart and impudent right to the end.

BATA. Erzi, I'm not blaming you. But my God, dying or not, Croz ought to have been compelled—(*he points to the great doors at*

the back which have so far remained closed throughout the play)
—to go out through there, through those doors; to drag himself
at his last gasp up the great staircase and to knock at the door
of the Lord High Chancellor, and humble himself there under
the forms of law.

PERSIUS. And he could have died after that, if he wanted to!

BATA. And where, where, I should like to know are we to have any
restitution for the offense against justice . . . ?

ERZI (*almost smiling, absently*). But it's Time, my dear friends, it is
Time that repairs all insults, and obliterates all scars. And besides,
in this case, since Nature has looked after Croz already, the only
thing that remains for us to do is to compensate Vanan for our
unjust suspicions by conferring some high distinction on him . . .
and also to nominate a new President. And I have a fancy that
at this minute the High Council is nominating . . . you, Cust.
The news should be here any minute now. I congratulate you,
Vanan. And you, Cust.

CUST (*staring before him with wide-open eyes*). The Council will nominate me President of this Court?

ERZI (*lightly and genially*). It's highly probable. The desk behind
which, from now onwards, you will cultivate your penetrating
thoughts will be very imposing and monumental.

CUST. Have you finished your inquiries?

ERZI. Their goal has been reached, and besides things are hurrying on,
everything is moving forward. The stone drops to the bottom, the
water becomes calm once more. Croz is dead, Ludvi-Pol is dead.
And they're not the only ones. The town is already turning to
other things. . . .

CUST (*almost to himself, pointing to the archives*). . . . Every trace
of the crime gone . . .

ERZI (*good-humoredly, jesting*). . . . Our good Vanan is at peace
with God, the tempest calmed . . . in a few moments workmen
will lower a number of levers and the lights will be extinguished;
and while dawn quickens over life's enchanting lake, now once
more blue and peaceful, we shall go home to bed, certain that the
affairs of this court . . . (*turning to* CUST) . . . are once more
in good hands.

BATA (*precipitating himself towards* CUST *with hand outstretched*).
Let me say, my dear Cust, that we're all proud and honored by
this nomination. I am sure there can be no doubt about it! Are
you glad?

CUST (*absently, nodding*). Very glad.

BATA. You'll be able to have a holiday now, won't you?

CUST. Yes, I could do with one. A holiday.

BATA. Well, goodbye for the present, my dear fellow. (*He goes out.*)

MAVERI (*promptly*). What is it, are you still a bit worried? No, no, don't worry, the nomination's certain. Well, so long. (*He goes out.*)

PERSIUS (*promptly*). Today you will reach the goal for which you have spent the best years of your life.

CUST. Yes, my whole life has been directed towards this moment.

PERSIUS (*watching him*). You will wait here for the news?

CUST (*absently*). Yes. Yes.

PERSIUS. Goodbye then. Till tomorrow. (*He goes out after colleagues.*)

CUST (*suddenly*). The stone dropping to the bottom . . . the lake becoming calm again . . . My God, Erzi! That image of yours . . .

ERZI. Is it that that's worrying you?

CUST. It's not that I'm worried . . . but I should like . . . (*with sudden anguish*) . . . to be able to understand; otherwise . . . It's difficult to rest. (*Suddenly pleading*) And God knows I have need of that . . .

MALGAI (*coming forward in his turn*). You're a bit exhausted, sir. A little rest and you'll be back in your old form again, quite recovered, Mr. . . . President! We can say that now, can't we? (*He goes out.*)

CUST (*in a low voice*). But I *am* recovered. (*He raises his hand, and rubs it with the familiar gesture.*) Look, for some days past I've kept wanting to do this. *I* have. I like it, it keeps me company. But now I'm beginning to forget to. Hours go by and I forget to do it. (*To* ERZI, *breathing heavily*) No, it's not that I'm worried, but certainly . . . there is something . . . that doesn't . . . (*with a cry*) doesn't fit, do you understand? (*Suddenly turning round*) Vanan! It's you who frighten me. When I look at you I feel that underneath this building, underneath you and me, a black gulf is opening!

ERZI (*his voice unexpectedly loud and severe*). What's the matter, Cust? What's the matter?

CUST (*frantically*). Vanan, the matter is the blood-stained face of your daughter! I can't find a single explanation on earth for that.

VANAN. My daughter died when she was a little girl . . . my daughter died when she was a little girl . . . it's so very long ago now . . .

CUST (*as before*). Vanan, suppose she . . . wanted to die . . . ? Suppose that was the terrible thing that happened? Suppose she threw herself down?

VANAN (*muttering*). You liar. You reptile. My poor Elena died when she was a little girl.

CUST (*with a cry*). Vanan, I fear . . . that when she shouted . . . she was asking something! Is it possible that no one heard? That no one answered? That that has not been inscribed on any register? That such an enormous question should remain unsolved?

ERZI (*suddenly, with sombre intensity*). Cust, I don't think that a man should be more stubborn than his little powers allow him to be! Administration: that is a human fact, its task is to smooth things out, not to dig things up, and turn them upside down! Nature: she heals her wounds so rapidly that perhaps the real truth is something else: that she is unaware of them. (*Dropping his voice*) And after all, if we want to talk about God . . .

VANAN (*suddenly interrupting, and then slowly making his way to the door*). . . . God is so good. He forgives. He forgets. And we too shall forget, in His blessedness. (*He goes out, supported by the* NURSE.)

ERZI. You are left alone to think about these things, Cust. You alone.

CUST (*almost to himself*). I alone. I alone. I alone. And when I too shall have turned my back and gone away . . .

ERZI. . . . what was done and what was left undone will all be the same. (*The* POLICE OFFICIAL *enters and hands* ERZI *a paper.* ERZI *looks at it. With a cry*) Cust! The Council . . . has nominated you! You've won. (*Approaching him, with sombre pity*) Poor Cust, you've almost changed in appearance during these last few days. In a short time you will have forgotten, exactly as Vanan has. The season granted to us is so brief, don't disturb it with your cries! Don't be stubborn. (*He points upwards.*) The Lord High Chancellor himself is happy that matters have been mended. He is very old; he is probably napping at the moment on his table. Pointless to go and disturb him. (*Moving towards the door*) Good-by, Cust, let the world roll on. That is mankind's job.

(*He goes out followed by the* OFFICIAL. *A silence.* MALGAI *reappears and begins putting out the lights one by one, preparing to close the place up and go away.*)

MALGAI (*moved by curiosity, and with rough kindliness*). You are all alone, Mr. President. Aren't you going home?

CUST. Yes. I shall go now as well. (*He goes slowly towards the corridor entrance; and suddenly stops. The room is almost dark.*)

MALGAI (*worried*). What's the matter? What are you waiting for?

CUST. (*His teeth are chattering slightly: he turns back.*) Because there is no argument on earth that would let me shut my eyes in peace tonight. I shall have to wake the Lord High Chancellor. I must confess the truth to him.

MALGAI. Shall I come with you, Mr. President?

CUST. No. I'm a bit frightened. But I know there is no one who can help me. (*He makes his way to the door which leads to the office of the Lord High Chancellor, and which has hitherto remained unopened. He throws the door open. Beyond it a long staircase is revealed going upwards;* CUST *begins to make his way up the stairs, very slowly, as*

Curtain

THE CHAIRS [1951]
A Tragic Farce

by Eugene Ionesco

translated by Donald M. Allen

Characters

OLD MAN, *aged ninety-five*
OLD WOMAN, *aged ninety-four*
THE ORATOR, *aged forty-five to fifty*
And many other characters

The Chairs, from *Four Plays* by Eugene Ionesco, translated by Donald M. Allen. Copyright © 1958 by Grove Press, Inc.

Scene. Circular walls with a recess upstage center. A large, very sparsely furnished room. To the right, going upstage from the proscenium, three doors. Then a window with a stool in front of it; then another door. In the center of the back wall of the recess, a large double door, and two other doors facing each other and bracketing the main door: these last two doors, or at least one of them, are almost hidden from the audience. To the left, going upstage from the proscenium, there are three doors, a window with a stool in front of it, opposite the window on the right, then a blackboard and a dais. Downstage are two chairs, side by side. A gas lamp hangs from the ceiling.

(*The curtain rises. Half-light. The* OLD MAN *is up on the stool, leaning out the window on the left. The* OLD WOMAN *lights the gas lamp. Green light. She goes over to the* OLD MAN *and takes him by the sleeve.*)

OLD WOMAN. Come my darling, close the window. There's a bad smell from that stagnant water, and besides the mosquitoes are coming in.

OLD MAN. Leave me alone!

OLD WOMAN. Come, come, my darling, come sit down. You shouldn't lean out, you might fall into the water. You know what happened to François I. You must be careful.

OLD MAN. Still more examples from history! Sweetheart, I'm tired of French history. I want to see—the boats on the water making blots in the sunlight.

OLD WOMAN. You can't see them, there's no sunlight, it's nighttime, my darling.

OLD MAN. There are still shadows. (*He leans out very far.*)

OLD WOMAN (*pulling him in with all her strength*). Oh! . . . you're frightening me, my darling . . . come sit down, you won't be able to see them come, anyway. There's no use trying. It's dark . . .

(*The* OLD MAN *reluctantly lets himself be pulled in.*)

OLD MAN. I wanted to see—you know how much I love to see the water.

OLD WOMAN. How can you, my darling? . . . It makes me dizzy. Ah! this house, this island, I can't get used to it. Water all around us . . . water under the windows, stretching as far as the horizon.

(*The* OLD WOMAN *drags the* OLD MAN *down and they move towards the two chairs downstage; the* OLD MAN *seats himself quite naturally on the lap of the* OLD WOMAN.)

OLD MAN. It's six o'clock in the evening . . . it is dark already. It wasn't like this before. Surely you remember, there was still daylight at nine o'clock in the evening, at ten o'clock, at midnight.

OLD WOMAN. Come to think of it, that's very true. What a remarkable memory you have!

OLD MAN. Things have certainly changed.

OLD WOMAN. Why is that, do you think?

OLD MAN. I don't know, Semiramis, sweetheart . . . Perhaps it's because the further one goes, the deeper one sinks. It's because the earth keeps turning around, around, around, around . . .

OLD WOMAN. Around, around, my little pet. (*Silence.*) Ah! yes, you've certainly a fine intellect. You are very gifted, my darling. You could have been head president, head king, or even head doctor, or head general, if you had wanted to, if only you'd had a little ambition in life . . .

OLD MAN. What good would that have done us? We'd not have lived any better . . . and besides, we have a position here. I am a general, in any case, of the house, since I am the general factotum.

OLD WOMAN (*caressing the* OLD MAN *as one caresses a child*). My darling, my pet.

OLD MAN. I'm very bored.

OLD WOMAN. You were more cheerful when you were looking at the water . . . Let's amuse ourselves by making believe, the way you did the other evening.

OLD MAN. Make believe yourself, it's your turn.

OLD WOMAN. It's your turn.

OLD MAN. Your turn.

OLD WOMAN. Your turn.

OLD MAN. Your turn.

OLD WOMAN. Your turn.

OLD MAN. Drink your tea, Semiramis.

(*Of course there is no tea.*)

OLD WOMAN. Come on now, imitate the month of February.

OLD MAN. I don't like the months of the year.

OLD WOMAN. Those are the only ones we have, up till now. Come on, just to please me . . .

OLD MAN. All right, here's the month of February. (*He scratches his head like Stan Laurel.*)

OLD WOMAN (*laughing, applauding*). That's just right. Thank you,

thank you, you're as cute as can be, my darling. (*She hugs him.*)
Oh, you are so gifted, you could have been at least a head general, if you had wanted to . . .

OLD MAN. I am a general, general factotum.
(*Silence.*)

OLD WOMAN. Tell me the story, you know *the* story: "Then at last we arrived . . ."

OLD MAN. Again? . . . I'm sick of it . . . "Then at last we arrived"? That again . . . you always ask for the same thing! . . . "Then at last we arrived . . ." But it's monotonous . . . For all of the seventy-five years that we've been married, every single evening, absolutely every blessed evening, you've made me tell the same story, you've made me imitate the same people, the same months . . . always the same . . . let's talk about something else . . .

OLD WOMAN. My darling, I'm not tired of it . . . it's your life, it fascinates me.

OLD MAN. You know it by heart.

OLD WOMAN. It's as if suddenly I'd forgotten everything . . . it's as though my mind were a clean slate every evening . . . Yes, my darling, I do it on purpose, I take a dose of salts . . . I become new again, for you, my darling, every evening . . . Come on, begin again, please.

OLD MAN. Well, if you want me to.

OLD WOMAN. Come on then, tell your story . . . It's also mine; what is yours is mine! Then at last we arrived . . .

OLD MAN. Then at last we arrived . . . my sweetheart . . .

OLD WOMAN. Then at last we arrived . . . my darling . . .

OLD MAN. Then at last we arrived at a big fence. We were soaked through, frozen to the bone, for hours, for days, for nights, for weeks . . .

OLD WOMAN. For months . . .

OLD MAN. . . . In the rain . . . Our ears, our feet, our knees, our noses, our teeth were chattering . . . that was eighty years ago . . . They wouldn't let us in . . . they might at least have opened the gate of the garden . . .
(*Silence.*)

OLD WOMAN. In the garden the grass was wet.

OLD MAN. There was a path which led to a little square and in the center, a village church . . . Where was this village? Do you recall?

OLD WOMAN. No, my darling, I've forgotten.

OLD MAN. How did we reach it? Where is the road? This place was called Paris, I think . . .

OLD WOMAN. Paris never existed, my little one.

OLD MAN. That city must have existed because it collapsed . . . It was the city of light, but it has been extinguished, extinguished, for four hundred thousand years . . . Nothing remains of it today, except a song.

OLD WOMAN. A real song? That's odd. What song?

OLD MAN. A lullaby, an allegory: "Paris will always be Paris."

OLD WOMAN. And the way to it was through the garden? Was it far?

OLD MAN (*dreaming, lost*). The song? . . . the rain? . . .

OLD WOMAN. You are very gifted. If you had had a little ambition in life you could have been head king, head journalist, head comedian, head general . . . All that's gone down the drain, alas . . . down the old black drain . . . down the old drain, I tell you. (*Silence.*)

OLD MAN. Then at last we arrived . . .

OLD WOMAN. Ah! yes, go on . . . tell me . . .

OLD MAN. (*While the* OLD WOMAN *begins to laugh softly, senilely, then progressively in great bursts, the* OLD MAN *laughs, too, as he continues.*) Then at last we arrived, we laughed till we cried, the story was so idiotic . . . the idiot arrived full speed, bare-bellied, the idiot was pot-bellied . . . he arrived with a trunk chock full of rice; the rice spilled out on the ground . . . the idiot on the ground too, belly to ground . . . then at last we laughed, we laughed, we laughed, the idiotic belly, bare with rice on the ground, the trunk, the story of sick from rice belly to ground, bare-bellied, all with rice, at last we laughed, the idiot at last arrived all bare, we laughed . . .

OLD WOMAN (*laughing*). At last we laughed like idiots, at last arrived all bare, we laughed, the trunk, the trunk full of rice, the rice on the belly, on the ground . . .

OLD MAN AND OLD WOMAN (*laughing together*). At last we laughed. Ah! . . . laughed . . . arrived . . . arrived . . . Ah! . . . Ah! . . . rived . . . arrived . . . arrived . . . the idiotic bare belly . . . arrived with the rice . . . arrived with the rice . . . (*This is all we hear.*) At last we . . . bare-bellied . . . arrived . . . the trunk . . . (*Then the* OLD MAN *and* OLD WOMAN *calm down little by little.*) We lau . . . Ah! . . . aughed . . . Ah! . . . arrived . . . Ah! . . . arrived . . . aughed . . . aughed.

OLD WOMAN. So that's the way it was, your wonderful Paris.

OLD MAN. Who could put it better?

OLD WOMAN. Oh! my darling, you are so really fine. Oh! so really, you know, so really, so really, you could have been anything in life, a lot more than general factotum.

OLD MAN. Let's be modest . . . we should be content with the little . . .

OLD WOMAN. Perhaps you've spoiled your career?

OLD MAN (*weeping suddenly*). I've spoiled it? I've spilled it? Ah! where are you, Mamma, Mamma, where are you, Mamma? . . . hi, hi, hi, I'm an orphan. (*He moans.*) . . . an orphan, dworfan.

OLD WOMAN. Here I am, what are you afraid of?

OLD MAN. No, Semiramis, my sweetheart, you're not my mamma . . . orphan, dworfan, who will protect me?

OLD WOMAN. But I'm here, my darling!

OLD MAN. It's not the same thing . . . I want my mamma, na, you, you're not my mamma, you . . .

OLD WOMAN (*caressing him*). You're breaking my heart, don't cry, my little one.

OLD MAN. Hi, hi, let me go, hi, hi, I'm all spoiled, I'm wet all over, my career is spilled, it's spoiled.

OLD WOMAN. Calm down.

OLD MAN (*sobbing, his mouth wide open like a baby*). I'm an orphan . . . dworfan.

OLD WOMAN (*trying to console him by cajoling him*). My orphan, my darling, you're breaking my heart, my orphan. (*She rocks the* OLD MAN *who is sitting on her knees again.*)

OLD MAN (*sobbing*). Hi, hi, hi! My mamma! Where is my mamma? I don't have a mamma anymore.

OLD WOMAN. I am your wife, I'm the one who is your mamma now.

OLD MAN (*giving in a little*). That's not true, I'm an orphan, hi, hi.

OLD WOMAN (*still rocking him*). My pet, my orphan, dworfan, worfan, morphan, orphan.

OLD MAN (*still sulky, but giving in more and more*). No . . . I don't wan't; I don't wa-a-a-ant.

OLD WOMAN (*crooning*). Orphan-ly, orphan-lay, orphan-lo, orphan-loo.

OLD MAN. No-o-o . . . No-o-o.

OLD WOMAN (*same business*). Li lon lala, li lon la lay, orphan-ly, or-phan-lay, relee-relay, orphan-li-relee-rela . . .

OLD MAN. Hi, hi, hi, hi. (*He sniffles, calming down little by little.*) Where is she? My mamma.

OLD WOMAN. In heavenly paradise . . . she hears you, she sees you, among the flowers; don't cry anymore, you will only make me weep!

OLD MAN. That's not even true-ue . . . she can't see me . . . she can't hear me. I'm an orphan, on earth, you're not my mamma . . .

OLD WOMAN. (*He is almost calm.*) Now, come on, calm down, don't

get so upset . . . you have great qualities, my little general . . .
dry your tears; the guests are sure to come this evening and they
mustn't see you this way . . . all is not lost, all is not spoiled,
you'll tell them everything, you will explain, you have a message
. . . you always say you are going to deliver it . . . you must
live, you have to struggle for your message . . .

OLD MAN. I have a message, that's God's truth, I struggle, a mission,
I have something to say, a message to communicate to humanity,
to mankind . . .

OLD WOMAN. To mankind, my darling, your message! . . .

OLD MAN. That's true, yes, it's true . . .

OLD WOMAN. (*She wipes the* OLD MAN's *nose, dries his tears.*) That's
it . . . you're a man, a soldier, a general factotum . . .

OLD MAN. (*He gets off the* OLD WOMAN's *lap and walks with short,
agitated steps.*) I'm not like other people, I have an ideal in life.
I am perhaps gifted, as you say, I have some talent, but things
aren't easy for me. I've served well in my capacity as general
factotum, I've always been in command of the situation, honor-
ably, that should be enough . . .

OLD WOMAN. Not for you, you're not like other people, you are much
greater, and moreover you'd have done much better if you had
got along with other people, like other people do. You've quar-
reled with all your friends, with all the directors, with all the
generals, with your own brother.

OLD MAN. It's not my fault, Semiramis, you know very well what he
said.

OLD WOMAN. What did he say?

OLD MAN. He said: "My friends, I've got a flea. I'm going to pay you
a visit in the hope of leaving my flea with you."

OLD WOMAN. People say things like that, my dear. You shouldn't have
paid any attention to it. But with Carel, why were you so angry
with him. Was it his fault too?

OLD MAN. You're going to make me angry, you're going to make me
angry. Na. Of course it was his fault. He came one evening, he
said: "I know just the word that fits you. I'm not going to say
it, I'll just think it." And he laughed like a fool.

OLD WOMAN. But he had a warm heart, my darling. In this life, you've
got to be less sensitive.

OLD MAN. I don't care for jokes like that.

OLD WOMAN. You could have been head admiral, head cabinet-maker,
head orchestra conductor.

(*Long silence. They remain immobile for a time, completely rigid
on their chairs.*)

OLD MAN (*as in a dream*). At the end of the garden there was . . . there was . . . there was . . . there was . . . was what, my dear?

OLD WOMAN. The city of Paris!

OLD MAN. At the end, at the end of the end of the city of Paris, there was, there was, was what?

OLD WOMAN. My darling, was what, my darling, was who?

OLD MAN. The place and the weather were beautiful . . .

OLD WOMAN. The weather was so beautiful, are you sure?

OLD MAN. I don't recall the place . . .

OLD WOMAN. Don't tax your mind then . . .

OLD MAN. It's too far away, I can no longer . . . recall it . . . where was this?

OLD WOMAN. But what?

OLD MAN. What I . . . what I . . . where was this? And who?

OLD WOMAN. No matter where it is—I will follow you anywhere, I'll follow you, my darling.

OLD MAN. Ah! I have so much difficulty expressing myself . . . but I must tell it all.

OLD WOMAN. It's a sacred duty. You've no right to keep your message from the world. You must reveal it to mankind, they're waiting for it . . . the universe waits only for you.

OLD MAN. Yes, yes, I will speak.

OLD WOMAN. Have you really decided? You must.

OLD MAN. Drink your tea.

OLD WOMAN. You could have been head orator, if you'd had more will power in life . . . I'm proud, I'm happy that you have at last decided to speak to every country, to Europe, to every continent!

OLD MAN. Unfortunately, I have so much difficulty expressing myself, it isn't easy for me.

OLD WOMAN. It's easy once you begin, like life and death . . . it's enough to have your mind made up. It's in speaking that ideas come to us, words, and then we, in our own words, we find perhaps everything, the city too, the garden, and then we are orphans no longer.

OLD MAN. It's not I who's going to speak, I've hired a professional orator, he'll speak in my name, you'll see.

OLD WOMAN. Then, it really is for this evening? And have you invited everyone, all the characters, all the property owners, and all the intellectuals?

OLD MAN. Yes, all the owners and all the intellectuals. (*Silence.*)

OLD WOMAN. The janitors? the bishops? the chemists? the tinsmiths?

the violinists? the delegates? the presidents? the police? the mer-
chants? the buildings? the pen holders? the chromosomes?

OLD MAN. Yes, yes, and the post-office employees, the inn-keepers, and
the artists, everybody who is a little intellectual, a little proprietary!

OLD WOMAN. And the bankers?

OLD MAN. Yes, invited.

OLD WOMAN. The proletarians? the functionaries? the militaries? the
revolutionaries? the reactionaries? the alienists and their alienated?

OLD MAN. Of course, all of them, all of them, all of them, since actually
everyone is either intellectual or proprietary.

OLD WOMAN. Don't get upset, my darling, I don't mean to annoy you,
you are so very absent-minded, like all great geniuses. This meeting is important, they must all be here this evening. Can you
count on them? Have they promised?

OLD MAN. Drink your tea, Semiramis. (*Silence.*)

OLD WOMAN. The papacy, the papayas, and the papers?

OLD MAN. I've invited them. (*Silence.*) I'm going to communicate the
message to them . . . All my life, I've felt that I was suffocating;
and now, they will know all, thanks to you and to the Orator,
you are the only ones who have understood me.

OLD WOMAN. I'm so proud of you . . .

OLD MAN. The meeting will take place in a few minutes.

OLD WOMAN. It's true then, they're going to come, this evening? You
won't feel like crying any more, the intellectuals and the pro-
prietors will take the place of papas and mammas? (*Silence.*)
Couldn't you put off this meeting? It won't be too tiring for us?
(*More violent agitation. For several moments the* OLD MAN *has
been turning around the* OLD WOMAN *with the short, hesitant steps
of an old man or of a child. He takes a step or two towards one
of the doors, then returns and walks around her again.*)

OLD MAN. You really think this might tire us?

OLD WOMAN. You have a slight cold.

OLD MAN. How can I call it off?

OLD WOMAN. Invite them for another evening. You could telephone.

OLD MAN. No, my God, I can't do that, it's too late. They've probably
already embarked!

OLD WOMAN. You should have been more careful.
(*We hear the sound of a boat gliding through the water.*)

OLD MAN. I think someone is coming already . . . (*The gliding sound
of a boat is heard more clearly.*) . . . Yes, they're coming! . . .
(*The* OLD WOMAN *gets up also and walks with a hobble.*)

OLD WOMAN. Perhaps it's the Orator.

OLD MAN. He won't come so soon. This must be somebody else. (*We hear the doorbell ring.*) Ah!

OLD WOMAN. Ah!

(*Nervously, the* OLD MAN *and the* OLD WOMAN *move towards the concealed door in the recess to the right. As they move upstage, they say*)

OLD MAN. Come on . . .

OLD WOMAN. My hair must look a sight . . . wait a moment . . .

(*She arranges her hair and her dress as she hobbles along, pulling up her thick red stockings.*)

OLD MAN. You should have gotten ready before . . . you had plenty of time.

OLD WOMAN. I'm so badly dressed . . . I'm wearing an old gown and it's all rumpled . . .

OLD MAN. All you had to do was to press it . . . hurry up! You're making our guests wait.

(*The* OLD MAN, *followed by the* OLD WOMAN *still grumbling, reaches the door in the recess; we don't see them for a moment; we hear them open the door, then close it again after having shown someone in.*)

VOICE OF OLD MAN. Good evening, madam, won't you please come in. We're delighted to see you. This is my wife.

VOICE OF OLD WOMAN. Good evening, madam, I am very happy to make your acquaintance. Take care, don't ruin your hat. You might take out the hatpin, that will be more comfortable. Oh! no, no one will sit on it.

VOICE OF OLD MAN. Put your fur down there. Let me help you. No, nothing will happen to it.

VOICE OF OLD WOMAN. Oh! what a pretty suit . . . and such darling colors in your blouse . . . Won't you have some cookies . . . Oh, you're not fat at all . . . no . . . plump . . . Just leave your umbrella there.

VOICE OF OLD MAN. Follow me, please.

OLD MAN (*back view*). I have only a modest position . . .

(*The* OLD MAN *and* OLD WOMAN *re-enter together, leaving space between them for their guest. She is invisible. The* OLD MAN *and* OLD WOMAN *advance, downstage, facing the audience and speaking to the invisible lady, who walks between them.*)

OLD MAN (*to the invisible lady*). You've had good weather?

OLD WOMAN (*to the lady*). You're not too tired? . . . Yes, a little.

OLD MAN (*to the lady*). At the edge of the water . . .

OLD WOMAN (*to the lady*). It's kind of you to say so.

OLD MAN (*to the lady*). Let me get you a chair.

(OLD MAN *goes to the left, he exits by door No. 6.*)

OLD WOMAN (*to the lady*). Take this one, for the moment, please. (*She indicates one of the two chairs and seats herself on the other, to the right of the invisible lady.*) It seems rather warm in here, doesn't it? (*She smiles at the lady.*) What a charming fan you have! My husband . . . (*The* OLD MAN *re-enters through door No. 7, carrying a chair.*) . . . gave me one very like it, that must have been seventy-three years ago . . . and I still have it . . . (*The* OLD MAN *places the chair to the left of the invisible lady.*) . . . it was for my birthday! . . .

(*The* OLD MAN *sits on the chair that he has just brought onstage, so that the invisible lady is between the old couple. The* OLD MAN *turns his face towards the lady, smiles at her, nods his head, softly rubs his hands together, with the air of following what she says. The* OLD WOMAN *does the same business.*)

OLD MAN. No, madam, life is never cheap.

OLD WOMAN (*to the lady*). You are so right . . . (*The lady speaks.*) As you say, it is about time all that changed . . . (*Changing her tone*) Perhaps my husband can do something about it . . . he's going to tell you about it.

OLD MAN (*to the* OLD WOMAN). Hush, hush, Semiramis, the time hasn't come to talk about that yet. (*To the lady*) Excuse me, madam, for having aroused your curiosity. (*The lady reacts.*) Dear madam, don't insist . . .

(*The* OLD MAN *and* OLD WOMAN *smile. They even laugh. They appear to be very amused by the story the invisible lady tells them. A pause, a moment of silence in the conversation. Their faces lose all expression.*)

OLD MAN (*to the invisible lady*). Yes, you're quite right . . .

OLD WOMAN. Yes, yes, yes . . . Oh! surely not.

OLD MAN. Yes, yes, yes. Not at all.

OLD WOMAN. Yes?

OLD MAN. No!?

OLD WOMAN. It's certainly true.

OLD MAN (*laughing*). It isn't possible.

OLD WOMAN (*laughing*). Oh! well. (*To the* OLD MAN) she's charming.

OLD MAN (*to the* OLD WOMAN). Madam has made a conquest. (*To the invisible lady*) My congratulations! . . .

OLD WOMAN (*to the invisible lady*). You're not like the young people today . . .

OLD MAN (*bending over painfully in order to recover an invisible object*

that the invisible lady has dropped). Let me . . . don't disturb
yourself . . . I'll get it . . . Oh! you're quicker than I . . .
(*He straightens up again.*)

OLD WOMAN (*to the* OLD MAN). She's younger than you!

OLD MAN (*to the invisible lady*). Old age is a heavy burden. I can only
wish you an eternal youth.

OLD WOMAN (*to the invisible lady*). He's sincere, he speaks from the
heart. (*To the* OLD MAN) My darling!

(*Several moments of silence. The* OLD MAN *and* OLD WOMAN, *heads
turned in profile, look at the invisible lady, smiling politely; they
then turn their heads towards the audience, then look again at the
invisible lady, answering her smile with their smiles, and her
questions with their replies.*)

OLD WOMAN. It's very kind of you to take such an interest in us.

OLD MAN. We live a retired life.

OLD WOMAN. My husband's not really misanthropic, he just loves
solitude.

OLD MAN. We have the radio, I get in some fishing, and then there's
fairly regular boat service.

OLD WOMAN. On Sundays there are two boats in the morning, one in
the evening, not to mention privately chartered trips.

OLD MAN (*to the invisible lady*). When the weather's clear, there is a
moon.

OLD WOMAN (*to the invisible lady*). He's always concerned with his
duties as general factotum . . . they keep him busy . . . On the
other hand, at his age, he might very well take it easy.

OLD MAN (*to the invisible lady*). I'll have plenty of time to take it easy
in my grave.

OLD WOMAN (*to the* OLD MAN). Don't say that, my little darling . . .
(*To the invisible lady*) Our family, what's left of it, my husband's
friends, still came to see us, from time to time, ten years ago . . .

OLD MAN (*to the invisible lady*). In the winter, a good book, beside the
radiator, and the memories of a lifetime.

OLD WOMAN (*to the invisible lady*). A modest life but a full one . . .
he devotes two hours every day to work on his message.

(*The doorbell rings. After a short pause, we hear the noise of a
boat leaving.*)

OLD WOMAN (*to the* OLD MAN). Someone has come. Go quickly.

OLD MAN (*to the invisible lady*). Please excuse me, madam. Just a
moment! (*To the* OLD WOMAN) Hurry and bring some chairs!

(*Loud ringing of the doorbell.*)

OLD MAN (*hastening, all bent over, towards door No. 2 to the right,
while the* OLD WOMAN *goes towards the concealed door on the*

left, hurrying with difficulty, hobbling along). It must be someone important. (*He hurries, opens door No. 2, and the invisible colonel enters. Perhaps it would be useful for us to hear discreetly several trumpet notes, several phrases, like "Hail the Chief." When he opens the door and sees the invisible colonel, the* OLD MAN *stiffens into a respectful position of attention.*) Ah! . . . Colonel! (*He lifts his hand vaguely towards his forehead, so as to roughly sketch a salute.*) Good evening, my dear Colonel . . . This is a very great honor for me . . . I . . . I . . . I was not expecting it . . . although . . . indeed . . . in short, I am most proud to welcome you, a hero of your eminence, into my humble dwelling . . . (*He presses the invisible hand that the invisible colonel gives him, bending forward ceremoniously, then straightening up again.*) Without false modesty, nevertheless, I permit myself to confess to you that I do not feel unworthy of the honor of your visit! Proud, yes . . . unworthy, no! . . .

(*The* OLD WOMAN *appears with a chair, entering from the right.*)

OLD WOMAN. Oh! What a handsome uniform! What beautiful medals! Who is it, my darling?

OLD MAN (*to the* OLD WOMAN). Can't you see that it's the colonel?

OLD WOMAN (*to the* OLD MAN). Ah!

OLD MAN (*to the* OLD WOMAN). Count his stripes! (*To the colonel*) This is my wife, Semiramis. (*To the* OLD WOMAN) Come here so that I can introduce you to the colonel. (*The* OLD WOMAN *approaches, dragging the chair by one hand, and makes a curtsey, without letting go of the chair. To the colonel*) My wife. (*To the* OLD WOMAN) The colonel.

OLD WOMAN. How do you do, Colonel. Welcome. You're an old comrade of my husband's, he's a general . . .

OLD MAN (*annoyed*). factotum, factotum . . .

(*The invisible colonel kisses the hand of the* OLD WOMAN. *This is apparent from the gesture she makes as she raises her hand toward his lips. Overcome with emotion, the* OLD WOMAN *lets go of the chair.*)

OLD WOMAN. Oh! He's most polite . . . you can see that he's really superior, a superior being! . . . (*She takes hold of the chair again. To the colonel*) This chair is for you . . .

OLD MAN (*to the invisible colonel*). This way, if you please . . . (*They move downstage, the* OLD WOMAN *dragging the chair. To the colonel*) Yes, one guest has come already. We're expecting a great many more people! . . .

(*The* OLD WOMAN *places the chair to the right.*)

OLD WOMAN (*to the colonel*). Sit here, please.

(*The* OLD MAN *introduces the two invisible guests to each other.*)

OLD MAN. A young lady we know . . .

OLD WOMAN. A very dear friend . . .

OLD MAN (*same business*). The colonel . . . a famous soldier.

OLD WOMAN (*indicating the chair she has just brought in to the colonel*). Do take this chair . . .

OLD MAN (*to the* OLD WOMAN). No, no, can't you see that the colonel wishes to sit beside the lady! . . .

(*The colonel seats himself invisibly on the third chair from the left; the invisible lady is supposedly sitting on the second chair; seated next to each other they engage in an inaudible conversation; the* OLD WOMAN *and* OLD MAN *continue to stand behind their chairs, on both sides of their invisible guests; the* OLD MAN *to the left of the lady, the* OLD WOMAN *to the right of the colonel.*)

OLD WOMAN (*listening to the conversation of the two guests*). Oh! Oh! That's going too far.

OLD MAN (*same business*). Perhaps. (*The* OLD MAN *and the* OLD WOMAN *make signs to each other over the heads of their guests, while they follow the inaudible conversation which takes a turn that seems to displease them. Abruptly*) Yes, Colonel, they are not here yet, but they'll be here. And the Orator will speak in my behalf, he will explain the meaning of my message . . . Take care, Colonel, this lady's husband may arrive at any moment.

OLD WOMAN (*to the* OLD MAN). Who is this gentleman?

OLD MAN (*to the* OLD WOMAN). I've told you, it's the colonel. (*Some embarrassing things take place, invisibly.*)

OLD WOMAN (*to the* OLD MAN). I knew it. I knew it.

OLD MAN. Then why are you asking?

OLD WOMAN. For my information. Colonel, no cigarette butts on the floor!

OLD MAN (*to colonel*). Colonel, Colonel, it's slipped my mind—in the last war did you win or lose?

OLD WOMAN (*to the invisible lady*). But my dear, don't let it happen!

OLD MAN. Look at me, look at me, do I look like a bad soldier? One time, Colonel, under fire . . .

OLD WOMAN. He's going too far! It's embarrassing! (*She seizes the invisible sleeve of the colonel.*) Listen to him! My darling, why don't you stop him!

OLD MAN (*continuing quickly*). And all on my own, I killed 209 of them; we called them that because they jumped so high to escape, however there weren't so many of them as there were flies; of course it is less amusing, Colonel, but thanks to my strength of character, I have . . . Oh! no, I must, please.

OLD WOMAN (*to colonel*). My husband never lies; it may be true that we are old, nevertheless we're respectable.

OLD MAN (*violently, to the colonel*). A hero must be a gentleman too, if he hopes to be a complete hero!

OLD WOMAN (*to the colonel*). I've known you for many years, but I'd never have believed you were capable of this. (*To the lady, while we hear the sound of boats*) I'd never have believed him capable of this. We have our dignity, our self-respect.

OLD MAN (*in a quavering voice*). I'm still capable of bearing arms. (*Doorbell rings.*) Excuse me, I must go to the door. (*He stumbles and knocks over the chair of the invisible lady.*) Oh! pardon.

OLD WOMAN (*rushing forward*). You didn't hurt yourself? (*The* OLD MAN *and* OLD WOMAN *help the invisible lady onto her feet.*) You've got all dirty, there's some dust. (*She helps brush the lady. The doorbell rings again.*)

OLD MAN. Forgive me, forgive me. (*To the* OLD WOMAN) Go bring a chair.

OLD WOMAN (*to the two invisible guests*). Excuse me for a moment. (*While the* OLD MAN *goes to open door No. 3, the* OLD WOMAN *exits through door No. 5 to look for a chair, and she re-enters by door No. 8.*)

OLD MAN (*moving towards the door*). He was trying to get my goat. I'm almost angry. (*He opens the door.*) Oh! madam, you're here! I can scarcely believe my eyes, and yet, nevertheless . . . I didn't really dare to hope . . . really it's . . . Oh! madam, madam . . . I have thought about you, all my life, all my life, madam, they always called you La Belle . . . it's your husband . . . someone told me, certainly . . . you haven't changed a bit . . . Oh! yes, yes, your nose *has* grown longer, maybe it's a little swollen . . . I didn't notice it when I first saw you, but I see it now . . . a lot longer . . . ah! how unfortunate! You certainly didn't do it on purpose . . . how did it happen? . . . little by little . . . excuse me, sir and dear friend, you'll permit me to call you "dear friend," I knew your wife long before you . . . she was the same, but with a completely different nose . . . I congratulate you, sir, you seem to love each other very much. (*The* OLD WOMAN *re-enters through door No. 8 with a chair.*) Semiramis, two guests have arrived, we need one more chair . . . (*The* OLD WOMAN *puts the chair behind the four others, then exits by door No. 8 and re-enters by door No. 5, after a few moments, with another chair that she places beside the one she has just brought in. By this time, the* OLD MAN *and the two guests have moved near the* OLD WOMAN.) Come this way, please, more guests have ar-

rived. I'm going to introduce you . . . now then, madam . . .
Oh! Belle, Belle, Miss Belle, that's what they used to call you . . .
now you're all bent over . . . Oh! sir, she is still Belle to me,
even so; under her glasses, she still has pretty eyes; her hair is
white, but under the white one can see brown, and blue, I'm sure
of that . . . come nearer, nearer . . . what is this, sir, a gift,
for my wife? (*To the* OLD WOMAN, *who has just come on with the
chair*) Semiramis, that is Belle, you know, Belle . . . (*To the
colonel and the invisible lady*) This is Miss, pardon, Mrs. Belle,
don't smile . . . and her husband . . . (*To the* OLD WOMAN)
A childhood friend, I've often spoken of her to you . . . and her
husband. (*Again to the colonel and to the invisible lady*) And her
husband . . .

OLD WOMAN (*making a little curtsey*). He certainly makes good introductions. He has fine manners. Good evening, madam, good evening, sir. (*She indicates the two first guests to the newly arrived
couple.*) Our friends, yes . . .

OLD MAN (*to the* OLD WOMAN). He's brought you a present. (*The* OLD
WOMAN *takes the present.*)

OLD WOMAN. Is it a flower, sir? or a cradle? a pear tree? or a crow?

OLD MAN (*to the* OLD WOMAN). No, no, can't you see that it's a painting?

OLD WOMAN. Oh! how pretty! Thank you, sir . . . (*To the invisible
lady*) Would you like to see it, dear friend?

OLD MAN (*to the invisible colonel*). Would you like to see it?

OLD WOMAN (*to Belle's husband*). Doctor, Doctor, I feel squeamish, I
have hot flashes, I feel sick, I've aches and pains, I haven't any
feeling in my feet, I've caught cold in my eyes, I've a cold in my
fingers, I'm suffering from liver trouble, Doctor, Doctor! . . .

OLD MAN (*to the* OLD WOMAN). This gentleman is not a doctor, he's a
photo-engraver.

OLD WOMAN (*to the first invisible lady*). If you've finished looking at
it, you might hang it up. (*To the* OLD MAN) That doesn't matter,
he's charming even so, he's dazzling. (*To the photo-engraver*)
Without meaning to flatter you . . . (*The* OLD MAN *and the* OLD
WOMAN *now move behind the chairs, close to each other, almost
touching, but back to back; they talk: the* OLD MAN *to Belle, the*
OLD WOMAN *to the photo-engraver; from time to time their replies,
as shown by the way they turn their heads, are addressed to one
or the other of the two first guests.*)

OLD MAN (*to Belle*). I am very touched . . . You're still the same, in
spite of everything . . . I've loved you, a hundred years ago . . .

But there's been such a change . . . No, you haven't changed a
bit . . . I loved you, I love you . . .

OLD WOMAN (*to the photo-engraver*). Oh! Sir, sir, sir . . .

OLD MAN (*to the colonel*). I'm in complete agreement with you on that
point.

OLD WOMAN (*to the photo-engraver*). Oh! certainly, sir, certainly, sir,
certainly . . . (*To the first lady*) Thanks for hanging it up . . .
Forgive me if I've inconvenienced you.

(*The light grows stronger. It should grow stronger and stronger
as the invisible guests continue to arrive.*)

OLD MAN (*almost whimpering to Belle*). Where are the snows of yester-
year?

OLD WOMAN (*to the photo-engraver*). Oh! Sir, sir, sir . . . Oh! sir . . .

OLD MAN (*pointing out the first lady to Belle*). She's a young friend
. . . she's very sweet . . .

OLD WOMAN (*pointing the colonel out to the photo-engraver*). Yes, he's
a mounted staff colonel . . . a comrade of my husband . . . a
subaltern, my husband's a general . . .

OLD MAN (*to Belle*). Your ears were not always so pointed! . . . My
Belle, do you remember?

OLD WOMAN (*to the photo-engraver, simpering grotesquely; she develops this manner more and more in this scene; she shows her
thick red stockings, raises her many petticoats, shows an under-
skirt full of holes, exposes her old breast; then, her hands on her
hips, throws her head back, makes little erotic cries, projects her
pelvis, her legs spread apart; she laughs like an old prostitute; this
business, entirely different from her manner heretofore as well as
from that she will have subsequently, and which must reveal the
hidden personality of the* OLD WOMAN, *ceases abruptly*). So you
think I'm too old for that, do you?

OLD MAN (*to Belle, very romantically*). When we were young, the
moon was a living star. Ah! yes, yes, if only we had dared, but
we were only children. Wouldn't you like to recapture those by-
gone days . . . is it still possible? Is it still possible? Ah! no, no,
it is no longer possible. Those days have flown away as fast as a
train. Time has left the marks of his wheels on our skin. Do you
believe surgeons can perform miracles? (*To the colonel*) I am a
soldier, and you too, we soldiers are always young, the generals
are like gods . . . (*To Belle*) It ought to be that way . . . Alas!
Alas! We have lost everything. We could have been so happy, I'm
sure of it, we could have been, we could have been; perhaps the
flowers are budding again beneath the snow! . . .

OLD WOMAN (*to photo-engraver*). Flatterer! Rascal! Ah! Ah! I look younger than my years? You're a little savage! You're exciting.

OLD MAN (*to Belle*). Will you be my Isolde and let me be your Tristan? Beauty is more than skin deep, it's in the heart . . . Do you understand? We could have had the pleasure of sharing, joy, beauty, eternity . . . an eternity . . . Why didn't we dare? We weren't brave enough . . . Everything is lost, lost, lost.

OLD WOMAN (*to photo-engraver*). Oh no. Oh! no, Oh! la la, you give me the shivers. You too, are you ticklish? To tickle or be tickled? I'm a little embarrassed . . . (*She laughs.*) Do you like my petticoat? Or do you like this skirt better?

OLD MAN (*to Belle*). A general factotum has a poor life!

OLD WOMAN (*turning her head towards the first invisible lady*). In order to make crepes de Chine? A leaf of beef, an hour of flour, a little gastric sugar. (*To the photo-engraver*) You've got clever fingers, ah . . . all the sa-a-ame! . . . Oh-oh-oh-oh.

OLD MAN (*to Belle*). My worthy helpmeet, Semiramis, has taken the *place of my mother*. (*He turns towards the colonel.*) Colonel, as I've often observed to you, one must take the truth as one finds it. (*He turns back towards Belle.*)

OLD WOMAN (*to photo-engraver*). Do you really really believe that one could have children at any age? Any age children?

OLD MAN (*to Belle*). It's this alone that has saved me: the inner life, peace of mind, austerity, my scientific investigations, philosophy, my message . . .

OLD WOMAN (*to photo-engraver*). I've never yet betrayed my husband, the general . . . not so hard, you're going to make me fall . . . I'm only his poor mamma! (*She sobs.*) A great, great (*She pushes him back.*), great . . . mamma. My conscience causes these tears to flow. For me the branch of the apple tree is broken. Try to find somebody else. I no longer want to gather rosebuds . . .

OLD MAN (*to Belle*). . . . All the preoccupations of a superior order . . .

(*The* OLD MAN *and* OLD WOMAN *lead Belle and the photo-engraver up alongside the two other invisible guests, and seat them.*)

OLD MAN AND OLD WOMAN (*to the photo-engraver and Belle*). Sit down, please sit down.

(*The* OLD MAN *and* OLD WOMAN *sit down too, he to the left, she to the right, with the four empty chairs between them. A long mute scene, punctuated at intervals with* "no," "yes," "yes." *The* OLD MAN *and* OLD WOMAN *listen to the conversation of the invisible guests.*)

OLD WOMAN (*to the photo-engraver*). We had one son . . . of course, he's still alive . . . he's gone away . . . it's a common story . . . or, rather, unusual . . . he abandoned his parents . . . he had a heart of gold . . . that was a long time ago . . . We loved him so much . . . he slammed the door . . . My husband and I tried to hold him back with all our might . . . he was seven years old, the age of reason, I called after him: "My son, my child, my son, my child." . . . He didn't even look back . . .

OLD MAN. Alas, no . . . no, we've never had a child . . . I'd hoped for a son . . . Semiramis, too . . . we did everything . . . and my poor Semiramis is so maternal, too. Perhaps it was better that way . . . As for me I was an ungrateful son myself . . . Ah! . . . grief, regret, remorse, that's all we have . . . that's all we have left . . .

OLD WOMAN. He said to me: "You kill birds! Why do you kill birds?" . . . But we don't kill birds . . . we've never harmed so much as a fly . . . His eyes were full of big tears. He wouldn't let us dry them. He wouldn't let me come near him. He said: "Yes, you kill all the birds, all the birds." . . . He showed us his little fists . . . "You're lying, you've betrayed me! The streets are full of dead birds, of dying baby birds." It's the song of the birds! . . . "No, it's their death rattle. The sky is red with blood." . . . No, my child, it's blue. He cried again: "You've betrayed me, I adored you, I believed you to be good . . . the streets are full of dead birds, you've torn out their eyes . . . Papa, Mamma, you're wicked! . . . I refuse to stay with you." . . . I threw myself at his feet . . . His father was weeping. We couldn't hold him back. As he went we could still hear him calling: "It's you who are responsible" . . . What does that mean, "responsible"?

OLD MAN. I let my mother die all alone in a ditch. She called after me, moaning feebly: "My little child, my beloved son, don't leave me to die all alone . . . Stay with me. I don't have much time left." Don't worry, Mamma, I told her, I'll be back in a moment . . . I was in a hurry . . . I was going to the ball, to dance. I will be back in a minute. But when I returned she was already dead, and they had buried her deep . . . I broke open the grave, I searched for . . . I couldn't find her . . . I know, I know, sons, always, abandon their mothers, and they more or less kill their fathers . . . Life is like that . . . but I, I suffer from it . . . and the others, they don't . . .

OLD WOMAN. He cried: "Papa, Mamma, I'll never set eyes on you again."

OLD MAN. I suffer from it, yes, the others don't . . .

OLD WOMAN. Don't speak of him to my husband. He loved his parents so much. He never left them for a single moment. He cared for them, coddled them . . . And they died in his arms, saying to him: "You have been a perfect son. God will be good to you."

OLD MAN. I can still see her stretched out in the ditch, she was holding lily of the valley in her hand, she cried: "Don't forget me, don't forget me" . . . her eyes were full of big tears, and she called me by my baby name: "Little Chick," she said, "Little Chick, don't leave me here all alone."

OLD WOMAN (*to the photo-engraver*). He has never written to us. From time to time, a friend tells us that he's been seen here or there, that he is well, that he is a good husband . . .

OLD MAN (*to Belle*). When I got back, she had been buried a long time. (*To the first invisible lady*) Oh, yes. Oh! yes, madam, we have a movie theatre in the house, a restaurant, bathrooms . . .

OLD WOMAN (*to the colonel*). Yes, Colonel, it is because he . . .

OLD MAN. Basically that's it.

(*Desultory conversation, getting bogged down.*)

OLD WOMAN. If only!

OLD MAN. Thus, I've not . . . I, it . . . certainly . . .

OLD WOMAN (*dislocated dialogue, exhaustion*). All in all.

OLD MAN. To ours and to theirs.

OLD WOMAN. So that.

OLD MAN. From me to him.

OLD WOMAN. Him, or her?

OLD MAN. Them.

OLD WOMAN. Curl-papers . . . After all.

OLD MAN. It's not that.

OLD WOMAN. Why?

OLD MAN. Yes.

OLD WOMAN. I.

OLD MAN. All in all.

OLD WOMAN. All in all.

OLD MAN (*to the first invisible lady*). What was that, madam?

(*A long silence, the* OLD MAN *and* OLD WOMAN *remain rigid on their chairs. Then the doorbell rings.*)

OLD MAN (*with increasing nervousness*). Someone has come. People. Still more people.

OLD WOMAN. I thought I heard some boats.

OLD MAN. I'll go to the door. Go bring some chairs. Excuse me, gentlemen, ladies. (*He goes towards door No. 7.*)

OLD WOMAN (*to the invisible guests who have already arrived*). Get up for a moment, please. The Orator will be here soon. We must ready the room for the meeting. (*The* OLD WOMAN *arranges the chairs, turning their backs towards the audience.*) Lend me a hand, please. Thanks.

OLD MAN (*opening door No. 7*). Good evening, ladies, good evening, gentlemen. Please come in.

(*The three or four invisible persons who have arrived are very tall, and the* OLD MAN *has to stand on his toes in order to shake hands with them. The* OLD WOMAN, *after placing the chairs as indicated above, goes over to the* OLD MAN.)

OLD MAN (*making introductions*). My wife . . . Mr. . . . Mrs. . . . my wife . . . Mr. . . . Mrs. . . . my wife . . .

OLD WOMAN. Who are all these people, my darling?

OLD MAN (*to* OLD WOMAN). Go find some chairs, dear.

OLD WOMAN. I can't do everything! . . .

(*She exits, grumbling, by door No. 6 and re-enters by door No. 7, while the* OLD MAN, *with the newly arrived guests, moves downstage.*)

OLD MAN. Don't drop your movie camera. (*More introductions.*) The Colonel . . . the Lady . . . Mrs. Belle . . . the Photo-engraver . . . These are the newspaper men, they have come to hear the Orator too, who should be here any minute now . . . Don't be impatient . . . You'll not be bored . . . all together now . . . (*The* OLD WOMAN *re-enters through door No. 7 with two chairs.*) Come along, bring the chairs more quickly . . . we're still short one.

(*The* OLD WOMAN *goes to find another chair, still grumbling, exiting by door No. 3, and re-entering by door No. 8.*)

OLD WOMAN. All right, and so . . . I'm doing as well as I can . . . I'm not a machine, you know . . . Who are all these people? (*She exits.*)

OLD MAN. Sit down, sit down, the ladies with the ladies, and the gentlemen with the gentlemen, or vice versa, if you prefer . . . We don't have any more nice chairs . . . we have to make do with what we have . . . I'm sorry . . . take the one in the middle . . . does anyone need a fountain pen? Telephone Maillot, you'll get Monique . . . Claude is an angel. I don't have a radio . . . I take all the newspapers . . . that depends on a number of things; I manage these buildings, but I have no help . . . we have to economize . . . no interviews, please, for the moment . . . later, we'll see . . . you'll soon have a place to sit . . . what can she be doing? (*The* OLD WOMAN *enters by door No. 8 with a chair.*) Faster, Semiramis . . .

OLD WOMAN. I'm doing my best . . . Who are all these people?

OLD MAN. I'll explain it all to you later.

OLD WOMAN. And that woman? That woman, my darling?

OLD MAN. Don't get upset . . . (*To the colonel*) Colonel, journalism is
a profession too, like a fighting man's . . . (*To the* OLD WOMAN)
Take care of the ladies, my dear . . . (*The doorbell rings. The*
OLD MAN *hurries towards door No. 8.*) Wait a moment . . . (*To
the* OLD WOMAN) Bring chairs!

OLD WOMAN. Gentlemen, ladies, excuse me . . .
(*She exits by door No. 3, re-entering by door No. 2; the* OLD MAN
*goes to open concealed door No. 9, and disappears at the moment
the* OLD WOMAN *re-enters by door No. 2.*)

OLD MAN (*out of sight*). Come in . . . come in . . . come in . . .
come in . . . (*He reappears, leading in a number of invisible
people, including one very small child he holds by the hand.*)
One doesn't bring little children to a scientific lecture . . . the
poor little thing is going to be bored . . . if he begins to cry
or to peepee on the ladies' dresses, that'll be a fine state of affairs!
(*He conducts them to stage center; the* OLD WOMAN *comes on with
two chairs.*) I wish to introduce you to my wife, Semiramis; and
these are their children.

OLD WOMAN. Ladies, gentlemen . . . Oh! aren't they sweet!

OLD MAN. That one is the smallest.

OLD WOMAN. Oh, he's so cute . . . so cute . . . so cute!

OLD MAN. Not enough chairs.

OLD WOMAN. Oh! dear, oh dear, oh dear . . .
(*She exits, looking for another chair, using now door No. 2 as
exit and door No. 3 on the right to re-enter.*)

OLD MAN. Hold the little boy on your lap . . . The twins can sit together in the same chair. Be careful, they're not very strong . . .
they go with the house, they belong to the landlord. Yes, my children, he'd make trouble for us, he's a bad man . . . he wants us
to buy them from him, these worthless chairs. (*The* OLD WOMAN
returns as quickly as she can with a chair.) You don't all know
each other . . . you're seeing each other for the first time . . .
you knew each other by name . . . (*To the* OLD WOMAN)
Semiramis, help me make the introductions . . .

OLD WOMAN. Who are all these people? . . . May I introduce you,
excuse me . . . May I introduce you . . . but who are they?

OLD MAN. May I introduce you . . . Allow me to introduce you . . .
permit me to introduce you . . . Mr., Mrs., Miss . . . Mr. . . .
Mrs. . . . Mrs. . . . Mr.

OLD WOMAN (*to* OLD MAN). Did you put on your sweater? (*To the
invisible guests*) Mr., Mrs., Mr. . . .
(*Doorbell rings again.*)

OLD MAN. More people!

(*Another ring of doorbell.*)

OLD WOMAN. More people!

(*The doorbell rings again, then several more times, and more times again; the* OLD MAN *is beside himself; the chairs, turned towards the dais, with their backs to the audience, form regular rows, each one longer as in a theatre; the* OLD MAN *is winded, he mops his brow, goes from one door to another, seats invisible people, while the* OLD WOMAN, *hobbling along, unable to move any faster, goes as rapidly as she can, from one door to another, hunting for chairs and carrying them in. There are now many invisible people on stage; both the* OLD MAN *and* OLD WOMAN *take care not to bump into people and to thread their way between the rows of chairs. The movement could go like this: the* OLD MAN *goes to door No. 4, the* OLD WOMAN *exits by door No. 3, returns by door No. 2; the* OLD MAN *goes to open door No. 7, the* OLD WOMAN *exits by door No. 8, re-enters by door No. 6 with chairs, etc., in this manner making their way around the stage, using all the doors.*)

OLD WOMAN. Beg pardon . . . excuse me . . . what . . . . oh, yes . . . beg pardon . . . excuse me . . .

OLD MAN. Gentlemen . . . come in . . . ladies . . . enter . . . it is Mrs. . . . let me . . . yes . . .

OLD WOMAN (*with more chairs*). Oh dear . . . Oh dear . . . there are too many . . . There really are too, too . . . too many, oh dear, oh dear, oh dear . . .

(*We hear from outside, louder and louder and approaching nearer and nearer, the sounds of boats moving through the water; all the noises come directly from the wings. The* OLD WOMAN *and the* OLD MAN *continue the business outlined above; they open the doors, they carry in chairs. The doorbell continues to ring.*)

OLD MAN. This table is in our way. (*He moves a table, or he sketches the business of moving it, without slowing down his rhythm, aided by the* OLD WOMAN.) There's scarcely a place left here, excuse us . . .

OLD WOMAN (*making a gesture of clearing the table, to the* OLD MAN). Are you wearing your sweater?

(*Doorbell rings.*)

OLD MAN. More people! More chairs! More people! More chairs! Come in, come in, ladies and gentlemen . . . Semiramis, faster . . . We'll give you a hand soon . . .

OLD WOMAN. Beg pardon . . . beg pardon . . . good evening, Mrs. . . . Mrs. . . . Mr. . . . Mr. . . . yes, yes, the chairs . . .

(The doorbell rings louder and louder and we hear the noises of boats striking the quay very close by, and more and more frequently. The OLD MAN *flounders among the chairs; he has scarcely enough time to go from one door to another, so rapidly do the ringings of the doorbell succeed each other.)*

OLD MAN. Yes, right away . . . are you wearing your sweater? Yes, yes . . . immediately, patience, yes, yes . . . patience . . .

OLD WOMAN. Your sweater? My sweater? . . . Beg pardon, beg pardon.

OLD MAN. This way, ladies and gentlemen, I request you . . . I re you . . . pardon . . . quest . . . enter,   enter . . . going   to show . . . there, the seats . . . dear friend . . . not there . . . take care . . . you, my friend?

(Then a long moment without words. We hear waves, boats, the continuous ringing of the doorbell. The movement culminates in intensity at this point. The doors are now opening and shutting all together ceaselessly. Only the main door in the center of the recess remains closed. The OLD MAN *and* OLD WOMAN *come and go, without saying a word, from one door to another; they appear to be gliding on roller skates. The* OLD MAN *receives the people, accompanies them, but doesn't take them very far, he only indicates seats to them after having taken one or two steps with them; he hasn't enough time. The* OLD WOMAN *carries in chairs. The* OLD MAN *and the* OLD WOMAN *meet each other and bump into each other, once or twice, without interrupting their rhythm. Then, the* OLD MAN *takes a position upstage center, and turns from left to right, from right to left, etc., towards all the doors and indicates the seats with his arms. His arms move very rapidly. Then, finally the* OLD WOMAN *stops, with a chair in one hand, which she places, takes up again, replaces, looks as though she, too, wants to go from one door to another, from right to left, from left to right, moving her head and neck very rapidly. This must not interrupt the rhythm; the* OLD MAN *and* OLD WOMAN *must still give the impression of not stopping, even while remaining almost in one place; their hands, their chests, their heads, their eyes are agitated, perhaps moving in little circles. Finally, there is a progressive slowing down of movement, at first slight: the ringings of the doorbell are less loud, less frequent; the doors open less and less rapidly; the gestures of the* OLD MAN *and* OLD WOMAN *slacken continuously. At the moment when the doors stop opening and closing altogether, and the ringings cease to be heard, we have the impression that the stage is packed with people.)*

OLD MAN. I'm going to find a place for you . . . patience . . . Semiramis, for the love of . . .

OLD WOMAN (*with a large gesture, her hands empty*). There are no more chairs, my darling. (*Then, abruptly, she begins to sell invisible programs in a full hall, with the doors closed.*) Programs, get your programs here, the program of the evening, buy your program!

OLD MAN. Relax, ladies and gentlemen, we'll take care of you . . . Each in his turn, in the order of your arrival . . . You'll have a seat. I'll take care of you.

OLD WOMAN. Buy your programs! Wait a moment, madam, I cannot take care of everyone at the same time, I haven't got thirty-three hands, you know, I'm not a cow . . . Mister, please be kind enough to pass the program to the lady next to you, thank you . . . my change, my change . . .

OLD MAN. I've told you that I'd find a place for you! Don't get excited! Over here, it's over here, there, take care . . . oh, dear friend . . . dear friends . . .

OLD WOMAN. . . . Programs . . . get your grams . . . grams . . .

OLD MAN. Yes, my dear, she's over there, further down, she's selling programs . . . no trade is unworthy . . . that's her . . . do you see her? . . . you have a seat in the second row . . . to the right . . . no, to the left . . . that's it! . . .

OLD WOMAN. . . . gram . . . gram . . . program . . . get your program . . .

OLD MAN. What do you expect me to do? I'm doing my best! (*To invisible seated people*) Push over a little, if you will please . . . there's still a little room, that will do for you, won't it, Mrs. . . . come here. (*He mounts the dais, forced by the pushing of the crowd.*) Ladies, gentlemen, please excuse us, there are no more seats available . . .

OLD WOMAN (*who is now on the opposite side of the stage, across from the* OLD MAN, *between door No. 3 and the window*). Get your programs . . . who wants a program? Eskimo pies, caramels . . . fruit drops . . . (*Unable to move, the* OLD WOMAN, *hemmed in by the crowd, scatters her programs and candies anywhere, above the invisible heads.*) Here are some! There they are!

OLD MAN (*standing on the dais, very animated; he is jostled as he descends from the dais, remounts it, steps down again, hits someone in the face, is struck by an elbow, says*). Pardon . . . please excuse us . . . take care . . . (*Pushed, he staggers, has trouble regaining his equilibrium, clutches at shoulders.*)

OLD WOMAN. Why are there so many people? Programs, get your program here, Eskimo pies.

OLD MAN. Ladies, young ladies, gentlemen, a moment of silence, I beg you . . . silence . . . it's very important . . . those people who've no seats are asked to clear the aisles . . . that's it . . . don't stand between the chairs.

OLD WOMAN (*to the* OLD MAN, *almost screaming*). Who are all these people, my darling? What are they doing here?

OLD MAN. Clear the aisles, ladies and gentlemen. Those who do not have seats must, for the convenience of all, stand against the wall, there, along the right or the left . . . you'll be able to hear everything, you'll see everything, don't worry, you won't miss a thing, all seats are equally good!

(*There is a great hullabaloo. Pushed by the crowd, the* OLD MAN *makes almost a complete turn around the stage and ends up at the window on the right, near to the stool. The* OLD WOMAN *makes the same movement in reverse, and ends up at the window on the left, near the stool there.*)

OLD MAN (*making this movement*). Don't push, don't push.

OLD WOMAN (*same business*). Don't push, don't push.

OLD MAN (*same business*). Don't push, don't push.

OLD WOMAN (*same business*). Don't push, ladies and gentlemen, don't push.

OLD MAN (*same business*). Relax . . . take it easy . . . be quiet . . . what's going on here?

OLD WOMAN (*same business*). There's no need to act like savages, in any case.

(*At last they reach their final positions. Each is near a window. The* OLD MAN *to the left, by the window which is beside the dais. The* OLD WOMAN *on the right. They don't move from these positions until the end.*)

OLD WOMAN (*calling to the* OLD MAN). My darling . . . I can't see you, anymore . . . where are you? Who are they? What do all these people want? Who is that man over there?

OLD MAN. Where are you? Where are you, Semiramis?

OLD WOMAN. My darling, where are you?

OLD MAN. Here, beside the window . . . Can you hear me?

OLD WOMAN. Yes, I hear your voice! . . . there are so many . . . but I can make out yours . . .

OLD MAN. And you, where are you?

OLD WOMAN. I'm beside the window too! . . . My dear, I'm frightened, there are too many people . . . we are very far from each other . . . at our age we have to be careful . . . we might get lost

. . . We must stay close together, one never knows, my darling,
my darling . . .

OLD MAN. Ah! . . . I just caught sight of you . . . Oh! . . . We'll
find each other, never fear . . . I'm with friends. (*To the friends*)
I'm happy to shake your hands . . . But of course, I believe in
progress, uninterrupted progress, with some jolts, nevertheless . . .

OLD WOMAN. That's fine, thanks . . . What foul weather! Yes, it's
been nice! (*Aside*) I'm afraid, even so . . . What am I doing
here? . . . (*She screams*) My darling, My darling! (*The* OLD
MAN *and* OLD WOMAN *individually speak to guests near them.*)

OLD MAN. In order to prevent the exploitation of man by man, we
need money, money, and still more money!

OLD WOMAN. My darling! (*Then, hemmed in by friends*) Yes, my husband is here, he's organizing everything . . . over there . . . Oh!
you'll never get there . . . you'd have to go across, he's with
friends . . .

OLD MAN. Certainly not . . . as I've always said . . . pure logic does
not exist . . . all we've got is an imitation.

OLD WOMAN. But you know, there are people who are happy. In the
morning they eat breakfast on the plane, at noon they lunch in
the pullman, and in the evening they dine aboard the liner. At
night they sleep in the trucks that roll, roll, roll . . .

OLD MAN. Talk about the dignity of man! At least let's try to save face.
Dignity is only skin deep.

OLD WOMAN. Don't slink away into the shadows . . . (*She bursts out
laughing in conversation.*)

OLD MAN. Your compatriots ask of me.

OLD WOMAN. Certainly . . . tell me everything.

OLD MAN. I've invited you . . . in order to explain to you . . . that
the individual and the person are one and the same.

OLD WOMAN. He has a borrowed look about him. He owes us a lot
of money.

OLD MAN. I am not myself. I am another. I am the one in the other.

OLD WOMAN. My children, take care not to trust one another.

OLD MAN. Sometimes I awaken in the midst of absolute silence. It's a
perfect circle. There's nothing lacking. But one must be careful,
all the same. Its shape might disappear. There are holes through
which it can escape.

OLD WOMAN. Ghosts, you know, phantoms, mere nothings . . . The
duties my husband fulfills are very important, sublime.

OLD MAN. Excuse me . . . that's not at all my opinion! At the proper
time, I'll communicate my views on this subject to you . . . I
have nothing to say for the present! . . . We're waiting for the

Orator, he'll tell you, he'll speak in my behalf, and explain everything that we hold most dear . . . he'll explain everything to
you . . . when? . . . when the moment has come . . . the moment will come soon . . .

OLD WOMAN (*on her side to her friends*). The sooner, the better . . .
That's understood . . . (*Aside*) They're never going to leave us
alone. Let them go, why don't they go? . . . My poor darling,
where is he? I can't see him any more . . .

OLD MAN (*same business*). Don't be so impatient. You'll hear my
message. In just a moment.

OLD WOMAN (*aside*). Ah! . . . I hear his voice! . . . (*To her friends*)
Do you know, my husband has never been understood. But at
last his hour has come.

OLD MAN. Listen to me, I've had a rich experience of life. In all walks
of life, at every level of thought . . . I'm not an egotist: humanity must profit by what I've learned.

OLD WOMAN. Ow! You stepped on my foot . . . I've got chilblains!

OLD MAN. I've perfected a real system. (*Aside*) The Orator ought to be
here. (*Aloud*) I've suffered enormously.

OLD WOMAN. We have suffered so much. (*Aside*) The Orator ought to
be here. It's certainly time.

OLD MAN. Suffered much, learned much.

OLD WOMAN (*like an echo*). Suffered much, learned much.

OLD MAN. You'll see for yourselves, my system is perfect.

OLD WOMAN (*like an echo*). You'll see for yourselves, his system is
perfect.

OLD MAN. If only my instructions are carried out.

OLD WOMAN (*echo*). If only his instructions are carried out.

OLD MAN. We'll save the world! . . .

OLD WOMAN (*echo*). Saving his own soul by saving the world! . . .

OLD MAN. One truth for all!

OLD WOMAN (*echo*). One truth for all!

OLD MAN. Follow me! . . .

OLD WOMAN (*echo*). Follow him! . . .

OLD MAN. For I have absolute certainty! . . .

OLD WOMAN (*echo*). He has absolute certainty!

OLD MAN. Never . . .

OLD WOMAN (*echo*). Ever and ever . . .

(*Suddenly we hear noises in the wings, fanfares.*)

OLD WOMAN. What's going on?

(*The noises increase, then the main door opens wide, with a
great crash; through the open door we see nothing but a very
powerful light which floods onto the stage through the main door*

and the windows, which at the entrance of the emperor are brightly lighted.)

OLD MAN. I don't know . . . I can scarcely believe . . . is it possible . . . but yes . . . but yes . . . incredible . . . and still it's true . . . yes . . . if . . . yes . . . it is the Emperor! His Majesty the Emperor!

(The light reaches its maximum intensity, through the open door and through the windows; but the light is cold, empty; more noises which cease abruptly.)

OLD MAN. Stand up! . . . It's His Majesty the Emperor! The Emperor in my house, in our house . . . Semiramis . . . do you realize what this means?

OLD WOMAN *(not understanding)*. The Emperor . . . the Emperor? My darling! *(Then suddenly she understands.)* Ah, yes, the Emperor! Your Majesty! Your Majesty! *(She wildly makes countless grotesque curtsies.)* In our house! In our house!

OLD MAN *(weeping with emotion)*. Your Majesty! . . . Oh! Your Majesty! . . . Your little, Your great Majesty! . . . Oh! what a sublime honor . . . it's all a marvelous dream.

OLD WOMAN *(like an echo)*. A marvelous dream . . . arvelous . . .

OLD MAN *(to the invisible crowd)*. Ladies, gentlemen, stand up, our beloved sovereign, the Emperor, is among us! Hurrah! Hurrah! *(He stands up on the stool; he stands on his toes in order to see the Emperor; the OLD WOMAN does the same on her side.)*

OLD WOMAN. Hurrah! Hurrah!

(Stamping of feet.)

OLD MAN. Your Majesty! . . . I'm over here! . . . Your Majesty! Can you hear me? Can you see me? Please tell his Majesty that I'm here! Your Majesty! Your Majesty!!! I'm here, your most faithful servant! . . .

OLD WOMAN *(still echoing)*. Your most faithful servant, Your Majesty!

OLD MAN. Your servant, your slave, your dog, arf, arf, your dog, Your Majesty! . . .

OLD WOMAN *(barking loudly like a dog)*. Arf . . . arf . . . arf . . .

OLD MAN *(wringing his hands)*. Can you see me? . . . Answer, Sire! . . . Ah, I can see you, I've just caught sight of Your Majesty's august face . . . your divine forehead . . . I've seen you, yes, in spite of the screen of courtiers . . .

OLD WOMAN. In spite of the courtiers . . . we're here, Your Majesty!

OLD MAN. Your Majesty! Your Majesty! Ladies, gentlemen, don't keep him—His Majesty standing . . . you see, Your Majesty, I'm truly the only one who cares for you, for your health, I'm the most faithful of all your subjects . . .

OLD WOMAN (*echoing*). Your Majesty's most faithful subjects!

OLD MAN. Let me through, now, ladies and gentlemen . . . how can I make my way through such a crowd? . . . I must go to present my most humble respects to His Majesty, the Emperor . . . let me pass . . .

OLD WOMAN (*echo*). Let him pass . . . let him pass . . . pass . . . ass . . .

OLD MAN. Let me pass, please, let me pass. (*Desperate*) Ah! Will I ever be able to reach him?

OLD WOMAN (*echo*). Reach him . . . reach him . . .

OLD MAN. Nevertheless, my heart and my whole being are at his feet, the crowd of courtiers surrounds him, ah! ah! they want to prevent me from approaching him . . . They know very well that . . . oh! I understand, I understand . . . Court intrigues, I know all about it . . . They hope to separate me from Your Majesty!

OLD WOMAN. Calm yourself, my darling . . . His Majesty sees you, he's looking at you . . . His Majesty has given me a wink . . . His Majesty is on our side! . . .

OLD MAN. They must give the Emperor the best seat . . . near the dais . . . so that he can hear everything the Orator is going to say.

OLD WOMAN (*hoisting herself up on the stool, on her toes, lifting her chin as high as she can, in order to see better*). At last they're taking care of the Emperor.

OLD MAN. Thank heaven for that! (*To the Emperor*) Sire . . . Your Majesty may rely on him. It's my friend, it's my representative who is at Your Majesty's side. (*On his toes, standing on the stool*) Gentlemen, ladies, young ladies, little children, I implore you.

OLD WOMAN (*echoing*). Plore . . . plore . . .

OLD MAN. . . . I want to see . . . move aside . . . I want . . . the celestial gaze, the noble face, the crown, the radiance of His Majesty . . . Sire, deign to turn your illustrious face in my direction, toward your humble servant . . . so humble . . . Oh! I caught sight of him clearly that time . . . I caught sight . . .

OLD WOMAN (*echo*). He caught sight that time . . . he caught sight . . . caught . . . sight . . .

OLD MAN. I'm at the height of joy . . . I've no more words to express my boundless gratitude . . . in my humble dwelling, Oh! Majesty! Oh! radiance! . . . here . . . here . . . in the dwelling where I am, true enough, a general . . . but within the hierarchy of your army, I'm only a simple general factotum . . .

OLD WOMAN (*echo*). General factotum . . .

OLD MAN. I'm proud of it . . . proud and humble, at the same time . . . as I should be . . . alas! certainly, I am a general, I might

have been at the imperial court, I have only a little court here to
take care of . . . Your Majesty . . . I . . . Your Majesty, I
have difficulty expressing myself . . . I might have had . . .
many things, not a few possessions if I'd known, if I'd wanted,
if I . . . if we . . . Your Majesty, forgive my emotion . . .

OLD WOMAN. Speak in the third person!

OLD MAN (*sniveling*). May Your Majesty deign to forgive me! You are
here at last . . . We have given up hope . . . you might not
even have come . . . Oh! Savior, in my life, I have been humiliated . . .

OLD WOMAN (*echo, sobbing*). . . . miliated . . . miliated . . .

OLD MAN. I've suffered much in my life . . . I might have been something, if I could have been sure of the support of Your Majesty
. . . I have no other support . . . if you hadn't come, everything
would have been too late . . . you are, Sire, my last recourse . . .

OLD WOMAN (*echo*). Last recourse . . . Sire . . . ast recourse . . .
ire . . . recourse . . .

OLD MAN. I've brought bad luck to my friends, to all those who have
helped me . . . Lightning struck the hand which was held out
toward me . . .

OLD WOMAN (*echo*). . . . hand that was held out . . . held out . . .
out . . .

OLD MAN. They've always had good reasons for hating me, bad reasons
for loving me . . .

OLD WOMAN. That's not true, my darling, not true. *I* love you, I'm your
little mother . . .

OLD MAN. All my enemies have been rewarded and my friends have
betrayed me . . .

OLD WOMAN (*echo*). Friends . . . betrayed . . . betrayed . . .

OLD MAN. They've treated me badly. They've persecuted me. If I com-
plained, it was always they who were in the right . . . Sometimes I've tried to revenge myself . . . I was never able to, never
able to revenge myself . . . I have too much pity . . . I refused
to strike the enemy to the ground, I have always been too good.

OLD WOMAN (*echo*). He was too good, good, good, good, good . . .

OLD MAN. It is my pity that has defeated me.

OLD WOMAN (*echo*). My pity . . . pity . . . pity . . .

OLD MAN. But they never pitied me. I gave them a pin prick, and they
repaid me with club blows, with knife blows, with cannon blows,
they've crushed my bones . . .

OLD WOMAN (*echo*). . . . My bones . . . my bones . . . my
bones . . .

OLD MAN. They've supplanted me, they've robbed me, they've assas-

sinated me . . . I've been the collector of injustices, the lightning
rod of catastrophes . . .

OLD WOMAN (*echo*). Lightning rod . . . catastrophe . . . lightning
rod . . .

OLD MAN. In order to forget, Your Majesty, I wanted to go in for
sports . . . for mountain climbing . . . they pulled my feet and
made me slip . . . I wanted to climb stairways, they rotted the
steps . . . I fell down . . . I wanted to travel, they refused
me a passport . . . I wanted to cross the river, they burnt my
bridges . . .

OLD WOMAN (*echo*). Burnt my bridges.

OLD MAN. I wanted to cross the Pyrenees, and there were no more
Pyrenees.

OLD WOMAN (*echo*). No more Pyrenees . . . He could have been,
he too, Your Majesty, like so many others, a head editor, a head
actor, a head doctor, Your Majesty, a head king . . .

OLD MAN. Furthermore, no one has ever shown me due consideration
. . . no one has ever sent me invitations . . . However, I, hear
me, I say this to you, I alone could have saved humanity, who is
so sick. Your Majesty realizes this as do I . . . or, at the least,
I could have spared it the evils from which it has suffered so much
this last quarter of a century, had I had the opportunity to communicate my message; I do not despair of saving it, there is
still time, I have a plan . . . alas, I express myself with difficulty . . .

OLD WOMAN (*above the invisible heads*). The Orator will be here, he'll
speak for you. His Majesty is here, thus you'll be heard, you've
no reason to despair, you hold all the trumps, everything has
changed, everything has changed . . .

OLD MAN. I hope Your Majesty will excuse me . . . I know you have
many other worries . . . I've been humiliated . . . Ladies and
gentlemen, move aside just a little bit, don't hide His Majesty's
nose from me altogether, I want to see the diamonds of the imperial crown glittering . . . But if Your Majesty has deigned to
come to our miserable home, it is because you have condescended
to take into consideration my wretched self. What an extraordinary
reward. Your Majesty, if corporeally I raise myself on my toes,
this is not through pride, this is only in order to gaze upon you!
. . . morally, I throw myself at your knees.

OLD WOMAN (*sobbing*). At your knees, Sire, we throw ourselves at your
knees, at your feet, at your toes . . .

OLD MAN. I've had scabies. My employer fired me because I did not bow
to his baby, to his horse. I've been kicked in the ass, but all this,

Sire, no longer has any importance . . . since . . . since . . .
Sir . . . Your Majesty . . . look . . . I am here . . . here . . .

OLD WOMAN (*echo*). Here . . . here . . . here . . . here . . . here
. . . here . . .

OLD MAN. Since Your Majesty is here . . . since Your Majesty will
take my message into consideration . . . But the Orator should
be here . . . he's making His Majesty wait . . .

OLD WOMAN. If your Majesty will forgive him. He's surely coming.
He will be here in a moment. They've telephoned us.

OLD MAN. His Majesty is so kind. His Majesty wouldn't depart just like
that, without having listened to everything, heard everything.

OLD WOMAN (*echo*). Heard everything . . . heard . . . listened to
everything . . .

OLD MAN. It is he who will speak in my name . . . I, I cannot . . .
I lack the talent . . . he has all the papers, all the documents . . .

OLD WOMAN (*echo*). He has all the documents . . .

OLD MAN. A little patience, Sire, I beg of you . . . he should be coming.

OLD WOMAN. He should be coming in a moment.

OLD MAN (*so that the Emperor will not grow impatient*). Your Majesty,
hear me, a long time ago I had the revelation . . . I was forty
years old . . . I say this also to you, ladies and gentlemen . . .
one evening, after supper, as was our custom, before going to bed,
I seated myself on my father's knees . . . my mustaches were
longer than his and more pointed . . . I had more hair on my
chest . . . my hair was graying already, but his was still brown
. . . There were some guests, grownups, sitting at table, who began to laugh, laugh.

OLD WOMAN (*echo*). Laugh . . . laugh . . .

OLD MAN. I'm not joking, I told them, I love my papa very much.
Someone replied: It is midnight, a child shouldn't stay up so
late. If you don't go beddy-bye, then you're no longer a kid. But
I'd still not have believed them if they hadn't addressed me as an
adult.

OLD WOMAN (*echo*). An adult.

OLD MAN. Instead of as a child . . .

OLD WOMAN (*echo*). A child.

OLD MAN. Nevertheless, I thought to myself, I'm not married. Hence,
I'm still a child. They married me off right then, expressly to prove
the contrary to me . . . Fortunately, my wife has been both
father and mother to me . . .

OLD WOMAN. The Orator should be here, Your Majesty . . .

OLD MAN. The Orator will come.

OLD WOMAN. He will come.

OLD MAN. He will come.

OLD WOMAN. He will come.

OLD MAN. He will come.

OLD WOMAN. He will come.

OLD MAN. He will come, he will come.

OLD WOMAN. He will come, he will come.

OLD MAN. He will come.

OLD WOMAN. He is coming.

OLD MAN. He is coming.

OLD WOMAN. He is coming, he is here.

OLD MAN. He is coming, he is here.

OLD WOMAN. He is coming, he is here.

OLD MAN AND OLD WOMAN. He is here . . .

OLD WOMAN. Here he is!

> (*Silence; all movement stops. Petrified, the two old people stare at door No. 5; this immobility lasts rather long—about thirty seconds; very slowly, very slowly the door opens wide, silently; then the* ORATOR *appears. He is a real person. He's a typical painter or poet of the nineteenth century; he wears a large black felt hat with a wide brim, loosely tied bow tie, artist's blouse, mustache and goatee, very histrionic in manner, conceited; just as the invisible people must be as real as possible, the* ORATOR *must appear unreal. He goes along the wall to the right, gliding, softly, to upstage center, in front of the main door, without turning his head to right or left; he passes close by the* OLD WOMAN *without appearing to notice her, not even when the* OLD WOMAN *touches his arm in order to assure herself that he exists. It is at this moment that the* OLD WOMAN *says:* "Here he is!")

OLD MAN. Here he is!

OLD WOMAN (*following the* ORATOR *with her eyes and continuing to stare at him*). It's really he, he exists. In flesh and blood.

OLD MAN (*following him with his eyes*). He exists. It's really he. This is not a dream!

OLD WOMAN. This is not a dream, I told you so.

> (*The* OLD MAN *clasps his hands, lifts his eyes to heaven; he exults silently. The* ORATOR, *having reached upstage center, lifts his hat, bends forward in silence, saluting the invisible Emperor with his hat with a musketeer's flourish and somewhat like an automaton. At this moment*)

OLD MAN. Your Majesty . . . May I present to you, the Orator . . .

OLD WOMAN. It is he!

> (*Then the* ORATOR *puts his hat back on his head and mounts the*

dais *from which he looks down on the invisible crowd on the* stage and at the chairs; he freezes in a solemn pose.)

OLD MAN (*to the invisible crowd*). You may ask him for autographs. (*Automatically, silently, the* ORATOR *signs and distributes number-less autographs. The* OLD MAN *during this time lifts his eyes again to heaven, clasping his hands, and exultantly says*) No man, in his lifetime, could hope for more . . .

OLD WOMAN (*echo*). No man could hope for more.

OLD MAN (*to the invisible crowd*). And now, with the permission of Your Majesty, I will address myself to all of you, ladies, young ladies, gentlemen, little children, dear colleagues, dear compatriots, Your Honor the President, dear comrades in arms . . .

OLD WOMAN (*echo*). And little children . . . dren . . . dren . . .

OLD MAN. I address myself to all of you, without distinction of age, sex, civil status, social rank, or business, to thank you, with all my heart.

OLD WOMAN (*echo*). To thank you . . .

OLD MAN. As well as the Orator . . . cordially, for having come in such large numbers . . . silence, gentlemen! . . .

OLD WOMAN (*echo*). . . . Silence, gentlemen . . .

OLD MAN. I address my thanks also to those who have made possible the meeting this evening, to the organizers . . .

OLD WOMAN. Bravo!

(*Meanwhile, the* ORATOR *on the dais remains solemn, immobile, except for his hand, which signs autographs automatically.*)

OLD MAN. To the owners of this building, to the architect, to the masons who were kind enough to erect these walls! . . .

OLD WOMAN (*echo*). . . . walls . . .

OLD MAN. To all those who've dug the foundations . . . Silence, ladies and gentlemen . . .

OLD WOMAN. . . . 'adies and gentlemen . . .

OLD MAN. Last but not least I address my warmest thanks to the cabinet-makers who have made these chairs on which you have been able to sit, to the master carpenter . . .

OLD WOMAN (*echo*). . . . penter . . .

OLD MAN. . . . Who made the armchair in which Your Majesty is sinking so softly, which does not prevent you, nevertheless, from maintaining a firm and manly attitude . . . Thanks again to all the technicians, machinists, electrocutioners . . .

OLD WOMAN (*echoing*). . . . cutioners . . . cutioners . . .

OLD MAN. . . . To the paper manufacturers and the printers, proof-readers, editors to whom we owe the programs, so charmingly decorated, to the universal solidarity of all men, thanks, thanks, to our country, to the State (*he turns toward where the Emperor is sitting*) whose helm Your Majesty directs with the skill of a true pilot . . . thanks to the usher . . .

OLD WOMAN (*echo*). . . . usher . . . rusher . . .

OLD MAN (*pointing to the* OLD WOMAN). Hawker of Eskimo pies and programs . . .

OLD WOMAN (*echo*). . . . grams . . .

OLD MAN. . . . My wife, my helpmeet . . . Semiramis! . . .

OLD WOMAN (*echo*). . . . ife . . . meet . . . mis . . . (*Aside*) The darling, he never forgets to give me credit.

OLD MAN. Thanks to all those who have given me their precious and expert, financial or moral support, thereby contributing to the overwhelming success of this evening's gathering . . . thanks again, thanks above all to our beloved sovereign, His Majesty the Emperor . . .

OLD WOMAN (*echo*). . . . jesty the Emperor . . .

OLD MAN (*in a total silence*). . . . A little silence . . . Your Majesty . . .

OLD WOMAN (*echo*). . . . jesty . . . jesty . . .

OLD MAN. Your Majesty, my wife and myself have nothing more to ask of life. Our existence can come to an end in this apotheosis . . . thanks be to heaven who has granted us such long and peaceful years . . . My life has been filled to overflowing. My mission is accomplished. I will not have lived in vain, since my message will be revealed to the world . . . (*Gesture towards the* ORATOR, *who does not perceive it; the* ORATOR *waves off requests for autographs, very dignified and firm.*) To the world, or rather to what is left of it! (*Wide gesture toward the invisible crowd.*) To you, ladies and gentlemen, and dear comrades, who are all that is left from humanity, but with such leftovers one can still make a very good soup . . . Orator, friend . . . (*The* ORATOR *looks in another direction.*) If I have been long unrecognized, underestimated by my contemporaries, it is because it had to be . . . (*The* OLD WOMAN *sobs.*) What matters all that now when I am leaving to you, to you, my dear Orator and friend (*The* ORATOR *rejects a new request for an autograph, then takes an indifferent pose, looking in all directions.*) . . . the responsibility of radiating upon posterity the light of my mind . . . thus making known to the universe my philosophy. Neglect none of the details of my private life, some laughable, some painful or heartwarming, of my tastes, my amusing gluttony . . . tell everything . . . speak of my helpmeet . . . (*The* OLD WOMAN *redoubles her sobs.*) . . . of the way she prepared those marvelous little Turkish pies, of her potted rabbit à la Normandabbit . . . speak of Berry, my native province . . . I count on you, great master and Orator . . . as for me and my faithful helpmeet, after our long years of labor in behalf of the progress of humanity during which we fought the good fight, nothing remains for us but to withdraw . . . immediately, in order to make the supreme sacrifice which no one demands of us but which we will carry out even so . . .

OLD WOMAN (*sobbing*). Yes, yes, let's die in full glory . . . let's die in order to become a legend . . . At least, they'll name a street after us . . .

OLD MAN (*to* OLD WOMAN). O my faithful helpmeet! . . . you who have believed in me, unfailingly, during a whole century, who have never left me, never . . . alas, today, at this supreme moment, the crowd pitilessly separates us . . .

> Above all I had hoped
> that together we might lie
> with all our bones together
> within the selfsame skin
> within the same sepulchre
> and that the same worms
> might share our old flesh
> that we might rot together . . .

OLD WOMAN. . . . Rot together . . .

OLD MAN. Alas! . . . alas! . . .

OLD WOMAN. Alas! . . . alas! . . .

OLD MAN. . . . Our corpses will fall far from each other, and we will rot in an aquatic solitude . . . Don't pity us over much.

OLD WOMAN. What will be, will be!

OLD MAN. We shall not be forgotten. The eternal Emperor will remember us, always.

OLD WOMAN (*echo*). Always.

OLD MAN. We will leave some traces, for we are people and not cities.

OLD MAN AND OLD WOMAN (*together*). We will have a street named after us.

OLD MAN. Let us be united in time and in eternity, even if we are not together in space, as we were in adversity: let us die at the same moment . . . (*To the* ORATOR, *who is impassive, immobile*) One last time . . . I place my trust in you . . . I count on you. You will tell all . . . bequeath my message . . . (*To the Emperor*) If Your Majesty will excuse me . . . Farewell to all. Farewell, Semiramis.

OLD WOMAN. Farewell to all! . . . Farewell, my darling!

OLD MAN. Long live the Emperor!

(*He throws confetti and paper streamers on the invisible Emperor; we hear fanfares; bright lights like fireworks.*)

OLD WOMAN. Long live the Emperor!

(*Confetti and streamers thrown in the direction of the Emperor, then on the immobile and impassive* ORATOR, *and on the empty chairs.*)

OLD MAN (*same business*). Long live the Emperor!

OLD WOMAN (*same business*). Long live the Emperor!

(*The* OLD WOMAN *and* OLD MAN *at the same moment throw themselves out the windows, shouting* "Long Live the Emperor." *Sudden silence; no more fireworks; we hear an "Ah" from both sides of the stage, the sea-green noises of bodies falling into the water. The light coming through the main door and the windows has disappeared; there remains only a weak light as at the beginning of the play; the darkened windows remain wide open, their curtains floating on the wind.*)

ORATOR. (*He has remained immobile and impassive during the scene of the double suicide, and now, after several moments, he decides to speak. He faces the rows of empty chairs; he makes the invisible crowd understand that he is deaf and dumb; he makes the signs of a deafmute; desperate efforts to make himself understood; then he coughs, groans, utters the guttural sounds of a mute.*) He, mme, mm, mm. Ju, gou, hou, hou. Heu, heu, gu gou, gueue. (*Helpless he lets his arms fall down alongside his body; suddenly, his face lights up, he has an idea, he turns toward the blackboard, he takes a piece of chalk out of his pocket, and writes, in large capitals:*

ANGELFOOD

then:

NNAA NNM NWNWNW V

He turns around again, towards the invisible crowd on the stage, and points with his finger to what he's written on the blackboard.)

ORATOR. Mmm, Mmm, Gueue, Gou, Gu. Mmm, Mmm, Mmm, Mmm. (*Then, not satisfied, with abrupt gestures he wipes out the chalk letters, and replaces them with others, among which we can make out, still in large capitals:*

ΛADIEU ΛDIEU ΛPΛ

Again, the ORATOR *turns around to face the crowd; he smiles, questions, with an air of hoping that he's been understood, of having said something; he indicates to the empty chairs what he's just written. He remains immobile for a few seconds, rather satisfied and a little solemn; but then, faced with the absence of the hoped for reaction, little by little his smile disappears, his face darkens; he waits another moment; suddenly he bows petulantly, brusquely, descends from the dais; he goes toward the main door upstage center, gliding like a ghost; before exiting through this door, he bows ceremoniously again to the rows of empty chairs, to the invisible Emperor. The stage remains empty with only the chairs, the dais, the floor covered with streamers and confetti. The main door is wide open onto darkness.*

We hear for the first time the human noises of the invisible crowd; these are bursts of laughter, murmurs, shh's, ironical coughs; weak at the beginning, these noises grow louder, then, again, progessively they become weaker. All this should last long enough for the audience—the real and visible audience—to leave with this ending firmly impressed on its mind. The curtain falls very slowly.) *

---

* In the original production the curtain fell on the mumblings of the mute Orator. The blackboard was not used.

THE ZOO STORY [1958]

A Play in One Scene

by Edward Albee

Players

PETER, *a man in his early forties, neither fat nor gaunt, neither handsome nor homely. He wears tweeds, smokes a pipe, carries horn-rimmed glasses. Although he is moving into middle age, his dress and his manner would suggest a man younger.*

JERRY, *a man in his late thirties, not poorly dressed, but carelessly. What was once a trim and lightly muscled body has begun to go to fat; and while he is no longer handsome, it is evident that he once was. His fall from physical grace should not suggest debauchery; he has, to come closest to it, a great weariness.*

The Zoo Story by Edward Albee. © 1959 by Edward Albee. Reprinted by permission of Coward-McCann, Inc. Notice: This play is the sole property of the author and is fully protected by copyright. It may not be acted by professionals or by amateurs without written consent. Public readings and radio or television broadcasts are likewise forbidden. All enquiries concerning rights should be addressed to the author's agent, the William Morris Agency, 1740 Broadway, New York 19, N.Y.

Scene. It is Central Park; a Sunday afternoon in summer; the present. There are two park benches, one toward either side of the stage; they both face the audience. Behind them: foliage, trees, sky. At the beginning, Peter is seated on one of the benches.

(*As the curtain rises,* PETER *is seated on the bench stage-right. He is reading a book. He stops reading, cleans his glasses, goes back to reading.* JERRY *enters.*)

JERRY. I've been to the zoo. (PETER *doesn't notice.*) I said, I've been to the ZOO. MISTER, I'VE BEEN TO THE ZOO!

PETER. Hm? . . . What? . . . I'm sorry, were you talking to me?

JERRY. I went to the zoo, and then I walked until I came here. Have I been walking north?

PETER (*puzzled*). North? Why . . . I . . . I think so. Let me see.

JERRY (*pointing past the audience*). Is that Fifth Avenue?

PETER. Why yes; yes, it is.

JERRY. And what is that cross street there; that one, to the right?

PETER. That? Oh, that's Seventy-fourth Street.

JERRY. And the zoo is around Sixty-fifth Street; so, I've been walking north.

PETER (*anxious to get back to his reading*). Yes; it would seem so.

JERRY. Good old north.

PETER (*lightly, by reflex*). Ha, ha.

JERRY (*after a slight pause*). But not due north.

PETER. I . . . well, no, not due north; but, we . . . call it north. It's northerly.

JERRY. (*Watches as* PETER, *anxious to dismiss him, prepares his pipe.*) Well, boy; *you're* not going to get lung cancer, are you?

PETER. (*Looks up, a little annoyed, then smiles.*) No, sir. Not from this.

JERRY. No, sir. What you'll probably get is cancer of the mouth, and then you'll have to wear one of those things Freud wore after they took one whole side of his jaw away. What do they call those things?

PETER (*uncomfortable*). A prosthesis?

JERRY. The very thing! A prosthesis. You're an educated man, aren't you? Are you a doctor?

PETER. Oh, no; no. I read about it somewhere; *Time* magazine, I think. (*He turns to his book.*)

JERRY. Well, *Time* magazine isn't for blockheads.

PETER. No, I suppose not.

JERRY (*after a pause*). Boy, I'm glad that's Fifth Avenue there.

PETER (*vaguely*). Yes.

JERRY. I don't like the west side of the park much.

PETER. Oh? (*Then, slightly wary, but interested*) Why?

JERRY (*offhand*). I don't know.

PETER. Oh. (*He returns to his book.*)

JERRY. (*He stands for a few seconds, looking at* PETER, *who finally looks up again, puzzled.*) Do you mind if we talk?

PETER (*obviously minding*). Why . . . no, no.

JERRY. Yes you do; you do.

PETER. (*Puts his book down, his pipe out and away, smiling.*) No, really; I don't mind.

JERRY. Yes you do.

PETER (*finally decided*). No; I don't mind at all, really.

JERRY. It's . . . it's a nice day.

PETER. (*Stares unnecessarily at the sky.*) Yes. Yes, it is; lovely.

JERRY. I've been to the zoo.

PETER. Yes, I think you said so . . . didn't you?

JERRY. You'll read about it in the papers tomorrow, if you don't see it on your TV tonight. You have TV, haven't you?

PETER. Why yes, we have two; one for the children.

JERRY. You're married!

PETER (*with pleased emphasis*). Why, certainly.

JERRY. It isn't a law, for God's sake.

PETER. No . . . no, of course not.

JERRY. And you have a wife.

PETER (*bewildered by the seeming lack of communication*). Yes!

JERRY. And you have children.

PETER. Yes; two.

JERRY. Boys?

PETER. No, girls . . . both girls.

JERRY. But you wanted boys.

PETER. Well . . . naturally, every man wants a son, but . . .

JERRY (*lightly mocking*). But that's the way the cookie crumbles?

PETER (*annoyed*). I wasn't going to say that.

JERRY. And you're not going to have any more kids, are you?

PETER (*a bit distantly*). No. No more. (*Then back, and irksome*) Why did you say that? How would you know about that?

JERRY. The way you cross your legs, perhaps; something in the voice. Or maybe I'm just guessing. Is it your wife?

PETER (*furious*). That's none of your business! (*A silence.*) Do you understand? (JERRY *nods.* PETER *is quiet now.*) Well, you're right. We'll have no more children.

JERRY (*softly*). That *is* the way the cookie crumbles.

PETER (*forgiving*). Yes . . . I guess so.

JERRY. Well, now; what else?

PETER. What were you saying about the zoo . . . that I'd read about it, or see . . . ?

JERRY. I'll tell you about it, soon. Do you mind if I ask you questions?

PETER. Oh, not really.

JERRY. I'll tell you why I do it; I don't talk to many people—except to say like: give me a beer, or where's the john, or what time does the feature go on, or keep your hands to yourself, buddy. You know—things like that.

PETER. I must say I don't . . .

JERRY. But every once in a while I like to talk to somebody, really *talk;* like to get to know somebody, know all about him.

PETER (*lightly laughing, still a little uncomfortable*). And am I the guinea pig for today?

JERRY. On a sun-drenched Sunday afternoon like this? Who better than a nice married man with two daughters and . . . uh . . . a dog? (PETER *shakes his head.*) No? Two dogs. (PETER *shakes his head again.*) Hm. No dogs? (PETER *shakes his head, sadly.*) Oh, that's a shame. But you look like an animal man. CATS? (PETER *nods his head, ruefully.*) Cats! But, that can't be your idea. No, sir. Your wife and daughters? (PETER *nods his head.*) Is there anything else I should know?

PETER. (*He has to clear his throat.*) There are . . . there are two parakeets. One . . . uh . . . one for each of my daughters.

JERRY. Birds.

PETER. My daughters keep them in a cage in their bedroom.

JERRY. Do they carry disease? The birds.

PETER. I don't believe so.

JERRY. That's too bad. If they did you could set them loose in the house and the cats could eat them and die, maybe. (PETER *looks blank for a moment, then laughs.*) And what else? What do you do to support your enormous household?

PETER. I . . . uh . . . I have an executive position with a . . . a small publishing house. We . . . uh . . . we publish textbooks.

JERRY. That sounds nice; very nice. What do you make?

PETER (*still cheerful*). Now look here!

JERRY. Oh, come on.

PETER. Well, I make around eighteen thousand a year, but I don't carry more than forty dollars at any one time . . . in case you're a . . . a holdup man . . . ha, ha, ha.

JERRY (*ignoring the above*). Where do you live? (PETER *is reluctant*.) Oh, look; I'm not going to rob you, and I'm not going to kidnap your parakeets, your cats, or your daughters.

PETER (*too loud*). I live between Lexington and Third Avenue, on Seventy-fourth Street.

JERRY. That wasn't so hard, was it?

PETER. I didn't mean to seem . . . ah . . . it's that you don't really carry on a conversation; you just ask questions. And I'm . . . I'm normally . . . uh . . . reticent. Why do you just stand there?

JERRY. I'll start walking around in a little while, and eventually I'll sit down. (*Recalling*) Wait until you see the expression on his face.

PETER. What? Whose face? Look here; is this something about the zoo?

JERRY (*distantly*). The what?

PETER. The zoo; the zoo. Something about the zoo.

JERRY. The zoo?

PETER. You've mentioned it several times.

JERRY (*still distant, but returning abruptly*). The zoo? Oh, yes; the zoo. I was there before I came here. I told you that. Say, what's the dividing line between upper-middle-middle-class and lower-upper-middle-class?

PETER. My dear fellow, I . . .

JERRY. Don't my dear fellow me.

PETER (*unhappily*). Was I patronizing? I believe I was; I'm sorry. But, you see, your question about the classes bewildered me.

JERRY. And when you're bewildered you become patronizing?

PETER. I . . . I don't express myself too well, sometimes. (*He attempts a joke on himself.*) I'm in publishing, not writing.

JERRY (*amused, but not at the humor*). So be it. The truth *is:* I was being patronizing.

PETER. Oh, now; you needn't say that. (*It is at this point that Jerry may begin to move about the stage with slowly increasing determination and authority, but pacing himself, so that the long speech about the dog comes at the high point of the arc.*)

JERRY. All right. Who are your favorite writers? Baudelaire and J. P. Marquand?

PETER (*wary*). Well, I like a great many writers; I have a considerable . . . catholicity of taste, if I may say so. Those two men are fine, each in his way. (*Warming up*) Baudelaire, of course . . . uh

. . . is by far the finer of the two, but Marquand has a place
. . . in our . . . uh . . . national . . .

JERRY. Skip it.

PETER. I . . . sorry.

JERRY. Do you know what I did before I went to the zoo today? I
walked all the way up Fifth Avenue from Washington Square;
all the way.

PETER. Oh; you live in the Village! (*This seems to enlighten* PETER.)

JERRY. No, I don't. I took the subway down to the Village so I could
walk all the way up Fifth Avenue to the zoo. It's one of those
things a person has to do; sometimes a person has to go a very
long distance out of his way to come back a short distance correctly.

PETER (*almost pouting*). Oh, I thought you lived in the Village.

JERRY. What were you trying to do? Make sense out of things? Bring
order? The old pigeonhole bit? Well, that's easy; I'll tell you.
I live in a four-story brownstone rooming-house on the upper
West Side between Columbus Avenue and Central Park West.
I live on the top floor; rear; west. It's a laughably small room,
and one of my walls is made of beaverboard; this beaverboard
separates my room from another laughably small room, so I
assume that the two rooms were once one room, a small room,
but not necessarily laughable. The room beyond my beaverboard
wall is occupied by a colored queen who always keeps his door
open; well, not always but *always* when he's plucking his eyebrows, which he does with Buddhist concentration. This colored
queen has rotten teeth, which is rare, and he has a Japanese
kimono, which is also pretty rare; and he wears this kimono to
and from the john in the hall, which is pretty frequent. I mean,
he goes to the john a lot. He never bothers me, and he never
brings anyone up to his room. All he does is pluck his eyebrows,
wear his kimono and go to the john. Now, the two front rooms
on my floor are a little larger, I guess; but they're pretty small,
too. There's a Puerto Rican family in one of them, a husband,
a wife, and some kids; I don't know how many. These people
entertain a lot. And in the other front room, there's somebody
living there, but I don't know who it is. I've never seen who it is.
Never. Never ever.

PETER (*embarrassed*). Why . . . why do you live there?

JERRY (*from a distance again*). I don't know.

PETER. It doesn't sound like a very nice place . . . where you live.

JERRY. Well, no; it isn't an apartment in the East Seventies. But, then
again, I don't have one wife, two daughters, two cats and two

parakeets. What I do have, I have toilet articles, a few clothes, a hot plate that I'm not supposed to have, a can opener, one that works with a key, you know; a knife, two forks, and two spoons, one small, one large; three plates, a cup, a saucer, a drinking glass, two picture frames, both empty, eight or nine books, a pack of pornographic playing cards, regular deck, an old Western Union typewriter that prints nothing but capital letters, and a small strongbox without a lock which has in it . . . what? Rocks! Some rocks . . . sea-rounded rocks I picked up on the beach when I was a kid. Under which . . . weighed down . . . are some letters . . . please letters . . . please why don't you do this, and please when will you do that letters. And when letters, too. When will you write? When will you come? When? These letters are from more recent years.

PETER. (*Stares glumly at his shoes, then*) About those two empty picture frames . . . ?

JERRY. I don't see why they need any explanation at all. Isn't it clear? I don't have pictures of anyone to put in them.

PETER. Your parents . . . perhaps . . . a girl friend . . .

JERRY. You're a very sweet man, and you're possessed of a truly enviable innocence. But good old Mom and good old Pop are dead . . . you know? . . . I'm broken up about it, too . . . I mean really. BUT. That particular vaudeville act is playing the cloud circuit now, so I don't see how I can look at them, all neat and framed. Besides, or, rather, to be pointed about it, good old Mom walked out on good old Pop when I was ten and a half years old; she embarked on an adulterous turn of our southern states . . . a journey of a year's duration . . . and her most constant companion . . . among others, among many others . . . was a Mr. Barleycorn. At least, that's what good old Pop told me after he went down . . . came back . . . brought her body north. We'd received the news between Christmas and New Year's, you see, that good old Mom had parted with the ghost in some dump in Alabama. And, without the ghost . . . she was less welcome. I mean, what was she? A stiff . . . a northern stiff. At any rate, good old Pop celebrated the New Year for an even two weeks and then slapped into the front of a somewhat moving city omnibus, which sort of cleaned things out family-wise. Well no; then there was Mom's sister, who was given neither to sin nor the consolations of the bottle. I moved in on her, and my memory of her is slight excepting I remember still that she did all things dourly: sleeping, eating, working, praying. She dropped dead on the stairs to her apartment, my apartment then, too, on the afternoon of my high school graduation. A terribly middle-European joke, if you ask me.

PETER. Oh, my; oh, my.

JERRY. Oh, your what? But that was a long time ago, and I have no feeling about any of it that I care to admit to myself. Perhaps you can see, though, why good old Mom and good old Pop are frameless. What's your name? Your first name?

PETER. I'm Peter.

JERRY. I'd forgotten to ask you. I'm Jerry.

PETER (*with a slight, nervous laugh*). Hello, Jerry.

JERRY. (*Nods his hello.*) And let's see now; what's the point of having a girl's picture, especially in two frames? I have two picture frames, you remember. I never see the pretty little ladies more than once, and most of them wouldn't be caught in the same room with a camera. It's odd, and I wonder if it's sad.

PETER. The girls?

JERRY. No. I wonder if it's sad that I never see the little ladies more than once. I've never been able to have sex with, or, how is it put? . . . make love to anybody more than once. Once; that's it. . . . Oh, wait; for a week and a half, when I was fifteen . . . and I hang my head in shame that puberty was late . . . I was a h-o-m-o-s-e-x-u-a-l. I mean, I was queer . . . (*very fast*) . . . queer, queer, queer . . . with bells ringing, banners snapping in the wind. And for those eleven days, I met at least twice a day with the park superintendent's son . . . a Greek boy, whose birthday was the same as mine, except he was a year older. I think I was very much in love . . . maybe just with sex. But that was the jazz of a very special hotel, wasn't it? And now; oh, do I love the little ladies; really, I love them. For about an hour.

PETER. Well, it seems perfectly simple to me. . . .

JERRY (*angry*). Look! Are you going to tell me to get married and have parakeets?

PETER (*angry himself*). Forget the parakeets! And stay single if you want to. It's no business of mine. I didn't start this conversation in the . . .

JERRY. All right, all right. I'm sorry. All right? You're not angry?

PETER (*laughing*). No, I'm not angry.

JERRY (*relieved*). Good. (*Now back to his previous tone*) Interesting that you asked me about the picture frames. I would have thought that you would have asked me about the pornographic playing cards.

PETER (*with a knowing smile*). Oh, I've seen those cards.

JERRY. That's not the point. (*Laughs.*) I suppose when you were a kid you and your pals passed them around, or you had a pack of your own.

PETER. Well, I guess a lot of us did.

JERRY. And you threw them away just before you got married.

PETER. Oh, now; look here. I didn't *need* anything like that when I got older.

JERRY. No?

PETER (*embarrassed*). I'd rather not talk about these things.

JERRY. So? Don't. Besides, I wasn't trying to plumb your post-adolescent sexual life and hard times; what I wanted to get at is the value difference between pornographic playing cards when you're a kid, and pornographic playing cards when you're older. It's that when you're a kid you use the cards as a substitute for a real experience, and when you're older you use real experience as a substitute for the fantasy. But I imagine you'd rather hear about what happened at the zoo.

PETER (*enthusiastic*). Oh, yes; the zoo. (*Then, awkward*) That is . . . if you. . . .

JERRY. Let me tell you about why I went . . . well, let me tell you some things. I've told you about the fourth floor of the rooming-house where I live. I think the rooms are better as you go down, floor by floor. I guess they are; I don't know. I don't know any of the people on the third and second floors. Oh, wait! I do know that there's a lady living on the third floor, in the front. I know because she cries all the time. Whenever I go out or come back in, whenever I pass her door, I always hear her crying, muffled, but . . . very determined. Very determined indeed. But the one I'm getting to, and all about the dog, is the landlady. I don't like to use words that are too harsh in describing people. I don't like to. But the landlady is a fat, ugly, mean, stupid, unwashed, misan-thropic, cheap, drunken bag of garbage. And you may have no-ticed that I very seldom use profanity, so I can't describe her as well as I might.

PETER. You describe her . . . vividly.

JERRY. Well, thanks. Anyway, she has a dog, and I will tell you about the dog, and she and her dog are the gatekeepers of my dwelling. The woman is bad enough; she leans around in the entrance hall, spying to see that I don't bring in things or people, and when she's had her midafternoon pint of lemon-flavored gin she always stops me in the hall, and grabs ahold of my coat or my arm, and she presses her disgusting body up against me to keep me in a corner so she can talk to me. The smell of her body and her breath . . . you can't imagine it . . . and somewhere, somewhere in the back of that pea-sized brain of hers, an organ developed just enough to let her eat, drink, and emit, she has some foul parody of sexual desire. And I, Peter, I am the object of her sweaty lust.

PETER. That's disgusting. That's . . . horrible.

JERRY. But I have found a way to keep her off. When she talks to me, when she presses herself to my body and mumbles about her room and how I should come there, I merely say: but, Love; wasn't yesterday enough for you, and the day before? Then she puzzles, she makes slits of her tiny eyes, she sways a little, and then, Peter . . . and it is at this moment that I think I might be doing some good in that tormented house . . . a simpleminded smile begins to form on her unthinkable face, and she giggles and groans as she thinks about yesterday and the day before; as she believes and relives what never happened. Then, she motions to that black monster of a dog she has, and she goes back to her room. And I am safe until our next meeting.

PETER. It's so . . . unthinkable. I find it hard to believe that people such as that really *are*.

JERRY (*lightly mocking*). It's for reading about, isn't it?

PETER (*seriously*). Yes.

JERRY. And fact is better left to fiction. You're right, Peter. Well, what I have been meaning to tell you about is the dog; I shall, now.

PETER (*nervously*). Oh, yes; the dog.

JERRY. Don't go. You're not thinking of going, are you?

PETER. Well . . . no, I don't think so.

JERRY (*as if to a child*). Because after I tell you about the dog, do you know what then? Then . . . then I'll tell you about what happened at the zoo.

PETER (*laughing faintly*). You're . . . you're full of stories, aren't you?

JERRY. You don't *have* to listen. Nobody is holding you here; remember that. Keep that in your mind.

PETER (*irritably*). I know that.

JERRY. You do? Good. (*The following long speech, it seems to me, should be done with a great deal of action, to achieve a hypnotic effect on Peter, and on the audience, too. Some specific actions have been suggested, but the director and the actor playing Jerry might best work it out for themselves.*) ALL RIGHT. (*As if reading from a huge billboard*) THE STORY OF JERRY AND THE DOG! (*Natural again*) What I am going to tell you has something to do with how sometimes it's necessary to go a long distance

out of the way in order to come back a short distance correctly;
or, maybe I only think that it has something to do with that. But,
it's why I went to the zoo today, and why I walked north . . .
northerly, rather . . . until I came here. All right. The dog, I
think I told you, is a black monster of a beast: an oversized
head, tiny, tiny ears, and eyes . . . bloodshot, infected, maybe;
and a body you can see the ribs through the skin. The dog is
black, all black; all black except for the bloodshot eyes, and
. . . yes . . . and an open sore on its . . . *right* forepaw; that
is red, too. And, oh yes; the poor monster, and I do believe it's an
old dog . . . it's certainly a misused one . . . almost always has
an erection . . . of sorts. That's red, too. And . . . what else?
. . . oh, yes; there's a gray-yellow-white color, too, when he
bares his fangs. Like this: Grrrrrrr! Which is what he did when
he saw me for the first time . . . the day I moved in. I worried
about that animal the very first minute I met him. Now, animals
don't take to me like Saint Francis had birds hanging off him
all the time. What I mean is: animals are indifferent to me . . .
like people (*He smiles slightly.*) . . . most of the time. But this
dog wasn't indifferent. From the very beginning he'd snarl and
then go for me, to get one of my legs. Not like he was rabid, you
know; he was sort of a stumbly dog, but he wasn't half-assed,
either. It was a good, stumbly run; but I always got away. He
got a piece of my trouser leg, look, you can see right here, where
it's mended; he got that the second day I lived there; but, I
kicked free and got upstairs fast, so that was that. (*Puzzles.*) I
still don't know to this day how the other roomers manage it, but
you know what I *think:* I think it had to do only with me. Cozy.
So. Anyway, this went on for over a week, whenever I came in;
but never when I went out. That's funny. Or, it *was* funny. I
could pack up and live in the street for all the dog cared. Well, I
thought about it up in my room one day, one of the times after
I'd bolted upstairs, and I made up my mind. I decided: First, I'll
kill the dog with kindness, and if that doesn't work . . . I'll just
kill him. (PETER *winces.*) Don't react, Peter; just listen. So, the
next day I went out and bought a bag of hamburgers, medium
rare, no catsup, no onion; and on the way home I threw away all
the rolls and kept just the meat. (*Action for the following, perhaps.*) When I got back to the roominghouse the dog was waiting
for me. I half opened the door that led into the entrance hall, and
there he was; waiting for me. It figured. I went in, very cautiously, and I had the hamburgers, you remember; I opened the
bag, and I set the meat down about twelve feet from where the

dog was snarling at me. Like so! He snarled; stopped snarling; sniffed; moved slowly; then faster; then faster toward the meat. Well, when he got to it he stopped, and he looked at me. I smiled; but tentatively, you understand. He turned his face back to the hamburgers, smelled, sniffed some more, and then . . . RRRAAAA-GGGGGHHHH, like that . . . he tore into them. It was as if he had never eaten anything in his life before, except like garbage. Which might very well have been the truth. I don't think the landlady ever eats anything but garbage. But. He ate all the hamburgers, almost all at once, making sounds in his throat like a woman. *Then,* when he'd finished the meat, the hamburger, and tried to eat the paper, too, he sat down and smiled. I think he smiled; I know cats do. It was a very gratifying few moments. Then, BAM, he snarled and made for me again. He didn't get me this time, either. So, I got upstairs, and I lay down on my bed and started to think about the dog again. To be truthful, I was offended, and I was damn mad, too. It was six perfectly good hamburgers with not enough pork in them to make it disgusting. I was offended. But, after a while, I decided to try it for a few more days. If you think about it, this dog had what amounted to an antipathy toward me; really. And, I wondered if I mightn't overcome this antipathy. So, I tried it for five more days, but it was always the same: snarl, sniff; move; faster; stare; gobble; RAAGGGHHH; smile; snarl; BAM. Well, now; by this time Columbus Avenue was strewn with hamburger rolls and I was less offended than disgusted. So, I decided to kill the dog. (PETER *raises a hand in protest.*) Oh, don't be so alarmed, Peter; I didn't succeed. The day I tried to kill the dog I bought only one hamburger and what I thought was a murderous portion of rat poison. When I bought the hamburger I asked the man not to bother with the roll, all I wanted was the meat. I expected some reaction from him, like: we don't sell no hamburgers without rolls; or, wha' d'ya wanna do, eat it out'a ya han's? But no; he smiled benignly, wrapped up the hamburger in waxed paper, and said: A bite for ya pussy-cat? I wanted to say: No, not really; it's part of a plan to poison a dog I know. But, you can't say "a dog I know" without sounding funny; so I said, a little too loud, I'm afraid, and too formally: YES, A BITE FOR MY PUSSY-CAT. People looked up. It always happens when I try to simplify things; people look up. But that's neither hither nor thither. So. On my way back to the roominghouse, I kneaded the hamburger and the rat poison together between my hands, at that point feeling as much sadness as disgust. I opened the door to the entrance hall, and there the monster was, waiting to take the offering and then jump me. Poor bastard; he never learned that the moment he took to smile before he went for me gave me time enough to get out of range. BUT, there he was; malevolence with an erection, waiting. I put the poison patty down, moved toward the stairs and watched. The poor animal gobbled the food down as usual, smiled, which made me almost sick, and then, BAM. But, I sprinted up the stairs, as usual, and the dog didn't get me, as usual. AND IT CAME TO PASS THAT THE BEAST WAS DEATHLY ILL. I knew this because he no longer attended me, and because the landlady sobered up. She stopped me in the hall the same evening of the attempted murder and confided the information that God had struck her puppy-dog a surely fatal blow. She had forgotten her bewildered lust, and her eyes were wide open for the first time. They looked like the dog's eyes. She sniveled and implored me to pray for the animal. I wanted to say to her: Madam, I have myself to pray for, the colored queen, the Puerto Rican family, the person in the front room whom I've never seen, the woman who cries deliberately behind her closed door, and the rest of the people in all roominghouses, everywhere; besides, Madam, I don't understand how to pray. But . . . to simplify things . . . I told her I would pray. She looked up. She said that I was a liar, and that I probably wanted the dog to die. I told her, and there was so much truth here, that I didn't want the dog to die. I didn't, and not just because I'd poisoned him. I'm afraid that I must tell you I wanted the dog to live so that I could see what our new relationship might come to. (PETER *indicates his increasing displeasure and slowly growing antagonism.*) Please understand, Peter; that sort of thing is important. You must believe me; it *is* important. We have to know the effect of our actions. (*Another deep sigh.*) Well, anyway; the dog recovered. I have no idea why, unless he was a descendant of the puppy that guarded the gates of hell or some such resort. I'm not up on my mythology. (*He pronounces the word myth-o-*logy.) Are you? (PETER *sets to thinking, but* JERRY *goes on.*) At any rate, and you've missed the eight-thousand-dollar question, Peter; at any rate, the dog recovered his health and the landlady recovered her thirst, in no way altered by the bow-wow's deliverance. When I came home from a movie that was playing on Forty-second Street, a movie I'd seen, or one that was very much like one or several I'd seen, after the landlady told me puppykins was better, I was so hoping for the dog to be waiting for me. I was . . . well, how would you put it . . . enticed? . . . fascinated? . . . no, I don't think so

. . . heart-shatteringly anxious, that's it; I was heart-shatteringly
anxious to confront my friend again. (PETER *reacts scoffingly*.)
Yes, Peter; friend. That's the only word for it. I was heart-
shatteringly et cetera to confront my doggy friend again. I came
in the door and advanced, unafraid, to the center of the entrance
hall. The beast was there . . . looking at me. And, you know, he
looked better for his scrape with the nevermind. I stopped; I
looked at him; he looked at me. I think . . . I think we stayed a
long time that way . . . still, stone-statue . . . just looking at
one another. I looked more into his face than he looked into mine.
I mean, I can concentrate longer at looking into a dog's face than
a dog can concentrate at looking into mine, or into anybody else's
face, for that matter. But during that twenty seconds or two hours
that we looked into each other's face, we made contact. Now,
here is what I had wanted to happen: I loved the dog now, and I
wanted him to love me. I had tried to love, and I had tried to kill,
and both had been unsuccessful by themselves. I hoped . . . and
I don't really know why I expected the dog to understand anything, much less my motivations . . . I hoped that the dog would
understand. (PETER *seems to be hypnotized*.) It's just . . . it's
just that . . . (JERRY *is abnormally tense, now*.) . . . it's just
that if you can't deal with people, you have to make a start somewhere. WITH ANIMALS! (*Much faster now, and like a conspirator*)
Don't you see? A person has to have some way of dealing with
SOMETHING. If not with people . . . if not with people . . .
SOMETHING. With a bed, with a cockroach, with a mirror . . .
no, that's too hard, that's one of the last steps. With a cockroach,
with a . . . with a . . . with a carpet, a roll of toilet paper . . .
no, not that, either . . . that's a mirror, too; always check bleeding. You see how hard it is to find things? With a street corner, and
too many lights, all colors reflecting on the oily-wet streets . . .
with a wisp of smoke, a wisp . . . of smoke . . . with . . .
with pornographic playing cards, with a strongbox . . . WITHOUT
A LOCK . . . with love, with vomiting, with crying, with fury
because the pretty little ladies aren't pretty little ladies, with making money with your body which is an act of love and I could
prove it, with howling because you're alive; with God. How about
that? WITH GOD WHO IS A COLORED QUEEN WHO WEARS A KIMONO
AND PLUCKS HIS EYEBROWS, WHO IS A WOMAN WHO CRIES WITH
DETERMINATION BEHIND HER CLOSED DOOR . . . with God who,
I'm told, turned his back on the whole thing some time ago . . .
with . . . some day, with people. (JERRY *sighs the next word
heavily*.) People. With an idea; a concept. And where better,

where ever better in this humiliating excuse for a jail, where better to communicate one single, simple-minded idea than in an entrance hall? Where? It would be A START! Where better to make a beginning . . . to understand and just possibly be understood . . . a beginning of an understanding, than with . . . (*Here* JERRY *seems to fall into almost grotesque fatigue*) . . . than with A DOG. Just that; a dog. (*Here there is a silence that might be prolonged for a moment or so; then* JERRY *wearily finishes his story.*) A dog. It seemed like a perfectly sensible idea. Man is a dog's best friend, remember. So: the dog and I looked at each other. I longer than the dog. And what I saw then has been the same ever since. Whenever the dog and I see each other we both stop where we are. We regard each other with a mixture of sadness and suspicion, and then we feign indifference. We walk past each other safely; we have an understanding. It's very sad, but you'll have to admit that it is an understanding. We had made many attempts at contact, and we had failed. The dog has returned to garbage, and I to solitary but free passage. I have not returned. I mean to say, I have *gained* solitary free passage, if that much further loss can be said to be gain. I have learned that neither kindness nor cruelty by themselves, independent of each other, creates any effect beyond themselves; and I have learned that the two combined, together, at the same time, are the teaching emotion. And what is gained is loss. And what has been the result: the dog and I have attained a compromise; more of a bargain, really. We neither love nor hurt because we do not try to reach each other. And, *was* trying to feed the dog an act of love? And, perhaps, was the dog's attempt to bite me *not* an act of love? If we can so misunderstand, well then, why have we invented the word love in the first place? (*There is silence.* JERRY *moves to* PETER'S *bench and sits down beside him. This is the first time* JERRY *has sat down during the play.*) The Story of Jerry and the Dog: the end. (PETER *is silent.*) Well, Peter? (JERRY *is suddenly cheerful.*) Well, Peter? Do you think I could sell that story to the *Reader's Digest* and make a couple of hundred bucks for *The Most Unforgettable Character I've Ever Met?* Huh? (JERRY *is animated, but* PETER *is disturbed.*) Oh, come on now, Peter; tell me what you think.

PETER (*numb*). I . . . I don't understand what . . . I don't think I . . . (*Now, almost tearfully*) Why did you tell me all of this?

JERRY. Why not?

PETER. I DON'T UNDERSTAND!

JERRY (*furious, but whispering*). That's a lie.

PETER. No. No, it's not.

JERRY (*quietly*). I tried to explain it to you as I went along. I went slowly; it all has to do with . . .

PETER. I DON'T WANT TO HEAR ANY MORE. I don't understand you, or your landlady, or her dog. . . .

JERRY. *Her* dog! I thought it was my . . . No. No, you're right. It *is* her dog. (*Looks at* PETER *intently, shaking his head.*) I don't know what I was thinking about; of course you don't understand. (*In a monotone, wearily*) I don't live in your block; I'm not married to two parakeets, or whatever your setup is. I am a *permanent transient,* and my home is the sickening roominghouses on the West Side of New York City, which is the greatest city in the world. Amen.

PETER. I'm . . . I'm sorry; I didn't mean to . . .

JERRY. Forget it. I suppose you don't quite know what to make of me, eh?

PETER (*a joke*). We get all kinds in publishing. (*Chuckles.*)

JERRY. You're a funny man. (*He forces a laugh.*) You know that? You're a very . . . a richly comic person.

PETER (*modestly, but amused*). Oh, now, not really (*still chuckling*).

JERRY. Peter, do I annoy you, or confuse you?

PETER (*lightly*). Well, I must confess that this wasn't the kind of afternoon I'd anticipated.

JERRY. You mean, I'm not the gentleman you were expecting.

PETER. I wasn't expecting anybody.

JERRY. No, I don't imagine you were. But I'm here, and I'm not leaving.

PETER (*consulting his watch*). Well, you may not be, but I must be getting home soon.

JERRY. Oh, come on; stay a while longer.

PETER. I really should get home; you see . . .

JERRY. (*Tickles* PETER'S *ribs with his fingers.*) Oh, come on.

PETER. (*He is very ticklish; as* JERRY *continues to tickle him his voice becomes falsetto.*) No, I . . . OHHHHH! Don't do that. Stop, Stop. Ohhh, no, no.

JERRY. Oh, come on.

PETER (*as* JERRY *tickles*). Oh, hee, hee, hee. I must go. I . . . hee, hee, hee. After all, stop, stop, hee, hee, hee, after all, the parakeets will be getting dinner ready soon. Hee, hee. And the cats are setting the table. Stop, stop, and, and . . . (PETER *is beside himself now*) . . . and we're having . . . hee, hee . . . uh . . . ho, ho, ho. (JERRY *stops tickling* PETER, *but the combination of the tickling and his own mad whimsy has* PETER *laughing almost hysterically. As his laughter continues, then subsides,* JERRY *watches him, with a curious fixed smile.*)

JERRY. Peter?

PETER. Oh, ha, ha, ha, ha, ha. What? What?

JERRY. Listen, now.

PETER. Oh, ho, ho. What . . . what is it, Jerry? Oh, my.

JERRY (*mysteriously*). Peter, do you want to know what happened at the zoo?

PETER. Ah, ha, ha. The what? Oh, yes; the zoo. Oh, ho, ho. Well, I had my own zoo there for a moment with . . . hee, hee, the parakeets getting dinner ready, and the . . . ha, ha, whatever it was, the . . .

JERRY (*calmly*). Yes, that was very funny, Peter. I wouldn't have expected it. But do you want to hear about what happened at the zoo, or not?

PETER. Yes. Yes, by all means; tell me what happened at the zoo. Oh, my. I don't know what happened to me.

JERRY. Now I'll let you in on what happened at the zoo; but first, I should tell you why I went to the zoo. I went to the zoo to find out more about the way people exist with animals, and the way animals exist with each other, and with people too. It probably wasn't a fair test, what with everyone separated by bars from everyone else, the animals for the most part from each other, and always the people from the animals. But, if it's a zoo, that's the way it is. (*He pokes* PETER *on the arm.*) Move over.

PETER (*friendly*). I'm sorry, haven't you enough room? (*He shifts a little.*)

JERRY (*smiling slightly*). Well, all the animals are there, and all the people are there, and it's Sunday and all the children are there. (*He pokes* PETER *again.*) Move over.

PETER (*patiently, still friendly*). All right. (*He moves some more, and* JERRY *has all the room he might need.*)

JERRY. And it's a hot day, so all the stench is there, too, and all the balloon sellers, and all the ice cream sellers, and all the seals are barking, and all the birds are screaming. (*Pokes* PETER *harder.*) Move over!

PETER (*beginning to be annoyed*). Look here, you have more than enough room! (*But he moves more, and is now fairly cramped at one end of the bench.*)

JERRY. And I am there, and it's feeding time at the lions' house, and the lion keeper comes into the lion cage, one of the lion cages, to feed one of the lions. (*Punches* PETER *on the arm, hard.*) MOVE OVER!

PETER (*very annoyed*). I can't move over any more, and stop hitting me. What's the matter with you?

JERRY. Do you want to hear the story? (*Punches* PETER'S *arm again.*)

PETER (*flabbergasted*). I'm not so sure! I certainly don't want to be punched in the arm.

JERRY. (*Punches* PETER'S *arm again.*) Like that?

PETER. Stop it! What's the matter with you?

JERRY. I'm crazy, you bastard.

PETER. That isn't funny.

JERRY. Listen to me, Peter. I want this bench. You go sit on the bench over there, and if you're good I'll tell you the rest of the story.

PETER (*flustered*). But . . . whatever for? What *is* the matter with you? Besides, I see no reason why I should give up this bench. I sit on this bench almost every Sunday afternoon, in good weather. It's secluded here; there's never anyone sitting here, so I have it all to myself.

JERRY (*softly*). Get off this bench, Peter; I want it.

PETER (*almost whining*). No.

JERRY. I said I want this bench, and I'm going to have it. Now get over there.

PETER. People can't have everything they want. You should know that; it's a rule; people can have some of the things they want, but they can't have everything.

JERRY. (*Laughs.*) Imbecile! You're slow-witted!

PETER. Stop that!

JERRY. You're a vegetable! Go lie down on the ground.

PETER (*intense*). Now *you* listen to me. I've put up with you all afternoon.

JERRY. Not really.

PETER. LONG ENOUGH. I've put up with you long enough. I've listened to you because you seemed . . . well, because I thought you wanted to talk to somebody.

JERRY. You put things well; economically, and, yet . . . oh, what is the word I want to put justice to your . . . JESUS, you make me sick . . . get off here and give me my bench.

PETER. MY BENCH!

JERRY. (*Pushes* PETER *almost, but not quite, off the bench.*) Get out of my sight.

PETER (*regaining his position*). God da . . . mn you. That's enough! I've had enough of you. I will not give up this bench; you can't have it, and that's that. Now, go away. (JERRY *snorts but does not move.*) Go away, I said. (JERRY *does not move.*) Get away from here. If you don't move on . . . you're a bum . . . that's what you are. . . . If you don't move on, I'll get a policeman here and make you go. (JERRY *laughs, stays.*) I warn you, I'll call a policeman.

JERRY (*softly*). You won't find a policeman around here; they're all over on the west side of the park chasing fairies down from trees or out of the bushes. That's all they do. That's their function. So scream your head off; it won't do you any good.

PETER. POLICE! I warn you, I'll have you arrested. POLICE! (*Pause.*) I said POLICE! (*Pause.*) I feel ridiculous.

JERRY. You look ridiculous: a grown man screaming for the police on a bright Sunday afternoon in the park with nobody harming you. If a policeman *did* fill his quota and come sludging over this way he'd probably take you in as a nut.

PETER (*with disgust and impotence*). Great God, I just came here to read, and now you want me to give up the bench. You're mad.

JERRY. Hey, I got news for you, as they say. I'm on your precious bench, and you're never going to have it for yourself again.

PETER (*furious*). Look, you; get off my bench. I don't care if it makes any sense or not. I want this bench to myself; I want you OFF IT!

JERRY (*mocking*). Aw . . . look who's mad.

PETER. GET OUT!

JERRY. No.

PETER. I WARN YOU!

JERRY. Do you know how ridiculous you look *now?*

PETER. (*His fury and self-consciousness have possessed him.*) It doesn't matter. (*He is almost crying.*) GET AWAY FROM MY BENCH!

JERRY. Why? You have everything in the world you want; you've told me about your home, and your family, and *your own* little zoo. You have everything, and now you want this bench. Are these the things men fight for? Tell me, Peter, is this bench, this iron and this wood, is this your honor? Is this the thing in the world you'd fight for? Can you think of anything more absurd?

PETER. Absurd? Look, I'm not going to talk to you about honor, or even try to explain it to you. Besides, it isn't a question of honor; but even if it were, you wouldn't understand.

JERRY (*contemptuously*). You don't even know what you're saying, do you? This is probably the first time in your life you've had anything more trying to face than changing your cats' toilet box. Stupid! Don't you have any idea, not even the slightest, what other people *need?*

PETER. Oh, boy, listen to you; well, you don't need this bench. That's for sure.

JERRY. Yes; yes, I do.

PETER (*quivering*). I've come here for years; I have hours of great
pleasure, great satisfaction, right here. And that's important to a
man. I'm a responsible person, and I'm a GROWNUP. This is my
bench, and you have no right to take it away from me.

JERRY. Fight for it, then. Defend yourself; defend your bench.

PETER. You've *pushed* me to it. Get up and fight.

JERRY. Like a man?

PETER (*still angry*). Yes, like a man, if you insist on mocking me even
further.

JERRY. I'll have to give you credit for one thing: you *are* a vegetable,
and a slightly nearsighted one, I think . . .

PETER. THAT'S ENOUGH. . . .

JERRY. . . . but, you know, as they say on TV all the time—you know
—and I mean this, Peter, you have a certain dignity; it surprises
me. . . .

PETER. STOP!

JERRY. (*Rises lazily.*) Very well, Peter, we'll battle for the bench, but
we're not evenly matched. (*He takes out and clicks open an ugly-
looking knife.*)

PETER (*suddenly awakening to the reality of the situation*). You *are*
mad! You're stark raving mad! YOU'RE GOING TO KILL ME! (*But
before* PETER *has time to think what to do,* JERRY *tosses the knife
at* PETER'S *feet.*)

JERRY. There you go. Pick it up. You have the knife and we'll be more
evenly matched.

PETER (*horrified*). No!

JERRY. (*Rushes over to* PETER, *grabs him by the collar;* PETER *rises;
their faces almost touch.*) Now you pick up that knife and you
fight with me. You fight for your self-respect; you fight for that
goddamned bench.

PETER (*struggling*). No! Let . . . let go of me! He . . . Help!

JERRY. (*Slaps* PETER *on each "fight."*) You fight, you miserable
bastard; fight for that bench; fight for your parakeets; fight for
your cats, fight for your two daughters; fight for your wife; fight
for your manhood, you pathetic little vegetable. (*Spits in* PETER'S
face.) You couldn't even get your wife with a male child.

PETER. (*Breaks away, enraged.*) It's a matter of genetics, not manhood,
you . . . you monster. (*He darts down, picks up the knife and
backs off a little; he is breathing heavily.*) I'll give you one last
chance; get out of here and leave me alone! (*He holds the knife
with a firm arm, but far in front of him, not to attack, but to
defend.*)

JERRY. (*Sighs heavily.*) So be it! (*With a rush he charges* PETER *and impales himself on the knife. Tableau: For just a moment, complete silence,* JERRY *impaled on the knife at the end of* PETER'S *still firm arm. Then* PETER *screams, pulls away, leaving the knife in* JERRY. JERRY *is motionless, on point. Then he, too, screams, and it must be the sound of an infuriated and fatally wounded animal. With the knife in him, he stumbles back to the bench that* PETER *had vacated. He crumbles there, sitting, facing* PETER, *his eyes wide in agony, his mouth open.*)

PETER (*whispering*). Oh my God, oh my God, oh my God. . . . (*He repeats these words many times, very rapidly.*)

JERRY. (JERRY *is dying; but now his expression seems to change. His features relax, and while his voice varies, sometimes wrenched with pain, for the most part he seems removed from his dying. He smiles.*) Thank you, Peter. I mean that, now; thank you very much. (PETER'S *mouth drops open. He cannot move; he is transfixed.*) Oh, Peter, I was so afraid I'd drive you away. (*He laughs as best he can.*) You don't know how afraid I was you'd go away and leave me. And now I'll tell you what happened at the zoo. I think . . . I think this is what happened at the zoo . . . I think. I think that while I was at the zoo I decided that I would walk north . . . northerly, rather . . . until I found you . . . or somebody . . . and I decided that I would talk to you . . . I would tell you things . . . and things that I would tell you would . . . Well, here we are. You see? Here we *are.* But . . . I don't know . . . could I have planned all this? No . . . no, I couldn't have. But I think I did. And now I've told you what you wanted to know, haven't I? And now you know all about what happened at the zoo. And now you know what you'll see in your TV, and the face I told you about . . . you remember . . . the face I told you about . . . my face, the face you see right now. Peter . . . Peter? . . . Peter . . . thank you. I came unto you (*He laughs, so faintly.*) and you have comforted me. Dear Peter.

PETER (*almost fainting*). Oh my God!

JERRY. You'd better go now. Somebody might come by, and you don't want to be here when anyone comes.

PETER. (*Does not move, but begins to weep.*) Oh my God, oh my God.

JERRY (*most faintly, now; he is very near death*). You won't be coming back here any more, Peter; you've been dispossessed. You've lost your bench, but you've defended your honor. And Peter, I'll tell you something now; you're not really a vegetable; it's all right, you're an animal. You're an animal, too. But you'd better hurry now, Peter. Hurry, you'd better go . . . see? (JERRY *takes a handkerchief and with great effort and pain wipes the knife handle clean of fingerprints.*) Hurry away, Peter. (PETER *begins to stagger away.*) Wait . . . wait, Peter. Take your book . . . book. Right here . . . beside me . . . on your bench . . . my bench, rather. Come . . . take your book. (PETER *starts for the book, but retreats.*) Hurry . . . Peter. (PETER *rushes to the bench, grabs the book, retreats.*) Very good, Peter . . . very good. Now . . . hurry away. (PETER *hesitates for a moment, then flees, stage-left.*) Hurry away. . . . (*His eyes are closed now.*) Hurry away, your parakeets are making the dinner . . . the cats . . . are setting the table . . .

PETER (*Off stage, a pitiful howl*). OH MY GOD!

JERRY. (*His eyes still closed, he shakes his head and speaks; a combination of scornful mimicry and supplication.*) Oh . . . my . . . God. (*He is dead.*)

Curtain